HUMAN RESOURCE MANAGEMENT
READINGS AND CASES

HUMAN RESOURCE MANAGEMENT
READINGS AND CASES

Tim O. Peterson
University of Tulsa

HOUGHTON MIFFLIN COMPANY   BOSTON
Dallas   Geneva, Illinois   Palo Alto   Princeton, New Jersey

Copyright © 1990 by Houghton Mifflin Company. All rights reserved.

No part of this work may be reproduced or transmitted in any form or by any means, electronic or mechanical, including photocopying and recording, or by any information storage or retrieval system without the prior written permission of the copyright owner unless such copying is expressly permitted by federal copyright law. With the exception of non-profit transcription in Braille, Houghton Mifflin is not authorized to grant permission for further uses of copyrighted selections reprinted in this text without the permission of their owners. Permission must be obtained from the individual copyright owners as identified herein. Address requests for permission to make copies of Houghton Mifflin material to College Permissions, Houghton Mifflin Company, One Beacon Street, Boston, MA 02108.

Printed in the U.S.A.

Library of Congress Catalog Card Number: 89-80934

ISBN: 0-395-47583-X

ABCDEFGHIJ-BP-96543210

This book is dedicated to my son, Todd, who by his every action reminds me that people are truly our most important resource.

CONTENTS

Preface xiii

I OVERVIEW AND INTRODUCTION 1

READINGS Evolution of Concept and Practice in Personnel Administration/Human Resource Management *Thomas A. Mahoney and John R. Deckop* 3

HIRS: Much More Than an Automated Filing Cabinet *Ellen J. Frank* 21

CASES The Midvale Plant (A): The Reorganized Personnel Department 26

Human Resource Management Is About People *Tim O. Peterson* 31

Readings for Professional Growth and Enrichment 34

II PLANNING FOR ORGANIZATIONS, JOBS, AND PEOPLE 35

READINGS The Design of a Career Oriented Human Resource System *Mary Ann Von Glinow, Michael J. Driver, Kenneth Brousseau, and J. Bruce Prince* 37

Skills Banks: From All According to Their Abilities *Ronald R. Knipling* 49

A "No Frills" Approach to Human Resource Planning *Lawrence M. Baytos* 59

Matching International Business Growth and International Management Development *Ruth G. Shaeffer* 67

vii

CASES Pacific Aircraft Company *Jeffrey A. McNally* 75

Weaver Rental *K. Michele Kacmar* 80

Readings for Professional Growth and Enrichment 82

III ORGANIZATIONAL ENTRY 83

READINGS Voluntary Affirmative Action and Preferential Treatment: Legal and Research Implications *Lawrence S. Kleiman and Robert H. Faley* 85

Installing a Realistic Job Preview: Ten Tough Choices *John P. Wanous* 99

Recruitment for Beginners *Lynda Farago, Phil Argyris, and Hung-Wei Chou* 114

Structured Interviewing: Raising the Psychometric Properties of the Employment Interview *Michael A. Campion, Elliott D. Pursell, and Barbara K. Brown* 118

Innovative Approaches to Personnel Selection and Performance Appraisal *H. John Bernardin* 133

Why Do Assessment Centers Work? The Puzzle of Assessment Center Validity *Richard Klimoski and Mary Brickner* 143

Employment Testing: The U.S. Job Service Is Spearheading a Revolution *Robert M. Madigan, K. Dow Scott, Diana L. Deadrick, and Jil A. Stoddard* 158

Development and Validation of a Computerized Interpretation System for Personnel Tests *C. David Vale, Laura S. Keller, and V. Jon Bentz* 167

Development and Validation of Minicourses in the Telecommunication Industry *Richard R. Reilly and Edmond W. Israelski* 181

CASES Freida Mae Jones *Martin R. Moser* 193

Harmard Industries *K. Michele Kacmar* 196

Readings for Professional Growth and Enrichment 200

IV DEVELOPING HUMAN RESOURCE PRODUCTIVITY 203

READINGS Kirkpatrick's Levels of Training Criteria: Thirty Years Later *George M. Alliger and Elizabeth M. Janak* 205

What's So Special About CBT? Making the Most of the Medium *Larry Brink* 214

Management Development *Kenneth N. Wexley and Timothy T. Baldwin* 225

Simulating the Consequences of Job Redesign *Nealia S. Bruning and Jay Weinroth* 242

The Effects of Psychologically Based Intervention Programs on Worker Productivity: A Meta-Analysis *Richard A. Guzzo, Richard D. Jette, and Raymond A. Katzell* 248

CASES TRW — Oilwell Cable Division *Michael G. Kolchin, Thomas J. Hyclak, and Sheree Demming* 262

A Change for the Better? *Mary K. Bargielski* 276

Readings for Professional Growth and Enrichment 278

V PERFORMANCE APPRAISAL AND REWARD SYSTEMS 281

READINGS Measure for Measure in Performance Appraisal *Jeffrey S. Kane* 283

Behind the Mask: The Politics of Employee Appraisal *Clinton O. Longenecker, Henry P. Sims, Jr., and Dennis A. Gioia* 294

Some Neglected Variables in Research on
Discrimination in Appraisals *Robert L. Dipboye* **308**

Training Programs for Performance Appraisal:
A Review *David E. Smith* **322**

The Cost of Alternative Comparable Worth Strategies
Richard D. Arvey and Katherine Holt **346**

Pay Concepts for the 1990s, Part 1
James L. Whitney **354**

Pay Concepts for the 1990s, Part 2
James L. Whitney **364**

Managing Corporate Culture Through Reward
Systems *Jeffrey Kerr and John W. Slocum, Jr.* **368**

CASES Chancellor State University *Thomas R. Miller* **381**

Redesigning Performance Appraisal at Citizens Bank
J. Gregory Chachere **384**

**Readings for Professional Growth
and Enrichment** **385**

VI MAINTAINING HUMAN RESOURCES 387

READINGS Labor Relations: Research and Practice in Transition
John A. Fossum **389**

Employee Fitness Programs: Their Impact on the
Employee and the Organization
Loren E. Falkenberg **407**

The Nature of Collective Bargaining
Betty W. Justice **420**

A Systems Model for Labor-Management Cooperation
David P. Swinehart and Mitchell A. Sherr **434**

The Process of Retirement: A Review and
Recommendations for Future Investigation
Terry A. Beehr **445**

How to Avoid Grievance Arbitration *Rebecca Ballard
and Michael D. Crino* **464**

Modeling the Skills Obsolescence Process: A Psychological/Economic Integration *John A. Fossum, Richard D. Arvey, Carol A. Paradise, and Nancy E. Robbins* **471**

After the Ax Falls: Job Loss as a Career Transition *Janina C. Latack and Janelle B. Dozier* **486**

CASES Southwestern Bell Telephone Company *Chimezie A. B. Osigweh and James Ball* **507**

Midsouth University *Fraya W. Andrews and Jon W. Beard* **513**

Readings for Professional Growth and Enrichment **516**

VII BEYOND FUNCTIONAL CONCERNS 519

READINGS The Strategic Implications of HR Planning *Barbara E. Heiken, James W. Randall, Jr., and Robert Lear* **521**

Linking Competitive Strategies with Human Resource Management Practices *Randall S. Schuler and Susan E. Jackson* **529**

The Performance Measurement and Reward System: Critical to Strategic Management *Paul J. Stonich* **547**

Human Resources: The Forgotten Factor in Mergers and Acquisitions *David L. Schweiger and John M. Ivancevich* **561**

Unions in the Next Century: An Exploratory Essay *Joseph Krislov* **572**

Balancing Work Life and Home Life: What Can Organizations Do to Help? *Douglas T. Hall and Judith Richter* **579**

A Role Model Approach to Sexual Harassment *Paula M. Popovich and Betty Jo Licata* **597**

Expatriate Assignments: Enhancing Success and Minimizing Failure *Rosalie L. Tung* **610**

CASES   A Management Dilemma: Regulating the Health of the
Unborn   *Donna M. Randall*   **624**

Decisions   *Shannon Himes Ratcliff*   **637**

**Readings for Professional Growth
and Enrichment**   **638**

PREFACE

The management of human resources is one of the major challenges organizations will face into the twenty-first century. Future managers and human resource specialists will need a clear understanding of the many tasks involved in effective human resource management. In the past, lip service has been paid to the importance of people to their organization. Today, more and more organizations are recognizing the importance of their employees and attempting to manage this valuable asset in a humane and effective manner.

Human Resource Management: Readings and Cases provides the human resource management (HRM) student with readings that enrich, extend, or expand on the topics discussed in the basic HRM textbook. Each section of the book also provides one long referred case and one short targeted case. By reading and discussing these cases, students will be able to apply the theories developed in the HRM textbook to real-world human resource problems. Each section ends with a list of additional readings for professional growth and enrichment. These readings provide supplemental material for increasing the depth and breadth of thought on the specific human resource topic covered in the section.

I am indebted to many of my academic colleagues for their inspiration, encouragement, and advice. Among those colleagues are: David Van Fleet, Ricky Griffin, Jon Beard, and Charlotte Sutton. I owe a special debt to Cynthia Fisher, who not only provided me with advice and comments on the material in this book, but who has, in her own special way, influenced my academic work.

In addition to my academic colleagues, I must thank those who have helped make this book a reality. Karen Marshall wrote many of the questions to the readings located in the instructor's manual. For one whole summer, Todd Peterson, Marijke Van Fleet, and Dirk Van Fleet copied articles and cases for me. Susan Leasure typed and organized all of the enrichment articles directly from my chicken scratching — no easy feat.

I am also grateful to the staff at Houghton Mifflin for their understanding. They were there when I needed them, as editors and as friends.

These acknowledgments would not be complete without thanking my wife, Claudette. She always encourages me to be my best, and she provides me with a family environment in which every day is a joy to be alive.

I

OVERVIEW AND INTRODUCTION

Readings

Evolution of Concept and Practice in Personnel Administration/Human Resource Management (PA/HRM)
Thomas A. Mahoney / John R. Deckop

This article reviews developments in personnel administration (PA) and human resource management (HRM), identifying major trends over the past 15–20 years and discussing state-of-the-art issues, all within editorial space constraints. We present our concept of the PA/HRM field at its current stage of development. Future reviews may revise, elaborate on, or propose correction of the interpretations presented here.

BACKGROUND

Something called personnel administration and/or human resource management (PA/HRM) exists as a function of managerial practice and as a focus for scholarship. Professional and scholarly associations (e.g., the American Society of Personnel Administration and the Personnel/Human Resource Division of the Academy of Management) attest to the identification of managers and scholars with the subject. Like various other fields of inquiry associated with managerial practice, PA/HRM has evolved over time in an eclectic manner, responding to changing issues, concepts, and challenges, rather than in a logical and deductive manner based on evolving disciplinary theory.

Understanding of the current status of the field as well as of changes over the past 20 years requires a brief review of the origins of PA/HRM (see Ling, 1965, for a full treatment of the subject). The emergence of PA/HRM as a function of managerial practice is usually attributed to the influence of scientific management. PA/HRM, like other functions of management, was identified as a field of practice requiring specialized attention (and, by inference, specialized study) to support it. PA/HRM is concerned with the recruitment, allocation, and utilization of human resources in employment. Taylor's (1911) account of his experiments with Schmidt shows the application of what are now called job design, selection, training, and motivation with compensation in the utilization of human resources.

Early publications concerning PA/HRM appeared in *The Annals* and in *Engineering Magazine* (1902–1905). A book, *Social Engineering* (Tolman, 1909), provided an account of personnel

Source: Thomas A. Mahoney and John R. Deckop, "Evolution of Concept and Practice in Personnel Administration/Human Resource Management (PA/HRM), *Journal of Management,* 1986, pp. 223–241. Reprinted by permission.

practices of employers. In 1916, *The Annals* published a full issue addressing "Personnel and Employment Problems in Industrial Management," and a textbook entitled *Personnel Administration* was published in 1920 (Tead & Metcalf, 1920). That book presented what was considered to be prevailing practice in employment, compensation, discipline, and related aspects of PA/HRM. Although most of the early development of PA/HRM was through practical experimentation, research in industrial psychology also began to affect practice, particularly concerning issues of fatigue, learning curves, employee selection, job analysis, vocational guidance, and, to a lesser extent, motivation. Industrial psychology research did not, however, provide any over-arching conceptual framework for PA. Rather, various specific conceptual models from psychology were applied to different issues of PA and employment.

Industrial sociology was a second scholarly discipline to be applied in research and to influence PA. Most commonly illustrated by the Hawthorne studies, sociological research began to address issues concerning the organizational work force and to emphasize concepts of social interaction, complementing the individual-based concepts of psychology (Roethlisberger & Dickson, 1939). Also, labor economics theory and research addressed collective bargaining and the operation of labor markets. The depression of the 1930s and the problems of labor mobilization for World War II provided challenges to improved functioning of labor markets as well as to personnel administration.

Following World War II, various scholars and practitioners considered the desirability of an interdisciplinary focus on labor and personnel problems. The term *industrial relations* was proposed to encompass labor market analysis, labor relations, and personnel administration, thereby relating research from psychology, sociology, and labor economics. A professional association of scholars and practitioners was initiated (Industrial Relations Research Association) and industrial relations centers for promoting interdisciplinary research were instituted at a number of universities.

Collegiate education in PA has been traced to a five-year course of study initiated at the Tuck School of Dartmouth in 1915 (Ling, 1965). Other programs of study developed in later years, but many of these reflected the sponsoring department's orientation (e.g., labor economics, industrial psychology, industrial sociology). Aligned with efforts in the late 1940s to bring an interdisciplinary focus to industrial relations, several schools began to offer study in the broader topic of industrial relations. Many, however, continued to offer courses in the more specialized areas of personnel administration, labor economics, industrial psychology, and industrial or occupational sociology. PA, as a field of professional study, remained separate from labor market analysis, public policy of collective bargaining, and related subjects.

PA, more narrowly defined than industrial relations, was also fragmented as a field of study and practice. This is evident particularly from textbooks and practitioner-oriented "handbooks" (Scott, Clothier, & Spriegel, 1961; Yoder, 1959; Yoder, Heneman, Turnbull, & Stone, 1958). Textbooks of the late 1950s and early 1960s identified the content domain of PA as reflective of business practice and were based on a functional approach to management. Activities that were people- or employee-centered were grouped together as PA (Scott et al., 1961). This definition was reflected in content chapters, each directed toward a different set of activities, such as recruiting, job evaluation, and training. The different chapters were largely unrelated to one another, with no apparent rationale for their ordering. The objective of the activities covered in a single chapter (e.g., recruiting) was relatively clear, but the overall objective of PA was not. Evidence of human relations concepts and values appeared in the stated objectives of "attaining maximum development, desirable working relationship ... and effective molding of human resources" (Scott et al., 1961, p. 11), and "provision of leadership and direction of people in their working ... relationship" (Yoder, 1959, p. 1). The overall focus was on people and relationships at work, with heavy concern for individual development and employee morale. PA/HRM of the 1950s can be characterized as administration of a collection of activities such as recruiting, selection, training, and compensation, each designed to accomplish some objective and often related to a disciplinary theoretical model, but lacking cohesion of objective and theory. Not surprisingly, the common term for organizational practice was personnel administration.

Around 1960, there was a movement to drastically revise the curriculums of schools of business (Gordon & Howell, 1959; Pierson, 1959). One aspect of this change was increased emphasis on theoretical contributions as related to managerial practice, particularly behavioral science theories. What are now termed the organization sciences (behavior, theory, development) then evolved rapidly. In general, the focus of the organization sciences was on understanding and managing the behavior of people as individuals, in groups, and in formal organizations. Both scholarship and practice shifted from design and administration of activities to managing a work force for the accomplishment of organizational objectives. Organizational effectiveness began to replace job performance as the object of understanding and achievement.

Personnel administration and organization sciences (OS) shared a scholarship domain for some time. Both have changed since 1960. Scholarship and research in both areas share common origins and this is reflected in citations. Interestingly, OS evolved as a field of scholarship without an associated field of practice (except organizational development); PA evolved as a field of practice without an integrated conceptual base. Knowledge derived from OS has application in PA and in general management, and some integration of PA and OS seems inevitable (Strauss, 1970). The organization sciences have application in several functional fields of management, particularly PA, but have no single field of direct application. With the occasional exception of organizational development, there are no managerial positions charged with direct application of OS.

Developments in PA/HRM over the past 20 years reveal the influence of scholarship in the organization sciences and the maturation of practice in personnel administration. Concepts identified in the 1950s are being rediscovered and employed in the development of a conceptual or theoretical basis for human resource management. In a sense, developments in organization science are contributing to rediscovery of concepts from interdisciplinary contributions to industrial relations in 1950 and 1960. These can provide the integration and focus to PA/HRM that have been missing.

The industrial relations concept of the 1940s and 1950s sought an interdisciplinary focus for labor economists, psychologists, and sociologists interested in human resources in employment. The concept of industrial relations was not well defined. Its domain was viewed as all of the relationships among individuals, employers, and unions that related to work. Labor economists identified largely with relationships in the labor market, and psychologists identified mainly with relationships in the employment context. PA activities related most closely to influences from psychology, and scholarship in PA evolved relatively ignorant of contributions from economics. Yoder (1962) sought an integration of PA activities within the framework of manpower management, but did not provide any conceptual basis for this integration. Thus, PA continued to evolve as a collection of activities, each associated with a particular model or theory from psychology.

Academic scholars apparently needed an integrating paradigm or model for research and instruction, and made efforts in the 1960s and 1970s to achieve this (Somers, 1969). Textbooks of PA published after 1960 attempted models analogous to systems models, trying to integrate the various activities of PA covered in individual chapters (Glueck & Milkovich, 1982; Heneman, Schwab, Fossum, & Dyer, 1983). None of these models truly provided integration of personnel activities, and, at most, suggested that the activities individually contributed to some set of outcomes for organizations. No integration was sought between labor market analysis and PA.

RECENT CHANGES

Several basic shifts in the orientation of PA/HRM have occurred during the last 20 years, all of them seen in changes in organizational practice, in professional associations, and in the literature of the field. These shifts relate in part to the parallel development of PA and OS mentioned above.

From PA to HRM

A change in terms from personnel to human resources in managerial functions as well as in textbook titles is more than fad and fashion. It signifies a shift from a human relations focus on people as such (although also as employees) to people as resources in an employing organization. This human resource focus was voiced by Yoder in 1959 but never exploited in textbooks or in corporate titles. A shift from PA to HRM in both theory and practice has become predominant.

From Administration to Management

The change in terms again signifies change in concept and practice. Administration typically connotes a professional/staff orientation and role, whereas management connotes a more general, line-management orientation. The newer terminology is aligned with the current focus on people as human resources, resources to be managed jointly with other resources of the organization. Interesting evidence of this shift appears in the introduction of a new course at the Harvard Business School with an associated new text entitled *Human Resource Management* (Beer, Spector, Lawrence, Mills, & Walton, 1985). Employees are increasingly being viewed as organizational resources to be utilized through management.

From Human Relations to Organizational Effectiveness

Twenty years ago, PA was dominated by concepts of human relations. Employee morale and job satisfaction were viewed as desirable ends. Increasingly, the objective of both practice and theory has shifted to organizational effectiveness. This change is partly due to the development of OS, with its focus on managing organizations rather than administering activities.

The basic trends or shifts in orientation noted above can be interpreted as evidence of the impact of the developing organization sciences upon theory and practice in personnel administration. We hypothesize that, as in past decades, the shifts were apparent in the practice of PA before appearing in conceptual analyses of the function. Managers were probably implementing concepts from OS regardless of their conceptual integration with PA concepts. For example, quality of work life (QWL) projects, work team organization, and programs to develop organizational cultures are all based on concepts from OS rather than on the more traditional disciplines supporting PA. Practitioners of PA have apparently been less constrained than academics by traditional disciplinary boundaries.

We interpret these shifts as also indicative of a search for an integrating conceptual framework for PA, an integration provided in part by the conceptual orientation of the organization sciences. Concepts developing in the organization sciences and popularized in recent managerial literature are reflective of 1940s and 1950s efforts to provide conceptual integration of industrial relations. Those concepts were proposed in the context of labor market analysis and have been largely ignored by psychologists focusing on PA activities. Re-emerging as concepts from OS, they may provide a framework for the conceptual integration of PA.

Concepts of Labor Market Structure

Writing as an institutionalist economist, Kerr (1954) observed that labor markets in practice often differ considerably from one another. At one extreme, he noted the unstructured labor market characterized by (a) lack of unions and any prioritizing criteria such as seniority; (b) a transitory, impersonal relationship between employer and employee; (c) relatively unskilled workers; (d) payment on the basis of unit of production; and (e) relatively little application of capital or machinery. His example of the unstructured labor market at that time was the agricultural harvest market.

More common, however, were the labor markets structured by institutional rules and traditions. Two different types of structured labor markets were identified, one associated with communal ownership of jobs by a craft, and the other associated with one person owning one job, or what Kerr called private property concepts of job ownership.

Communal ownership is characterized by crafts or professions being associated with a set of unique jobs. Craftsmen or professionals alone are qualified to staff and perform an identifiable set of jobs. Kerr, for example, would characterize the labor market for typographers as one where entry involves qualification and often certification for the craft. Once certified, often demonstrated by union membership, the individual worker has access to a relatively standard job in a variety of employing organizations. Others are forbidden access through lack of certification. Employee mobility is horizontal from employer to employer within the craft or profession.

Private property forms of labor markets employ the concept of job ownership by the individual incumbent of the job. Individuals assigned to jobs literally own their jobs until transferred or terminated. Ownership rights change with job mobility and are governed by various rules for prioritizing movement. For example, employees might progress from one job to another with an employer on the basis of seniority. In the event of a layoff, ownership rights would be expressed in rules for bumping employees with less seniority. Mobility is more often vertical with a single employer than horizontal within a single craft or profession.

Kerr's (1954) concept of structured labor markets was based on observation of employment practices related to the traditions of craft and industrial unions. His observation was empirical and unrelated to normative prescriptions concerning PA activities. The concept appeared in later economic analysis (Doeringer & Piore, 1971), but was not incorporated into concepts of PA. Interestingly, Kerr's distinction between craft or organizationally open labor markets and private property or organizationally closed internal labor markets has reappeared in popular treatises on managerial practice based on concepts from the organization sciences (Ouchi, 1981; Peters & Waterman, 1982). Whereas Kerr's observation was empirical and lacked normative connotations, the modern treatments tend to promote adoption of the private property or organizationally closed model as opposed to the unstructured model; the craft or organizationally open labor market structure is largely ignored in popular management literature.

In summary, several stages in the evolution of PA/HRM over the past 50 years are apparent. What we know as PA/HRM began as activities practiced by employers, activities functionally linked as relating to people. Probably due to growing scholarly interest, a conceptual integration was attempted in the 1940s with the concept of industrial relations. That attempt at cohesion was unsuccessful. PA remained a collection of activities, each buttressed with theoretical models, scholarship, and professional orientation. The parallel development of OS addressed issues of managing individuals, groups, and organizations. OS influenced the practice of PA more than its conceptual framework, and HRM replaced PA in functional corporate titles before it did so in textbook titles. We perceive PA as seeking conceptual integration more in line with these shifts, and suggest that a basis for at least partial integration lies in concepts enunciated in 1954 and rediscovered recently in OS. In many ways, the conceptual evolution of PA/HRM has lagged behind managerial practice.

SPECIFIC CHANGES AND DEVELOPMENTS

The general changes in the PA/HRM field described above have been reinforced by more specific changes which have occurred in the last 20 years. These developments also suggest a merging of OS concepts and PA/HRM practices.

Evidence of these developments can be found in journal publications, texts, conference topics and presentations, and descriptions of practice. The specific subjects discussed here are our personal choice and were not derived from an exhaustive study of all potentially feasible data sources.

From Human Resource Planning to Strategy

What is known today as human resource planning has its roots in the early practice of employment planning. As it matured in practice, employment planning broadened in focus, shifting away from a specific concern for forecasting to a more inclusive, strategic perspective.

Prior to the late 1950s and early 1960s, most of the attention given to human resource planning was limited to manning tables. Concern for management development and succession and for professional staffing grew significantly in the late 1950s (Mahoney, 1961). Sophisticated forecasting and planning models developed in operations research were then being translated into applications for human resource forecasting (Grinold & Marshall, 1979). Military sponsors in particular encouraged the application of advanced forecasting and decision-making models in human resource planning (Charnes, Cooper, & Niehaus, 1972).

In its early stages, human resource planning addressed the forecasting of supply of and demand for human resources; relatively little was available by way of formal models concerning actions to reconcile supply and demand forecasts. Reconciliation of these forecasts was typically addressed by calling out possible actions like recruiting, promotion, and layoff, but not much guidance was available for evaluating such alternative actions (Milkovich & Mahoney, 1979). Some of the forecasting models found application in the simulation of recruitment and promotion policies, particularly as related to affirmative action programs (Churchill & Shank, 1976). Doubtless, some of the monitoring and reporting requirements for Equal Employment Opportunity Commission (EEOC) compliance encouraged the continued development and application of human resource planning.

Problem diagnosis and resultant contingency plans could not be accomplished, however, unless broader, more strategic concerns were considered. Diagnosis presumes prior identification of problems, and selection of contingent actions presumes earlier specification of objectives. Human resource policy and program planning presume prior specification of human resource goals and organizational strategies. Rather predictably, human resource planning evolved from a focus on forecasting to a concern for human resource links with organizational strategy. Today, there is considerable effort to establish these linkages (DeVanna, Fombrun, & Tichy, 1981; Dyer, 1983). There is not an accepted conceptual framework as yet. Various scholars are actively seeking to develop conceptual frameworks to integrate human resource activities with organizational strategy.

From Labor Relations to Governance

Labor relations or collective bargaining has always been one of the many activities related to the personnel function. The orientation to the topic, however, appears to have been changing to focus more broadly on issues of work-force governance rather than on the process of contract negotiations.

An early rationale for examination of labor relations was that organizational as well as individual relationships were included in the content domain of industrial relations. An intellectual rationalization was less important in the world of practice, and labor relations was a necessary activity in an employing organization whose work force was represented by a union. So-called personnel and labor relations were not well integrated, however, in practice or in conceptual analysis. In practice, the two sets of activities were headed by positions equal in power and responsibility. In conceptual analysis and text examination, labor relations was viewed as a process of negotiations and contract administration and as lacking a content domain. The present series of reviews perpetuates the distinction between PA/HRM and labor relations; as authors of the first review, we violate that distinction and intentionally attempt an overview of the entire domain of HRM, including labor relations.

The change to a more general conception of governance exemplifies the evolution of Dunlop's (1958) concept of "web of rules," and the incorporation of influences from themes of participative management, organizational development, and QWL experiments. Labor relations's relatively narrow focus on contract negotiations, contract administration, and conflict resolution has broadened to focus on determination and administration of the web of rules governing human resource management, or what we term work-force governance.

Related literature of the past two decades has addressed contract negotiation techniques and processes (Bazerman & Neale, 1982), reasons why employees join unions (Brett, 1980), processes of arbitration and conflict resolution (Grigsby & Bigoness, 1982; Neale, 1984), and, more recently, alternative forms of employee influence (Kochan, Katz, & Mower, 1984). Considerable research and conceptualization in QWL experimentation (Goodman, 1979), Japanese management styles (Ouchi & Jaeger, 1978), and participative management also relate to the change in focus and orientation. Conceptualization of personnel issues has traditionally been dominated by models of individual motivation and behavior, whereas labor relations has been conceptualized as interorganizational relations. The importance of groups, unionized or not, is being recognized more and more in both research and practice. For example, quality control (QC) circle experiments appear to be an effort to promote employee participation through QC circles at least as much as an effort to generate improved productivity through production suggestions. Similarly, QWL experiments appear, in many cases, to be an effort to provide a vehicle for employee participation. Not surprisingly, various spokesmen for organized labor have viewed QC circles and QWL experiments as threats to labor relations (Kochan et al., 1984). These activities are perceived as providing channels for employee influence apart from the collective bargaining relationship.

Many aspects of traditional PA/HRM view the employee as an individual (selection, training, compensation), and conceptual analysis of these topics employs models of individual behavior. Employee influence models, however, address issues from the standpoint of the entire work force and therefore require models more related to societal analysis. Concern for labor law and bargaining processes has evolved into concern for work-force participation and involvement in work decisions. In certain QWL experiments, for example, the content of the collective bargaining agreement has been excluded from consideration, illustrating how QWL efforts effectively expand work-force involvement and participation beyond the traditional issues of collective bargaining. Labor relations is no longer the only mode of work-force participation in governance. Collective bargaining is increasingly being perceived as merely one of several modes of work-force influence.

What we term work-force governance emerges from a combination of traditional labor relations and various OS concerns, particularly organizational behavior. The conceptual framework of labor relations in earlier decades addressed relationships between two parties, the employer and the union. Attention was focused on the behavior of these two parties in a negotiation context. Behavioral science influenced the analyses of individual participation in labor unions that began to enlarge the conceptual domain of labor relations (Klandermans, 1984; Ladd, Gordon, Beauvais, & Morgan, 1982). At the same time, behavioral scientists addressed issues of employee participation in management outside the context of collective bargaining. It became apparent in experiments in participative management that collective bargaining was merely one means of participation in decision making over content concerns of PA/HRM. Managers and union leaders are particularly aware of the various alternatives to collective bargaining. With this broadened focus, the dominant model of labor relations has changed from a process model of relationships between two parties to a model of work-force influence and participation in decision making.

From Morale to Climate to Culture

As an outgrowth of the human relations movement, morale came to attention as a characteristic of the work force that could potentially influence performance. Morale was loosely defined in the texts of the period as "a condition in which individuals and groups voluntarily make a reasonable subordination of their personal objectives to the ... objectives of their organization" (Davis, 1951, p. 802), and as the "feelings of employees toward work and working relationships with the employer and with other employees" (Yoder, 1959, p. 445). So-called morale surveys attempted to assess morale through measures of employee attitudes and opinions. Morale was often conceptualized as a group construct, although measured as a summation of individual opinions. Concern for morale stemmed from a presumed relationship between morale and productive performance, not unlike the presumed linkage of job satisfaction and performance. Although the satisfaction-performance hypothesis was typically attributed to human relations influences, it could possibly reflect operationalization of the work-force morale-performance hypothesis. Morale, conceptualized as a work-force characteristic, was defined and addressed as an individual characteristic of job satisfaction.

What is known today as organizational behavior concerned psychological constructs associated with aspects of PA. Morale and job satisfaction were two such constructs. Research in morale was flagging; interest in job satisfaction continued. However, job satisfaction remained a construct at the individual level. In place of morale, organizational climate emerged as a group-level construct. Climate was loosely conceptualized as aspects of work and the organizational environment influencing the beliefs, attitudes, and motivation of employees. Climate generally referred to the psychological environment of work and membership in an organization. The idea of organizational climate emerged along with that of organizational behavior, and, like morale, focused on a group or organizational variable as opposed to the individual constructs of psychology. Climate was viewed as a group psychological state which both reflected individual attitudes and influenced those attitudes and behavior (Taguiri & Litwin, 1968).

Attempts to measure climate proved difficult. Group measures such as absenteeism and turnover rates were invariably behavioral measures, and summarized individual behaviors presumed to be affected by morale and climate. Measures of individual attitudes and perceptions were often summarized in average scores, but were again presumed to reflect the unmeasured environment. Measures of more objective organizational characteristics, such as structure, were not correlated closely enough with perceptual measures to qualify as objective measures of climate. And despite considerable investment in research, the difficulties encountered in defining climate discouraged further investment (Payne & Pugh, 1976).

Most recently, the concept of climate has re-emerged as organizational culture, a mélange of beliefs, rituals, and traditions which characterize an organization (Deal & Kennedy, 1982). Organizational culture appears in such objective characteristics as dress, mannerisms, behavior, and titles, as well as in stories told by organizational members. Consistent with traditional approaches in anthropological research, culture is assessed through observation rather than through statistical summarization of self-report measures of attitude. Conceptually, organizational culture represents an evolution of the climate construct. Methodologically, it represents a shift from individual to group measurement. The culture construct also has roots in the early work of Whyte (1955) and others, just as models like Theory Z relate back to Kerr (1954).

Although the culture construct enjoys wide popularity at the moment in management circles, it is not clear what will be its lasting impact, if any, on management thought and practice. It does seem to represent, however, a further broadening and extension of the concept of climate, just as climate evolved from previous concerns for morale.

From Individual Job to Teamwork

Developing from the traditions of scientific management, the concept of tasks grouped into a job to be performed by an individual lay at the base of PA. Job analysis was a core activity resulting in job descriptions which formed the basis for selection, training, appraisal, compensation, and all staffing decisions. This model still pervades much of the conceptualization of HRM as well as the rationalization of specific practices.

Concepts of job enlargement and job enrichment have emerged from theories of motivation in organizational behavior. A body of research focusing on job design has also developed (Hackman & Oldham, 1980). These ideas have had notable impact on managerial practice, but are only slowly being integrated into conceptualizations of HRM. Models of selection, training, appraisal, and compensation are still closely tied to the concept of jobs being performed by individuals; reorientation of these models to accommodate teamwork can be anticipated in the future. At the same time, we can expect to see the concept of a job becoming less fixed and defined. Instead, organizations will be more likely to view a job as a variable, defined more by the skills and desires of the incumbent than by a rigid organizational specification.

From Problem Focus to Accountability Focus

In line with the shift from administration to management comes a related change from an activity focus to an organizational outcome focus.

Traditional concerns focused on problems such as turnover, absenteeism, and job satisfaction. With a problem focus, various activities or practices were viewed as solutions and evaluated in terms of their effect on problem measures.

Developments in recent years have shifted the focus from problem solution to assessment of organizational outcomes and of multiple outcomes of a program. Utility analysis studies financial impacts as opposed to behavioral effects (Cascio, 1982). Utility theory proposes a methodology for translating traditional human resource measures such as turnover, job performance, and training effectiveness into organizationally relevant measures of cost and profit. Beginning with analyses of selection practices (e.g., Schmidt, Hunter, McKensie, & Muldrow, 1979), utility analysis has been extended to the assessment of human resource transactions from selection to separation (Boudreau & Berger, 1985), training (Schmidt, Hunter, & Pearlman, 1982), performance evaluation (Landy, Farr, & Jacobs, 1982), and employment planning (Steffy & Werling, 1985). Utility analysis illustrates the evolution from a professional/activity orientation to a managerial/organizational orientation. Further evidence of change is a growing concern to relate HRM to organizational productivity (Schneider, 1985). Productivity has long been a concern of human resource managers and others, but coupled with utility analysis, productivity assessment may become operational as the rationale for HRM.

From Training to Development

The traditional activity of training has evolved over the years into what is now termed development. Training is still an element of HRM, but employee development, which includes training, has surpassed it in interest and attention.

Training focuses on the learning of skills and teaches specific patterns of behavior. Training aims at reducing the variance of behavior among employees performing a specific task or job. Development, however, addresses the elaboration or enhancement of basic, underlying aptitudes or abilities. Given some distribution of abilities, development seeks to increase the variance among individuals as they are developed to their fullest potential.

Training is typified by learning models (McGehee & Thayer, 1961) and development by models of growth (Sonnenfeld, 1984). Training is accomplished in controlled settings, whereas development is subject to a far wider set of experiences. Management development in the 1950s and 1960s was clearly differentiated from training and was viewed as the full range of experiential influences in employee staffing and performance (Mahoney, 1961).

Training continues as an interest of HRM, but it has increasingly been integrated with the broader concern of employee development. Today, issues of career development (Sonnenfeld, 1984), stress (Latack, 1984), chemical dependency (Dickman & Emener, 1982), and employee counseling (Cairo, 1983) are integrated with training as part of overall employee development. This concern for development parallels heightened interest in lifetime employment and what has been termed "performance oriented paternalism" (Dyer, Foltman, & Milkovich, 1984). In brief, the orientation is toward development of the individual's full potential for employment rather than toward provision of specific, job-oriented skills.

PA/HRM ACTIVITIES IN NEED OF INTEGRATION

Various developments and changes in PA/HRM have been noted. Although all of these occurred relatively independently of one another, we interpret them as symptomatic of a search for a unifying framework focusing on human resources in the accomplishment of organizational performance.

Until recently, PA could be characterized as a functional collection of managerial activities and practices directed at people as employees. Conceptual theory (where available) and managerial practice in an activity were relatively independent of other activities. Each discipline, for example, applied disciplinary models or paradigms to analysis of specific human resource issues. Employee compensation was viewed as a market phenomenon by labor economists and as a reward influencing individual motivation by industrial psychologists. Employee selection was approached as an application of psychometric classification and prediction. Employee training and development was viewed as the application of learning theory. Personnel administration involved the application of theories and models of basic social science disciplines to the management of people at work, and there was no framework unifying the different models or their applications.

Absence of a unifying theory or framework was not troublesome as long as thinking proceeded linearly from practice or intervention to effect, without consideration of interaction effects. It became troublesome, however, as diagnostic analysis emerged. Analysis backward from effect to cause could identify many branches which interacted in producing a particular effect. Thus, for example, high turnover might be attributed to improper selection, inadequate training, and/or low wages. Further, the interventions of selection, training, and compensation are interrelated; training effects depend critically on the quality of the trainee, and the size and potential of the pool for selection depends on the relative level of wages. Attempts at diagnostic and contingency analysis clearly indicated the lack of a unifying theory for HRM.

The absence of a theoretical framework was doubtless more disturbing to scholars than to practitioners. Human resource managers appear to have sought integration of activities with organizational outcomes through human resource planning and cost effectiveness assessments (Cheek, 1973). Most recently, the concept of a closed or organizational career labor market popularized in the management literature has provided a basis for integration of PA/HRM activities. PA/HRM activities have been designed to develop and promote a Theory Z model. An alternative approach to integration pursued by some scholars and practitioners is to design PA/HRM activities to support specific corporate strategies.

The integration of PA/HRM activities within the context of corporate strategy holds appeal (Angle, Manz, & Van de Ven, 1985). Imposing "prospector" and "defender" strategy concepts could provide a framework for integrating PA/ HRM activities (Miles & Snow, 1984). Certainly, the orientation toward recruitment, selection, training and development, and compensation would vary depending on basic strategic orientation, which would provide a basis for integration of PA/HRM activities. Unfortunately, there is as yet no accepted, finite set of strategic orientations.

We suggest that the roots of a conceptual framework for the integration of PA/HRM already exist. They are evident in Kerr's (1954) concepts of labor market structure, especially as elaborated in popular management literature, and in prevailing PA/HRM practice. Much of current practice is already integrated around these different labor market structures. Theory and research have not yet incorporated the related concepts, which could help in unifying PA/HRM. These concepts might be viewed as PA/HRM strategies, each of which could be aligned with different corporate strategies. Given an organizational orientation toward (a) a craft or job structure (Kerr's communal structure), (b) an organizational career structure (Kerr's private property structure), or (c) an unstructured market, choice among the variants of practice in PA/HRM activities would be constrained, and each would have to support the basic orientation.

Craft or Job Structure

The craft or job structure depends on a supply of qualified candidates for employment, candidates who can be presumed qualified for minimal performance upon hiring. This presumption is most valid for an occupation and/or industry where jobs are relatively standard among employers, permitting easy transferability of skills. General training is obtained at the employee's expense prior to employment, and some form of skill certification is desired. Traditional examples of craft workers would include electricians and heavy equipment operators, whose training is obtained through an apprenticeship program and whose qualifications are certified by licensure; modern examples would include teachers, nurses, and engineers. Such workers can move relatively easily from one employer to another with ready transferability of skills.

Selection strategies in such cases would emphasize skill level rather than developmental potential and would typically rely heavily on assessments of prior training and experience. Approaches to job design would be somewhat constrained, because easy mobility among employers is contingent on relatively standard jobs among employing organizations. The employer's training activities would focus on orientation to employer practices and on unique job elements, not on the development of general skills transferable to other employers. Aspects of compensation most relevant in this structure would be competitive comparability with other employers and specific performance incentives; compensation structure would be less relevant because employees would not seek advancement within the organization. Market-based wage structures would probably be the norm.

The craft or job structure would be most feasible in a fairly structured setting where employment demands are variable. Examples would include engineers in the aerospace industry, crafts people in the construction industry, and nurses in health care. Employees are hired and terminated relatively easily as demands vary. Some occupations and industries have even developed association-wide systems of pensions and benefits which accommodate easy employer mobility (e.g., construction and teaching).

For the occupational/industry examples above, implementation of a craft or job structure depends on external performance of certain HRM functions such as education and training, certification, and even benefit administration. The employing organization adapts to the existing external structure and/or contributes to its design and maintenance. This external structure, although supportive of the internal HRM structure, also constrains the design of internal HRM strategy and practice.

Organizational Career Structure

The organizational career structure of PA/HRM illustrates many of the concepts of OS, particularly as popularized in management literature. Employees are hired in entry-level positions and advance within the organization through training and development. Specialized knowledge of the organization and its configurations of jobs is more critical to performance than general knowledge of standardized skills available through prior training. Consequently, there are fewer opportunities to move from one employer to another, and employment security is emphasized.

Recruitment and selection identify employees who have developmental potential and who are unlikely to terminate. Extensive training and development activities at all levels assure potential candidates for promotion. Succession planning and employee appraisal are likely to be important functions as well. Maintenance of an equitable, rewarding, internal compensation structure would probably be more critical than alignment with external market rates, because recruiting is restricted to entry-level jobs. Concepts of job design and/or teamwork have more application in the career structure than in the job structure because of relaxation of the constraint of standardized jobs; the organization of work in the career structure can be designed and altered to fit organizational characteristics over time.

Examples of PA/HRM career structures are organizations such as Hewlett Packard and IBM, and managerial occupations in many organizations. The career structure of PA/HRM for managerial and administrative positions probably evolved without much conscious thought, whereas the Hewlett Packard and IBM structures appear to have resulted from conscious choice. We can speculate that for managers and administrators, organizational knowledge is more important to performance than is professional knowledge; presumed benefits for Hewlett Packard and IBM may include improved cooperation, loyalty, and work-force flexibility.

Adoption of a career structure would appear to be most feasible where employment levels are reasonably stable or growing at a steady rate; wild fluctuations in employment or growth at a rate faster than people could be developed would be difficult to accommodate. A PA/HRM career structure would appear to be congruent only with product and market strategies which would permit the planning and commitments involved.

Both job and career structures as well as combinations of both concepts can be observed in a single organization. For example, university faculty members are employed within a job structure, whereas university administrators are employed within a career structure. Alternatively, production employees in the steel industry were employed for decades in a system incorporating both job and career elements. Production workers were hired into a labor pool and advanced through seniority in any of a number of career sequences, but jobs were relatively standardized across the industry as well. The concepts of job and career structures are probably best viewed as archetypes, not as a finite set of PA/HRM structures and strategies.

Unstructured Market

What Kerr (1954) called the unstructured labor market is a third alternative strategy and conforms to what economists term the secondary labor market. The other HRM structures involve a commitment to either occupation or organization; commitment in the unstructured market is minimal and revolves around a wage contract only. Jobs may be structured or unstructured, but make almost no demands on skill or ability. Jobs are often entry jobs without any significant career potential. Neither the employee nor the employer invests significantly in education or training and development. Compensation may be based on production, but is more commonly based on time worked, and working hours are adjusted with production demands.

The feasibility of an unstructured approach to HRM would vary with the availability of a continuing pool of ready workers and the existence of jobs with varying demands for labor. A work process depending on a series of jobs being staffed every day could not be easily managed without more commitment than is achieved in the unstructured setting. Examples of application of the unstructured approach would include unskilled counter help at fast-food outlets, delivery of telephone directories, and agricultural harvesting and canning. Agencies for temporary help illustrate institutional bridging of unstructured and structured labor markets; the hiring of temporary agency employees permits employers the flexibility of the unstructured market for jobs which may require considerable training. Traditional HRM functions of training, appraisal, and recruiting are performed by the temporary agency, leaving the employer with only a wage commitment.

FUTURE DIRECTIONS

Much experimentation in HRM has already occurred in practice. We already find employers utilizing a mix of craft, career, and unstructured HRM approaches for different segments of their work forces. These approaches have evolved over time without conscious thought for the integration of HRM activities. The popularization of OS concepts integrated into Theory Z or other alternative models has contributed to an awareness of potential choices among HRM approaches. Similarly, recognition of alternative organizational cultures has fostered awareness of choices and the opportunity to shape cultures. Unfortunately, there is little in HRM theory and research to guide those choices; most theory and research has been confined to individual HRM components such as selection validity, job evaluation, and training evaluation. Reformulation of HRM theory and research to align with alternative HRM strategies or approaches could advance both scholarship and practice.

The three HRM models reviewed above are posed as HRM strategy alternatives. Each appears to require unique variants of traditional HRM practices; practices in selecting, compensating, and training are designed to complement the particular strategy. Each also appears to align with particular environmental variations of product demand, industry standardization, educational support, and the like. Yet these environment-strategy-practice links are only commonsensical and lack both theoretical rationalization and empirical verification.

Imposing an HRM strategy concept upon the analysis of HRM activities could provide a framework for at least partial integration of HRM theory and practice, integration within an HRM strategy focus. Instead of a functional orientation (e.g., employee selection with multiple adaptations to different situations), the orientation would be HRM strategy relating functional concerns within a strategy category. Attention would be directed toward such questions as, "Given an organizational career strategy, what mix of HRM policies and practices is required to support that strategy?" and, "Within what set of organizational and environmental constraints is a given HRM strategy likely to be most effective?" Conceptual integration would be enhanced and empirical research would be redirected from investigation of individual practice variants to a more aggregated level of programmatic variants.

The basic shifts from personnel to human resources, from administration to management, and from human relations to organizational effectiveness have already been accomplished, although not yet effectuated throughout history. Integration of OS and PA/HRM concepts has probably been advanced more in practice than in scholarship. We foresee continued integration, and propose a focus on HRM strategy as a means of integration. The HRM strategic orientations advanced here themselves represent integration of the organizational career strategy popularized by OS with the wider range of strategies advanced in the 1950s from a different perspective. Future reviews of this type can report on the predictive validity of our projections.

REFERENCES

Angle, H., Manz, C., & Van de Ven, A. (1985). Integrating human resource management and corporate strategy: A preview of the 3M story. *Human Resources Management, 24*(1), 51–68.

Bazerman, M., & Neale, M. (1982). Improving negotiation effectiveness under final offer arbitration: The role of selection and training. *Journal of Applied Psychology, 67*(1), 45–52.

Beer, M., Spector, B., Lawrence, P. R., Mills, D. Q., & Walton, R. E. (1985). *Human resource management*. New York: The Free Press.

Boudreau, J., & Berger, C. (1985). Decision-theoretic utility analysis applied to employee separations and acquisitions. *Journal of Applied Psychology, 70*(3), 581–612.

Brett, J. (1980). Why employees want unions. *Organizational Dynamics, 8*(4), 47–59.

Cairo, P. (1983). Counseling in industry: A selected review of the literature. *Personnel Psychology, 36,* 1–18.

Cascio, W. (1982). *Costing human resources: The financial impact of behavior in organizations.* Boston: Kent.

Charnes, A., Cooper, W., & Niehaus, R. (1972). *Studies in manpower planning.* Washington, DC: Department of Navy.

Cheek, L. M. (1973). Cost effectiveness comes to the personnel function. *Harvard Business Review, 51*(3), 96–105.

Churchill, N., & Shank, J. (1976). Affirmative action and guilt-edged goals. *Harvard Business Review, 54*(2), 111–116.

Davis, R. C. (1951). *The fundamentals of top management.* New York: Harper.

Deal, T., & Kennedy, A. (1982). *Corporate cultures.* Reading, MA: Addison-Wesley.

DeVanna, M., Fombrun, C., & Tichy, N. (1981). Human resources management: A strategic perspective. *Organizational Dynamics, 9*(3), 51–67.

Doeringer, P., & Piore, M. (1971). *Internal labor markets and manpower analysis.* Lexington, MA: D.C. Heath.

Dunlop, J. (1958). *Industrial relations systems.* New York: Henry Holt.

Dyer, L. (1983). Bringing human resources into the strategy formulation process. *Human Resource Management, 23* (Fall), 257–271.

Dyer, L., Foltman, F., & Milkovich, G. (1984). Contemporary employment stabilization practices. In T. Kochan & T. Barocci (Eds.), *Human resource management and industrial relations* (pp. 203–213). Boston: Little, Brown.

Glueck, W. F., & Milkovich, G. T. (1982). *Personnel: A diagnostic approach.* Plano, TX: Business Publications.

Goodman, P. (1979). *Assessing organizational change: The Rushton quality of work experiment.* New York: Wiley.

Gordon, R. A., & Howell, J. (1959). *Higher education for business.* New York: Columbia University Press.

Grigsby, D., & Bigoness, W. (1982). Effects of mediation and alternative forms of arbitration on bargaining behavior: A laboratory study. *Journal of Applied Psychology, 67*(5), 549–554.

Grinold, R., & Marshall, K. (1979). *Manpower planning models.* New York: Elsevier North-Holland.

Hackman, J., & Oldham, G. (1980). *Work redesign.* Reading, MA: Addison-Wesley.

Heneman, H. G., III, Schwab, D. P., Fossum, J. A., & Dyer, L. D. (1983). *Personnel/human resource management.* Homewood, IL: Richard D. Irwin.

Kerr, C. (1954). The Balkanization of labor markets. In E. W. Bakke, P. M. Hauser, G. L.

Palmer, C. A. Myers, D. Yoder, & C. Kerr (Eds.), *Labor mobility and economic opportunity* (pp. 93–109). New York: Wiley.

Klandermans, P. (1984). Mobilization and participation in trade union action: An expectancy-value approach. *Journal of Occupational Psychology, 57*(2), 107–120.

Kochan, T., Katz, H., & Mower, N. (1984). *Worker participation and American unions*. Kalamazoo, MI: W.E. Upjohn Institute.

Ladd, R., Gordon, M., Beauvais, L., & Morgan, R. (1982). Union commitment: Replication and extension. *Journal of Applied Psychology, 67*(5), 640–644.

Landy, F., Farr, J., & Jacobs, R. (1982). Utility concepts in performance measurement. *Organizational Behavior and Human Performance, 30,* 15–40.

Latack, J. (1984). Career transitions within organizations: An exploratory study of work, nonwork, and coping strategies. *Organizational Behavior and Human Performance, 34,* 296–322.

Ling, C. (1965). *The management of personnel relations*. Homewood, IL: Richard D. Irwin.

Mahoney, T. (1961). *Building the executive team: A guide to management development*. Englewood Cliffs, NJ: Prentice-Hall.

McGehee, W., & Thayer, P. (1961). *Training in business and industry*. New York: Wiley.

Miles, R., & Snow, C. (1984). Designing strategic human resource systems. *Organizational Dynamics, 13*(8), 36–52.

Milkovich, G., & Mahoney, T. (1979). Human resource planning and PAIR policy. In D. Yoder & H. Heneman (Eds.), *ASPA handbook of personnel and industrial relations* (pp. 2–1 to 2–30). Washington, DC: Bureau of National Affairs.

Neale, M. (1984). The effects of negotiation and arbitration cost salience on bargaining behavior: The role of the arbitrator and constituency on negotiator judgment. *Organizational Behavior & Human Performance, 34*(1), 97–111.

Ouchi, W. G. (1981). *Theory Z*. Reading, MA: Addison-Wesley.

Ouchi, W., & Jaeger, A. (1978). Type Z organization: Stability in the midst of mobility. *Academy of Management Review, 3,* 305–314.

Payne, R., & Pugh, D. (1976). Organizational structure and climate. In M. Dunnette (Ed.), *Handbook of industrial and organizational psychology* (pp. 1125–1174). Chicago: Rand McNally.

Peters, T. J., & Waterman, R. H. (1982). *In search of excellence*. New York: Harper & Row.

Pierson, F. C. (1959). *The education of American businessmen*. New York: McGraw-Hill.

Roethlisberger, F. J., & Dickson, W. J. (1939). *Management and the worker*. Cambridge, MA: Harvard University Press.

Schmidt, F., Hunter, J., McKensie, R., & Muldrow, T. (1979). Impact of valid selection procedures on work-force productivity. *Journal of Applied Psychology, 64,* 609–626.

Schmidt, F., Hunter, J., & Pearlman, K. (1982). Assessing the economic impact of personnel programs on workforce productivity. *Personnel Psychology, 35,* 333–347.

Schneider, B. (1985). Organizational behavior. *Annual Review of Psychology, 36,* 573–611.

Scott, W. D., Clothier, R. C., & Spriegel, W. R. (1961). *Personnel management*. New York: McGraw-Hill.

Somers, G. (1969). *Essays in industrial relations theory*. Ames, IA: Iowa State University Press.

Sonnenfeld, J. (1984). *Managing career systems: Channeling the flow of executive careers*. Homewood, IL: Richard D. Irwin.

Steffy, B., & Werling, S. (1985). Incorporating human resource planning models into utility analysis to determine the long-term impact of selection and training. In R. Robinson & J. Pearce (Eds.), *Proceedings of the 45th annual meeting of the Academy of Management* (pp. 279–283). San Diego, CA.

Strauss, G. (1970). Organizational behavior and personnel relations. In W. L. Ginsburg, E. R. Livernash, H. S. Parnes, & G. Strauss (Eds.), *A review of industrial relations research* (pp. 145–206). Madison, WI: Industrial Relations Research Association.

Taguiri, R., & Litwin, G. (1968). *Organizational climate: Exploration of a concept*. Cambridge, MA: Harvard University Press.

Taylor, F. W. (1911). *The principles of scientific management*. New York: Harper & Bros.

Tead, D., & Metcalf, A. C. (1920). *Personnel administration*. New York: McGraw-Hill.

Tolman, W. H. (1909). *Social engineering*. New York: McGraw-Hill.

Trice, H., Beyer, J., Dickman, F., & Emener, W. G. (1982). Employee assistance programs: Basic concepts, attributes and an evaluation. *Personnel Administrator,* August, 55–66.

Whyte, W. F. (1955). *Money and motivation*. New York: Harper.

Yoder, D. (1959). *Personnel principles and policies*. Englewood Cliffs, NJ: Prentice-Hall.

Yoder, D. (1962). *Personnel management & industrial relations* (5th ed.). Englewood Cliffs, NJ: Prentice-Hall.

Yoder, D., Heneman, H., Jr., Turnbull, J., & Stone, C. (1958). *Handbook of personnel management and labor relations.* New York: McGraw-Hill.

Thomas A. Mahoney and John R. Deckop are affiliated with Vanderbilt University. Preparation of this article was supported by the Dean's Research Fund of the Owen Graduate School of Management, Vanderbilt University.

HRIS: Much More Than an Automated Filing Cabinet
Ellen J. Frank

Every detail of HR data is a piece of a gigantic and complex companywide information jigsaw puzzle. HR managers who correctly select and relate those pieces of information can directly support companywide growth and development.

HRISs that best contribute to companywide management share the following two basic capabilities:

- They can expand individual employee records to accept additional data fields — HR software should facilitate data sorting on any combination of data fields. The system's contribution to managerial decision making and personnel research increases dramatically if the HRIS has the power to select and define subsets of employees.
- They can format HR data so it can be readily analyzed for all possible organizational levels (e.g., division, location, department, and job title) — By means of a coded message, this function, whose design requires the most thought, can identify each of the company's job positions and can categorize employees' records into as many meaningful subgroups as are required to study personnel problems.

The number of fields required by an employee's identification code (ID) depends on an organization's complexity. For example, a large, geographically dispersed organization might use IDs arranged in seven sectors that reflect the same structure defined by the organization's reporting chart (see Exhibit 1).

If a job classification system is part of the compensation plan, or if budget account codes identify positions for financial planning, it should be incorporated into each employee's ID whenever possible. And by overlapping the personnel ID number with other corporate information systems, data sets can be merged when needed, thereby serving the greatest number of users companywide.

ORGANIZATIONAL CENSUS

Just as governments monitor changes in the composition of their national populations, senior executives should monitor their own constituencies. Employee biographical data analyzed in conjunction with employee behavior patterns or

Source: Ellen J. Frank, "HRIS: Much More Than an Automated Filing Cabinet." Reprinted from *Computers in Personnel* (New York: Auerbach Publishers). © 1988 Warren, Gorham & Lamont, Inc. Used with permission.

EXHIBIT 1
ID Fields Corresponding to an Organization Chart

Region: Eastern, North America
Location: New York City, Building 2
Division: Consumer Products, Personnel
Department: Compensation, Purchasing
Section: Wage and Hours, Subcontracting
Classification: Clerical, Union, Technical, Professional
Job Title: Secretary II, Warehouse Worker

---

performance measures can help identify those employees who require additional management attention.

Census data (e.g., age, sex, race, marital status, number of dependents, education, date of hire, and date of termination) is fundamental to any HRIS. Employees' salary and performance-appraisal data should also be included in a format suitable for analysis and cross tabulating with other HR and performance variables.

A practical use for census data is tracking the results of EEO/AAPs (equal employment opportunity/affirmation action plans). The following questions could reveal information that would be helpful to any manager:

- What is the percentage of middle-level managers in each department who are women?
- What is the number of minority-group employees hired in the last 12 months for technical positions?
- What is the number of employees 40 years of age and older who left the company involuntarily?

Managers can generate the answers to these questions by specifying the appropriate parameter values for employees' IDs and by sorting and cross tabulating the appropriate data fields.

Compensation managers might use census data from an HRIS to study the contingency relationships between employees' performance and their salaries. Or they might compare average salaries with industrywide salary surveys and then compare these results with company turnover figures to determine whether employees are leaving the organization because of perceived inequities in compensation.

Recruitment and selection managers might want to generate the following information about job seekers as well as their own companies' successful new hires:

- The biographic profiles of the people applying for entry-level production jobs in the company.
- The educational level of clerical employees.
- The average age of the work force.
- How employees in Location A compare with employees doing the same job in Location B.

Benefits managers could use a census to help create optimal benefits packages. For example, if the census shows that increasing numbers of women with children are being hired, HR managers would probably investigate day-care programs. Or they can use the HR data to determine which benefits to emphasize in a forthcoming employee-relations campaign. If the census indicates an aging work force, HR managers might stimulate better attendance and performance through increased medical and pension benefits.

Managers administering performance appraisals could use a flexible HRIS to monitor evaluation results and identify which groups of employees generally are receiving low supervisory ratings. Managers might also query the system regarding distribution of appraisals (e.g., Do departments use the full range of performance categories, or do they instead show leniency error?). Performance evaluations are poor — or even useless — motivators if all employees receive similar ratings despite any variation among their actual performances.

The only problem in using organizational HR census data to improve managerial effectiveness is that all kinds of managers generate census-related questions with increasing volume and frequency.

TRAINING AND DEVELOPMENT

It would be helpful to leaders of orientation programs and new sales training courses to know what previous trainees thought of the programs.

An HRIS can help track training needs through a training coding system. For example, it may be beneficial to track all in-service courses that employees have attended during their employment. In many cases, however, tracking an employee's two or three most recent courses is sufficient to identify future training needs.

As employees complete training programs, the code number and date of completion (in sortable form) should be entered into their individual files. If, for example, a companywide orientation program is coded "02," the training department can request a list of all names not followed by the "02" code. If the old sales program is coded "07," the training department can request names with "07" and a year. If a company decides to establish a course to retrain older employees, the system can be used to update and monitor the progress of both presentations and employees.

When the training and development department prepares its year-end training report, it can easily include quantitative information beyond simple attendance records. It might consider reporting head counts according to the length of the training course attended, department or unit, EEO category, or other subgroupings that give top management an accurate idea of the value of training to the organization.

TURNOVER

An HRIS can be instructed to answer several significant questions about employee turnover, such as the following:

- What are the two most frequently given reasons for resignation by salespeople about to leave the company?
- Which production units suffer the greatest turnover?
- Do younger workers leave more often than older workers?

If your company never established an exit interview procedure, you may want to consider developing one and collecting the information in the HRIS. Properly handled — in a nonthreatening environment — employees who are about to leave can provide valuable insight into organizational deficiencies. Enlightened management should consider negative comments as potential symptoms of serious productivity and morale problems.

Exit interviews can provide most of the information needed to generate a list of reasons for resignations. This list can be supported by some basic library research or by requesting information from professional associations. Although resigning employees should be asked to complete a brief exit interview form, face-to-face interviews are preferable because the information can be more substantial. (You might consider asking for two or three reasons for the resignation; in many cases, leaving a job involves a combination of circumstances.)

At the end of the quarter — or end of the year, depending on company size — a summary report of the exit interviews can be generated, listing conditions most frequently cited as a cause for leaving and identifying which departments have a pattern of turnover that might reflect a need for additional investigation and organizational change. This report might also point out patterns of biographical characteristics of resigning employees (e.g., age, sex, marital status, education level, and average seniority). For example, an effort should be made to overcome a pattern of resignations by young, well-educated and ambitious professionals.

INTERNAL RECRUITMENT

Answers to the following questions, generated by manipulating HRIS data fields, can support internal transfer and promotion decisons:

- Which employees want to be considered for specific jobs when they become available?
- Who would accept a transfer to another region?
- Who has the experience necessary for a new job?

An internal recruiting system requires that employees be asked periodically to update their answers to availability questions, such as:

- For which available jobs would you like to be considered, given that you have the basic qualifications? Your responses can be entered using the fields of ID code that specify each position.
- Are you willing to relocate to other company locations or to work alternative shifts?
- Which hobbies and outside interests might you translate into full-time jobs that could benefit both you and the organization?

An internal recruiting system gains power and flexibility when employees' previous ID numbers are retained as part of their personnel file. The old IDs are a means of tracking an individual employee's career movement. For example, if a position for sales manager requires sales and supervisory experience in the western region, the company's recruiting department could request a list of names of those employees who are willing to work in the western region, who have ID history files indicating sales and sales-supervisor experience, who have indicated an interest in moving to a managerial position, and who have received outstanding performance evaluations.

CORPORATE CREDIBILITY

For decades, HR departments were stereotyped as performing only clerical or recordkeeping activities. Now, HR professionals can earn the same status, respect, and salary as other departmental VPs and can make contributions to major corporate decisions. HRISs must also earn that same type of organizational credibility by being more than big electronic file cabinets. These systems integrated into senior management's countrywide decision making can gain respect as a resource that readily provides the data needed to improve organizational productivity.

Ellen J. Frank is associate professor of management at Southern Connecticut State University, New Haven.

Cases

The Midvale Plant (A): The Reorganized Personnel Department

The Midvale plant of the Abacus Corporation is located in a suburb of Metro City, some fifteen miles from the corporate main office and major manufacturing facilities in the central city. The plant was established as the principal source of small coil windings and subassemblies for the company's radio and television production. In its first fifteen years of operation, the plant experienced a slow, steady growth to a size of three hundred employees, twenty-five of whom were management or supervisory personnel. Many technical and managerial services were provided by home-office personnel, whom the Midvale people referred to as "city folk" located at "the city."

The plant manager at Midvale, George Whitfield, had twenty-five years with the corporation and had been on his present job for eleven years. He was interested primarily in the production work at the plant, constantly striving for increased output, and he displayed very little interest in personnel administration. He left routine personnel matters in the plant to the supervisors and his secretary, Miss Martin.

The employee group at Midvale consisted primarily of production workers, a majority of whom were female. The plant was not highly regarded by employees in the company because many of them felt that Midvale was a "dumping ground" and that anyone assigned to it probably had little future with the company. Until two years ago employees at the plant had resisted all attempts to be organized by labor unions. About that time, however, the morale of most departments was not good, and a majority of the employees felt a need for some form of union representation. One of the unions that represented employees in the main plant became interested in the group at Midvale and determined to organize them. The union-organizing campaign met little resistance, and a short time later the union won recognition from the company as the bargaining agent for Midvale production employees. The union-relations and collective-bargaining activities were carried on by management representatives from the central manufacturing office.

PLANT GROWTH AND REORGANIZATION

The Midvale plant started to grow rapidly. In three years' time, production at

Source: Raymond L. Hilgert, Sterling H. Schoen, and Joseph W. Towle, Cases and Policies in *Personnel/Human Resources Management,* 5th ed. Boston: Houghton Mifflin Company, 1986. Reprinted by permission.

All names and places are disguised.

the plant almost doubled. The payroll of production employees grew to 650; the management group increased to 60 personnel, of whom over half were female supervisors and managers. This growth necessitated the expansion of manufacturing facilities, which formerly occupied a one-story building. An adjoining two-story warehouse was taken over by the Midvale plant, and several new production units were installed in it. Once the decision to expand was made, major changes occurred frequently in every department and unit. Many times the employees found that their workbenches or desks had been moved or their supervisors changed before adequate explanations were made to them. Situations of this kind often had to be handled by the union as complaints or grievances discussed with the plant manager.

As a result of rapid growth and many personnel changes in the plant, a complete reorganization of line-and-staff functions took place. The parent Abacus Corporation sent several new managerial people to Midvale from other manufacturing plants. George Whitfield, who previously had had four departments and the office manager reporting to him, was relieved of all other responsibility and was given supervision over the assembly department. He moved his office from the attractive quarters in the front of the plant to a small room in the warehouse building where the assembly department was relocated. Two of the men who assumed departmental supervisory jobs in the new organization were brought in from other company plants.

A new plant manager and experienced manufacturing executive, Oliver Hawk, was transferred from the company's main office to Midvale. After participating in the reorganization of other Abacus plants, Mr. Hawk had become a strong proponent of decentralization in management and organization. He insisted on the transfer of accounting, production control, labor relations, and personnel functions from the home office to the Midvale plant. In addition, he appointed one of his former assistants to the position of plant controller, with responsibility for certain records, bookkeeping, and cost and payroll activities. Some of these functions, especially payroll and employee records, had been handled by the office manager, whose responsibilities after the reorganization were reduced to office services, the purchase of supplies, and the stenographic pool.

In spite of these changes and rapid growth, the work in the plant continued to be handled quite well. Production and financial results improved each year even though the changes taking place had created many problems.

PERSONNEL MANAGEMENT

Before the reorganization, the personnel work in the plant, consisting primarily of hiring, general wage and salary administration, union relations, and the like, was theoretically provided by the industrial-relations section in the home office. Actually, the department heads at Midvale employed most of their workers personally, even though the paperwork and formal procedures required services from the employment office at "the city." Over the years the majority of the work concerning routine salary and wage administration, employee benefits, vacations, incidental absences, and so forth, had been handled by Miss Martin, George

EXHIBIT 1
The Midvale Plant Organization Chart Before Reorganization

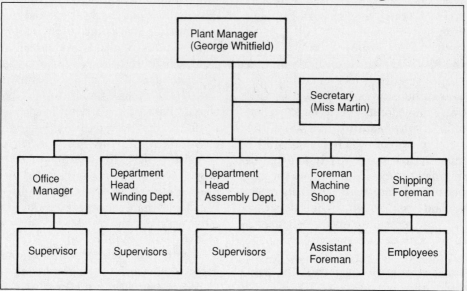

Whitfield's secretary, who acted as an unofficial chief clerk. Everyone at Midvale had come to look to her for answers to routine personnel questions, and she had accepted these responsibilities willingly. She took a great deal of pride in being "busy," and she derived pleasure from telling her associates that she did not "know what they would do without her." With Miss Martin assuming authority and responsibility in routine personnel matters, supervisors usually did not try to answer questions from their employees involving personnel policies, but instead referred them to Miss Martin. Few of Miss Martin's rulings, procedures, and practices were in writing, and she stated frequently that she preferred to keep most personnel policies "flexible, and juggle them around in my head as needed." Miss Martin was well liked by the union stewards at Midvale, and most union grievances were minor and quickly settled.

At the time of the reorganization, Mr. Hawk decided that a full-time personnel supervisor was needed in the plant. A young man named Tom Jones, a college-educated junior executive having several years' experience with the parent company, was appointed to this new post. Most department heads and supervisors at Midvale welcomed this appointment because they believed that Tom Jones would handle all their problems in much the same way that Miss Martin had previously done, and with more expertise.

Tom Jones was given wide latitude in setting up the personnel department. A general description of his authority, provided by Mr. Hawk, was as follows:

To be responsible for labor-relations activities and to represent the company in bargaining with the union. To be responsible for the hiring, placement, and induction of employees in the plant. To be responsible for wage and salary administration. To be responsible for the liaison of all plant matters with the benefit department in the home office. To be responsible for employee activities, leaves of absence, disability, incidental absence, and so on, and to act in a staff capacity.

In setting up the new department, Tom Jones appointed a personnel assistant, Ethel Asper, and delegated most of the responsibility related to employment of workers to her. In addition, Miss Martin was assigned to the personnel office and given the title of chief clerk. In terms of her salary, this was not a demotion, but neither was it a promotion. Miss Martin did not look on it too kindly, and she appeared to be envious of the new personnel assistant. She decided to retire a few months earlier than necessary. Miss Martin left the company shortly after Tom Jones arrived to assume his responsibilities. He promptly appointed June Eiler to the chief clerk's job. June, naturally, was entirely unfamiliar with the work that had been handled by Miss Martin.

ORGANIZATIONAL RELATIONS

The majority of the managers and supervisors in the plant had been trained under George Whitfield and believed that technical and production aspects of their jobs were more important than personnel and human-relations problems. One department head, Alice Jeffries, was quoted as having said, "I hope this new fellow Jones doesn't hold a lot of meetings and keep my people off the job." However, the newer supervisors and department heads who had transferred into Midvale had worked in plants that had personnel supervisors. They seemed to be more accustomed to the new organization and the services available from a personnel department.

After assuming his job as personnel supervisor, Tom Jones found that the new chief clerk, June Eiler, was being consulted on routine personnel matters as Miss Martin had. He was disturbed by a telephone call from George Whitfield, who said, "Tom, I know that you are new on this job, but you'll have to do something about vacation plans. One of our women on the assembly line was told by Miss Martin that she could take her vacation in May, and now your chief clerk says she had to wait until June. You'll probably have to talk to her.

"And there's another thing. A month ago we started to hire a young fellow named Jorgenson for benchwork, filing, polishing, and miscellaneous work. Miss Martin and I thought we had him hired, but the employment office over at the city stopped it, saying we can't hire anyone who's not a high school graduate. Why in hell does a filer have to be a high school graduate? Now this applicant isn't a relative or a friend or anything special, but I have a supervisor who's going to be very unhappy until we get that young guy on the payroll. You're going to have to do something about these problems and get them handled the way Miss Martin used to do."

Tom tried to interrupt and answer but Whitfield went right on talking. "And I think you ought to know that the union reps are stirring up a fuss about some of the things going on around here. The

EXHIBIT 2

The Midvale Plant Organization Chart after Reorganization

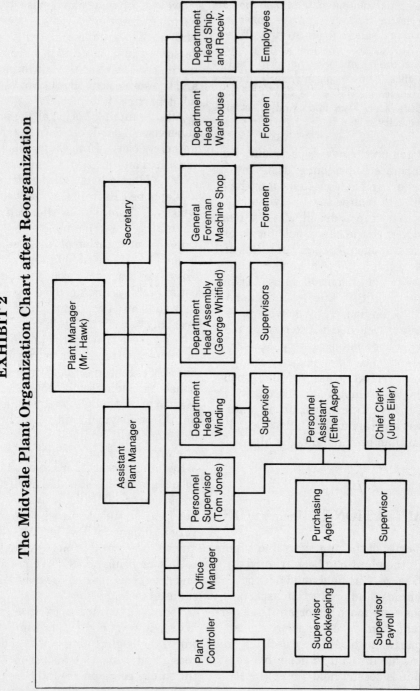

stewards in my department are concerned that you haven't met with them and talked about union problems, grievances, and negotiations. They think you've got the company bighead and that personnel problems are going to be hard to settle around here without Miss Martin."

During the telephone conversation Tom Jones tried to explain several new policies designed by the home office to upgrade Abacus plant personnel. For example, the company management had decided that for an indefinite period of time only high school graduates were to be employed for all jobs other than custodial work. Tom was not successful in convincing Whitfield of the merits of this policy. Upon completing the call, Tom decided to make a list of matters pertaining to plant personnel relations that he should discuss with Mr. Hawk.

Human Resource Management Is About People
Tim O. Peterson

Brian Van Patton leaned back in his office chair and sipped on his morning coffee. He had finally made it. He was the assistant vice-president for personnel at Eagle Express. Eagle Express was a medium-sized electronic job shop employing 750 skilled and semiskilled technicians. Annual revenues were $12.3 million, up 17.6 percent over last year's revenues.

Brian was truly excited about his new job. He had just completed his bachelor's degree in human resource management at Metro State University. He had worked full time while he had attended State, first as a short-order cook, then as a night watchman, and finally as a sales representative at a rental car agency. Now Brian was going to get to do what he liked best: work with people. That was why he had majored in human resources management. This was going to be great!

With that thought in mind, Brian picked up the first memo in his in basket (see following pages). "No time like the present to get started," he thought.

After reading the memos, Brian sat at his desk with a blank stare. What had he gotten himself into? Was this working with people? He remembered when State had offered the elective on human resource information systems. He had told his friends, "Human resource management is about people, not computers. I don't need any of that stuff." Now his words were coming back to haunt him.

Tim O. Peterson is associate professor of management at the University of Tulsa.

From the Desk of Raymond Maywoods
Vice-President for Personnel

June 13

Brian,

    The big boss just saw a presentation on Human Resource Information Systems at the Executive Development Forum he attends every month.
    He is real excited about this idea. He says we could improve our human resource planning and training programs with a system like this. He said it can be used for selection, making job assignments, safety reporting, and lots of other things. (See his memo to me.)
    He wants you to look into getting us a system like this. Why don't you start by answering the questions in his memo.

Ray

P.S. What is a Human Resource Information System anyway? Before you talk to the boss, please run the information by me so I can get smart too. Welcome to the team, Brian!

President's Office

June 11

Ray,

    We had a very interesting Executive Forum this week. Our guest speaker spoke about human resource information systems and their impact on business.

    These systems can be used for many different types of personnel activities like human resource planning, training, selection, making assignments, safety and health reporting, EEO tracking, absentee tracking, etc.

    It seems like these systems are a good investment. I think we need one. What do you think? Why don't you put Brian on this? It's a hot new topic in personnel. Brian probably studied this when he was at State. The speaker at the forum said that State offered an elective on the topic last year.

    Could you get Brian to answer the following questions for me?

1. Can you give me a good working definition for a human resource information system?
2. What type of data do we need to have on our people to make one of these systems useful?
3. Could we get a better handle on our turnover problem with a system like this?
4. How do you see us using the system?
5. How does it contribute to the company's management of its people?
6. What's the first step in getting a human resource information system rolling here at Eagle Express?

    This looks like an important issue, and we need to explore it completely. Tell Brian that the ball is in his court.

Tony

Readings for Professional Growth and Enrichment

Beer, M., and B. A. Spector (1984). "Human Resources Management: The Integration of Industrial Relations and Organization Development." In R. M. Rowland and G. R. Ferris (eds.), *Research in Personnel and Human Resources Management,* Vol. 2. Greenwich, Conn.: JAI Press.

Brixcoe, D. R. (1982). "Human Resource Management Has Come of Age." *Personnel Administrator* 27: 75–83.

DeSanctis, G. (1986). "Human Resource Information Systems: A Current Assessment." MIS Quarterly (March): 15–27.

Landy, F. J., and J. Vasey (1984). "Theory and Logic in Human Resources Research." In K. M. Rowland and G. R. Ferris (eds.), *Research in Personnel and Human Resources Management,* Vol. 2. Greenwich, Conn.: JAI Press.

Laurent, A. (1986). "The Cross-Cultural Puzzle of International Human Resource Management." *Human Resource Management* 25: 91–102.

Magnus, M. (1983). "Trends and Issues in Personnel Management." *Personnel Journal* 62 (March): 238–242.

Miles, R. E., and H. R. Rosenberg (1982). "The Human Resource Approach to Management: Second-Generation Issues." *Organizational Dynamics* 10: 26–41.

Walker, A. J. (1982). "The Newest Job in Personnel: Human Resources Data Administrator." *Personnel Journal* 61 (December): 924–928.

II

PLANNING FOR ORGANIZATIONS, JOBS, AND PEOPLE

Readings

The Design of a Career Oriented Human Resource System
Mary Ann Von Glinow / Michael J. Driver / Kenneth Brousseau / J. Bruce Prince

In recent years considerable interest and attention have been paid to careers and career-related phenomena in corporate America. Nowhere has this interest been more apparent than in human resource (HR) departments of large companies (Walker & Gutteridge, 1979). This heightened interest has resulted in numerous theories touting the importance of career planning to human resource management (Dyer, 1976; Hall, 1976; Walker, 1978). Despite the acclaim, however, little is known about actual company experiences with career planning or what career planning really means to individuals (Walker & Gutteridge, 1979). Further, very little is known about the impact of individual careers on the organization's HR system. The purpose of this research effort, therefore, is to organize and extend the impact that current career literature has on modern HR systems by the development of a taxonomy of career-sensitive HR system properties.

CURRENT CAREER THINKING

A number of empirical and in-depth case studies have provided some insight into the ways in which careers are initially conceived and subsequently pursued, the way careers evolve over time, and the ways in which individuals change during the course of their working lives as a result of their careers (Hall, 1976; Schein, 1978; Super, 1980).

Driver (1979) developed a career concept model that suggests that individuals possess different ideas about how their careers should develop. These concepts are based on past career movement and act as internal gyroscopes that appear to guide career decisions. This model and recent empirical findings (Olson, 1979; Prince, 1979) suggest that many view their careers as ideally consisting of a series of steps up an organizational ladder — the linear career concept. However, others view their careers as a lifelong commitment to a job or field — the steady state concept. Still others see their career as a series of infrequent but major shifts to new occupations or functional domains — the spiral concept. Finally, there are those who view their career as a series of frequent moves between jobs that are unrelated — the transitory concept.

Similarly, Schein (1978) attributes differences in the ways that individuals

Source: Mary Ann Von Glinow, Michael J. Driver, Kenneth Brousseau, and J. Bruce Prince, "The Design of a Career Oriented Human Resource System," *Academy of Management Review,* 1983, pp. 23–32. Reprinted by permission.

pursue their careers to career "anchors" that form the motivational foundations of career aspirations. He notes that some individuals organize their careers around themes of creativity and autonomy. Others are attracted to occupations and organizations that emphasize technical competence. Driver (1979) notes that career concepts appear to be integrally linked to key motives, or career anchors. There is some empirical support (Driver, 1981; Olson, 1979; Prince, 1979) to suggest that the steady-state career concept may be based on the basic need for security and for a clearly recognized, valued role in society. The linear concept appears linked to the need for achievement and power. The spiral concept appears to be related to growth needs, and transitories appear to be motivated by the need for identity and challenge. Though still exploratory, the use of career motives in explaining variance surrounding career choices appears feasible.

In addition to motives, careers may be examined from a temporal perspective. Dalton, Thompson, and Price (1977) show how individuals frequently move through a series of career stages over time that involve substantive changes in the role requirements, as well as in the types of skills, knowledge, and work orientations that the role requires. Similarly, others have shown how work values and personal expectations and aspirations tend to shift in predictable ways as people move through successive stages of life (Gould, 1972; Levinson, 1977; Super, 1980). Consistent with this growing awareness that career orientations are susceptible to changes over time, researchers increasingly are focusing on the dynamic interplay that takes place between the types of work that an individual performs and his or her work values, temperament, and outlook (Brousseau, 1978; Brousseau & Prince, 1981; Kohn & Schooler, 1978).

Implications for Human Resource Management Development

These findings concerning careers have far-reaching implications for the design of human resource practices in organizations. Schein (1978), for example, spoke of the need for "total systems" capable of identifying, developing, and managing human resources throughout the entire career cycle. These total systems for human resource planning and development would include methods for linking various organizational and personnel functions such as strategic planning, human resource planning, performance appraisal, personnel assessment, and career planning in ways that facilitate the matching of organizational and individual needs over time.

Similarly, Driver's (1978) career concept model serves as a framework for diagnosing and designing career management practices in organizations, and it requires consideration of a total system of organizational and personnel functions. The career concept model includes analysis of frequency of job changes, direction of the job change (i.e., vertical or lateral), and motives that guide the individual's job and occupational choice. Therefore, to create and maintain congruence between individual career concepts and organizational practices, there is a need for long range, consistent integration in recruiting strategies, job assignment and sequencing methods, training programs, performance appraisal procedures, rewards, and organizational structure (Driver, 1979).

Typically, personnel and human resource practices change as the organization evolves, new personnel specialists are hired, and new policies and procedures are adopted. Consequently, the various functions that have been designed and implemented at different times, by different people, and in response to different needs may not operate in unison to achieve common objectives. As previously noted, numerous human resource functions are involved in the management and development of careers. Therefore, situations in which human resource functions do not fit together logically are at odds with the career development strategies that career theorists and career-oriented models suggest. If, for example, people were recruited for work on the basis of creativity, but are subsequently evaluated on accuracy, career problems would be likely to arise.

Current career management and development models promote a *systems* view of human resource management. When viewed systematically, the management of career development is not just another HR function operating independently of other HR functions. Instead, the management of career development is seen as a process involving organizational and human resource functions that collectively compose a system of interacting parts. Unfortunately, few conceptual tools exist to meet the need for systemic diagnosis and/or design of career-oriented human resource systems.

Most HR systems in reality are a discrete collection of components (i.e., recruiting, training, performance appraisal) and rarely have been designed from a "total systems" perspective. Walker and Gutteridge note that of the 225 organizations they surveyed that have some type of career development/planning function, most of the HR systems have fragmented career orientations. They note further that:

> By far the strongest factor associated with effective career planning is its integration with existing personnel systems. When such systems as performance appraisal, training and development programs, rotational programs, information systems and skills inventories, and management succession planning are in place and linked to career planning practices, the overall effectiveness is considered high (1979, p. 4).

Therefore, in response to this need for a systems view of human resource management, a basic HR system is presented here — a system with a set of properties or parameters that can be utilized for diagnostic and design purposes. The authors suggest how this framework can be used as a guide for designing a career-sensitive human resource system.

An Integrated Human Resource System

Figure 1 depicts a basic HR system, designed to chart essential information flows concerning the management of human resources throughout the organization. An integrated HR system is defined here as one in which HR activities are holistically interdependent and connected, each of which informs the design and implementation of particular activities. More specifically, individuals and organizational parts are aware of and are actively involved with each other.

This model was conceptualized as

FIGURE 1
Integrated Human Resource System

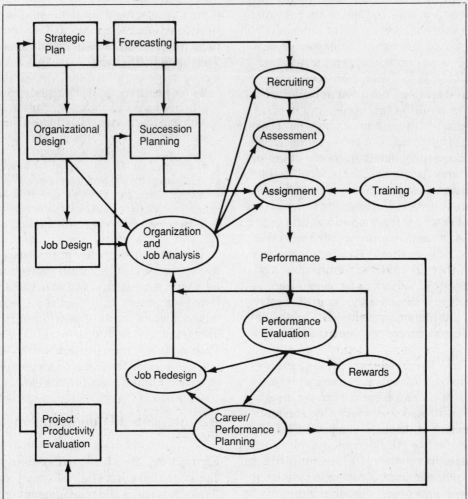

having distinct personnel as well as organizational functions. The circular components represent the traditional personnel functions most frequently dealt with by HR personnel. The boxes represent organizational functions not dealt with traditionally by personnel policies or practices. It is believed that the components represented in Figure 1 represent a minimal set of critical functions necessary for appropriate functioning of any HR system, not just one that encourages a career orientation. These functions have been linked by arrows not to indicate causality but to indicate minimally necessary information flows between these components.

For example, in Figure 1, should the organization's *strategic plan* call for expansion into new technologies or markets, this information can be used to forecast for compatible expertise and career orientations. *Forecasts* developed in this manner should be used to guide recruiting. When recruiting is predicated on accurate organizational forecasting information, the recruiting and forecasting functions become linked in this HR system based on the need for information.

Recruiting should be linked to *assessment;* the same criteria used in recruiting must be carried over to assessment. An integrated HR system also would assess these individuals according to criteria appropriate for career guidance and in accordance with the job analysis.

Organization and job analysis (a traditional personnel function) and *succession planning* (a traditional organizational function) should each impact *assignment* policies. This suggests that an integrated HR system should assign individuals to jobs, positions, and training based not only on assessment, but on what the organization plans for top management succession. In addition, assignment should be grounded in thorough job analysis that lends credibility to the assignment policies. In addition to informing the short and long run manpower forecasts, the strategic plan should be linked to *organizational design* and *job design,* two important organizational functions reliant on the organization's business strategy for appropriate integration. A fully integrated HR system considers these components and informational linkages, not based on individual concerns solely, but because effective and efficient systems must be informed at the organizational level as well.

Once assessed, the individual should be assigned to a particular job classification or sent to *training* to develop, upgrade, or learn new skills. Assignment is not identical to assessment. Assignments can be based on factors other than a person's assessed qualities (e.g., necessity). Training and assessment should be integrally linked; each supplies important information for the other.

Performance is the key criterion in this system affected by assignment of individuals to jobs. Performance most directly depends on the capability of the individual assigned to a particular job completing the task(s) at hand. Hence the arrow from assignment to performance. The *performance evaluation* results from performance and continues, along with the reward subsystem, to be the most controversial of all HR subsystems. This is so primarily because performance evaluation, when called into question, must be proved valid by the employing organization. Of crucial importance here are linkages to job analysis and individual assessment. This focuses attention on whether individual concerns are integrated with organizational concerns.

The *rewards* function of most organizations, in an integrated HR system, should derive from as well as influence the performance evaluation. Hence the double arrows. There is general recognition that rewarding the individual's performance must be predicated on accurate measurement and evaluation of that performance if it is to be considered a viable part of the HR system (Kerr, 1975). Similarly, the individual needs to be given rewards consistent with his/her reward preferences. In addition, the reward system should be consistent with the way in which performance evaluation occurs, as well as with the characteristics of the person in that job.

Performance evaluation should activate a *career planning* function, as well as a *performance planning* function, consistent with maximizing individual potential and organizational objectives. Career planning enhances the performance of future assignments. It therefore should be linked to performance as well as training; performance planning indicates immediate performance objectives. Should the need for *job redesign* result from either performance planning or performance evaluation, the design effort also should be contingent on outputs from the previously mentioned HR functions and should inform the organization and job analysis component. Career/performance planning, rewards, and job redesign are exceptionally complex components of an integrated HR system. They have not been systematically dealt with, either by organizations in their hiring policies or by external agencies such as EEOC. As such, few prescriptions exist for organizations caught in the midst of the changing demographics of the work force. An integrated HR system must consider all of these functions as systematically and holistically interdependent with one another.

Enhanced productivity at the individual level should lead to enhanced project productivity. *Project productivity evaluation* should inform the organization's strategic plan and, as such, both ideally are linked to one another in this HR system design. Project productivity serves as one index of how the HR system is functioning.

In summary, Figure 1 represents key components of an integrated HR system. To show the impact of career thinking on HR systems, a set of dimensions characterizing properties of the system, or system parameters, is offered. The impact of career thinking is felt on these parameters, and not on the HR functions (recruiting, assessment, etc.) per se. These parameters are unique in their configuration and serve as the basis for systematic diagnosis of *any* human resource system.

CAREER-SENSITIVE HR SYSTEM PARAMETERS

The HR system of an organization, as previously mentioned, is viewed as having General System Theory (Miller, 1965; Von Bertalanffy, 1952) properties that here are termed HR system parameters. Human resource system parameters enable one to analyze any HR system, as well as design new HR systems. The system parameters most clearly linked to a career focus fall into four categories: (1) structure, (2) process, (3) boundary, and (4) human. These parameters are shown in Table 1.

Structural

Structural factors reflect a basic system property—complexity. As has been illustrated at the individual (Driver & Streufert, 1969) and the organizational (Lawrence & Lorsch, 1969) levels, structural complexity is defined to include

TABLE 1
Basic HR System Parameters Showing Expected Patterns Given a Career Orientation

Parameters	Career Orientation
I. Structure	
A. Integration	
1. Connectivity	High
2. Consistency	High
B. Differentiation: diversity	High
II. Process	
A. Self-reflexive	High
B. Innovative	High
C. Developmental orientation	High
III. Boundary	
A. Strategic linkage	High
B. Environmental sensitivity	High
IV. Human	
A. Person vs. organization centered	High
B. Nonwork focus	High
C. Objectivity	Moderate
D. Use of behavioral science	Moderate

differentiation and integration. Differentiation refers to the number of parts in a system and/or the degree of difference among parts. Integration refers to the connection among parts.

In the context of career-oriented HR systems, integration is viewed along two parameters: connectivity and consistency. Connectivity is the degree to which relevant information from one part of the HR system is used in other parts. When two functions are connected in some way (e.g., forecasting and recruiting), they begin to take on the characteristics of an integrated HR system. Figure 1 illustrates connectivity through the use of arrows. For instance, connectivity occurs when job analysis results in the screening of job applicants for job-related traits, or when the use of training results in better assignment. In examining connectivity, it is useful to distinguish between formal and informal connectivity. Formal connectivity refers to any connection covered by explicit rules and procedures, whereas informal connectivity covers sporadic or spontaneous connections. By noting the lack of a formal connection, one can often detect weak links or troublesome spots in an HR system.

A second aspect of integration is dimensional consistency. This refers to how much an HR system uses a consistent set of dimensions across varied functions. For example, does the system select, train, and reward people on the same aptitude or personality dimensions? Does job analysis yield job dimensions that can be used to select individuals on matching personality attributes?

A second major structural system parameter is differentiation, operationalized here as system diversity. The diversity parameter is concerned with how varied HR practices are across units. Diversity also is concerned with the degree to which individual employees establish unique personal arrangements as are found occasionally in MBO or cafeteria-reward plans.

HR system complexity, then, is an interaction of connectivity, consistency, and diversity. In actual practice, many systems aim at simplicity because simple systems are inexpensive and do not require highly skilled experts to design and manage them. The benefits of simplicity are obvious. The costs, however, may be substantial if the impact of careers on organizational performance is taken into consideration.

Process

All systems including HR systems are not merely static, but operate on input to produce output. Several process parameters deserve attention within the career context. The most basic process parameter inherent in the integrated HR system is termed self-reflexivity. A self-reflexive system is one that examines feedback on its performance and alters not only strategies, but also goals and objectives if warranted. Self-reflexivity implies collection of two forms of evaluative data: (a) data on the operating efficacy of the current function (e.g., evaluation of training program effectiveness) and (b) evaluation of employee, work, or environmental factors relevant to the design of new functions (e.g., surveying labor markets to design a recruiting program). The opposite of a self-reflexive system is a reactive system, which corrects only when things are seriously wrong. As with structural simplicity, non-self-reflexive systems have the advantage of less immediate costs and competence demands. However, HR system planners have noted that the long-term costs of the non-self-reflexive systems become staggering.

A second process parameter is innovation. Systems may be self-reflexive but not innovative, using only tried and true procedures to examine their processes. Complexity of the issues HR systems must deal with often require the development of new methods. Off-the-shelf, widely used approaches simply cannot be expected to resolve unique and complex problems. But, here again, such an approach has cost and competence demands that must be considered.

The final process parameter is termed developmental orientation and refers to the nature of goals in the system. Some systems possess "status quo" goals, aimed at maintenance of the present state of affairs. Typical of these goals are maintenance of the labor force at optimal turnover, offsetting obsolescence, and maintaining current levels of productivity. A developmental orientation requires variable standards — that is, goals frequently are reset at different levels. Often these goals concern increased complexity or self-reflexivity of the total system or its units. A developmental orientation refers to goals stressing maximum development of individual as well as organizational potential.

Boundary

Boundary parameters deal with the nature of transactions or connections across the boundary between the system and the outside environment. Two boundary parameters deserve attention: strategic linkage and environmental sensitivity. Strategic linkage refers to whether the HR system is linked to the organizational strategy function for dealing with the environment. There are many forms of strategic linkage. For example, a reactive strategic linkage is one in which the organization strategies dictate HR function outcomes and may treat HR system conditions as constraints on strategic choices. A proactive linkage is one in which human resources become positive inputs into strategic decisions about goals and plans of the whole system (e.g., labor or management competencies or values determine product decisions). To the extent that an HR system is not strategically linked, it may be buffered from environmental forces that may result in a lack of realism.

Direct environmental sensitivity is the extent to which the HR system scans and responds to external forces outside the organization (e.g., changes in labor supply, governmental regulations). Absence of sensitivity is referred to as system closure. A closed system is self-contained and ignores external phenomena. An open system allows external factors to penetrate the HR system. There are costs associated with either extreme. The present authors advocate a partially open system, which is consistent with the developmental orientation because it permits enough instability and pressure from the external environment to keep the HR system from becoming rigid (Jantsch, 1973). A partially open system also permits rational self-reflexivity (e.g., setting new goals based on events or trends).

Human

The final set of parameters specifically concerns human-based systems. These are human factor parameters, the most obvious of which is the degree to which the HR system is person centered as compared with organization centered. A highly person-centered system is concerned with the needs of each individual employee. A highly organization-centered system is employee concerned only to the extent that the employees are instrumental in meeting company goals. Clearly, there are many middle positions, blending people and organizations differently (Argyris, 1962).

Resembling the person-centered parameter is a related parameter dealing with the extent to which the organization becomes involved with employee, family, avocational, and other nonwork activities (Evans & Bartolome, 1980; Sundby, 1980). With the advent of dual-career couples entering corporations, low involvement postures appear to be less feasible as a corporate strategy.

Finally, two parameters concern the HR system analysis of its personnel. The first, objectivity, refers to the degree to which people are assessed and dealt with in an objective, replicable manner, as opposed to the use of subjective and intuitive personnel judgments. Objectivity is especially sought by agencies such as EEOC, though counterarguments exist for the "social reality" of subjective judgments.

The second parameter stems from the first. The use of objective methods presupposes knowledge and use of behavioral science methods and theories (e.g., in tests). Subjective approaches often rely on common sense, though they may be informed by behavioral science knowledge just as some objective methods can bear little or no relationship to scientific inquiry (e.g., certain background requirements).

EXPECTED CAREER IMPACT ON HR SYSTEM PARAMETERS

The basic impacts of career thinking on system structure are presented in Table 1. One major impact of a career orientation is the increase in system complexity, especially integration. Because a career orientation focuses on employees over long periods of time, lack of integration in an HR system is inconceivable. In a non-career-oriented HR system, people are seen as short run assets. Therefore, a lack of *connection* between assessment and rewards might pose little or no threat. However, if it is expected that employees should be motivated and developed over time, each part of the HR system should be connected and consistent. In fact, the authors view a lack of consistency across the HR system as a major contributor to career distress. How can a person (or an organization) engage in intelligent career development or planning when signals for success vary from one function to another (e.g., when a person is trained for precision only to find that creativity is rewarded in the performance evaluation)?

Diversity is also expected to be high in a career-oriented HR system because individuals appear to possess different career orientations (Driver, 1979; Schein, 1978). Uniform assumptions about employees have led many organizations to treat all individuals equally, though not necessarily equitably. General panaceas often have led to outcomes that fall so far short of so many peoples' needs that they react with aversion to any new approaches. In a career-oriented HR system, the establishment of tolerance of individual diversity is a prerequisite to effective outcomes.

Concerning the process parameters highlighted in Table 1, a career-oriented HR system would most likely be both self-reflexive as well as innovative. Because individual career patterns change over one's life stages (Dalton et al., 1977), a career-oriented HR system is likely to be self-reflexive. Only self-reflexive HR systems can alter policies and procedures as needed in anticipation of work force changes. Like self-reflexivity, innovation also seems necessary insomuch as career patterns appear to be evolving in new directions (Driver, 1981; Hall, 1976; Von Glinow, 1982) that require new procedures (e.g., new structures to accommodate career-oriented individuals).

A developmental orientation seems equally essential in a career-oriented HR system (Brousseau, 1978; Brousseau & Price, 1981). Development is focused primarily at the individual level, though an integrated HR system is concerned with organizational development as well. There are, however, certain persons who are not particularly in need of development. These pockets of stasis amidst development are simply reflexive of the HR system's tolerance for diversity, and as such they differentiate the uniqueness of this integrated HR system from others.

A career-oriented HR system needs to be closely linked to the organization's business strategy. Career aspirations can hardly be met if strategic needs and career needs are not synchronized. If people, for example, with long-term stability orientations are integrated into an operation whose strategy is to develop short-term projects, dysfunctional outcomes would be expected.

Environmental sensitivity would need to be partially open in a career-oriented HR system. New trends in labor markets, work values, and personnel practices obviously must be incorporated. Excessive openness is not advocated, however, because continuity of practice is vital, particularly to certain career orientations.

In a career-oriented HR system, an orientation that includes both individual and organizational interests seems essential. For careers to be meaningful at the organizational level, they cannot be exclusively person-centered or organization-centered. It is significant that organizations that do not attend to promotional and career opportunities run risks such as withdrawal and decreased performance as well as turnover (Mohrman & Von Glinow, 1981). Inattention to career forecasting may prompt a totally ineffective long-term strategy. Similarly, a purely organization-centered HR system can significantly alienate both white- and blue-collar workers.

Nonwork factors are intricately intertwined in a career-oriented HR system. Careers have evolved for reasons other than the Protestant work ethic (Evans & Bartolome, 1980). Clearly, there are trade-offs among work, family, avocation, and marriage that must be sensed and responded to by the career-oriented HR system.

Pure objectivity in the HR system is not advocated, because subjective factors often are critical to career success. Creativity and subtlety often argue in favor of greater subjective approaches. However, purely subjective systems are not advocated, because of problems such as perceptual bias, occasional lapses of system equity, and lack of realism. Therefore, a system that combines both subjective and objective methods of evaluation in a self-reflexive manner, aimed at maximum effectiveness, appears most appropriate to a career-oriented HR system. Finally, attention to behavioral science seems to be an essential requirement for a career-oriented HR system. The behavioral sciences are helping to provide "informed choice" and essential tools for person, job, and organizational analysis (Weiss & Bucuvalas, 1980).

CONCLUSIONS AND IMPLICATIONS

In an attempt to extend current thinking on the need for integration within the HR function, an integrated HR system with system parameters that is career-oriented has been developed. In addition, the system parameters presented are offered as both a diagnostic and a system design aid. The use of the parameter analysis in enriching applied and theoretical HR system thinking has several implications and suggestions for future use. In terms of practical suggestions for HR system designers, the parameter analysis can be used:

1. As a measurement and diagnostic tool to examine any system within the organization (e.g., HR system, control system).
2. To design specific decision subsystems (e.g., management identification and development) within the overall HR system.
3. To design HR systems that are maximally sensitive to internal and external demands (e.g., environment, individual careers, organizational concerns of efficiency) through attention to system parameters.
4. As a tool for longitudinally tracking individual career change. Similarly, such analyses can be used to change the system and the individuals within that system over time. The usefulness of a careers perspective allows practitioners to establish conditions suitable for individual change to occur, which otherwise may not be amenable to monitoring (e.g., creating conditions whereby individual careers are encouraged to

change within the framework of career concept diversity).
5. As a basis for initially measuring the individual's perception (e.g., of career planning) and subsequently comparing that perception with the objective properties of the system.

In terms of future research, two essential questions are suggested by the career sensitive HR system described:

1. Do the parameters described in Table 1 lead to more effective career management in organizations?
2. Does more effective career management lead to enhanced individual performance and organizational productivity?

These research questions serve as a preliminary basis on which to begin testing hypotheses relating to effective career management. This taxonomy of expected patterns, given a career orientation, serves as an initial guide to allow researchers concerned with "total systems" as well as individual careers to begin to structure research through a multilevel, multiparameter analysis.

Such diagnosis and design of career-oriented systems is a lengthy process best conducted through longitudinal inquiries and not particularly amenable to cross-sectional research using only paper and pencil tests. It should be noted that the integrated HR system and parameter analysis represents a general analytic approach designed for analysis of any system. The career configuration is but one configuration of this general analytical approach. Clearly, future research is needed in the design of career-oriented human resource systems in organizations.

REFERENCES

Argyris, C. *Interpersonal competence and organizational effectiveness.* Homewood, Ill.: Dorsey Press, 1962.

Brousseau, K. R. Personality and job experience. *Organizational Behavior and Human Performance,* 1978, 22, 235–252.

Brousseau, K. R., & Prince, J. B. Job-person dynamics: An extension of longitudinal research. *Journal of Applied Psychology,* 1981, 66 (1), 59–62.

Dalton, G. W., Thompson, P. H., & Price, R. Career stages: A model of professional careers in organizations. *Organizational Dynamics,* Summer 1977, 19–42.

Driver, M. J. Career concepts and organizational development. Paper presented at the Academy of Management Meeting, San Francisco, 1978.

Driver, M. J. Career concepts and career management in organizations. In C. L. Cooper (Ed.), *Behavioral problems in organizations.* Englewood Cliffs, N. J.: Prentice-Hall, 1979, 79–139.

Driver, M. J. Demographic and societal factors affecting the linear career crisis. Unpublished manuscript, Graduate School of Business Administration, University of Southern California, 1981.

Driver, M. J., & Streufert, S. Integrative complexity: An approach to individuals and groups as information processing systems. *Administrative Science Quarterly,* 1969, 14, 272–285.

Dyer, L. *Careers in organizations.* Ithaca, N. Y.: State School of Industrial and Labor Relations, Cornell University, 1976.

Evans, P., & Bartolomè, F. The relationship between professional life and private life. In B. Derr (Ed.), *Work, family and the career.* New York: Praeger, 1980, 281–317.

Gould, R. L. The phases of adult life: A study in developmental psychology. *American Journal of Psychiatry,* 1972, 129, 521–531.

Hall, D. T. *Careers in organizations.* Pacific Palisades, Cal.: Goodyear, 1976.

Jantsch, E. *Design for evolution.* New York: George Brazilios, 1973.

Kerr, S. On the folly of rewarding A while hoping for B. *Academy of Management Journal.* 1975, 18, 769–783.

Kohn, M. L., & Schooler, C. The reciprocal effects of the substantive complexity of work and intellectual flexibility: A longitudinal assessment. *American Sociological Review,* 1978, 84, 97–118.

Lawrence, P., & Lorsch, J. *Organization and environment.* Homewood, Ill.: Irwin, 1969.

Levinson, D. The mid-life transition: A period in adult psychosocial development. *Psychiatry,* 1977, 40, 104.

Miller, J. G. Living systems. *Behavioral Science,* 1965, 10, 337–412.

Mohrman, S. A., & Von Glinow, M. A. A dynamic approach to employee attachment and withdrawal. Unpublished working manuscript, University of Southern California, 1981.

Olson, T. Career concepts and decision styles. Paper given at the National Academy of Management Meeting, Atlanta, 1979.

Prince, B. An investigation of career concepts and career anchors. Paper given at the Western Academy of Management Meeting, Portland, Oregon, 1979.

Schein, E. H. *Career dynamics: Matching individual and organizational needs.* Reading, Mass.: Addison-Wesley, 1978.

Sundby, D. The career quad: A psychological look at some divergent dual career families. In B. Derr (Ed.), *Work, family and the career.* New York: Praeger, 1980.

Super, D. A life-span, life-space approach to career development. *Journal of Vocational Behavior,* 16, 1980, 282–298.

Von Bertalanffy, L. *Problems of life.* New York: Harper & Row, 1952.

Von Glinow, M. A. Integrating human resource management policies with career concepts: The case of the dual career couple. In B. Gutek (Ed.), *Sex role stereotyping and affirmative action policy,* UCLA Institute of Industrial Relations, 1982, 164–182.

Walker, J. W., & Gutteridge, T. G. Career planning practices: An AMA survey report. New York: AMACOM, 1979.

Walker, J. W. Does career planning rock the boat? *Human Resource Management,* Spring, 1978, 2–8.

Weiss, C., & Bucuvalas, M. *Social science research and decision making.* New York: Columbia University Press, 1980.

Mary Ann Von Glinow is Assistant Professor of Management and Organization in the Graduate School of Business, University of Southern California. Michael J. Driver is Professor of Management and Organization in the Graduate School of Business, University of Southern California. Kenneth Brousseau, Principal Partner in Decision Synergistics, is an Adjunct Research Scientist in the Center for Effective Organizations, University of Southern California. J. Bruce Prince is a doctoral student in Organization Behavior in the Graduate School of Business, University of Southern California and an Assistant Professor at Concordia University.

Skills Banks: From All According to Their Abilities
Ronald R. Knipling

HR professionals in project-oriented business environments (e.g., training, HR systems, telecommunications systems) find it increasingly difficult to define their companies' employees' professional identities. After years of working on projects, individual employees possess an often complex collection of professional skills. Managers who develop numerous projects and oversee numerous subordinates may have trouble matching projects with people and may be ignorant of their own organizations' available knowledge and skills and the weaknesses that must be corrected.

Source: Ronald R. Knipling: "Skills Banks: From All According to Their Abilities." Reprinted from *Computers in Personnel* (New York: Auerbach Publishers). © 1988 Warren, Gorham & Lamont Inc. Used with permission.

PROFICIENCY PROFILE

A skills bank is a data base designed to capture each employee's proficiency profile, including information about education, experience, skills, knowledge, professional contacts, and other characteristics useful to an organization and its work. A typical skills bank requires a microcomputer, commercially available software (either a general data base management system (DBMS) or a specific skills bank application), and a skills inventory questionnaire that is completed by each employee.

Applications A data base that includes this background information enables managers to support and improve staff placement and project assignments, companywide training programs, individual training needs assessment, individual development plans, marketing of staff capabilities, and professional staff recruiting. If, for example, an organization has 50 professional employees and 50 relevant, identifiable skills, the skills bank provides managers with 2,500 pieces of information regarding staff strengths and weaknesses. If current proficiencies do not match organizational needs, this shortfall can be incorporated into a detailed staff development plan.

Who needs it? Not every organization needs a skills bank. If jobs are well-defined and generally remain unchanged, traditional placement and staff training needs assessment approaches will be adequate. Candidate organizations for skills banks share some or all of the following characteristics:

- More than 25 employees.
- Project-oriented employees.
- Multidisciplinary projects.
- New and changing professional skills, often due to technological change and shifts in business direction.
- Staff specialists in various knowledge and skill areas.
- Anticipated changes in staff skills.
- Moderate to high staff turnover.
- New managers or management.

THE PROTOTYPE

This article is based largely on the author's experience developing a skills bank for the Consulting Services Division (CSD) of the Financial Management Service of the US Department of the Treasury. As an external consultant working closely with the Financial Management Service's technical and HR development staffs, the author created a skills bank and used it to assess CSD employees' skills and need for training. CSD's mission focused on system development and functional requirements analysis for large automated financial systems (e.g., electronic funds transfer systems). Most CSD staff members had strong backgrounds in accounting but were new to systems development and large computer and telecommunications systems. CSD met virtually all the organizational criteria for developing a useful skills bank.

Staff Relations

Well-conceived and benign skills banks are good for everyone — as an MIS for managers and as a way to improve employees' assessments and enhance their professional development. But, in spite of these good intentions, a skills bank can cause a potentially negative staff reaction if the concept is not introduced properly. For example, if employees perceive that the skills bank can be used against them to identify poor performance they may resist or rebel against the system.

To prevent a negative reaction, management should seek to maximize employee participation in the job analysis process and in the development of the skills inventory questionnaire. An in-house liaison should be assigned to handle most staff interaction throughout this development process. The ideal candidate is trusted, nonthreatening, and holds a mid-level position. If the organization is large or distributed at many sites, several liaisons should be assigned. Every employee completing a form should have the opportunity to discuss it with a skills bank liaison. All communications to employees regarding the skills bank should emphasize that their questionnaire answers will be confidential and that the skills bank will be used fairly and appropriately for optimal employee placement and professional development.

Data Collection Instrument

The most important component of a skills bank is the data collection instrument, the skills inventory questionnaire (SIQ). It must ask the right organization-specific questions (data base input) for the skills bank to generate useful organization-specific answers (data base output). The SIQ should be designed to capture each employee's educational profile, work experiences, job-relevant knowledge or skills, project assignment history within the organization, and, perhaps, preferred areas of work. The SIQ should cover all knowledge, skill, and experience areas important to the organization.

Job analysis and KSCs Like any good HR development intervention (e.g., selection system development), a skills bank should be based on job analyses. Job analyses determine major job functions and identify required knowledge, skills, and competencies (KSCs). The following job analysis techniques are probably the most useful:

- A thorough review of such organizational documentation as job descriptions, organization charts, and organizational capability statements.
- Structured interviews with managers, incumbents, HR professionals, and consultants.

A job analysis will reveal dozens — as many as 100 — important KSCs, which can usually be grouped into major categories or clusters. For example, in our CSD project, the job analysis revealed 95 specific KSCs in four areas. The following are the first two KSC categories:

- Process — Project management, oral presentation, questionnaire and structured interview design, negotiation, personal facility with office automation software, and training development and conduct.
- Computer science and information systems — Specific hardware or software systems, data communications and telecommunications, mass data storage, DP security, and AI and decision support systems.

The third and fourth KSC categories were specific to CSD's mission of system development and requirements analysis:

- Systems development life cycle — Requirements analysis, cost/benefit analysis, preparation of system development project plans, analysis of baseline systems.
- Systems operations — Financial, manufacturing, and inventory. Respondents rated their skills in 46 specific functional areas relating to the specific types of financial systems under development (e.g., accounting, auditing, disbursing, and cash management).

KSCs organized into this classification scheme will make the SIQ easier to complete and the skills bank data base easier to analyze. Whatever form a KSC list takes, space should be left at the end for write-in KSCs. No matter how exhaustive a KSC list seems, employees will make worthwhile contributions if given the chance. And write-in KSCs reassure employees that the data base will serve their personal interests as well as the business needs of their organization.

Core and specialized KSCs Skills banks are typically developed by organizations that comprise numerous employees and project teams, each working on specialized projects. In addition to differentiated skills, most organizations also require from their employees certain basic proficiencies that are often called core skills.

Core skills are the KSCs that every staff member must have. For example, all employees in a company that develops telecommunications systems should have a technical understanding of telecommunications, proficiency in specific methods of systems development, and the requisite process skills. For example, CSD required at least a moderate proficiency in 16 divisionwide core KSCs. Moderate was defined as a self-rating of 2 on a scale of 0 to 5. All CSD employees initially possessed this skill level, but the skills bank helped establish this level as an organizational goal — and an individual goal for every employee.

Specialized skills are needed by only a few staff experts. For example, in telecommunications, only a few experts must know encryption techniques or queueing theory. A single expert will suffice if the topic is relatively obscure. Managers and technical gurus identify the necessary specialization skills as well as the required number of experts. This type of planning shows how the skills bank is used for strategic staff management. In profit-making organizations, glamour staff KSCs, such as those relating to marketing and client demand, must also be identified.

Managers can use the skills bank data base to systematically compare their actual staff to an ideal staff. Shortfalls in required specialization skills justify advanced staff training and development.

Skills Questionnaire

The SIQ helps determine which KSCs are needed most in an organization. Because there may be no further opportunities for postimplementation analysis of the skills bank data base, every important question should be written into the SIQ before it is administered.

Not only should the SIQ ask the right questions, it should ask the questions right. The SIQ must be understandable,

EXHIBIT 1
Sample SIQ Cover Page Instructions

Introduction

This skills inventory questionnaire will be used to build the staff skills bank. Employees do one or more things very well; the purpose of this questionnaire is for you to identify those skills. When all skills are identified, a training plan will be developed to train those skills for which there is a clear need.

Generally, employees will be able to rate themselves high (3, 4, or 5) in only a few categories. Most employees know a little about a lot of different job-relevant topics but have advanced or extensive knowledge and experience in only a few. Don't let the length of the form intimidate you. It covers most areas that we may need expertise in from our employees; no one is expected to have advanced knowledge and skill in a large number of areas.

Your answers to this questionnaire will be kept confidential. The self-assessment of your skills — along with the skills of your coworkers — will make up the skills bank data base. Information from this data base will assist management in staffing projects and preparing individual development plans (IDPs) for all employees. The skills bank is intended to prepare you for your job responsibilities and to apply your talents and skills within the organization.

Instructions

This form will take 60 to 90 minutes to complete. Although all sections are important, Section III, "Knowledge/Skill/Competence (KSC) Inventory" will require you to rate your personal proficiency in a number of areas. Self-rating will be based on a scale of 0 to 5.

If you have any questions regarding this questionnaire or the skills bank in general, please contact the staff liaison. Please return the completed form by next Thursday.

Thank you for your time and care in completing this questionnaire.

---

explicit, and easy to complete. It must contain clear instructions and correct formatting (see Exhibit 1 for sample cover page instructions).

The SIQ should be consistent with the planned data base. Variables include text (e.g., name, college), category (e.g., branch or project team), quantitative data, yes/no responses, and dates.

The SIQ should determine each employee's level of proficiency in each KSC. This information can be determined through self-ratings, supervisor or manager ratings, operational measures (e.g., years of experience), and a combination of these approaches. Our CSD project used the self-rating approach. For employees to rate themselves reliably, they must first be convinced that they should be candid and objective through a precise, numerical proficiency scale they can apply to their own skills. We used the following six-point scale:

0 = No training or experience
1 = Basic knowledge or skill
2 = Moderate knowledge or skill
3 = Advanced knowledge or skill
4 = Technical subject matter expert
5 = Experienced project leader or contributing professional

The definitions of the scale values should be expanded, and sample instructions should accompany the KSC inventory (see Exhibit 2). The majority of respondents in our experience rated themselves realistically and candidly. In extreme cases of over- or underrating, the skills bank liaison can request that employees review the scale and consider revising their ratings. This issue should not be handled contentiously. Some inconsistencies across the ratings are more acceptable than problems in staff relations and administration caused by unhappy employees whose self-ratings were challenged.

Besides KSC inventory, the following employee data should also be requested:

- General information (e.g., job title, years of service, education).
- Specific company project experience.
- Organizations previously worked for.
- Specific professional training programs attended.
- Years of experience in specialty areas (particularly useful if this information is required for proposals).
- Special-interest areas for professional specialties.

Although completed SIQs are concise, they are still comprehensive, and managers can learn a lot about their employees through these documents. This type of relational data base also reveals much about the organization by comparing KSCs or other skills bank variables.

An SIQ is best developed through an iterative approach. After the first draft, several managers and employees should be asked to review it and offer comments. Include job incumbents, executives, middle managers, technical specialists, training and HR professionals, and consultants.

To test a draft, as many as 15 employees not previously involved in the project should be asked to complete the draft SIQ and provide feedback on problems (e.g., mistakes, ambiguities, contradictions, or omissions). After the trial run and revisions, real data can be collected.

Staff time invested in setting up a skills bank not only enhances the accuracy of the data base but fosters a sense of ownership and acceptance by the employees.

SIQ administration In a cover letter or in the introductory instructions to the SIQ, management should inform employee respondents approximately how much time the form should take to complete, usually 90 minutes at most. If it cannot be completed in less than 90 minutes, it is probably too long. Allow two-week turnaround. Turnaround longer than two weeks will probably result in employees setting the questionnaire aside and forgetting about it.

The skills bank staff liaison distributes the forms individually and briefly discusses them with each employee. Completed SIQs should be returned to the

EXHIBIT 2
Sample KSC Proficiency Scale

Instructions

Please rate your proficiency (i.e., knowledge, skill, and competency, or KSC) for each of the areas listed on the following pages. Use the 0 to 5 scale to rate your KSCs. Employees should apply the self-ratings carefully and in accordance with the scale's definitions. Inflated self-ratings will hide a training need. Deflated self-ratings may recommend you for training that you don't need or may force you to miss project assignments that you are qualified for. Please study the scale and apply it rigorously.

KSC Scale

Scale Value	Proficiency Level	Definition
0	No formal training or experience	Minimal knowledge of area or knowledge limited to very general concepts.
1	Basic knowledge or skill	Have been exposed to fundamentals of the field (e.g., one course or part of course or indirect job experience) but would not feel comfortable working in this area without relevant training.
2	Moderate knowledge or skill	Some formal education (e.g., 2 to 4 academic courses), some job experience (e.g., one project), or other equivalent combination of education and experience. Would feel comfortable being assigned to project in this area without preparatory training, but still learning large parts of the field.
3	Advanced knowledge or skill	Have had formal training (e.g., 5 or more courses) or specific job experience (e.g., 2 or more projects). Have no need for training in basic or fundamental concepts; only training required would be in advanced, specialized aspects of this field.
4	Technical subject matter expert	Through education and extensive experience, have command of virtually all basic concepts and techniques in this area. Have the knowledge or skill to act as project leader or principal technical consultant in this area.
5	Experienced project leader or contributing professional	Subject matter expertise plus experience in instructing, directing, or coaching others in this area. Have authored publications or technical reports in the area, led major projects, or otherwise have been a contributing professional in the field.

Reminder

You should expect to have more KSCs in the 0 to 2 range than in the 3 to 5 range. Most employees have a general knowledge of many topics relevant to their work but advanced and specialized knowledge and experience in only a few areas. Don't be intimidated if most of your responses are in the 0 to 2 range. This is expected.

liaison, who checks each form to see that directions were followed completely. Although the liaison reviews the KSC self-ratings to spot misinterpretations, it's important not to create friction over self-aggrandizement or self-effacement. These errors will be the exception rather than the rule, and the skills bank will be useful despite slight variations in employees' interpretations of the rating scale.

Data input, a mechanical step, must still be planned carefully. Optical character readers are practical only for very large organizations using SIQs that consist entirely of multiple choice questions. Most skills banks require manual data entry, which is time-consuming. Every extra variable increases the data input and error-checking work load.

A second employee should check the data for errors. Input errors could harm relations between employees or even lead to employees being overlooked for training programs that they deserve and need.

MANAGEMENT APPLICATIONS

A skills bank can be used to assign and train employees, formulate individual development plans (IDPs), prepare marketing proposals, and recruit and select new employees (see Exhibit 3).

Project assignments Aided by a skills bank, managers can quickly and confidently select the best employees for development projects. For example, a new project requires a mix of six key skills, with advanced-level competence in two KSCs. There are 100 employees to select from — half of whom are barely known.

EXHIBIT 3

Skills Bank Applications

Project assignments
Retrieve by skill
Retrieve by skill and rating ($R \geq x$)
Retrieve by multiple skills and ratings

Organizationwide training needs assessment
Core skills
Specialization skills
Staff cross-training plans

Individual development plans (IDPs)
Core skill deficiencies
Current specialization skills
Potential and future specialization skills

Marketing proposal preparation
Select the best résumés for proposals
Screen for years of experience or academic degree RFP requirements

Recruiting and selection
Recruiting needs assessment
Selection of new employees (based on modified SIQ completed by applicants)

Without a skills bank, this staff placement might require tedious meetings, memos, and résumé reviews. The skills bank can quickly provide comprehensive information. A single data base retrieval could list all the employees and their KSC ratings for each specific KSC of interest. A better approach might be to list the KSC ratings for all six skills for each employee. A review of these printouts narrows the search to 10 or 15 top prospects.

The data base will allow retrieval of names and relevant KSC ratings for employees whose ratings meet a certain criteria (e.g., $R \geq 4$ in the two critical skills and $R \geq 2$ in the other four areas).

Project assignment searches need not be limited to skills bank KSC inventory data. For example, searches can focus on information relating to clients served or on similar previous projects on which employees worked. When making project assignment decisions, managers will also rely on such intangible factors as personality and recent performance. The skills bank doesn't dictate the decision, but delivers information to support the decision process.

Few managers can freely choose among all their employees for a particular assignment. The skills bank doesn't solve the availability problem but facilitates use of specific staff experience as a factor in project assignments. In addition to finding hidden candidates, the skills bank could identify other employees who are committed to continuing projects but can offer specific expertise in a part-time advisory role.

Training assessment Suppose that spreadsheets are rapidly becoming a company's basic business tools. Spreadsheets are therefore designated as a core KSC, and the skills bank can retrieve the names of all employees who have indicated little or no proficiency with spreadsheets (e.g., KSC self-ratings of $R \leq 1$). Basic training on spreadsheets can be given to these employees.

If an organization must staff new projects in many areas of specialization, its skills bank can be asked how many experts are available in specific topics. A manager may determine that the organization needs experts with $R \geq 4$ in Topic X. The skills bank will identify the current experts as well as candidates with the potential (e.g., $R = 3$) to become experts with additional professional development in that area.

If the specialization KSC concept applies to an organization, all employees can be assigned one or more specialization areas in which they can stay or get smart. The assignments will be based on employees' current strengths and interests and the organization's strategic needs. Employees gain an increased sense of importance in and commitment to their organization and a better focus on their own professional growth. And the organization gains experts in key areas of specialized knowledge and skill.

To establish a cross-training program, all staff members who are above a junior level should be assigned one or more areas of cross-training responsibility. They will become gurus in their assigned topics. Training sessions can be held during lunch hours, evenings, or in one-on-one mentor-trainee conferences.

A large organization consisting of several branches can classify KSCs in the following five categories:

- Common core KSCs — Proficiencies needed by each staff member, regardless of branch assignment.
- Branch-specific core KSCs — Proficiencies needed by each staff member of one or more branches.
- Branch-specific specialization KSCs — Proficiencies for which one or more branches require one or more experts.
- Non-branch-specific specialized KSCs — Proficiencies for which the organization requires experts, who need not be attached to any particular branch.
- Other KSCs — Proficiencies that may be important to the organization for certain projects, but which are not designated as a core or specialization skill either at branch or organizational levels.

Depending on an organization's geographical distribution or the autonomy of its individual branches, the training needs assessment may be performed as an organizationwide analysis or as a series of separate reports addressing individual branches.

Individual development plan An organizationwide training needs assessment looks at the aggregate use of staff skills to determine overall training needs relating to both core and specialized KSCs. But the same data may also be applied to individual development plans. A by-product of the organizational training needs assessment should be a statement of an ideal but attainable KSC profile for each staff member. A simple comparison of the actual and the ideal KSC profile identifies core skill deficiencies to be corrected, current specialized skills to be sustained, and potential specialized skills to be developed. It is an explicit statement of employees' weaknesses, strengths, and areas to improve.

An IDP comprises an individual assessment plus a training and development plan for that assessment. However, an assessment should undergo a subjective review before it is translated into individual development goals.

Marketing In order to identify the most qualified and impressive employees for a proposed project, KSC searches can reveal an organization's top people. The best employees for a job may not always have the most impressive résumés. Requests for proposals (RFPs) may specify particular academic degrees, years of experience, or prior service in support of the client organization. These variables included in the SIQ can be used to select the strongest employees for an assignment.

Information from the skills bank will also help impress prospective clients by detailing range and quality of an organization's human resources. Although a prospective client won't be handed a skills bank printout, the vendor will at least know what talents it can advertise.

Recruiting and selection Recruiting needs assessment is an extension of training needs assessment. A staff training needs assessment may reveal that the actual training shortfall for some specialized KSCs is too great to be eliminated through staff training. The training problem becomes a recruiting problem. Small to moderate shortfalls indicate training needs; large shortfalls (in the proficiency levels of particular skills, the number of individuals with these skills, or both) indicate recruiting needs. Recruits must strengthen key areas of specialization without weakening the core areas. Junior-level recruitment may best focus on core skills rather than on specialization skills.

A modified version of the skills bank form may be useful for employment applications. To prevent exaggeration, applicants could be instructed to identify a number of their strongest KSCs from a list. For example, the instructions might say: "From the following list of 100 knowledges, skills, or competencies, identify up to 20 which you would be most qualified to contribute to our organization." If nothing else, this information would support job interviews.

The skills bank in various modified formats can also supplement and focus other selection procedures (e.g., résumé review, transcript evaluation, interviews, and reference checking). A skills bank should supplement, not substitute, these traditional selection methods.

SKILLS BANK MISAPPLICATIONS

Data confidentiality is fundamental to the system's integrity; skills bank data, especially the KSC self-ratings, should be used only on a need-to-know basis. Otherwise, self-ratings should never be posted or disclosed.

Skills banks should not be used for such employee administrative actions as promotions, demotions, or terminations. Although KSC self-ratings are generally reliable, they should not be used to directly compare or evaluate employees for administrative purposes.

Skills bank data should not be cranked out mechanically. Skills banks are decision aids, not decision makers.

Support and Maintenance

Skills bank operators and administrators should be assigned to produce reports for management and to maintain and update the data base. In some cases, a staff development coordinator could also be the administrator, though the coordinator position usually requires more interpersonal and organizational skills and a greater understanding of skills bank applications. The coordinator manages such key skills bank applications as annual staff IDPs, organizational training needs assessment, marketing assessments, and internal cross-training plans.

Ronald R. Knipling, PhD, is a principal of the Singer Company's Allen Division in Alexandria, Virginia.

A "No Frills" Approach to Human Resource Planning
Lawrence M. Baytos

Strategic human resource planning has become quite fashionable, as evidenced by the epidemic of conferences on the subject. Many companies have added one or more HR professionals with the term "planning" in their titles. Consultants have picked up on the HR planning theme and repackaged their programs for that market. University professors are fine-tuning their theoretical planning models, hoping for commercial application.

I view the explosive growth of HR planning with mixed emotions. Certainly it is a discipline that is sorely needed by many, if not most, organizations. On the other hand, there are some potential risks involved.

- It may become a fashionable personnel fad and quickly pass into disuse, like many others before.
- Initial planning attempts can become so complex and cumbersome that the resulting plan has little day-to-day value as a management tool.
- In a highly volatile economy, many companies have found their strategic business plans to be of limited value. Little is gained by grafting a HR plan to an unreliable business plan.

Source: Lawrence M. Baytos, "A 'No Frills' Approach to Human Resource Planning," *Human Resource Planning,* 1984, pp. 39–46. Reprinted by permission.

In our own [Quaker Oats's] HR planning efforts, we were acutely conscious of these dangers. Nevertheless, the potential was most appealing and achievable provided we were able to develop a pragmatic "no-frills" approach.

SOME BASIC ASSUMPTIONS

In structuring our efforts, some basic decisions had to be made at the outset.

1. We would not have a HR planning "guru." To take planning responsibility out of the hands of our key HR functional specialist and generalists would diminish their jobs and reduce their commitment to the end product.
2. The HR plan would not be elaborate, especially in its early form. A ponderous document would simply turn off senior management and gather dust.
3. We were wary of investing too heavily in outside help. Our focus was to develop the broad general themes. A healthy application of old-fashioned common sense, business judgment, and traditional corporate values were sufficient to bring the issues into focus.
4. We did not want to get excessively preoccupied with HR planning. HR strategies can affect business strategies, but they are seldom the drivers. One only has to read the daily announcements of layoffs, bankruptcies and mergers for verification of this reality.
5. Our "no-frills" approach pales by comparison with the sophisticated and comprehensive approaches used by GE, Honeywell and others. However, it is consistent with our view that HR planning is simply another management tool and not an end in itself. We felt it was better to have managers asking for more planning rather than complain about too much.

Adaptation of a planning process to the company's style and philosophy was not an easy task. We did have the benefit of an informal, but relatively strong pro-employee philosophy of management. The philosophy was supported by some thoughtful and effective programs, particularly among our larger and older profit centers. On the other hand, there were some significant impediments to developing a useful overall strategic approach. Since these deterrents are typical of many major companies today, they are worthy of consideration.

1. We have a decentralized approach to profit center management, requiring careful selling of any planning concepts emanating from headquarters.
2. About 45% of our employees are based outside the U.S., creating concerns about cross-cultural application of specific principles.
3. The level of commitment and sophistication of HR programs (but not professionals) varied widely. These variations were accounted for by how long the profit center had been a part of the company (ranging from 105 years to a few months) and differing needs resulting from industry characteristics (food, toys, specialty retailing, chemicals, etc.)

Given the diversity of the company, any attempt to impose a rigid set of objectives and timetables would be greeted with passive, nonviolent yet total resistance.

RELATING HR PLAN TO FINANCIAL/OPERATING PLANS

At Quaker the key planning medium is a three-year operating/financial plan. In the company's early planning efforts, longer time periods were utilized. However, in a rapidly changing economic and competitive environment, the projections beyond the third year proved to be of limited value. The process can be represented as shown here:

financial plans permits us to develop appropriate HR plans. Furthermore, if a specific HR issue can affect achievements of financial plans, it would be introduced. An example of the latter would be highlighting the risks of a rapid expansion program when there has been inadequate time to develop key managers.

THE PLANNING FORMAT

The HR planning process we used was very straightforward. It does not require a mastery of a specific behavioral science or strategic planning theory. The process is represented in Figure 1. Specific steps (A–E) are keyed to the chart.

A. Where we are The review of the current status made us acutely aware of the

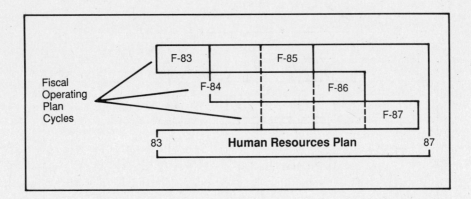

Conceptually, the HR plan supports and helps bind the operating plans together. There are some major differences between the two plans in content and approach.

We have not incorporated our specific HR plans into the financial planning documents. However, a knowledge of the

widely varying degrees of sophistication in our current programs. The needs of our high-tech plastic molding plan in New York State are very different from our recently acquired orange juice processor in Florida. To some extent, these differing needs are a permanent condition.

Plan Characteristics

Strategic/Financial	Human Resource	Rationale for HR Difference
a) Financial or operational in nature, SBU specific	Broadly defined	Based on general principles which apply across business/country lines
b) 3-year cycles repeated annually	Longer cycles, less frequent iteration	Makeup and attitudes of a large work force can be changed only slowly and slightly
c) Finite performance measures; ROE, market shares, EPS growth	Softer performance measures, e.g. percentage openings filled internally, "quality" of the work force, etc.	Progress harder to measure, numbers may not be as important as qualitative evaluation

FIGURE 1

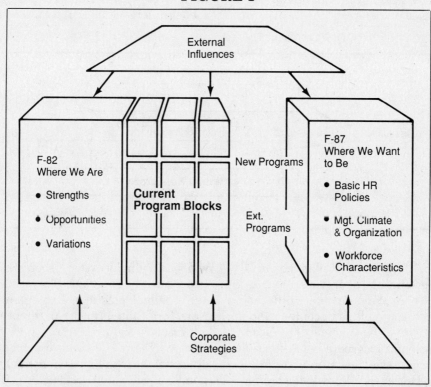

FIGURE 2
HR Building Blocks

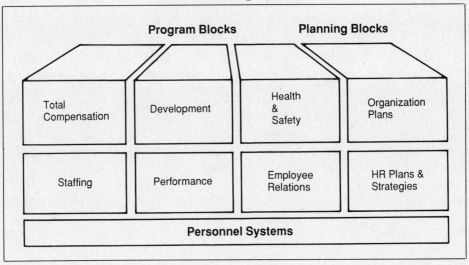

B. Program review Our approach to reviewing current HR programs involved a liberal adaptation of Dr. James Walker's HR building blocks. This proved to be helpful for participants to develop a conceptual understanding of what we were trying to accomplish. (See Figure 2.)

Our review led to the addition of the employee relations and health and safety program blocks, which are not included in Dr. Walker's model. Since these are an important part of our total HR management responsibility, we felt their inclusion and integration were important. Our visual model also reduces the predominance of the planning activities. We felt this to be more consistent with our organizational realities.

C. Corporate business strategies Quaker has done an effective job in the development and broad communication of overall financial goals and operating strategies. Our task was to determine how these would affect HR objectives and programs. Our preparation included the presentation on the corporate plan by the planning department head. Some examples of the issues that emerged included the following:

- The need for white-collar productivity improvements to help meet ambitious earnings growth targets in a soft economy.
- Need for more intensive management development to meet the demands of international businesses that have been in a high growth mode.
- The need to prepare for the HR aspects of rapidly developing a new business segment.

Quaker's strategies have remained reasonably steady for years and have been met on a relatively consistent basis. Therefore, the assessment of the internal impact was relatively straightforward. A more difficult challenge is the assessment of the external environment.

D. *External* It was easy enough to see that many of the HR programs we have, and will want to have, have been shaped by forces outside the company. A thorough analysis of the external forces is costly, and organizations offering "environmental scans" are popping up. However, we found that most of what we needed to know is available in government publications and the business press supplemented by studies such as the Yankelovich "New Values" reports. Eventually, we managed to group the major categories, as follows:

External environment
- Demographics
- Economic Conditions
- Sociological Trends
- Technology
- Regulatory Environment
- Union Initiatives

We attempted to identify major developments very broadly and trace their logical implications for HR programs. A package of reading materials was provided to those providing input to the process so that we might approach the effort with similar outlooks.

The analysis of external impact is not a highly refined part of our planning process. Nor is refinement a high priority, since our product mix and range of talent needed suggest that we can accommodate moderate disruptions or directional changes in the environment influences. The same assessment will not hold true for many companies. For example, trends in the number of electronic engineering graduates may be of critical importance to a computer manufacturer.

E. *The resulting objectives* A summary of the principal areas covered by statements of objectives is shown in Figure 3. The review process led to a variety of reactions. Business areas which had an effective HR function for some years may have felt the objectives were not challenging enough, while some of our recently acquired units may view them as nearly impossible. One manager stated the objectives seemed like ordinary "common sense." The point is, however, that

FIGURE 3
Human Resource Objectives

I. **Individual Performance and Growth**
 1. Productivity Improvement — Employee Involvement
 2. Individual Performance Against Objectives (Fair Appraisals)
 3. Recruitment and Personnel Development

II. **Meeting Employee Needs**
 1. Competitive Compensation, Equitable Pay Opportunities
 2. Comprehensive Benefits, Financial Protection
 3. Employment Continuity
 4. Employee Safety and Health

III. **Working Relationships**
 1. Teamwork
 2. Two-Way Communication (Union-Free Status)
 3. Creativity/Innovation

IV. **Method of Operation**
 1. Organization Structure
 2. Employee Ownership Perspective

we have broad agreement on what represents "common sense" for management of human resources. The leaders could go beyond the basic standards setting the pace for the rest of the corporation.

F. Filling the gap   The last step in the process is to fill the gap between where we are and where we want to be by the end of the plan cycle. This is the prioritization phase. This gap may be filled by expanding current programs or creating entirely new ones.

Filling Need Areas	Needs Addressed	Example
Expand Current Programs	Frequency Content Quality	Assign U.S. trainers to meet international needs
Create New Programs	Current Emerging Future	Training and organization planning to enhance creativity and innovation

The priorities that were developed were company-wide in nature. Consistent with the varying degrees of sophistication, the prioritization phase was carried out through our numerous profit centers. I find the long-term objectives especially helpful in visits to our various international subsidiaries. Working from the same overall framework, the process of determining current status and future priorities is greatly facilitated.

COMMUNICATING OBJECTIVES

We felt it was extremely important to communicate our HR objectives to those employees throughout the world whose personnel actions affect employee perceptions and progress toward our goals. For example, there are literally thousands of our managers who do performance appraisals. If we did not clearly communicate our goals regarding appraisals, how could we expect our managers to work toward them?

This approach is strongly supported by Ouchi's description of a "Theory Z" company. Ouchi's examples are mostly anecdotal. However, in *Corporate Cultures,* by Deal and Kennedy, some very strong evidence was cited for building a values-centered corporate culture.

In their study they profiled 80 prominent companies.

- 24 of 80 companies had a clearly articulated philosophy
- 18 of these 24 had communicated the philosophy broadly
- All 18 companies had outstanding performance records

We found this data quite compelling; and since it fit with basic corporate philosophies, communication will be a key element in the package.

Our communication package will combine the three major blocks of corporate objectives: basic corporate values, financial objectives and human resource objectives. Some example objectives are shown in Figure 4.

FIGURE 4
Communication Program

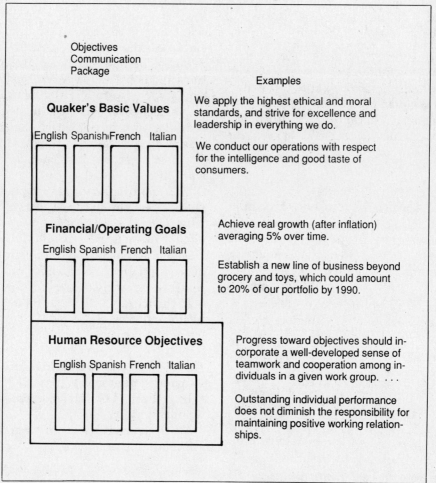

CONCLUSION

Development of the first cycle of our long-term HR objectives is almost complete. Our objectives were not nearly as specific as we had envisioned, but we can see that our newly articulated objectives have already proven to be of great value in helping to prioritize the activities of the HR departments in our several dozen subsidiaries. When there may be 50 or more "programs" that HR is responsible for developing and administering in a given profit center, it is most helpful to have agreement on the ten or so broad issues which are really important to the company. Already some new and unexpected initiatives have resulted. However, like any other planning process, the value of HR planning can only be proven when a new plateau of performance is achieved and then sustained for an extended period of time. Time will tell if we have adopted a very useful management tool, or simply fallen prey to "just another fad."

Lawrence M. Baytos is Vice President, Corporate Personnel, at Quaker Oats Company, Chicago.

Matching International Business Growth and International Management Development
Ruth G. Shaeffer

Traditionally, American companies have focused most of their attention on doing business right in their own backyard. The U.S. market for goods and services is huge and until the early 1980s most American firms believed it provided ample opportunities for profitable growth.

Doing business overseas was almost an after-thought — but a very appealing one. For several decades following World War II, there was unusually strong demand for U.S. products abroad. Most of the other industrialized countries of the world were still rebuilding from the war and U.S. companies also had the advantage of major economies of scale that permitted lower prices.

This *extra* business was generally handled on an *export* basis — back in those days we dominated world trade. As time went on, whenever the volume of business in a given foreign country warranted it, the parent corporation might establish an overseas production and sales subsidiary in that country to provide essentially the same kinds of goods and services it had already developed for the U.S.

In other words, even though a U.S. company might have subsidiaries in many major countries of the world, these businesses were not likely to be free-standing. They were *add-ons* — satellite businesses that owed their continuing existence to new products and marketing approaches developed for the firm's U.S. market. They were, if you will, the *tail* of the dog — a friendly tail that wagged a lot but not an integral part of the dog's body.

OLD STYLE MANAGEMENT DEVELOPMENT

Under such circumstances, it is not surprising that U.S. companies focused virtually all their management development efforts on their U.S. managers.

Source: Ruth G. Shaeffer, "Matching International Business Growth and International Management Development," *Human Resource Planning,* Volume 12, Number 1, pp. 29–35. Reprinted by permission.

Without even thinking very much about it, they just assumed that all their future key executives would be Americans. (The same thing was true of companies headquartered in other countries. British firms expected to have British executives; French firms French ones; and so on.)

There were other ways in which these companies assumed the *status quo* would continue indefinitely. For example, they expected that:

- The company would continue to grow and prosper simply by providing much of the same kinds of goods and services it had in the past.
- Replicating the staffing of the existing organization — including maintaining much the same perspectives, know-how, and skills at various levels — would keep the company on track.
- The firm's management development efforts would therefore be considered successful if they produced what we might call *clones* — almost identically qualified replacements for individual executives whenever they might be needed.

Going along with their expectation that they were running a *steady-state* organization, most chief executives also assumed that:

- The best and most efficient way to manage the company was through a top-down, vertical chain-of-command. All major decisions would be made at corporate headquarters by the CEO and his staff (or, in the case of European companies, by the Managing Board).
- Line managers at lower organization levels were expected to manage the day-to-day operation of their assigned units in accordance with uniform company policies and directives, including detailed operating plans and budgets. They were not expected to concern themselves with any broader, more long-range issues.

Of course, not all companies were quite this rigid, but, in retrospect, many will admit they really were.

THE SHIFT TO STRATEGIC BUSINESS MANAGEMENT

Today, of course, the situation looks quite different. The environment for business has become turbulent, fast-paced, fiercely competitive, and increasingly global in scope; companies headquartered all over the world are being forced to change. They all need to manage their affairs in a much more flexible dynamic way. They are focusing on what, when, and how to *change* rather than on how to maintain the *status quo*. And, since their primary objective is to be a prosperous, growing enterprise, it has been back to *business* management basics for them:

- To decide what range of businesses they now need to be in for competitive reasons. And to consider how these businesses should be defined and interrelated.
- To formulate and implement viable competitive strategies — possibly

global strategies — for each of those businesses.
- To be aware of and flexibly responsive to changing markets and changing technologies all over the world.
- To become more agile and resilient in dealing with unexpected political, economic, and competitive challenges and opportunities.

Accomplishing all this requires a very different overall management system: The new approach to managing that they are using provides much greater autonomy at lower levels and is much less rigid.

- Major strategic decision-making responsibilities are being distributed to teams of line executives in charge of business units throughout the organization (including those overseas). Each organization level deals with a different set of strategic issues and so adds value in a different way. An interactive dialogue then takes place between the various parts and levels of the organization to reach agreement on appropriate strategies and to allocate available resources.
- Information-gathering and information-sharing become integral parts of each line manager's job, whether at home or abroad.
- Close *team work* is needed in planning and smoothly implementing strategically necessary change without undermining the viability of on-going operations.
- And strong *personal leadership* is needed to build consensus and to inspire commitment to making strategic change happen.

It is obvious this new way of managing calls for different perspectives, for different information, for different skills, and for much greater tolerance for ambiguity and uncertainty. These new requirements must, of course, be taken into account in planning all management selection and development efforts, regardless of whether they take place in the U.S. or abroad.

STAGES OF INTERNATIONAL BUSINESS DEVELOPMENT

Doing business internationally is becoming much more important competitively. As U.S. firms get more involved, their approach tends to evolve through four distinct stages.

For most companies, *international sales* — the exporting of products to dealers, distributors, or end users in various countries — is usually the first step. As the business grows, however, they usually move on to the next stage.

They set up *multinational operations* — operations in certain specific foreign countries to make as well as to sell certain products. These foreign subsidiaries are often expected to broaden their activities to include all the major businesses the parent corporation is in. When this is the case, a mother/daughter relationship is established, with the overseas daughter looking very much like the mother company at home. But the company's French daughter will have no dealings with its German daughter or its English daughter. Each will stay within its national boundaries. (Some people think we should use the term *multidomestic* rather than *multinational* to describe this form of country-by-country organization.)

As I have already mentioned, such country organizations are not usually free-standing businesses, but now that companies have shifted to strategic *business* management, the country organizations do plan their own competitive product/market strategies and often make some minor product adaptations to fit local market needs.

There are some kinds of businesses in which it is almost essential to be organized by country. Insurance is one, for it is heavily regulated at the country level. So, I believe, are pharmaceuticals. And, even though McDonald's seems to have universal appeal — I have seen them in Europe and also in Japan—many food businesses and restaurant chains limit their operations to certain specific countries.

Comparatively speaking, the markets served by country-by-country operations are small so that no significant economies of scale can be achieved. Furthermore, insufficient funds are generated to support much R & D.

But the barriers separating national economic systems are breaking down and thanks to such wonders as movies, satellite television, global journalism, and instant telecommunications, much broader markets are indeed developing.

- The European Economic Community, for example, is truly becoming a tariff-free *regional* economy in which it is possible to produce goods for the whole Community in one country and market them in all the others.

  A maker of dog food was telling me what a great advantage this offers in competing against odd-line national companies. His company uses different labels, brand names, and advertising for different companies but all the product is produced in one place. As he put it, "The dogs don't care."

  But notice we are now talking about *whole dogs* — not about tails. This is a free-standing business that is virtually independent of its parent company. It is even large enough to support most of its own product and market R & D.
- Closer to home, the trade barriers between Canada and the United States have just been reduced again. North America, not including Mexico, is increasingly being treated as a single strategic business region.
- There may soon be a barrier-free zone in Southeast Asia too.

These changes are leading some diversified companies to restructure on the basis of *regional businesses* instead of lumping all the company's businesses together in country organizations. They may still have operations in all the same countries, but each country will be producing a given product for the whole region, not just for itself. Moreover, the key strategic planning will now be done at the regional level.

To add even further complexity, manufacturing firms all over the world are making extensive use of parts and components from low-wage areas in Asia, Mexico, and South America. As one U.S. auto parts manufacturer put it, "We have a big operation in Korea. We never expected to, but our biggest U.S. customer asked us to go there to supply his new Korean plant. Of course we did, and now we are supplying our other customers back home with Korean-made parts too."

As business activities all over the world become more and more intertwined, and as foreign firms continue to make competitive inroads worldwide, the executives who head the major business units within large American companies are increasingly being given *global business charters*. Having already pruned, delayered, and strengthened their U.S. business to fight off foreign competition at home, they are now being charged with formulating and implementing *global* business expansion strategies. The Japanese have already given us a lesson or two in how it is done. Sometimes it is possible to market the identical quality product worldwide. But often it requires knowing enough about local markets to identify profitable niches and tailor the basic product to them.

The decline in the value of the dollar will help our exports somewhat. But the recognition that international business growth has its own stages and imperatives will have much greater impact.

- Just as much, if not more, attention must now be given to the cultures of different countries, the changing needs of foreign markets, the changing economic and political situations of various countries and the changing technologies being developed in other parts of the world.
- And just as much, if not more, attention must be given to the selection and development of international business managers. They must now do far more than manage the company's existing overseas operations. They are key to identifying and taking timely action to grasp the strategic opportunities in their areas. Working closely with their U.S.-based counterparts, these overseas executives may well be able to turn the company into the multi-regional or global success story it hopes to become.

As the proportion of a company's revenues and profits from the other parts of the world increases, it makes sense to include more executives with international business experience in the top management group. A substantial number of leading companies are already working very hard to achieve this outcome. Meanwhile, they are taking every opportunity they can to broaden the perspectives of current top-level executives and to enhance their understanding of cross-cultural differences. For example, one company has instituted a mandatory Senior Executive Program which lasts one week each year. The meetings take place all over the world and the priority topic at each one is the business environment and the strategy being followed in that area.

MATCHING INTERNATIONAL BUSINESS GROWTH AND INTERNATIONAL MANAGEMENT DEVELOPMENT?

You bet! In fact, you had best be ahead of the game. How else can you provide those international businesses with solid management expertise as they come on stream?

But much more than that, how else

can you start up the powerful innovating engine your company needs to take advantage of emerging opportunities and to drive strategic growth all over the world? Strategy, structure, and staffing must all be interrelated to achieve organization effectiveness — and in many cases the staffing must come first. The managers you help develop are the ones who will choose the strategy and design the structure.

- *Expect to be a U.S. business with international sales through sales reps, joint ventures, or distributor relationships?* Fine. Businesses in this category generally limit their management development efforts to their own U.S. managers, but some also offer to help develop their partner's managers. Moreover, if you see these export arrangements as temporary — as steppingstones leading toward country businesses or mother/daughter organizations, you may also want to provide some business management training and development to your sales reps, to your key liaison executives or even to the heads of various partner organizations. Assuming they have all lived in the particular country, these are high potential candidates to head up your next stage organization. They already know the territory and the business; they need opportunities to develop their strategic leadership skills and their general operating management skills.
- *Expect to be a U.S. business with multinational subsidiaries?* Because of the current emphasis on the management of *businesses,* country organizations are now likely to be represented on several lines of business strategy teams. Sometimes it is necessary to have a U.S. executive head up a country organization at first, but there is general agreement that just as soon as possible, virtually all the managers should be from the country. They, of course, need to learn how your company operates and to develop the skills required to fulfill their managerial roles. And it is important to remember that they too will soon have strategic planning responsibilities that require special tools and perspectives.

Furthermore, in preparation for the day when the company decides to establish *regional businesses,* the business managers within various country organizations might now begin to meet with each other to discuss recent developments and mutual problems, to share ideas and information and possible solution suggestions, and to begin to understand the reasons for their differing points of view. Some companies are also providing for temporary transfers between country organizations.

- *Expect to be a company comprised of regional businesses?* If the top two executives have lived in different countries within the region, there will be a constant reminder of the cultural and geographic differences that must be balanced in arriving at overall strategies and business plans for the region. If a company is expecting a U.S. executive to head up some regional business in Europe or Asia in four years or so, that person should be overseas *right now*. That company should also begin developing a foreign national as a teammate. Future regional managers will also benefit from heavy developmental emphasis on strategic leadership skills and a solid background in financial analysis. Team leadership skills are essential, for one of the first tasks will probably be to rationalize the production and distribution setup in the region to make it most cost effective.

Major regional businesses may well be a part of *global* businesses. Certainly the regional business leaders cannot be indifferent to what is happening elsewhere in the world. For example, when Proctor and Gamble lost market share in Japan because of the technological improvement in disposable diapers that a Japanese company had made, P & G did far more than improve its own product in Japan. It immediately advised all regions of the new technology and it was installed worldwide so that no competitor could cut into P & G's market share in any other region.

In the future, the executives who head major regional businesses are likely to be prime candidates to become CEO's of those same businesses on a global scale. To prepare them for that possibility and to ensure that current global business strategies appropriately balance the interests of all regions, leading edge companies are including their regional business leaders as members of the top management teams that run each of their global businesses.

- *Expect to be a world-class company with several global businesses?* In terms of further management development, companies report the need to emphasize worldwide information sharing on economic, social, political, technological, and market trends, and to focus on building teamwork across related business lines as well as across functional lines and country-regional lines. It is by no means an easy job to run a global business successfully even when it is done on a multi-discipline team basis. Sometimes, a truly transnational organization producing products globally may make sense for competitive reasons.

But of course, the real world is even more complex than this rather simple progression for categorizing international business development options and international management development options makes it seem. For example:

- Some of the company's businesses can best be organized one way and some another.
- Businesses may need to be set up differently in one country, say Japan, than they are in the rest of the world.
- The appropriate organization form for a business may change drastically, say from global to multidomestic, if it shifts to a niche strategy. What then? One of the best things that has happened since companies stopped relying on a top-down management system is they now place less emphasis on uniformity and symmetry. Each business unit is much more free to organize its affairs to meet its own strategic needs and to build its own relationships with other parts of the company. Moreover, in addition to participating in some corporate-wide executive development programs, it is free to focus on meeting its own special development needs.

If you, as a human resource development specialist or a human resource planner, are aware of the competitive imperatives that underlie international business development you will readily understand how crucial your role is in making strategic change happen. You will also understand how important it is to take a proactive role in preparing for organization change rather than simply responding to it after the fact.

It is often said and it is, of course, true that the company's CEO is key. More and more CEOs are using the people who will be most affected by a major change — both line and staff — to get together as a team to figure out what needs to be done, how, by whom, and when so the responding change will be supported and implemented smoothly. The goal is to help the company achieve profitable growth by responding effectively to the challenges and opportunities posed by the changing environment.

Will *you* be the one who sits back and says that it is what everyone else in my company should do? Or will you be right out there on the team that is making strategic change happen?

Ruth G. Shaeffer is employed by The Conference Board.

Cases

Pacific Aircraft Company
Jeffrey A. McNally

You have just been selected as a human resources consultant advising the president, Mr. William H. Wilson, of the Pacific Aircraft Company (PAC), a medium-sized aircraft manufacturing company located in the suburbs of Los Angeles, California. At the present time you are meeting with Mr. Wilson for the first time, and he is giving you some background information about the company before you meet with the personnel staff members later in the day. Mr. Wilson, the founder and principal stockholder of the company, is a man of about forty-five who seems to have a considerable amount of personal pride and satisfaction in his firm. Mr. Wilson, nervously swiveling and rocking in his chair, says to you:

"This company is where it is today because of the direction and guidance I have provided over the past fifteen or so years. My primary personnel staff members have all been personally selected by me, and I've watched them grow into their jobs. You are the first 'outsider' hired by Pacific, so you might find some of our folks a bit suspicious of your motives. I hope not though. But I'm beginning to get the feeling that we really have a good deal less management control than we might have had a few years back. We've made a number of costly personnel mistakes recently, and we've never done that before. I'm beginning to feel that we're really not doing the sort of comprehensive personnel planning we should be doing. We've also had a higher than usual turnover rate with some of our new employees, and this is starting to worry me too. Well, we'll be meeting with the personnel staff members shortly, so let me give you some background data that you should find useful."

1. *Size* — Approximately 1,550 employees; approximately 125 white-collar employees and approximately 1,325 blue-collar employees.
2. *Sales* — *FY 76–77*, 148.7 million; *FY 77–78*, 153.2 million; *FY 78–79*, 152.9 million; *FY 79–80*, 158.6 million.
3. *Profits* — *FY 76–77*, 13.9 million; *FY 77–78*, 15.4 million; *FY 78–79*, 14.9 million; *FY 79–80*, 16.2 million.
4. *Technology* — assembly line production with highly specialized tooling and assembly. Heavy emphasis on quality control.

This case was prepared by Jeffrey A. McNally as a basis for class discussion rather than to illustrate effective or ineffective handing of an administrative situation.

Source: Raymond L. Hilgert, Sterling H. Schoen, and Joseph W. Towle, *Cases and Policies in Personnel/Human Resources Management*, 5th ed. Boston: Houghton Mifflin Company, 1986. Reprinted by permission.

5. *Goals* — To increase sales and profits by a minimum of 25 percent within the next fiscal year.
6. *Market* — Small- to medium-sized airlines and private aircraft owners located primarily on the West Coast.

A little later on this first day you and Mr. Wilson arrive at the conference room at the PAC headquarters for your scheduled meeting, and Mr. Wilson begins things by making the following introductory remarks:

"For the benefit of our new human resources consultant, I have asked each of our personnel staff members to present a very candid overview of their particular area of concern. As the head of Pacific, let me get the ball rolling by saying that from where I sit, this firm has come a long way, but that doesn't mean that there's not still a long way to go. I honestly believe that we are now in a position to really make our move and expand our markets. I see us positioned to make really significant growth in the upcoming fiscal year.

"We need to get that fighting spirit, that competitive edge, back into Pacific, because it seems we've begun to stagnate, and I think we need a revitalization of our primary business interests. 'Future shock' seems to have set in, and we appear to have been passed by. I am somewhat concerned by many of the economic signals I've been reading lately. It seems that we may be dipping into another recession, this time possibly a much more prolonged one, and if I'm reading the tea leaves correctly, interest rates may be going even higher. Let's also consider our operating costs. I have been reviewing the printouts recently, and I notice that our absenteeism, tardiness, and even quality control wastage rates are climbing dramatically. I think we should all consider adopting some of the stringent methods of accountability some other successful firms use. Believe me, we need to streamline our operations to cut out the fat and save as much as possible in those areas for which we are responsible. Now is the time! Not only do our internal operations require some changes, but I also think it's time for all of us to think creatively about ways to develop and expand our markets.

"I've talked more than enough for one meeting, and our real purpose today is to discuss the myriad of personnel management issues which face Pacific, and I know you people are in the best position to do this. Let's have a very informal, free-flowing, give-and-take session today.

"For the benefit of our human resources consultant, let me introduce each of you and then we can begin to roll up our sleeves and get to work. First, our Vice President of Personnel, Ms. Donna Gregory. Next, Donna's primary assistant, Mr. Patrick Brace, and last, but certainly not least, Mr. Jeffrey Walker. Donna, let me ask you to begin."

"Bill, I have to agree with you that we need to do something to energize Pacific, and that's why I'm anxious to have this fresh look to help us analyze the personnel management processes of the company. From my perspective, one thing which has been causing me headaches lately is our community relations. Various groups are exerting considerable pressure on me, because they say we have to hire some minorities. I know from talking to manufacturing that they're also receiving outside pressure about our alleged pollution of Lake Winemea. I have one thing to say to all of these groups . . . Poppycock! No one, but no one, tells Pacific Aircraft Company how to run our business. We are today, as we have always been, in the business of making money by making our customers happy. Our responsibility is to our customers, workers, and ourselves — nobody else.

"The other big area of concern pressuring our personnel office is governmental interference with our internal affairs, specifically from the EEOC. Some of their publications seem arbitrary and contradictory, and they are making life quite difficult for us. Things change constantly. I'm spending an increasing amount of time answering correspondence and providing data for federal agencies and commissions. We have to insure that we are complying with all the relevant regulations or else we'll be sued and perhaps even have to pay substantial fines. As a matter of fact, I spent a great deal of time preparing that written Affirmative Action plan for the EEOC. I don't know how much time we wasted on establishing employment goals and then writing plans designed to meet those goals. I don't know where the report is right now, but I probably could locate it if our new consultant would be interested.

"I too have noticed the rather high turnover and absentee rates production has been experiencing, and as you know I was able to find replacements for everyone we lost. It seems to me that we may be better off without these people, because for the most part they are a bunch of malcontents who want something for nothing. The 'work ethic' seems to be a thing of the past, particularly with the sector of society that typically enters this company. The average age of our blue-collar worker is twenty-four, with ten years of formal education, and only 28 percent of the entire work force is married, most of whom are our more stable white-collar employees.

"Mr. Wilson, we have another problem I probably should mention. We may be losing that large government contract we picked up last year. We really don't have the trained personnel to meet the contract specifications. We have to furnish records to the government to demonstrate that we have an adequate number of employees with the right technical qualifications who meet the mandated government equal employment opportunity goals. I simply don't have those kinds of records available at a moment's notice. You know I asked you to give me the go ahead on an employment planning information system, and some of the things Pat Brace is working on sound pretty good, but that will not help us with the loss of this contract.

"Bill, while we've got you here, I wonder if you think we should schedule a trip to the State University as we did last year. It seemed to be worth the time and effort, and it really wasn't all that costly. [As you observed, Bill thought for several minutes and then nodded his approval.] How many people should we recruit and what types?"

Mr. Wilson replied: "That's not an easy question to answer. Although I like having college graduates around, I am a little concerned that we are approaching this unsystematically. I think we first need to determine our requirements. Let's start by having all the department heads submit a list of their needs over the next six-month, one-year, and two-year time frames as far as college graduates go. Then we can consolidate the requirements and know what we are looking for. When you talk to these individuals, remember to emphasize how great the aircraft industry is. If we can get them to want to be involved with the aircraft industry, it will be that much easier to get them to Pacific. This is especially important because some of our problems with EEOC and some recent bad publicity may turn off some of these potential employees. When we get them here I hope they are satisfied; therefore, it might be a good idea to show them in advance job descriptions of the jobs they would be performing."

The next personnel staff member to talk was Ms. Gregory's primary assistant, Mr. Patrick Brace.

"My primary responsibility at Pacific Aircraft is to read applicable regulations and complete most of the correspondence coming out of the personnel department. My major project right now is the complete preparation of job analyses for all the white-collar positions in the company. I've been working on this for about nine months now. First of all, I examined job descriptions used for similar jobs elsewhere which are listed in the *Dictionary of Occupational Titles*. I found that adequate job descriptions and job specifications exist for about 85 percent of our employees. For those jobs which are unique to Pacific, I have interviewed current and former job occupants. When I combine the data they provide me with my own observations of their performance on the job, I think I'm able to write a pretty good job description and specification. Now that I have most of them written, I'd like to see them used throughout Pacific. In particular, I would like to see you use them in the selection and recruiting process, which is so important to us. I would like next to turn it over to Jeff Walker."

"At Pacific Aircraft Company my area is selection of employees, and unlike Patrick, I know what I'm doing in the company is *essential* to our future. The government has nothing to do with selection, so we do this because the selection of the most highly qualified employees is in our best interests. Important as this work is, though, I'd be less than honest if I didn't admit that we've been having some problems in selection over the past several months. Mr. Wilson already alluded to this, but I've been keeping track of some of the most recent problems.

"1. One woman we hired is doing a great job for us. Then we accidentally found out she has a prison record for a felony committed twelve years ago. Her supervisor wants to know how we missed this and wants to let her go. We have no policy on this, but I feel she's more than proven herself in three years on the job at PAC.

"2. One of our best managerial candidates refused to undergo our two-day battery of psychological testing. He said it was an 'invasion of his privacy.'

"3. PAC also requires a polygraph test for all of the blue-collar males who apply to the company. We've had a few refuse to take it. Our thefts are high, but I wonder if this test is any good. Personally, I feel it's essential.

"4. Our turnover has been high, as has been mentioned. We think it may be because we aren't matching the best people to the right jobs. We set our standards for selection as high as possible, and this is easier to do with unemployment rates so high.

"Maybe our consultant can shed some light on these problems, because I don't know what, if anything, we're doing wrong. We have each employee fill out a nine-page application blank which asks about the potential employee's job experiences, educational background, age, sex, marital status, number of children, and so forth, so I don't think there are any problems here. Once we get a sufficiently large stack of applications, Patrick, Donna, and I sit down together and decide who will be selected to take our battery of psychological tests and the polygraph test. Based upon the results of these, we vote to make our selections. I know I speak for the entire personnel staff; we'd certainly appreciate your analysis."

Mr. Wilson concluded the meeting by thanking everyone for their preparation and candor. He concluded that it was a good meeting and that it was now time to let you get to work.

As any good human resources consultant, you want to spend some time observing firsthand the operations at Pacific. Here are some of the situations you observe.

As everyone begins to file out of the conference room, you overhear a hushed conversation between Patrick and Jeffrey. "Where did Donna get those figures about the average age of our blue-collar workers being twenty-four, ten years of formal education, and 28 percent of the work force married? Those numbers don't seem even close to being correct. She's always trying to look good in front of the old man."

As you walk toward the personnel office, you observe an individual rushing through the swinging doors. He joined a group of five other people who were apparently sitting there waiting for their new employee orientation to begin. One of the secretaries welcomed the new employees to Pacific Aircraft, and then the "paper blitz" began. In the next thirty minutes she gave them a lot of paper and forms — work rules, benefits packages available, pay and insurance forms to fill out, and so on. Then each new employee received a slip of paper with the name and location of their new supervisor, and they were told to report to their supervisor. As you observed this individual as he attempted to find Andrew Villaneuva, his new supervisor, he seemed very lost. Finally he found Andrew, who took him around the immediate work area for a couple of minutes, pointed out his new workbench, then wished him good luck.

As you continue to walk around Pacific, you observe a young, very well-dressed individual walk into the personnel department. The individual begins to talk to Patrick, and as you listen he explains that he is about to graduate from pharmacy school. He is very interested in working somewhere in this area, because he feels the L.A. area is a very exciting place to live and work. Patrick begins to explain to the young man that it is quite unlikely that Pacific would really be the best place for a pharmacology graduate, when Mr. Wilson walks into the room.

"Patrick, I'll take care of this young man. You look just like the bright kind of person we're looking for around here. Come on into my office and we'll see what we can do."

As you meander through other areas of the organization, you observe a very homogeneous group of employees. Of course, you don't see everyone, but you see primarily white, middle-aged, male employees with the exception of the female secretaries in the front office. Employee morale seems to be fairly good from what you can see. You also observe that some of the employees eye you rather suspiciously. Mr. Wilson had mentioned this possibility.

As a human resources consultant, you, of course, realize that it would be nice to spend more time at Pacific, but you also realize that the meter is always running, and PAC is only one of your clients. You're not completely sure what Mr. Wilson will want to discuss at your next meeting, so you want to be certain that you analyze the Pacific Aircraft Company as thoroughly as possible.

Jeffrey A. McNally (Lieutenant Colonel, U.S. Army) is affiliated with the Department of Behavioral Sciences and Leadership, U.S. Military Academy.

Weaver Rental
K. Michele Kacmar

Surveying the five neat piles of paper on her desk, Pam Ritter sighed. Would she really ever be able to decide which of the five job analysis techniques she should select for her company, Weaver Rental? It all had seemed so easy when her boss, Rick Jacobi, approached her with the assignment. All she had to do was prepare a report indicating the most appropriate job analysis technique for the company and support her decision with facts. But then she began researching available job analysis techniques.

Without much effort, Pam was able to locate five different techniques that companies use frequently: the Position Analysis Questionnaire (PAQ), Guidelines Oriented Job Analysis (GOJA), Functional Job Analysis (FJA), Job Element Method (JEM), and Iowa Merit Employment Systems (IMES).

Whereas each method is similar — all are job analysis techniques — Pam soon found that each also has unique characteristics. The Position Analysis Questionnaire has the largest research base, with over twenty-five years of research findings. PAQ is a structured job analysis questionnaire that can be used to analyze a wide spectrum of jobs. The Guidelines Oriented Job Analysis is relatively new, and generally used to develop a job-relevant selection system. GOJA can be used for job analysis purposes, however, if only the first few steps in the procedure are used. The Functional Job Analysis is an extremely thorough procedure that applies a standardized language for describing and measuring a worker's tasks. Two different types of task information — what a worker does and how a task is performed — are generated when FJA is used. The Job Element Method focuses on worker-oriented behaviors in order to identify characteristics of superior workers on the job. These characteristics, called job elements, are further analyzed and divided

"Weaver Rental" by K. Michele Kacmar is reprinted by permission of the author.

into subelements. Because of its nature, JEM is a means of developing worker specifications as well as performing a job analysis. The Iowa Merit Employment Systems, like GOJA, provide a series of steps to follow to develop selection tests. If only the first few steps are performed, a job analysis results. To perform the job analysis, a workbook-like questionnaire is completed by individuals who understand the job.

Pam also found it fairly easy to develop a list of specific requirements for the job analysis technique Weaver Rental needed:

1. a fairly easy-to-use system that required limited training
2. a system that could be easily tailored to Weaver's needs
3. a system that could analyze all jobs at Weaver
4. comparability and reliability of data collected at various points in time
5. no minimum size of available job incumbents
6. a system applicable to other HR needs, such as developing selection tests and doing performance appraisals
7. reasonable cost

With all this information in front of her, Pam sat down and produced a table that indicated whether or not each of the five techniques met the specific requirements. Based on the results from the table, she ranked all the methods. Now all she had to do was write the report. But she just couldn't shake the thought that she had overlooked something in her investigation. With this thought in mind, before she started the report, she began reanalyzing the piles of papers in an attempt to convince herself that her analysis was correct.

Comparison of Available Job Analysis Techniques

Characteristics	Job Analysis Technique				
	PAQ	GOJA	FJA	JEM	IMES
Ease of use	2	1	2	1	1
Tailorability	3	3	2	1	1
Range of jobs	3	3	3	3	3
Comparability of data	3	1	2	3	1
Reliability of data	3	1	3	3	1
Incumbents needed	2	3	3	1	1
Applicability to HR needs	3	3	2	3	3
Cost	2	2	2	1	2
Total	21	17	19	16	13
Rank	1	3	2	4	5

K. Michele Kacmar is assistant professor at Rensselaer Polytechnic Institute.

Readings for Professional Growth and Enrichment

Ash, R. A., E. L. Levine, and F. Sistrunk (1983). "The Role of Jobs and Job-based Methods in Personnel and Human Resources Management." In K. M. Rowland and G. R. Ferris (eds.), *Research in Personnel and Human Resources Management,* Vol. 1. Greenwich, Conn.: JAI Press.

Baird, L., I. Meshoulam, and G. De Give (1983). "Meshing Human Resources Planning with Strategic Business Planning: A Model Approach." *Personnel* 60: 14–25.

Bamberger, W. (1983). "Understanding and Applying Demographic Information and Techniques." *Personnel Journal* 62 (January): 865–870.

Drzysofia, F., and J. Newman (1982). "Evaluating Employment Outcomes: Availability Models and Measures." *Industrial Relations* 21: 277–292.

Ghorpade, J., and T. J. Atchison (1980). "The Concept of Job Analysis: A Review and Some Suggestions. "*Public Personnel Management Journal* 9: 134–144.

Green, S. B., and T. Stutzman (1986). "An Evaluation of Methods to Select Respondents to Structured Job-Analysis Questionnaires." *Personnel Psychology* 39: 543–564.

Kaufman, D. J. (1984). "Planning: Strategic, Human Resources, and Employment: An Integrated Approach." *Management Planning* 32: 24–29.

Leigh, D. R. (1984). "Business Planning Is People Planning." *Personnel Journal* 63: 44–50.

Markowitz, J. (1981). "Four Methods of Job Analysis." *Training and Development Journal* (September): 112–121.

Miller, E. L., and E. H. Burack (1981). "A Status Report on Human Resource Planning from the Perspective of Human Resource Planners." *Human Resource Planning* 4: 33–40.

Russ, C. F., Jr. (1982). "Manpower Planning Systems: Part I." *Personnel Journal* 61: 40–45.

Russ, C. F., Jr. (1982). "Manpower Planning Systems: Part II." *Personnel Journal* 61: 119–123.

Scarborough, N., and T. W. Zimmerer (1982). "Human Resources Forecasting: Why and Where to Begin." *Personnel Administrator* 27: 55–61.

Schuster, F. E. (1982). "A Tool for Evaluating and Controlling the Management of Human Resources." *Personnel Administrator* 27 (October): 63–69.

Thompson, D. E., and T. A. Thompson (1982). "Court Standards for Job Analysis in Test Validation." *Personnel Psychology* 35: 865–874.

ORGANIZATIONAL ENTRY

Readings

Voluntary Affirmative Action and Preferential Treatment: Legal and Research Implications
Lawrence S. Kleiman / Robert H. Faley

Organizational attempts to ensure a balanced work force can result in employment practices that give some members of protected classifications preferential treatment. Often this preferential treatment is a result of the implementation of a voluntary affirmative action plan (AAP). The purpose of this paper is to examine the legal and research implications stemming from the implementation of such plans. By "voluntary" we mean an AAP that is neither required by Executive Order 11246 (which applies to government contractors) nor "court ordered." As such, voluntary AAPs can fall along a broad continuum including, for example, programs that result from an organization's formal analysis comparing work force availability with organizational utilization of specific protected subgroups, AAPs that are the product of a negotiated collective bargaining agreement between union and management, and AAPs that are based on consent decrees negotiated between plaintiff and defendant under the auspices of the court.

While the practice of implementing voluntary AAPs in the employment setting is fraught with ethical and political issues (especially when the AAP includes the use of preferential treatment), the focus of the present paper is on legal issues. It reviews important Supreme Court decisions in which "reverse discrimination" charges have been lodged against organizations for their alleged use of preferential treatment stemming from the implementation of voluntary AAPs.

THE *STEELWORKERS* DECISION

Claims of reverse discrimination brought before the courts have been adjudicated on the basis of statutory law (viz., Title VII of the Civil Rights Act of 1964) and Constitutional law (generally the Fourteenth Amendment). The first AAP-related claim of reverse discrimination in employment was addressed by the Supreme Court in *U.S. Steelworkers v. Weber* (1979), a Title VII case. The high court, in approving the defendant's AAP-based preferential treatment of

---

Source: Lawrence S. Kleiman and Robert H. Faley, "Voluntary Affirmative Action and Preferential Treatment: Legal and Research Implications," *Personnel Psychology,* 1988, 41, pp. 481–496. Reprinted by permission of *Personnel Psychology.*

An earlier version of this paper was presented at the second annual conference of the Society for Industrial and Organizational Psychology, April, 1987.

minorities (which called for a 50% quota for selecting blacks into an apprenticeship training program) devised a four-part test for judging the AAP's legality (i.e., whether the plan was "bona fide"). First, the Court ruled that an employer must demonstrate that the purpose of its AAP was remedial in nature. Second, the Court ruled that the plan must not unnecessarily trammel the interests of other (i.e., nonminority) employees. Third, the plan must not exclude non-covered group members as a class. And fourth, the Court ruled that the elements of the plan must be "reasonable."

In *Steelworkers*, the "remedial need" requirement was satisfied by evidence of the existence of a "conspicuous imbalance" that reflected underrepresentation of minorities in traditionally segregated job categories, which the AAP was designed to remedy. It is important to note the Court did not require that the employer acknowledge responsibility for the imbalance; the Supreme Court noted that companies need not admit to discrimination to take responsible affirmative action. As evidence that the second part of the test had been satisfied, the Court determined that the AAP did not require the discharge of nonminority employees or their replacement by minorities (i.e., "displacement"). The third part of the test (i.e., group exclusion) was satisfied by evidence indicating that 50% of those admitted to the apprenticeship training program were nonminority employees. Thus, the plan did not create an absolute bar to their advancement. Last, the elements of the plan were deemed "reasonable" on the basis of evidence that the plan was temporary in nature. Once established goals were met, the plan would be dismantled.

POST-*STEELWORKERS* DECISIONS

Since 1979 several other AAP-related reverse discrimination claims have been brought before the courts; some of these cases have reached the Supreme Court. In these cases the Supreme Court has reaffirmed, as well as further clarified, the Title VII standards originally set forth in *Steelworkers*. It has also dealt with previously unaddressed constitutional standards. All the Supreme Court decisions subsequent to *Steelworkers* and involving charges of reverse discrimination stemming from the implementation of a voluntary AAP (as well as two Supreme Court cases involving court-ordered AAPs) are reviewed in this section. Case summaries are presented in Table 1.

The Adjudication Process

In an EEO lawsuit, an employer's actions may be adjudicated on the basis of either the disparate treatment (intentional) or disparate impact (unintentional) theories of discrimination. Only the procedure for establishing disparate treatment will be discussed here since all Supreme Court decisions bearing on the legality of voluntary AAPs have dealt exclusively with such claims.

In adjudicating reverse discrimination disparate treatment cases, the courts have followed a three-step procedure that assesses (1) whether the plaintiff has successfully met its burden of establishing a prima facie case, (2) whether, if a prima facie case has been established, the defendant has successfully demonstrated that its actions were based on

TABLE 1
Summary of Post-Steelworkers Supreme Court Decisions

Case	Basis for Claim	Plaintiff's Allegation	Prevailing Party
Johnson (1987)	Title VII	A white male was passed over for promotion in favor of a less qualified female. The employer impermissibly took sex into account in making the promotion	Defendant
Paradise (1987)	Constitution	An AAP specifying a one-to-one black/white promotion quota impermissibly led to the rejection of four white applicants	Defendant
Sheet Metal Workers (1986)	Title VII Constitution	The lower court's actions violated the remedial provision of Title VII by ordering race-conscious relief benefitting individuals who were not *identified* victims of unlawful discrimination	Defendant
Cleveland (1986)	Title VII	The provisions of a consent decree violated the remedial provision of Title VII by benefitting individuals who were not *identified* victims of the defendant's discriminatory practices	Defendant
Wygant (1986)	Constitution	AAP impermissibly gave preference to minorities in layoff decisions	Plaintiff
Stotts (1984)	Title VII	The court improperly modified a consent decree in order to permit preferential treatment in layoff decisions	Plaintiff

legitimate, nondiscriminatory reasons, and (3) whether the plaintiff has successfully demonstrated that the "legitimate" reason advanced by the defendant was merely a pretext for discrimination. Figure 1 illustrates this adjudication process relative to AA complaints.

The focus of this paper centers on the second step of this procedure (viz., the employer's burden of demonstrating a legitimate nondiscriminatory reason for its AAP). Steps 1 and 3 are excluded because they have not as yet been addressed by the Supreme Court (see *Kromnick v. School District of Philadelphia,* 1984, and *Parker v. B & O Railroad Co.,* 1981, for lower-court decisions addressing the issue of prima facie evidence; see *Sester v. Novack Investment Co.,* 1981, and *Lehman v. Yellow Freight System,* 1981, for lower-court decisions addressing the issue of pretext).

The AAP Defense

This section focuses on the standards formulated by the courts for establishing that an AAP is a "legitimate, nondiscriminatory reason" for granting preferential treatment. Specifically addressed is the manner in which subsequent courts have interpreted and clarified the four-part test enumerated in *Steelworkers*. Evidence pertaining to the first part of the test is examined in the next section; evidence pertaining to the latter

FIGURE 1
Court's Adjudication Process for Affirmative Action Complaints

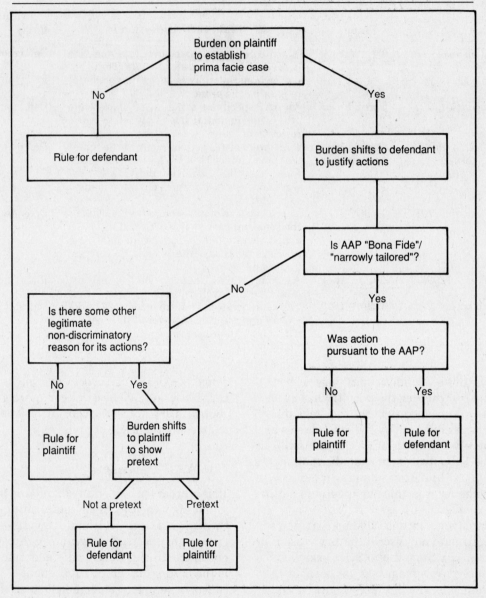

three parts are examined in subsequent sections.

Remedial purpose The criteria for meeting the remedial purpose portion of the four-part *Steelworkers* test differed depending on whether the plaintiff's action was based on Title VII or the *Constitution* (usually the Fourteenth Amendment). The issue was addressed in four post-*Steelworker* Supreme Court cases. *Wygant v. Jackson Board of Education* (1986) and *U.S. v. Paradise* (1986) were Fourteenth Amendment cases, and *Johnson v. Santa Clara County* (1987) and *Firefighters v. City of Cleveland* (1986) were Title VII cases.

The *Wygant* case focused on those provisions of a collective bargaining agreement that were meant to preserve minority hiring gains in the event of layoffs. The collective bargaining agreement stipulated that teachers with the most seniority would be retained unless the percentage of minority personnel laid off was greater than the percentage of minorities employed at that time. As a result of this, nonminorities were laid off while minority teachers with less seniority were retained. While claiming that it had not previously discriminated against minorities, the defendant attempted to demonstrate the remedial purpose of its AAP on the basis of prior *societal* rather than *employer-imposed* discriminatory actions. The core of its argument was that, due to the effects of societal discrimination, the percentage of minority teachers was less than that of minority students. These percentages, it was argued, needed to be equated in order to provide a sufficient number of minority teachers to serve as role models for minority students. The lower courts ruled in favor of the defendant, stating that it was unnecessary for the defendant to demonstrate prior discrimination in order to satisfy the remedial purpose requirement; a showing of societal discrimination based solely on a racial imbalance would be sufficient.

This decision was reversed by the Supreme Court, which stated that:

> The Court never has held that societal discrimination alone is sufficient to justify a racial classification. Rather, the Court has insisted upon some showing of prior discrimination by the government unit involved before allowing limited use of racial classifications in order to remedy such discrimination. (p. 6)

In *Paradise,* also a Fourteenth Amendment case, there was overwhelming evidence that the defendant had a prior history of discrimination against blacks who had applied for state trooper positions and had "dragged its feet" when forced by the court to rectify its past behavior. Among the past discriminatory actions were the use of unvalidated employment tests with adverse impact and discrimination against blacks at the trooper training academy. After 12 years of litigation, the defendant agreed to follow two consent decrees (which it had previously ignored) stipulating that blacks be given preferential treatment based on hiring and promotion quotas. Four white applicants, who were denied promotion to corporal as a result of the quota system, filed a class-action reverse discrimination suit.

The Supreme Court ruled in favor of the defendant, stating that the use of a quota system was acceptable under such adverse conditions.

We conclude that the relief ordered survives even strict scrutiny standards . . . for almost four decades the department had excluded blacks from all positions, including jobs in the upper ranks. Such egregious discriminatory conduct was "unquestionably a violation of the Fourteenth Amendment" . . . the pervasive, systematic, and obstinate discriminatory conduct of the Department created a profound need and a firm justification for the race-conscious relief ordered by the District Court. (p. 15)

In *Johnson,* a Title VII case, the defendant gave preference to a female over a male who had scored slightly higher (two points) on the selection criteria for a skilled craft worker position. The Supreme Court ruled that the AAP served a remedial purpose since it helped rectify a "conspicuous imbalance" in the defendant's work force that reflected underrepresentation of women in traditionally segregated job categories. As evidence of this "conspicuous imbalance," the court noted that none of the 238 skilled craft worker positions were held by females at the time the AAP was adopted. The Court stated that such evidence was sufficient in lieu of more direct evidence of past discrimination.

In *Cleveland,* a consent decree that provided for the use of preferential treatment and other affirmative action was the substantive issue. As evidence that the AAP resulting from the consent decree served a remedial need (as required by Title VII), the Court looked both at statistical evidence of a "conspicuous imbalance" and at the defendant's admission that it had previously engaged in discriminatory practices against Hispanics and blacks.

Some tentative conclusions may be drawn regarding the evidence and proof necessary to sustain the defendant's burden related to establishing remedial purpose. First of all, the basis for the plaintiff's claim is important since differences clearly exist in the way the courts adjudicate Title VII and constitutional cases. As noted by the Supreme Court in *Johnson,* "we do not regard as identical the constraints of Title VII and the federal *Constitution* on voluntarily adopted affirmative action plans" (p. 14).

The standards for establishing remedial purpose in a Title VII case were most fully articulated in *Johnson.* Here the majority opinion stated that a defendant could establish remedial purpose in a Title VII case by demonstrating that the AAP was implemented to correct a "manifest imbalance." To establish a manifest imbalance, the Court ruled the defendant had to demonstrate that the percentage of minorities it employed at the time the AAP was implemented was "unduly" low. Specifically, the defendant had to demonstrate a discrepancy between the percentage of minorities in its work force (in the job in question) and the percentage of minorities in the "relevant" labor market. The Court noted that the area labor market or the general labor market (rather than the skilled labor market) could be used for comparison purposes if the job in question required no special expertise or if the job was a "traditionally segregated" one (i.e., one minorities or women had been traditionally excluded from because of "societal influences"). The Court's rationale for using the general or area labor market as a basis for determining whether a manifest imbalance existed for jobs requiring no special expertise was that it was from these labor markets that unskilled applicants were typically selected. Thus, absent discrimination, the proportion of minorities in the employer's work force in such jobs would be expected to match the proportion of minorities within the general or area labor market. The *Johnson* Court also discussed its rationale for using the general or area labor market as a basis for determining whether a manifest imbalance existed in a "traditionally segregated job category." Referring to *Steelworkers,* the *Johnson* Court noted that "such an approach reflected a recognition that the proportion of black craft workers in the local labor force was likely as minuscule as the proportion in Kaiser's work force" (p. 15). If employers were not permitted through their affirmative action efforts to hire minorities for traditionally segregated jobs in percentages that exceeded those in the skilled labor market, "industries in which discrimination has been most effective would be precluded from adopting [AAPs]" (p. 15). However, where the job at issue required special expertise and was not a traditionally segregated one, the Court noted "the comparison should be with those in the labor force who possess the relevant qualifications" (p. 14).

In the instant case, the *Johnson* Court concluded that the skilled craft worker position in question was a traditionally segregated one because females constituted only 5% of the local skilled craft worker labor force. Therefore, in judging whether there was a manifest imbalance in the defendant's work force, the Court compared the percentage of females employed by the organization as skilled craft workers (0%) with the percentage of females in the area labor market (36%).

The size of the discrepancy between the work force and labor force percentages that would be needed to sustain a remedial purpose claim was not clearly delineated in the *Johnson* opinion. The disparity was quite large in both *Johnson* and *Steelworkers*. At what point the Court would consider the disparity to be "insignificant" remains to be seen. Hopefully, future courts will more fully delineate the criteria for determining when the difference between the two percentages is sufficient to establish remedial need; possibly the use of the four-fifths rule or a finding of a statistically significant difference may become the answer(s).

By allowing an organization to implement an AAP without being required to admit to past discrimination, the Supreme Court has provided a means by which employers can implement voluntary AAPs without simultaneously subjecting themselves to other Title VII claims. As noted in *Johnson,* requiring that employers admit to past discrimination "could inappropriately create a significant disincentive for employers to adopt an affirmative action plan" (pp. 14–15).

It should be noted, of course, that there are many instances where an employer's manifest imbalance may be sufficiently flagrant to also establish a prima facie case of discrimination under Title VII. This occurred in *Sheet Metal Workers v. EEOC* (1986) and *Cleveland*. As noted in *Johnson,* "when there is sufficient evidence to meet the more stringent 'prima facie' standard, be it statistical, nonstatistical, or a combination of the two, the employer is free to adopt an affirmative action plan" (p. 15).

The criteria for judging the remedial purpose defense become more stringent when reverse discrimination claims are brought under the Fourteenth Amendment. As noted by the *Johnson* Court,

> The dissent maintains that the obligations of a public employer under Title VII must be identical to its obligations under the *Constitution,* and that a public employer's adoption of an affirmative action plan therefore should be governed by *Wygant* . . . [however], the fact that a public employer must also satisfy the *Constitution* does not negate the fact that the *statutory* prohibition with which the employer must contend was not intended to extend as far as that of the *Constitution.* (pp. 9–10)

In order to establish a remedial purpose under a Fourteenth Amendment claim, an employer must provide evidence of prior discrimination since "the compelling government interest" served by the AAP is the eradication of discrimination in the employment setting. As noted in *Wygant,*

> a public employer . . . must insure that, before it embarks on an affirmative action program, it has convincing evidence to justify the conclusion that there has been *prior discrimination* (italics added). (p. 9)

Evidence that the employer's AAP satisfied a "compelling government interest" would include, for example, a statistical imbalance that meets the Title VII prima facie standard (as occurred in *Sheet Metal Workers*), admission of past discriminatory actions by the employer (as occurred in *Cleveland*), a history of prior court decisions against the employer (as occurred in *Paradise*), or a combination of the above.

Other evidence of a well-conceived AAP
Once it has been shown that preferential treatment has occurred (a prima facie case has been established) and that its occurrence was triggered by an AAP based on a remedial purpose or a compelling government interest, the Court's attention turns to other important aspects of a "bona fide" or "narrowly tailored" AAP. "Bona fide" refers to Title VII and "narrowly tailored" to constitutional cases. The standards for a "bona fide" AAP have been noted above in *Steelworkers;* the standards for a "narrowly tailored" AAP are well summarized in *Paradise* (reflecting the factors Justice Powell articulated in *Sheet Metal Workers*)

> In determining whether race-conscious remedies are appropriate [in constitutional cases], we look to several factors, including the necessity for the relief and the efficacy of alternative remedies; the flexibility and duration of the relief, including the availability of waiver provisions; the relationship of the numerical goals to the relevant labor market; and the impact of the relief on the rights of third parties. (p. 19)

Although "bona fide" and "narrowly tailored" standards may appear to be different on the surface, they have been interpreted by the courts to be essentially substantive extensions of one another and will be treated here as such. For example, the analogue to the constitutional "impact on third parties" standard would include the Title VII standards that a "bona fide" AAP not unnecessarily trammel the interests of other employees and not exclude noncovered group members as a class. Or the Title VII analogue to the constitutional standard that a "narrowly tailored" AAP be flexible and of a particular duration would be that a "bona fide" AAP be reasonable (i.e., temporary in nature). The manner in which each of the standards articulated in *Sheet Metal Workers* has been addressed by the Supreme Court is examined below.

Necessity and efficacy of alternatives
The Supreme Court addressed this issue in *Wygant*. Here the Court stated that an employer must consider, prior to implementing an AAP, whether alternative and less restrictive means that would accomplish the intended purpose of the AAP are available. The Court noted it

> should give particularly intense scrutiny to whether a nonracial approach or a more narrowly tailored racial classification could promote the substantial interest about as well and at tolerable administrative expense. (p. 11)

In addition to concluding that a remedial need did not exist, the *Wygant* court ruled that the Board of Education's AAP was established without first considering viable alternatives to layoffs (viz., hiring quotas). The AAP would have been struck down on either account.

The issue of alternatives also arose in *Paradise* and *Sheet Metal Workers*, cases that involved the use of quotas in hiring and/or promotion. Several possible alternatives to a quota system were discussed in these cases (e.g., the use of injunctions, fines, consent decrees, tests with less adverse impact). In each instance, however, the Supreme Court ruled that the use of quotas was the only viable way of eliminating discrimination. These decisions were due, in large part, to the defendants' poor "track records," which led the Court to conclude that nothing short of extreme remedies (i.e., quotas) would be successful.

Interestingly, in *Cleveland,* the Court noted that the alternatives issue was satisfied since the defendant's AAP was itself one of many alternatives that the defendant explored, and it was judged by the defendant to be the most viable.

Flexibility   It is quite clear that the courts look favorably on AAPs that are flexible. Flexibility may be indicated by a number of factors. These include, among others, an organization's willingness to modify its AAP when conditions warrant (i.e., the availability of waiver provisions), the use of protected group status as only one of several factors used in making the employment decision, and an organization's intent to utilize the AAP as a temporary measure.

In both *Paradise* and *Sheet Metal Workers* the Supreme Court judged the employers' AAPs to be "flexible." Although both cases involved court-ordered AAPs, these decisions nonetheless add clarity to the Supreme Court's operational definition of flexibility.

In *Paradise,* the Supreme Court's judgement that the AAP was flexible was based partly on the presence of a provision that stipulated that quotas would be waived if no qualified blacks were available in the applicant pool. Moreover, the AAP did not require gratuitous promotions of blacks, but rather, was to be used only when the defendant *needed* to make promotions. That the AAP would endure only until the defendant devised an alternative promotion procedure with no adverse impact was also viewed favorably by the Court.

In *Sheet Metal Workers,* the Court concluded that the AAP was implemented in a flexible manner by the lower court, as indicated by the lower court's willingness to adjust the deadline imposed upon the union for meeting its black membership goals. Moreover, flexibility was evidenced since the lower court was also willing to modify the class size requirements in light of prevailing economic conditions, which would have prevented the targets of the AAP from being met. The Supreme Court further noted that the AAP was temporary in nature, "scheduled to terminate when petitioners achieve the membership goal, and the Court determines that it is no longer needed to remedy past discrimination" (p. 53).

The Supreme Court's view on the issue of flexibility is further clarified in the *Johnson* decision. Here, the Court noted several flexible features of the defendant's AAP. For example, the plan took into account the limited availability of women in the local labor pool and avoided the use of strict numerical standards; sex was considered as one of several factors in the employment decision. The Court also noted that the difference in qualifications between Johnson and the successful female applicant was minimal. Unfortunately, the decision gave no indication of how great a difference in qualifications had to exist in order to warrant a decision of "inflexibility."

Numerical goals Two main issues have been addressed with respect to numerical goals. The first deals with issues related to the relevant labor market used as a benchmark to establish the long-term or ultimate selection goal(s) of the defendant's plan. In *Wygant,* for instance, goals were set on the basis of the "role model theory" (i.e., the AAP attempted to match the percentage of minority teachers with the percentage of minority students within the school district). The Supreme Court ruled that this procedure was misguided; the defendant should have used as a benchmark the qualified public school teacher population in the relevant labor market. Interestingly, in its rejection of the "role model theory," the Supreme Court noted that under certain circumstances this theory could be used to allow an organization "to escape the obligation to remedy [discriminatory] practices by justifying the small percentage of black teachers by reference to the small percentage of black students" (p. 7).

The second issue pertaining to numerical goals involved the *magnitude* of the short-term or interim goals of the defendant's AAP. Interim goals were challenged in both *Paradise* and *Sheet Metal Workers*. In *Paradise,* the AAP called for a 50% interim goal to be implemented until the long-term goal of 25% black representation was reached. In *Sheet Metal Workers,* the long-term goal was to increase the percentage of minority union members from 10 to 29%. Rather than setting specific interim goals, the AAP set a time limit (six years) for achieving this percentage figure. Given that there were over 3,000 union members, the union would obviously have needed to utilize yearly goals that were far greater than the 29% long-term goal. In both of these cases it was argued that the interim goals were too high as well as arbitrary; they should be "narrowly tailored" to the relevant work force population.

In addressing these types of magnitude-related issues, the Supreme Court stated that the size of the interim goal merely dictated the *speed* at which the long-term goals were to be met and, thus, could exceed the long-term goals of the AAP. As noted by Justice Brennan in *Paradise,* the defendants' "argument ignores that the 50% figure is not itself a goal; rather it represents the speed at which the goal of 25% will be achieved" (p. 28). The Court further noted that speed was an important factor in both of these cases because of the long history of the defendants' discrimination, as well as the defendants' past unwillingness to remedy it. Whether speed-related interim goals set as high as 50% would be allowable under less compelling circumstances is questionable. It should be noted that in none of the cases reviewed did the interim goal exceed 50%.

Impact on third parties As indicated by the Supreme Court in *Paradise,* the courts must examine the impact of an AAP on the rights of "innocent third parties." A plan that *unjustly* burdens third parties would be legally unacceptable. As argued by the plaintiffs in *Cleveland,* the granting of preferential treatment to minorities unjustly hurts nonminorities (i.e., those who would have been hired had it not been for the AAP) and who bear no direct blame for past discrimination (the "innocent victims theory"). The Supreme Court, however, rejected this argument by concluding it was not unreasonable to require nonminority firefighters who had committed no wrong to bear some burden of the remedy. After all, reasoned the Court, these individuals had benefited from the effects of past discrimination.

Another argument used by plaintiffs regarding the impact of AAPs on third parties arose in *Cleveland* and *Sheet Metal Workers*. An issue in these cases was whether Section 706(g) of Title VII precludes a court from awarding relief that would benefit individuals who were not the actual (i.e., identified) victims of the employer's discrimination. Awarding relief to unidentified minority victims, defendants argued, would unjustly burden nonminorities.

In *Cleveland,* the dictum of the court was in the form of a consent decree. Here, the Supreme Court ruled that Section 706(g) did not apply to consent decrees, since a consent decree is "before litigation" and thus may go beyond what Section 706(g) allows; a consent decree may exceed the relief that a court could award after a trial. Thus, the Court gave tacit approval for class-wide relief (including relief to unidentified victims) where the AAP is voluntary in nature.

The argument that class-wide relief is not available under Section 706(g) was also rejected by the Court in *Sheet Metal Workers*. Unlike the *Cleveland* case, *Sheet Metal Workers* involved the use of a *court-ordered* AAP. In interpreting Section 706(g), the Court stated that

> Our examination of the legislative history of Title VII convinces us that, when examined in context, the statements relied upon by petitioners and the Solicitor General do not indicate that Congress intended to limit relief under 706(g) to that which benefits only the actual victims of unlawful discrimination. (p. 27)

There are several other circumstances under which a voluntary AAP may be judged to have an unfair impact on third parties. One such circumstance, first articulated in *Steelworkers* and later reaffirmed in *Cleveland, Paradise,* and *Johnson,* occurs when the AAP provides an "absolute bar" to the advancement of nonminorities.

As reported in *Johnson,* the defendant "had pursued a moderate, gradual approach ... which visits minimal intrusion on the legitimate expectations of other employees" (p. 22). Moreover, the Court noted that the defendant's AAP "requires women to compete with all other qualified applicants. No persons are automatically excluded from consideration; all are able to have their qualifications weighted against those of other applicants" (p. 20). While no court has precisely defined the term "absolute bar," none of the challenged AAPs have been found to violate this requirement.

Another circumstance under which an AAP would be judged as having an unfair impact on third parties is when its use results in the hiring of unqualified minorities. This view was expressed by the Supreme Court in *Paradise*.

> Finally, the basic limitation, that black troopers promoted must be qualified, remains. Qualified white candidates simply have to compete with qualified black candidates. (p. 31)

Thus, while it is permissible to select a minority applicant who is less qualified than a nonminority one, the minority must at least meet the minimum qualifications for the job. Interestingly, in none of the cases reviewed did the plaintiffs raise the argument that the minorities selected as the result of an AAP were unqualified.

A third circumstance that would invalidate an AAP due to its impact on third parties is when its use results in the displacement of nonminorities. Originally addressed in *Steelworkers,* the Supreme Court further clarified the issue of displacement in *Wygant* and *Firefighters v. Stotts* (1984). In these cases the Court expressed concern that the displacement of nonminorities imposed by preferential layoff policies placed an unfair burden on innocent third-parties. As stated in *Wygant,*

> Though hiring goals may burden some individuals, they simply do not impose the same kind of injury that layoffs impose. Denial of future employment opportunity is not as intrusive as loss of an existing job. (p. 14)

The Court thus concluded that the burden caused by preferential layoffs was too intrusive, and that less intrusive alternatives must be used.

The fourth circumstance that invalidates the use of an AAP due to its unfair impact on third parties arose in *Stotts*. At issue was a consent decree that was later modified by the district court (over the City's objection) to include preferential layoffs to preserve the AAP's minority hiring gains. The Supreme Court ruled that such a modification was improper since it was inconsistent with the provisions of a bona fide seniority system. Moreover, the Court ruled the district court did not have authority to override this system by awarding seniority to individuals who were not proven victims of discrimination.

That employers should avoid AAPs with preferential layoff provisions appears to be a reasonable conclusion to draw from these decisions, especially since in both *Stotts* and *Wygant* the Court expressly pointed out there were less burdensome alternatives to layoffs that the employer could have enacted to preserve minority hiring gains. Moreover, avoiding AAPs with preferential layoffs provisions would be especially appropriate when the layoff provisions violate the provisions of a bona fide seniority system.

DISCUSSION

The principal goal of voluntary AAPs is to remedy work-place inequities that have resulted from the discriminatory policies, procedures, and practices of employers (Sowell, 1983). With this goal apparently in mind, the courts have sanctioned the legality of AAPs, as long as they are implemented within the fairly strict set of parameters outlined above. However, although granting preferential treatment as part of an AAP may help remedy discriminatory inequities at the workplace, it also may affect other important societal and organizational outcomes, creating a "rippling effect."

Unfortunately, there is a dearth of research that examines the unintended consequences of AAPs. As noted by Sowell (1983), many of the hypotheses concerning the benefits of AAPs, while reasonable, are simply that — hypotheses; it is unreasonable to view these hypotheses as axioms in the absence of corroborative research findings.

One area of needed research concerns the impact of preferential treatment on the attitudes and behavior of all employees — both those receiving and those denied such treatment. The scant research findings accumulated thus far raise some important concerns. For example, females knowingly selected for a position on the basis of their sex were found to view themselves and their job performance less positively than females knowingly selected on the basis of merit (Heilman, Simon, & Repper, 1987); females who believed their gender substantially influenced their hiring possessed less organizational commitment and job satisfaction and experienced greater stress (Chacko, 1982).

Preferential treatment may also have a negative impact on the attitudes of other employees toward those receiving such treatment. As noted by Jacobson and Koch (1977), female supervisors were found to be viewed more negatively by their subordinates if the supervisors had attained their positions as the result of preferential treatment.

Research assessing the impact of AAP-related preferential treatment on organizational utility is also needed. For example, the implementation of an AAP is very likely to affect an organization's recruitment costs since organizations that attempt to meet AA goals often need to greatly expand their recruitment efforts. As noted by Kroeck, Barrett, and Alexander (1983), a hiring quota only *slightly* in excess of a minority group's representation in the relevant labor market was found to substantially increase an organization's recruitment costs. Little, if anything, is known about other organizational costs and benefits attributable to AAPs, however (e.g., the cost of AAP-triggered ligation, of bypassing more qualified applicants; the benefits of improved company image, of a decreased likelihood of an EEO charge being filed by a minority).

An additional area of needed research is the assessment of the extent to which the occupational advancement of various minority groups has, in fact, been improved as the result of AAPs. Based on an assessment of data collected by the U.S. Census Bureau and the Equal Employment Opportunity Commission, several researchers (Faley & Froggatt, 1987; Ledvinka, 1982; Milkovich & Newman, 1984; Thurow, 1983) have concluded that, at best, only moderate aggregate gains in employment opportunities have been made by blacks and females since the advent of affirmative action. Unfortunately, using such data to infer causality (i.e., to infer that these gains are due to AAPs) is wrought with methodological difficulties — which makes it impossible to clearly discern the "main effect" of AAPs on pay and other employment-related outcomes. For example, the slight gains achieved thus far may be attributable to a host of other factors, such as the impact of other EEO policies and programs, improved educational opportunities for minorities, economic realities such as the necessity of the two-income family, and so on. Clearly, further and better research is needed to more fully understand the impact of AAPs on the employment opportunities of each protected classification.

Without further research into these and other AAP-related areas, organizations choosing to implement an AAP will continue to do so within a vacuum of knowledge regarding the linkages that may exist between AAPs and important organizational (and societal) outcomes. As researchers, it is critical that we take this opportunity to intensify our efforts to develop research strategies that could help provide a better picture of the extent to which AAPs act as panaceas for the effects of past and present discrimination. Until more is known about these linkages, an employer choosing to implement a voluntary AAP would be well advised to select a strategy in which the degree of preferential treatment is commensurate with the severity of the problem that necessitates it (see Ledvinka, 1975, for a discussion of various AAP implementation strategies).

REFERENCES

Chacko, T. I. (1982). Women and equal employment opportunity: Some unintended effects. *Journal of Applied Psychology, 67,* 119–123.

Faley, R. H., Froggatt, K. L. (1987). A longitudinal examination of the membership patterns of minorities and women in referral unions. *Journal of Labor Research, 8* (1), 93–101.

Firefighters v. City of Cleveland, No. 84-1999, slip op. (U.S. July 2, 1986).

Firefighters v. Stotts, 34 FEP Cases 1702 (1984).

Heilman, M. E., Simon, M. C., Repper, D. P. (1987). Intentionally favored, unintentionally harmed? Impact of sex-based preferential selection on self-perceptions and self-evaluations. *Journal of Applied Psychology, 72,* 62–68.

Jacobson, M. B., Koch, W. (1977). Women as leaders: Performance evaluation as a function of method of leader selection. *Organizational Behavior and Human Performance, 20,* 149–157.

Johnson v. Santa Clara County No. 85-1129, slip op. (U.S. March 25, 1987).

Kroeck, K. G., Barrett, G. V., Alexander, R. A. (1983). Imposed quotas and personnel selection: A computer simulation study. *Journal of Applied Psychology, 68,* 123–136.

Kromnick v. School District of Philadelphia, 35 FEP Cases 1 (1984).

Ledvinka, J. (1975). Technical implications of equal employment law for manpower planning. PERSONNEL PSYCHOLOGY, *28,* 299–323.

Ledvinka, J. (1982). *Federal regulation of personnel and human resource management.* Boston: Kent.

Lehman v. Yellow Freight System, 26 FEP Cases 75 (1981).

Milkovich, G. T., Newman, J. M. (1984). *Compensation.* Plano, TX: Business Publications.

Parker v. B & O Railroad Co., 25 FEP Cases 889 (1981).

Sester v. Navack Investment Co., 26 FEP Cases 513 (1981).

Sheet Metal Workers v. EEOC No. 84-1656, slip op. (U.S. July 2, 1986).

Sowell, T. (1983). A dissenting opinion about affirmative action. In Pearlman, K., Schmidt, F.L., Hamner, W. C. (Eds.), *Contemporary problems in personnel* (pp. 459–470). New York: Wiley & Sons.

Thurow, L. C. (1983). The economic progress of minority groups. In Pearlman, K., Schmidt, F.L., Hamner, W. C. (Eds.), *Contemporary problems in personnel* (pp. 451–458), New York: Wiley & Sons.

U.S. v. Paradise, No. 85-999, slip op. (U.S. February 25, 1987).

U.S. Steelworkers v. Weber, 20 FEP Cases 1 (1979).

Wygant v. Jackson Board of Education, No. 84-1340, slip op. (U.S. May 19, 1986).

Lawrence S. Kleiman is in the Department of Management at the University of Tennessee at Chattanooga. Robert H. Faley is in the Graduate School of Management at Kent State University.

Installing a Realistic Job Preview: Ten Tough Choices
John P. Wanous

It has been over thirty years since Weitz (1956) described the first published account of a realistic job preview (RJP) experiment. A review and meta-analysis of 21 experiments (Premack & Wanous, 1985) concluded that RJPs lower initial expectations ($r = -.17$, with a 95% confidence interval of $-.10$ to $-.24$) and increase job survival ($r = .06$). A utility analysis of the RJP's effect on job survival indicated that the amount of replacement-cost savings varies with the severity of an organization's turnover problem. Specifically, it was estimated that 12% could be saved for an organization with a 50% survival rate and 6% for one with an 80% survival rate (Premack & Wanous, 1985). Most of the nonmilitary RJP experiments fell into the 50–80% job survival rate, but those of military recruits going through basic training or attending West Point had survival rates in the 85–95% range, and thus, the effect of the RJP on military job survival was less (Wanous & Colella, in press).

The attention given to research accounts of RJP experiments accelerated dramatically in the 1980s. Specifically, a recent review (Wanous & Colella, in press) found a total of 38 reports of RJP research, of which 25 (66%) were done in the 1980s. However, the attention given to practical issues of how to do an RJP has been almost nonexistent. Except for one account of an RJP experiment at the Southern New England Telephone Company (Wanous, 1975, 1980), virtually

John P. Wanous is in the College of Business, Ohio State University.

Source: John P. Wanous, "Installing a Realistic Job Preview: Ten Tough Choices," *Personnel Psychology,* 1989, 42, pp. 117–133. Reprinted by permission of *Personnel Psychology.*

nothing has been written on the many implemenation issues that must be faced. As Dunnette (1986) has so nicely stated, "knowing psychology isn't the same as knowing how to do psychology." It is the issue of "how to do" RJPs that is addressed here.

Identified are ten "tough choices" that run the gamut from initiation through the development and implementation of an RJP. They are labeled as such because they mostly appear as choices between two desirable alternatives.

Some may object that framing these issues as choices overstates the degree to which one must really choose one over the other. In some instances, it may be possible to do both and avoid the tough choice. However, these are usually tough choices because of organizational politics or limited resources. In my own experience with an eastern telephone company, a midwestern bank, and the U.S. military I have found them typically to be "either/or" choices. In the written accounts of other RJP experiments, usually only one course of action is taken for each of these choices. Avoiding choices is possible, but it is the exception.

Thus, the use of "tough choices" here meets two objectives. First, it is an accurate description of practical issues facing the installation of an RJP. Second, it is a literary device that sharpens the focus on each of the issues by framing them as mutually exclusive choices.

This paper is organized into two sections. First, the ten tough choices are presented, and this presentation is followed by recommendations for each one. Since these "tough choices" are simply decisions that one must make, a basic theoretical framework for assessing decision effectiveness should be used as a guide for making the specific choices. The one chosen is based on group decision effectiveness (Vroom & Yetton, 1973):

$$\frac{\text{Quality} \times \text{Acceptance}}{\text{Costs}}$$

In the Vroom and Yetton version of this framework, the time used to make a decision is the only cost considered. In the present case, however, the time taken to develop and implement an RJP is only one type of cost. In the present case "acceptance" refers to acceptance by top management (i.e., what they are willing to do with regard to RJP implementation). The quality "criterion" was defined on the basis of those factors that the best available research and theory suggest are likely to increase the RJP's effectiveness in enhancing job survival. When issues of a job candidate's "accepting" the message of an RJP arise, they are considered part of the quality criterion.

TEN TOUGH CHOICES

Tough Choice 1: Getting Started — Reaction or Proaction?

Unless one is doing a lab study, there are usually two quite different motivations for initiating an RJP. The more common of the two is reaction to a current problem of too much turnover among one's new hires. There are three advantages to starting this way. First, it is usually easy to get top management approval quickly. Second, the project will have reasonably high internal visibility. Third, because turnover is a problem, the utility of the RJP is likely to be higher than when job survival rates are lower (Premack & Wanous, 1985).

These three advantages of reacting to a problem must be weighed against its two disadvantages. First, management's commitment to the RJP may be thin and may evaporate when the job survival problem goes away. Years of social-psychological research on commitment show that it increases when there are fewer (or no apparent) external reasons to undertake a course of action (e.g., Salancik, 1977). Second, there is a risk that some turnover problems will diminish in intensity by the time one is actually ready to begin the RJP. This can be an important problem when turnover is closely linked to the business cycle, which is the case for much turnover, particularly that of entry-level employees (Mobley, 1982).

Alternatively, an organization might choose to begin an RJP to avoid a future problem. Although proaction is much less common, a recent project conducted at the Long Beach Naval Shipyard (Wanous & Baker, 1987) helps to identify the issues here. By developing RJPs for a situation without a pressing turnover problem, one gains two advantages. First, commitment to the project is probably deeper, and second, it can be designed and installed prior to the beginning of a retention problem. The disadvantages are that one might get off to a slower start without a crisis to motivate, that the project will have low visibility, and that the RJP's utility is lower when there is lower turnover. (See Premack & Wanous, 1985, p. 716, for a utility analysis. Briefly, the higher an organization's "normal" rate of newcomer job survival, the smaller the percentage increase in job survival resulting from an RJP.)

Tough Choice 2: Diagnosis — Structured or Unstructured?

Diagnosing an organization is the first step in the development of an RJP (Wanous, 1980). It might be tempting to draw an analogy between RJP diagnosis and that done to justify the content of a selection test or a needs analysis for the design of a training program. This may be unwise since the legal status of the RJP as "a test" has yet to be established. Thus, the procedures used to do an organizational diagnosis have yet to be scrutinized in ways similar to job analysis in selection testing (Arvey & Faley, 1988). It is unlikely that RJPs will be considered as "tests" because they are not used as ways to reject applicants. They are designed only to facilitate self-selection.

The organizational diagnosis must concern specific job duties, broader organizational characteristics, and ways the typical employee reacts to both. This means a combination of descriptive material (similar to a job analysis) and evaluative reactions (similar to employee attitude surveys) must be gathered.

The tough choice here is whether to gather extensive data in a systematic way that yields quantifiable results or whether to do the diagnosis in a much more unstructured way. The structured approach is typified by using a large representative sample of employees and a systematic method of gathering data (almost always a questionnaire, sometimes a combination of interview and questionnaire), and results can be presented to top management in a written report using both descriptive and inferential statistics. It is the approach to data gathering closest to "normal science" in our field. It is what most I/O psychologists would call "good" research, and it is the method of choice if one wants to publish results in a research journal.

The unstructured approach is in many ways the antithesis, but it comes from a different tradition in the social sciences (i.e., OD rather than I/O psychology). Interviews are almost always used here, although a combination of questionnaires and interviews is not uncommon (e.g., Alderfer & Brown, 1972). Thus, while both approaches often use a combination of methods, the structured approach almost always uses a questionnaire, whereas the unstructured approach almost always uses interviews.

The biggest advantage to the structured approach is the quality of the diagnostic data, and this can be important when trying to gain top management acceptance of the final product. (Credibility to job applicants is a quality issue and is considered in choices 5 and 6 below.) The cost of such data can be high in terms of both money and time, as can be seen by reading the methods section of Dean and Wanous (1984). Specifically, it took about one year to complete the structured diagnosis. This was because 100 bank teller job incumbents were first interviewed in order to design an "empathic" questionnaire (see Alderfer & Brown, 1972). Following approval of the diagnostic questionnaire by top management, a survey of all other tellers ($N = 850$ at more than 100 branch locations) was undertaken. Senior managers also met with the researchers to provide their perceptions of the particular job being studied.

The unstructured approach is weakest where the structured is strongest, and vice versa. Top officials who see the RJP as potentially exposing their leadership failures may criticize the sample of interviewees as unrepresentative. To minimize this, it is wise to have management select at least some of the people to be interviewed. Another strategy is to do the inteviews in groups. If the group members concur in their opinions, credibility will be increased. The cost savings are a definite advantage because the unstructured diagnosis can be done in one or two days rather than months.

As someone who has done both structured (Dean & Wanous, 1984) and unstructured (Wanous & Baker, 1987) diagnoses, I believe either approach can yield sufficiently valid data to construct a useful RJP. From the preceding analysis it should be clear that the structured approach is more likely to generate data that most I/O psychologists would call high quality. Thus, the only obvious weakness of the structured approach is its higher cost, which results from doing a complete "organizational analysis" (Schneider, 1976; Schneider & Schmitt, 1986) that includes not only elements of a job analysis, but also information about organizational climate/culture.

Tough Choice 3: Content — Descriptive or Judgmental?

This choice strikes at the core of what is meant by "reality" in an RJP. One might suppose that the only way to construct an accurate RJP would be to include mostly descriptive material (e.g., starting salaries, average length of time to a promotion, hours of work). There are two advantages to this approach. First, it is usually easier to defend descriptive material as being unbiased by individual differences in what people will find satisfying. This is because job satisfaction is usually thought of as a reaction to a comparison of two elements: (1) the perception of what one is receiving and (2) what is desired (see Wanous & Lawler, 1972, for a review). Second, as a result of the above, acceptance by top management is likely to be more forthcoming.

An alternative view of an RJP is that one should try to maximize the degree of judgmental information (i.e., things that satisfy and dissatisfy employees). There are several reasons for this approach. First, the objective of the RJP is to increase job survival. If one does not focus on those factors that cause turnover, the RJP will not be very effective. To do so, one must include the most important assets and liabilities of a particular work situation and explicitly identify them as such.

The second reason to maximize judgmental content is that naive job candidates need to be given the "richer" material that only judgmental information provides. However, maximizing judgmental information does increase the risk of RJPs being seen as biased, resulting in the possibility of increased management resistance to them.

There are two ways that judgmental information has been presented in RJPs. The first is to present information that might appear to be descriptive but is actually judgmental. For example, telling job candidates that first-level supervisors monitor employee behavior very closely may sound descriptive. However, if most employees are dissatisfied with close supervision, this is actually communicating judgmental information.

The second approach is more explicit. Taking the close supervision example from above, the RJP would also include statements about how the typical employee feels about such supervision. This could be done by reporting results from a questionnaire survey if a structured diagnosis has been done, or by having a person speak as a typical employee (in a video RJP) if an unstructured diagnosis has been done.

It must be noted that including judgmental information does not imply that one should exclude descriptive material. The statements about what is typically satisfying or dissatisfying must refer to something descriptive in nature. Thus, a judgmental RJP would go beyond merely saying "you will work on the weekend but get Monday and Tuesday off." The judgmental approach would go on to describe typical feelings about such a work schedule.

Tough Choice 4: Content — Extensive or Intensive?

This choice concerns the degree to which one constructs an "extensive" or an "intensive" RJP. One view is that the RJP should include all pertinent information, so that it is not a "deficient" view of reality. In addition, the extensive RJP includes at least some material that will be relevant to almost all job candidates. A good example of an extensive RJP is the booklet used by Ilgen and Seely (1974) in their study of new cadets at West Point. It is a 10-page, single-spaced preview that includes both detailed information (typical schedule for a day) and less specific warnings (e.g., "beast barracks," little time to yourself, being rated by other cadets as to your "aptitude for service").

In contrast, the intensive RJP runs the risk of omitting information that is important to some people. However, it has two advantages. First, the most severe problems causing turnover are readily understood by job candidates because they are not "lost" amidst other information. Second, retention of the few key points is easier. The best examples of intensive RJPs are those currently being used throughout the Canadian Forces (Flynn & Ellis, 1984; Flynn, Ellis, & Zuliani, 1984). These are short videos (five minutes) tailored for every military specialty (rifleman, tank crew member, etc.). They make only a few points, but they try to make them as forcefully as possible.

Sometimes one can freely choose between the extensive and intensive approaches, but at other times certain organizational constraints may effectively limit the option to use one or the other. For example, the West Point situation mentioned above was one where the newcomer recruits had plenty of time to digest information about West Point during the summer vacation after high school graduation. In contrast, the Canadian Forces frequently encounter time constraints. For example, a potential recruit may be undecided about a military specialty. Thus, the only way to provide a preview is to keep it short enough to allow a review of several options.

There will almost always be some situational constraints favoring one or the other of these options. Besides those mentioned above, the degree of job complexity is probably the best example. Although it would not make sense to develop an extensive RJP for a simple job (and an uncomplicated organizational culture), the reverse is not necessarily true. That is, it can make good sense to use an intensive RJP in a complicated situation by focusing only on those factors that are (1) most important, (2) correlated with turnover, (3) most misperceived by recruits.

Tough Choice 5: Content — High or Medium Negativity?

The amount of negative information is clearly not a dichotomous choice, although for the sake of clarifying some issues it will be treated as such here. The choice, then, is between a medium and a high degree of negativity.

A high degree of negative information is exemplified by how easy it is to be maimed or killed on the job, sexism at work, "games" people play at work, or potential health hazards. This can be contrasted with a more moderate degree of negativity typified by the hours of work, how unchallenging the work is, lack of praise (but lots of criticism), long tenure to promotions, having to stand while at work, and so forth. The former refers to potentially illegal and dangerous facets of work, whereas the latter are not illegal and dangerous, although they may be dissatisfying.

In earlier writing on RJPs (Wanous, 1980) I said that the preview should try to mirror both the job itself and the organizational climate or culture. In other words, the degree of negativity should reflect that discovered in one's diagnosis. This may appear to imply that there is no discretion left for someone installing an RJP. However, I believe there is some latitude for choice without violating the general principle of the RJP being matched to organizational realities.

The examples listed at the beginning of this section epitomize the choice here.

That is, how far can one really go in formally documenting certain dangerous or potentially illegal factors? Is it desirable to admit that asbestos may still be part of the physical working environment?

To date, however, I have not seen a single case where someone actually chose the "high" negativity option — based on my recent review of 38 RJP accounts (Wanous & Colella, in press). Thus, the "choice" remains hypothetical as of this writing. Nevertheless, it is one worth thinking about for the reasons discussed below.

A high degree of negative information may be more effective at triggering self-selection among job candidates. However, this advantage must be weighed against its two liabilities. First, too many people might be discouraged. (This is hypothetical because no documented RJP has yet caused this to happen.) Second, the RJP could be used as evidence of management's negligence in a lawsuit. (This too is hypothetical, since the most damning material is almost always edited. Nevertheless, the "raw" diagnostic data could be subpoenaed, but this too is hypothetical since no such action has yet happened.)

A medium amount of negative information, typical of all the RJPs I have seen, usually encourages a modest degree of self-selection. Specifically, the average effect of an RJP on self-selection was calculated as $r = .06$, the same effect as the RJP on job survival (Premack & Wanous, 1985).

Although self-selection is modestly affected, a medium amount of negativity could increase a job candidate's ability to cope with newcomer stress. The research evidence on this possibility is, however, mixed. On the one hand, four studies that used questionnaire measures of coping found no evidence of self-selection being increased by an RJP (Premack & Wanous, 1985). On the other hand, those studies that presented the RJP after candidates had accepted job offers could be interpreted as supporting the coping hypothesis. This is because self-selection is eliminated as an underlying cause of increased job survival. The support is somewhat ambiguous, however, because other hypotheses such as increased trust or met expectations also are viable for RJPs given after job choice (Wanous & Colella, in press).

Although I have previously suggested that self-selection and coping are alternative ways that RJPs increase job survival (Wanous, 1980), it is quite possible that they might actually cancel each other out. This could happen if a high degree of negativity encouraged self-selection but made coping seem impossible. In contrast, medium negativity could encourage coping strategies, which, in turn, would reduce the degree of self-selection. The possibility that self-selection and coping have offsetting effects has yet to be examined because high versus medium negativity has not been manipulated in an experiment.

Tough Choice 6: Medium Used — Written or Audio-Visual?

According to the published research accounts, RJPs have been presented in three ways: brochures, audio-visual methods (A-V), and in-person interviews. Brochures and A-V methods dominate, however. Thus, the choice appears to be between them. However, it should be noted that presenting realistic job information during job interviews may be the most popular choice among those who have informal or unsystematic approaches and whose efforts have not been chronicled for others to read. In-person, two-way RJPs during the job interview could be the unpublished "iceberg" to the published "tip" represented by booklets and videos.

Written brochures have the distinct advantage of being much lower in cost than A-V methods, and they are easier to change. Editing on a word processor cannot be compared to editing a videotape. A second advantage is that the job candidate can re-read the RJP, since it is "hard copy."

A written brochure is compatible with an RJP that emphasizes descriptive (choice 3) and extensive content (choice 4). In contrast, the A-V approach is compatible with an RJP that maximizes judgmental content and limits the information to a few key points (Popovich & Wanous, 1982).

The A-V method has two distinct advantages. First, one can usually be more certain that a job candidate has seen and heard one of these, since they are frequently monitored by company personnel. Handing out brochures is no guarantee that they will be read. Second, comprehension of A-V RJPs is not constrained by the reading skills of some job candidates, although having a limited vocabulary could be a limitation.

Only a handful of studies used the job interview as an RJP (see Wanous & Colella, in press, for a review), and only one of the field experiments (Colarelli, 1984) compared the interview with an alternative method (a booklet). Thus, our knowledge of interviews-as-RJPs is quite limited, although Colarelli's study found it to be significantly more effective than either the brochure or control groups (which were not significantly different from each other). Because so little research has been done on the effectiveness of the interview as a medium for the RJP, the choice appears to remain between booklets and the A-V, at least for the time being, until further research is completed. An interesting line of research into the untapped potential of interviews is discussed in the concluding section of this paper.

Tough Choice 7: Message Source — Actors or Job Incumbents?

This choice primarily applies to those who have selected an A-V method. Basically, the choice is between using job incumbents and using others (actors or other company personnel) to present the message. This is raised as an issue because job candidates make source attributions based on how polished or scripted the RJP appears to be. When the RJP is an edited videocassette compilation of representative comments from job incumbents, it has a totally different "look" than when it is scripted and acted. When I have shown both types to students or personnel managers, virtually everyone could see the difference. Of course, their task was made easier because they had the advantage of seeing both types, so the contrast effect probably helped their judgments. Nevertheless, I firmly believe job candidates can attribute the source correctly without the benefit of a contrast effect, even though I know of no study designed to assess this particular issue.

The single, but important, advantage of using job incumbents is that they are more credible sources. There are three reasons for this greater credibility: (1) incumbents are seen as having more expertise, (2) incumbents are trusted more, and (3) incumbents are liked more due to a similar-to-me effect (Popovich & Wanous, 1982).

The disadvantages of incumbents become the advantages of using actors or other nonincumbents. First, they typically read from a script, so it is easier to organize, edit, and control what is being included. Second, using edited interviews of job incumbents is no guarantee they will be candid in discussing the most important problems for new employees. Third, incumbents look more amateurish, even beyond that which can be edited out of the final version. Basically, the choice is one of credibility versus style. In other words, it is between something that looks like a "television news" interview and something that looks like a commercial.

Tough Choice 8: Timing — Late or Early?

For the purposes of argument, this decision has been dichotomized into a choice between early and late presentation of the RJP. As has been the case in most of the previous choice points, the advantages and disadvantages of one alternative are the mirror reflection of the other.

If one chooses to position the RJP relatively late in the organizational entry process, there are two advantages. First, the costs are usually lower because fewer viable job candidates remain. Second, it is usually easier to get top management to approve negative material because far fewer people will see, hear, or read it. Since most or all of the rejections have been made by the organization, top management is usually more comfortable showing negative material to those receiving (or about to receive) job offers.

Showing the RJP early has the advantage of possibly affecting a job candidate's self-selection decision. This is because the effort involved in going through the organizational entry process tends to increase the chances of a person accepting a job offer. Effort expenditure builds commitment, as has been shown many times throughout psychology (e.g., Lewis, 1965).

Tough Choice 9: Getting Started — Pilot Study or Policy?

The choice here is doing the RJP as a pilot project versus installing it as a component of one's normal recruiting practice. The primary advantage of doing a pilot experiment is that the commitment to the project involves fewer people and less money and, for these reasons, may be easier to get approved. A secondary advantage of a pilot study is its usefulness as a "manipulation check" of the RJP. This would involve primarily a test of the RJP's effect on initial expectations rather than its effect on subsequent job survival.

Installing an RJP as part of the normal recruitment/selection process has, however, two distinct advantages. First, one does not face the ethical dilemma implicit in using a control group. The argument is that withholding something beneficial from employees (or even potential employees) is unethical, and must not be done even if the scientific method requires the use of a control group.

The second advantage of going ahead on a large scale is that one probably cannot trust the data from a single small-scale study, as has been forcefully pointed out in the area of selection testing (e.g., Hunter, Schmidt, & Jackson, 1982). The argument here is that one can trust the results of a meta-analysis more than a "local" research study. Since the results of RJPs have been subjected to meta-analysis (Premack & Wanous, 1985), this argument suggests that delays in full-scale implementation in order to do a pilot study represent an opportunity cost.

Tough Choice 10: Sharing Results — Proprietary Secret or Disseminate Results?

Regardless of whether one conducts a pilot experiment or launches into a full-scale use of RJPs, there are going to be results of one sort or another. Thus, the choice here is whether or not to share these with those outside the organization. The advantage in privacy is that competitors do not know what has been done. This disadvantage is that you, in turn, cannot profit from the efforts of others.

As is sometimes the case, this choice can be constrained by certain situational factors. There may not be any "rewards" for writing up the results of an RJP for nonacademics. When coupled with a low probability of getting a manuscript published, the combination leads to very low motivation in expectancy theory terms (Vroom, 1964).

RECOMMENDATIONS

Table 1 summarizes the ten tough choices in one column and indicates the recommended alternatives in the other. Remember that the contrasted alternatives of each choice tend to be the mirror opposites of each other. The advantages of one are the disadvantages of the other. Because of this, this section will explain why the advantages of one may outweigh those of the other.

TABLE 1
Recommended Solutions to Tough Choices

Tough Choice	Alternatives	Recommended Alternative
1. Getting started:	Reaction or proaction?	Proactive whenever possible
2. Diagnosis:	Structured or unstructured?	Either is effective; unstructured when possible
3. Content:	Descriptive or judgmental?	Judgmental content
4. Content:	Extensive or unstructured?	Intensive content
5. Content:	High or medium negativity?	Medium negativity
6. Medium used:	Written or audio-visual?	Audio-visual
7. Message source:	Actors or job incumbents?	Job incumbents
8. Timing:	Late or early?	Early
9. Getting started:	Pilot study or policy?	Policy
10. Sharing results:	Proprietary secret or disseminate the results?	Disseminate the results

Ideally, the recommendations made in Table 1 should be guided by the accumulated research. However, the most recent reviews (Premack & Wanous, 1985; Wanous & Colella, in press) do not yield sufficiently precise conclusions that can be applied to the ten tough choices, except for choice number 6. At the present time the data seem to show that A-V RJPs are more effective at enhancing job performance than are written RJPs. This conclusion is based on a relatively small subset of studies, so it must be considered quite tentative until further research is conducted. Furthermore, the moderating effect was not found for job survival, which is the more theoretically relevant criterion.

In order for the research literature to inform one's choice at a particular point, there must be at least some variance across the studies that have been done. Unfortunately, this does not appear to be the case for tough choices 1, 5, 9, and 10. Of the 27 "field" studies of RJPs, virtually all of them are reactions (number 1) using medium negativity (number 5) as part of an experimental pilot study (number 9) where the results were published or at least available in written form (number 10).

Besides having variance in a factor across studies, a second condition is necessary for research to inform one's choice. That is, when there is variance in a factor, the reviewer should be able to accurately record the variance. This was not the case for choice number 2, because the various "methods" sections are not sufficiently precise to code the degree of "structure" used in each job/organizational diagnosis. A reading of the methods sections does suggest there is a range of unstructured to structured diagnoses, but the typical account is insufficient for reliable and accurate coding. A meta-analysis of RJPs (Premack & Wanous, 1985) found no situational moderators with respect to their effects on job survival. Thus, the apparent variance in diagnostic methods does not appear to be related to RJP effectiveness — which supports my earlier claim that diagnostic methods are substitutable for each other.

The remaining choice points (numbers 3, 4, 7, & 8) all tend to be confounded with other factors, making it virtually impossible to untangle their effects via meta-analysis or any other review method. For example, all seven military studies of RJPs were done "late," that is, after one's organizational choice (Wanous & Colella, in press). This lateness is confounded with the generally much higher job survival rates found in the military.

From the above discussion it should be clear that recommendations for virtually all of the tough choices cannot be directly derived from the research that has been done. Thus, the recommendations made below are probably more subjective than would be desirable. In making them, I try to be explicit about the relative weight assigned to each of the three general criteria used here: quality, acceptance, and costs.

Whenever possible one should try to proact on the environment by developing RJPs even when there is no current turnover problem. The delays in starting after turnover becomes a problem can be considerable, reducing the utility of the RJP. In two personal cases (Dean & Wanous, 1984; Wanous, 1973) it took over one year to launch the RJP, resulting in a missed opportunity to affect the highest turnover period facing each organization during that year. Such "opportunity costs" can be estimated if one knows average replacement costs in hiring. (See Dean & Wanous, 1984, for the replacement costs for a bank teller and Cascio, 1987, for a more general treatment.)

Having done both structured and unstructured organizational diagnoses, both seem effective, so the recommendation at this choice point is the most equivocal of all ten. Unless one has good reason to anticipate a lot of resistance to the RJP or legal challenges, the unstructured approach is much more time and cost effective. In other words, I see the choice here as a trade-off between acceptance and cost, where quality is a less important consideration in making the choice.

Including as much judgmental material in an RJP as possible is usually a good idea. Naive job candidates do not have the ability to interpret the meaning of purely descriptive material. The best example of this was when I examined the effects of an on-site job visit used to recruit telephone operators (Wanous, 1973, 1980). One might assume that nothing could be more "real." However, the visit did not communicate how experienced employees felt about the job. As a result, it tended to inflate expectations, which was just the opposite from its intended purpose.

The content of RJPs should also be intensive (i.e., focused on a few key factors). The two basic criteria for selecting these are (1) do people have inaccurate expectations about this factor, and (2) is the factor important enough to affect one's decision to quit or stay. The extensive RJP may appear to be more "complete" to someone in a personnel department, who is in a position to make such an assessment. However, it is the mind of the job candidate that is the key here. It is the message that is "received and comprehended" that will affect self-selection decisions, not necessarily the message that was "sent" (Hovland, Janis, & Kelly, 1953; Popovich & Wanous, 1982). The present state of RJP research (Premack & Wanous, 1985; Wanous & Colella, in press) is not sufficiently detailed to decide this issue, however. This design facet is too frequently confounded with others to be untangled at the present time.

A reviewer of this article does not believe that a five-minute RJP could be either intensive or extensive. I agree that five minutes is usually too short for an extensive RJP — unless the job is very simple. I do not agree that five minutes is necessarily too short for an intensive RJP, because that would depend on how many important and inaccurate areas needed to be included, as indicated by one's diagnosis.

The third aspect of RJP content is how much negative information to include. As a general rule, the balance of positive and negative information should reflect that balance indicated by the organizational diagnosis. However, this is often a lot easier to espouse as an objective than to accomplish in practice. In order to obtain top management acceptance, one should strive for a medium level of negative content, keeping in mind the two criteria suggested above for selecting specific factors: they should be inaccurately perceived and should be important to most job candidates.

Two of the content choices (judgmental

and intensive) are compatible with the audio-visual method, which is recommended over booklets. It is much easier to communicate strong feelings about a job in an A-V format than in a booklet. And as Madison Avenue has known for years, you only try to present one or two key points in a television commercial. Research has also shown that complex messages are better understood in a written form (Chaiken & Eagly, 1976). So, if one wanted to ignore these recommendations, it would still be "internally consistent" to use a booklet for an extensive and mostly descriptive RJP.

An intriguing research possibility concerns the use of the two-way interview. Besides being underrepresented in the RJP research to date, it may be the method of choice for the future — this speculation is based on the latest developments in research on persuasion (i.e., Petty & Cacioppo, 1986).

When RJP research was linked to research on attitude change and persuasion (Popovich & Wanous, 1982), the "classical" framework developed by Hovland et al. (1953) was used. The Hovland school is described by Petty and Cacioppo as emphasizing "peripheral routes" to persuasion (e.g., the source of the message, its content, the medium/channel used, or the characteristics of the receiver. In contrast, Petty and Cacioppo advocate their "central route" to attitude change, which emphasizes the extent to which receivers carefully and thoughtfully assess and elaborate on the merits of the message. They summarize an extensive program of research showing the superiority of the central route for producing larger and more lasting attitude changes (Petty & Cacioppo, 1986). Much of this research has only been done recently, which accounts for why it has yet to be incorporated into the RJP literature.

The factors likely to trigger a central route are high involvement of the receiver, low distraction, moderate message repetition, more than one message source, and high need for cognition on the part of the receiver. It seems to me that the face-to-face nature of an interview is more conducive to achieving some of these factors than either booklets or videos.

It must be remembered, however, that the peripheral route is still a viable method and will be the relevant route when the central route is not triggered by the above factors. Nevertheless, the Petty and Cacioppo work suggests the possibility of increased RJP effectiveness, if their research on attitude change translates to the employment context.

When presenting video RJP material to job candidates, the strong recommendation is to use current job incumbents, not actors. It is even better to let them speak in their own words, since a nonactor trying to be an actor is the worst of both worlds. The credibility gained in this way is invaluable compared with the potential disadvantages and is supported by years of research on the classical peripheral route to attitude change (Hovland et al., 1953; Popovich & Wanous, 1982).

Showing the RJP as early as possible in the organizational entry process is also very desirable. The chance to influence self-selection decisions should not be lost by delaying the RJP. Even though the administrative costs are higher, replacement costs for personnel who quit very early are going to be even greater (Cascio, 1987).

Enough research has been published to date so that one probably does not have to rely on a pilot study to initiate an RJP program. Relying on a pilot study is risky because the small sample sizes usually found are insufficient for providing good estimates of the true effect of an RJP. Research summaries across large numbers of studies (e.g., Premack & Wanous, 1985; Wanous & Colella, in press) are preferable since the much larger sample size found in a research summary gives a more accurate estimate of the degree to which job survival will be enhanced by an RJP.

On the other hand, if one's purpose is only to do a manipulation check on the RJP, then a pilot study could be useful. If the study were limited primarily to the RJP's effect on initial expectations, then it could be completed more quickly than if one were to wait months longer to gather turnover data. This would reduce some of the opportunity cost of not installing the RJP immediately. Whether or not such a pilot study is necessary should depend on both the quality of one's initial diagnosis and its acceptance by management.

The RJP is so tailor-made for a specific job in a specific organization that there is little to fear from the sharing of one's results. The concept of RJPs in recruitment has been in the public arena, and it is a low-tech concept not at all similar to computer technology, gene splicing, and so forth. It seems clear there is much to be gained from the experiences of others by sharing information.

As a final note, a reviewer suggested the addition of an eleventh choice concerned with one's "activity versus passivity" toward what top management considers to be "acceptable." The reviewer thought that the whole tone of this article was too passive.

I agree that there has been no explicit discussion of strategies for dealing with top management in this regard. This seemed beyond the scope of what was intended, and it has been dealt with to some extent in the literature on OD (e.g., Bennis, 1987). On the other hand, the specific arguments listed for each choice represent what could be said in an effort to be actively persuasive. For example, if a reluctant boss objects to the inclusion of some material, one could try to counter this with such arguments as "look at the extensiveness of our diagnosis" (choice number 2), "it's really crucial to tell naive candidates how the typical person feels" (choice number 3), or "we have to be fairly negative or else we won't get certain people to drop out" (choice number 5). In a sense, then, the arguments presented here could be used to "frame" top management's thinking about what constitutes a high quality and acceptable RJP.

REFERENCES

Alderfer, C. P., Brown, L. D. (1972). Designing an "empathic" questionnaire for organizational research. *Journal of Applied Psychology, 56,* 456–460.

Arvey, R. D., Faley, R. H. (1988). Fairness in selecting employees (2nd ed.). Reading, MA: Addison-Wesley.

Bennis, W. (1987). Using our knowledge of organizational behavior: The improbable task. In Lorsch, J.W. (Ed.), *Handbook of organizational behavior* (pp. 29–49). Englewood Cliffs, NJ: Prentice-Hall.

Cascio, W. F. (1987). *Costing human resources: The*

financial impact of behavior in organizations. Boston: PWS-Kent.

Chaiken, S., Eagly, A. H. (1976). Communication modality as a determinant of message persuasiveness and message comprehensibility. *Journal of Personality and Social Psychology, 34,* 605–614.

Colarelli, S. M. (1984). Methods of communication and mediating processes in realistic job previews. *Journal of Applied Psychology, 69,* 633–642.

Dean, R. A., Wanous, J. P. (1984). The effects of realistic job previews on hiring bank tellers. *Journal of Applied Psychology, 69,* 61–68.

Dunnette, M. D. (1986, August). *Being there.* Presented at the annual convention of the American Psychological Association, Washington, DC.

Flynn, J. A., Ellis, R. T. (1984). *The effectiveness of the orientation video in enhancing career information gain* (Working Paper 84-11). Willowdale, Ontario: Canadian Forces Personnel Applied Research Unit.

Flynn, J. A., Ellis, R. T., Zuliani, R. A. (1984). *Content validation of the orientation video* (Working Paper 84-12). Willowdale, Ontario: Canadian Forces Personnel Applied Research Unit.

Hovland, C. I., Janis, I. L., Kelly, H. H. (1953). *Communication and persuasion.* New Haven, CT: Yale University Press.

Hunter, J. E., Schmidt, F. L., Jackson, G. B. (1982). *Meta-analysis: Cumulating research findings across studies.* Beverly Hills, CA: Sage Publications.

Ilgen, D. R., Seeley, W. (1974). Realistic expectations as an aid in reducing voluntary resignations. *Journal of Applied Psychology, 59,* 452–455.

Lewis, M. (1965). Psychological effect of effort. *Psychological Bulletin, 64,* 183–190.

Mobley, W. H. (1982). *Employee turnover: Causes, consequences, and control.* Reading, MA: Addison-Wesley.

Petty, R. E., Cacioppo, J. T. (1986). *Communication and persuasion: Central and peripheral routes to attitude change.* New York: Springer-Verlag.

Popovich, P., Wanous, J. P. (1982). The realistic job preview as a persuasive communication. *Academy of Management Review, 7,* 570–578.

Premack, S. L., Wanous, J. P. (1985). A meta-analysis of realistic job preview experiments. *Journal of Applied Psychology, 70,* 706–719.

Salancik, G. R. (1977). Commitment and the control of organizational behavior and belief. In Staw, B. M., Salancik, G. R. (Eds.), *New directions in organizational behavior* (pp. 1–54). Chicago: St. Clair Press.

Schneider, B. (1976). *Staffing organizations.* Pacific Palisades, CA: Goodyear.

Schneider, B., Schmitt, N. (1986). *Staffing organizations* (2nd ed.). Glenview, IL: Scott, Foresman Company.

Vroom, V. H. (1964). *Work and motivation.* New York: Wiley.

Vroom, V. H., Yetton, P. W. (1973). *Leadership and decision making.* Pittsburgh, PA: University of Pittsburgh Press.

Wanous, J. P. (1973). Effects of a realistic job preview on job acceptance, job attitudes, and job survival. *Journal of Applied Psychology, 58,* 327–332.

Wanous, J. P. (1975). Tell it like it is at realistic job previews. *Personnel, 52*(4), 50–60.

Wanous, J. P. (1980). *Organizational entry: Recruitment, selection, and socialization of newcomers.* Reading, MA: Addison-Wesley.

Wanous, J. P., Baker, H. G., Jr. (1987, May). *Development of realistic job previews for the Long Beach Naval Shipyard* (Technical Note 87-24). San Diego, CA: Navy Personnel Research and Development Center.

Wanous, J. P., Colella, A. (in press). Future directions in organizational entry research. In Rowland, K., Ferris, G. (Eds.), *Research in personnel/human resource management* (Vol. 7). Greenwich, CT: JAI Press.

Wanous, J. P., Lawler, E. E. III. (1972). The measurement and meaning of job satisfaction. *Journal of Applied Psychology, 56,* 95–105.

Weitz, J. (1956). Job expectancy and survival. *Journal of Applied Psychology, 40,* 245–247.

John P. Wanous is in the College of Business, Ohio State University. The author would like to thank Arnon Reichers and Benjamin Schneider for their helpful comments.

Recruitment for Beginners
Lynda Farago / Phil Argyris / Hung-Wei Chou

The old biweekly jobs-posting list, which made the rounds of the HR department's recruiters and regularly included over 300 positions, was worked over by the recruiters — typically with illegible, scrawled handwriting — and was then handed to a secretary for typing and production. There was also a weekly, manually produced report called "The Number of Days to Fill Positions," based on the same data, although the numbers never seemed to add up. The letters that offered the jobs were typed forms with fill-in-the-blanks spaces into which personal information — name, salary, and position titles — was added by hand.

Three logs were maintained simultaneously: one by the receptionist across whose desk the requisitions had to pass; another by the secretary who distributed the requisitions to the recruiters; and another by the recruiters themselves, who tracked the positions they were responsible for filling.

Early management predictions anticipated an automated system that would save at least 0.5 full-time equivalents of a recruiter's time.

The Medical Center's systems department supported only Burroughs (now Unisys) microcomputers; HR had to develop a homegrown alternative to commercial software that would not only meet HR's needs but that could be supported by the systems department.

HR designed a requisition tracking system that would function like an automated log book to inventory all position requisitions and the resulting hire information. In addition, it would organize the information into various reports, listings, and letters, including biweekly job postings, open requisition reports, lists of requisitions by recruiter, sources of new-hire reports, new-hire orientation reports, and management reports. The system runs on a Burroughs (B-20) microcomputer network under the BTOS operating system, a derivative of CTOS from Convergent Technologies in San Jose, CA. But this application could be developed to run on any microcomputer.

The system presents to recruiter uses a series of menus, beginning with a screen that requests a password. After entering an acceptable word, a user is brought to the system's main menu, which offers five functional options:

- Enter or view data.
- Edit dictionaries.
- Print reports.
- Create offer or benefits letters.
- Perform system maintenance functions.

Selection of a desired option brings the user to the appropriate screen to perform the desired task (see Exhibit 1). Exiting the system is accomplished by pressing FINISH to reach the computer's command prompt.

The system was put together by a de-

Source: Lynda Farago, Phil Argyris, and Hung-Wei Chou, "Recruitment for Beginners." Reprinted from *Computers in Personnel* (New York: Auerbach Publishers). © 1988 Warren, Gorham & Lamont Inc. Used with permission.

EXHIBIT 1
Functional Options and How to Select Them

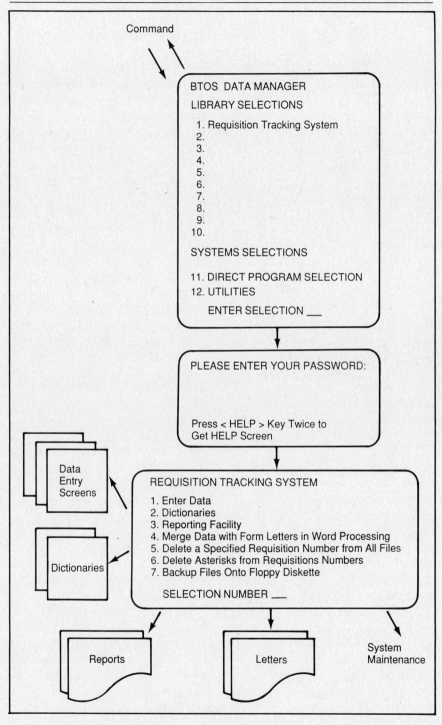

signer and two programmers to be used by nontechnical HR professionals. HELP screens are associated with each of the menus. Data is stored in four data files and three dictionaries: category-code dictionary, job-code grade dictionary, and source-of-hire dictionary. Data can be changed in or deleted from each of the files, separately or simultaneously. The dictionaries can be modified to reflect new salary ranges for jobs. The system is now used independently of other systems. But with new network software, the department will soon upload the new-hire information into the HR mainframe, thus saving an additional keypunch step.

WORK FLOW

The system is configured as a single master station and three slaves networked together, one slave for each of the recruiters. All three recruiters as well as the system coordinator can enter data into the system or perform an inquiry without interfering with other users.

The system's work flow, as shown in Exhibit 2, is initiated when a new requisition is handed to the system coordinator, who starts the requisition process by entering all relevant data on the master terminal. The coordinator then produces a report called the employment rep log, which shows all open requisitions by recruiter and gives recruiters their assigned lists of positions to fill.

For newly listed jobs, a recruiter logs onto the system, then enters the appropriate job description and other relevant information about the job. When the position is filled, the recruiter enters all new-hire information and instructs the system to produce an offer letter, a benefits letter, and new-hire-orientation reports (given to new hires on their first day).

Twice each week, the system coordinator produces the jobs-posting list, which is updated regularly by each of the recruiters and shows all open positions at that time. Only unfilled jobs appear on this list. On request, the system coordinator also produces various management and statistical reports, including a monthly report showing the average number of days individual recruiters needed to fill positions.

The system is meant to eliminate the redundant and time-consuming paper recordkeeping needed to track a requisition's progress through the HR office. By automating routine functions, the system allows HR professionals to perform those creative tasks that computers cannot:

- Developing novel approaches to recruiting.
- Employment planning.
- Integrating recruitment with other HR functions.

The system still needs some fine-tuning, but the benefits are obvious. Job-posting lists are now up to date and generated easily by recruiters maintaining their assigned hire and requisition data. There is a general sense of excitement throughout the department about using computers and calling up information through a screen, rather than turning pages in logs. Recruiters' jobs are now considerably more interesting and fun, and communications to new employees are accurate and professional looking.

Letting go of manual recordkeeping takes time and requires the patience of

EXHIBIT 2
Requisition System Work Flow

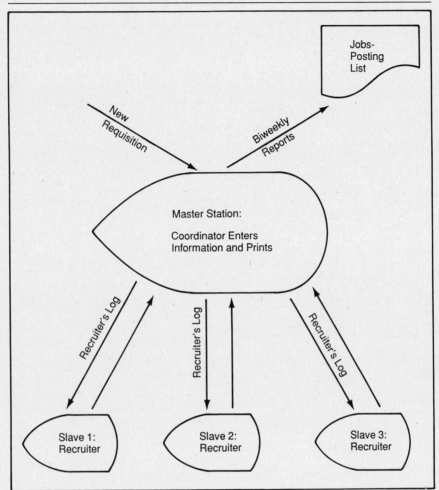

both HR professionals and hospital employees as well as a trustworthy and responsive system to soften users' resistance to new processes and routines. Although the system is straightforward and easy to use, the department depends on users' progress, needs, and suggestions to assist in the emotional process of change.

ONE FUNCTION LEADS TO ANOTHER

Staff members are beginning to analyze their work for future automation applications. They now ask the kind of questions that could motivate the department to automate more recruitment functions as well as other HR applications:

- Can this report be keyed in and printed automatically?
- Why am I entering this data if no one will ever refer to it again?
- Can correspondence be centralized on the master station to save time?
- When will the benefits managers be able to access this system?
- If the information in this report could be sorted by department, would it be more useful to me?

The systems analyst's job is much easier because the users are thinking and contributing so much. HR's latest challenge is to stay no more than one step behind the ideas from the recruiters-turned-analysts.

Lynda Farago is the manager of human resource systems and Phil Argyris and Hung-Wei Chou are senior programmer/analysts at the New England Medical Center in Boston.

Structured Interviewing: Raising the Psychometric Properties of the Employment Interview
Michael A. Campion / Elliott D. Pursell / Barbara K. Brown

The reliability and validity of the employment interview has been questioned throughout the history of industrial psychology, starting early in the century (e.g., Hollingworth, 1922; Scott, 1915) and in every review since (Arvey & J. Campion, 1982; Carlson, Thayer, Mayfield, & Peterson, 1971; J. Hunter & R. Hunter, 1984; Mayfield, 1964; Reilly & Chao, 1982; Schmitt, 1976; Ulrich & Trumbo, 1965; Wagner, 1949; Webster, 1964; O. Wright, 1969). Structuring the interview has often been proposed as a means of improvement, but the operationalization of structure has varied widely across studies, with at least three different forms observed. First, many studies developed semistructured interviews in that the process was not completely specified but some form of assistance was provided in conducting the interview or evaluating responses. Yonge (1956) used an outline and rating scale. Barrett, Svetlik, and Prien (1967) had interviewers take notes during the interview and make ratings afterwards. Landy (1976) used dimensional rating scales and an interview panel. Mayfield, Brown, and Hamstra (1980) developed an interview guide and summary form with suggested questions. Zedeck, Tziner, and Middlestadt (1983) made evaluations on behaviorally anchored rating scales. Arvey, Miller, Gould, and Burch (1987) developed a job-analysis-based interview schedule. In addition, many other studies provided some form of structure for the interview, but the detail given was insufficient for understanding the nature or degree of the structure (e.g., Albrecht, Glaser, & Marks, 1964; Borman, 1982; Campbell, Prien, & Brailey, 1960; Free-

Source: Michael A. Campion, Elliott D. Pursell, and Barbara K. Brown, "Structured Interviewing: Raising the Psychometric Properties of the Employment Interview," *Personnel Psychology,* 1988, 41, pp. 25–42. Reprinted by permission of *Personnel Psychology.*

man, Manson, Katzoff, & Pathman, 1942; Gardner & Williams, 1973; Ghiselli, 1966; Glaser, Schwarz, & Flanagan, 1958; Huse, 1962; Tubiana & Ben-Shakhar, 1982).

Second, some studies "patterned" the interview as suggested by McMurry (1947). With this approach, the interviewer did not have to ask the same questions of each candidate but, instead, selected from an array (or pattern) of questions. Maas (1965) improved the patterned interview by using behavioral expectation scales (Smith & Kendall, 1963). Janz (1982) and Orpen (1985) evaluated a further variant called the "patterned behavior description interview," which involved a critical incident job analysis (Flanagan, 1954), recorded responses, and rating scales. Finally, Schwab and Heneman (1969) and Heneman, Schwab, Huett, and Ford (1975) enhanced structure in a manner similar to patterning, in which interviewers could not deviate from a predetermined job-analysis-based interview format (i.e., application form).

Third, Latham, Saari, Pursell, and M. Campion (1980), Latham and Saari (1984), and recently, Weekley and Gier (1987) evaluated an approach called "situational" interviewing. This approach was more structured than previous efforts in that it used the same questions for each candidate, anchored rating scales, and an interview panel to record and evaluate responses. On the basis of the goal-setting assumption that intentions are related to behavior (Locke, 1968), candidates' responses as to what they would do in hypothetical job situations were hypothesized to be predictive of what they would actually do on the job. Situations were generated using critical incident job analyses (Flanagan, 1954).

PURPOSE OF THIS STUDY

This study extends previous research in four ways. First, it presents a more highly structured interviewing technique than most other efforts. Previously this technique was only described in a nonresearch journal (Pursell, M. Campion, & Gaylord, 1980) and in unpublished sources (M. Campion & Pursell, 1981; Pursell & Gaylord, 1976). This technique begins with the same research theme as Latham et al. (1980), but it extends the methodology to other question types in addition to situational questions. Also included are job knowledge, worker requirements, and job sample and simulation questions. Second, more so than with other approaches to interviewing, greater explicit attention is afforded to the guidelines on test development from both the professional perspective (*Validation Principles,* Society of Industrial and Organizational Psychology, Inc., 1987) and the legal perspective (*Uniform Guidelines;* Equal Employment Opportunity Commission, Civil Service Commission, Department of Labor, & Department of Justice, 1978) in order to enhance the likelihood of validity and legal defensibility. Third, aside from presenting the usual psychometric quality indicators of interrater reliability and predictive validity, this study also presents evidence of test fairness and utility. Fourth, a battery of typical employment aptitude tests are examined to determine whether the psychometric properties of the interview can be raised to the level of these traditional selection devices and to explore the constructs measured by the interview.

OVERVIEW OF THE STRUCTURED INTERVIEWING TECHNIQUE

Both the *Uniform Guidelines* (p. 38296) and the *Validation Principles* (p. 1) consider interviews to require validation just as any other selection procedure. The aforementioned common belief in the lack of validity of the traditional unstructured interview, along with its inherent subjectivity and apparent susceptibility to bias, may make it particularly vulnerable to legal attack (Arvey, 1979). The proposed approach to interviewing attempts to reduce subjectivity and inconsistency by highly structuring the process with the following six steps.

Step 1: Develop questions based on a job analysis. Adequate job analysis for any selection procedure is not only encouraged by the *Uniform Guidelines* (pp. 38304–38306) and *Validation Principles* (pp. 5–6), but there is evidence of its importance both in court decisions (Kleiman & Faley, 1985) and in avoiding bias (Kesselman & Lopez, 1979). All questions must be clearly job related. Any method of job analysis can be used, as long as it includes a determination of knowledge, skills, abilities, and other requirements upon which to base interview questions. There should be a measure of importance of job tasks so that questions only assess prerequisites for performing critical work (*Uniform Guidelines*, p. 38302; *Validation Principles*, pp. 22–23). Additionally, questions should not generally be based on the requirements of higher-level jobs (*Uniform Guidelines*, p. 38298; *Validation Principles*, pp. 13–14) or on knowledge or skills the employee will learn with brief training or experience on the job (*Uniform Guidelines*, p. 38298; *Validation Principles*, p. 22).

A variety of question types can be used, including situational questions as described above (Latham et al., 1980), questions on job knowledge that is related to performance, and job sample or simulation questions where possible. These latter questions can range from actually performing part of the job to mockups of job tasks, or to simply phrasing questions in terminology and examples from the job. It is important, however, that they assess requirements at the same complexity level as that needed on the job (*Uniform Guidelines*, pp. 38305–38306). Samples and simulations not only enhance content and face validity but, when properly developed, can exhibit criterion-related validity (J. Campion, 1972) and avoid bias (Brugnoli, J. Campion, & Basen, 1979; Schmidt, Greenthal, J. Hunter, Berner, & Seaton, 1977). Finally, other worker requirement questions also are included. They frequently involve questions on background (e.g., experience, education) or "willingness" questions (e.g., shift work, travel). They also serve as warm-up questions at the beginning of the interview, and as realistic job previews (Wanous, 1980).

Aside from the criteria already mentioned, questions should be reviewed to make certain they are accurate, complete, and unambiguous. Furthermore, they should be reviewed by independent job experts who are members of protected groups to check for any potential for bias or misinterpretation.

Step 2: Ask the same questions of each candidate. All candidates are asked the same questions. There is no prompting or follow-up questioning, although the questions can be repeated.

Step 3: Anchor the rating scales for scoring answers with examples and illustrations. A scoring system is developed for each question by generating examples or definitions for *good* (5), *marginal* (3), and *poor* (1) answers. One approach is to ask job experts for example answers they have actually heard that subsequently distinguished different levels of performers on the job (Latham et al., 1980). A simpler approach is to brainstorm potential answers with experts and personnel representatives familiar with the job and with interviewing comparable candidates. Often both approaches are used to generate potential answers. Either way, example answers must be scaled to the requirements of the job so that good answers do not far exceed the requirements, and poor answers are not so low that they do not help distinguish between candidates. Predetermined answer-rating scales enhance consistency across interviews and objectivity of judging candidate responses. Making the scoring system explicit is essential to justifying the content validity of assessment procedures (Sackett, 1987; *Validation Principles,* p. 24). In addition, developing example answers serves as an evaluation of the questions; difficulty in generating answers suggests that restructuring or elimination of the questions may be warranted.

Step 4: Have an interview panel record and rate answers. Using an interview panel reduces the impact of idiosyncratic biases that single interviewers might introduce (*Validation Principles,* p. 12). If possible, the panel should consist of a subset of the job experts who helped analyze the job and develop the interview questions because they are most familiar with the job and the questions. Three members are typically used, including supervisors of the job to be filled and a personnel representative. It is advisable to use the same members for all interviews to enhance consistency. However, an excessively large number of interviews or other constraints (e.g., turnover) may make this infeasible. The panel assembles in advance to review job duties and requirements, questions and answers, the interview process, and ways to avoid rating errors that can bias evaluations (Latham, Wexley, & Pursell, 1975). Application forms are not reviewed prior to the interview to avoid influencing the evaluation process (cf. Dipboye, Fontenelle, & Garner, 1984; Tucker & Rowe, 1977). All members independently record and rate each candidate's answers during the actual interview.

Step 5: Consistently administer the process to all candidates. The same panel member should conduct all interviews and ask all questions. Panel members do not discuss questions, answers, or candidates between interviews in order to avoid potential bias from changing standards or comparisons among candidates. After all interviews are complete for a given job, any large discrepancies between ratings are discussed (Thornton & Byham, 1982; but cf. Sackett & Wilson, 1982). Memory decay for candidate answers is avoided by the extensive note taking of panel members. The ratings and items are averaged to ensure equal weighting because differential weighting schemes are generally not preferred (Einhorn & Hogarth, 1975; Wainer, 1976). Differences in importance between job requirements is addressed by the number of items assessing each requirement. Every attempt is made to conduct interviews in as nonstressful a manner as possible (e.g., introductions of panel members, comfortable interview setting, only one member asks all questions). Candidates are allowed to ask questions in a subsequent nonevaluation interview with a personnel representative.

Step 6: Give special attention to job relatedness, fairness, and documentation in accordance with testing guidelines. Consideration of the *Uniform Guidelines* and *Validation Principles* has been noted throughout the process. Components needing documentation include the job analysis and interview development procedure, candidate responses and scores, evidence for content or criterion-related validity, adverse impact analyses, and other aspects as appropriate.

METHOD

Setting and Sample

The structured interview was used for hiring entry-level labor-pool employees in a large pulp and paper mill located in the rural Southeast. The traditional unionized facility placed new employees in bottom-level jobs in the various union lines of progression throughout the mill. Interest was in selecting employees with the basic skills needed to perform any of these entry-level jobs.

Of the 243 applicants interviewed, 149 were hired. The hires were 37.6% minority and 20.1% female, which was representative of the community work force and likely future candidates (*Uniform Guidelines*, p. 38301; *Validation Principles*, p. 12). Age averaged 30.4 ($SD = 7.9$) and education averaged 12.2 ($SD = 2.1$) years. Adequate statistical power was ensured (*Validation Principles*, p. 8) by the fact that the 149 hires provided 90% power to detect an observed correlation of .24 (i.e., uncorrected for range restriction and criterion unreliability; $p < .05$, one-tailed test; Schmidt, J. Hunter, & Urry, 1976).

Structured Interview

Analyses of the labor pool revealed that a subset of 17 jobs were most frequently staffed by entry-level employees. Job analysis conferences were conducted with incumbents and supervisors for each job. Lists of duties and requirements were generated, and duties were evaluated in terms of importance and time spent. The jobs were highly similar in terms of 25 shared requirements (i.e., knowledge, skills, abilities, and other worker characteristics), which suggested support for a job family for selection purposes (Pearlman, 1980; *Uniform Guidelines*, p. 38304). Interview questions were developed to assess the requirements needed to perform the most important and time-consuming duties. Detailed content validity procedures and analyses were described in M. Campion and Pursell (1981).

The developmental procedures described above were followed, and a 20-item interview resulted. All the previously mentioned question types were included, with most questions representing a combination of the various types. Three examples provided below illustrate the range of questions.

a. Job knowledge question assessed mechanical comprehension: "When putting a piece of machinery back together after repairing it, why would you clean all the parts first?"
    (5) Particles of dust and dirt can cause wear on moving parts. Need to have parts clean to inspect for wear and damage.
    (3) Parts will go together easier. Equipment will run better.
    (1) So it will all be clean. I don't know.
b. Simulation question assessed low level reading ability: "Many of the jobs require the operation of a forklift. Please read this (90-word) forklift checkout procedure aloud."
    (5) Reads fluently pronouncing all words accurately.
    (3) Can read most words but hesitates.
    (1) Reads with great difficulty.
c. Worker characteristic or willingness question assessed fear of heights: "Some jobs require climbing ladders to a height of a five-story building and going out on a catwalk to work. Give us your feeling about performing a task such as this."
    (5) Heights do not bother me. I have done similar work at heights in the past (and gives examples).
    (3) I do not think I am afraid of heights. I know that this would have to be done as part of the job.
    (1) I am afraid of heights. I would do it if absolutely necessary.

A cutting score of 4.0 was set for the interview based on a modified Angoff (1971) procedure. Job experts judged the minimum acceptable performance level on each item, and the average across the items was used as the cutting score. This helped ensure that the interview assessed requirements at a similar complexity level to the job (*Uniform Guidelines,* pp. 38305–38306).

Because of the magnitude of this hiring program, many interview panel members were needed. But in all cases, the three panel members included two supervisors familiar with the different entry-level jobs and a personnel representative. Interviews lasted approximately 30 minutes.

Performance Criterion

Behavioral observation scales (Latham & Wexley, 1977, 1981) were developed because more objective, behavioral, and job-analysis-based performance appraisals may be more legally defensible (Kleiman & Faley, 1985; *Uniform Guidelines,* p. 38300). This procedure began with a critical incident job analysis (Flanagan, 1954), which was separate from the analysis used to develop the interview. Content coverage was ensured by collecting 6,150 critical incidents from 100 supervisors describing the performance of 393 employees. Incidents were condensed into 75 items and coupled with 5-point frequency scales to constitute the behavioral observation instrument. Reproducibility was demonstrated by having an independent analyst reclassify a 9% sample of the critical incidents into the 75 items. Approximately 96% accuracy was observed. Total scores were calculated as sums of the items. Internal consistency reliability (Cronbach, 1951) was .99, indicating substantial homogeneity. Interrater reliability between independent supervisory evaluations over a one-month time period on a sample of 30 employees was .76 ($p < .05$).

All supervisors using the instrument were given a half-day training program on minimizing rating errors (Latham et al., 1975). Appraisals were conducted after six months of employment. To avoid potential bias, in no case were the same supervisors involved in both the interviews and performance appraisals (Schoorman, 1988; *Uniform Guidelines,* p. 38300; *Validation Principles,* p. 14).

Employment Aptitude Tests

Before starting work, all candidates hired were examined on an experimental battery of four typical paper-and-pencil employment tests, which were chosen to assess cognitive aptitudes suggested by the job analysis.

1. Mathematical aptitude was measured with the Flanagan Industrial Test — Arithmetic (Form A). Its 60 items measured ability to perform simple addition, subtraction, multiplication, and division of whole numbers (Flanagan, 1975). A time limit of 15 minutes was allowed, and the score was the number correct. The manual reported an alternative forms reliability of .79.

2. Mechanical aptitude was measured with the mechanical knowledge test of the SRA Mechanical Aptitudes battery (Form AH). Its 45 items measured ability to recognize a variety of common tools (Richardson, Bellows, Henry, & Company, Inc., 1947). It was timed at 10 minutes and scored in terms of number correct. The manual only reported internal consistency reliability, which was inappropriate for speeded tests (Nunnally, 1978).

3. Following oral instructions was measured with the Personnel Tests for Industry — Oral Directions Test (Form S). Its 16 items measured ability to follow oral instructions on a 15-minute audio tape (Langmuir, 1974). The score was a weighted total of number correct (39 maximum). The manual reported a mean corrected split-half reliability of .80 and a mean retest reliability of .84.

4. Reading scales was measured by the 12-item Can You Read a Scale? test, which assessed ability to read standard scales or rules (Lawshe, 1943). It was timed at four minutes and scored as number correct. No manual was available.

RESULTS

All measures appeared to have substantial range and variation (Table 1). Internal consistency reliability of the structured interview was .72, indicating some heterogeneity among the 20 items. Interrater reliability (intraclass correlation) among the three raters was quite high at .88. The reliability of the mean of the three raters was very high at .96 (Cronbach, Gleser, Nanda, & Rajaratnam, 1972). Interrater agreement was also examined (Tinsley & Weiss, 1975) because hiring decisions were made based on the absolute level of interview scores. Agreement among interviewers was within a criterion of .5 points on the total scores in 95% of the cases ($p < .05$; Lawlis & Lu, 1972).

The validity coefficient between the structured interview and performance

TABLE 1

Means, Standard Deviations, and Correlations among the Measures

	n	M	SD	Correlations[a]					
				1	2	3	4	5	6[b]
1. Structured interview	149	4.21	.39		40	70	52	66	49/56
2. Mathematical aptitude	140	53.95	7.18	27		38	58	51	33/38
3. Mechanical aptitude	140	27.16	8.25	54	27		45	74	45/52
4. Following oral instructions	140	32.72	4.74	37	53	31		63	40/46
5. Reading scales	140	6.95	3.77	50	44	64	54		44/51
6. Performance appraisal	149	278.30	53.42	34	25	32	30	32	

a. Decimals omitted. All significant at $p < .05$. Correlations below the diagonal are uncorrected; those above are corrected for range restriction. Corrections involving the interview are for direct restriction, while those not involving interview are for indirect restriction (Guilford, 1965, pp. 343 and 344, respectively).

b. Correlations to left of slash (/) corrected for range restriction; those to right also corrected for criterion unreliability (Guilford, 1965, p. 487).

appraisal was .34 ($p < .05$). Correcting for direct range restriction caused by selection based on the interview (restricted SD in the sample hired of .39 versus unrestricted SD in the total sample interviewed of .60) and criterion unreliability (interrater $r = .76$) yielded correlations of .49 and .39, respectively (Guilford, 1965, pp. 343 and 487). Correcting for both factors yielded a correlation of .56 (Schmidt et al., 1976).

Test fairness was evaluated using a moderated regression strategy, which assessed equality of intercepts and slopes (Bartlett, Bobko, Mosier, & Hannan, 1978). In the equation in which the interview is used to predict the performance appraisal, intercept differences were tested by adding race to the equation, and the slope differences were tested by also adding race by interview interaction to the equation. A similar analysis was performed for sex. Results showed a significant intercept difference for race (incremental R squared $= .11$, $F = 20.30$, $df = 1,146$, $p < .05$), but a plot of the separate regression lines indicated that a common line slightly overpredicted (i.e., was not unfair) for minorities. No slope differences were observed for race, and no intercept or slope differences were observed for sex ($p > .05$).

Gain in utility from using the structured interview over random selection (*Validation Principles,* pp. 17–18) was estimated using formulas and procedures from Schmidt, J. Hunter, McKenzie, and Muldrow (1979). Relevant data included interviewer time and administrative costs of $30 per applicant, selection ratio of .62, average standard score on the interview of those selected of .42, and validity coefficients of .34 uncorrected and .56 corrected. The standard deviation of job performance in dollar terms was estimated at $5,000 per year by supervisors using the Schmidt et al. direct estimate technique. This value was 33% of annual mean wages, which was slightly below the 40% estimate often discussed in utility research (Schmidt & J. Hunter, 1983; Schmidt, J. Hunter, Outerbridge, & Trattner, 1986). Using these figures, the one-year utility from the 149 hires was estimated at approximately $100,000 using the uncorrected validity and $168,000 using the corrected validity. Assuming a 10% annual interest rate and no separations (Boudreau & Berger, 1985), the estimated gain in 10 years would be over $1 million in net present value in the year 1980. Precise development costs were unknown, but they would be small compared with this gain in utility (e.g., $20,000 to $30,000 in salaries).

The four employment aptitude tests were also positively correlated with the performance appraisal (Table 1). Correcting for indirect range restriction caused by the interview substantially increased their size (Guilford, 1965, p. 344). Although the correlations were slightly smaller than the interview, none were significantly smaller ($p > .05$).

Test fairness analyses of the tests resulted in findings similar to the interview with regard to race. No slope differences occurred, but intercept differences were significant in all cases (incremental R squared = .07 to .11, F = 12.02 to 18.46, $df = 1,137, p < .05$). Again, plots of the separate regression lines indicated that a common line slightly overpredicted (i.e., was not unfair) for minorities. With regard to sex, the tests showed no slope differences, but intercept differences were significant for the mechanical aptitude and following oral directions tests (incremental R squared = .06 and .05, respectively, F = 9.86 and 8.28, $df = 1,137, p < .05$). Plots of regression lines indicated that the common line slightly overpredicted (i.e., was not unfair) for females.

Gain in utility from using the tests over random selection was analyzed assuming the same selection ratio, standard score for selectees, and standard deviation of job performance in dollars, but administrative costs of only $5 per applicant. The one-year gain in utility ranged from approximately $77,000 to $100,000 using the uncorrected validities and from $118,000 to $160,000 using the corrected validities. These values were slightly smaller than those with the interview. Therefore, even though the tests would have reduced development costs (i.e., job analysis still required, but no instrument development costs), the tests and interview would likely have comparable utility.

An examination of incremental value revealed that the tests explained additional variance in the performance appraisal beyond that explained by the interview (incremental R squared = .07, F = 11.17, $df = 4,135, p < .05$), but the interview did not explain additional variance in the appraisal beyond that explained by the tests combined (incremental R squared = .01, F = 2.30, df = 1,135, n.s.). Consequently, the interview would not have incremental utility beyond the tests, and there may even be a slight negative utility because of the development costs of the interview.

Correlations between the interview and tests were positive and moderate to large in size (Table 1), with a multiple of .59 (F = 17.99, $df = 4,135, p < .05$). Correcting for range restriction on the interview substantially increased their size and resulted in a multiple correlation of .75. This suggested a strong cognitive aptitude component to the interview.

DISCUSSION

This article presents a highly structured interviewing technique that includes the following steps: (1) develop questions based on a job analysis, (2) ask the same questions of each candidate, (3) anchor the rating scales for scoring answers with examples and illustrations, (4) have an interview panel record and rate answers, (5) consistently administer the process to all candidates, and (6) give special attention to job relatedness, fairness, and documentation in accordance with testing guidelines. In a field study, an interview developed using this technique demonstrates interrater reliability, predictive validity, test fairness for minorities and females, and cost/benefit utility.

Paper-and-pencil cognitive aptitude tests have historically been viewed as the best predictors of job performance (J. Hunter & R. Hunter, 1984; Reilly & Chao, 1982). Four typical employment tests are used to determine whether highly structuring the interview can raise its psychometric properties to the levels of these traditional selection instruments. The level of reliability of the interview seems comparable to those of the tests, to the extent that reliabilities for the tests are available in the manuals. The level of validity of the interview is slightly larger than the tests, but not significantly so. The corrected interview validity of .56 is also quite similar to the mean validity of .53 for cognitive aptitude predictors in general, and far larger than the mean validity of .14 for traditional interviews, for entry-level jobs as discovered in a large-scale meta-analytic study (J. Hunter & R. Hunter, 1984). Test fairness analyses yield similar results for both the interview and tests with regard to race, with a slight overprediction for minorities. While the interview shows no difference for sex, however, the tests slightly overpredict females. Intercept differences are a frequent form of differential prediction (Bartlett et al., 1978), but slight overprediction is not unfair to minorities and females. Finally, the utilities of the interview and the tests are quite comparable, even with the larger development costs of the interview. Using expectancy tables (Taylor & Russell, 1939) and assuming base rates and selection ratios of 50%, the traditional interview ($r = .14$) yields 55% successful employees, and this structured interview ($r = .56$) yields nearly 70% successful employees.

The effectiveness of this approach to structured interviewing may be explained in terms of both method and content. Both clearly represent characteristics that are central to professional and legal testing guidelines. The methods used to structure the interview give it an advantage in terms of standardization (*Uniform Guidelines,* p. 38298; *Validation Principles,* pp. 7 and 14). Having multiple interviewers consistently evaluate candidates on the same questions using the same criteria may reduce idiosyncratic biases of interviewers, as well as their susceptibility to order or contrast effects among the candidates. Other methodological features may also enhance validity. All the question types have some prior empirical validity evidence: situational (e.g., Latham et al., 1980), knowledge (e.g., J. Hunter, 1986), sample/simulation (e.g., J. Campion, 1972), and worker requirements (e.g., Wanous, 1980). Content validity may be enhanced by attempting to assess requirements at the same complexity level as needed on the job (*Uniform Guidelines,* pp. 38305–38306) and by explicitly predetermining the scoring system (Sackett, 1987). Training interviewers to avoid common response errors (Latham et al., 1975) may also help improve validity (Pursell, Dossett, & Latham, 1980).

The content of the structured interview may make it effective in that it is based on job analysis (*Uniform Guidelines,* pp. 38304–38306; *Validation Principles,* pp. 5–6). Examination of a battery of typical environment aptitude tests bears on the content of the interview by providing an assessment of the constructs it taps. The large correlations suggest that the interview has a substantial job knowledge or cognitive ability component. Thus, the content of the structured interview may be more like that of an orally administered cognitive ability test. The predictability of job performance through measures of job knowledge or general cognitive ability is well documented (Gottfredson, 1986; J. Hunter, 1986).

The superiority of structured interviews over unstructured interviews and the potential method versus content explanations for that superiority have also been noted by recent unpublished meta-analytic studies (McDaniel et al., 1987; Wiesner & Cronshaw, 1987; P. Wright, Lichtenfels, & Pursell, 1987). It is important to attend to the constructs underlying interviews in meta-analyses. Lumping cognitive-oriented with motivation-oriented interviews would be misleading.

Further analyses of the employment aptitude tests reveal that they also predict the performance criterion, and they add incrementally to the prediction beyond the interview but not the reverse. This raises the question of why spend the additional effort and expense of using a structured interview, when commercially available and inexpensive paper-and-pencil ability tests predict just as well. At least three explanations can be offered. First, many (if not most) managers believe in the value of interviews, and they will frequently conduct interviews and allow them to influence hiring decisions, even when other more valid selection devices are available. In fact, there is no evidence that the continual warnings of researchers over the last 40 years about the limitations of the traditional interview have decreased its prevalence. Structured interviewing allows managers to take part in the selection process in an interviewer role, yet it gives the usually haphazard interview psychometric qualities comparable to a cognitive ability test.

Second, the development procedures of the structured interview may make it easier to content validate than commercial available written tests, which makes the technique especially appealing to small employers (Robinson, 1981). Third, there is some evidence that content-oriented job sample tests are perceived by both minority and majority applicants as fairer and more appropriate than written tests (Schmidt et al., 1977). Thus, the structured interviewing approach in this study may have greater face validity to applicants than commercially available aptitude tests.

At least four directions for future research can be suggested. First, future research could explore the usefulness of this structured interviewing technique for other jobs and settings. Both this study and research on the highly similar situational interview (Latham et al., 1980; Latham & Saari, 1984) have focused on jobs in the forest products industry. With the exception of small samples of foremen and hourly workers in Latham et al. and a small sample of sales people in the recent study by Weekley and Gier (1987), most data have come from entry-level hiring. Although the authors are aware of many other applications with different and higher-level jobs, further reliability and validity evidence is needed. It may be that higher-level jobs (e.g., management) would require some probing and follow-up questioning. Perhaps coding schemes for recording probes can be borrowed from survey interviewing research (e.g., Survey Research Center's Interviewing Manual, 1976). In addition, employment interviewing research might benefit by consideration of other findings in survey interviewing research, such as the importance of interviewer–interviewee interactions and nonverbal behavior (e.g., Beed & Stimson, 1985; Kahn & Cannell, 1957; Warwick & Lininger, 1975).

Second, future research could examine the relative effectiveness of the various types of questions. In the present study, most questions represented combinations of situational questions, job knowledge questions, sample/simulation questions, and worker requirement questions. But research on purer forms, such as the Latham et al. (1980) study on situational questions, could be undertaken.

Third, a potential advantage of the proposed form of structured interviewing is management acceptance. This is not the case if selection programs are too cumbersome (Mayfield et al., 1980). The experience of the authors is that managers appreciate the obvious fairness of asking the exact same questions of all candidates and having predetermined answer-rating scales. Participation in the interview panel is an interesting and involving experience for the managers. They feel the process makes an otherwise subjective and "soft" interview seem more objective and worthwhile. Although this structured interview may be somewhat constraining relative to traditional interviews (e.g., no follow-up questions, one member asking all questions), there is an unpublished study suggesting managers and attorneys view structured interviews as more practical and defensible (Latham & Finnegan, 1987). That study also found that employee hires did not differ in preferences for types of interviews, but student applicants believed the unstructured interview was advantageous in winning a lawsuit. This latter finding, along with the enhanced fairness perceptions of content-oriented measures observed by Schmidt et al. (1977), suggests candidate reactions to structured interviewing may also be favorable for the company. Future research could further explore both managerial and candidate reactions to structured interviews.

Fourth, future research could examine underlying mechanisms. Is this highly structured interviewing technique effective because of its degree of standardization and other methodological advantages; is it effective because it is job related and taps general cognitive ability which is predictive of performance on most jobs; or are both mechanisms operating?

REFERENCES

Albrecht, P. A., Glaser, E. M., Marks, J. (1964). Validation of a multiple-assessment procedure for managerial personnel. *Journal of Applied Psychology, 48,* 351–360.

Angoff, W. H. (1971). Scales, norms, and equivalent scores. In Thorndike, R.L. (Ed.), *Educational measurement* (2nd ed., pp. 508–600). Washington, DC: American Council on Education.

Arvey, R. D. (1979). Unfair discrimination in the employment interview: Legal and psychological aspects. *Psychological Bulletin, 86,* 736–765.

Arvey, R. D., Campion, J. E. (1982). The employment interview: A summary and review of recent research. PERSONNEL PSYCHOLOGY, *35,* 281–322.

Arvey, R. D., Miller, H. E., Gould, R., Burch, P. (1987). Interview validity for selecting sales clerks. PERSONNEL PSYCHOLOGY, *40,* 1–12.

Barrett, G.V., Svetlik, B., Prien, E. P. (1967). Validity of the job-concept interview in an industrial setting. *Journal of Applied Psychology, 51,* 233–235.

Bartlett, C. J., Bobko, P., Mosier, S. B., Hannan, R. (1978). Testing for fairness with a moderated multiple-regression strategy: An alternative to differential analysis. PERSONNEL PSYCHOLOGY, *31,* 233–241.

Beed, T. W., Stimson, R. J. (Eds.). (1985). *Survey interviewing: Theory and techniques.* Sydney, Australia: George Allen & Unwin.

Borman, W. C. (1982). Validity of behavioral assessment for predicting military recruiter performance. *Journal of Applied Psychology, 67,* 3–9.

Boudreau, J. W., Berger, C. J. (1985). Decision-theoretic utility analysis applied to employee separations and acquisitions [Monograph]. *Journal of Applied Psychology, 70,* 581–612.

Brugnoli, G. A., Campion, J. E., Basen, J. A. (1979). Racial bias in the use of work samples for personnel selection. *Journal of Applied Psychology, 64,* 119–123.

Campbell, J. T., Prien, E. P., Brailey, L. G. (1960). Predicting performance evaluations. PERSONNEL PSYCHOLOGY, *13,* 435–440.

Campion, J. E. (1972). Work sampling for personnel selection. *Journal of Applied Psychology, 56,* 40–44.

Campion, M. A., Pursell, E. D. (1981). *Plymouth fiber extraboard validation report: Content and criterion-related validation of a structured interview and written test battery for an entry-level production job family.* Plymouth, NC: Human Resources Research, Weyerhaeuser Company.

Carlson, R. E., Thayer, P. W., Mayfield, E. C, Peterson, D. A. (1971). Improvements in the selection interview. *Personnel Journal, 50,* 268–275, 317.

Cronbach, L. J. (1951). Coefficient alpha and the internal structure of tests. *Psychometrika, 16,* 297–334.

Cronbach, L. J., Gleser, G. C., Nanda, H., Rajaratnam, N. (1972). *The dependability of behavioral measurements: Theory of generalizability for scores and profiles.* New York: Wiley.

Dipboye, R. L., Fontenelle, G. A., Garner, K. (1984). Effects of previewing the application on interview process and outcomes. *Journal of Applied Psychology, 69,* 118–128.

Einhorn, H. J., Hogarth, R. M. (1975). Unit weighting schemes for decision making. *Organizational Behavior and Human Performance, 13,* 171–192.

Equal Employment Opportunity Commission, Civil Service Commission, Department of Labor, Department of Justice. (1978). Adoption by four agencies of uniform guidelines on employee selection procedures. *Federal Register, 43,* 38290–38315.

Flanagan, J. C. (1954). The critical incident technique. *Psychological Bulletin, 51,* 327–358.

Flanagan, J. C. (1975). *Flanagan industrial tests examiner's manual.* Chicago: Science Research Associates.

Freeman, G. L., Manson, G. E., Katzoff, E. T., Pathman, J. H. (1942). The stress interview. *Journal of Abnormal and Social Psychology, 37,* 427–447.

Gardner, K. E., Williams, A. P. O. (1973). A twenty-five year follow-up of an extended interview selection procedure in the Royal Navy. *Occupational Psychology, 47,* 1–13.

Ghiselli, E. E. (1966). The validity of a personnel interview. PERSONNEL PSYCHOLOGY, *19,* 389–394.

Glaser, R., Schwarz, P. A., Flanagan, J. C. (1958). The contribution of interview and situational performance procedures to the selection of supervisory personnel. *Journal of Applied Psychology, 42*, 69–73.

Gottfredson, L. S. (1986). The *g* factor in employment [Special issue]. *Journal of Vocational Behavior, 29*(3).

Guilford, J. P. (1965). *Fundamental statistics in psychology and education* (4th ed.). New York: McGraw-Hill.

Heneman, H. G., Schwab, D. P., Huett, D. L., Ford, J. J. (1975). Interviewer validity as a function of interview structure, biographical data, and interviewee order. *Journal of Applied Psychology, 60*, 748–753.

Hollingworth, H. L. (1922). *Judging human character*. New York: Appleton.

Hunter, J. E. (1986). Cognitive ability, cognitive aptitudes, job knowledge, and job performance. *Journal of Vocational Behavior, 29*, 340–362.

Hunter, J. E., Hunter, R. F. (1984). The validity and utility of alternative predictors of job performance. Psychological Bulletin, 96, 72–98.

Huse, E. F. (1962). Assessments of higher-level personnel: IV. The validity of assessment techniques based on systematically varied information. PERSONNEL PSYCHOLOGY, 15, 195–205.

Janz, T. (1982). Initial comparisons of patterned behavior description interviews versus unstructured interviews. *Journal of Applied Psychology, 67*, 577–580.

Kahn, R. L., Cannell, C. F. (1957). *The dynamics of interviewing*. New York: Wiley.

Kesselman, G. A., Lopez, F. E. (1979). The impact of job analysis on employment test validation for minority and nonminority accounting personnel. PERSONNEL PSYCHOLOGY, 32, 91–108.

Kleiman, L. S., Faley, R. H. (1985). The implications of professional and legal guidelines for court decisions involving criterion-related validity: A review and analysis. PERSONNEL PSYCHOLOGY, 38, 803–833.

Landy, F. L. (1976). The validity of the interview in police officer selection. *Journal of Applied Psychology, 61*, 193–198.

Langmuir, C. R. (1974). *Personnel tests for industry — Oral directions test manual*. New York: Psychological Corporation.

Latham, G. P., Finnegan, B. J. (1987). *The practicality of the situational interview*. Unpublished manuscript.

Latham, G. P., Saari, L. M. (1984). Do people do what they say? Further studies on the situational interview. *Journal of Applied Psychology, 69*, 569–573.

Latham, G. P., Saari, L. M., Pursell, E. D., Campion, M. A. (1980). The situational interview. *Journal of Applied Psychology, 65*, 422–427.

Latham, G. P., Wexley, K. N. (1977). Behavioral observation scales for performance appraisal purposes. PERSONNEL PSYCHOLOGY, 30, 255–268.

Latham, G. P., Wexley, K. N. (1981). Increasing productivity through performance appraisal. Reading, MA: Addison-Wesley.

Latham, G. P., Wexley, K. N., Pursell, E. D. (1975). Training managers to minimize rating errors in the observation of behavior. *Journal of Applied Psychology, 60*, 550–555.

Lawlis, G. I., Lu, E. (1972). Judgment of counseling process: Reliability, agreement, and error. *Psychological Bulletin, 78*, 17–20.

Lawshe, C. F. (1943). Can you read a scale? In Tiffin, J. (Ed.), *Purdue vocational series*. West Lafayette, IN: University Book Store.

Locke, E. A. (1968). Toward a theory of task motivation and incentives. *Organizational Behavior and Human Performance, 3*, 157–189.

Maas, J. B. (1965). Patterned scaled expectation interview: Reliability studies on a new technique. *Journal of Applied Psychology, 49*, 431–433.

Mayfield, E. C. (1964). The selection interview — A re-evaluation of published research. PERSONNEL PSYCHOLOGY, 17, 239–260.

Mayfield, E. C., Brown, S. H., Hamstra, B. W. (1980). Selection interviewing in the life insurance industry: An update of research and practice. PERSONNEL PSYCHOLOGY, 33, 725–739.

McDaniel, M. A., Whetzel, D. L., Schmidt, F. L., Hunter, J. E., Maurer, S., Russell, J. (1987). *The validity of employment interviews: A review and meta-analysis*. Manuscript submitted for publication.

McMurry, R. N. (1947). Validating the patterned interview. *Personnel, 23*, 263–272.

Nunnally, J. C. (1978). *Psychometric theory* (2nd ed.). New York: McGraw-Hill.

Orpen, C. (1985). Patterned behavior description interviews versus unstructured interviews: A comparative validity study. *Journal of Applied Psychology, 70*, 774–776.

Pearlman, K. (1980). Job families: A review and discussion of their implications for personnel selection. *Psychological Bulletin, 87*, 1–28.

Pursell, E. D., Campion, M. A., Gaylord, S. R. (1980). Structured interviewing: Avoiding selection problems. *Personnel Journal, 59*, 907–912.

Pursell, E. D., Dossett, D. L., Latham, G. P. (1980). Obtaining valid predictors by minimizing rating errors in the criterion. PERSONNEL PSYCHOLOGY, *33*, 91–96.

Pursell, E. D., Gaylord, S. R. (1976). *Structured interviewing*. Tacoma, WA: Organizational Effectiveness, Weyerhaeuser Company.

Reilly, R. R., Chao, G. T. (1982). Validity and fairness of some alternative employee selection procedures. PERSONNEL PSYCHOLOGY, *35*, 1–62.

Richardson, Bellows, Henry, & Company, Inc. (1947). *SRA mechanical aptitudes*. Chicago: Science Research Associates.

Robinson, D. D. (1981). Content-oriented personnel selection in a small business setting. PERSONNEL PSYCHOLOGY, *34*, 77–87.

Sackett, P. R. (1987). Assessment centers and content validity: Some neglected issues. PERSONNEL PSYCHOLOGY, *40*, 13–25.

Sackett, P. R., Wilson, M. A. (1982). Factors affecting the consensus judgment process in managerial assessment centers. *Journal of Applied Psychology, 67*, 10–17.

Schmidt, F. L., Greenthal, A. L., Hunter, J. E., Berner, J. G., Seaton, F. W. (1977). Job sample vs. paper-and-pencil trades and technical tests: Adverse impact and examinee attitudes. PERSONNEL PSYCHOLOGY, *30*, 187–197.

Schmidt, F. L., Hunter, J. E. (1983). Individual differences in productivity: An empirical test of estimates derived from studies of selection procedures utility. *Journal of Applied Psychology, 68*, 407–414.

Schmidt, F. L., Hunter, J. E., McKenzie, R. S., Muldrow, T. W. (1979). The impact of valid selection procedures on work force productivity. *Journal of Applied Psychology, 64*, 609–626.

Schmidt, F. L., Hunter, J. E., Outerbridge, A. N., Trattner, M. H. (1986). The economic impact of job selection methods on size, productivity, and payroll costs of the federal work force: An empirically based demonstration. PERSONNEL PSYCHOLOGY, *39*, 1–29.

Schmidt, F. L., Hunter, J. E., Urry, V. W. (1976). Statistical power in criterion-related validity studies. *Journal of Applied Psychology, 61*, 473–485.

Schmitt, N. (1976). Social and situational determinants of interview decisions: Implications for the employment interview. PERSONNEL PSYCHOLOGY, *29*, 79–101.

Schoorman, F. D. (1988). The escalation bias in performance appraisal: An unintended consequence of supervisor participation in hiring decisions. *Journal of Applied Psychology, 73*.

Schwab, D. P., Heneman, H. G. (1969). Relationship between interview structure and interviewer reliability in an employment situation. *Journal of Applied Psychology, 53*, 214–217.

Scott, W. D. (1915). The scientific selection of salesmen. *Advertising and Selling, 25*, 5–6, 94–96.

Smith, P. C., Kendall, L. (1963). Retranslation of expectations: An approach to the construction of unambiguous anchors for rating scales. *Journal of Applied Psychology, 47*, 149–155.

Society of Industrial and Organizational Psychology, Inc. (1987). *Principles for the validation and use of personnel selection procedures* (3rd ed.). College Park, MD: Author.

Survey Research Center, University of Michigan. (1976). *Interviewer's manual* (rev. ed.). Ann Arbor, MI: Institute for Social Research.

Taylor, H. C., Russell, J. T. (1939). The relationship of validity coefficients to the practical effectiveness of tests in selection: Discussion and tables. *Journal of Applied Psychology, 23*, 565–578.

Thornton, G. C., Byham, W. C. (1982). *Assessment centers and managerial performance*. New York: Academic Press.

Tinsley, H. E. A., Weiss, D. J. (1975). Interrater reliability and agreement of subjective judgments. *Journal of Counseling Psychology, 22*, 358–376.

Tubiana, J. H., Ben-Shakhar, G. (1982). An objective group questionnaire as a substitute for a personal interview in the prediction of success in military training in Israel. PERSONNEL PSYCHOLOGY, *35*, 349–357.

Tucker, D. H., Rowe, P. M. (1977). Consulting the application form prior to the interview: An essential step in the selecting process. *Journal of Applied Psychology, 62*, 283–287.

Ulrich, L., Trumbo, D. (1965). The selection interview since 1949. *Psychological Bulletin, 63*, 100–116.

Wagner, R. (1949). The employment interview: A critical summary. PERSONNEL PSYCHOLOGY, *2*, 17–46.

Wainer, H. (1976). Estimating coefficients in linear models: It don't make no nevermind. *Psychological Bulletin, 83*, 213–217.

Wanous, J. P. (1980). *Organizational entry: Recruitment, selection, and socialization of newcomers*. Reading, MA: Addison-Wesley.

Warwick, D. P., Lininger, C. A. (1975). *The sample survey: Theory and practice*. New York: McGraw-Hill.

Webster, E. C. (1964). *Decision making in the employment interview*. Montreal: Eagle.

Weekley, J. A., Gier, J. A. (1987). Reliability and validity of the situational interview for a sales position. *Journal of Applied Psychology, 72*, 484–487.

Wiesner, W. H., Cronshaw, S. F. (1987). *The moderating impact of interview format and degree of structure on interview validity*. Manuscript submitted for publication.

Wright, O. R. (1969). Summary of research on the selection interview since 1964. PERSONNEL PSYCHOLOGY, 22, 391–413.

Wright, P. M., Lichtenfels, P. A., Pursell, E. D. (1987). *The structured interview: Additional studies and a meta–analysis*. Manuscript submitted for publication.

Yonge, K. A. (1956). The value of the interview: An orientation and a pilot study. *Journal of Applied Psychology, 40*, 25–31.

Zedeck, S., Tziner, A., Middlestadt, S. E. (1983). Interviewer validity and reliability: An individual analysis approach. PERSONNEL PSYCHOLOGY, 36, 355–370.

Michael A. Campion and Barbara K. Brown are in the Krannert School of Management, Purdue University. Elliott D. Pursell is employed by Human Resource Systems, New Bern, North Carolina. Special thanks to Chris J. Berger, James E. Campion, Michael M. Harris, Judith L. Komaki, James S. Russell, and two anonymous reviewers for their comments on this manuscript.

Innovative Approaches to Personnel Selection and Performance Appraisal
H. John Bernardin

Despite considerable research in the prediction of job effectiveness, the variance which is unaccounted for still exceeds that which is explained. Many researchers attribute this situation to a lack of reliability, relevance, or validity of the criterion. The research indicates that Murphy's Law is alive and well with regard to performance measurement (Bernardin, in press-b). Others concede that even with regard to the most simplistic predictive equation — that performance is a function of Individual Ability × Motivation — our understanding of the latter is superficial. Thus, although the predictive value of cognitive ability tests for virtually any job is now clear, an understanding of the ubiquitous motivational components of the equation is very elusive.

The purpose of this article is to suggest new approaches for the study and measurement on both the predictor and the criterion side of research in human resource management. The motivational components of worker characteristics are explored through the thesis that the compatibility between worker preferences for job characteristics and actual job characteristics is correlated with job effectiveness. Through the Job Characteristics Questionnaire (JCQ), an application of this notion to actual personnel selection is proposed and illustrated. For the

Source: From "Innovative Approaches to Personnel Selection and Performance Appraisal" by H. John Bernardin, *Journal of Management Systems,* Vol. 1, No. 1, pp. 25–36. Copyright 1989 by Maximillian Press. Reprinted by permission.

criterion, a revolutionary approach to the measurement of human performance, Performance Distribution Assessment (PDA; Kane, 1986), is described and evaluated in the context of the current state of performance measurement and appraisal.

The current research on the JCQ and PDA is very active and promising. There is, however, a great deal more to be done. Hopefully this article will stimulate the critical research that is needed before definitive conclusions can be drawn about the efficacy of these innovative approaches to personnel selection and the measurement of job performance. Let us begin on the predictor side of the equation.

JCQ: AN INTERACTIONIST PERSPECTIVE ON PERSONNEL SELECTION

Considerable research has established that workers' preferences or interests are related to job performance, employee absences, job satisfaction, and voluntary termination (e.g., Bernardin & Bownas, 1985; Mobley, 1982; Patsfall & Feimer, 1985; Steers & Mowday, 1981). However, little information is included in this literature which has implications for personnel selection. The evidence of inventories designed to assess motivation, interest, and personality, for example, shows low validity for such instruments when they are empirically validated with an applicant sample (Anastasi, 1985; Guion, 1965; Hough, 1987).

Numerous studies have used motivational instruments to examine the compatibility of employee needs or preferences with the characteristics of the job (e.g., Stone, 1986). These compatibility indices are often statistically related to outcome measures such as turnover, job satisfaction, and job performance (e.g., Abdel-Halim, 1980). However, the most frequently studied instruments related to job characteristics, such as the Job Diagnostic Survey (Hackman & Oldham, 1974), the Job Characteristics Inventory (Sims, Szilagyi, & Keller, 1976), and the Survey of Work Values (Wollack, Goodale, Wijting, & Smith, 1971), have little or no utility for actual personnel decisions because of the transparent nature of the scoring keys. In general, transparent, nonverifiable instruments assessing motivation or personality have limited utility for actual employment decisions (e.g., Bernardin, 1987; Wanous, 1980; Wesman, 1952).

A major problem in personnel selection with measuring compatibility is that applicant motivation to obtain a job may offset negative emotion regarding the job characteristics. One theoretical explanation for the utility of realistic job previews, for example, is that they allow individuals to self-select out of jobs that do not satisfy their needs or preferences (Breaugh & Billings, 1986). However, for situations in which applicants are highly motivated to obtain a job, the self-selection process may never occur. Job seekers, eager for gainful employment, often ignore discomforting characteristics of a job. Deliberate distortion of applicant responses is one of the most serious problems in the use of instruments purported to measure personality, motivation, or job preferences for employment decisions (Bernardin & Bownas, 1985). In order to obtain employment, applicants often complete instruments with their conception of the most desirable answers from the employer's perspective in mind. Once employed, incompatibilities between employee needs and preferences and actual job characteristics may affect job satisfaction and performance and, assuming more attractive options are available, perhaps foster voluntary termination (Mobley, 1977).

Forced-choice methodology was developed to control this type of response distortion. Such instruments designed to measure job performance have resulted in higher validities than other formats for real employment decisions (Bernardin & Beatty, 1984, p. 190) and have been effective in reducing distortion on personality instruments (Anastasi, 1985). However, there has been little application of the methodology outside of performance appraisal and clinically oriented tests of personality or motivation such as the Sixteen Personality Factors Questionnaire (16PF; Cattell, Eber, & Tatsuoka, 1970). In general, the nature of clinically oriented instruments limits their ability to predict critical criteria in specific job situations; criterion-related validities are generally unimpressive (Patsfall & Feimer, 1985).

Although there are several explanations for the relatively low validities in addition to response distortion (e.g., small sample sizes, criterion bias, and predictor unreliability), the underlying theory of trait-based personality instruments has also been questioned (e.g., Bernardin, 1987; Karren & Hannan, 1986). Virtually all standardized personality and motivational instruments assume that work motivation is a function of stable or static needs, motives, or values within the individual. This so-called *person-centered* approach to personnel selection has dominated the research, which has attempted to predict work motivation and job performance. An interactionist perspective assumes that work motivation is a function of the "interactions" of these needs, motives, and such with the characteristics of the job. Variables related to the tasks to be performed, the work environment in general, the work schedule, the characteristics of the co-workers, supervisors, clients and customers, and the compensation system have all been studied extensively and successfully correlated with job performance, job satisfaction, turnover, and absenteeism. In their review of the person-environment fit literature, Patsfall and Feimer (1985) concluded that "congruence between the needs of individuals and the characteristics of an organizational setting will determine the individual's behavior. The extant empirical evidence generally supports this view" (p. 76).

Although there has been abundant research on employee compatibility with the work environment and the congruence of employee needs with job characteristics (e.g., Abdel-Haim, 1980; Holland, 1976; Lofquist & Dawis, 1969; Patsfall & Feimer, 1985), except for the disappointing attempts to measure compatibility through employment interviews (Hunter & Hunter, 1984), there have been few applications of this approach to actual personnel selection. However, the limited attempts to predict job performance and turnover with an interactionist perspective have shown great promise (e.g., Bernardin, 1987; Cleff, 1973; Hannan, 1979; Karren & Hannan, 1986). Hannan (1979), for example, computed a measure of congruence between personality characteristics of police officers and subjective perceptions of the work environment. The congruence measure predicted subsequent performance ratings and outpredicted all cognitive selection tests. Karren and Hannan (1986) developed an "expected motivation" questionnaire for border patrol officers based on a similar congruence theory. Scores on the congruence measure predicted performance in a training program. Bernardin (1987) developed a forced-choice "Discomfort Scale" based on a job analysis that identified particularly negative characteristics of a job with very high turnover. Scores on the Discomfort Scale were significantly correlated with subsequent turnover and job satisfaction.

Based on the success of the Discomfort Scale and recent criticisms of available measures of job characteristics (e.g., Stone & Guetal, 1985), Bernardin and Johnson (1987) developed the JCQ, a 400-item instrument designed to measure job factors shown by previous research to be correlated with one or more effectiveness criteria (e.g., performance, turnover, absenteeism, and job satisfaction). With the JCQ, incumbents are asked to indicate the extent to which each item is characteristic of the position(s) to be filled. The item characteristic ratings are then used to group items into forced-choice tetrads comprised of two valid items (i.e., those reliably judged to be highly characteristic of the job) and two invalid items (not characteristic of the job); all items of the tetrad are equivalent on desirability.

Although research on the ability of the forced-choice method to reduce or eliminate deliberate response distortion has been equivocal (Anastasi, 1985), the tetradic format has proven superior compared to other formats (Berkshire & Highland, 1953). Bernardin (1987), for example, found no differences in response patterns between incumbents and applicants on the Discomfort Scale. In the same study, there was significantly greater response distortion on the 16PF for the applicant sample compared to incumbent participants. Thus, the tetradic, forced-choice format appeared to effectively hide the scoring key of the Discomfort Scale and control deliberate response bias for the applicant population. Concurrent validation strategies may thus be appropriate with similar instruments.

Reliability indices on the characteristic and desirability ratings have been acceptable across a variety of occupations and data collection methods. Research is currently being conducted on the incremental validity of scoring keys derived for specific positions to be filled within a job class versus a generalized key developed for a job class.

The JCQ is designed to yield an overall applicant profile compatibility score plus factor scores on task requirements, physical environment, customer characteristics, coworker characteristics, leader characteristics, compensation preferences, task variety, physical demands and potential danger, work schedule and job autonomy. The next section describes the basic methodology.

BASIC METHODOLOGY

Job Analysis to Derive Ratings of the Characteristics

The JCQ is administered to job incumbents who are very familiar with either a specific position to be filled and/or a target job under study. Respondents are asked to indicate the extent to which each JCQ item is characteristic of the job or position under study. For example, respondents are asked to indicate the extent to which the following items are characteristic of the job:

1. Working alone all day.
2. Having different projects which challenge the intellect.
3. Staying physically active all day.
4. Working at my own pace.
5. Being able to choose the order of my work tasks.
6. Working under the constant threat of danger.
7. Having to copy or post numerical data all day.
8. Having to make public speeches.
9. Working under extreme time pressure.
10. Having an opportunity to be creative at work.

The average time required to complete the JCQ is 15 minutes and can be reduced by removing specific variables and items that do not apply to the job (e.g., customer characteristics). There is also a provision for adding important characteristics that are not covered in the JCQ.

Items Grouped to Form Tetrads

Based on the ratings just mentioned and desirability ratings already available on the items (Bernardin & Johnson, 1987), items are then grouped into tetrads using the following criteria: (a) equal desirability scores, and (b) two items with high characteristic ratings and two items with low characteristic ratings. Once the characteristic ratings are entered, a simple computer program derives the tetrads. The tetrads are then assembled to form the tailored JCQ for the position under study, with two valid and two invalid items per tetrad.

Based on reliability studies, it is recommended that a minimum of 20 desirable and 20 undesirable tetrads be used. Thus, there are a minimum total of 80 compatible job characteristics with approximately eight valid items for each of the a priori factors. Scoring yields scores ranging from 0 to 8 on each factor and a total profile compatibility score based on unit weights for the 80 valid or characteristic items.

Directions to Respondents

Job applicants are asked to select the two job characteristics from each tetrad they would find most or least desirable in a work situation. For example, respondents may be asked to select two of the following items they consider most desirable in a job:

1. Being able to choose the order of my work tasks.
2. Having different and challenging projects.
3. Staying physically active on the job.
4. Clearly seeing the effects of my hard work.

For tetrads comprised of four undesirable characteristics, job applicants would also indicate which two of the four items they would consider least desirable in a job.

PRELIMINARY RESULTS AND CONCLUSION

The initial test of the JCQ methodology has been very successful in a study of fast food counter personnel. Using "intentions to quit" as the criterion, a measure which has proven to be a highly reliable predictor of subsequent turnover (Bernardin, 1987), the composite JCQ compatibility score correlated .58 with intentions to turn over. It is important to note that there were no racial or sex differences on the JCQ. A predictive validity study relating JCQ scores to actual turnover, productivity, and absenteeism is underway in the same setting.

Although the validity of cognitive ability tests for predicting job performance is now well recognized (Hunter & Hunter, 1984), our ability to predict and understand employee motivation on the job is far less clear despite the unanimous acceptance that job performance is a function of both an individual's ability and motivation. The use of personality and motivational instruments in personnel selection has been disappointing and controversial. The JCQ was introduced as a methodology to accommodate the interactionist perspective on work motivation. Preliminary results show the method has great promise. Obviously, considerable research needs to be done.

PERFORMANCE DISTRIBUTION ASSESSMENT: CHANGING THE WAY WE CONCEPTUALIZE AND MEASURE PERFORMANCE

No single topic in personnel/human resources has been the subject of more research and writing than performance appraisal. I can think of eight books published on the topic in the last 6 years, with others on the way. There are over 100 new empirical pieces on the subject in major journals since 1984 (Bernardin, in press-b). Yet despite this plethora of attention, it is easy to single out the most innovative and exciting stream of research which has the potential to substantially change the way performance is measured and appraisal is conducted. I am referring to the work by Kane (1986) on "Performance Distribution Assessment" (PDA). Kane developed a new theoretical model of performance measurement called the *distributional measurement model* and a computerized rating system based on the model called the *Performance Review and Information Standardizing Method* (PRISM; Kane, 1987).

There is little argument that performance appraisal is a critical component of the human resource system. Almost all human resource functions are in some way linked to performance measurement. Because of this great need, there have been numerous attempts to develop a methodology that could solve the myriad of problems identified in the literature (Bernardin & Beatty, 1984). No method has proven successful, and many have been utter disasters.

Problems with Current Appraisal Methods

There are five major problems with the existing performance appraisal methods which seriously undermine their usefulness. First, rating errors, such as halo and leniency, beset even the seemingly most sophisticated systems, such as forced-choice, management-by-objectives (MBO), and behaviorally anchored scales (BARS; Bernardin & Beatty, 1984). Second, none of the methods previously proposed allow for the legitimate comparability of performance scores across jobs. Particularly for administrative decisions, such as merit pay, scores should be produced which are universally comparable across jobs and work units. Third, none of the systems formally corrects ratings in order to hold ratees accountable for only that portion of performance which was feasible, given the situation. Rather, this critical consideration is left to the whim of the rater. Fourth, no rating methods attempt to measure the distribution of an individual's performance, that is, the consistency of performance across an appraisal period. And fifth, most of the most highly touted appraisal methods today require a great deal of paperwork for rating and data storage. This paper shuffling is often cited as a major cause of poor attitudes toward the appraisal process.

At least as it is proposed, Kane's (1986) PDA and (1987) PRISM are designed to overcome these five critical shortcomings. Through its scoring procedure, PDA should control or reduce unintentional errors in rating such as halo and intentional distortion. The frequency response format and the computerized documentation required for rating should not only inhibit error but provide a methodology for correcting it as well.

PDA also provides for the simultaneous assessment of performance on highly specific aspects of a job while producing scores on aspects of performance that are comparable across jobs and units. This latter feature of PDA, in combination with the specificity of the content, may be its most important feature because other methods designed to increase rating accuracy through content specificity cannot yield comparable scores across jobs.

A great deal of research now documents the importance of constraints and perceptions of constraints on performance in the appraisal process. For example, Bernardin and Villanova (1986) identified perceptions of external constraints on performance as the major correlate of discrepancies between self and supervisory ratings. A majority of rated employees cite the failure of raters to adequately take into account those factors that are beyond the performer's control and impede maximum performance. Among the factors are: failure to receive critical equipment or raw materials, inferior materials, and absences/turnover of key personnel. Bernardin (in press-a) illustrated the pervasiveness of the problem in several settings. The PDA method records the rater's assessment of the effects of these external factors and adjusts scores to reflect the extent to which the factors affected performance. No other appraisal system formally assesses an individual's actual performance outcomes in the context of the best record, which was feasible under the circumstances. Thus, the method should increase perceptions of fairness, because it holds employees accountable for only that performance which was feasible.

Although all other appraisal methods measure only an "average" or "typical" level of performance on each dimension, PDA yields other parameters as well. With methods such as BARS and BOS, variability around the average level is assumed to be in error, despite the truism that individuals differ on their consistency in performance. Some people are very consistent, and their performance outcomes are all very similar. Others perform around a wide band of performance. This consistency/inconsistency parameter is a measurable and reliable phenomenon. The PDA method measures average performance, consistency of performance, and what Kane refers to as the "negative range avoidance," which is an employee's success in avoiding particularly harmful, costly outcomes.

Although the usefulness of the two additional parameters has yet to be determined, the incorporation of consistency and "negative range avoidance" into a performance measurement system makes strong theoretical sense.

With the development of PRISM (Kane, 1987), the PDA method almost completely eliminates the paperwork which plagues most other appraisal methods. With the advent of computerized appraisal, the data should be more accessible for important administrative decisions, such as promotions and merit pay, and allow human resource specialists to derive aggregate measures of performance for purposes of assessing group, division, or company performance.

PRISM scores are derived from ratings on each job function that were feasible to achieve in a particular job situation. The extent to which a rater achieved what was feasible is expressed on a scale ranging from 0% to 100%. Unlike all other appraisal methods, because of the way it is derived, the percentage score has precisely the same meaning for all jobs and in all rating situations, that is, the percentage of best feasible performance achieved.

The PDA Rating Process

As is discussed next, the rating process for PDA and PRISM is complicated. The rater must make judgments of frequency on not only exhibited behavior, but also the feasibility of performing at specified levels of performance. Considerable time is also required in the development of the performance dimensions to be rated. But Kane's argument is that more time is exactly what is required in order to increase the effectiveness of performance appraisal systems. Given the plethora of research pointing to the ineffectiveness of the simple approaches, it appears that the time has come to try an approach more meticulously developed and administered. Here is a summary of the steps involved in the development and use of PDA.

1. Performance level descriptors are written by prospective raters and ratees. The "descriptors" describe performance representing low-, middle-, and high-outcome levels for each performance dimensions. For example, for the managerial dimension entitled "Organizing," the *low-level descriptor* is defined as "the system was completely illogical and incapable of producing the intended products or services" (Kane, 1988). Each descriptor reflects only one of six possible aspects of value for the outcome. The six aspects are quality, quantity, timeliness, cost effectiveness, need for supervision, and impact on coworkers (the descriptor just presented reflects the "quality" aspect). However, not all six aspects of value are necessarily relevant to each performance descriptor. For example, for the Organizing example, only the quality, quantity, and impact aspects of value may be relevant.

If the rating system is computerized, as is PRISM, the descriptors are entered into the computer program so they can be retrieved during the rating process. Although the development of the low-, middle-, and high-level descriptors for each relevant value on each dimension is obviously time consuming, the process is almost therapeutic in terms of its ability to get raters and ratees to focus on the important outcomes for a given job. Raters and ratees should be very familiar with the descriptors before the appraisal period begins. In addition to the development of the descriptors, utility scale values are also derived to reflect the differences between the values of the outcome levels on each dimension.

2. During the rating process, the rater responds to two sets of four questions for each dimension. The first set of questions concerns the feasibility of performing at each outcome level. Raters are asked to indicate the percentage of times it was feasible to perform at (or better than) a specified level.

The final set of four questions call for the rater to record the ratee's actual record of performance on that dimension.

Each of these questions is displayed in succession on the PRISM screen along with the minimum and maximum percentages possible given the responses to the "feasibility" questions.

Each value aspect for a given dimension requires responses to the eight questions. Kane (1987) estimated that it takes about 3 minutes for a rater to go through the eight questions for one aspect of one dimension. After the rater completes this process for each relevant dimension and aspect and enters the ratings, the computer program derives the scores.

3. The computerized scoring process yields an overall score on the best possible performance achieved on each dimension across the three parameters, plus separate scores on each of them (i.e., average outcome level, consistency, and negative range avoidance). The report form can also reflect performance on each specific aspect of value. The specificity of the scoring thus enables supervisors to identify those dimensions, aspects of value, and parameters on which employees were particularly strong or weak. The feedback is thus very useful for improving performance in the most important areas.

CONCLUSION

Although there are now several microcomputer-based appraisal systems available, PRISM is easily the most thoroughly developed and theoretically justified. The most critical problem with PRISM is the time that is necessary for each rater to complete a set of ratings. In order to control for constraints on performance that are beyond the control of the ratee, raters must not only rate actual performance on each function but the percentage of times various outcome levels are feasible. This does take considerable time, particularly given normal spans of control. However, given the plethora of studies documenting the poor reliability and validity of other appraisal methods, Kane's (1986) contention that supervisors need to pay more attention to performance seems warranted. The key, however, is to contravene a naive management principle that the essence of effective performance appraisal is to "keep it simple." Although the cognitive demands on the rater are quite simple, PRISM is not perceived as simple relative to those appraisal methods that are popular (Bernardin & Klatt, 1985). However, PRISM has the potential for revolutionizing the whole approach to performance measurement and, for the first time, clearly integrating the process of appraisal with other components of the human resource system, particularly compensation, succession planning, productivity measurement, and performance enhancement.

There is now considerable research being done on the PDA method. One of the first applications of the method has been successful. Deadrick (personal communication, June 13, 1987) reported that raters preferred the PDA method to a graphic format and considered it to be a fairer and more valid form of performance appraisal.

REFERENCES

Abdel-Halim, A. A. (1980). Effects of person-job compatibility on managerial reactions to role ambiguity. *Organizational Behavior and Human Performance, 26,* 193–211.

Anastasi, A. (1985). The use of personality assessment in industry: Methodological and interpretive problems. In J. Bernardin & D. Bownas (Eds.), *Personality assessment in organizations* (p. 120). New York: Praeger.

Berkshire, J. R., & Highland, R. W. (1953). Forced-choice performance rating: A methodological study. *Personnel Psychology 6,* 355–378.

Bernardin, H. J. (1985). *A multi-faceted approach to the improvement of customer service representative performance and the reduction of turnover* (Final Tech. Report) Boca Raton, FL: College of Business, Florida Atlantic University.

Bernardin, H. J. (1987). Development and validation of a forced-choice scale to measure job-related discomfort among customer service representatives. *Academy of Management Journal, 30,* 162–173.

Bernardin, H. J. (in press-a). Attribution bias in the workplace: Implication for the strategic planners. *Human Resource Planning Journal.*

Bernardin, H. J. (in press-b). *Performance appraisal: Assessing human behavior at work.* Boston: PWS-Kent.

Bernardin, H. J., & Beatty, R. W. (1984). *Performance appraisal: Assessing human behavior at work.* Boston: Kent-Wadsworth.

Bernardin, H. J., & Bownas, D. (Eds.). (1985). *Personality assessment in organizations.* New York: Praeger.

Bernardin, H. J., & Johnson, D. (1987). *The development of the Job Characteristics Questionnaire.* Unpublished manuscript. (Available from J. Bernardin, College of Business, Florida Atlantic University, Boca Raton, FL 33431)

Bernardin, H. J., & Klatt, L. (1985). Managerial appraisal systems: Has practice caught up with the 'state of the art'? *Personnel Administrator, 30,* 79–86.

Bernardin, H. J., & Villanova, P. (1986). Performance appraisal. In E. Locke (Ed.), *The generalizability of laboratory experiments: An inductive survey* (pp. 43–62). Lexington, MA: Lexington Books.

Breaugh, J. A., & Billings, R. S. (1986). The realistic job preview: Five key elements and their importance for research and practice. *Proceedings of the Academy of Management,* 240–244.

Cattell, R. B., Eber, H. W., & Tatsuoka, M. (1970). *Handbook for the Sixteen Personality Factor Questionnaire.* Champaign, IL: Institute for Personality and Ability Testing.

Cleff, S. J. (1973). Computer-assisted job matching. In W. C. Byham & D. Bodin (Eds.), *Alternatives to paper and pencil testing* (pp. 124–138). Pittsburgh: University of Pittsburgh.

Guion, R. M. (1965). *Personnel testing.* New York: McGraw-Hill.

Hackman, J. R., & Oldham, G. R. (1974). *The job diagnostic survey: An instrument for the diagnosis of jobs and the evaluation of job redesign projects.* New Haven, CT: Yale University Press.

Hannan, R. L. (1979). *Work performance as a function of the interaction of ability, work values, and the perceived work environment* (Doctoral dissertation). College Park, MD: University of Maryland Press.

Holland, J. L. (1976). Vocational preferences. In M. D. Dunnette (Ed.), *Handbook for industrial and organizational psychology* (pp. 521–570). Chicago: Rand-McNally.

Hough, L. M. (1987, August). *Overcoming objections to the uses of temperament variables in selection.* Paper presented at the 95th annual meeting of the American Psychological Association, New York.

Hunter, J. E., & Hunter, R. E. (1984). Validity and utility of alternative predictors of job performance. *Psychological Bulletin, 96,* 72–98.

Kane, J. (1986). Performance distribution assessment. In R. Berk (Ed.), *Performance assessment* (pp. 237–274). Baltimore: Johns Hopkins University Press.

Kane, J. (1987). Measure for measure in performance appraisal. *Computers in Personnel, 1,* 31–39.

Kane, J. (1988). *The PRISM demonstration package.* Amherst, MA: Performances Sciences International.

Karren, R., & Hannan, R. (1986). *The development and evaluation of an expected-motivation questionnaire for selection.* Unpublished manuscript, Department of Management, University of Massachusetts, Amherst, MA.

Lofquist, L. H., & Dawis, R. V. (1969) *Adjustment to work.* New York: Appleton-Century-Crofts.

Mobley, W. H. (1977). Intermediate linkages in the relationship between job satisfaction and employee turnover. *Journal of Applied Psychology, 62,* 237–240.

Mobley, W. H. (1982). *Employee turnover: Causes, consequences and control.* Reading, MA: Addison-Wesley.

Patsfall, M., & Feimer, N. (1985). The role of person-environment fit in job performance and satisfaction. In J. Bernardin & D. Bownas (Eds.), *Personality assessment in organizations* (pp. 53–81). New York: Praeger.

Sims, H. P., Szilagyi, S., & Keller, R. T. (1976). The measurement of job characteristics. *Academy of Management Journal, 19,* 195–212.

Steers, R. M., & Mowday, R. T. (1981). Employee turnover and postdecision accommodation processes. In L. L. Cummings & B. M. Staw (Eds.), *Research in organizational behavior* (pp. 225–280). Greenwich, CT: JAI.

Stone, E. F. (1986). Job scope-job satisfaction and job scope-job performance relationships. In E. A. Locke (Ed.), *Generalizing from laboratory to field settings* (pp. 189–206). Lexington, MA: Lexington Books.

Stone, E. F., & Guetal, H. G. (1985). An empirical derivation of the dimensions along which characteristics of jobs are perceived. *Academy of Management Journal, 28,* 376–396.

Wanous, J. P. (1980). *Organizational entry.* Reading, MA: Addison-Wesley.

Wesman, A. G. (1952). Faking personality test scores in a simulated employment situation. *Journal of Applied Psychology, 36,* 112–113.

Wollack, S. Z., Goodale, J. G., Wijting, J., & Smith, P. C. (1971). Development of the survey of work values. *Journal of Applied Psychology, 55,* 331–338.

H. John Bernardin is professor of management and director of research for the College of Business and Public Administration at Florida Atlantic University.

Why Do Assessment Centers Work? The Puzzle of Assessment Center Validity
Richard Klimoski / Mary Brickner

Assessment centers appear to be the modern enigma in human resource practices. The use of assessment center procedures for assessments of managerial potential is prevalent in corporations, large and small. Although assessment centers are generally considered valid predictors of managerial success, the nature of those predictions and the underlying dynamics of assessment center practices remain a puzzle. A number of questions surrounding assessment

Source: Richard Klimoski and Mary Brickner, "Why Do Assessment Centers Work? The Puzzle of Assessment Center Validity," *Personnel Psychology,* 1987, 40, pp. 243–260. Reprinted by permission of *Personnel Psychology.*

centers have been raised. In this paper we will try to piece the assessment center picture together by considering questions that surround assessment center practices.

DO ASSESSMENT CENTERS WORK?

A number of articles on assessment center validity have appeared in the literature. Meta-analyses of assessment center research results have been reported by Schmitt, Gooding, Noe, & Kirsch (1984), Hunter & Hunter (1984), and by Gaugler, Rosenthal, Thornton & Bentson (1985). Early summaries of research (Cohen, 1980; Klimoski & Strickland, 1977) reported moderate to high validity coefficients for assessment center predictions. More recently, Schmitt, Gooding, et al. (1984) compared validity studies for different types of performance predictors. Their reported mean predictive validity for assessment centers was .407. Meta-analyses by Hunter & Hunter (1984) and Gaugler and her colleagues reported validities in the range of 37–43.

Given the predictive validities consistently reported in reviews, we would have to conclude that indeed assessment centers do work. Assessment centers are useful tools for predicting the future success of potential managers.

FOR WHOM DO ASSESSMENT CENTERS WORK?

Available studies demonstrate the usefulness of assessment centers for predicting managerial success regardless of educational level (Huck, 1973), prior assessment center experience (Struth, Frank, & Amato, 1980), race (Huck & Bray, 1976; Moses, 1973), or gender (Moses, 1973; Moses & Boehm, 1975). These studies supported the usefulness of assessment centers in predicting managerial success fairly regardless of membership in subgroups.

WHERE DO ASSESSMENT CENTERS WORK?

Assessment centers have been used in a wide variety of organizational settings. This selection tool has been effectively utilized in manufacturing companies (Turnage & Muchinsky, 1982), government (Struth et al., 1980), military services (Borman, 1982, Tziner & Duran, 1982), utility companies (Schmitt, 1977), oil companies (Norton, 1977), educational institutions (Schmitt, Noe, Merritt, & Fitzgerald, 1984) and by the FBI (Neidig, Martin, & Yates, 1979).

FOR WHAT PURPOSES DO ASSESSMENT CENTERS WORK?

Assessment centers have proven to be useful for a variety of purposes beyond promotion and selection (Cascio & Silbey, 1979). They are useful in training and development (Lorenzo, 1984), for career planning (Gaugler, Rosenthal, Thornton, & Bentson, 1985), and in improving important managerial skills in assessors (Lorenzo, 1984). However in the few comparative studies they have been most predictive of advancement criteria (Klimoski & Strickland, 1981; Turnage & Muchinsky, 1984).[1]

WHY DO ASSESSMENT CENTERS WORK?

The studies reviewed above establish that the assessment center is a useful tool for predicting managerial success, across organizations and types of employees and for a number of purposes. Given the extensive literature, however, we believe it appropriate (even long overdue) to ask "Why?"

As straightforward as this question must seem, it appears to us that no firm answer is yet available. Quite the contrary, given the nature of assessment center research and the evidence generated in the last ten years, there appear to be several plausible explanations.

The traditional explanation Assessment centers have been designed to predict managerial success by providing raters with an opportunity to infer personal qualities and traits that have been determined, through careful job analysis, to be relevant to success (Byham, 1980). That is, assessment centers are standardized devices to allow assessments of traits, which are then used for predicting future success on the job. The traditional argument is that assessment centers work because they do a good job of measuring and integrating information regarding an individual's traits or qualities (Byham, 1980). But do they?

The evidence for the construct validity of the dimensions used in assessment centers is not encouraging. The bulk of the reported literature shows little support for the view that assessment center procedures do in fact produce scores that serve as valid representations of separate constructs or that those constructs are used in evaluation decisions in the manner proposed by assessment center designers.

Sackett and Hakel (1979) examined how individuals used assessment center information in forming overall ratings. They found that assessors used only a small number of dimensions although they had been instructed to use all of them in making their judgments. Three dimensions (leadership, organizing and planning, and decision making) accurately predicted overall ratings. Considered pessimistically, their results imply the existence of only general and diffuse measurements of behaviors. Alternatively, it may be that the dimensionality of effectiveness is not that complex. In either case, this raises real questions about both the need and the potential for centers to discriminate among a large number of dimensions.

Turnage and Muchinsky (1982) reported that assessment center trait ratings gave little help beyond what could be obtained from a global rating. The average correlation between dimension ratings and the overall rating was .91. They reported a lack of discriminant validity and high levels of convergent validity across traits. This was considered an

---

1. The above findings should not be used to conclude that assessment centers are performing better than alternatives in predicting these different criteria. The limited number of comparative studies which contrast alternative predictions suggest that they are not (cf. Borman, 1982; Hinrichs, 1978; Hunter & Hunter, 1984; Klimoski & Strickland, 1981).

indication that assessors were making global evaluations rather than differentiating among traits.

Sackett and Dreher (1982) studied the interrelationships among dimensions between and within assessment center exercises in three different organizations. In all three organizations they found within-exercise ratings correlated more highly with each other than did dimensional ratings across exercises. In two of the organizations there was no convergence among the various measures of a dimension (the average correlation was zero). Method variance predominated over the shared variance of measures of a single trait. In the third organization, all ratings were highly correlated with all other ratings. This indicates a lack of discriminant validity for the dimensions considered. They concluded that there was little evidence that assessment center ratings accurately reflect the complex traits that they purport to measure (p. 401).

Russell (1985, 1986) sought to further our understanding of the decision-making processes of assessors in assessment centers. His findings were consistent with previous research (Sackett & Hakel, 1979): assessors did not use specific dimensions in making their judgments. In his study, assessors' perceptions of center participants were strongly affected by an underlying factor (either interpersonal skills or problem-solving skills). In his later study, halo across the six dimensions assessed in two exercises was great. Russell suggests that "the best guesses of assessment center architects and job analysts should not be expected necessarily to exhibit rigorous evidence of construct validity" (Russell, 1985, p. 743). He too emphasizes that the bases for the predictive validity of assessment centers are not understood.

The available research consistently demonstrates a lack of evidence for the construct validity of assessment center dimension ratings. Moreover, it convinces us that assessment centers are *not* working as designed. If they have predictive validity, it is not because they are effectively measuring and using traits (Zedeck & Cascio, 1984). We must look elsewhere for the answer.

Some alternative explanations A variety of alternative explanations for why assessment centers appear to work can be gleaned from the literature. The following are presented as possibilities. In many cases they appear as suggestions made by various writers. Few have been carefully evaluated.

Actual criteria contamination explanation The apparent predictive validity of assessment centers could arise out of the unintended but real possibility that promotions in organizations (or other criterion decisions) are partially based on assessment center judgments. Thus, individuals who get favorable ratings are considered for promotion over those who do not. A future analysis of the relationship between center assessments and promotions would then appear to show a correspondence between assessment center ratings and success criteria.

In the early literature (e.g., Kraut & Scott, 1972), this dynamic was popularly referred to as the "crown prince (princess)" system of promotions. In true predictive studies (e.g., Bray & Grant, 1966), of course, this type of criterion contamination is not possible (unless the assessment center ratings are allowed to be "leaked out"). However, in many studies (e.g., Klimoski & Strickland, 1981) data are gathered from operational centers. That is, assessment center evaluations are obtained and used for purposes of administrative action (e.g., selecting individuals for promotions). Under these circumstances criterion contamination is quite possible.

As of 1974, Howard listed ten studies reporting validity data in which center ratings had been used for promotions. Not surprisingly, all of these showed significant relationships. She argued, however, that while such contamination could indeed artificially inflate the apparent validity of center predictions, it was not a major problem because center ratings would be used less frequently as a basis for advancement in later years. Kraut and Scott (1972) were similarly reassuring. They maintained that a favorable rating was not sufficient to be promoted, with the "possible exception of the top 5% who receive the very highest rating" (p. 128). If some companies use center ratings for promotions, however, it is only for the initial move. Beyond this, other dynamics operate to determine who gets ahead (Stumpf & London, 1981). Silzer (1985) reported that 73% of those providing on-the-job ratings had never seen assessment reports; 9% had seen them three to nine years before providing criterion information. Finally, Gaugler et al. (1985) found little support for the actual contamination hypotheses. In their meta-analysis, study design did not moderate assessment center validity. Specifically, reports from operational centers did not show higher validities than those where center ratings (as potential predictors) were thought not to be used. Nevertheless, in the face of so little research to test this notion specifically, it cannot be ruled out as a potential explanation for apparent center validity.

"Subtle" criterion contamination Klimoski and Strickland (1977) proposed the notion that assessment center validity might be affected by a form of criterion contamination that operates in an indirect or subtle fashion. Their reasoning was based on the fact that a great deal of evidence for the validity of assessment centers was based on predictions of promotions or promotion-linked criteria (e.g., salary growth). They proposed that, instead of looking for behavioral evidence of specific traits or personal qualities, assessment center staff in fact observe and evaluate candidates on the basis of their knowledge of those factors needed to get ahead in the company. Instead of systematically evaluating each person on the dimensions created for the center, they attempt to perform a policy-capturing function and to mimic what future decision makers might do in making a promotion decision. This may or may not be based on performance. Thus, judgments made by center staff would tend to correlate with judgments made by managers in the field.

Once again there is little definitive research on this potential explanation; most evidence is circumstantial. For example, if this dynamic were operating, assessment center validities would be higher for promotion criteria than for other success indicators (e.g., performance in grade). As mentioned, this does appear to be the case. Similarly, the explanation implies that assessment center staff characteristics would affect the magnitude of the validities obtained. That is, staff who come from or who have intimate knowledge of the corporate setting into which center participants will go after being assessed should be better able to predict (or anticipate) the promotion criteria and processes. They should produce judgments with higher validities than outsiders or consultants. Silzer (1985) did find higher validities for staff who had greater familiarity with norms in one versus another company. In fact, he agrees with Holt (1970) that such knowledge is an indispensable feature of a good clinical prediction paradigm. In contrast, Gaugler et al. (1985) reported in their meta-analysis that validities were higher when assessors were psychologists rather than managers. Presumably the former would have less familiarity with organizational decision making about promotions than the latter. Still other studies have reported equivocal results (e.g., Borman, Eaton, Bryan, & Rosse, 1983).

One other line of evidence relevant to the argument that subtle criterion contamination may be operating has been raised by Dunnette & Borman (1979). They observed that assessments of overall performance or potential in assessment centers tend to correlate more highly with organizational success criteria than do ratings of specific dimensions. Moreover, the average validity coefficients for dimension ratings are much lower than those obtained for overall ratings (e.g., Turnage & Muchinsky, 1984). They reason that overall assessment ratings are thus likely to be influenced by factors that are presumably linked to success in the company but not reflected in the dimensions (e.g., proper background, appearance, etc.). In our opinion, the subtle criterion contamination hypothesis of Klimoski and Strickland can not be ruled out as a significant contributor to assessment center validity.

Self-fulfilling prophecy explanation Another possible explanation for the apparent validity of assessment centers relates to a self-fulfilling prophecy dynamic operating for assessees. It could be argued that being selected to participate in an assessment center may reinforce the feelings of self-efficacy for competent managerial candidates. Bandura (1982) notes that judgments of self-efficacy affect how much effort a person will direct toward a goal and how long he or she will persist in striving to attain a goal. He suggests that if a person has a strong sense of self-efficacy, that person will exert more effort and be more persistent in meeting a challenge. Moreover, competent managerial candidates, after experiencing success on assessment center tasks, may also have increased feelings of self-efficacy. This state results in the candidate directing more effort toward the development of skills and abilities that are important to managerial success. In this way, the selection of competent people for participation in the assessment center becomes a self-fulfilling prophecy. Even if individuals are put through centers as a matter of course (as a result of seniority or a court ruling), receiving favorable feedback on performance in the center would reinforce an "effective-manager" self-image. This, in turn, would result in greater effort and persistence in developing the managerial skills and abilities important to managerial success. Such increased effort in the development of managerial skills should result (given the assessed capacity), in greater managerial capability. Finally, higher levels of managerial skill would increase the probability of selection or promotion to a managerial position. In a sense, the assessee can make the staff prediction come true.

Both Russell (1986) and Gaugler, et al. (1985) refer to these notions and the potential role of self-efficacy. Moreover, we know that expectations for high performance on the part of others can be communicated and do have an impact (Rosenthal & Jacobson, 1968). For example, in a field experiment in a training context, Eden found that staff members who believed in the high potential of their trainees (regardless of their actual capabilities) had classes with disproportionate numbers of high performers. More to the point, this high performance continued even when the original trainers had been transferred for administrative reasons (Eden & Ravid, 1982; Eden & Shani, 1982). Thus, instructor expectancies appeared to have been perceived, reinforced, and internalized as part of the trainees' self-images, with positive outcomes as a result (see also Crawford, Thomas, & Fink, 1980). While little data to test this notion in an assessment center context are available, we do know that center participation alone can change or reinforce self-perceptions (Schmitt, et al., 1986).

Performance consistency explanation
Judgments in assessment centers are supposed to be based on trait inferences made from observations of behavior elicited by the center exercises and tasks.

It is possible, however, that a different process might be operating. That is, staff may be evaluating the past and present performance of individuals and basing overall assessments on these, thus bypassing the judgment of traits entirely.

High performers in the centers are thus predicted to be high performers in future managerial roles.

This explanation is based on certain features of the typical assessment center. One is that a great deal of achievement-relevant background information in the form of autobiographical information is available to staff before they make assessment evaluations. This information is gathered at a number of points in the center process, most notably in the extensive, in-depth interviews that are usually conducted. The vast literature on the value of biodata for predicting job success (Campbell, Dunnette, Lawler & Weick, 1970; Childs & Klimoski, 1986; Owens, 1976) makes it clear that the validity of staff predictions could be enhanced by relying on such information. Past history of successes would thus be expected to relate to future success.

As straightforward as this explanation is, it is also true that there seems to be little evidence available to evaluate it. Studies have attempted to examine components of the assessment center for their contributions to the center's prediction of success (e.g., Hinrichs & Haanpera, 1976; Wollowick & McNamara, 1969), but the biodata component has rarely been explicitly considered. Borman (1982) found little evidence of the predictive validity of a structured interview in an assessment center created for evaluating Army recruiters. But it is not clear how much biodata was actually obtained in the interviews conducted for the study.

On the other hand, Hinrichs (1969) noted that data from existing personnel records were highly predictive of overall ratings obtained from a two-day assessment center program. He suggested that a careful evaluation of personnel records and employment history could provide much of the same information (or at least the predictive power) as a lengthy and expensive assessment program (p. 431). Turnage & Muchinsky (1984) did use assessment center data in which there was a biodata component, but the results (with the exception of age) were not that supportive of the past history explanation of center ratings.

Alternatively, the predictive validity of assessment centers may rest on a second feature, the fact that center exercises serve as job samples. To the extent that the exercises (as job samples) reflect behavior and performance that is relevant and representative of future managerial job requirements, evaluations should be related to and predict managerial success. Such evaluations, however, would serve as indications of current levels of performance (a sample) rather than assessments of managerial potential (a sign; Wernimont & Campbell, 1968). To phrase it differently, present performance (in center exercises) predicts future performance (as managers).

The designs of most assessment centers are based on the results of job analyses (Byham, 1980). Most specialists would agree that this is a necessary step in the development of any center. Nevertheless, there is some controversy as to just how job analysis information is to be used. Traditionally, it has provided the bases for the identification of managerial job requirements — the traits or qualities to be assessed. In fact, it serves to produce what is usually referred to as the construct validity for assessment centers (Sackett & Dreher, 1984). But job analysis can also be the source of information for creating the actual simulations used. That is, it can be the basis for establishing a center's content validity. For example, Neidig and Neidig (1984) contend that an accurate sampling of relevant work situations in a center is critical for establishing the job relatedness of the assessment center. In this way job analysis can ensure that good performance on the exercises will relate to good on-the-job performance because the candidate is presumed to have the requisite knowledge, abilities, and traits if he/she does well. But it should be stressed that the measurement of performance levels on samples (as predictors) need not even involve the notion of underlying constructs (see, e.g., Campion, 1972).

We will not attempt to restate, much less resolve, the arguments about whether assessment centers should have construct validity or content validity (or both). The interested reader is referred to Brush and Schoenfeldt (1977), Byham (1980), Dreher and Sackett (1981), Neidig and Neidig (1984), Norton (1977, 1981), and Sackett and Dreher (1982, 1984). The point is that most centers *do* involve the use of apparently content (face?) valid exercises or simulations (i.e., job samples). Assessment centers may work (be valid) because levels of performance on these exercises, not inference with regard to particular traits, form the bases for predicting managerial job success.

A managerial intelligence explanation
A final hypothesis with regard to the reasons for assessment center validity bears some relationship to the subtle criterion contamination notion. It is sufficiently distinct, however, to merit special mention. To put it simply, assessment centers may predict managerial success

because the ratings obtained reflect the level of intellectual functioning of candidates.

There seems to be no doubt that intelligence is important for managerial effectiveness. Most analyses of managerial job requirements refer to the importance of verbal skills (manifested in oral and written communications), analytic or reasoning skills, the regular use of short- and long-term reasoning, including well-developed plans or routines (for example, scripts) for the combining of information. Effective managerial functioning is also thought to involve what has been called the application of "tacit knowledge" (Wagner & Sternberg, 1985). Research suggests that tacit knowledge appears to be acquired and developed by intellectually more capable individuals. In short, intelligence can be defined by that old phrase, "What one needs when you don't know what to do." Given the nature of managerial work, intelligence must be viewed as a major determinant of managerial success (Lord, DeVader, & Alliger, 1986; Yukl, 1981).

Actually, the empirical relationship between intelligence and managerial performance has long been established (Ghiselli, 1966, 1971, 1973; McCormick & Tiffin, 1974; Miner, 1957). Ghiselli (1966) reported intelligence tests as the best predictors of future performance for foremen, managers, administrators, and executives. Moderate correlations (.25–.30) between intelligence and performance are frequently obtained. In his (1971) study of managerial talent he was also able to report moderate correlations (.28–.45) between intelligence and performance for managers and personnel officers. Lower correlations (.01–.07), however, were found in studies of line managers in packing plants. Similarly, in 1973, Ghiselli determined that intelligence tests were useful for predicting trainability, job proficiency, and performance among foremen, administrators, and executives (correlation ranging from .28–.36). These data provide evidence for the consistent relationship observed between intelligence and effective managerial performance. Miner also (1957) reviewed a number of studies of intelligence and success in military contexts.

The importance of intelligence has also been recognized explicitly by the assessment center literature. To begin with, it is frequently part of the measurement plan of assessment centers. Thornton and Byham (1982) refer to a number of centers that incorporated intelligence measures. Bray and Grant (1966) used three intelligence tests in their famous Management Progress Study.

Scores from these tests all correlated significantly with staff predictions of success for managers. Moses (1973) found that SCAT scores were significantly correlated with intelligence in a longitudinal study of assessment center evaluations and managerial performance. Huck (1973) reported moderate correlations (.40) between SCAT test scores and overall assessment ratings. And Carleton (1970) found moderate correlations between intelligence test scores and a composite criterion of behavioral ratings in assessment centers. This was also true of a recent study by Wolfson (1985) at IBM. Schmitt (1977) reported high correlations between intelligence test scores (SCAT) and overall dimension ratings.

Finally, the observed predictive validity of assessment centers may be attributable, in part, to assessment centers as measures of intelligence. For example,

Tziner and Dolan (1982) compared assessment center results with some traditional forms of evaluation (i.e., tests of verbal intelligence, supervisory evaluation, evaluations for selection interviews). They found that verbal intelligence scores were highly predictive of future performance. In fact, these scores were better than individual exercises and overall assessment ratings for predicting future performance. Intelligence scores accounted for the largest portion of variance. Moreover, Klimoski and Strickland (1981) found that paper and pencil measures of intelligence predicted future managerial performance ratings better than did assessment centers.

All this is not to argue that measures of intelligence are superior to assessment centers as predictors or that assessment ratings are to be characterized as perfect surrogates for intelligence tests. In fact, the evidence is too equivocal to do this. The interested reader can contrast the findings of Schmitt, Gooding, et al. (1984), Turnage and Muchinsky (1984), Russell (1985), and Gaugler et al. (1985).

What does seem clear, however, is that both center behavior and assessor judgments are influenced in part by the level of general intellectual functioning of assessees. Further, the on-the-job performance of these same individuals is likely to be similarly affected. If assessment centers predict job success, their apparent validity may be due, in part, to this underlying nomological network. At this point, however, we just don't know the extent of this happening.

In this section we have discussed several possible explanations for the predictive validity that is so characteristic of assessment center predictions. These explanations (or hypotheses) include criterion contamination, policy capturing, self-fulfilling prophecies for assessees, construct and context capturing capacity, and assessment centers as measures of intelligence. These explanations are not mutually exclusive and are probably not equally complete or plausible. However, they do provide implications for both practice and future research.

IMPLICATIONS FOR PRACTICE

The various explanations for the mechanisms by which assessment centers appear to obtain their validity would seem to make a difference for practices in this area. That is to say, the beliefs of and assumptions made by managers would guide choices among different assessment center formats and the likelihood of their use.

Managers frequently have a real need to assess or inventory the personal traits or qualities of individuals. For example, they may wish to provide accurate and specific developmental feedback to employees. Thus, they might well turn to assessment centers as the technique of choice. The available research evidence suggests it would be a mistake to do this. They might be better advised to consider alternative devices (e.g., standardized paper-and-pencil instruments, clinical inferences by trained professionals).

If, however, managers believe that the assessment center has the potential to be construct valid, certain steps are warranted. They might start by limiting the number of dimensions or qualities to be assessed. The latter could be selected to reflect higher order constructs or broader attributes than is usually the case (e.g., interpersonal skill vs. behavior flexibility), thus acknowledging both the ecological relationship among human traits and the limits of human (assessor) capacities to discriminate. For example, Barr and Hitt (1986) reported that experienced managers used substantially fewer factors yet produced decisions with more explanatory power than did naive subjects.

Furthermore, staff might be given longer periods of training than seem to be the case with centers set up more recently. Similarly, individuals might be given extended "tours of duty" as staff assessors. In this regard, it is interesting to note that in the classical (or AT&T) model, assessor assignments could last as long as a year. In such cases, the expertise developed and the resultant capacities to discriminate among traits would seem to be much greater than would occur among individuals serving as staff at a center set up for a single group of candidates. In any event, during training and throughout the life of the center, staff judgments should be calibrated against other construct valid indicators.

Finally, several suggestions (even programs) can be found in the literature for how one might improve the validity of trait judgments, depending on whether the problem is believed to derive from human information-processing errors occurring during the encoding of behavioral information (McElroy & Downey, 1982; Nathan & Alexander, 1985) or when it is retrieved at the time assessment ratings are made (Alba & Hasher, 1983; Johnson & Raye, 1981).

In contrast, the manager may not be that concerned about constructs but may still be interested in valid prediction; our review implies several alternatives. If an assessment center format is to be retained (and for procedural justice reasons we can see why this might be the case), a content-based model might be followed. Assessment center exercises would be designed as work-sample tests. As is frequently the case anyway, the major tasks to be performed in the managerial role would be simulated in the center. In contrast with present practices, however, the way candidate performance is assessed and scored would be different. Instead of obtaining staff ratings on behavioral dimensions, points would be allocated for appropriate actions taken by candidates. Staff would no longer be required to provide inferences about a candidate on some underlying construct but would only have to record whether or not something actually occurred (see Campion, 1972, and Schmitt & Ostroff, 1986, for an example of how such work samples might be scored).

The dynamics of some of the other "explanations" could actually be utilized to meet the needs of the organization — or attempts might be made to mitigate them. For example, high levels of (practical) intelligence might be recognized as relevant and appropriate in managerial candidates. Standardized measures could then be used as the preferred assessment tool (Sternberg, 1979). Similarly, high performers in the center might be encouraged to take pride in this accomplishment and to do things to strengthen this self-image. On the other hand, if subtle criterion contamination is felt to be a problem, it may be wise to use individuals as assessors who have limited knowledge of the organization. In fact, candidates might be sent to "generic" centers conducted by specialized consulting firms or sponsored by industry groups.

IMPLICATIONS FOR RESEARCH

While the above advice might be given to practitioners, it must frequently be based on inferences from the available research literature. The fact is, most evidence for the alternative dynamics of center validity is circumstantial. Thus, almost any of the suggestions provided should be considered tentative and the starting point for research.

In terms of priorities, however, given the real need of organizations to assess potential (apart from competencies), it would seem most important to establish if, or under what conditions, assessment centers can be made to produce valid measures of constructs. Given what we now know about human judgment and social cognition, there is some reason to be optimistic about finding a solution. Recent theories in these areas should be applied to the assessment center process (see Zedeck, 1986, for an excellent treatment of this).

Specifically, numerous and potentially relevant variables could be experimentally manipulated to determine their impact on discriminant and convergent validities of staff ratings. For example, Silverman, Dalessio, Woods, and Johnson (1986) predicted on the basis of current models of cognitive processing that there would be differences in the dimensionality and construct validity of assessments made by staff who were instructed to form dimension ratings right after each center exercise (a common practice) and by those who would have to postpone making such judgments until all the exercises had been completed. This was indeed found to be true. Unfortunately, the authors did not go on to see to what extent criterion-related validities were similarly affected. Turnage and Muchinsky (1982) also stressed the potential impact of limiting the number of dimensions to be assessed on construct validity.

Similarly, Zajonc's (1960) concept of cognitive tuning implies that individuals have a tendency to simplify social information and to reduce or minimize attention to discrepant information. This is especially true when we expect to have to pass on impressions to other people. If this is occurring in assessment centers, perhaps centers should be redesigned so that certain staff would provide the behavioral information but others would actually make the dimension rating. To take this one step further, one might speculate on the consequences for better construct validity if separate staff were used to make the overall assessment ratings or predictions of likely success with trait ratings as input from others.

Research on the impact of staff specialization (with regard to dimensions) or exercise specialization (e.g., where exercises are designed to produce behavior relevant to a single dimension) might reveal advantages of these approaches (see Cohen & Sands, 1978, for a parallel example). Finally, alternative methods of reaching overall assessment ratings might be examined. Instead of having staff follow a majority or consensus-decision rule, dialectical or devil's advocacy models could be incorporated. There is some evidence that the latter would produce better quality (more construct valid) evaluations (Schweiger, Sandberg, & Ragan, 1986; Zedeck, 1986). Other suggestions for research on the potential impact on group processes on overall assessment ratings can be found in the work of Klimoski, Friedman, and Weldon (1980).

But studies may reveal that it is just

not possible to establish assessment centers as valid measures of constructs (at least in the number and variety of interest to managers). If this were to be the case, there would still appear to be any number of programs of research that could be built around some of the alternative explanations for the assessment center's apparent predictive validity as presented in this paper. The point is, to establish the correctness of one or more of these would lead to sound recommendations for practice. This in turn, would increase our confidence that we actually know what we are doing in the use of whatever selection/promotion devices we end up with. It should also reduce the nagging feeling (as reported by one reviewer of this paper) that when assessment centers actually work, one has just been through some sort of a "voodoo rite."

CONCLUSION

For all we do know about assessment centers, we don't know enough. We know that these procedures are useful for predicting managerial success. Nevertheless, the predictive validity of assessment centers remains a puzzle. We agree with Russell (1985) when he states, "although assessors are apparently not doing what assessment center architects thought they were doing, the reasons behind assessment center predictive validity remain unknown" (p. 743).

In this paper we have attempted to define some of the pieces used in putting the assessment center picture together. By identifying some of the possible explanations for the predictive validity of assessment centers, we believe we provide a framework for a better understanding of the assessment center method.

REFERENCES

Alba, J. W., Hasher, L. (1983). Is memory schematic? *Psychological Bulletin, 92,* 203–231.

Bandura, A. (1982). Self-efficacy mechanism in human agency. *American Psychologist, 37,* 122–147.

Barr, S. H., Hitt, M. A. (1986). A comparison of selection decision models in manager versus student samples. PERSONNEL PSYCHOLOGY *39,* 599–618.

Borman, W. C. (1982). Validity of behavioral assessment for predicting military recruiter performance. *Journal of Applied Psychology, 67,* 3–9.

Borman, W. C., Eaton, N. K., Bryan, J. D., Rosse, R. L. (1983). Validity of Army recruiter behavioral assessment: Does the assessor make a difference? *Journal of Applied Psychology, 68,* 415–419.

Bray, D. W., Grant, D. L. (1966). The assessment center in the measurement of potential for business management. *Psychological Monographs, 80* (17 whole No. 625).

Brush, D. H., Schoenfeldt, L. F. (1980, May–June). Identifying managerial potential: An alternative to assessment centers. *Personnel,* pp. 68–76.

Byham, W. C. (1980, February). Starting an assessment center the correct way. *Personnel Administrator,* pp. 27–32.

Campion, J. E. (1972). Work sampling for personnel selection. *Journal of Applied Psychology, 56,* 40–44.

Campbell, J. P., Dunnette, M. D., Lawler, E. E. III, Weick, K. B., Jr. (1970). *Managerial behavior, performance, and effectiveness.* New York: McGraw-Hill.

Carlton, F. O. (1970). *Relationships between follow-up evaluations and information developed in a management assessment center.* Paper presented at the annual meeting of the American Psychological Association, Miami Beach, FL.

Cascio, W. F., Silbey, V. (1979). Utility of the assessment center as a selection device. *Journal of Applied Psychology, 64,* 107–118.

Childs, A., Klimoski, R. J. (1986). Successfully predicting career success: An application of biographical inventory. *Journal of Applied Psychology, 71*, 3–8.

Cohen, S. L. (1980, February). The bottom line on assessment center technology. *Personnel Administrator*, pp. 50–56.

Cohen, S. L., Sands, L. (1978). The effects of order of exercise presentation on assessment center performance: one standardization concern. PERSONNEL PSYCHOLOGY *31*, 35–46.

Crawford, K. S., Thomas, B. D., Fink, J. J. (1980). Pygmalion at sea: Improving the work effectiveness of low performers. *Journal of Applied Behavioral Science, 16*, 482–505.

Dunnette, M. D., Borman, W. C. (1979). Personnel selection and clarification systems. *Annual Review of Psychology, 30*, 477–525.

Dreher, G. F., Sackett, P. R. (1981). Some problems with applying content validity evidence to assessment center procedures. *Academy of Management Review, 6*, 551–560.

Eden, D., Ravid, G. (1982). Pygmalion versus self-expectancy: Effects of instructor and self-expectancy on trainee performance. *Organizational Behavior and Human Performance, 30*, 352–364.

Eden, D., Shani, A. (1982). Pygmalion goes to boot camp: Expectancy, leadership and trainee performance. *Journal of Applied Psychology, 67*, 194–199.

Gaugler, B. B., Rosenthal, D. B., Thornton, G. C. III, Bentson, C. (1985). *Meta-analyses of assessment center validity*. Paper presented at the annual meeting of the American Psychological Association, Los Angeles.

Ghiselli, E. E. (1966). *The validity of occupational aptitude tests*. New York: Wiley & Sons.

Ghiselli, E. E. (1971). *Explorations in managerial talent*. New York: Springer Publishing Co.

Ghiselli, E. E. (1973). The validity of aptitude tests in personnel selection. PERSONNEL PSYCHOLOGY *26*, 461–477.

Hinrichs, J. R. (1969). Comparison of "real life" assessments of management potential with situational exercises, paper-and-pencil ability tests, and personality inventories. *Journal of Applied Psychology, 53*, 425–432.

Hinrichs, J. R. (1978). An eight-year follow-up of a management assessment center. *Journal of Applied Psychology, 63*, 596–601.

Hinrichs, J. R., Haanpera, S. (1976). Reliability of measurement in situational exercises: An assessment of the assessment center method. PERSONNEL PSYCHOLOGY *29*, 31–40.

Holt, R. R. (1970). Yet another look at clinical and statistical prediction: Or is clinical psychology worthwhile. *American Psychologist, 25*, 337–349.

Howard, A. (1974). An assessment of assessment centers. *Academy of Management Journal, 17*, 115–134.

Huck, J. R. (1973). Assessment centers: A review of the external and internal validities. PERSONNEL PSYCHOLOGY *26*, 191–212.

Huck, J. R., Bray, D. W. (1976). Management assessment center evaluations and subsequent job performance of white and black females. PERSONNEL PSYCHOLOGY *29*, 13–30.

Hunter, J. E., Hunter, R. F. (1984). Validity and utility of alternative predictors of job performance. *Psychological Bulletin, 96*, 72–98.

Johnson, M. K., Raye, C. L. (1981). Reality monitoring. *Psychology Review, 88*, 67–85.

Klimoski, R. J., Friedman, B. A., Weldon, E. (1980). Leader influence in the assessment of performance. PERSONNEL PSYCHOLOGY *33*, 389–401.

Klimoski, R. J. & Strickland, W. J. (1977). Assessment centers — valid or merely prescient. PERSONNEL PSYCHOLOGY *30*, 353–361.

Klimoski, R. J., Strickland, W. J. (1981). *A comparative view of assessment centers: A case analysis*. Unpublished manuscript.

Kraut, A. I., Scott, G. J. (1972). Validity of an operational management assessment program. *Journal of Applied Psychology, 56*, 124–129.

Lord, R. G., DeVader, C. L., Alliger, G. M. (1986). A meta-analysis of the relation between personality traits and leadership perceptions: An application of validity generalization procedures. *Journal of Applied Psychology, 71*, 402–410.

Lorenzo, R. V. (1984). Effects of assessorship on managers' proficiency in acquiring, evaluating, and communicating information about people. PERSONNEL PSYCHOLOGY *37*, 617–634.

McCormick, E. J., Tiffin, J. (1974). *Industrial psychology*. Englewood Cliffs: Prentice Hall, Inc.

McElroy, J. C., Downey, H. K. (1982). Observation in organization research: Panacea to the performance-attribution effect? *Academy of Management Journal, 25*, 822–835.

Miner, J. B. (1957). *Intelligence in the United States*. New York: Springer Publishing Co.

Moses, J. L. (1973). The development of an assessment center for the early identification of supervisory potential. PERSONNEL PSYCHOLOGY *26*, 569–580.

Moses, J. L., Boehm, V. R. (1975). Relationship of assessment center performance to management progress of women. *Journal of Applied Psychology, 60,* 527–529.

Nathan, B. R., Alexander, R. A. (1985). The role of inferential accuracy in performance rating. *Academy of Management Review, 10,* 109–115.

Neidig, R. D., Martin, J. C., Yates, R. E. (1979). The contribution of exercise skill ratings to final assessment center evaluations. *Journal of Assessment Center Technology, 2,* 21–23.

Neidig, R. D., Neidig, P. J. (1984). Multiple assessment center exercises and job relatedness. *Journal of Applied Psychology, 69,* 182–186.

Norton, S. D. (1977). The empirical and content validity of assessment centers vs. traditional methods for predicting managerial success. *Academy of Management Review, 2,* 442–452.

Norton, S. D. (1981). The assessment center process and content validity: A reply to Dreher and Sackett. *Academy of Management Review, 6,* 561–566.

Owens, W. A. (1976). Background data. In Dunnette, M. D. (Ed.) *Handbook of industrial and organizational psychology* (pp. 609–644). Chicago: Rand McNally.

Rosenthal, R., Jacobson, L. (1986). *Pygmalion in the classroom.* New York: Holt.

Russell, C. J. (1985). Individual decision processes in an assessment center. *Journal of Applied Psychology, 70,* 737–746.

Russell, C. J. (1986). *An examination of person characteristic vs. role congruency explanations for post exercise assessment center ratings.* Unpublished manuscript.

Sackett, P. R., Dreher, G. F. (1982). Constructs and assessment center dimensions: Some troubling empirical findings. *Journal of Applied Psychology, 67,* 401–410.

Sackett, P. R., Dreher, G. F. (1984). Situation specificity of behavior and assessment center validation strategies: A rejoinder to Neidig and Neidig. *Journal of Applied Psychology, 69,* 187–190.

Sackett, P. R., Hakel, M. D. (1979). Temporal stability and individual differences in using assessment information to form overall ratings. *Organizational Behavior and Human Performance, 23,* 120–137.

Schmitt, N. (1977). Interrater agreement in dimensionality and combination of assessment center judgments. *Journal of Applied Psychology, 63,* 171–176.

Schmitt, N., Ford, J. K., Stultz, D. M. (1986). Changes in self-perceived ability as a function of performance in an assessment center. *Journal of Occupational Psychology, 59,* 327–335.

Schmitt, N., Gooding, R. Z., Noe, R. A., Kirsch, M. (1984). Meta-analysis of validity studies published between 1964 and 1982 and the investigation of study characteristics. PERSONNEL PSYCHOLOGY *37,* 407–422.

Schmitt, N., Noe, R. A., Meritt, R., Fitzgerald, M. P. (1984). Validity of assessment center ratings for the prediction of performance ratings and school climate of school administrators. *Journal of Applied Psychology, 69,* 207–213.

Schmitt, N., Ostroff, S. (1986). Operationalizing the "behavioral consistency" approach: Selection test development based on a content-oriented strategy. PERSONNEL PSYCHOLOGY, *39,* 91–108.

Schweiger, D., Sandberg, W. R., Ragan, J. W. (1986). Group approaches for improving strategic decision making: A comparative analysis of dialectical inquiry, devil's advocacy, and consensus. *Academy of Management Journal, 29,* 51–71.

Silverman, W. H., Dalessio, A., Woods, S. B., Johnson, R. L. (1986). Influence of assessment center methods on assessor ratings. PERSONNEL PSYCHOLOGY *39,* 565–579.

Silzer, R. E. (1985). Assessment center validity across two organizations. In symposium, *Assessment center validity: Recent data and current status.* Presented at annual meeting of the American Psychological Association, Los Angeles, CA.

Sternberg, R. J. (1979). The nature of mental abilities. *American Psychologist, 34,* 214–230.

Struth, M. R., Frank, F. D., Amato, A. (1980). Effects of assessor training on subsequent performance as an assessee. *Journal of Assessment Center Technology, 3,* 17–22.

Stumpf, S. A., London, M. (1981). Management promotions: Individual and organizational factors influencing the decision process. *Academy of Management Review, 6,* 539–549.

Thornton, G. C. III, Byham, W. C. (1982). *Assessment centers and managerial performance.* New York: Academic Press.

Turnage, J. J., Muchinsky, P. M. (1982). Transitutional variability in human performance with assessment centers. *Organizational Behavior and Human Performance, 30,* 174–200.

Turnage, J. J., Muchinsky, P. M. (1984). A comparison of the predictive validity of assessment center evaluations versus traditional measures in forecasting supervisory job performance: Interpretive implications of criterion distortion for the assessment center. *Journal of Applied Psychology, 69,* 595–602.

Tziner, A., Dolan, S. (1982). Validity of an assessment center for identifying future female officers in the military. *Journal of Applied Psychology, 67,* 728–736.

Wagner, R. K., Sternberg, R. J. (1985). Practical intelligence in real world pursuits: The role of tacit knowledge. *Journal of Personality and Social Psychology, 49,* 436–458.

Wernimont, P. R., Campbell, J. P. (1968). Signs, samples and criteria. *Journal of Applied Psychology, 52,* 372–376.

Wolfson, A. (1985). Assessment centers ten years later. In symposium, *Assessment center validity: Recent data and current status.* Presented at the annual meeting of the American Psychological Association, Los Angeles, CA.

Wollowick, H. B., McNamara, W. J. (1969). Relation of components of an assessment center to management success. *Journal of Applied Psychology, 53,* 348–352.

Yukl, G. A. (1981). *Leadership in organizations.* Englewood Cliffs: Prentice Hall, Inc.

Zajonc, R. B. (1960). The process of cognitive timing in communications. *Journal of Abnormal and Social Psychology, 61,* 159–167.

Zedeck, S. (1986). A process analysis of the assessment center method. In Staw B., Cummings L. L. (Eds.), *Research in organizational behavior, 8,* 259–296.

Zedeck, S., Cascio, W. F. (1984). Psychological issues in personnel decisions. *Annual Review of Psychology, 35,* 461–518.

Richard Klimoski is affiliated with Ohio State University. Mary Brickner is affiliated with the University of Akron.

The authors would like to acknowledge the helpful comments of Walter Borman, Neal Schmitt, and an anonymous reviewer on an earlier draft of this paper.

Employment Testing: The U.S. Job Service Is Spearheading a Revolution
Considering Validity Generalization in Employment Decisions
Robert M. Madigan / K. Dow Scott / Diana L. Deadrick / Jil A. Stoddard

For most of the past 20 years, the use of psychological tests in selection and promotion has diminished steadily. Faced with the difficult and often expensive task of developing evidence of test validity, employers frequently have opted to discontinue or forego testing. This trend is now being reversed. Surprisingly, impetus for this resurgence in testing is partially attributable to a federal agency, the U.S. Employment Service (USES). The validity generalization (VG) testing program currently being implemented by USES through local Job Service offices in many areas of the country sharply contradicts prevailing beliefs regarding the use of employment tests. The central tenets of the program are that standardized ability tests are fair and valid predictors of performance for all jobs, and that such tests provide employers (and the nation) with a powerful tool

Source: From "Employment Testing: The U.S. Job Service is Spearheading a Revolution: Considering Validity Generalization in Employment Decisions" by Robert M. Madigan, K. Dow Scott, Diana L. Deadrick and Jil A. Stoddard, *Personnel Administrator,* September 1986. Reprinted by permission of the authors.

for improving work force productivity. This article provides an overview of the VG program, its relationship to current employment testing regulations, the potential benefits to employers of using VG, and some issues associated with the program.

VALIDITY GENERALIZATION

The term "validity generalization" is drawn from an extensive and controversial stream of research launched in the 1970s by John E. Hunter (Michigan State University) and Frank L. Schmidt (then of the U.S. Office of Personnel Management). Their conclusion that standardized tests of cognitive (mental) ability are generally valid for employment selection decisions provides the basis (and the name) for the USES program. A brief overview of their research and findings as they apply to the USES program is provided here.[1]

The research by Hunter and Schmidt can be described as a reinterpretation of findings from previous investigations of the validity of employment tests. Thousands of validation studies have been conducted over the past 50 years, but the findings have been inconsistent. Similar tests for similar (or identical) jobs in different settings often yielded widely varying validity coefficients (correlations between test scores and job performance). This apparent inconsistency led to the generally accepted conclusion that the validity of an employment test for a particular job is specific to the situation. As a result, employers usually have been required to develop evidence of the validity of any tests used, regardless of findings elsewhere.

Hunter and Schmidt tested an alternative explanation for the historical inconsistency in test validation studies. Noting that the number of workers (sample size) in most previous studies was relatively small, and that the results of such studies are potentially influenced by a variety of technical deficiencies, they reasoned that inconsistent findings could be primarily attributable to statistical errors. Using a meta-analysis research method that provides a means to correct or adjust for such sources or error, Schmidt, Hunter and associates developed a persuasive body of evidence that the validity of ability tests for employment screening is relatively stable across jobs and organizations. Subsequent studies also strongly indicated that the validity of ability tests is generally higher than that of other selection procedures such as interviews, reference checks, experience ratings, etc.

In one study, Hunter cumulated the results of 515 studies of the validity of the General Aptitude Test Battery (GATB) carried out over a 45-year period by the Employment Service.[2] Three general abilities (cognitive, perceptual, and psychomotor) derived from GATB scales were found to be valid predictors of job proficiency for all jobs. Moreover, although there was considerable variation in the validity of these three abilities across jobs, the differences were adequately accommodated by grouping all jobs into five broad job families reflecting a hierarchy of job complexity. Since this job sample was representative of the 12,000 jobs included in the *Dictionary of Occupational Titles*,[3] the findings in this study were generalized to all jobs.

In a series of related studies, Hunter and the Employment Service addressed the topic of the fairness of psychological tests. The issue of test fairness actually consists of two distinct questions: (1) is the test fair in the sense that it is an accurate estimate of job performance ability for all applicant sub-groups? and (2) does use of the test adversely (disproportionately) limit job opportunities for minority group members?

Research evidence pertaining to question (1) is overwhelmingly positive. Virtually all studies conducted over the past 15 years by numerous researchers have concluded that ability tests are fair to minority groups. In fact, with respect to the GATB, an analysis of 51 studies showed that use of the GATB to predict job performance was likely to overestimate, rather than underestimate, the job performance of blacks.[4]

The answer to question (2) depends upon the extent of the difference in average test scores between nonminority and minority members on the particular tests. Significant differences in ability test scores between groups are nearly universal; the GATB is no exception. Although these differences vary by minority group and type of ability, the difference in average scores between nonminorities and blacks is substantial for all three general abilities. For example, if the cutoff score on cognitive ability was set at the average of the majority group, only 23 percent of black applicants would pass. The figures for perceptual abilities and psychomotor abilities are 25 percent and 41 percent, respectively.[5] Thus, use of the three general ability scores based on the GATB could be expected to produce a racially unbalanced work force.

In summary, the validity generalization program is based on the following research findings:

1. GATB scores are valid predictors of job proficiency although validity varies somewhat by type of job.
2. GATB scores fairly estimate job abilities for all groups.
3. Use of unadjusted GATB scores will adversely affect job opportunities for minorities.

THE GATB

The General Aptitude Test Battery was put into use in 1947 by state employment services offices after an extensive developmental research effort. It has been the focus of a continuing program of research to refine the tests and validate their use for vocational counseling and employee selection. Hence the GATB has a broad research record for many occupational classifications, and is probably the best validated multiple aptitude test battery in existence for employment applications.

The test battery consists of 12 timed tests (parts) — eight paper and pencil tests and four apparatus tests. Each part requires performance of familiar tasks such as name comparisons, arithmetic computations and reasoning, form perceptions, pegboard manipulations, etc. The 12 parts yield eight specific aptitude scores: verbal aptitude, numerical aptitude, spatial aptitude, form perception, clerical perception, motor coordination, finger dexterity, and manual dexterity. In addition, a general intelligence or learning ability score is derived from the arithmetic reasoning, vocabulary, and spatial perception test scores. These nine aptitudes measure basic abilities or capacities to learn various jobs.

Past research on the GATB had concentrated on developing norms (standards) for specific occupations and identifying patterns of aptitudes for occupational families. Norms were developed by identifying the specific aptitudes most relevant to particular occupations, and determining the degree to which these aptitudes related to proficiency in job performance or success in occupational training. A minimum or "cutting" score for each aptitude was set at the level that would effectively screen out a majority of the potentially unsuccessful workers for that occupation. The combination of aptitudes and minimum scores that comprised a norm differed for each occupation.

Use of GATB data in the VG program differs from the historical approach in three key respects. First, specific aptitude scores are combined into the three general ability scores noted above. These ability scores are then weighted and combined to produce overall aptitude scores for each of the five broad job families that Hunter had previously identified. Thus, minimum or critical scores on any specific aptitude are eliminated. Second, the overall score for each job family is converted to a percentile score to facilitate the use of a top-down hiring strategy (hire the best qualified), as opposed to use of the test scores to screen out the unqualified. Third, separate rankings (within-group percentiles) are computed for nonminorities, blacks, and hispanics. In effect, this procedure adjusts the GATB scores of minorities to eliminate adverse impact.

THE JOB SERVICE PROGRAM

Implementation of VG in local offices of the Job Service currently varies within and between states. For example, local Job Service offices in Michigan tested 73,600 applicants during 1985, and over 26,000 VG-selected applicants were referred to employers. Other states are just beginning to implement the program, but at least 25 states offer VG testing in some locations. A number of localities are following the "full implementation" model piloted in Roanoke, Virginia, and recommended by USES. In this approach, testing replaces interviews by local office personnel as the basic tool for all applicant screening and referral activities. As a consequence, significant operational changes are required, both in the nature and mode of service to applicants, and in the role of the local office staff.

To achieve maximum efficiency, the Roanoke office tailored all internal procedures around VG. Because the GATB is most efficiently administered in groups, individual applicant registration and interviewing were replaced by group registration (intake) and testing sessions. In the daily intake sessions, new applicants are given assistance in completing the necessary forms, and an orientation to program procedures and the nature of the GATB is provided. All applicants are encouraged to take the GATB, which is administered daily at a centrally located testing center.

As of January 1986, 80 percent of applicants were being tested. Results of the testing are entered into the local office records (computer files), and applicants are sent a report of their percentile rank for each of the five job families. These percentiles are interpreted as an indicator of the applicant's relative suitability (aptitude) for jobs of that type. When a job order is received, the job family to which it belongs is determined and a file search is initiated to identify and rank applicants for referral to the job. Other criteria established by the employer and preferences of the applicant also are considered in making referrals. For instance, an employer might require a specific type of training or experience, or an applicant's availability for certain hours or types of work could be restricted. Referrals would then be based on percentile ranking within these constraints.

Implementation of the VG program significantly changes the role and activities of Job Service interviewers. Much of the time formerly spent on initial assessment interviews is devoted to matching applicants' records with employer requirements. Interviewers are encouraged to become more knowledgeable of the particulars of the jobs they fill and the employers they serve. In order to facilitate this, Roanoke interviewers are designated as "account representatives" for specific employers, with responsibility for all transactions with that employer. According to officials in the Roanoke office, these changes have resulted in increases in the number and quality of candidates who are referred to employers. This improved responsiveness to employer needs has led to increased use of the job service by employers.

VG AND THE "UNIFORM GUIDELINES"

The VG program appears to challenge standards in the *Uniform Guidelines for Employee Selection Procedures* in a number of key respects. First, as noted above, the basic premise that the validity of ability tests is specific to particular situations is rejected. Employers using the VG program are informed that the VG testing program is valid and fair. Hence, they are relieved of the burdensome responsibility for conducting validation studies (of the GATB) in their organizations.

Second, because the three general abilities are believed to be valid predictors of success for all jobs, the detailed job analysis required by the guidelines is unnecessary. The analysis need only be sufficient to classify jobs into their appropriate job family. Since the worker function ratings in the occupation code of the *Dictionary of Occupational Titles* (DOT) provided the original basis for grouping jobs into five families, and the 515 jobs in the study were representative of the 12,000 jobs in the DOT, the basic job analysis for most jobs in the U.S. economy already exists.

Third, the VG program uses test scores to rank applicants. Research by USES has shown that ability test performance is directly related to job performance, i.e., as test scores increase there is a corresponding increase in average job performance. This finding appears to provide adequate justification for a "top-down" selection strategy. On the other hand, the thrust of the guidelines has been to "encourage" use of the minimum score (low cutoff) method.

Finally, the use of within-group percentile scores for nonminorities, blacks, and hispanics appears to be proscribed by the disparate treatment provision of the guidelines. Separate rankings are clearly a case of subjecting different racial groups to different standards (albeit for the purpose of eliminating adverse impact). The guidelines appear to allow use of different standards only in situations where a test is potentially unfair.

In short, the VG program is consistent with the ultimate objective of the EEOC, to increase employment opportunities for minorities. In fact, if the VG program is used to supplant less objective screening procedures, the overall selection ratio of minorities should increase over current levels. However, this is accomplished by means of a race-conscious hiring procedure based on premises that have heretofore been explicitly rejected by the EEOC. It is conceivable that the VG program, or more specifically, the procedures and findings of Hunter and Schmidt, will be defined as new, "professionally acceptable techniques" (under Sec. 14 of the guidelines). However, the silence of the EEOC to date and the continuing debate over validity generalization within the academic community suggest that this is unlikely.

BENEFITS TO EMPLOYERS

Few employers would challenge the proposition that the productivity of good workers significantly exceeds that of poor workers. The difference in productivity between top and bottom workers can vary widely by job or organization, but research findings suggest the ratio is about two to one for the typical job. Since valid ability tests increase the probability of selecting successful employees (better than other known selection devices), it follows that the use of valid tests to rank applicants provides an economic benefit to employers.

Documentation of the dollar value of productivity improvement attributable to testing has been difficult and expensive to develop in the past. Attempts to translate productivity differences among employees into dollar terms required detailed cost accounting procedures, and this approach was only applicable to a limited range of jobs. However, reasonable (conservative) estimates are now readily calculated for most jobs by means of recently developed procedures.[6] Hence, analyses of the monetary value (utility) of VG testing to individual employers will be forthcoming as the program is implemented more widely.

Application of this type of analysis to federal hiring data for 1980 indicates that optimal use of the GATB for all hiring decisions in that year would have had a value to the government of over $1 billion, or approximately 16 percent of total wages. Although an estimate of this magnitude naturally invites skepticism, it is actually based on *conservative* assumptions regarding the validity of VG test scores and variance in worker productivity. Furthermore, the figure escalates substantially if the continuing effects of improved selection (average tenure) are included in the calculation. Thus, the economic benefits of testing are likely to be much larger than was previously believed.

To some employers, a promise of increased worker productivity through better selection of qualified applicants will be viewed with misgiving or disinterest. Productivity improvement often is primarily a function of technology, and in some instances the contribution of workers to total productivity is virtually impossible to determine. However, cost reduction is of interest to all employers, and there is solid logic and evidence to support the use of VG to reduce costs. For instance, the validity of the GATB (and other ability tests) for predicting successful performance of applicants in various types of training programs is well established. Improved selection of trainees results in fewer failures, which translates directly into savings in training and employment costs. Similar reports of the effectiveness of VG have been received by the authors from Roanoke area employers, and are frequently reported in other VG pilot project areas. For example, a study by Philip Morris found a significant increase in the rate of training success for employees hired via a selection procedure incorporating VG over that of two comparison groups.[7]

The VG program offers other possible monetary and intangible benefits to employers. For example, one Roanoke area employer attributes a dramatic reduction in turnover of reduced administrative costs by using the Job Service as a sole source of job applicants. Fewer applicants are processed by the company and the quality of referrals has often increased, as evidenced by a reduction in the number of referrals per placement for many of these employers. Furthermore, the close working relationship between employer and Job Service personnel engendered by this procedure facilitates responsiveness to employer needs by the local Job Service office.

While the potential benefits appear to be significant, employers must recognize that the VG program is not a panacea. Test information is only one factor in employment decisions. The organization also must improve validity and fairness in other aspects of the selection decision process. Moreover, ability is only one component in the employee performance equation. Management practices often determine whether those abilities are properly developed, and whether the employee's energies are focused and tapped. In other words, tests might be valid predictors of job performance and training success, but the extent to which organizations capitalize on improved selection procedures depends to a large degree on how well they manage their human resources.

A standard caveat pertaining to the use of employment tests also applies to the VG program. To state that ability tests have high validity for predicting successful job performance is not to imply that they are perfect predictors. On the contrary, it merely suggests that the probability of mistakes in assessing the relative abilities of applicants is reduced. Predictions for particular applicants will sometimes be wrong, but over the long run the proportion of "correct" decisions will exceed that of decisions made without benefit of test information. Hence, organizations with a high level of employment activity will more quickly realize the benefits of VG screening.

ISSUES

Surprisingly little discussion or debate over the consequences of nationwide implementation of the VG program has surfaced in the professional or popular press (perhaps the program has not yet captured sufficient attention). Whatever the reason, VG testing is likely to renew or reinvigorate debate over some basic policy issue.

For example, the use of within-group percentiles to rank applicants appears to be at odds with the position taken by other federal agencies. Not only could separate rankings for nonminorities, blacks, and hispanics constitute disparate treatment, but this procedure also raises the more emotion-laden issue of preferential treatment. Given equivalent qualifications (in terms of test performance) for a minority and a nonminority candidate, the minority candidate will be ranked higher. This procedure is a logical and reasonable compromise between the conflicting national goals of economic efficiency (hire the best qualified) and equal economic opportunity for members of minority groups. However, by explicitly using different standards, the program also appears to be inviting charges of reverse discrimination. It is interesting to speculate how the current leadership of the EEOC and the Justice Department might view this particular form of quota in view of their adamant opposition to preferential hiring under any conditions.

A second issue pertains to the basic mission of the Job Service. The VG program very closely aligns the agency with employer perspectives and values. Obviously, job orders from employers are necessary to meet the needs of job seekers, and VG holds considerable promise for expanding the number and type of job orders placed with local offices. However, the emphasis on identifying the best qualified means some less qualified (in terms of test performance) individuals will be excluded from referral to jobs that they could perform successfully. The question boils down to one of the proper role of the public employment system. Should the Employment Service focus primarily on those most in need? (This was its function in the '70s, and it was not a marked success. Individuals most in need often are not competitive in the job market. As a result, employers found they could get better applicants elsewhere.) Or, should the Employment Service concentrate on helping employers make optimal use of the nation's human capital? An affirmative answer here raises a question of individual rights: Should a government agency be so closely identified with employer interests in decisions that affect people's life chances?

From the perspective of individual applicants, there is little doubt that widespread adoption of VG will directly affect the distribution of economic winners and losers. Some of the able, but chronically unemployed, will have opportunities that were previously denied them. (The Roanoke Job Service staff can attest to this fact.) On the other hand, top-down referral of applicants based on VG scores will exclude people who would have been considered if minimum standards were used. The consequences for the less able (and the developmentally disabled) could be severe. Moreover, extensive use of VG testing could exacerbate the "permanent underclass" problem in our society by creating a new class of stigmatized unemployed, the "low scorers" (some of whom will be erroneously labelled).

If the VG program is to be successfully implemented on a national level, problems of this genre will need to be addressed. While such problems will undoubtedly prove difficult to resolve, they must be kept in perspective. The previous approach based on interviewing was less effective and was plagued with similar and equally formidable problems. On the other hand, VG testing holds the promise of significantly contributing to productivity improvement, one of the keys to stemming the flow of jobs offshore. If this is borne out, the net effect of nationwide implementation of VG on job opportunities could be positive.

CONCLUSIONS

From the perspective of individual employers, the VG program appears to be one of those rare "no lose" opportunities. It offers a number of potential benefits with little perceptible risk or cost. As noted above, the extent to which a particular employer can realize benefits from the program depends on a number of factors.

However, from the evidence to date it appears that the majority of employers would be well advised to take two actions. First, they should carefully reexamine their beliefs and/or practices with respect to the use of ability tests in employment decisions. If employment activity is high, they could be missing an opportunity to significantly improve the quality of selection decisions.

Second, employers should reevaluate their use of the Job Service. They might be underutilizing a valuable resource. With the advent of the VG program, many local Job Services offices can provide a comprehensive applicant screening service at no cost.

REFERENCES

1. Readers unfamiliar with this research can find a thorough summary and extensive references in the USES Test Research Reports 45–49 available through the Job Service officials in their area. Also, *Personnel Psychology,* Winter 1985, provides an overview of many of the issues raised with respect to VG in a question-and-answer format.
2. J. E. Hunter, *The Dimensionality of the General Aptitude Test Battery and the Dominance of General Factors over Specific Factors in the Prediction of Job Performance.* Washington, DC: U.S. Employment Service, 1982.
3. U.S. Department of Labor, *Dictionary of Occupational Titles,* 1977.
4. U.S. Dept. of Labor, Employment and Training Administration, *Fairness of the General Aptitude Test Battery: Ability Differences and Their Impact on Minority Hiring Rates,* USES Test Research Report No. 46, Washington, DC, 1983.
5. *Ibid.*
6. Wayne F. Cascio, *Costing Human Resources: The Financial Impact of Behavior in Organizations.* Boston: Kent Publishing Co., 1982.
7. Dennis L. Warmke, "Successful Implementation of the 'New' GATB in Entry-Level Selection," paper presented at the ASPA Region IV Conference, October 15, 1984.

Robert M. Madigan and K. Dow Scott are assistant and associate professors of management, respectively, at Virginia Polytechnic Institute (VPI) and State University in Blacksburg, Virginia. Diana L. Deadrick is a doctoral candidate in human resource management at VPI, and Jil A. Stoddard is an employee relations representative at Philip Morris USA in Richmond, Virginia.

Development and Validation of a Computerized Interpretation System for Personnel Tests
C. David Vale / Laura S. Keller / V. Jon Bentz

Tests of mental ability, personality characteristics, interests, values, and specific job-relevant skills have long been used as aids in personnel selection. In the ideal situation, scores from such tests can be entered into empirically developed equations to predict important job-performance criteria, allowing selection decisions to be made statistically. For some jobs, however, it is not feasible to collect the data required to develop these equations. This is especially true for executive and management positions, where each job may be unique. In these cases, a more clinical approach must be taken. Clinical assessment data typically do not lend themselves to regression approaches. The services of an expert test interpreter (usually a psychologist) are thus required to translate test scores into a narrative report directly addressing the information needed by personnel managers to make an actual selection decision.

While narrative interpretive reports are an efficient way of integrating the expertise of the psychologist and the personnel specialist, obtaining an expert interpretation of every job candidate's test scores can be prohibitively expensive and time consuming. Computerization of the interpretive process can maintain the advantages of expert interpretive input to selection decisions while offering increased efficiency, standardization, accuracy, and permanence. This paper describes the development and validation of a computerized narrative interpretation system for a battery of psychological tests used by a large national retail merchandising organization. The process used to develop this system is applicable to other test batteries used for personnel decisions.

SOME ADVANTAGES OF COMPUTERIZING A NARRATIVE TEST REPORT

The computer is markedly more efficient at performing certain tasks than is a human. This efficiency can result in time, personnel, and of course, financial savings. Test interpretation is a complex process that requires the human expert to have had considerable professional education in testing and many hours of training specific to the test battery in use. The substantial investment in terms of educational costs and the training time required of both trainer and trainee is greatly reduced if a few resident experts can teach their interpretive system to a computer. Training time is shorter, and training is a one-time process instead of being repeated for every new human interpreter. An added advantage is that the computer version can do the

---

Source: C. David Vale, Laura S. Keller, and V. Jon Bentz, "Development and Validation of a Computerized Interpretation System for Personnel Tests," *Personnel Psychology,* 1986, 39, pp. 525–542. Reprinted by permission of *Personnel Psychology.*

same work that previously required many individual test experts.

For example, it may require a human test expert a minimum of two hours to produce a narrative interpretation for a comprehensive test battery. At a conservative estimate of $20 per hour for the expert's time, the report would cost $40. Once an automated interpretive system has been programmed, the cost of computer time to produce a similar report is approximately 25 cents. If the computerized report is as useful to the personnel decision-maker as the human expert's report, the efficiency gain is about 16,000%.

Standardization is a second advantage of computerized interpretive systems. If two human interpreters write reports on the same set of test scores, it is highly unlikely that their interpretations will be identical. This inconsistency can be problematic if it results in different personnel decisions being made from the same scores. In theory, standardization could be achieved if all tests were interpreted by a single expert, but this is impractical in most settings. In addition, even a single expert's interpretive strategy may vary from one report to another. A computerized system achieves perfect standardization; it applies its programmed decision rules with total reliability, guaranteeing that all interpretations resulting from the same scores will be identical.

A third potential advantage of an automated system is accuracy. Even if a single interpreter could produce perfectly reliable reports, it is likely that personal biases or interpretive errors would compromise the report's accuracy, at least to some extent. Additional errors are likely to creep in as a result of burnout; rarely can any human interpreter mass-produce interpretations without fatigue and boredom affecting accuracy. Assuming that all interpreters are experts in the field, report accuracy could be increased by having several experts work on a consensual interpretation, thus balancing out individual errors and biases. Although the use of multiple human experts to interpret every individual score profile is impractical, a computerized system can incorporate the expertise of a large number of test experts. A consensually developed automated system of interpretations is thus likely to result in a more accurate final report.

Another important advantage of computerization is permanence. Human interpreters may quit their jobs, be transferred, or retire, taking all of their interpretive expertise with them. A computerized interpretive system is permanent until it is purposely replaced by an improved version.

METHODS FOR DEVELOPING A COMPUTERIZED INTERPRETATION

Until very recent years, applications of computer technology to standard psychological testing practices were confined to test scoring and, occasionally, to test administration. Both of these uses capitalize on the computer's speed and reliability at performing clerical functions without infringing on the interpretive tasks traditionally performed by an assessment expert. A significant broadening of sanctioned roles for the computer assessment expert is in progress, however (cf. Butcher, Keller, & Bacon,

1985). Increasingly, the computer is functioning as an "expert clinician" by generating narrative interpretive reports based on psychological test scores.

There are several ways in which a computer program can be designed to generate test interpretations. While it is technically feasible to use the computer's learning capacity to generate new interpretive rules for standard assessment devices, the majority of contemporary applications follow established practice in being either (a) descriptive, (b) clinician-modeled, or (c) clinical-actuarial in nature (Roid & Gorsuch, 1984).

A descriptive interpretive program consists of a series of sentences or phrases, each interpreting a different single test or scale score. Programs of this type differ in how much effort is put into tailoring the report for the individual through such devices as gender-specific statements, and the phrases may or may not be put together in a narrative form. The earliest example of such a system was the Minnesota Multiphasic Personality Inventory (MMPI) report developed at the Mayo Clinic (Rome et al., 1962); the computer generated a profile of scale scores and several intepretive phrases, each based on single-scale elevations. The descriptive approach is the simplest method of computerizing test interpretations, but it tends to be overly simplistic. Configural (score pattern) interpretations are not included, and narrative reports based on single-scale elevations alone tend to be choppy to read and prone to internal contradictions.

Clinician-modeled programs use a method analogous to that employed in the development of several automated psychiatric interviews (Erdman, Klei, & Greist, 1985). The expert test interpreter is viewed as "an information-processing organism who has collected direct observations, interviews, and tests as 'inputs' that he must process (analyze, organize, and integrate) prior to 'outputting' his recommendation or prediction" (Kleinmuntz, 1969, p. 85). Thus, if the interpretive expert's strategy can be made explicit, the computer can be programmed to model his or her decision process.

One method used to model the clinician's judgmental process employs a logical decision tree to successively rule out potential classifications and converge on a final category. This approach has been used in computerized diagnostic interview systems (cf. Fleiss, Spitzer, Cohen, & Endicott, 1972). The validity of such programs is usually evaluated by comparing their diagnoses with those of clinicians working from the same input data. While the extent of agreement is not particularly impressive, the correlations are comparable to those of clinicians with each other (Hedlund, Evenson, Sletten, & Cho, 1980). Such programs are limited by the difficulty of making interpretive experts' judgmental rules explicit and often by the unreliability of the tests or diagnostic rules on which these systems are based.

Another method of modeling the clinician uses statistical analyses of expert judgments, rather than trusting the experts to be able to clearly delineate their own interpretive strategies. Goldberg (1970), for example, developed mathematical models of the prediction process of clinical psychologists attempting to classify MMPI profiles as either neurotic or psychotic. He found that after the human experts' classification rules were specified and programmed, the computerized model outperformed the original clinicians. The automated formula removed human unreliability from application of the "hopefully, somewhat valid judgmental strategy" (p. 423).

The validity of a computerized system developed by either of the pure clinician-modeled strategies rests on an assumption that must be justified: that the strategy of the clinician being modeled is actually valid in predicting relevant criteria. The third major category of strategies for developing an automated interpretive system, the clinical-actuarial model, tries to avoid this problem by basing all narrative statements on empirical research findings for various test-scale elevations or configurations. For example, a system developed to intepret the MMPI would employ only descriptors that have been empirically determined to characterize persons with certain highpoint scale combinations, or "codetypes."

In actual practice there are no purely actuarial automated interpretive reports. This is because such actuarial systems require empirical data in an amount that increases geometrically with the number of variables and levels considered by the system. Thus available actuarial systems either leave a large percentage of examinees unclassified or use such broad categories that fine interpretations are impossible. Even those systems written for well-researched personality instruments such as the MMPI are actually a mixture of rules based on actuarially validated relationships and other rules pulled from established clinical lore or from the expert author's personal experience with the test.

Given these constraints, at the present time the best method for developing an automated system for an established test or test battery would seem to be a mixed strategy employing both actuarial and clinician-modeled approaches. The MMPI report developed at Assessment Systems Corporation for National Computer Systems (1982), while modeled on the judgmental strategy of one interpretive expert, was also actuarial in that this expert attempted to incorporate all the accepted actuarial data, as well as his personal clinical experience, into his interpretation. The program was built hierarchically around codetype interpretations: if an examinee's profile fit an established score pattern for which actuarially validated descriptors were available, a standard narrative was invoked fitting that configuration (with a few modifications based on other moderating scale elevations).

The mixed strategy used in developing the MMPI computer interpretation was modified somewhat in developing the interpretive system described below. The codetype structure was not generalizable to the new test batteries, and the use of only one interpretive expert's judgmental strategy introduced the possibility of idiosyncratic biases. Wiggins (1980) has pointed out that pooling the judgments of several clinicians into a composite model can improve a computer algorithm's predictive power by reducing the effects of such individual biases and unreliability.

These considerations were incorporated into the development of the retail merchandising company's computerized interpretive system. A committee of testing experts was consulted in designing the report structure and was responsible for approving all interpretations included in the final statement library as well as participating in validation of the computer-generated reports. Although one senior interpretive expert served as the primary source of information about the test scores and their possible interpretations, the overall program was designed as an "answer-to-question mapping system" rather than an automated version of one person's report-writing style. The committee provided a comprehensive list of questions that should be answered by a good interpretive report, scales were selected from the test battery as necessary to answer each of these questions, and a computer statement library was written around this pre-ordained structure. The following sections will describe the development and validation of this system in more detail.

DEVELOPMENT OF A COMPUTERIZED NARRATIVE INTERPRETATION FOR AN EXECUTIVE SCREENING BATTERY

Development of the Initial Question List

The first step in a structured approach to development of a computerized interpretation system is specification of the questions to be answered by the final narrative report. The initial question list for this company's system was developed by a committee of interpretive experts and program designers working from samples of narrative reports already used by the company in making personnel selection decisions. Four broad content areas to be covered by the final report were identified: mental ability, business motivation, personal characteristics, and emotional adjustment. Mental ability was later broken down into overall, quantitative, and verbal abilities for the final report format. In all, approximately 60 questions were developed to adequately cover the information contained in these six areas.

The question list provided a complete description of the content and overall structure of the statement library to be developed for the computer. The next step was to decide which scale scores from the test battery were relevant to the provision of answers to each of the questions. The company's senior expert's judgment provided the initial direction for this: For each question the report was to address, he suggested a scale or set of scales as the source of information pertaining to that issue. (Information on the tests composing the battery and their validity for executive screening can be found in Bentz, 1983). For example, the question list developed for the Quantitative Skills section of the report asked the following questions:

1. Quantitative Ability
   a. How does his/her quantitative ability compare to that of other company executives?
   b. Can he/she handle complex quantitative material?
2. Does he/she like to use his/her quantitative skills?
   a. Does he/she enjoy computational tasks?
   b. Can he/she tolerate routine, detailed, or repetitive work?
   c. Does he/she have careful work habits?
   d. Does he/she like to have variety and change in his/her work?

Development of the Preliminary Statement Library

After the overall structure was determined through the list of questions and associated scales, the statement library was developed by writing sets of answers to each question for several levels of the relevant scales. Further interpretive information was obtained from a training manual provided by the testing experts. This manual included brief definitions of the battery's scales, the relevance of each to executive behavior, sets of interpretations considered appropriate for scores falling at the 10th, 25th, 50th, 75th, and 95th percentiles on each scale, and a refined list of concise statements designed to assist in developing a narrative report. The manual also included some brief descriptions of important scale combinations, including a few scale configurations particularly relevant to executive selection, and mentioned some scales that might have a moderating effect on the interpretation of other scales.

These statements and scale descriptions provided a basic outline, which was used to develop the computerized statement library. However, the information provided in this manual was often incomplete, and the sample interpretive statements did not always directly address the issues raised in the question list. Thus, the library writers modified and extrapolated from this basic material in order to address the specific content areas mandated by the question list. The interpretive material provided in the manual was expanded to provide a richer variety of interpretive statements and finer gradations of interpretive possibilities within each scale. Using the training manual's statements as anchor points, the range of interpretations was expanded to approximately 10 levels per scale. The statements at each of these levels provided a slightly different answer to the question being addressed.

The preliminary version of the statement library consisted primarily of sets of statements corresponding to all possible score levels of single scales. For example, the first set of statements in the library was composed of 10 different answers to the question, "How does this person's overall mental ability compare to that of company executives?" These 10 answers each corresponded to a different score range on the scale relevant to this question (Overall Mental Ability). Obviously, only one of these statements would be invoked for any particular examinee. Most of the library was composed of similar sets of statements providing different answers to one particular question based on the score level of a single scale. At this point in the developmental process, the actual score levels to which the statements were to correspond were not specified; the goal was simply to develop a set of statements reflecting progressively higher elevations on the scale in question.

The preliminary library also included some sections that were more complicated in structure. According to the interpretive manual and the senior expert, several interpretations depended on combinations of two or more scales rather than the elevations of single scales alone. Three different strategies were used to deal with these situations. In the simplest case, a set of statements was written for a particular scale, but a few words of some of the statements were deleted, modified, or added, depending on the level of another scale. For example, a set of statements was written for varying levels of one scale, but the word "volatile" was added to some of these descriptors only if the score on another scale was also high. Another example of this strategy was the ubiquitous use of transitional phrases throughout the library. In order to create a final narrative report that would read smoothly, it was necessary to add a few words at several points in the library providing bridges between contiguous statements. Transitions such as "nevertheless," "however," "in addition," and "on the other hand" were employed to improve the readability of the final narrative.

The second strategy was to write two or more entire sets of statements for a single scale, with the two sets differing as a function of the score level of another scale. For example, there were substantially different sets of statements for Self-confidence depending on whether the Sociability score was low, medium, or high.

The third strategy, a configural approach, was to write statements to be invoked only by the simultaneous occurrence of several scale score elevations in specified ranges. This type of strategy is a form of the codetype narrative used in the MMPI system.

The preliminary statement library reflected a collaborative and iterative process of consultation among the senior expert and the library writers. While the question list and interpretive manual provided basic guidance, the expansion of the range of statements and the modification of the manual's interpretations to fit the needs of this system necessitated the development of a substantial amount of new and original interpretive material. The validity and appropriateness of the new material was continually reviewed through consultations with the senior expert, and his editorial comments were incorporated into the library.

Committee Revision and Editing of Statement Library

The next step in the development process was to meet with the other interpretive experts to develop a final, consensually acceptable form of the statement library that would be useful in a variety of the company's personnel settings. The entire staff of experts met with the library writers to edit and revise the preliminary statement library — this is a developmental step that is seldom included in computerized interpretation systems currently available. The experts went back to the original question list and eliminated a few areas that had proved to be redundant when the longer report was developed. The statement library was modified to reflect these deletions.

Using the revised question list as a guide to the content and organization to be achieved in the final library, the experts were then asked to edit all the statement sets for content, wording, and proper ordering. They also examined all configural statements to see whether the interpretations added anything unique that could not be obtained using simpler single- or two-scale combinations. If not, they were instructed to change the configuration to a simpler rule. Otherwise, they were told to make sure that the list of scales contributing to the configuration was correct.

Many of the editing changes involved relatively minor changes in wording, but there were a few modifications made in statement order as well. Several statements were deleted because the experts believed the subdivisions were too fine for the range of interpretations that could be accurately derived from that particular scale. All of the approved revisions were then incorporated into the final statement library.

Assignment of Score Ranges to Statements

The final statement library, after the editing changes, consisted of many sets of statements ordered according to scale elevations but without actual score ranges assigned. The next step was to insert the logic invoking the statements according to score levels agreed upon by the experts. To achieve maximal accuracy in assigning score levels and to minimize the idiosyncrasies of individual experts, the final score levels were assigned on the basis of group averages. Each expert was asked to examine every interpretive statement included in the library and to provide "ratings" (more accurately, score ranges on the particular scale in question) for which that statement was most appropriate. Thus, for each set of statements reflecting progressively higher elevations on a particular scale, the experts provided a series of score "cutoffs" or "bounds," reflecting both the range of scores for which a statement was appropriate and the point at which the next contiguous statement in the set became more appropriate.

Mean ratings were computed for each statement, and their standard errors were examined as indices of rater agreement. Values of 3.5 for percentile scores and .35 for decile scores were selected as the largest standard errors indicating acceptable rater agreement. When the standard error of the mean rating was less than these values, the mean rating was adopted as the cutoff score to be used in the final statement library. Mean ratings possessing standard errors greater than or equal to these values were examined further. It was first determined whether any particular expert had contributed a rating that was markedly discrepant from the others; if so, that expert was sent a new rating form and asked to reconsider his or her ratings, checking that he or she had read the instructions thoroughly and had not made errors in recording the chosen cutoff scores. This resolved a few of the discrepancies.

When the rating discrepancies appeared to reflect general disagreement rather than a particular rater's outlying scores, the entire set of statements surrounding the problematic statement(s) was examined to see whether adding another interpretive level or rewording the existing statements would help to resolve the differences. If such action appeared useful, it was taken. The experts then rated the revised statement set.

The results of the initial ratings and the effects of the re-rating process can most easily be evaluated on the 34 answers to questions that involved only a single scale (i.e., excluding those that considered scales in interaction). On these answers, interrater reliability estimates could be obtained on the cutting scores separating each of the statements. Intra-class correlations were computed using the sample formula for the reliability of an average rating (Winer, 1971, pp. 283–289). The reliabilities of the initial averate ratings ranged from .759 to .998 with a mean of .978; after re-rating, they ranged from .875 to .998 with a mean of .985. These differences were due to changes in 4 of the 34 answer sets. The average reliability to these four sets changed from .878 to .936. It should be noted that the high levels of interrater agreement observed on all answer sets were due in part to the fact that the statements were ordered by score level before they were given to the experts for rating.

The few remaining discrepancies were submitted to the senior expert for a final ruling. Where he believed that the mean expert rating was appropriate, it was adopted as the final cutoff score despite its large standard error. In a few cases, he believed that the mean value was inappropriate, and a rating between the group mean and his own rating was adopted.

After the rating process was complete, computerized interpretive reports were generated for a variety of score profiles provided by the company to test the system. These reports were reviewed for overall structure, grammar, spelling, smoothness of transitions, and content. A few changes in wording were made, and the cutoffs were modified on some of the configural statements so that they would be invoked more often for particularly outstanding executive candidates.

A section from a sample computer-generated narrative report that answers the quantitative-skills questions listed above is reproduced below. The complete interpretive narrative is approximately two pages of narrative followed by a profile page plotting the candidate's actual test scores.

QUANTITATIVE SKILLS AND THEIR USE

Mr. Alpha has exceptionally fine quantitative ability. He is capable of working with highly complex and abstract numerical material, reasoning through problems and solving them very rapidly.

Despite his good numerical ability, Mr. Alpha very strongly dislikes computational work and will avoid numerical tasks whenever possible. He also strongly dislikes repetitive, detailed, or routine tasks and will have no tolerance for such assignments. When he does engage in quantitative work, his need for change and variety is likely to interfere with careful and conscientious attention to detail.

VALIDATION OF THE COMPUTERIZED INTERPRETIVE SYSTEM

Method

A narrative report's function is to interpret test-score data in a way that can be easily understood by laypersons and still be considered accurate by test experts. Evaluation of the computerized interpretation system thus focused on the accuracy and readability of the reports. Specifically, these characteristics of the computer-generated narratives were compared with those of reports generated by experts. Because this system was developed to generate interpretive statements that had already been empirically validated for the test battery (see Bentz, 1983), it was not considered necessary to evaluate the accuracy of the report's statements against external job-performance criteria. The goal of validation was to examine whether the computerized reports provided the same (or better) selection information as human experts could derive from the same scores. Obviously, this validation strategy would be inappropriate for a computerized version of any test battery that had not already been shown to be valid for personnel selection.

A set of 18 score profiles was chosen from company archives by the senior expert as representative of the range of ability and personal characteristics typical of the executive candidate population and representing configurations of scores that a competent company psychologist should be able to interpret. Three profiles were sent to each of six interpretive experts, who were asked to generate narrative interpretations for them. All 18 profiles were also submitted to the computerized system for interpretation. Seventeen profiles were returned by the experts in proper form; these 17 and their corresponding computer versions were used in the validation study. (The one not returned resulted from an error in the distribution of materials to experts.)

The expert-generated reports were edited to make their formats similar to the computer-generated reports. The text itself was not changed except to correct obvious typographical errors. In general, the expert-generated reports' formats differed sufficiently from the computer-generated reports for it to be relatively easy to distinguish them; this was an undesirable, but unavoidable, consequence of allowing individualized report styles.

The reports were then distributed to the experts for evaluation. Each expert received all of the report pairs (expert- and computer-generated) except those that he or she had interpreted. Thus, each expert received 28 or 30 reports. The experts were first asked to estimate the values of each of the scores that led to the report (they had never been shown the actual scale scores for these narratives). They did this by checking a point on a graphic rating scale. In addition, they were asked to rate the thoroughness, readability, and coherence of the reports. For thoroughness they were asked to evaluate "How completely does it cover the important information and issues that should be included in an interpretation of the Executive Screening Battery?" on a five-point scale ranging from (1) "Leaves out essential information" to (5) "Extremely thorough." For readability they were asked to evaluate "Is it well organized and is the information presented in a clear manner" on a scale ranging from (1) "Very unclear and difficult to read" to (5) "Excellent narrative style." For coherence they were asked to evaluate "How well does the report present a coherent picture of the individual's character?" on a scale ranging from (1) "Presentation is inconsistent and contradictory" to (5) "Excellent synopsis of the individual's character."

The accuracy of the interpretations was evaluated by comparing the estimated scores based on reading the narratives to the actual test scores underlying them. The experts were told to make estimates of the scores if they could infer any information about the scales from the report, but they were not compelled to guess scores on every scale in the absence of data. Since there were five potential raters for each report, and each score on each profile was estimated by at least one expert, the number of estimates for each score of each profile ranged from 1 to 5, depending on how many of the experts believed they had sufficient data on which to base an estimate. The means of each of these sets of estimates were computed and were compared to the actual underlying scores. This resulted in comparisons for 29 test scores on each of 34 profiles. The differences between underlying and estimated scores were summarized by computing the average absolute differences between the average estimated scores and the scores used to produce the interpretation.

Responses to the questions regarding thoroughness, readability, and coherence were summarized by computing means for the expert- and computer-generated reports.

Results

Of the 170 reports sent to the experts, 164 were returned. The remaining 6 were unrated, apparently because of insufficient time on the part of a rater. Table 1 shows the results of these analyses. The first two columns show the means and standard deviations of the scores and of the average of all scores. Note that all scores have been expressed on a percentile scale for comparability (i.e., all decile scores were multiplied by ten). Columns three and four show the average absolute errors between the mean estimated scores and the scores that generated the interpretations for the expert and computer interpretations. The remaining columns show the results of correlated t tests contrasting the magnitude of the errors between expert and computer interpretation.

For all scores except Agreeableness and Scientific and Artistic Interest, the experts were able to estimate actual test scores from the computer-generated reports with less error than from the human-generated reports. Seven of the comparisons of individual scores favoring the computer-generated reports and the comparison of the average of all scores were statistically significant at the 5% level. None of the comparisons favoring the accuracy of the manually developed interpretations were statistically significant. The error of the average score was approximately two score points less for the computer-generated reports than for the manually generated reports.

A wide range of error levels is apparent in Table 1. This appears to reflect the relative prominence of the scales in the reports. The scales with the largest errors are Musical and Artistic Interests. These scales receive little mention in the computerized report and apparently also received little mention in the expert-generated reports, giving the experts minimal data on which to base score estimates. The ability and personality variables, which receive relatively thorough treatment in both types of reports, have uniformly smaller errors.

Table 2 presents the mean ratings for the three evaluation questions. The computer-generated reports received a mean thoroughness rating 0.480 points higher on the 5-point scale than the expert-generated reports. This difference is significant at the 5% level and is in line with the finding of greater accuracy for the computer-generated reports and the fact that they were usually longer than the expert-generated ones.

Both types of reports were rated approximately 3.4 on readability. Although the expert-generated reports were rated 0.065 points higher, this was not statistically significant and does not seem a substantial difference. Both types were considered adequately readable.

The expert-generated reports were considered somewhat more coherent than their computer-generated counterparts.

TABLE 1
Results of Score Reproduction Analysis

	True Scores		Absolute Error		Error of Diff.	t	p
	Mean	SD	Expert	Comp.			
Mental ability							
Quantitative	58.353	24.546	5.465	2.985	1.204	2.06	.056
Linguistic	54.353	23.436	5.344	3.688	.750	2.21	.042*
Overall	57.941	17.782	3.615	2.965	.856	.76	.458
Personality							
Sociability	71.706	14.123	3.718	2.962	.923	.82	.425
Reflectiveness	52.941	9.196	3.554	3.397	.871	.18	.859
Optimism	76.471	14.116	5.488	3.171	.967	2.40	.029*
Emotional control	72.353	13.005	5.050	3.324	1.250	1.38	.186
Serious vs. carefree	54.118	12.277	3.691	3.382	.615	.50	.622
General activity	64.118	14.603	4.829	3.382	.638	2.27	.038*
Social leadership	71.118	12.041	4.572	3.750	.764	1.06	.308
Self-confidence	74.529	17.454	4.518	3.621	.972	.92	.370
Composure	65.294	11.789	5.912	3.003	.982	2.96	.009**
Objectiveness	68.824	14.951	4.088	2.079	.856	2.35	.032*
Agreeableness	50.000	12.748	4.137	4.750	.988	−.62	.544
Tolerance	67.588	21.275	4.944	2.941	.804	2.49	.024*
Values and interests							
Analytical	59.941	25.413	11.380	7.343	3.647	1.11	.285
Economic	81.118	21.595	5.244	3.765	.828	1.79	.093
Aesthetic	16.529	14.655	15.569	10.468	3.890	1.31	.208
Social	44.176	24.306	12.567	11.387	2.391	.49	.629
Political	74.235	22.507	5.777	3.441	1.708	1.37	.190
Mechanical	32.706	21.840	15.804	13.020	2.573	1.08	.295
Computational	55.706	26.865	9.588	6.756	2.851	.99	.335
Scientific	36.000	20.890	16.441	17.486	4.495	−.23	.819
Persuasive	84.353	15.095	7.720	5.003	1.400	1.94	.070
Artistic	37.353	24.326	22.431	24.608	3.783	−.58	.573
Literary	46.235	23.832	13.845	6.027	2.909	2.69	.016*
Musical	56.647	25.797	35.196	34.020	3.150	.37	.714
Social service	52.235	28.066	8.398	6.385	1.547	1.30	.212
Clerical	52.353	23.617	10.983	6.290	2.829	1.66	.117
All scores	58.132	5.315	8.961	7.083	.339	5.54	<.001**

Note. All scores have been converted to percentiles for comparability. All *t* statistics have 16 degrees of freedom.

* $p < .05$; ** $p < .01$.

TABLE 2
Ratings of Validation Questions

	Mean		Error of Difference	t	p
	Expert	Computer			
Thoroughness	3.588	4.068	.136	−3.53	.003**
Readability	3.438	3.373	.096	.68	.504
Coherence	3.371	3.077	.134	2.19	.044*

* $p < .05$; ** $p < .01$

While the computerized reports were rated 3.076, the expert-generated reports were rated 0.295 points higher, a statistically significant difference. Although both types were considered "adequately consistent," the experts appeared to do a somewhat better job of capturing the "essential character" of the individual in a concise manner.

CONCLUSIONS

The results of this effort suggest that a computerized interpretation can produce narrative reports that are at least as good as those produced by the typical human interpretive expert. The two types of reports may excel in different areas, however. Whereas the computerized version appears to be more thorough and accurate, the human experts may be able to assemble a more coherent and integrated summary of an individual's salient personality features. This might be due in part to the human expert's ability to choose to exclude inconsistent information or to emphasize unusual score configurations, whereas the more thorough and reliable computerized report will always print every interpretation invoked by the candidate's scale scores without highlighting some over others. It is possible to restructure the computer program to provide more summary statements emphasizing important constellations of attributes. It is also possible, however, that the coherence of the human experts' interpretations results from forcing reality into a convenient conceptual mold. If this is the case, greater coherence could be imposed on the computerized interpretation only at the expense of accuracy.

The general development approach used here appeared to work quite well with a committee of experts. Focusing first on the list of questions to be answered provided a good structure in which to integrate the content. The average ratings used as cut points for the answers apparently provided accurate and reliable decision rules. The success of this use of average ratings, however, was due in part to the fact that this was not an extensively configural interpretation. It is unclear to what degree the structure of the development process was responsible for the infrequency of configural interpretations and how much was due to the application itself. Although average ratings were used to obtain the final cuts for the configural answers, the configurations were developed prior to that process by group consensus. In a more configural interpretation developed by a committee, a consensual process might be more efficient for setting the cutting scores as well as defining the configurations.

This approach to validation, although concise and efficient, provides supportive rather than definitive evidence of validity. The design rests to some degree on the integrity of the researcher. One could, for example, produce an interpretation that simply listed the scores in narrative terms; profile reproduction would be quite good. A similar situation exists in test development, however, in which the internal consistency of a test can be maximized by repeating a single question for the full length of the test. In the design reported, the safeguard against this is the subjective evaluation by experts of the thoroughness of the report.

Some additional deficiencies in the developmental approach taken here have been discussed by Vale and Keller (1987). Issues not explicitly considered in the development of this interpretation were statement utility and safety. In an interpretation intended for nonprofessional consumers, it is important that each statement present something of value to the consumer and that no statement present information, whether correct or not, that the consumer might misconstrue or should not have access to. Although a great deal of informal attention was given to these matters during the development of this interpretation, if the approach used here was to be adopted as a general method, explicit consideration should be given to each of these points. Regarding utility, a sample of consumers should review each question in the list to verify that the information that will be provided is indeed useful. Similarly, regarding safety, the original experts or an independent panel of professionals should review each of the statements and note any that contain information that a consumer should not have access to.

The availability of a panel of experts to interpret a comprehensive battery such as this may be relatively rare. The utility of the technology of test interpretation is not limited to traditional psychological tests, however. It is applicable to any situation where configurations of numbers need to be explained. In general, the technology is most beneficial when there is a body of expertise that is frequently applied. For example, the technology could be applied to survey-based management-development programs that use standard questionnaires to evaluate and their results to modify the behavior of managers. Where a facilitator is typically required to interpret the survey results, a narrative report could substitute, at least in part, for the facilitator. Similarly, an interpretation system could be developed to explain the details of a corporate benefit package to a new employee, the details tailored to the employee's specific situation and needs. When the expertise is well defined and the application is routine, the technology of test interpretation can result in substantial cost savings.

REFERENCES

Bentz, V. J. (1983, May). *Research findings from personality assessment of executives*. Paper presented at the Sixth Annual Symposium on Applied Behavioral Science, Blacksburg, VA.

Butcher, J. N., Keller, L. S., Bacon, S. F. (1985). Current developments and future directions in computerized personality assessment. *Journal of Consulting and Clinical Psychology, 53,* 803–815.

Erdman, H. P., Klein, M., Greist, J. H. (1985). Direct patient computer interviewing. *Journal of Consulting and Clinical Psychology, 53,* 760–773.

Fleiss, J. L., Spitzer, R. L., Cohen, J., Endicott, J. (1972). Three computer diagnosis methods compared. *Archives of General Psychiatry, 27,* 643–649.

Goldberg, L. R. (1970). Man vs. model of man: A rationale, plus some evidence, for a method of improving on clinical inferences. *Psychological Bulletin, 73,* 422–432.

Hedlund, J. L., Evenson, R. C., Sletten, I. W., Cho, D. W. (1980). The computer and clinical prediction. In Sidowski, J. B., Johnson, J. H., Williams, T. A. (Eds.), *Technology in mental health care delivery systems* (pp. 201–235). Norwood, NJ: Ablex.

Kleinmuntz, B. (Ed.). (1969). *Clinical information processing by computer: An essay and selected readings.* New York: Holt, Rinehart & Winston.

National Computer Systems. (1982). *User's guide for the Minnesota report.* Minneapolis: Author.

Roid, G. H., Gorsuch, R. L. (1984). Development and clinical use of test-interpretive programs on microcomputers. In Schwartz, M. D. (Ed.), *Using computers in clinical practice* (pp. 141–149). New York: Haworth.

Rome, H. P., Swenson, W. M., Mataya, P., McCarthy, C. E., Pearson, J. S., Keating, F. R., Hathaway, S. R. (1962). Symposium on automation techniques in personality assessment. *Proceedings of the Staff Meetings of the Mayo Clinic, 37,* 61–82.

Vale, C. D., Keller, L. S. (1987). Developing expert computer systems to interpret psychological tests. In Butcher, J. N. (Ed.), *The practitioner's guide to computer-based psychological testing.* New York: Basic Books.

Wiggins, J. S. (1980). *Personality and prediction: Principles of personality assessment.* Menlo Park, CA: Addison-Wesley.

Winer, B. J. (1971). *Statistical principles in experimental design.* New York: McGraw-Hill.

C. David Vale is employed by Assessment Systems Corporation, St. Paul, Minnesota. V. Jon Bentz is a retired employee of Sears, Roebuck and Company. The authors would like to thank Greg Allen, Charlotte Campbell, Helen Holz, Grace Inman, Curt Pradelt, and Bruce Ward for their assistance in the development of this system.

Development and Validation of Minicourses in the Telecommunication Industry
Richard R. Reilly / Edmond W. Israelski

Beginning in the early 1970s the Bell System began moving toward the implementation of a variety of electronic digitally based systems. Some of these systems were designed to replace electromechanical, analog equipment, such as in the telephone switching area. Other systems were designed to computerize what had been largely clerical or testing functions. Each of these systems brought with it changes in job performance requirements and a consequent need for new and extensive training. For all of the target positions in question there was no trained labor pool to draw from, so that selection procedures such as job

Source: Reilly, R. R. and Israelski, E. W., 1988, "Development and Validation of Minicourses in the Telecommunications Industry." *Journal of Applied Psychology,* Vol. 73, No. 4, 721–726. Copyright 1988 by the American Psychological Association. Reprinted by permission.

knowledge tests or work sample proficiency tests were not viable options. The training programs themselves were lengthy and costly to administer. For example, training for the electronic switching and minicomputer maintenance positions could take as long as one full year.

At least two other factors also had to be considered. First, the new technology would eventually result in a decrease in the total number of positions. From an organizational point of view, then, it was desirable to move as many of the current employees into these positions as possible. All of these people, however, had been trained in the older technology, which in most cases shared few features with the new systems. Procedures that could identify current employees that would most likely be successful in training and on the job were required. Second, many of the target jobs had few or no incumbents at the time that test development was initiated. Thus, approaches that could be taken to produce valid and cost-effective selection procedures on a timely basis were constrained by an inability to observe and survey employees in the target positions.

This combination of circumstances led to an approach that became known in the Bell System of the 1970s as the minicourse approach to selection. The minicourse approach is similar to miniaturized training as discussed by Siegal and Bergman (1975) and to trainability testing as discussed by Robertson and Downs (1979). This approach has been a highly successful method of selecting personnel for new jobs or for jobs that have changed significantly because of the implementation of new technology. The purpose of this article is to describe some of the unique characteristics of the minicourse approach as it has been used in the telecommunications industry and to present some of the empirical results that have been obtained.

MINICOURSE DEVELOPMENT

In a minicourse a job candidate is given a standardized sample of programmed training material relevant to the target position. Each minicourse unit or module is followed by a test designed to measure learning of the material. Although a typical minicourse has a 6-hr time limit, some have had a limit of 2 hrs and others have taken as long as 3 days. The major objective of minicourses is to place the candidate in a context that closely approximates the training setting, so that the ability to learn material critical to completing the full training course and to performing the job can be assessed.

Work on the first minicourse, designed to select Electronic Switching System (ESS) personnel, was begun in the early 1970s. The ESS Minicourse in its early developmental stages was self-paced and took up to 5 days to complete; it consisted of seven modules presented in self-paced instruction format with feedback. At the end of each module the candidate was administered a timed test that included open-ended questions. Although the implementation of the ESS Minicourse was highly successful, both from the point of view of field acceptance and documented reduction in training costs, the expense and cumbersome nature of administration as well as the difficulty of scoring the open-ended questions led to changes in subsequent minicourse development. One change was to limit the amount of administration time to a maximum of 1 day. A second change was to develop only multiple-choice, end-of-module tests, thereby eliminating the need for expert scoring.

Over the years the steps in the minicourse development process have become fairly well-defined and include the following: (a) job analysis, (b) review and analysis of training, (c) development of draft minicourse material, (d) linking of minicourse content to training content and job performance requirements, (e) pretest of minicourse to develop initial normative data, conduct item analysis, and make any necessary revisions, and (f) implementation and small-sample, criterion-related validation where possible.

Job Analysis

The job analysis step in minicourse development involves defining the specific tasks performed and collecting subject matter expert (SME) judgments of task importance. In some cases, minicourses have been planned and developed for jobs in which there were few or no incumbents. In these instances, SMEs consisted of job planners and technical personnel familiar with the requirements of the job. In addition, training developers served as SMEs. Where incumbents were available, formal task surveys have been used to collect task importance and frequency ratings.

Review and Analysis of Training

The analysis of training content focuses primarily on the relationship between training material and job tasks. That is, a determination is made as to which tasks are represented by the various components of training. In addition, emphasis is placed on identifying the materials that do not require specialized previous training or knowledge to learn. Thus, minicourses can be administered to applicants with no previous experience with the technology being addressed. For reasons of administrative feasibility, minicourses have tended to focus on conceptual material as opposed to hands-on training. All minicourses are administered in employment offices by personnel without any specialized technological expertise. Because of this, emphasis is placed on identifying aspects of training that result in the knowledge necessary to perform specific tasks on the job as opposed to actual task performance. In some cases, analyses of training have included the use of taxonomies (e.g., Bloom, 1974), so that minicourse content could be systematically compared with full training course content.

Development of Minicourse Content

Two types of minicourse materials have been developed. The first type is highly specific material that matches training content very closely. An example would be material relevant to a specific piece of equipment. This type of material is obviously extremely face-valid for the job in question and results in a good match between the selection procedure content and the training content. A drawback of highly specific content is that it may quickly become obsolete as technology changes (e.g., the equipment changes). The second type of material tends to be more generic in nature and has a longer "half-life," in the sense that it will remain relevant despite technological change. For example, a minicourse module on understanding binary, octal, hexadecimal, and decimal numbering systems was developed for one minicourse. This type of module is generic enough to survive specific changes in technology, yet still results in a strong relationship between minicourse content, training content, and job content.

Minicourses are typically divided into a number of specific modules that are presented to the candidate in the form of programmed instruction. Each module includes the opportunity for the candidate to practice answering questions with feedback. A timed, end-of-module test accompanies each specific module and has consisted primarily of multiple-choice questions. Material tends to be introductory in nature with respect to the technology addressed for obvious reasons. Minicourses are administered to candidates with a wide variety of backgrounds, and no prior specialized knowledge is assumed. For this reason it is difficult to go too far beyond the introductory stage in a minicourse. Although minicourses are generally much longer than the usual paper-and-pencil test, it is desirable for administrative reasons to keep minicourse length under 1 working day. This constraint limits the amount of material that can be effectively presented to about four modules.

Linking Minicourse Content to Training and Job Content

SMEs are used to quantify the linkage between specific minicourse content (including test items) to training content and to specific tasks performed on the job. If possible, incumbents, supervisors, or both serve as SMEs for this linkage process. For jobs without any current incumbents, experts have included system designers, training developers, and others familiar with the job and training. The end product of this analysis is a table indicating the linkages among minicourse content, training content, and specific job tasks.

Pretesting

Once minicourse materials have been developed, reviewed, and edited, a sample of candidates is identified and asked to take the minicourse under pretest conditions. The policy established for use of the resulting test scores has typically been advantageous to these volunteer candidates. Candidates who pass the test are considered passing in the full operational sense; candidates who fail are given an opportunity to retake the test with no penalty as soon as the minicourse is implemented. Pretest data are used to conduct item analyses and generate normative data for scaling purposes. It should be noted that for some minicourses an equally weighted combination of time-to-complete and test performance has been used as a scoring metric. Thus, in some cases both time-to-complete data and test performance are included in the analysis.

Implementation and Criterion-Related Validation

After analysis of pretest data has been completed, interim passing scores are set and the minicourse is implemented. The interim cutoffs are set on a strictly normative basis, because no criterion data are available. If possible, follow-up criterion-related validation is done, with a recognition that restriction in range because of explicit selection has occurred. Criteria for the studies have included both training performance measures and job performance. Sample sizes have typically been fairly small because they are dependent on the flow of candidates into the job. On completion of the criterion-related study, SMEs are asked to review the results and reconsider the interim cutoffs. In practice, the final selection ratios have ranged from .5 to .2.

The developmental strategy that is followed allows minicourses to be implemented almost simultaneously with the introduction of a new position and a new training course. A major advantage of minicourses is this feature of implementation on a timely basis. The follow-up criterion-related validity studies have been done, where possible, to lend further support to the content validation strategy that is followed in minicourse development.

So far, American Telephone and Telegraph (AT&T) and the divested Bell System companies have had experience with seven different minicourse-type selection procedures: (a) the Electronic Switching Systems (ESS) Minicourse for central office switching technicians, (b) the Electronic System Minicourse (ESM), a more generic minicourse for all technicians working on digital, electronic equipment, (c) the Digital Cable Technologies Minicourse (DCTM) designed for technicians working on fiber optic and digital transmission systems, (d) the Special Services Minicourse (SSC) for technicians working on private and special customer circuits, (e) the Maintenance Administrator Minicourse (MAC) for technical clerks who test local subscriber lines, (f) the Loop Assignment Center (LAC) Minicourse designed to select personnel who deal with a computerized system that handles the assignment of circuits and other telephone network facilities, and (g) the Berger Aptitude for Programming Test (BAPT; Berger, 1987) used to select software support-technicians and programmers. The BAPT is one exception to the general rule of minicourse development, in that it is a standardized selection procedure that was developed outside of AT&T. It was included, however, because it shares common elements with the other minicourses, principally the presentation of content-relevant material and the assessment of examinee learning of this material. Table 1 summarizes descriptive data for each minicourse, including the length of the minicourse, the number of modules included, and the target jobs for each minicourse.

RESULTS FOR CRITERION-RELATED VALIDATION OF MINICOURSES

Although the approach outlined above for minicourse development has been largely adhered to in the developmental process, it has not been possible to do empirical criterion-related validation studies for all of the minicourses. The reliabilities for minicourses are generally high, typically averaging in the high .80s to the low .90s, when parallel forms are compared. A number of predictive validity studies have been done and are

TABLE 1
Summary of Minicourses Developed at AT&T and Bell Companies

Minicourse	Length	Modules	Target/Job
ESS-MC	3 days	7	ESS switching techs
ESM	6 hr	4	ESS, PBX minicomputer Techs
DCTM	6 hr	4	Cable repair techs, fiber optics, loop electronics
SSC-MC	6 hr	5	Special services testers
MA-MC	4 hr	4	Loop testers
BAPT (Psychometrics)	2 hr	3	Software support techs programmers
LAC	3 hr	4	Facilities assigners

Note. ESS-MC = Electronic Switching Systems Minicourse; ESM = Electronic Systems Minicourse; DCTM = Digital Cable Technologies Minicourse; SSC = Special Service Center; MA = Maintenance Administrator; BAPT = Berger Aptitude for Programming Test; LAC = Loop Assignment Center.

TABLE 2
Results of Criterion-Related Validity Studies of AT&T and Bell Minicourses

Minicourse	Criterion	N	Validity
ESS	Time to complete training	51	.59
EMS	Electronics training performance	68	.50
LAC	LAC training performance	109	.60
LAC	Job performance rating	77	.39
BAPT	Performance in programmer training	44	.72
ESM	Performance in programmer training	36	.56

Note. All validity coefficients are significant ($p < .01$). ESS = Electronic Switching Systems; ESM = Electronic Systems Minicourse; LAC = Loop Assignment Center; BAPT = Berger Aptitude for Programming Test.

summarized in Table 2. The criteria for these studies included time-to-complete, self-paced training in electronics (ESS and ESM), programming proficiency measures (ESM and BAPT), and ratings of training performance and job proficiency (LAC minicourse). The average coefficient for the validity studies was .62, which includes one coefficient for actual on-the-job performance ($r = .39$).

Minicourses are ideally designed to be second-stage selection procedures and, in fact, are used this way within AT&T. One might question whether minicourses add anything to prediction beyond a first-stage general ability test. In order to answer this question it is necessary to test the incremental validity that is due to the addition of minicourse scores to general ability test scores. Unfortunately, the data necessary to test this hypothesis were available for only two of the cases presented in Table 2. In both cases, programming proficiency was the criterion. A general ability test battery used to select technical personnel was entered first, and the incremental variance explained when each of two minicourses added was tested. The general ability test had a correlation of .54 with the criterion and correlations of .57 and .60 with BAPT and ESM, respectively. The increment in the squared multiple correlation because of the addition of ESM was .09, $F(1, 31) = 4.34, p < .05$. The addition of the BAPT as the second predictor resulted in an increment in R^2 of .25, $F(1, 41) = 22.59, p < .001$. Thus, in the two instances where it was possible to assess them, the contributions of minicourses added significantly to prediction.

As noted earlier, the scoring system for most of the minicourses was a combination of time-to-complete and total score. Candidates taking minicourses under these conditions were required to have a minimum of approximately 60% correct on each module test in order to proceed to the next unit. This requirement obviated the potential strategy of applicants rushing through the entire minicourse to maximize the speed component of their score. Previous research (Reilly & Manese, 1979) had indicated that time-to-complete and test performance had extremely low correlations, providing for an optimal predictive contribution of each variable.

GENERALIZABILITY OF THE AT&T FINDINGS: A META-ANALYSIS

Minicourses are one example of an approach more generally defined as *trainability testing*. The concept of trainability testing has some historical antecedents in the research of McGehee (1948), who reported biserial correlations ranging from .60 to .84 between quantity of output in eight successive production periods during on-the-job training and the time required to reach a learning criterion. A later study by Gordon and Cohen (1973) found that early performance in a welding program was a good predictor of the time taken to complete the entire training course. Moreover, Siegal and Bergman (1975) demonstrated a significant relationship between a sample of training performance and on-the-job performance. Subsequent reports by Robertson and Downs (1979), Robertson and Mindel (1980), and Siegal (1983) further supported this approach.

A review of published and unpublished validity studies in various data bases was conducted to identify coefficients for trainability tests. All coefficients were reported for independent samples with the exception of two coefficients reported by Muller (1983) that were based on two overlapping samples. In samples where more than one criterion was available, validities were averaged, or, if a summary criterion was included, that validity was analyzed. The most frequent criterion of training performance was rated training proficiency (20 coefficients). Of the remaining coefficients, 10 represented correlations with time-to-complete, self-paced training, and 2 were based on correlations with objective proficiency measures. Of the 13 coefficients with job performance, 11 were based on correlations with supervisory ratings, and 2 were based on correlations with objective performance measures. The Appendix lists the sources of all validity coefficients analyzed.

All studies included in the meta-analysis had a trainability test as a predictor. For purposes of inclusion in the meta-analysis, a trainability test was defined as a measure derived from the performance of an examinee on a content-oriented sample of training tasks or material. A large number of coefficients came from studies done in the United Kingdom (e.g., Robertson & Downs, 1979), where trainability tests have been developed by governmental agencies. The remaining coefficients came from studies done in the U.S. military, AT&T, and miscellaneous studies published in journals.

A total of 51 coefficients, including the AT&T coefficients, was identified. Over all samples and all criteria the average validity was .46. For validities with on-the-job performance as a criterion the average validity was .39, and for studies where training performance was the criterion the average validity was .49. None of these coefficients were corrected for restriction in range, but it should be noted that the job performance criterion studies were not only subject to the usual explicit and incidental selection occurring at the time of employment but were also subject to further restriction in range because of dropout and failure in training. Table 3 summarizes the meta-analytic results (Hunter, Schmidt, & Jackson, 1982) with respect to these 51 coefficients. It can be seen that sampling error explained only 27% of the variance in coefficients overall, 33% of the variance in validities when training performance was the criterion, but 70% when job performance was the criterion. The contributions of range restriction and criterion error of measurement to variance were not analyzed because these data were rarely reported and it was not felt that any other assumed distributions would be suitable.

The results suggest that validities are more generalizable for job performance criteria than for training criteria. This finding is not surprising, because all trainability tests measure some general learning ability that has been demonstrated to be a good predictor of job performance in almost all settings (Hunter, 1986). The larger amount of situation-specific validity for training criteria might be due to the quality of the mini-course content, the quality of training, or to a combination of these factors. In any case, the average uncorrected validities for training criteria are large enough to indicate generalizability despite the large amount of situation-specific variance.

Under the same assumptions used by Hunter and Hunter (1984), the average validities were corrected for criterion error of measurement. Training criterion reliability was assumed to have an upper limit of .8, and job performance criterion reliability was assumed to have an upper limit of .6. The corrected coefficients are nearly identical with those reported by Hunter and Hunter (1984) for work sample and ability tests. For training criteria the average corrected validity was .55, and for job performance the corrected validity was .50. Over all samples the average corrected weighted validity was .53, as compared with the averages of .54 for work samples and .53 for ability tests reported by Hunter and Hunter (1984). The 90% credibility values of .35 overall performance, .41 for job performance, and .36 for training performance (see Table 3) lend further support to the generalizability of trainability test validity.

DISCUSSION

The similarity of the average coefficients to work sample and ability tests should

TABLE 3
Summary of Meta-Analysis Results

Sample	$\bar{r}$	$\bar{\rho}$	S_r^2	σ_ρ^2	%	Σn_i	k	σ_ρ	90% credibility value
Criterion									
Job performance	.39	.50	.017	.005	70	800	13	.071	.41
Training performance	.49	.55	.032	.021	33	2089	38	.146	.36
Total	.46	.53	.030	.019	27	2889	51	.137	.35

Note. $\bar{r}$ = mean uncorrected validity weighted by sample size; $\bar{\rho} = r$ corrected for criterion unreliability; S_r^2 = variance of validities weighted by sample size; σ_ρ^2 = variance of validities corrected for sampling error; Σn_i = total sample size; k = number of coefficients; % = percentage of variance explained by sampling error.

not be surprising because trainability tests share elements of both types of selection procedures. Minicourse performance, as noted above, is partly a function of general learning ability. Minicourses can also be viewed as one form of a work sample test. As Asher and Sciarrino (1974) have noted, the more features there are in common between the predictor and the criterion, the higher the validity is likely to be. The AT&T model, which derives the minicourse content directly from training, resulted in relatively high coefficients when the criterion was training performance.

The constraints operating for the target jobs at AT&T made it difficult for even so large an employer to conduct criterion-related validity studies. However, it was felt to be important to do criterion-related studies despite the imperfect circumstances. Guion (1978) has noted the problem of inferring validity from content relevance alone, and Tenopyr (1977) has noted that a central issue in content-oriented validity is the extent to which content-relevance provides evidence of construct validity. Thus, the minicourse approach at AT&T, which includes criterion-related followups if possible, addresses the issues of predictive and construct validity as well as content validity.

The empirical results shown in Table 2 are only a small part of the overall AT&T experience with the minicourse approach. Some of the other outcomes are more difficult to quantify. For example, although no minicourse has been directly challenged in court, there have been a few labor arbitration hearings on the subject of minicourse validity, and in every one that has been heard the use of the minicourse by the company to make promotion and transfer decisions has been upheld. (Traditionally, AT&T labor contracts have provided for the selection of the most-senior qualified candidate, where qualifications may be based on test performance.) Minicourses also have extremely good face validity because they involve learning the actual concepts and technology that are used in training and on the job. This face validity may account for the relative lack of legal challenges to minicourse validity. Properly developed minicourses also possess a solid base of content validity. Finally, the acceptance by the field of the minicourse approach has been remarkably good. This has been most clearly manifested by the continuing requests received by AT&T's Human Resources Department to develop minicourses for specific technologies within the predivestiture Bell System.

Two other aspects of the application of minicourses within AT&T should be noted. The first is the realistic preview aspect of the minicourses. Because a minicourse exposes individuals to the same technology that they will encounter on the job, it does give individuals a certain amount of realistic exposure to job content. Although only anecdotal evidence of this realistic preview feature of minicourses exists at this time, reports from both AT&T and elsewhere (Downs, Farr, & Colbeck, 1978) suggest that applicants taking trainability tests are, in many cases, better able to make informed decisions about their suitability for a particular job.

The economic benefits of minicourses are considerable even considering the fairly expensive (approximately $100 per applicant) cost of administration. Not only is job performance improved, resulting in gains from increased productivity, but more immediate benefits are observed in training. Decreased failure rates and shorter time to complete self-paced training result in direct savings that can be easily documented (Israelski, 1987; Reilly and Manese, 1979). It should be noted that minicourses as they have been used at AT&T are second-stage selection devices. Normally, applicants pass a general ability battery before reaching a minicourse test. Thus, a relatively inexpensive paper-and-pencil measure is used to prescreen for the more expensive minicourse procedures.

The question as to whether minicourses, in the long run, can add anything to general ability tests could not be answered conclusively using these data, but some data were presented suggesting an affirmative conclusion. In another direct comparison, Gordon & Kleiman (1976) found a trainability test to be superior to an aptitude test for predicting training performance in a police academy.

The estimates of population validity offer another way of answering this question. Trainability tests have a population validity approximately equal to the population validity for cognitive tests reported by Hunter and Hunter (1984). Even with relatively high intercorrelations between the two types of measures, trainability tests would lead to a substantial increment in the multiple correlation. With an intercorrelation of .6 between ability and trainability tests, for example, the increment in the squared multiple correlation would be .07, an increment large enough to be significant with samples as small as 50 subjects. Given the approximately equal population validities for general ability and trainability tests, it can be argued that, unless there is complete overlap (excepting error of measurement) between the two types of measures, trainability tests will add to validity. It is reasonable to assume that some of the additional variance explained by trainability tests is a function of the close match between tests and training or job tasks.

The AT&T experience shows that minicourses are a valid alternative to other types of predictors for jobs that have few or no incumbents and involve learning new technology. A few important disadvantages of minicourses should be noted, however. One obvious disadvantage is the time and cost to administer the AT&T-type minicourse. The administrative requirements can be even more burdensome if time is used as a performance metric. This requires logging each candidate's start and finish time for each module. A second disadvantage to minicourses is more serious and concerns the "half-life" of the typical minicourse. Because minicourse content is intended to reflect the requirements of training and the job, changes in technology may decrease the content relevance of the minicourse. Minicourse content must be periodically reviewed and compared with job requirements and updated if necessary. As changes become more and more extensive it may be necessary to renorm and possibly to revalidate the minicourse. Another disadvantage lies in the similarity of the minicourse materials with the actual training material. If job candidates are current employees, some of whom may gain access to the training materials, there is a possibility that some applicants may gain what may be perceived as an unfair advantage on the minicourse. This problem is probably best handled by sacrificing content relevance to some extent and not making the minicourse exactly the same as the training. In any event, test items used in training should not be used in the minicourse.

REFERENCES

Asher, J. J., & Sciarrino, J. A. (1974). Realistic work sample tests: A review. *Personnel Psychology, 27,* 519–533.

Berger, F. R. (1987). *Research information on the Berger Aptitude for Programming Test.* Sherman Oaks, CA: Psychometrics.

Bloom, B. S. (Ed.). (1974). *Taxonomy of educational objectives: Handbook I. Cognitive domain.* New York: McKay.

Downs, S., Farr, R. M., & Colbeck, L. (1978). Self-appraisal: A convergence of selection and guidance. *Journal of Occupational Psychology, 51,* 271–278.

Gordon, M. E., & Cohen, S. L. (1973). Training behavior as a predictor of trainability. *Personnel Psychology, 26,* 261–272.

Gordon, M. E., & Kleiman, L. S. (1976). The prediction of trainability using a work sample test and an aptitude test: A direct comparison. *Personnel Psychology, 29,* 243–253.

Guion, R. M. (1978). Scoring of content domain samples: The problem of fairness. *Journal of Applied Psychology, 63,* 499–506.

Hunter, J. E. (1986). Cognitive ability, cognitive aptitudes, job knowledge and job performance. *Journal of Vocational Behavior, 29,* 340–362.

Hunter, J. E., & Hunter, R. F. (1984). Validity and utility of alternative predictors of job performance. *Psychological Bulletin, 96,* 72–98.

Hunter, J. E., Schmidt, F. L., & Jackson, G. B. (1982). *Meta-analysis: Cumulating research findings across studies.* Beverly Hills, CA: Sage.

Israelski, E. W. (1987, April). *AT&T experience with minicourses as selection devices.* Paper presented at the 2nd Annual Convention of the Society for Industrial and Organizational Psychology, Atlanta, GA.

McGehee, W. (1948). Cutting training waste. *Personnel Psychology, 1,* 331–340.

Muller, M. J. (1983). *Prediction of training performance for the software support technician position.* Unpublished manuscript, American Telephone & Telegraph, Short Hills, NJ.

Reilly, R. R., & Manese, W. R. (1979). The validation of a minicourse for telephone company switching technicians. *Personnel Psychology, 32,* 83–90.

Robertson, I., & Downs, S. (1979). Learning and the prediction of performance: Development of trainability testing in the United Kingdom. *Journal of Applied Psychology, 64,* 42–50.

Robertson, I., & Mindel, R. M. (1980). A study of trainability testing. *Journal of Occupational Psychology, 53,* 131–138.

Siegal, A. F. (1983, August). *Job sample miniature training and evaluation.* Paper presented at the

91st Annual Convention of the American Psychological Association, Anaheim, CA.

Siegal, A. F., & Bergman, B. A. (1975). A job learning approach to performance prediction. *Personnel Psychology, 28,* 325–339.

Tenopyr, M. L. (1977). Content–construct confusion. *Personnel Psychology, 30,* 47–54.

APPENDIX: STUDIES CONTRIBUTING COEFFICIENTS FOR THE META-ANALYSIS
(Number of Coefficients Shown in Parentheses)

Fiks, A. I., Bawden, H., Davies, S., Gaspari, J., Meek, A., & Weinstock, A. (1976). Public assistance worker job trial. (Final Technical Report). Philadelphia, PA: Jewish Employment and Vocational Service, Job Trials Research Center. (1)

Gordon, M. E., & Cohen, S. L. (1973). Training behavior as a predictor of trainability. *Personnel Psychology, 26,* 261–272. (3)

Gordon, M. E., & Kleiman, L. S. (1976). The prediction of trainability using a work sample test and an aptitude test: A direct comparison. *Personnel Psychology, 29,* 243–253. (4)

Maclane, C. N. (1980, September). *A miniature training and evaluation approach to entry-level selection.* Paper presented to the 88th Annual Convention of the American Psychological Association, Montreal, Quebec, Canada. (1)

Muller, M. J. (1983). *Prediction of training performance for the software support technician position.* Unpublished manuscript, American Telephone & Telegraph Co., Short Hills, NJ. (2)

Reilly, R. R. (1985). *Documentation of validity for the Electronic Systems Minicourse.* Unpublished manuscript, American Telephone & Telegraph Co., Short Hills, NJ. (4)

Reilly, R. R., & Manese, W. R. (1979). The validation of a minicourse for telephone company switching technicians. *Personnel Psychology, 32,* 83–90. (1)

Robertson, I., & Downs, S. (1979). Learning and the prediction of performance: Development of trainability testing in the United Kingdom. *Journal of Applied Psychology, 64,* 42–50. (22)

Robertson, L., & Mindel, R. M. (1980). A study of trainability testing. *Journal of Occupational Psychology, 53,* 131–138. (6)

Siegal, A. I. (1983). *Trainability testing for Navy selection and classification (NPRDC.TR 85-25).* San Diego, CA: Navy Personnel Research and Development Center. (3)

Siegal, A. F., & Bergman, B. A. (1975). A job learning approach to performance prediction. *Personnel Psychology, 28,* 325–339. (2)

Zink, D. L. (1987). *Validation of the FACS-LAC Minicourse.* Unpublished manuscript, Bellcore, Inc., Livingston, NJ. (2)

Richard R. Reilly is affiliated with Stevens Institute of Technology. Edmond W. Israelski is employed by American Telephone and Telegraph, Morristown, New Jersey. The authors thank Mary L. Tenopyr for her help and guidance in conducting the test development and validation work at AT&T and for her helpful comments on an earlier version of this article. They also thank all of the consultants and AT&T personnel who worked on various minicourses.

Cases

Freida Mae Jones
Martin R. Moser

Freida Mae Jones was born in her grandmother's Georgia farmhouse on June 1, 1949. She was the sixth of George and Ella Jones's ten children. Mr. and Mrs. Jones moved to New York City when Freida was four because they felt that the educational and career opportunities for their children would be better in the North. With the help of some cousins, they settled in a five-room apartment in the Bronx. George worked as a janitor at Lincoln Memorial Hospital, and Ella was a part-time housekeeper in a nearby neighborhood. George and Ella were conservative, strict parents. They kept a close watch on their children's activities and demanded they be home by a certain hour. The Joneses believed that because they were black, the children would have to perform and behave better than their peers to be successful. They believed that their children's education would be the most important factor in their success as adults.

Freida entered Memorial High School, a racially integrated public school, in September 1963. Seventy percent of the student body was Caucasian, 20 percent black, and 10 percent Hispanic. About 60 percent of the graduates went on to college. Of this 60 percent, 4 percent were black and Hispanic and all were male. In the middle of her senior year, Freida was the top student in her class. Following school regulations, Freida met with her guidance counselor to discuss her plans upon graduation. The counselor advised her to consider training in a "practical" field such as housekeeping, cooking, or sewing, so that she could find a job.

George and Ella Jones were furious when Freida told them what the counselor had advised. Ella said, "Don't they see what they are doing? Freida is the top-rated student in her whole class and they are telling her to become a manual worker. She showed that she has a fine mind and can work better than any of her classmates and still she is told not to become anybody in this world. It's really not any different in the North than back home in Georgia, except that they don't try to hide it down South. They want her to throw away her fine mind because she is a black girl and not a white boy. I'm going to go up to her school tomorrow and talk to the principal."

As a result of Mrs. Jones's visit to the principal, Freida was assisted in applying to ten Eastern colleges, each of which offered her full scholarships. In September 1966, Freida entered Werbley Col-

---

Source: From "Freida Mae Jones" by Martin R. Moser, *Journal of Management Case Studies.* Copyright Martin R. Moser, 1985. Reprinted by permission of the author.

All names in this article are fictitious.

lege, an exclusive private women's college in Massachusetts. In 1970, Freida graduated summa cum laude in history. She decided to return to New York to teach grade school in the city's public school system. Freida was unable to obtain a full-time position, so she substituted. She also enrolled as a part-time student in Columbia University's Graduate School of Education. In 1975 she had attained her Master of Arts degree in Teaching from Columbia but could not find a permanent teaching job. New York City was laying off teachers and had instituted a hiring freeze because of the city's financial problems.

Feeling frustrated about her future as a teacher, Freida decided to get an MBA. She thought that there was more opportunity in business than in education. Churchill Business School, a small, prestigious school located in upstate New York, accepted Freida into its MBA program.

Freida completed her MBA in 1977 and accepted an entry-level position at the Industrialist World Bank of Boston in a fast-track management development program. The three-year program introduced her to all facets of bank operations, from telling to loan training and operations management. She was rotated to branch offices throughout New England. After completing the program she became an assistant manager for branch operations in the West Springfield branch office.

During her second year in the program, Freida had met James Walker, a black doctoral student in business administration at the University of Massachusetts. Her assignment to West Springfield precipitated their decision to get married. They originally anticipated that they would marry when James finished his doctorate and could move to Boston. Instead, they decided he would pursue a job in the Springfield–Hartford area.

Freida was not only the first black but also the first woman to hold an executive position in the West Springfield branch office. Throughout the training program Freida felt somewhat uneasy although she did very well. There were six other blacks in the program, five men and one woman, and she found support and comfort in sharing her feelings with them. The group spent much of their free time together. Freida had hoped that she would be located near one or more of the group when she went out into the "real world." She felt that although she was able to share her feelings about work with James, he did not have the full appreciation or understanding of her coworkers. However, the nearest group member was located one hundred miles away.

Freida's boss in Springfield was Stan Luboda, a fifty-five-year-old native New Englander. Freida felt that he treated her differently than he did the other trainees. He always tried to help her and took a lot of time (too much, according to Freida) explaining things to her. Freida felt that he was treating her like a child and not like an intelligent and able professional.

"I'm really getting frustrated and angry about what is happening at the bank," Freida said to her husband. "The people don't even realize it, but their prejudice comes through all the time. I feel as if I have to fight all the time just to start off even. Luboda gives Paul Cohen more responsibility than me and we both started at the same time, with the same amount of training. He's meeting customers alone and Luboda has accompanied me to each meeting I've had with a customer."

"I run into the same thing at school," said James. "The people don't even know that they are doing it. The other day I met with a professor on my dissertation committee. I've known and worked with him for over three years. He said he wanted to talk with me about a memo he had received. I asked him what it was about and he said that the records office wanted to know about my absence during the spring semester. He said that I had to sign some forms. He had me confused with Martin Jordan, another black student. Then he realized that it wasn't me, but Jordan he wanted. All I could think was that we all must look alike to him. I was angry. Maybe it was an honest mistake on his part, but whenever something like that happens, and it happens often, it gets me really angry."

"Something like that happened to me," said Freida. "I was using the copy machine, and Luboda's secretary was talking to someone in the hall. She had just gotten a haircut and was saying that her hair was now like Freida's — short and kinky — and that she would have to talk to me about how to take care of it. Luckily, my back was to her. I bit my lip and went on with my business. Maybe she was trying to be cute, because I know she saw me standing there, but comments like that are not cute, they are racist."

"I don't know what to do," said James. "I try to keep things in perspective. Unless people interfere with my progress, I try to let it slide. I only have so much energy and it doesn't make sense to waste it on people who don't matter. But that doesn't make it any easier to function in a racist environment. People don't realize that they are being racist. But a lot of times their expectations of black people or women, or whatever, are different because of skin color or gender. They expect you to be different, although if you were to ask them they would say that they don't. In fact, they would be highly offended if you implied that they were racist or sexist. They don't see themselves that way."

"Luboda is interfering with my progress," said Freida. "The kinds of experiences I have now will have a direct effect on my career advancement. If decisions are being made because I am black or a woman, then they are racially and sexually biased. It's the same kind of attitude that the guidance counselor had when I was in high school, although not as blatant."

In September 1980, Freida decided to speak to Luboda about his treatment of her. She met with him in his office. "Mr. Luboda, there is something that I would like to discuss with you, and I feel a little uncomfortable because I'm not sure how you will respond to what I am going to say."

"I want you to feel that you can trust me," said Luboda. "I am anxious to help you in any way I can."

"I feel that you treat me differently than you treat the other people around here," said Freida. "I feel that you are overcautious with me, that you always try to help me, and never let me do anything on my own."

"I always try to help the new people around here," answered Luboda. "I'm not treating you any differently than I treat any other person. I think that you are being a little too sensitive. Do you think that I treat you differently because you are black?"

"The thought had occurred to me," said Freida. "Paul Cohen started here the same time that I did and he has much more responsibility than I do." (Cohen was already handling accounts on his own, while Freida had not yet been given that responsibility.)

"Freida, I know you are not a naive person," said Luboda. "You know the way the world works. There are some things which need to be taken more slowly than others. There are some assignments for which Cohen has been given more responsibility than you, and there are some assignments for which you are given more responsibility than Cohen. I try to put you where you do the most good."

"What you are saying is that Cohen gets the more visible, customer contact assignments and I get the behind-the-scenes running of the operations assignments," said Freida. "I'm not naive, but I'm also not stupid either. Your decisions are unfair. Cohen's career will advance more quickly than mine because of the assignments that he gets."

"Freida, that is not true," said Luboda. "Your career will not be hurt because you are getting different responsibilities than Cohen. You both need the different kinds of experiences you are getting. And you have to face the reality of the banking business. We are in a conservative business. When we speak to customers we need to gain their confidence, and we put the best people for the job in the positions to achieve that end. If we don't get their confidence they can go down the street to our competitors and do business with them. Their services are no different than ours. It's a competitive business in which you need every edge you have. It's going to take time for people to change some of their attitudes about whom they borrow money from or where they put their money. I can't change the way people feel. I am running a business, but believe me I won't make any decisions that are detrimental to you or to the bank. There is an important place for you here at the bank. Remember, you have to use your skills to the best advantage of the bank as well as your career."

"So what you are saying is that all things being equal, except my gender and my race, that Cohen will get different treatment than me in terms of assignments," said Freida.

"You're making it sound like I am making a racist and sexist decision," said Luboda. "I'm making a business decision utilizing the resources at my disposal and the market situation in which I must operate. You know exactly what I am talking about. What would you do if you were in my position?"

Martin R. Moser is professor of business policy, College of Management Science, University of Lowell.

Harmard Industries
K. Michele Kacmar

It was well past midnight on a Friday night when Chuck Burns, director of personnel selection for Harmard Industries, closed his briefcase and prepared to head for the parking lot. His work schedule had been hectic ever since he had been

"Harmard Industries" by K. Michele Kacmar is reprinted by permission of the author.

informed of the decision to update the company's selection procedures. With the written proposal due first thing Monday morning, however, this would be one of his last late evenings.

When Chuck was first told of the decision to update the selection procedures, he thought the decision was a good one. After all, no changes to the procedures had been made in over five years and an update was in order. Nevertheless, the nature of the change that he was asked to investigate caused him to have second thoughts.

Whereas current tests and procedures used to screen applicants would be examined and revised, the major change would be the addition of a physical examination. The need for this addition surfaced when the bill for the group insurance policy for the new fiscal year arrived.

Over the last few years, the cost of insurance coverage for employees had increased at a phenomenal rate. One of the major causes, according to a report provided by the insurance company, was long-term illnesses. Specifically, long-term hospitalization for such diseases as cancer, emphysema, and heart trouble had increased the average hospital stay from four days to twenty-four days over the past three years. The cost of this increase was being passed on to Harmard.

One solution to the high premium cost was to require a physical examination for all new employees. If a company required a pre-employment physical, the insurance company would discount the rate charged to employers. To qualify for the discounted rate, however, the physical examination had to include not only tests for heart trouble, cancer, and emphysema, but also a test for acquired immune deficiency syndrome (AIDS).

According to the insurance company's report, The American Council of Life Insurance had found that individuals who test positive for the AIDS antibody have a twenty times greater chance of dying within five years than those who do not. The insurance company also presented evidence indicating that health benefit claims were heavily concentrated in the first and second year after the issuance of policies.

Chuck was troubled by considerations other than lower insurance costs. Could the company legally use the test results as a screening technique? He knew that a June 1986 Justice Department memorandum stated that acting on the fear of contagion was not prohibited by federal law nor was it considered discrimination. However, he also knew that thousands of people were fighting for the rights of AIDS patients and that over twenty states and cities have legislated to make AIDS a protected handicap.

Further, because the insurance company refused to offer the discounted rate to anyone who was not tested or who tested positive for AIDS, Harmard would have to pay a much higher insurance premium for those individuals if they were hired. Would Harmard's top management be willing to accept this alternative?

To determine the feasibility of adding a physical examination to the selection procedure, Chuck decided to perform a cost analysis. His first step was to send letters to local physicians in an effort to determine their level of interest in providing pre-employment physical examinations. Over the past month, Chuck had been contacting and interviewing the physicians who had responded to the letter. With every interview, new problems arose.

One recurring problem was the lack of enthusiasm the physicians showed when the AIDS test was mentioned. They were reluctant to agree to provide an AIDS test due to the complications that arose when a test came back positive, such as who was responsible for informing the person of the test results.

As a second step in his cost analysis, Chuck wanted to determine how the applicants might respond to being asked to submit to an AIDS test. To answer this question, he surveyed the current employees to determine how they would have felt if they had been asked to submit to such a test prior to employment. Respondents were assured that they would not be required to submit to an examination because they were already insured by the insurance company, and that their answers were simply to help determine the impact of requiring this type of test.

Results from the survey indicated that more than 75 percent would be offended if asked to submit to an AIDS test. Also, more than 35 percent would have refused to take the test and would not have elected to work for the company.

Chuck's third step in analyzing the costs was to speak with several corporate lawyers concerning the possibility of legal actions against Harmard if individuals were asked to submit to an AIDS test. Testing was not recommended. Violation of individual's confidentiality, especially because a positive test does not mean that the person will develop AIDS, was the reason most often cited for not recommending an AIDS test.

With his analysis complete, Chuck assembled the information and tried to make sense of it. The first thing he needed to determine was how much the addition of a pre-employment physical examination would increase the costs of the Harmard's selection procedures. There were several costs to consider: examination costs, human resource costs, insurance costs, and potential legal costs.

The examination costs would include the fee for the physician performing the examination as well as any laboratory fees for tests. The physicians that Chuck interviewed returned price quotes that ranged from $150 to $225 plus lab fees. Lab fees were estimated to range from $75 to $150.

Human resource costs were harder to determine. As Chuck ascertained from the survey of current employees, approximately one-third of the employees would have opted to not accept the job offer if they had been asked to submit to an AIDS test. If these employees could be considered representative of new recruits, the number of employees to be recruited would increase by one-third in order to fill all the open jobs. This will add to overall recruitment costs.

An additional human resource cost would be the cost of replacing current staff who quit when they realize that they are working side by side with AIDS victims. Even though there have been no reported cases of AIDS caused by casual contact, people have irrational fears. For example, parents have fought to keep children with AIDS out of their children's classrooms.

The increased costs for insurance would depend on the number of individuals who tested positive for AIDS. In March 1987, Chuck read in *Business Week* that the Centers for Disease Control in Atlanta estimated that 1.5 million Americans already carry the AIDS virus. The article also indicated that by 1991 about 5 percent of the AIDS cases will be heterosexuals who do not use intravenous drugs and who have not received a blood transfusion.

The legal costs would also be difficult to determine. The number of lawsuits are sure to rise given the constantly changing legal grounds concerning AIDS. With the number of court cases currently being argued, what was deemed legal on Monday may be discriminatory on Wednesday and legal again on Friday. The cheapest solution for legal costs would be for Harmard to retain a lawyer on staff to protect Harmard's interests constantly. The average starting salary for a corporate lawyer, not including benefits, is approximately $85,000.

K. Michele Kacmar is assistant professor at Rensselaer Polytechnic Institute.

Readings for Professional Growth and Enrichment

Adler, P., C. K. Parsons, and S. B. Zolke (1985). "Employee Privacy: Legal and Research Developments and Implications for Personnel Administration." *Sloan Management Review* 26: 13–22.

Arvey, R. D. (1979). "Unfair Discrimination in the Employment Interview: Legal and Psychological Aspects." *Psychological Bulletin* 86: 736–765.

Ayton, E., and J. A. Belohlav (1982). "Equal Opportunity Laws: Some Common Problems." *Personnel Journal* 61: 282–285.

Baker, D. D., and D. E. Terpstra (1982). "Employee Selection: Must Every Job Test Be Validated?" *Personnel Journal* 61: 602–605.

Breauch, J. A. (1983). "Realistic Job Previews: A Critical Appraisal and Future Research Directions." *Academy of Management Review* 8: 612–619.

Breaugh, J. A. (1981). "Relationships Between Recruiting Sources and Employee Performance, Absenteeism, and Work Attitudes." *Academy of Management Journal* 24: 142–147.

Cascio, W. F., and N. F. Phillips (1979). "Performance Testing: A Rose among Thorns?" *Personnel Psychology* 32: 751–755, 759–766.

Cornelius, E. T. III (1983). "The Use of Projective Techniques in Personnel Selection." In K. M. Rowland and G. R. Ferris (eds.), *Research in Personnel and Human Resource Management*, Vol. 1. Greenwich, Conn.: JAI Press.

Curry, T. H. (1981). "A Common Sense Management Approach to Employee Selection and EEO Compliance for the Smaller Employer." *Personnel Administrator* (April): 35–38.

Heilman, M. E. (1983). "Sex Bias in Work Settings: The Lack of Fit Model." In L. L. Cummings and B. M. Staw (eds.), *Research in Organizational Behavior*, Vol. 5. Greenwich, Conn.: JAI Press.

Hogan, J., and A. M. Quigley (1986). "Physical Standards for Employment and the Courts." *American Psychologist*, 41 (November): 1193–1217.

Lowell, R. S., and J. A. De Loach (1982). "Equal Employment Opportunity: Are You Overlooking the Application Forms?" *Personnel* 59 (July–August): 49–55.

Lubliner, M. J. (1981). "Developing Recruiting Literature That Pays Off." *Personnel Administrator* (February): 51–54, 95.

Mangum, S. L. (1982). "Recruitment and Job Search: The Recruitment Tactics of Employers." *Personnel Administrator* 27: 96–102.

Michaels, P. T. (1980). "Seven Questions That Will Improve Managerial Hiring Decisions." *Personnel Journal* 59 (March): 199.

Muchinsky, P. M. (1986). "Personnel Selection Methods." In C. L. Cooper and I. T. Robertson (eds.), *International Review of Industrial and Organizational Psychology*. New York: John Wiley & Sons.

Nemec, M. M. (1981). "Recruitment Advertising — It's More than Just Help

Wanted!" *Personnel Administrator* (February): 57–60.

Pinkpank, J. C. (1983). "Preventing and Defending EEO Charges." *Personnel Administrator* 28: 35–40.

Schmidt, F. L., and J. E. Hunter (1981). "Employment Testing: Old Theories and New Research Findings." *American Psychologist* 36 (October): 1128–1137.

Schmitt, N., and B. W. Coyle (1976). "Applicant Decisions in the Employment Interview." *Journal of Applied Psychology* 61: 184–192.

Schmitt, N., and R. A. Noe (1986). "Personnel Selection and Equal Employment Opportunity." In C. L. Cooper and I. T. Robertson (eds.), *International Review of Industrial and Organizational Psychology*. New York: John Wiley & Sons.

Schmitt, N., and B. Schneider (1983). "Current Issues in Personnel Selection." In K. M. Rowland and G. R. Ferris (eds.), *Research in Personnel and Human Resources Management,* Vol. 1. Greenwich, Conn.: JAI Press.

Taylor, S. M., and D. W. Schmidt (1983). "A Process Oriented Investigation of Recruitment Source Effectiveness." *Personnel Psychology* 36: 343–354.

IV

DEVELOPING HUMAN RESOURCE PRODUCTIVITY

Readings

Kirkpatrick's Levels of Training Criteria: Thirty Years Later
George M. Alliger / Elizabeth A. Janak

About 30 years ago, Kirkpatrick published a series of articles in which he outlined four categories of measures of the effectiveness of training outcomes (Kirkpatrick, 1959a, 1959b, 1960a, 1960b). Each category was termed a "step." Step 1 was termed *reactions* and defined as trainees' "liking of" and "feelings for" a training program. Note that a reaction measure is conceived in attitudinal rather than behavioral terms. Step 2, *learning*, was defined as "principles, facts, and techniques understood and absorbed" by the trainees. Step 3 was *behavior*, defined as "using [learned principles and techniques] on the job." Step 4, *results*, was spoken of simply as the ends, goals, or "results desired . . . reduction of costs; reduction of turnover and absenteeism; reduction of grievances; increase in quality and quantity of production; or improved morale."

This proposed model or taxonomy of training evaluation criteria clearly met a felt organizational need for it quickly became well known in training departments around the country. Moreover, the field of industrial/organizational psychology has largely accepted this framework (Cascio, 1987).

The power of Kirkpatrick's model is its simplicity and its ability to help people think about training evaluation criteria. In other words, it provides a vocabulary and rough taxonomy for criteria. At the same time, Kirkpatrick's model, through its easily adopted vocabulary and a number of (often implicit) assumptions, can tend to misunderstandings and overgeneralizations. We discuss the model in the light of three assumptions that appear to be largely implicit in the minds of researchers and trainers, although to all appearances unintended by Kirkpatrick himself when the model was proposed. These three assumptions, however, have been endorsed or can be identified in the literature.

The first assumption is that the "steps" are arranged in ascending value of information provided (Newstrom, 1978). A measure of learning provides more information than does a measure of reaction, and so forth. It is, in fact, now common to see the term "levels" of criteria referred to instead of the more purely procedural term "steps" (Goldstein, 1986a; we use the term "levels" in the remainder of the article). The second assumption is that these levels of evaluation are causally linked. For example, Hamblin (1974) states, "training leads to reactions which lead to learning which leads to changes in job behavior which lead to changes in

Source: George M. Alliger and Elizabeth A. Janak, "Kirkpatrick's Levels of Training Criteria: Thirty Years Later." *Personnel Psychology* 1989, Vol. 42, pp. 331–342. Reprinted by permission of *Personnel Psychology*.

the organization." A third assumption is that the levels are positively intercorrelated. That is, a set of essentially positive interrelationships, or "positive manifold," is posited to exist among levels of training evaluation (cf. Newstrom, 1978). Each of these three assumptions about Kirkpatrick's steps appears to be codified in what has been termed the "hierarchical model" of training evaluation (Hamblin, 1974; Noe & Schmitt, 1986), where "favorable outcomes at the lowest criterion level are seen to be necessary for favorable outcomes to occur at the next higher level, and so on" (Clement, 1982).

EXAMINING THE ASSUMPTIONS

It is our belief that each of these assumptions about levels of training evaluation is problematic. We address each theoretically and then discuss a literature overview, including relevant correlations from the literature to further examine the third assumption.

Assumption 1: Each succeeding level is more informative than the last. This assumption has the flavor of reasonableness, which may explain a nearly absolute lack of discussion about it in the literature. There are, however, some questions that can be raised in regard to it. First, it is not clear that all training in organizations is meant to effect change at all four levels. Some training may be largely rewarding, spirit-building, or perquisite in nature. For example, programs designed to instill company pride or rejuvenate employees may be realistically expected to have impacts at the reaction level only. Similarly, training that is limited to inculcation of company history or philosophy may, in some cases, be best and most appropriately measured by growth in knowledge: the goal may be a knowledgeable manager, and attendant behavior change, for example, may not be of immediate interest to the evaluator.

A point worth making in this regard is that Assumption 1 can lead to a perception of Level 4 results as invariably the "best" measure, since it is highest in the hierarchy. Advocacy of the "dollar criterion" (Brogden & Taylor, 1950), having been championed in research journals (e.g., Reilly & Smither, 1985; Weekly, Frank, O'Connor, & Peters, 1985), now appears in popular practitioner journals (e.g., Fitz-enz, 1985; Sheppeck & Cohen, 1985) and management textbooks (e.g., Hall & Goodale, 1986). Such sources promise that techniques for dollar estimation of intervention effectiveness will help HRM managers to "strengthen their power and influence" (Hall & Goodale, 1986). Estimating intervention value in dollars is thus enthusiastically presented as one way to emerge from the dark ages of the "personnel" function and move into the new era of the "human resources" department, which is (in theory) happily revenue producing instead of resource draining. Nonetheless, even when practically possible, there may be times when dollar estimation is inappropriate, as when the plant manager argued against quantitative evaluation because it was important to keep the idea of the intervention in the fore (Saporito, 1986). That there is a tendency for the purely quantitative, as dollars surely are, to obscure the field of possible approaches to issues such as evaluation is attested to by Goldstein (1986b, p. 22):

> It is startling to discover that most I/O psychologists still believe that quantitative models are good while qualitative research models do not contribute. . . . [But] the continuum from good to bad does not have anchors with quantitative on the good side and qualitative on the bad side.

Assumption 2: Each level is caused by the previous level. Causality is difficult to prove or disprove. Several questions can be raised about this assumption, however. The first question is one of temporality. While Level 3 and 4 measures occur at some time after training, Levels 1 and 2 usually are administered directly after training (as well as possibly before, in the case of Level 2). Indeed, a single instrument may measure both reactions and learning (Alliger & Horowitz, 1989). There would seem, then, to be no temporal distinction between reactions and learning as far as their assessment. Why then assume the former causes the latter? Probably the rationale is that those students reacting well to training are attending to the training as well. But Lewicki's (1986) studies, for example, indicate that attending can be deleterious to learning; other psychologists have argued that people are not good at reporting their experiences of learning (Hofstadter & Dennett, 1981; Thorndike, 1935). Moreover, perhaps it is only when trainees are challenged to the point of experiencing the training as somewhat unpleasant that they learn: In such a case learning and reactions might be *negatively* correlated. Such negative correlations between Level 1 and Level 2 measures have in fact been found in educational classroom research (Remmers, Martin, & Elliot, 1949; Rodin & Rodin, 1972). Or consider that humorous lectures are liked better (Level 1) but do not cause more learning (Level 2) (Kaplan & Pascoe, 1977).

There is some reason to believe, then, that reactions may not be expected to cause learning. (This is of course more likely to the extent that reaction measures are attitudinally and not behaviorally based.) At the same time, among learning, behavior, and results, some causal links should exist. Learning often should relate to behavior since, in some cases, grasp of some principle, sequence, or facts can be important to behavior. Level 3, behaviors, should cause Level 4, results. In a reverse causality, Level 4, results, should be important to the maintenance of Level 3, behaviors, since people will tend to continue behaviors that are perceived to be effective. That is, feedback sustains the behavior-results link. Figure 1 illustrates both the traditional hierarchical causal model (Clement, 1982) and this alternative proposed causal linking among levels of criteria, where Level 1 is unrelated to the other levels, Level 2 to some degree is important in the causality of Levels 3 and 4, and Levels 3 and 4 are causally interdependent.

Assumption 3: Each succeeding level is correlated with the previous level; or, more generally, there exists a "positive manifold": all correlations among levels are positive. This assumption is clearly linked to the previous one. If each level is causally linked to the previous level, then positive correlations among measures should exist. But, considering the points already made about causal linking among levels, to what extent, is it in fact

FIGURE 1

(a) The Causality in the Hierarchical Model and (b) an Alternative Model of Causality among Kirkpatrick's Four Levels of Training Criteria

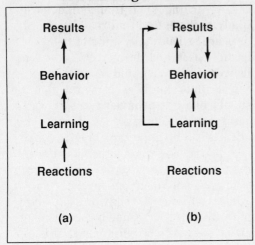

logical to assume this set of positive relationships? For example, it has been argued that perhaps no positive relationship should be predicted between reactions and learning. On the other hand, our theoretical expectations are that Levels 2, 3, and 4 would be intercorrelated.

To some degree, evidence against the validity of Assumption 3 is seen in the literature. Many evaluation studies that have evaluated training on two or more of Kirkpatrick's levels have reported different effects of training for different levels (e.g., Campion & Campion, 1987; Decker, 1982; Meyer & Raich, 1983; Moffie, Calhoon, & O'Brien, 1964; Russell, Wexley, & Hunter, 1984). This provides indirect evidence against the likelihood of finding high positive intercorrelations among levels. An examination of correlations among levels, which provide a more direct examination of Assumption 3, follows.

AN EXAMINATION OF THE INTERCORRELATION AMONG LEVELS

One way to examine empirically the accuracy of the above assumptions is to review the literature for reported correlations among criteria, categorized by Kirkpatrick's levels. Accordingly, a citation search was conducted on Kirkpatrick (1959a, 1959b, 1960a, 1960b, 1967, 1976, 1977, 1978, 1979, 1985) for the years 1969 to the present (the Social Science Citation Index began in 1969). Of the 55 articles so located, only 8 dealt with the actual evaluation of a training program; none reported correlations between levels. Consequently, a literature search was conducted for any article dealing with evaluation of a training program in several journals that might be expected to publish such articles. Journals were reviewed from 1959 to the present, if possible. Specifically, we reviewed *Academy of Management Journal, Academy of Management Review* (first published in 1976), *Journal of Applied Behavioral Science, Journal of Applied Psychology, Personnel Psychology, Personnel,* and *Training and Development Journal (Journal of ASTD* until 1966). Table 1 shows the number of articles found by journal and category. Only one relevant article was found in *Academy of Management Review;* it did not report criteria, and so that journal is not included in Table 1.

TABLE 1
Breakdown of Literature Review by Journal and Level of Criteria

	Journal						
	AMJ	JABS	JAP	PP	P	TDJ	Total
Years reviewed	59–88	65–88	59–88	59–88	59–88	60–88	
No. articles reporting training evaluation results	18	41	79	21	10	32	201
Criteria levels used							
1	1	1	2	—	1	6	11
2	8	9	29	9	2	4	61
3	5	16	34	4	2	5	66
4	—	5	3	—	2	1	11
1, 2	1	1	6	3	—	2	13
1, 3	—	6	—	1	1	10	18
1, 4	—	—	—	1	—	1	2
2, 3	1	1	4	1	—	1	8
2, 4	—	—	—	—	—	—	0
3, 4	1	1	—	—	1	—	3
1, 2, 3	1	—	1	—	1	—	3
1, 2, 4	—	—	—	—	—	—	0
1, 3, 4	—	1	—	—	—	1	2
2, 3, 4	—	—	—	—	—	—	0
1, 2, 3, 4	—	—	—	2	—	1	3
Design							
Field	14	33	38	19	10	30	144
Laboratory	4	8	41	2	0	2	57

Note: AMJ = *Academy of Management Journal,* JABS = *Journal of Applied Behavioral Science,* JAP = *Journal of Applied Psychology,* PP = *Personnel Psychology,* P = *Personnel,* TDJ = *Training and Development Journal.*

Table 1 illustrates some interesting facts. First, most articles in the journals reviewed look at a single level of evaluation. Second, in contrast to the results of Catalanello & Kirkpatrick's (1968) and Kirkpatrick's (1978) industry surveys, most studies do not focus on reactions alone. In all probability this reflects the difference between practice and publishing: in practice, most training is evaluated on the reaction level only, while editors for the reviewed journals may look for evaluation results measuring learning, behavior, or results. Third, field studies are well represented (70% of total). It should also be noted that our search turned up numerous articles that addressed training evaluation but that did not report an evaluation study. For example, *Training and Development Journal* actually published in this time period 214 articles on training evaluation; only the 32 shown in Table 1 reported an evaluation study.

Unfortunately, of the articles in Table 1, only eight reported intercorrelations among two or more levels of evaluation. Consequently, we widened our search again by following leads from reference lists in these articles and appropriate other articles and books. In the end, we found 16 articles reporting 30 appropriate correlations. Four of these articles were academic samples relating teacher ratings and student evaluations; our interest was in industrial training. Consequently, our final data set consisted of only 12 articles reporting 26 correlations. Although disappointed in this small number of usable results, we felt our search was relatively successful, given the apparent sparsity of correlational data of this type: Clement (1982) reported being unable to locate in the literature *any* correlations between levels of Kirkpatrick's model. Actually, the fact that the vast majority of articles reviewed did not report inter-level correlations, even when it was highly likely the data would have allowed such correlations to be calculated, may signify that the hierarchical model is simply assumed to be correct. Table 2 provides a list of the 11 articles, and information about the samples studied. Table 3 provides the correlations between levels of evaluation, listed in descending magnitude. Sample size-weighted mean correlations for each pair of levels are found in parentheses.

RESULTS AND DISCUSSION

As can be seen, the number of available correlations between pairs of levels ranged from one to eight. This small number of correlations means, obviously, that generalizations should be made with care. An examination of the mean sample size-weighted correlations for each cell in Table 3 indicates that Level 1 may tend to correlate only slightly with the other levels: $r_{1.2} = .07$; $r_{1.3} = .05$; and $r_{1.4} = .48$ (but this last is based on a single correlation). On the other hand, the weighted mean correlations among Levels 2, 3, and 4 could be said to be slightly larger: $r_{2.3} = .18$; $r_{2.4} = .40$; and $r_{3.4} = .19$. Is it in fact possible that attitudinal reactions to training should be considered in a category independent from such constructs as learning or behavior, as these mean correlations might suggest and as is depicted in Figure 1? The data from our literature search certainly do not warrant a definite answer to this question. For example, it is certainly possible that some of these correlations are artifactually small, due to the reduced variance typical of reaction measures (cf. Alliger & Horowitz, 1989). The variance of the reaction measures was available for only five of the articles listed in Table 2; when we examined the variance relative to the means for those measures, reduced reaction measure variance could be concluded as probable in some cases but not in others. In any case, the proposed model of Figure 1 may perhaps stand as an alternative that, even if ultimately incorrect, may stimulate further research. Such research would seem useful, since practitioners and researchers in training are often faced with decisions regarding the nature of training evaluation data.

Clement (1982) has stated that correlations that do not support the hierarchical model fail to do so because of noise from intervening variables such as motivation, context of transfer, trainee attitudes, and so forth. No doubt these variables account for some of the variation among correlations in Table 3.

In this regard, one question that might

TABLE 2
Articles Reporting Correlations Between Levels of Evaluation

Author(s)	N	Type of Sample	Description of Measures (Level: Type)
Alliger	90	1st- to 5th-level managers	2: Posttest 3: Questionnaire
Alliger & Horowitz	1,259	1st-level managers	1: Questionnaire 2: Pre-posttest
Bolman	118	Workers (type unspecified)	1: Questionnaire 2: Self-ratings
Clement	50	1st-level supervisors	1: Questionnaire 2: Pre-posttest 3: Self-ratings 4: Subordinate ratings
Eden & Shani	105	Male soldiers	1: Questionnaire 2: Posttest
Miles	34	School Principals	2: Observer ratings 3: Peer ratings
Noe & Schmitt	60	School Administrators	1: Questionnaire 2: Observer ratings 3: Observer ratings 4: Supervisor ratings
Reeves & Jensen	173	Workers (type unspecified)	1: Questionnaire 3: Self-ratings
Severin	50[a]	——[a]	2: Training grades 3: Supervisor ratings 4: Production records
Smith	60	Branch office managers	2: Pre-posttest 4: Customer satisfaction
Stroud	103	Supervisors	1: Questionnaire 3: Self-ratings Supervisor ratings
Wexley & Baldwin	256	Management students	1: Questionnaire 2: Posttest 3: Self-ratings Observer ratings

a. Severin's article was itself a compendium of many studies; the median N was 50, and the nature of the samples varied.

TABLE 3
Correlations Between Levels of Evaluation

	Level 2	Level 3	Level 4
Level 1	.79[e]	.12[k]	.48[g]
	.50[d]	.04[l]	
	.35[c]	.06[g]	
	.17[g]	.01[h]	
	.07[l]	(.04)	
	−.03[b]		
	(.03)		
Level 2		.74[j]	.53[g]
		.40[d]	.24[i]
		.16[a]	(.40)
		.06[f]	
		.06[l]	
		−.02[d]	
		−.05[d]	
		−.15[g]	
		(.18)	
Level 3			.48[i]
			.41[g]
			.20[d]
			.00[d]
			−.07[d]
			(.19)

Note: For Noe and Schmitt data, original study correlations determined by adding residual to reproduced correlations; for Reeves & Jensen, an average r is presented; for Severin, and Wexley & Baldwin, median correlations are reported; for Stroud, correlation in table represents midpoint of range reported (.036 to .211). Mean sample size-weighted correlations for each cell are in parentheses.

a. Alliger (1988); b. Alliger & Horowitz (1989); c. Bolman (1971); d. Clement (1982); e. Eden & Shani (1982); f. Miles (1965); g. Noe & Schmitt (1986); h. Reeves & Jensen; i. Severin (1952); j. Smith (1976); k. Stroud (1959); l. Wexley & Baldwin (1986).

be raised from Assumptions 2 and 3 is whether all correlations in Table 3 may be seen as arising from a single distribution, sampling error accounting for differences among correlations. That is, if all levels are intercorrelated to about the same degree, then sampling error might be the only source of variance among correlations within and among levels. However, predicted variance due to sampling error accounts for less than 15% of the variance of the distribution consisting of all correlations in Table 3.

An issue of interest not addressed in this article is the relationship among criteria *on the same level*. Should researchers be satisfied that a single criterion on a given level will completely capture that level, or that other criteria on that level would have told the same story about training effectiveness? We would like to suggest that caution is needed here: the measurement of different criteria on the same level could show different results. Consider, for example, that behavior learned in a training class might be differentially displayed to, and evaluated by, superiors, peers, or subordinates.

Kirkpatrick's model may never have been meant to be more than a first, global heuristic for training evaluation. As such it has done well. There are, in fact, several other models of training evaluation criteria, most of them very similar to Kirkpatrick's (e.g., Jackson & Kulp, 1978; Warr, Bird, & Rackham, 1970). However, we have proposed that each of three assumptions apparently implicit in the general understanding of Kirkpatrick's model, and in that of most other models as well, can be logically questioned. We have also shown that much of the literature available underscores the problematic nature of these assumptions.

REFERENCES

Alliger, G. M. (1988). [Evaluating training effectiveness for upper-level managers.] Unpublished raw data.

Alliger, G. M., Horowitz, H. M. (1989). IBM takes the guessing out of testing. *Training and Development Journal, 43*(4), 69–73.

Bolman, L. (1971). Some effects of trainers on their t-groups. *Journal of Applied Behavioral Science, 7*, 309–326.

Brogden, H. E., Taylor, E. K. (1950). The dollar criterion — Applying the cost accounting concept to criterion construction. PERSONNEL PSYCHOLOGY, *3*, 133–154.

Campion, M. A., Campion, J. E. (1987). Evaluation of an interviewee skills training program in a natural field setting. PERSONNEL PSYCHOLOGY, *40*, 675–691.

Cascio, W. F. (1987). *Applied psychology in personnel management* (3rd ed.). Englewood Cliffs, NJ: Prentice-Hall.

Catalanello, R. F., Kirkpatrick, D. L. (1968). Evaluating training programs — The state of the art. *Training and Development Journal, 22*(5), 2–9.

Clement, R. W. (1982). Testing the hierarchy theory of training evaluation: An expanded role for trainee reactions. *Public Personnel Management Journal, 11*, 176–184.

Decker, P. J. (1982). The enhancement of behavior modeling training of supervisory skills by the inclusion of a retention process. PERSONNEL PSYCHOLOGY, *35*, 323–332.

Eden, D., Shani, A. B. (1982). Pygmalion goes to boot camp: Expectancy, leadership, and trainee performance. *Journal of Applied Psychology, 67*, 194–199.

Fitz-enz, J. (1985). HR measurement: Formulas for success. *Personnel Journal, 64*(10), 53–60.

Goldstein, I. R. (1986a). *Training in organizations: Needs assessment, development, and evaluation*. Pacific Grove, CA: Brooks/Cole.

Goldstein, I. R. (1986b). *Presidential address to the Society of Industrial-Organizational Psychology*. Washington, DC.

Hall, D. T., Goodale, J. G. (1986). *Human resource management: Strategy, design, and implementation*. Glenview, IL: Scott, Foresman and Company.

Hamblin, A. C. (1974). *Evaluation and control of training*. New York: McGraw-Hill.

Hofstadter, D. R., Dennett, D. C. (1981). *The mind's I: Fantasies and reflections on self and soul*. New York: Bantam Books

Jackson, S., Kulp, M. J. (1978). Designing guidelines for evaluating the outcomes of management training. In Peterson, R. O. (Ed.), *Determining the payoffs of management training* (pp. 1–42). Madison, WI: ASTD.

Kaplan, R. M., Pascoe, G. C. (1977). Humorous lectures and humorous examples: Some effects upon comprehension and retention. *Journal of Educational Psychology, 69*, 61–65.

Kirkpatrick, D. L. (1959a). Techniques for evaluating training programs. *Journal of ASTD, 13*(11), 3–9.

Kirkpatrick, D. L. (1959b). Techniques for evaluating training programs: Part 2 — Learning. *Journal of ASTD, 13*(12), 21–26.

Kirkpatrick, D. L. (1960a). Techniques for evaluating training programs: Part 3 — Behavior. *Journal of ASTD, 14*(1), 13–18.

Kirkpatrick, D. L. (1960b). Techniques for evaluating training programs: Part 4 — Results. *Journal of ASTD, 14*(2), 28–32.

Kirkpatrick, D. L. (1967). Evaluation of training. In Craig, R. L., Bittel, L. R. (Eds.), *Training and development handbook* (pp. 87–112). New York: McGraw-Hill.

Kirkpatrick, D. L. (1976). Evaluation. In Craig, R. L. (Ed.), *Training and development handbook* (pp. 301–319). New York: McGraw-Hill.

Kirkpatrick, D. L. (1977). Evaluating training programs, evidence vs. proof. *Training and Development Journal, 31*(11), 9–12.

Kirkpatrick, D. L. (1978). Evaluating in-house training programs. *Training and Development Journal, 32*(9), 6–9.

Kirkpatrick, D. L. (1979). Techniques for evaluating training programs. *Training and Development Journal, 33*(6), 78–92.

Kirkpatrick, D. L. (1985). Effective training and development, Part 2: In-house approaches and techniques. *Personnel, 62*(1), 52–56.

Lewicki, P. (1986). *Nonconscious social information processing*. New York: Academic Press.

Meyers, H. H., Raich, M. S. (1983). An objective evaluation of a behavior modeling training program. PERSONNEL PSYCHOLOGY, *36*, 755–761.

Miles, M. B. (1965) Changes during and following

laboratory training: A clinical experimental study. *Journal of Applied Behavior Science, 1,* 215–242.

Moffie, D. J., Calhoon, R., O'Brien, J. K. (1964). Evaluation of a management level program. PERSONNEL PSYCHOLOGY, *17,* 431–440.

Newstrom, J. W. (1978). Catch-22: The problems of incomplete evaluation of training. *Training and Development Journal,* 32(11), 22–24.

Noe, R. A., Schmitt, N. M. (1986). The influence of trainee attitudes on training effectiveness: Test of a model. PERSONNEL PSYCHOLOGY, *39,* 497–523.

Reeves, E. T., Jensen, J. M. (1972). Effectiveness of program evaluation. *Training and Development Journal,* 26(1), 36–41.

Reilly, R. R., Smither, J. W. (1985). An examination of two alternative techniques to estimate the standard deviation of job performance in dollars. *Journal of Applied Psychology, 70,* 651–661.

Remmers, H. H., Martin, D., Elliot, D. N. (1949). *Student achievement and instructor evaluations in chemistry: Studies in higher education.* West Lafayette, IN: Purdue University.

Rodin, M., Rodin, B. (1972). Student evaluations of teachers. *Science, 177,* 1164–1166.

Russell, J. S., Wexley, K. N., Hunter, J. E. (1984). Questioning the effectiveness of behavior modeling training in an industrial setting. PERSONNEL PSYCHOLOGY, *37,* 465–481.

Saporito, B. (1986). The revolt against working smarter. *Fortune, 114*(2), 58–67.

Sheppeck, M. A., Cohen, S. L. (1985). Put a dollar value on your training program. *Training and Development Journal, 39*(11), 59–62.

Severin, D. (1952). The predictability of various kinds of criteria. PERSONNEL PSYCHOLOGY, *5,* 93–104.

Smith, P. E. (1976). Management modeling training to improve morale and customer satisfaction. PERSONNEL PSYCHOLOGY, *29,* 351–359.

Stroud, P. (1959, November/December). Evaluating a human relations training program. *Personnel, 36,* pp. 52–60.

Thorndike, E. L. (1935). *The psychology of wants, interests, and attitudes.* New York: Appleton-Century.

Warr, P., Bird, M., Rackham, N. (1970). *Evaluation of management training.* London: Gower Press.

Weekly, J. A., Frank, B., O'Connor, E. J., Peters, L. H. (1985). A comparison of three methods of estimating the standard deviation of performance in dollars. *Journal of Applied Psychology, 70,* 122–126.

Wexley, K. N., Baldwin, T. T. (1986). Post training strategy for facilitating positive transfer: An empirical exploration. *Academy of Management Journal, 29,* 503–520.

George M. Alliger and Elizabeth A. Janak are affiliated with the State University of New York at Albany.

The authors wish to thank Michael Britt for aiding in the literature search and Steven Cronshaw, Kevin Williams, Wilson Wong, and the editor Paul Sackett and an anonymous reviewer for their helpful comments on an earlier version of this article.

What's So Special About CBT? Making the Most of the Medium
Larry Brink

"The market for CBT is on the verge of stalling out. The systems have improved, the costs have declined, the equipment has become more widespread, and people's awareness of the medium has increased. Yet CBT has a bad reputation because there is so much awful courseware. And companies are still drawing their courseware developers from the programmer-technician ranks. Very few

"What's So Special About CBT? Making the Most of the Medium" by Larry Brink is reprinted by permission of the author.

people have the skills and the instructional design background necessary to make use of the sophisticated features of modern authoring systems.... The typical pattern is for the unskilled courseware developer to spend some period of time producing unimaginative page-turners and then to blame the authoring system when the much-wanted benefits of CBT aren't realized."

That comment from an observer of the computer-based training field was the stimulus for this article. Whether or not you agree that the market is stalling out (I do not!), most professionals familiar with the field would have difficulty challenging the other assertions. "Buyers" (clients, prospective clients, or whoever is asking for the CBT product) are certainly aware of CBT and are receptive to its use. The technology and tools for developing and delivering CBT are refined and reasonably priced; they surely offer more sophistication than most course developers utilize. And it is also true that the majority of instructional programs developed in the CBT medium are downright disappointing.

As a principal in a training company and a developer of computer-based instructional materials, I am vitally interested in and concerned about this problem. What is it about CBT that's so different? Do CBT developers require special instructional design skills because of the unique attributes of the meaning? Or do most of the people creating CBT simply not have *any* instructional design background? What are some of the symptoms of inadequate CBT, and how do they relate to CBT's unique attributes? Finally, are there ways to remedy the situation and improve the quality of CBT products? Let's begin by examining why the CBT field finds itself in its current predicament.

WHAT'S TO BLAME?

Attention to the Medium

CBT has received a great deal of attention in the past three to five years, perhaps because some have hailed it as the medium of the future. Everybody, it seems, is talking or writing about CBT, and high visibility always brings with it the opportunity for adverse comment. Careful review of products in *any* medium will reveal variations in quality. So some negative reaction to some CBT products must be expected — there are bad products in all formats.

High Expectations and Unsubstantiated Claims

The history of instructional technology demonstrates that most "new" systems are hyped as the ultimate solution to every challenge. This isn't new behavior — after introducing motion picture technology, Thomas Edison modestly proclaimed that film would replace the need for classroom teachers.

In the case of CBT, claims are regularly made for more efficient and effective learning, shorter development times, and lower costs. Assurances are given that anyone with even modest knowledge of course content can create outstanding CBT products. Forgetting to consider things like time for testing *all* program branches, CBT proponents promise the elimination of production cycles. They also proclaim that "one person can do it all." In short, too much is claimed too often, to the enormous detriment of everyone involved.

Widespread Use of CBT as a Relatively Recent Phenomenon

Anytime people work with something new, they have to invest a lot of time in it before they can do really good work. This is particularly relevant with CBT, since so many products are "first generation." Furthermore, there are currently no established standards for the development of CBT, no tested models to follow, and very few examples for designers to analyze and study. Think for a moment. Can you easily name six or seven CBT products that you'd recommend to a new CBT designer as exemplars of the medium?

Even when such examples are available, their underlying structure and organization are difficult to observe, since branching is invisible. CBT products are also generally expensive and require hardware that is not always readily available. So designers interested in studying worthwhile examples of CBT find themselves in a much more difficult situation than when they are looking for print, video, or workshop products.

Predisposition to Negative Reactions

Although I am unaware of any hard evidence, computers seem to evoke more negative reactions from users than other instructional media do. These reactions stem first from general uneasiness with computers. Many people who consider themselves managers, not "techies," don't want to be seen in the vicinity of a computer. And perhaps they sense that CBT, given the current state of the art, is something to stay away from.

The varied nature of the training audience comes into play here too. Studies in programmed instruction have shown that learners who are high achievers tend to like to move freely and explore or otherwise control the learning situation. They dislike learning situations that don't provide those opportunities. How often do you faithfully complete a tutorial before beginning to work with a new application?

But one can certainly think of CBT applications that would be challenging and exciting to even the brightest learners. Interactive case studies are an excellent example of successful CBT application. Learners are provided with data and are then asked to make choices based on the approach they'd like to follow. Think of how involved people get in playing computer games like *Zork* (interactive fiction products) or *Flight Simulator*. CBT products that reflect a higher quality of design and implementation will go a long way toward eliciting more positive reactions.

Bad Media Selection Decisions

No question about it — much of what ends up as CBT has no business using the computer as the medium of instruction. Subject matter that demands extensive background reading, for example, belongs in a book. Too often, knowledgeable, well-intentioned designers are forced to use CBT due to *a priori* marketing decisions. While such decisions may make sound business sense, they don't help designers who must actually deal with the selected medium.

In many such situations, learners don't know that business objectives dictated the choice of CBT. If courses are inadequate, the designers and the medium itself are often seen as the problem when inappropriate media selection is actually to blame. I am not suggesting that designers should refuse to consider business factors — only that such factors often make the task of product design much more difficult. This tension between marketing and instructional decision-making criteria is one that must be honestly addressed by all parties.

Complexity of the Medium and Lack of Skilled Designers

This is a critical part of the problem, and one that designers can do something about. Two major categories contribute to the difficulty of developing CBT programs.

- Technical complexities require that designers master the use of hardware and software in order to understand what the total system can do and how it can be manipulated.
- Instructional design complexities require that designers understand and master special skills that are particularly germane to CBT development.

Every medium of instruction requires designers to maintain and exercise a unique repertoire. None of us should be surprised by this. Yet with CBT, people fail to pay sufficient attention to this issue. Therefore, there is a dearth of experienced and skilled designers.

People with little or no instructional design background cannot be expected to develop superior training, CBT or otherwise. Of course, some people without such training will develop good products, but a vast majority will not. People who possess a basic set of instructional design skills have an *essential* but *insufficient* background for dealing effectively with CBT. These designers should presumably develop higher quality CBT products as they become more knowledgeable about the medium. So it's true that the use of designers from the programmer-technician ranks contributes to the preponderance of mediocre courseware. It is also true that an increased understanding of the medium will allow qualified designers to do a better job.

Let's give some more consideration to a number of instructional design issues as they relate specifically to the complexity of the CBT medium.

CBT'S UNIQUE ATTRIBUTES

The seven characteristics of CBT discussed below offer unique instructional opportunities and require special attention from designers.

1. *Interactivity* is perhaps the most talked about and least understood attribute of CBT. Since the computer presumably offers "intelligence" — power to analyze and interpret, ability to compare and respond, and many other capabilities — buyers and users expect that such capabilities will be part of all CBT. Computer-based simulations and various computer games, both educational and recreational, use interactivity effectively.

People often confuse pressing keys other than RETURN or the SPACE BAR, asking and answering questions, or entering a single word or number with true interactivity. But it is cognitive activity, not physical activity, that is important to learning. Designers must be concerned with "minds-on," not simply "hands-on," activities. True interactivity demands quite powerful tools and a great deal of development time. It also demands attention to the desired learning outcomes and an appropriate budget to cover the design, testing, and revision of courseware.

Designers are *underutilizing* the CBT medium when they don't exploit this attribute to enhance instruction. But CBT that is low in interactivity should not immediately be dismissed as substandard. Such courseware simply misses taking advantage of a unique capability. Just because an instructional film doesn't use animation (a unique attribute of film), it doesn't mean the film is a failure. Interactive CBT is complex and difficult to design. That's why we see so little of it.

2. *Control of sequence and timing* means the ability to specify how and when pieces of information will be revealed. When presenting instruction through a computer, the designer has complete control of the sequence in which the learner receives information. First some data, then a graphic, then a learner interaction requiring a proper response, then another piece of information, and so on. The designer can also control the rate at which information appears on the screen and the amount of time the student has to respond. This kind of control is unique to CBT and skilled designers can use it to manipulate the conditions of learning.

Student or learner control is another much talked about aspect of CBT. Designers may choose to allow learners to determine how material is presented. They may demand that certain parts of a lesson are taken in a predetermined sequence or they may permit users to select entry and exit points. Based on analysis of learner responses, designers may elect to force learners into remediation paths or may simply point out deficiencies for future attention. In order to properly evaluate design assumptions related to control, sufficient try-out and revision cycles must be built into CBT product developmental schedules and budgets.

3. CBT offers the capacity to guide learners through the performance of activities. This is the attribute of *"doing"* versus *"reading."* Whether learners are entering data to control an on-screen function, moving through an interactive case study, or responding to a set of conditions and making judgments, they are doing something other than reading. Learners are able to practice a performance, and the CBT is designed to guide, monitor, and evaluate this performance. Use of this capacity can lead to extremely effective instruction.

However, people sometimes place a premium on physical activity because it is so easily observed and evaluated. Use of the "doing versus reading" attribute, then, doesn't in and of itself, guarantee learning. "Doing" must be properly positioned, meaningful to the learner, and appropriate to the learning task. We must not lose sight of the fact that while reading is usually physically passive, it often stimulates significant cognitive activity, which is ultimately responsible for learning.

4. The medium of CBT offers designers unique opportunities to *question* learners, *evaluate* learners' progress, and *provide specific feedback* based on learner responses. Such questions and feedback may be embedded at the most appropriate location within the sequence of instruction, allowing designers to immediately inform a learner of an error or deficiency. These attributes allow CBT

developers to individualize instruction through differential branching.

Through careful use of questions, evaluation, and feedback, CBT courses can become more diagnostic and prescriptive than other forms of instruction, and a number of recent CBT products have taken this direction.

5. *Individualization,* a much talked-about capability, involves tailoring instruction to the individual through the development of multiple learning paths. At the lowest level, CBT can offer immediate feedback to learners based on their individual responses to questions. At the highest level, pre-testing can be used to identify appropriate learner characteristics which then dictate specific paths to be taken. Within these paths, analysis of individual learner progress allows designers to build appropriate branching to support the required level of individualization.

The attributes of CBT that permit individualization are answer judging, answer analysis, and branching. As with other capabilities, the extent to which individualization is used depends on many factors. These include instructional rationale and philosophy, system capabilities (e.g., memory available for storage of significant data), time and money available for development, and knowledge of audience characteristics.

6. *Remediation* allows designers to individualize courseware by taking the learner to specific sequences of instruction after determining that the learner has not adequately understood certain content. Moving the learner from location to location, providing reviews of previously presented instruction, and providing unique remediation paths are sophisticated capabilities in the hands of a skilled designer. When combined with powerful response tracking, differential remediation can be provided as errors occur. Full, effective use of this attribute demands high level instructional design.

7. *Screen format and design* are crucial. The medium offers the developer many opportunities to design the visual display. These include techniques and methods of information presentation (windowing, colors, type style, type size, graphics style), techniques for gaining the learners' attention (animation, color changes, variable positioning of data), and methods that allow the use of alternate user input devices (keyboard, mouse, touch screen, light pen). Thoughtful consideration of screen format and design is critical for successful CBT — perhaps equal in importance to actual course content. Poor screen design by itself can cause product failure.

EXPLOITING THE MEDIUM

Even this short list of capabilities and attributes may seem overwhelming to some. Each item demands that the designer make specific, conscious choices. In order to exploit any of them, designers must carefully plan their instruction with full understanding of the implications for the CBT development effort. For example, if there is reason to believe that different groups in the audience will require or benefit from alternate instructional treatments, what amount of individualization will be included? Will all learners receive selected instructional sequences? Will learners be given the opportunity to skip over certain parts of lessons? How will that affect individualized paths? How much information can you store on the delivery system?

Will you have the opportunity to test your draft instruction thoroughly enough to determine how well it matches your hypothesized learner differences?

One can go on and on with such questions. The challenge is not to come up with the longest list of questions, but rather to be certain that your use of unique CBT attributes is appropriate, meaningful, and relevant to the particular instructional situation you face. The primary question in your mind should be "how can I utilize the unique attributes of CBT to best meet my training objectives?" In order to develop quality CBT, the medium must be exploited properly. It's easy to disappoint buyers and users; it's not so easy to produce an outstanding course.

Becoming aware of the attributes that set CBT apart from other media is a fundamental requirement for those who want to understand how to fully use the medium. Examination of common mistakes that CBT designers make is invaluable for avoiding similar traps. Such errors can be significantly reduced when the development effort includes a proper planning phase. This is particularly important in CBT since the cost of mistakes is quite high.

INAPPROPRIATE INTERACTION AND COURSES OUT OF CONTROL

A basic mistake is building a course that totally lacks interaction when it is appropriate for satisfying the objectives of the course. The best example is the classic page-turner, displaying screen after screen of text. A sales skills course that doesn't allow learners to practice the skills is another example of this deficiency. Practice through interactive case studies would be highly appropriate in such a course.

On the other hand, including perfunctory interaction *for interaction's sake alone* is a certain way to damage a course. As mentioned earlier, confusing physical activity with cognitive interactivity is another sure sign of failure to use CBT appropriately. Although touch screens are fun to use, touching the screen to continue a lesson is no more interactive than pressing RETURN. Such action should not be confused with true *interaction*.

Another common error is the assumption that isolated questions somehow satisfy the desire for interaction. Formulaic use of questions (three screens, a question, three more screens, and another question) quickly becomes repetitious and boring. And using the number of screens since the last question or evaluation point as a rule for determining when to insert another question is just as mindless. However, when questions are used creatively, as in the interactive case study, they can be an outstanding way to build meaningful activity.

In the realm of controlling events, a common symptom of inadequate design is failure to allow learners to easily exit and reenter courseware. Although it is generally unacceptable, courses often force learners to go back to the beginning of a sequence after any exit. Another extreme, giving learners too much control, can also cause problems. For example, allowing learners to randomly display screens of their choice can be dangerous. When learners have the ability to take a course in any desired sequence, designers must be certain that learners don't miss critical information. Jumping into the middle of a lesson can obviously cause difficulties for the learner.

ACTIVITY TRAPS AND FEEDBACK FAILURE

A classic mistake is the failure to include activities that allow learners to practice the task they are learning. Think of the CBT products that purport to teach learners how to use a computer application like word processing or spreadsheets but consist entirely of a diatribe with no activity or practice. When practice *is* included, a common mistake is a simulation that is not faithful to that which it is simulating. When the learner is misled, confused, or frustrated by such an activity, the course is obviously deficient. A final error is trapping a learner within an activity. Designers must provide ways for the learners to say, "I don't know how to proceed." There is nothing more frustrating than being unable to continue but having no options other than exiting the training altogether.

Another deficiency has to do with the use of poorly designed questions and feedback. Many training developers do not understand question construction principles. With CBT, this is troublesome indeed. For example, the effect of poorly worded distractors in a multiple choice question is compounded when feedback for every answer must be included and presented to the learner. While all distractors — even illogical ones — can go without explanation on a standard paper and pencil test, in CBT they all require explanations *and* transitional branches to the rest of the course. Designers tend to rely on comprehension and memorization questions rather than on questions that test the learners' ability to *apply* what they have learned. Again, this is not a mistake peculiar to CBT, but it's one that is exacerbated by the formulaic use of questions for interaction.

Failure to present meaningful feedback (I include "Incorrect. Try Again." and other such phrases) is another symptom of poor design. Two associated problems are the failure to make feedback sufficiently specific and the failure to present feedback immediately after the occurrence of an error. Feedback is much less useful when it is presented after too long an interval and when it is not explicit enough to help the learner move forward in the training.

Another mistake occurs when questions are used for the purpose of evaluation or any activity other than testing *per se* — demanding that the learner return to the question for another try after giving an incorrect response. Sometimes it is more appropriate to track attempts and intervene after a given number of incorrect responses. Other useful techniques include simply providing the correct answer within a feedback path as part of the explanation, moving to a parallel form of the question, or branching to a remediation path.

ARBITRARY INDIVIDUALIZATION AND INCONSISTENT REMEDIATION

Attempting to build an individualized course without a precise rationale and a thorough understanding of your audience's characteristics can lead to difficulties. A course is in trouble when learners feel as though they are being arbitrarily pigeonholed. Use of trite comments ("Well, Jim . . ." "I'm sorry, Jim . . ." and so on) simply misses the instructional point behind individualization. I once heard a marketing person suggest that a CBT course be designed to trick the learners into feeling as though the course would relate to their individual backgrounds, experience levels, and subject knowledge. In essence, the suggestion was to query learners up front and then simply ignore their responses. The presumption was that learners would be led to believe that the course was tailored to them even though it was not. We all use a variety of tricks to make the task of course design more manageable, efficient, and effective, but we must not go so far as to deceive the audience.

Issues such as depth and frequency must be dealt with when a designer chooses to put remediation to use. Inconsistent use of remediation can confuse learners who come to expect a certain treatment and then find additional instruction lacking. Problems will certainly develop when designers incorrectly assume that the learners are in need of remediation based on the analysis of a single response. Any time a significant amount of remediation seems to be called for, a second question or activity which further clarifies and substantiates the error condition should be presented, and the second response should be analyzed for consistency with the first. Sending a learner into an eight-minute review branch based on a faulty design assumption is an unfortunate waste of time. When this happens, a real error might go undetected. Learners lose in two ways — time is wasted and a true learning problem may not be remediated. Remediation that is too lengthy, complex, or general is also symptomatic of inadequate design.

SETTING UP THE SCREEN

There are numerous symptoms of inadequate screen design. Three types that come to mind have to do with physical size of the screen, display of information, and flow from screen to screen.

Because CBT designers must contend with rather severe space limitations on most computer displays, it is not unusual to see screens that are much too densely packed with information. Screens must be clear and readable. Sufficient amounts of "white" space must be left on the display. Designers must also be careful to position instructions, feedback, and other data consistently. Efficiency of programs is reduced when learners have to hunt for the next instruction.

The availability of a great many screen attributes allows designers freedom in displaying information. Frequently, though, designers don't develop a clear plan for taking advantage of screen attributes. Too many colors, attractive but unreadable fonts, inappropriate blinking, or too many changes in brightness levels can cause visual fatigue. Overly complex screens can also confuse learners.

The failure to impose clear distinctions between different types of instructional screens can be a troublesome design deficiency. For example, insufficient distinctions between menu and question screens may contribute to learner confusion. Careful attention to screen format and design can smooth the flow of a course and increase a learner's sense of comfort and control. Good use of screen design attributes can help designers make transitions from one piece of information to the next. This is particularly the case when a screen change is required. What to erase and display, where to display, how to stop and start again — these are all controllable factors that demand the attention of the designer. Screen formatting and design can be manipulated to have positive effects on transition points.

WHERE TO FROM HERE?

Many factors affect the design, development, implementation, and delivery of CBT products. This medium of instruction is a demanding one. It's understandable that CBT products and producers are raising some eyebrows. There are questions to ask, judgments to make, and criticisms to answer. But the current state of affairs can be explained and solutions to most problems can be found.

That the medium demands skilled designers is clear. Even seasoned designers must attend to CBT's special characteristics and attributes. Let's not expect that everyone is up to the task of producing award-winning courseware. Awards are reserved for a few, but a majority of instructional designers are capable of developing *respectable* CBT products that achieve results.

A number of principles and guidelines have been sprinkled throughout this article. Some of the suggestions listed below are restatements of ideas alluded to earlier; others are presented here as summary thoughts.

- Those of us who are serious about CBT have several obligations. We must sell people on the medium, but we have to be careful not to oversell. We have to educate buyers and users so that unreasonable expectations are brought into line, unsubstantiated claims are dealt with properly, and inappropriate media selection decisions are minimized.
- Negative criticism and predisposition will tend to fade as quality products come into the marketplace. Meanwhile, those who can use the medium to produce exemplary (or even good) courses will benefit from attention and visibility.
- There is no formula for the development of CBT. Designers must study the medium and its attributes and apply fundamental instructional design principles to the task of course development. Many basic design principles apply to CBT just as they do to other media, but designers must also try to utilize that which is special about CBT in meeting training objectives.
- When the capabilities of an instructional medium are underutilized, buyers and users may be disappointed. When video is used to present a "talking head," criticism is to be expected. Clear rationale for the use of CBT will help to minimize this disappointment. Thoughtful planning is the best investment one can make in development of CBT courseware. Spend adequate time determining which characteristics of CBT will form the structure of the course. Be certain that everyone

understands the investment (dollars and beyond) necessary for the specified product.
- During early phases of the course development process, think of ways to exploit the medium. The interactive case study, for example, is an excellent way to accomplish a number of goals. Learners are in control, interactivity is the prominent instructional vehicle, learning is evaluated based on application of concepts and skills, and the course is individualized. Remember that it is not necessary to employ every aspect of the medium in every CBT course. Don't complicate the design task by forcing in every characteristic and attribute. This can make for an unmanageable project. Worse, it can reduce the quality of the course.
- Careful screen formatting and design are critical to the success of CBT products. This single aspect of courseware design can literally make or break a product. Computer-generated graphics permit designers to clarify points of instruction and improve the appearance of CBT courseware. For example, the use of screen headers can link a sequence of screens together in a meaningful way. They serve as placemarkers which keep learners aware of where they are within a lesson. Use of color for coding or cueing of information can produce subtle yet meaningful effects. Attention to information display should not be given back seat status. This is a part of CBT courseware design for which it may be worthwhile to hire outside graphic design experts.
- Careful analysis and thorough understanding of audience characteristics are very important. Certain instructional strategies are rooted in audience definitions and needs. You cannot, for example, build individualized tracks of instruction without concise user specifications. The amount of control to be passed to the learner and the best way to remediate errors must be based, to some extent at least, on the nature of the training audience.

There are no quick-acting prescriptions — no magical lists that guarantee success. As in similar endeavors, there is a certain mixture of art and science here. There are some people who have a knack for CBT design and others who simply shouldn't get involved. Most designers fall somewhere in between these extremes. A proper blend of skill and experience is what you want to strive to obtain.

How do you improve your CBT skills? One way is to become aware of those aspects of CBT that are special. Another way is to practice. You can, for example, practice building interactive sequences of instruction. You can commit to paper several methods of handling certain types of remediation. You can begin to catalog screen attributes that are available on your system and develop prototype screen formats. You can solicit user reaction to your prototypes and systematically refine these screens for use within courseware. By challenging yourself to tackle selected aspects of the medium, you can refine your skill base and add to your repertoire.

Attending professional seminars and conferences can also be helpful, although your success at such meetings will depend on the quality of those who run the sessions. Professional gatherings are often terrific opportunities to review and study CBT courseware that may otherwise be unavailable to you. Forming alliances with other designers and examining their CBT products can be helpful as well. Tennis players say that to improve your game you must compete against players more skillful than you. If you are able to work with skilled designers and development groups, jump at the opportunity. Quality apprenticeships can be an excellent learning vehicle.

Tools, techniques, and methods will change as the CBT arena matures. The reality of the situation is that product quality will continue to fluctuate. With time, more experienced and skillful designers will enter the marketplace. As the percentage of unqualified personnel decreases, product quality will increase and stabilize. As the nature and function of the computer as a training tool evolves, designers must be willing to take on the challenge of growing alongside the medium.

Larry Brink is currently a principal of Apogee Training and Development, Inc., in Woburn, Massachusetts.

Management Development
Kenneth N. Wexley / Timothy T. Baldwin

In 1954, Peter Drucker stated that the manager is the dynamic, life-giving element in every business organization. Indeed, in today's competitive environment, the quality and performance of an organization's managers may determine its very survival. It may have once been generally believed that managers were born and not made, but now there is increasing acceptance of the idea that managerial knowledge, skills, and abilities can be learned and improved (Campbell, Dunnette, Lawler, & Weick, 1970). Interest in fostering managerial talent has led to a burgeoning body of articles and books devoted to what might be termed *management development*. In addition, many American organizations expend huge amounts of time, money, talent, and energy to develop their managerial talent. For the purposes of this review, management development is defined as the whole, complex process by which individuals learn, grow, and improve their abilities to perform professional management tasks (Bennett, 1982; Hawrylyshyn, 1975). A good overview of this area is offered by Boyatzis (1982), Cox & Beck (1984), and London (1985).

Despite considerable recent attention to the topic, management development may still be one of the most ill-defined and variously interpreted concepts in the management literature. Many researchers view management development as involving formalized education designed to develop a broad range of abilities which would enable managers to cope with a large variety of tasks in diverse organizational contexts. Others speak of management development as instruction in highly specific managerial skills (e.g.,

Source: Kenneth N. Wexley and Timothy T. Baldwin, "Management Development," *Journal of Management,* 1986, pp. 277–294. Reprinted by permission.

time management, delegation, managing conflict) which would be immediately applicable in a particular organizational setting. Still others consider development synonymous with career planning, job rotation, on-the-job experience, and coaching. In this review we take a broad perspective, consistent with our definition of management development. We view management education, management training, and both planned and unplanned on-the-job experiences as all being potentially important inputs for a manager's development. Although the exact relationships among the components of development await empirical specification, this three-part framework (i.e., management education, management training, and on-the-job experiences) underlies our discussion of issues, topics, controversies, and strategies in management development.

In order to uncover relevant literature, we searched all academic and practitioner journals related to management development. In addition, we requested all members of the Management Education and Development Division of the Academy of Management to send us any articles, technical reports, or unpublished papers pertaining to management development. We also contacted other researchers and practitioners known to have an interest in this subject.

Our search resulted in a voluminous and unusually diverse set of articles. We have incorporated a wide variety of research, which we feel reflects the extremely broad nature of this field. To make the review as current as possible, we have emphasized works that have appeared since 1980, but have also included earlier articles in order to adequately uncover key issues and document trends.

Finally, our goal was to provide breadth of coverage, but not to make the review exhaustive. Rather, articles were selected for their ability to best convey the state of manuscript development research and to stimulate readers' ideas for future research and practice.

MANAGEMENT EDUCATION

Management education denotes those activities traditionally conducted by colleges and universities that focus on developing a broad range of managerial knowledge and general conceptual abilities. Unquestionably, the major issue in management education today is the curriculum offered in our business schools, and this concern has been labeled *the competency movement*. This movement has been fueled by increasing criticism of the quality of education received by our nation's graduating BBA and MBA students. It asks a fundamental question: "Should management education be directed toward the development of specific managerial skills and competencies or should it continue to focus on providing a general education?" Advocates of the competency movement argue that managers and managers-to-be emerge from our management education programs insensitive to the nuances of organizational culture, lacking a true interest in managing, and, most important, deficient in the skills thought essential for effective management (Behrman & Levin, 1984; Heisler & Lasher, in press; Livingston, 1971).

Researchers also argue that educators have focused more on teaching individuals about management rather than how to manage, and that management students get few opportunities to learn about, practice, and become competent in the behavioral skills essential for good management (Badawy, 1982; Heisler & Lasher, in press; Waters, 1980). The traditional management education curriculum, as presently constituted, may not be adequately preparing individuals for the challenges they experience as professional managers (Pfeffer, 1977).

Responding to this perceived inability of business schools to teach managerial competencies, American business has increased its capacity to be its own educational provider (Eurich, 1985). Companies have long been educating their own in some way, but the new corporate classrooms for managers in such organizations as McDonald's, Texas Instruments, Kimberly-Clark, and Polaroid attempt to teach the types of managerial competencies students are reportedly not gaining in universities. In addition, the focus of some existing corporate management education is changing. Corporations are demanding education that is result-oriented and aimed at implementing business strategy and corporate objectives, rather than that focusing on the development of general knowledge and administrative concepts (Bolt, 1985). Although some popular literature has begun to look to successful organizations for development ideas (Digman, 1978; Peters & Waterman, 1982), more attention should be devoted to how developmentally oriented, effective firms are structuring their management education.

Further indication of the impact of the competency movement is reflected in the advent of journals and books devoted solely to the issue of competency-based education (Blank, 1982; Whetten & Cameron, 1984). Models and frameworks of requisite management competencies (Cameron & Whetten, 1983; Powers, 1983) and new academic programs (Damm, 1983; Faerman, Quinn, & Thompson, 1985) have also been proposed.

However, several writers have pointed to problems in the teaching of managerial competencies. Bradford (1983), although an advocate of the competency movement, has noted three potential difficulties associated with competency-based education: how such specific competency-based teaching can be framed vis-à-vis the rest of the business curriculum, how course content can avoid being too narrow, and how to ensure that instructors have the needed desire and skills to implement such courses. Vaill (1983) has attacked the competency movement on a fundamental level, arguing that the movement is essentially a theory of managing which lacks validation. He has seriously questioned whether a skills-list definition of competency would accurately reflect how effective managers actually function. Other skeptics have contended that the role of education in general, and that of management education in particular, should be much broader than the teaching of specific competencies (Johnston, 1986).

Both conceptual and competency-based courses should have a meaningful place in management education. Providing students with a balanced curriculum that emphasizes both conceptual understanding and more specific competencies is perhaps the best strategy.

Certainly, the optimal business school curriculum is not the only important issue in management education today. Other significant issues include instructional effectiveness, evaluation of alternative teaching methodologies, and ways of fostering stronger alignment between university and business community goals. Unfortunately, research on these topics is just beginning (e.g., see Bednar & Heisler, 1985; Heisler & Lasher, in press). They urgently need more attention.

MANAGEMENT TRAINING

Management training differs from management education in that training covers those activities designed to impart specific managerial skills (e.g., time management, delegation) which would be immediately applicable in a particular organizational setting. Training may also focus on a manager's level of self-awareness or motivation (Wexley & Latham, 1981).

Unlike the competency movement in management education, no particular issue stands out in the literature on management training. Instead, the recent empirical and conceptual research might be categorized into the general topic areas traditionally used by personnel training reviewers: needs assessment, training content and methods, maximizing learning and transfer, evaluation, and special target groups (McGehee & Thayer, 1961; Wexley, 1984).

Needs Assessment

Various methods of assessing management development needs have been summarized previously by other authors (Digman, 1980; Moore & Dutton, 1978). Recent work has included an innovative approach by Yukl (1982), who focused attention on observable managerial behaviors rather than on what he considered abstract skills. He used a typology of managerial behavior consisting of 23 behaviors measured by the Managerial Behavior Survey (MBS) (Yukl & Van Fleet, 1982). Respondents (e.g., subordinates, peers, and superiors), who had had ample opportunity to observe a manager's behavior, were asked to describe that behavior using the MBS. The same respondents also filled out a parallel questionnaire on which they indicated what level of behavior was optimal for managerial effectiveness in that particular position. The discrepancy between actual and ideal behavior could then be computed. Whenever a discrepancy occurred, it could simply indicate that the manager was unaware of how important a particular behavior was, or, more important, it could signal a need for additional training. In a similar vein, Klimoski (1982) focused on a manager's subordinates and peers as sources of training-needs information. Subordinates rated their manager's job behavior using Yukl's management categories, and peers rated the same manager using dimensions derived from the assessment center literature.

Byham (1983) has discussed how assessment centers can be useful for identifying individual management development needs. He has argued that although assessors have typically been used solely for selection or promotability information, they are also valuable for detailing the strengths and weaknesses of each participant and making specific developmental recommendations.

Finally, self-assessment of training needs has been a popular topic in the management literature (Oppenheimer, 1982). Empirical research has focused on the conditions under which self-assessments can be expected to be most accurate. For example, one recent study has suggested that self-assessments will be most accurate when a manager has a positive attitude toward the usefulness of training (Ford & Noe, 1985).

Training Content and Methods

Campbell et al. (1970) classified off-the-job management training activities into two basic types: (a) information presentation techniques (e.g., lectures and programmed instruction) and (b) simulation methods (e.g., case studies and business games). Recent investigations have focused almost exclusively on the second type, an example being the current attention devoted to behavior modeling (Goldstein & Sorcher, 1974). Thousands of organizations now use some variant of behavior modeling (Parry & Reich, 1984), and research evidence generally supports its utility for improving the human-relations skills of managers (Birkenbach, Kamfer, & Morshuizen, 1985; Latham & Saari, 1979; Meyer & Raich, 1983). Most of the evidence to date has been obtained using soft criteria (i.e., reactions and learning), although there are some studies (e.g., Meyer & Raich, 1983) in which hard criteria (i.e., changes in behavior and/or results) were positively affected by this training method.

Despite the evidence cited above, some writers have questioned how well behavior modeling fits in with the goals of adult education (Robinson, 1980), and others have concluded that behavior modeling may not always produce behavior change or improved performance results (e.g., Russell, Wexley, & Hunter, 1984).

Although business games (Keys, in press) and the case method (Berger, 1983) continue to receive conceptual support in the literature, rigorous evaluative research on these two techniques is sorely needed. Argyris (1980) has criticized the case method on a fundamental level by arguing that it may facilitate learning that does not question the underlying values of managers or the policies of their organization. It may also inhibit the learning that would enable managers to question these basic factors and to improve the application of new learning in their home organization.

Several additional methods involving simulation have emerged in the popular literature, such as intensive athletic competition (Wellemeyer, 1983) and wilderness experiences (Van Zwieten, 1984). After reviewing a variety of these techniques, Newstrom (1985a) concluded that support for such methods consists solely of participant testimonials and lacks empirical evidence.

Our attempt to categorize the plethora of subjects falling under the broad umbrella of management training was a virtually impossible task. Subjects ranged from the very straightforward (e.g., problem solving, communications, time management) to unusual topics like image improvement and minimizing stage fright. Other nontraditional training topics receiving attention in the literature include: creativity (Payne & Pettingill, in press), performance rating (Bernardin & Buckley, 1981), harnessing pygmalion (Eden, 1984), complicated understanding (Bartunek, Gordon, & Weathersby, 1983), strategic thinking (Easterby-Smith & Davies, 1983), and efficacy training (Gist, 1986). Clearly, however, those management programs most frequently taught, and having the most empirical and/or theoretical support, remain those familiar to management development writers and practitioners. These include managerial motivation, leadership style, decision making, and supervisory interpersonal skills (e.g., see Blake & Mouton, 1978; Fiedler, Chemers, & Mahar, 1976; Goldstein & Sorcher, 1974; Hersey & Blanchard, 1981; Kepner & Tregoe, 1981; Miner, in press; Vroom & Yetton, 1973).

Surprisingly little research is being conducted on the use of computer training for managers and new technologies in management development. The overriding claim for computer use in management development is that it can individualize the learning experience for each learner in terms of pace and style of approach (Cooper, 1983). Future research is needed to support this claim and to better understand the match between managerial characteristics (e.g., abilities, personality characteristics, educational backgrounds) and various computerized instructional strategies.

Maximizing Learning and Transfer

Some of the most promising conceptual and empirical work in management training sheds light on ways of maximizing learning and/or transfer by focusing on the nature of the managerial skills taught, the management trainee, or the organizational environment. Waters (1980) classified managerial skills according to behavioral specificity and relative time interval, which resulted in three main types of skills: practice, context, and insight. He suggested that practice skills be learned first, because they can enhance insight and context skills. Brush and Licata (1983) went a step further and argued that each of these skills is really a composite of behavioral and knowledge components combined with an underlying noncognitive base. If managerial training is to be effective, each skill must be microanalyzed in terms of these components. Brush and Licata also argued that those managerial skills which are primarily influenced by noncognitive (i.e., attitudinal and affective) components will be less learnable and less likely to be improved by management training interventions.

With regard to the management trainee, research suggests that individual factors such as intelligence level (Gill, 1982), cognitive style (Mezoff, 1982), learning style (Kolb, 1981; Robey & Taggart, 1981), and trainee motivation and personality (Baumgartel, Reynolds, & Pathan, 1984; Campbell & Van Velsor, 1985) may affect management training outcomes. Lists of organizational factors that may constrain or facilitate positive transfer of learning (e.g., climate, reward systems) have also been proposed (Goldstein, 1985; Newstrom, 1985b).

Other authors have offered various strategies for facilitating positive transfer from management training (Kelley, Orgel, & Baer, 1985; Leifer & Newstrom, 1980). One innovative strategy for maximizing transfer is Marx's (1982) relapse prevention model, which incorporates a set of self-control techniques. In a recent empirical study, Wexley and Baldwin (in press) compared the relative effectiveness of three strategies (relapse prevention, assigned goal setting, and participative goal setting) in maximizing the positive transfer of time management skills. Both goal-setting strategies were found to be beneficial in facilitating transfer. Although the relapse prevention strategy was somewhat problematic in this study, additional research on this innovative approach is highly recommended.

Evaluation

As Kirkpatrick (1967) pointed out almost 20 years ago, the effectiveness of training programs should be evaluated in terms of reactions, learning, behavior, and/or results. Yet, writers have continually maintained that actual management training program evaluation is still in its infancy (Campbell et al., 1970; Clement, 1981). Critics have argued that most evaluations fail to go beyond trainee reactions and learning (Goldstein, 1980), are characterized by low methodological rigor (Stone, 1982), and may even be discouraged in the organization (Guyot, 1978). Nevertheless, recent research gives reason to be somewhat optimistic about the future of managerial training program evaluation.

The most significant development in the area of evaluation has centered on the estimation of the dollar value or utility of training interventions (Cascio, 1982; Spencer, 1984). Equations have been derived for evaluating the utility of a single intervention compared to a control group, an intervention readministered periodically (e.g., yearly), and a comparison among two or more training interventions (Schmidt, Hunter, & Pearlman, 1982). Cascio & Gilbert (1980) described the evaluation of a health services management training program in terms of its return on investment. Benefits were documented via trainee interviews, monthly productivity reports, and other file information. The validity of the results clearly hinged on the accuracy of the cost and benefit estimations of the trainees, but the findings showed that the benefits to the organization outweighed the costs by a ratio of 6:1.

If the effects of management training programs are to be examined clearly, rigorous experimental designs are essential, as is the measurement of individual- and group-level change or gain. Stone (1982) has offered excellent recommendations for improving the internal, external, statistical, and construct validities of true- and quasi-experimental designs. Other authors have suggested various methods for improving the measurement of change by focusing on retrospective pretests and the distinction between alpha, beta, and gamma change. (For a discussion of these evaluation issues see Howard, Ralph, Gulanick, Maxwell, Nance, & Gerber, 1979; Terborg, Howard, & Maxwell, 1980). Russell, Terborg, and Powers (1985) have demonstrated how training programs can be evaluated using organizational-level measures of performance.

Special Target Groups

In recent years, management training articles have often concentrated on segments of the managerial population thought to require some type of special managerial training. Three such target groups are women, small business owners/entrepreneurs, and international managers.

Women Although women currently comprise over 43% of the American work force, a figure that is expected to increase to 47% by 1995, they hold no more than 5–10% of all managerial and administrative positions (Trafford, 1984). This discrepancy exists partly because all women do not necessarily desire to occupy managerial and administrative roles. Even so, there remains a large discrepancy between the proportion of women in the work force and the proportion of women who are managers (Smith & Langrish, 1984). Research has shown that there are few fundamental differences between men and women on any mental, physical, or motivational capacities of consequence to effective management (Reif, Newstrom, & Monczka, 1975; Ritchie & Moses, 1983). Minor differences do exist, but mostly in ways that increase the probability of women succeeding in management.

Because of these reported similarities between women and men, the question is whether special efforts are really necessary for the management training of women. Should the design and content of training programs for women be different from those for men? Some evidence shows that no special efforts need to be made for developing female managers, and that our present training efforts in this area are successful (Alpander & Gutman, 1976). Several authors have contended, however, that although women and men do not basically differ in their managerial potential, women have certain internal and external barriers that need to be dealt with during management training (Larwood, Wood, & Inderlied, 1978). The principal internal barriers concern role conflicts, such as feminine versus managerial roles and family versus work and career roles (McLane, 1980). Major external barriers include stereotypical prejudgment of women and lack of role models and mentors within organizations.

The existence of these barriers suggests that management training programs should be undertaken for female managers, but an additional issue is the content of these special training efforts. Several authors have suggested that these programs include career awareness education; education of women in the perceptions, strategies, and behavioral skills needed in the corporate arena; identification and removal of stereotypical behaviors blocking the career paths of women; and a strong emphasis on mentoring, coaching, and positive role modeling for success (White, Crino, & DeSanctis, 1981). Apparently, the real challenge in female managerial training may be as much one of managerial socialization as it is of skill training.

Small business owners/entrepreneurs
As the small business environment grows more complex and challenging, the importance of formal education for small business owners/entrepreneurs increases. Unfortunately, researchers and practitioners alike have traditionally shown almost no interest in the educational problems of the small business enterprise (McGuire, 1976). However, a recent survey conducted by Kiesner (1984) suggests that academic institutions as well as trade and professional associations are beginning to provide more offerings relevant to small business management. For example, Tyler and Barbato (1984) reported on the design and implementation of a small business executive development program conducted at the Rochester Institute of Technology. This program covers such diverse topics as information systems, personnel relations, and negotiation strategies for small business man-

agers. In addition, the Irish Management Institute (Smyth, 1975) has identified a list of 15 problems that occur particularly in managing small business enterprises and has developed a program designed to deal with these problems.

International managers Intercultural awareness is becoming increasingly important because international contacts enable the pursuit of new markets and open avenues for multinational business operations (Bogorya, 1985). Factors such as increased foreign competition, greater reliance on overseas subsidiaries, and more American managers living overseas further underscore the need for cross-cultural training (Dotlich, 1982). Yet, a recent survey of 105 American organizations operating abroad revealed that only 32% of them had formal training programs to prepare managers for overseas work. The remaining 68% reported having no formal training programs for this purpose (Tung, 1981). This paucity of intercultural training may be due to trainers' uncertainty about appropriate content and methods, as well as to skepticism regarding the potential effectiveness of such programs. With the exception of research conducted on the culture assimilator (O'Brien & Plooij, 1977), we have found no additional evaluative research in this area. However, a few recent articles concern appropriate content and methods. A needs analysis conducted at Honeywell Corporation surveyed employees who traveled extensively or who lived abroad, in order to determine cultural, language, and communication barriers affecting managerial performance in host countries. Results suggested that cross-cultural training programs should focus as much on helping managers identify their own cultural paradigms (values, assumptions, and beliefs) as on the presentation of both general and specific information about the host countries (Dotlich, 1982).

ON-THE-JOB EXPERIENCES

Although off-the-job management education and management skill training have dominated the management development literature, a recurring theme has long been that most management development may occur on the job itself (Digman, 1978; Drucker, 1954; Mintzberg, 1973; Zemke, 1985). Writers have contended that many valuable lessons are learned directly from one's years of managerial experiences, and some recent research has attempted to maximize the value of these experiences. Several approaches have been suggested for structuring and improving the developmental yield of on-the-job managerial experience.

One such approach is known as action learning (Foy, 1977; Peddler, 1983). Developed in England and apparently quite popular throughout the world, action learning is similar to the more familiar strategy of job rotation. It places managers in unfamiliar jobs and/or unfamiliar settings. This may involve moving managers from one division of a giant company to another, or exchanging managers across several companies. Some additional strategies for structuring job experiences are: providing more autonomy in achieving one's job goals (Davies & Easterby-Smith, 1984); exposure to good and bad role models (Lombardo & McCall, 1983); and ensuring job assignments characterized by high stakes, trying circumstances, exhausting work loads, and learning new skills on the run (Lombardo, 1985).

More self-control by managers themselves (e.g., Luthans & Davis, 1979; Manz & Sims, 1980) and how managers can foster self-control in their employees' jobs (e.g., Sims, 1985) and also received attention in the literature. Writers have discussed how managers need to be taught to "push" themselves to do unattractive but necessary tasks, "pull" themselves to perform naturally enjoyable tasks, and use the practice of "unleading" to foster their employees' development. Specifically, managers and employees need training in self-observation, self-goal setting, self-reward and punishment, and behavior self-rehearsal.

Mentoring can be defined as a relationship in which an individual takes a personal interest in another's career and guides or sponsors that person (Roche, 1979). Although typically discussed in relation to female managerial development, mentoring is a critical on-the-job management development tool for both males and females. Despite the perceived importance of mentoring for management development, formalized mentoring programs have shown mixed results, with programs sometimes resulting in less than expected levels of learning and/or trainee satisfaction (Klauss, 1981; Kram, 1985).

In an effort to improve the mentoring process, recent empirical research has focused primarily on two basic questions: (a) What critical factors in the mentor-protégé relationship lead to positive mentoring outcomes? (b) What factors influence managers' desire to involve themselves in mentoring others? Research indicates that protégé learning increases when both parties exhibit high levels of trust, informality, openness with information, interaction frequency, and people orientation tempered with professional orientation (Clawson, 1980; Kram, 1985). Further, belief in career planning, career satisfaction, a high level of education, and previous benefit from a mentor have been found to be positively related to managers' willingness to mentor others (Campion & Goldfinch, 1983; Roche, 1979). This growing body of empirical research is important for increasing our understanding of mentoring, but more theorizing is needed in this area to direct and integrate research findings. Hunt and Michael (1983) and Clawson (1985) have suggested frameworks that should help in identifying key research questions as well as strategies for improving the implementation of mentoring programs.

The growing awareness of the opportunities for development present in managers' on-the-job work activities is a movie in the right direction (McCauley, 1986). The intuitive appeal of on-the-job development approaches, however, must not preclude using the same rigorous research methods as should be used to evaluate off-the-job training. Clearly, we still know far too little about how to maximize managers' development through on-the-job experiences. This subject calls for field research and experimentation.

FUNDAMENTAL CONCERNS

Several fundamental concerns regarding research and practice warrant further discussion. First, management includes a variety of occupations, each of which involves different responsibilities, skills, attitudes, and values. As Schein (1984) has noted, "management" is a catch-all phrase used to depict such diverse positions as supervisor, functional manager, general manager, entrepreneur, and chief executive officer (CEO). In addition, there are those individual contributors who manage projects, budgets, or portfolios, but not people. These individuals may or may not have the title of "manager." Despite the multitude of meanings of this term, much of the literature we reviewed either ignores this issue or attempts to circumvent it by claiming that management is management wherever one finds it. Considering the enormous diversity of managerial positions, it is unlikely that the same content, methods, learning principles, transfer strategies, and evaluation procedures will always be optimal in all situations. Therefore, we contend that more attention should be devoted to clarifying the broad domain of managerial work, and, in particular, to identifying the crucial dimensions which will allow us to distinguish one type of managerial position from another. Subsequent research can then proceed more judiciously to investigate which particular management development practices will be most appropriate for each type of managerial position. Contingency approaches and models of management development are sorely needed (e.g., see Randolph & Posner, 1979).

Second, the field of management development is extremely atheoretical in nature. This has resulted in a body of literature that can generally be described as descriptive, anecdotal, nonempirical, and faddish. Although some empirical research has demonstrated that specific developmental techniques work, too little research has emanated from a valid theory of effective management. Part of this problem is because there is no comprehensive theory of managerial effectiveness (Norden, 1981). Several writers have generated lists of requirements for effective management (e.g., Bennis & Nanus, 1985; Sank, 1974; Stewart, 1984), but, interestingly, these lists vary greatly from author to author.

We do have traditional developmental approaches that are well grounded in the particular theories of their developers (e.g., Fiedler, Chemers, & Mahar, 1976; Goldstein & Sorcher, 1974; Vroom & Yetton, 1973), but each of these approaches represents a rather narrow component of the broad spectrum of managerial effectiveness. For instance, some are directed at improving leadership style, others at improving managerial decision making, and still others at enhancing managerial motivation. Although these attempts to generate theory-based approaches and comprehensive lists are commendable, we still do not know much about how different aspects of managerial effectiveness (e.g., leadership style and decision making) fit together to form a comprehensive whole.

IMPLICATIONS FOR PRACTICE

Clearly, Drucker's (1954) notion of the critical importance of effective managers is widely accepted in American organizations today. Hundreds of millions of dollars are spent annually on management development and the volume of work on it is massive. In this era of increasing international competitiveness and market maturity, organizations seem more aware than ever that they must take an active stance and cannot leave the development of their managerial talent to chance.

The interest in and resources devoted to management development continue to grow, and the existing literature suggests some very general issues that we think have significant implications for the practice of management development.

First, management development is a multifaceted, complex, and long-term process, and there is no quick or simple answer to the question, "How should we best develop our managers?" However, many practitioners and practice-oriented writers ignore this basic point. For example, those concerned with improving business curriculum relevance rarely consider how such changes might interact with existing management training programs or on-the-job activities. Similarly, management trainers often design and conduct their programs as if they existed in a vacuum totally unaffected by the day-to-day managerial experiences that have preceded and/or will follow the training. That development can take place over an individual's entire career should be recognized by those responsible for management development in our organizations. It may begin with an individual's basic educational experiences, continue with the person's progressive career experiences, and be augmented with periodic training programs that the individual attends throughout his or her organizational tenure. Regardless of the combination of development inputs, however, a holistic and integrative perspective is a necessity if management development is to be an effective and vital stimulus for increased organizational effectiveness. In short, there is no one best way of management development. It includes a huge variety of activities and events that span an individual's entire career and is contingent on numerous factors in the individual, the type of managerial job, and the organization. (For an example of this type of approach, see London, 1985.)

Second, organizations should also pay more attention to systematically identifying their own specific developmental objectives and evaluating the outcomes of their developmental programs. Too much of existing management development seems to be exclusively concerned with techniques and methods of the "train and hope" variety. As a first step, developers should attempt, prior to any training, to determine objectives for managers' development and to link these objectives to sources of evidence (appraisals, records, documents) that might indicate to what extent the objectives have been met. It is important to be as concerned with what is to be learned as with the hardware and techniques involved to achieve that learning. Utility analysis is a promising direction for evaluating the bottom-line impact of our developmental activities, but it is contingent on the existence of this first step.

Third, management development activities should not take place independent of, or worse, in conflict with, organizational objectives. We concur with those writers who stress the need for a more explicit linkage between the developmental function and general organizational strategic objectives (Hayes, 1985). Tichy, Fombrun, & Devanna (1982) have described a number of U.S. companies (e.g., Exxon, IBM, General Motors) that are currently attempting to strategically manage the development of their executive talent.

A final important issue, and one which we are certainly not the first to lament (Campbell, 1971; Goldstein, 1980; Wexley, 1984), is that the utility of management education, training, and experience still remains more an article of faith rather than an empirical fact. We concur with Freedman and Stumpf's (1982) observation that the field has stressed the development of techniques and instruments that are often of dubious validity and rarely generalizable beyond the organizational sites in which they were developed. Given the value and costs of management development activities (Huber, 1985), it is unsettling that so little evaluative evidence exists and that so many people question whether these efforts do anything to upgrade actual managerial performance (Hoffman, 1983). If we are to progress in our knowledge and understanding of how to effectively develop managers, considerably more attention must be devoted to this most fundamental of issues.

REFERENCES

Alpander, G. G., & Gutman, J. E. (1976). Contents and techniques of management development programs for women. *Personnel Journal, 55*(2), 76–79.

Argyris, C. (1980). Some limitations of the case method: Experiences in a management development program. *Academy of Management Review, 5,* 291–298.

Badawy, M. K. (1982). *Developing managerial skills in engineers and scientists.* New York: Van Nostrand Reinhold.

Bartunek, J. M., Gordon, J. R., & Weathersby, R. P. (1983). Developing "complicated" understanding in administrators. *Academy of Management Review, 8,* 273–284.

Baumgartel, H. J., Reynolds, M. J. I., & Pathan, R. Z. (1984). How personality and organizational climate variables moderate the effectiveness of management development programmes: A review and some recent research findings. *Management and Labour Studies, 9*(1), 1–16.

Bednar, D. A., & Heisler, W. J. (1985). Relationships between communicator style and instructional effectiveness in an industrial training setting. In R. B. Robinson, Jr. & J. A. Pearce II (Eds.), *Proceedings of the 45th Annual Meeting of the Academy of Management* (pp. 421–424). San Diego, CA.

Behrman, J. N., & Levin, R. I. (1984). Are business schools doing their job? *Harvard Business Review, 62*(1), 140–147.

Bennett, R. (1982). Management development for real. *Journal of Management Development, 1*(4), 38–51.

Bennis, W., & Nanus, B. (1985). *Leaders: The strategies for taking charge.* New York: Harper & Row.

Berger, M. A. (1983). In defense of the case method: A reply to Argyris. *Academy of Management Review, 8,* 329–333.

Bernardin, H. J., & Buckley, M. R. (1981). Strategies in rater training. *Academy of Management Review, 6,* 205–212.

Birkenbach, X. C., Kamfer, L., & Morshuizen, J. D. (1985). The development and the evaluation of a behaviour-modeling training programme for supervisors. *South African Journal of Psychology, 15,* 11–19.

Blake, R. R., & Mouton, J. S. (1978). *The new managerial grid.* Houston, TX: Gulf Publishing.

Blank, W. E. (1982). *Handbook for developing competency-based training programs.* Englewood Cliffs, NJ: Prentice Hall.

Bogorya, Y. (1985). Intercultural training for managers involved in international business. *Journal of Management Development, 4*(2), 17–25.

Bolt, J. F. (1985). Tailor executive development to strategy. *Harvard Business Review, 63*(6), 168–179.

Boyatzis, R. E. (1982). *The competent manager: A model for effective performance.* New York: Wiley.

Bradford, D. L. (1983). Some potential problems with the teaching of managerial competencies. *The Organizational Behavior Teaching Journal, 8*(2), 45–49.

Brush, D. H., & Licata, B. J. (1983). The impact of skill learnability on the effectiveness of managerial training and development. *Journal of Management, 9,* 27–39.

Byham, W. C. (1983). The use of assessment centers in management development. In B. Taylor & G. L. Lippitt (Eds.), *Management development* and training handbook — 2nd edition (pp. 222–244). London: McGraw-Hill.

Cameron, K. S., & Whetten, D. S. (1983). A model for teaching management skills. *The Organizational Behavior Teaching Journal, 8*(2), 21–27.

Campbell, J. P. (1971). Personnel training and development. *Annual Review of Psychology, 22,* 565–602.

Campbell, J. P., Dunnette, M. D., Lawler, E. E., & Weick, K. E. (1970). *Managerial behavior, performance, and effectiveness.* New York: McGraw-Hill.

Campbell, D., & Van Velsor, E. (1985). The use of personality measures in a management development program. In H. J. Bernardin & D. A. Bownas (Eds.), *Personality assessment in organizations* (pp. 193–216). New York: Praeger Press.

Campion, M. A., & Goldfinch, J. R. (1983). Mentoring among hospital administrators. *Hospital and Health Services Administration, 28*(4), 77–93.

Cascio, W. (1982). *Costing human resources: The financial impact of behavior in organizations.* Boston: Kent.

Cascio, W. J., & Gilbert, G. R. (1980). Making dollars and sense out of management development. In R. C. Huseman (Ed.), *Proceedings of the 40th Annual Meeting of the National Academy of Management* (pp. 95–98). Detroit, MI.

Clawson, J. G. (1980). Mentoring in managerial careers. In C. B. Derr (Ed.), *Work, family and the career* (pp. 144–165). New York: Praeger Special Studies.

Clawson, J. G. (1985). *Coaching, chemistry, and contingency theory. A theory of developmental relationships in organizations.* Unpublished manuscript, University of Virginia, Darden School of Business, Charlottesville.

Clement, R. W. (1981). Evaluating the effectiveness of management training: Progress during the 1970's and prospects for the 1980's. *Human Resource Management, 20*(4), 8–13.

Cooper, A. (1983). New technologies in management education. In B. Taylor & G. L. Lippitt (Eds.), *Management development and training handbook — 2nd edition* (pp. 245–306). London: McGraw-Hill.

Cox, C., & Beck, J. (1984). *Management development: Advances in practice and theory.* New York: Wiley.

Damm, R. C. (1983). Measuring skills: The University of Pittsburgh experience. *The Organizational Behavior Teaching Journal, 8*(2), 35–36.

Davies, J., & Easterby-Smith, M. (1984). Learning and developing from managerial work experiences. *Journal of Management Studies 21*(2), 169–183.

Digman, L. A. (1978). How well-managed organizations develop their executives. *Organizational Dynamics, 7*(2), 63–80.

Digman, L. A. (1980). How companies assess management development needs. In R. C. Huseman (Ed.), *Proceedings of the 40th Annual Meeting of the National Academy of Management* (pp. 99–103). Detroit, MI.

Dotlich, D. (1982). International and intracultural management development. *Training and Development Journal, 36*(10), 26–31.

Drucker, P. (1954). *The practice of management.* New York: Harper & Row.

Easterby-Smith, M., & Davies, J. (1983). Developing strategic thinking. *Long Range Planning, 16,* 39–48.

Eden, D. (1984). Self-fulfilling prophecy as a management tool: Harnessing pygmalion. *Academy of Management Review, 9,* 64–73.

Eurich, N. P. (1985). *Corporate classrooms: The learning business.* Princeton, NJ: Carnegie Foundation for the Advancement of Teaching.

Faerman, S. R., Quinn, R. E., & Thompson, M. P. (1985, June). *Management theory and management development: A 3.5 million dollar experiment.* Paper presented at the Organizational Behavior Teaching Conference, Charlottesville, VA.

Fiedler, F. E., Chemers, M. M., & Mahar, L. (1976). *Improving leadership effectiveness: The leader match concept.* New York: Wiley.

Ford, J. K., & Noe, R. (1985). *The impact of managerial level, function and attitude on the self-assessment of training needs.* Unpublished manuscript, Michigan State University, Department of Psychology, East Lansing.

Foy, N. (1977). Action learning comes to industry. *Harvard Business Review, 55*(5), 158–168.

Freedman, R. D., & Stumpf, S. A. (1982). Management education: Its theory, research and practice. In R. D. Freedman, C. J. Cooper, & S. A. Stumpf (Eds.), *Management education* (pp. 3–22). New York: Wiley.

Gill, R. W. T. (1982). A trainability concept for management potential and an empirical study of relationship with intelligence for two managerial skills. *Journal of Occupational Psychology, 55,* 139–147.

Gist, M. E. (1986). *A field experiment examining the*

effects of efficacy-based training on subsequent training task performance among managers. Unpublished manuscript, University of North Carolina, Department of Organizational Behavior, Chapel Hill.

Goldstein, A. P., & Sorcher, M. (1974). *Changing supervisory behavior*. New York: Pergamon Press.

Goldstein, I. L. (1980). Training in work organizations. *Annual Review of Psychology, 31*, 229–272.

Goldstein, I. L. (1985, August). *Organization analysis and evaluation models*. Paper presented at the Annual Meeting of the American Psychological Association, Los Angeles, CA.

Guyot, J. F. (1978). Management training and the post-industrial apologetics. *California Management Review, 20*(4), 84–93.

Hawrylyshyn, B. (1975). Management education — a conceptual framework. In B. Taylor & G. L. Lippitt (Eds.), *Management development and training handbook* (pp. 169–181). London: McGraw-Hill.

Hayes, M. (1985). Developing managers for strategic management. In W. D. Guth (Ed.), *Handbook of business strategy* (pp. 420–444). Boston: Warren, Gorham, & Lamont Publishing.

Heisler, W. J., & Lasher, H. J. (in press). The business of management development and management education: A call for increased collaboration. *Journal of Management Development*.

Hersey, P., & Blanchard, K. H. (1981). So you want to know your leadership style? *Training and Development Journal, 35*(6), 34–54.

Hoffman, F. O. (1983). Is management development doing the job? *Training and Development Journal, 37*(1), 34–39.

Howard, G. S., Ralph, K. M., Gulanick, N. A., Maxwell, S. E., Nance, D. W., & Gerber, S. R. (1979). Internal invalidity in pretest-posttest self-report evaluations and a re-evaluation of retrospective pretests. *Applied Psychological Measurement, 3*, 1–23.

Huber, V. L. (1985). Training and development: Not always the best medicine. *Personnel, 62*(1), 12–15.

Hunt, D. M., & Michael, C. (1983). Mentorship: A career training and development tool. *Academy of Management Review, 8*, 475–485.

Johnston, J. S., Jr. (1986). *Educating managers: Executive effectiveness through liberal learning*. San Francisco: Jossey Bass.

Kelly, A. I., Orgel, R. F., & Baer, D. M. (1985). Seven strategies that guarantee training transfer. *Training and Development Journal, 39*(11), 78–82.

Kepner, C. H., & Tregoe, B. B. (1981). *The new rational manager: A systematic approach to problem solving and decision making*. New York: McGraw-Hill.

Keys, B. (in press). Total enterprise simulation gaming for management development. *Journal of Management Development*.

Kiesner, W. F. (1984, June). *Small business course content, timing, and other critical factors in the success of small business training courses*. Paper presented at the 29th Annual Conference of the International Council for Small Business, Chicago, IL.

Kirkpatrick, D. L. (1967). Evaluation of training. In R. L. Craig (Ed.), *Training and development handbook* (pp. 18-1 to 18-27). New York: McGraw-Hill.

Klauss, R. (1981). Formalized mentor relationships for management and executive development programs in the federal government. *Public Administration Review, 41*(4), 489–496.

Klimoski, R. J. (1982, August). *Needs assessment for management development*. Paper presented at the Annual Meeting of the American Psychological Association, Washington, DC.

Kolb, D. A. (1981). Experimental learning theory and the learning style inventory: A reply to Freedman and Stumpf. *Academy of Management Review, 6*, 289–296.

Kram, K. E. (1985). *Mentoring at work: Developmental relationships in organizational life*. Glenview, IL: Scott Foresman.

Larwood, L., Wood, M. M., & Inderlied, S. D. (1978). Training women for management: New problems, new solutions. *Academy of Management Review, 3*, 584–593.

Latham, G. P., & Saari, L. M. (1979). Application of social-learning theory to training supervisors through behavior modeling. *Journal of Applied Psychology, 64*, 239–246.

Leifer, M. S., & Newstrom, J. W. (1980). Solving the transfer of training problem. *Training and Development Journal, 34*(8), 42–46.

Livingston, J. S. (1971). Myth of the well educated manager. *Harvard Business Review, 49*(1), 79–89.

Lombardo, M. M. (1985). Five challenging assignments. *Issues and Observations, 5*(2). Available from Center for Creative Leadership, Greensboro, NC.

Lombardo, M. M., & McCall, M. W. (1983). Great truths that may not be. *Issues and Observations,*

3(2). Available from Center for Creative Leadership, Greensboro, NC.

London, M. (1985). *Developing managers.* San Francisco: Jossey-Bass.

Luthans, F., & Davis, T. R. V. (1979). Behavioral self-management (BSM): The missing link in managerial effectiveness. *Organizational Dynamics, 8*(1), 42–60.

Manz, C., & Sims, H. P. (1980). Self-management as a substitute for leadership: A social learning theory perspective. *Academy of Management Review, 5,* 361–367.

Marx, R. D. (1982). Relapse prevention for managerial training: A model for maintenance of behavior change. *Academy of Management Review, 7,* 433–441.

McCauley, C. D. (1986). *Development experiences in managerial work: A literature review* (Tech. Rep. No. 36). Available from Center for Creative Leadership, Greensboro, NC.

McGehee, W., & Thayer, P. W. (1961). *Training in business and industry.* New York: Wiley.

McLane, H. J. (1980). *Selecting, developing, and retaining women executives: A corporate strategy for the eighties.* New York: Van Nostrand Reinhold.

McGuire, J. W. (1976). The small enterprise in economics and organization theory. *Journal of Contemporary Business, 5*(2), 115.

Meyer, H. H., & Raich, M. S. (1983). An objective evaluation of a behavior modeling program. *Personnel Psychology, 36,* 755–762.

Mezoff, B. (1982). Cognitive style and interpersonal behavior: A review with implications for human relations training. *Group and Organization Studies, 7*(1), 13–32.

Miner, J. B. (in press). Managerial role motivation training. *Journal of Management Development.*

Mintzberg, H. (1973). *The nature of managerial work.* New York: Harper & Row.

Moore, M. L., & Dutton, P. (1978). Training needs analysis: Review and critique. *Academy of Management Review, 3,* 532–545.

Newstrom, J. W. (1985a). "Mod" management development: Does it deliver what it promises? *Journal of Management Development, 4*(1), 3–11.

Newstrom, J. W. (1985b). *A contingency model for addressing the impediments to transfer of training.* Paper presented at the 45th Annual Meeting of the Academy of Management, San Diego, CA.

Norden, P. V. (1981). A framework for educating managers. In R. D. Carter (Ed.), *Future challenges in management education* (pp. 5–14). New York: Praeger Publishing.

O'Brien, G. E., & Plooij, D. (1977). Comparison of programmed and prose culture training upon attitudes and knowledge. *Journal of Applied Psychology, 62,* 499–505.

Oppenheimer, R. J. (1982). An alternative approach to assessing management development needs. *Training and Development Journal, 36*(3), 72–76.

Parry, S. B., & Reich, L. R. (1984). An uneasy look at behavior modeling. *Training and Development Journal, 38*(3), 57–62.

Payne, S. L., & Pettingill, B. F. (in press). Improving student creativity in management education. *Journal of Business Education.*

Peddler, M. (1983). *Action learning in practice.* Aldershot, England: Gower Publishing.

Peters, T. J., & Waterman, R. H. (1982). *In search of excellence.* New York: Harper & Row.

Pfeffer, J. (1977). Effects of an MBA and socioeconomic origins on business school graduates' salaries. *Journal of Applied Psychology, 62,* 698–705.

Powers, E. A. (1983). The AMA management competency program: A developmental process. *The Organizational Behavior Teaching Journal, 8*(2), 16–20.

Randolph, W. A., & Posner, B. Z. (1979). Designing meaningful learning situations in management: A contingency, decision-tree approach. *Academy of Management Review, 4,* 459–467.

Reif, W. E., Newstrom, J. W., & Monczka, R. M. (1975). Exploding some myths about women managers. *California Management Review, 17*(4), 72–79.

Ritchie, R. J., & Moses, J. L. (1983). Assessment center correlates of women's advancement into middle management: A 7-year longitudinal analysis. *Journal of Applied Psychology, 68,* 227–231.

Robey, D., & Taggart, W. (1981). Measuring managers' minds: The assessment of style in human information processing. *Academy of Management Review, 6,* 375–383.

Robinson, J. (1980). Will behavior modeling survive the 80's? *Training and Development Journal, 34*(1), 22–28.

Roche, G. (1979). Much ado about mentors. *Harvard Business Review, 57*(1), 14–24.

Russell, J. S., Terborg, J. R., & Powers, M. L. (1985). Organizational performance and organizational level training and support. *Personnel Psychology, 38,* 849–863.

Russell, J. S., Wexley, K. N., & Hunter, J. E. (1984). Questioning the effectiveness of behavior modeling training in an industrial setting. *Personnel Psychology, 37,* 465–481.

Sank, L. (1974). Effective and ineffective managerial traits obtained as naturalistic descriptions from executive members of a super corporation. *Personnel Psychology, 26,* 432–444.

Schein, E. H. (1984, August). *Management development: What is management? What is development?* Paper presented at the 44th Annual Meeting of the National Academy of Management, Boston, MA.

Schmidt, F. L., Hunter, J. E., & Pearlman, K. (1982). Assessing the economic impact of personnel programs on workforce productivity. *Personnel Psychology, 35,* 333–347.

Sims, H. P. (1985, August). *Leading others to lead themselves: pitfalls along the path.* Paper presented at the 45th Annual Meeting of the National Academy of Management, San Diego, CA.

Smith, M., & Langrish, S. (1984). The task for the 80's: Training women managers. In C. Cox & J. Beck (Eds.), *Management development: Advances in practice and theory* (pp. 67–80). New York: Wiley.

Smyth, G. F. (1975). Identifying and developing the entrepreneur. In B. Taylor & G. Lippitt (Eds.), *Management development and training handbook* (pp. 135–148). London: McGraw-Hill.

Spencer, L. M. (1984). How to calculate the costs and benefits of an HRD program. *Training, 21*(7), 40–51.

Stewart, R. (1984). The nature of management? A problem for management education. *Journal of Management Studies, 21*(3), 323–330.

Stone, E. F. (1982). Research design: Issues in studies assessing the effects of management education. In R. D. Freedman, C. L. Cooper, & S. A. Stumpf (Eds.), *Management education* (pp. 87–132). New York: Wiley.

Terborg, J. R., Howard, G. S., & Maxwell, S. E. (1980). Evaluating planned organizational change: A method for assessing alpha, beta, and gamma change. *Academy of Management Review, 5,* 109–121.

Tichy, N. M., Fombrun, C. J., & Devanna, M. A. (1982). Strategic human resource management. *Sloan Management Review, 23*(2), 47–61.

Trafford, A. (1984, August). She's come a long way — or has she? *U.S. News and World Report,* p. 44.

Tung, R. L. (1981). Selection and training of personnel for overseas assignments. *Columbia Journal of World Business, 16*(1), 68–78.

Tyler, P., & Barbato, R. (1984, June). *Designing, marketing and conducting a successful small business executive development program.* Paper presented at the 29th Annual Conference of the International Council on Small Business, Chicago, IL.

Vaill, P. (1983). The theory of managing in the managerial competency movement. *The Organizational Behavior Teaching Journal, 8*(2), 50–54.

Van Zwieten, J. (1984). Training on the rocks. *Training and Development Journal, 38*(1), 26–33.

Vroom, V. H., & Yetton, P. W. (1973). *Leadership and decision making.* Pittsburgh: University of Pittsburgh Press.

Waters, J. A. (1980). Managerial skill development. *Academy of Management Review, 5,* 449–453.

Wellemeyer, M. (1983, October). Triathletes of business. *Fortune,* pp. 193–194.

Wexley, K. N. (1984). Personnel training. *Annual Review of Psychology, 35,* 519–551.

Wexley, K. N., & Baldwin, T. T. (in press). Strategies for facilitating the positive transfer of training: An empirical exploration. *Academy of Management Journal.*

Wexley, K. N., & Latham, G. P. (1981). *Developing and training human resources in organizations.* Glenview, IL: Scott Foresman.

Whetten, D. S., & Cameron, K. S. (1984). *Developing managerial skills.* Glenview, IL: Scott Foresman.

White, M. C., Crino, M. D., & DeSanctis, G. L. (1981). *A critical review of female performance, performance training and organizational initiatives designed to aid women in the work-role environment. Personnel Psychology, 34,* 227–248.

Yukl, G. (1982). *A behavioral approach to needs assessment for managers.* Paper presented at The 42nd Annual Meeting of The Academy of Management, New York.

Yukl, G., & Van Fleet, D. D. (1982). Cross-situational, multi-method research on military leader effectiveness. *Organizational Behavior and Human Performance, 30,* 87–108.

Zemke, R. (1985). The Honeywell studies: How managers learn to manage. *Training, 22*(8), 46–51.

Kenneth N. Wexley is affiliated with Michigan State University; Timothy T. Baldwin is affiliated with Indiana University.

Simulating the Consequences of Job Redesign
Nealia S. Bruning / Jay Weinroth

Researchers can create computer simulations of complex employment and production systems by first analyzing an organization as an interrelated set of subsystems.[1] Independent models for each subsystem can be programmed and tested; these separate but related models can later be combined in order to simulate entire organizations. Turnover, absenteeism and tardiness, production of units of output, production of defective units, and termination of part-time substitute workers are examples of elements that can be modeled separately and combined to produce a complete simulation.

Unlike most operations-research methods, simulation does not first specify fixed conditions and then require analysts to estimate the effect of their absence.[2] Simulation seeks to represent organizational systems as is (to the extent that the model has been developed correctly).

The method is experimentation. Before any job-change intervention takes place, hypothetical variables can be altered, observed, and analyzed in the simulated system. If the simulated system accurately portrays an organization, the changes made in the model should represent the effects of job changes in that organization.

NINE-STEP PROCEDURE

This article outlines the procedure we developed to estimate the effectiveness of an intervention:[3]

1. Develop a model of the existing organizational system.
2. Develop a theoretical model to identify the potential results and economic value of each potential intervention.
3. Develop a computerized simulation model that incorporates the organizational model and summarizes the cumulative effect of various decisions.
4. Validate the model against the organizational system it is intended to represent.
5. Conduct a pilot intervention in a specific company unit.
6. Compare the results of the pilot program with the projected simulation results.
7. Revise the simulation model to more accurately reflect the relationships established in the pilot project.
8. Rerun the simulation to generate a more accurate estimate of the value of broad organizational intervention.
9. Decide whether to implement the job-change intervention.

Source: Nealia S. Bruning and Jay Weinroth, "Simulating the Consequences of Job Redesign." Reprinted from *Computers in Personnel* (New York: Auerbach Publishers). © 1988 Warren, Gorham & Lamont Inc. Used with permission.

Implementation of this procedure requires integration of an HR manager's organizational knowledge with simulation modeling software written by a competent programmer.

A Manufacturer's Application

A medium-sized midwestern manufacturer and fabricator of printed circuit boards and circuit board components provided the initial data for our research. The company's senior management sought to improve productivity through employee participation and involvement. Because management expected employees' suggestions to concern changes in the repetitive nature of their work, it wanted to determine the potential value of participation and the usefulness of proposed job changes.

Organizational Models   Organizational models can be created through various methods, including data collection from company departments and empirically derived reporting relationships, experts' representations of the existing system, and the previously defined system models.

We took a general view of the company, using a behavioral model called the job characteristics model, which focused on workers' attitudes and behavior. Developed by Richard Hackman and Greg Oldham,[4] this model defines certain general job characteristics important to workers. As these job characteristics improve, the employees' job satisfaction, motivation, and performance should improve as well.

The manufacturing company's employees were surveyed to determine their attitudes on various job components, including job characteristics (e.g., skill variety, autonomy, job identity, task significance, and feedback), perceived work-related competence (e.g., degree of achievement and need fulfillment), job satisfaction, and intention to leave the organization. Relationships between these components were derived through statistical analysis.[5]

Supplemental data was collected through other organizational studies (e.g., the relationships between job satisfaction and turnover and between job satisfaction and absenteeism).[6]

Theoretical Models   In order to determine the job redesign's potential value, we created a theoretical model in which job characteristics were expected to lead to job satisfaction, which in turn, was expected to lead to higher productivity, lower turnover, and lower absenteeism (see Exhibit 1). The following results were derived from the model:

- The number of units produced.
- Overall turnover.
- The average number of employees absent each day.
- The lower productivity level of replacement personnel.
- Inventory.
- Product reject rates.
- Total costs (including material, labor, overhead, and administration).
- Profit.

When the data needed to determine these results was not available (e.g., demand for products), estimates were made.

This theoretical model helped

EXHIBIT 1
Theoretical Model of Results of Job Characteristics and Satisfaction

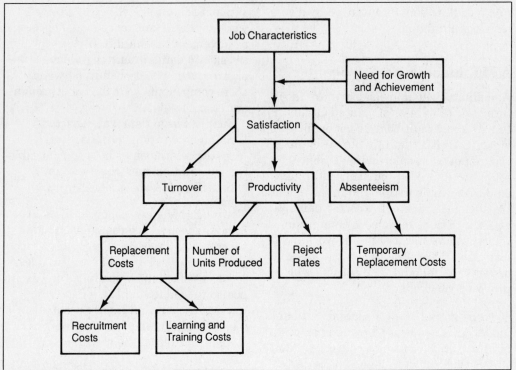

determine the factors that contributed to productivity and profit within the manufacturing company. At this stage, an HR manager or researcher should also determine the relationship between the intervention and the company's structure and culture. Exhibit 1 shows the elements of the theoretical model; the intervention's effect on job characteristics should alter the results at the base of the model.

This theoretical model should be reviewed with managers familiar with the system because their support is needed to establish the validity of any simulation model. If the organization contracts for a simulation study, key managers or decision makers should be involved in the development and evaluation of the model from its early stages through completion.[7] In the case of the manufacturing company, however, the model builders developed the simulation to support the company's HR research.

Simulation Model The theoretical model is the software that enables a computer to simulate actual work processes. Simulated workers in the model are assigned characteristics of real employees (e.g., growth needs, turnover and absenteeism propensity, and expertise). These workers then perform work on the basis of dependencies established for the model.

In the manufacturing company simulation, the simulated workers performed their jobs for nine months (182 work days), were absent or late, left the organization, and were replaced; the effects on the number of units produced were calculated and stored. Productivity statistics for the period were aligned with the corresponding workers' characteristics. This simulation model represented the organization as it appeared before any intervention was proposed.

Model Validation and Experimentation
Before attempting to predict productivity-related results from the various interventions, the model builders first determined that the model will simulate the organization's daily behavior without interventions. The objective of this determination is to ensure that there are no errors in the software. We then compared the model's profile of job characteristics, perceived competence, and satisfaction characteristics with those of the organization's population of workers.

Ideally, model builders should also be able to compare the modeled projections of such components as absenteeism rates, turnover rates, actual units produced, and reject and defect rates with actual organization records. In this case, however, the broader organizational data was not directly available. (The data that could be compared matched up well with the actual worker characteristics, but further development of this validation step is needed.)

Following development and validation of the model, we introduced two policy interventions into the simulation to determine the expected costs and benefits of job changes. Some expected results were lower absenteeism, lower turnover, lower reject and defect rates, and increased motivation. These results were then reviewed in the simulation study to determine the overall benefit of the intervention to the organization. To determine whether the change produced a net benefit, the cost of the change was subtracted from the amount of the overall benefit.

The first policy change introduced into the manufacturing company was an increase in employees' perceived competence levels. This change was the first to be made, because it had the greatest effect on the results identified in the preliminary study. This increase in perceived competence can be accomplished either through training or the organization's selection practices.

The second policy change was an increase in the perceived level of job characteristics for those tasks rated as inadequate. This increase was added to the increase in competence. It could be implemented by redesigning the jobs or by hiring replacement employees with more positive attitudes than the current employees. These policy changes helped increase productivity by as much as 4%. (Estimation of the actual net costs or benefits of the intervention was prevented, however, by a unionization drive. A net benefit would have justified undertaking the next step in the modeling process as previously outlined.)

A simulation's credibility can be established through the following three fundamental procedures:

- Running the model several times to generate representative outcome

averages — Means and standard deviations constitute the simulation's predicted system behavior.[8]
- Comparing the means obtained from the previous step and the distribution patterns of desirable results with known means and distributions in the actual system.
- Determining whether relationships between important elements (e.g., effect of satisfaction on turnover) are modeled correctly in the simulation software — This determination may be achieved by changing the average values of these elements, one at a time, and then observing whether all other elements change proportionately in the simulated results.

A sensitivity analysis is also performed this way in order to determine whether changes in model output correspond proportionally to changes in input. For example, simulated turnover in our model should change proportionately as the mean for workers' sense of competence is manipulated, following the degree of change expected in the actual system. The model can also change or improve our understanding of the expected behavior of an actual system.

Pilot Intervention After projecting an intervention's net benefits, HR should initiate a pilot program to further validate and refine the model. This pilot should be representative of the organization. The pilot's design should help ensure that results obtained in the organization's test section are compatible with those obtained throughout the company. At least one company control group that does not experience an intervention should be established to compare with those that do.

Pilot Results Compared with Simulation Projections The results of the pilot should be measured after the related intervention has taken effect. The time period depends on the type of intervention planned. If the model's support role is successful, the results of the model and the pilot program should be similar enough to predict the accuracy of the model so far.

The success of the model in predicting the outcome of a pilot program is the strongest evidence for the validity of that program. In the validation procedure, a small-scale intervention can be made to improve the model in order to make large-scale projections possible.

Simulation Model Revision When the results of the pilot program are compared with the simulated projections, major differences must be reconciled. This reconciliation can be carried out by adjusting the simulation model where it appears to be faulty and by improving the intervention itself. Because the simulation model is based on the underlying relationships between the system's behavioral elements, the intervention must alter the elements in the causal chain; a serious difference between the results of the pilot program and the simulation model could indicate a faulty model or a failure in the job-change intervention.

If there seems to be a mismatch between model output and pilot program results, the numbers produced by each should be contrasted and analyzed. If the fault lies somewhere in the logic of the simulation software, a trail can be charted back to the errors. The model can then be corrected and run again.

Rerun the Simulation Model The revised simulation model should be rerun to understand the effect of the intervention on the organization. Estimates of the costs of the intervention must also be included to estimate the costs and benefits involved.

Implementation Decision The refined and validated simulation model should now allow company decision makers to assess the expected results of its implementation. They will be able to answer whether a job change that requires costly equipment and training will benefit workers' performance, absenteeism, and turnover sufficiently to justify the intervention. The simulation process will also compel decision makers to examine the assumed relationships between the variables and the actual effect of the intervention.

The simulation software's flexibility and capacity for interaction add to its usefulness to HR management. For example, GPSS/PC (General Purpose Simulation System), from Digital Equipment Corp. of Maynard, MA, includes debugging aids, graphics, and animation screens for management presentations.

GPSS simulations can be halted when desired, and the speed of simulated events can be varied to reveal how the model's interactions occur. Animation and graphics displays can simulate such HR measures as absenteeism, production levels, reject rates, changes in inventory level, back ordering, and work in process. They aid communication between managers and model builders, and they promote the credibility and accuracy of the models.

These tools, however, should be used with caution. Animation, for example, is persuasive because it is dynamic and colorful. Managers should be sure to include quantitative details to support the validity of their model's performance.

Only the later stages of modeling and intervention produce fairly precise simulations and behavioral predictions. Because there will always be some unanticipated results from any intervention, revisions of the simulation model and the intervention strategy may be required throughout the intervention process.

The value of the simulation process is derived not only from the added information produced for decision makers but from the analytical effort required to model an organization. HR managers can apply these models to help determine the results of organizational change.

NOTES

1. J. Dutton and W. G. Briggs, "Simulation Model Construction," *Computer Simulation of Human Behavior,* eds. J. Dutton and W. Starbuck (New York: John Wiley & Sons, 1973), pp. 103–126.
2. J. W. Schmidt, "Fundamentals of Digital Simulation Modeling," *Proceedings of the 1981 Winter Simulation Conference,* eds. T. I. Oren; C. M. Delfosse; and C. M. Shub (San Diego, CA: Society for Computer Simulation, 1981), pp. 13–21.
3. A. M. Law, "Introduction to Simulation: A Powerful Tool for Analyzing Complex Manufacturing Systems," *Industrial Engineering* 18, no. 5 (1986), pp. 46–63; Schmidt, 1981; Schmidt, "Introduction to Systems Analysis, Modeling and Simulation."
4. J. R. Hackman and G. R. Oldham, "Motivation Through the Design of Work: Test of a Theory," *Organizational Behavior and Human Performance* 16 (1976), pp. 250–279; Hackman and Oldham, *Work Redesign* (Reading, MA: Addison-Wesley, 1980).
5. Satisfaction was predicted by entering the sum of the job characteristics (JOBC), competence (COMP), and the interaction between JOBC and COMP into a single term. (See Cohen & Cohen, 1975, for more detail on this procedure.) The multiple R^2 was .46 ($F = 68.08$; $p < .01$). The F-tests for JOBC, COMP, and the

interaction term beta weights were all statistically significant ($p < .01$). The standardized beta weight values of these tests were B = .95 (F = 10.10) for JOBC, B = .96 (F = 28.00) for COMP, and B = .99 (F = 6.01) for the interaction term.

6. M. M. Petty; G. W. McGee; and J. W. Cavender, "A Meta-analysis of the Relationships Between Individual Job Satisfaction and Individual Performance," *The Academy of Management Review* 9 (1984), pp. 712–721; W. H. Mobley, *Employee Turnover: Causes, Consequences and Control* (Reading, MA: Addison-Wesley, 1982).

7. O. Balci, "Credibility Assessment of Simulation Results," *Proceedings of the 1986 Winter Simulation Conference,* eds. J. Wilson; J. Henricksen; and S. Roberts (San Diego, CA: Society for Computer Simulation, 1986), pp. 38–44; Balci, *Guidelines for Successful Simulation Studies* (Blacksburg, VA: Virginia Institute, Department of Computer Science, 1986); J. S. Carson, "Convincing Users of Model's Validity Is Challenging Aspect of Modeler's Job," *Industrial Engineering* 18 (1986), pp. 74–85; D. A. Koskossidis and B. J. Davies, "Validation and Verification of Job Shop Simulation Models," *Proceedings of the 1984 Winter Simulation Conference,* ed. W. Wade (San Diego, CA: Society for Computer Simulation, 1984), pp. 252–255; R. G. Sargent, "An Expository of Verification and Validation of Simulation Models," *Proceedings of the 1985 Winter Simulation Conference,* eds. D. Gantz; G. Blais; and S. Solomon (San Diego, CA).

8. D. W. Kelton, "Analysis of Simulation Output Data," *Proceedings of the 1985 Winter Simulation Conference,* eds. D. Gantz; G. Blais; and S. Solomon (San Diego, CA: Society for Computer Simulation, 1985), pp. 33–35; Kelton, "Statistical Design and Analysis," *Proceedings of the 1986 Winter Simulation Conference,* eds. J. Wilson; J. Henricksen; and S. Roberts (San Diego, CA: Society for Computer Simulation, 1986), pp. 45–51; Sargent, 1985; Schmidt, 1981; and Shannon, 1985.

RECOMMENDED READINGS

GPSS/PC Reference Manual. Stow, MA: Minuteman Software, 1986.

Law, A. M., "Pitfalls in the Simulation of Manufacturing Systems." In *Proceedings of the 1986 Winter Simulation Conference,* eds. J. Wilson; J. Henricksen; and S. Roberts. San Diego, CA: Society for Computer Simulation, 1986.

Nealia S. Bruning is an associate professor of administrative sciences at Kent State University. Jay Weinroth is an assistant professor of administrative sciences at Kent State University.

The Effects of Psychologically Based Intervention Programs on Worker Productivity: A Meta-Analysis
Richard A. Guzzo / Richard D. Jette / Raymond A. Katzell

The practical importance of increased worker productivity is widely recognized. Psychological theories and principles of human performance have led to a number of intervention programs designed to serve that end. A matter of great concern to both theory and practice is the extent to which such programs actually increase productivity. This paper presents evidence on that question based on a quantitative analysis of nearly one hundred published reports of such efforts.

Moreover, this analysis compares the effects of different programs, whereas

Source: Richard A. Guzzo, Richard D. Jette, and Raymond A. Katzell, "The Effects of Psychologically Based Intervention Programs on Worker Productivity: A Meta-Analysis," *Personnel Psychology,* 1985, 38, pp. 275–291. Reprinted by permission of *Personnel Psychology.*

most previous evaluations dealt with one or another improvement strategy. Examples include reviews of the effects of incentives as used in the Scanlon Plan (White, 1979), of flexitime and other alternative work schedules (Nollen, 1982; Ronen, 1981), of organization development (Nicholas, 1982), and of management by objectives (Kondrasuk, 1981).

A previous review that did furnish comparative information was that of Locke, Feren, McCaleb, Shaw, and Denny (1980). That paper examined the relative impact of four techniques for raising work motivation: financial incentives, goal setting, participation, and job enrichment. The present study goes beyond that review by comparing the relative effects of a great number, wider variety, and more recent set of programs, and it does so on the basis of a more precise method of analysis, meta-analysis.

Meta-analysis is a statistical technique for integrating findings across numerous studies (Glass, McGaw, & Smith, 1981; Hunter, Schmidt, & Jackson, 1982). It involves the calculation of effect sizes, which are quantified estimates of the impact of a treatment (or intervention program) on a dependent variable such as productivity. Effect size estimates also can be statistically corrected for artifactual variance, such as variance due to sampling error. Through meta-analysis, a common yardstick for measuring the results of different studies is obtained that furnishes a level of integration of studies not possible through traditional judgmental ways of reviewing a body of literature. In fact, proponents of meta-analysis have criticized traditional literature review methods for their susceptibility to bias and insensitivity to artifactual sources of differences in results (Glass et al., 1981; Hunter et al., 1982).

This study applies meta-analysis to literature already reviewed by traditional methods of narrative description of findings and tabulation of the frequency of significant and nonsignificant findings. That literature comprises a set of worker productivity experiments published during the period 1971–81 and reviewed by Katzell, Bienstock, and Faerstein (1977) and Guzzo and Bondy (1983). In a summarization of those reviews, Katzell and Guzzo (1983) reported that for 207 productivity experiments reported during the period, 87% found evidence of improvement in at least one aspect of productivity. That finding represents a substantial rate of success, a rate that was found to vary somewhat by type of productivity measure and type of intervention program. Katzell and Guzzo reported "no discernible differences in the results of productivity experiments according to type of worker, type of organization, or other study characteristics," however (1983, p. 471). (They also cautioned that the success rate may have been inflated if unsuccessful experiments were more often unreported.)

Applying meta-analysis to that set of productivity experiments presents an opportunity to test for the possible effects of reviewer bias or insensitivity in those earlier analyses. Comparing the conclusions reached through those reviews with those reached through meta-analysis of the same literature should serve either to confirm or question those conclusions. It will also permit a judgment of the relative power of the two approaches. Meta-analysis may also provide more refined information, such as estimates of the strength of effect of programs, rather than merely rates of success, as well as estimates of artifactual variability in findings.

Thus, this study was undertaken to accomplish three objectives through meta-analysis: (1) to compare conclusions yielded by traditional methods of literature reveiw with those yielded by meta-analysis; (2) to see whether earlier published conclusions regarding productivity improvement programs require revision; and (3) to furnish new information regarding the relative magnitudes of the effects of those programs and the possible moderating effects of study parameters.

TYPES OF INTERVENTION PROGRAMS

By "intervention program" we mean the introduction of an experimental treatment or change in one or more independent variables. The taxonomy of intervention programs used by Katzell et al. (1977) and Guzzo and Bondy (1983), as outlined below, has been adopted here.

Recruitment and Selection

The literature on this subject consists almost entirely of correlational studies. The only actual interventions reported in the review period involved providing realistic job previews.

Training and Instruction

Included here are a wide variety of practices designed to enhance worker performance through learning, including the use of behavior modeling, human relations programs, management seminars, etc. Excluded are programs aimed at changing supervisory styles, which are grouped below under Supervisory Methods.

Appraisal and Feedback

This category consists of practices designed to provide employees with more frequent or extensive feedback about their job performance. The sources of such feedback are, in some instances, formal appraisals and appraisal interviews. In other instances, feedback is made available to employees through increased capacity for self-monitoring or by access to performance data previously available only to their superiors.

Management by Objectives

Management by objectives (MBO) may be considered a species of the preceding, but MBO emphasizes the specification of work objectives, monitoring of accomplishments, reward attainment when objectives are met, and participation in the setting and review of work objectives.

Goal Setting

Goal setting is related to both MBO and feedback techniques. Its central focus, however, is the specification of difficult but attainable goals for limited but important aspects of job performance. Worker participation in establishing or negotiating goals is not a necessary component; neither is any formal tying of goal attainment to performance appraisal or reward.

Financial Compensation

This type of program for improving productivity typically ties monetary rewards to individual, group, or organization-wide performance.

Work Redesign

This approach seeks to raise productivity by enriching jobs with qualities that enhance worker interest and motivation.

Decision Making Techniques

A growing field of interest is that of decision making in organizations, especially by managers. Programs for improving decision making in organizations have been devised and implemented. At present, only a few studies of the impact of decision making interventions exist.

Supervisory Methods

Although supervisors are centrally involved in the implementation of other programs (e.g., MBO), this category is used for programs intended to change the general patterns of supervision, usually by broad retraining or the redefinition of roles. Increasing participation is a major example.

Work Rescheduling

Recent innovations in work scheduling practices have mainly concerned the establishment of flexible working hours or the redistribution of hours in a workweek.

Socio-Technical Interventions

Programs of this sort involve a number of integrated changes in the human resource management practices of organizations. They focus on a joint consideration of technological and social demands at work and, typically, are implemented over a considerable period of time. Socio-technical interventions usually involve several of the types of programs already described. The term "organization development" is often employed in the same way.

It should be noted that this taxonomy is not inclusive of all possible types of intervention programs that can be applied to improve worker productivity. The focus of this paper is on only those programs with bases in behavioral science and those for which a sufficient number of applications were reported between 1971 and 1981 from which to estimate program effects reliably.

HYPOTHESES AND QUESTIONS

Two broad hypotheses were tested through the meta-analysis of productivity experiments. The first was that the average effect of intervention programs is significantly different from zero. The second was that the effects of intervention programs will vary according to certain situational factors. The former hypothesis is consistent with the success rate of intervention effects reported by Katzell and Guzzo (1983). The latter hypothesis is consistent with the assertion that there exist meaningful differences in organizational contexts that determine the consequences of changes made in those contexts (e.g., Katzell, 1962) — that hypothesis could be tested only crudely in the reviews of Katzell et al. (1977) and Guzzo and Bondy (1983), and it was expected that the power of meta-analysis would permit a more sensitive test.

In addition to testing those general hypotheses, meta-analysis addressed other research questions of interest, including differences among intervention programs in the magnitude of their productivity effects, differences in effects according to nature of the productivity criterion, joint effects of multiple simultaneous interventions, and the relationship between methodological features of studies and the findings they report. This last issue is one which has generated controversy in discussions of the integration of findings across studies. Some assert that studies of lesser methodological rigor should be given less weight than studies of greater methodological rigor (e.g., Hunter et al., 1982), whereas others believe that all studies should be recognized equally (Glass et al., 1981). The final research question, as discussed previously, concerned possible differences in substantive conclusions reached through a literature review performed via meta-analysis versus one performed through traditional means.

METHOD

Selection of Studies

Data for this study came from the reports of productivity experiments initially reviewed by Katzell et al. (1977) and Guzzo and Bondy (1983). Those reports had the following characteristics: (1) The reports were of experiments, defined here as a planned change of some feature or practice in a workplace with systematic observation and measurement of the consequences of the change. (2) The results of the study pertained to an objectively measured aspect of productivity. (3) The experiment took place in enduring organizations with missions to provide goods or services and in which workers were gainfully employed; thus, reports of simulations, laboratory studies, and research in other than field settings were excluded. (4) Each was a publicly available report of a productivity experiment carried out in the United States. (5) The date of publication was between 1971 and 1981, inclusive.

Of the 207 reports meeting those criteria, only 98 contained sufficient information for the calculation of an effect size, which is the dependent variable in meta-analysis. For those 98 reports, 330 effect sizes were calculated using the procedures described below. Those effect sizes were calculated over 37,371 measurements of worker productivity, which constituted the basic data of this study.

Productivity Measures

The productivity outcomes reported in the 98 usable studies were classified under one of three rubrics. The three types, reflecting different aspects of productivity, were output, withdrawal, and disruption, the same classification used by Katzell and Guzzo (1983). Output measures included those of quantity and quality of production and of cost effectiveness. Withdrawal measures typically consisted of turnover and absenteeism. Measures of disruption included accidents, strikes, and other costly disturbances.

An overall index of productivity also was formed by combining all measures of productivity. The overall measure was employed in certain of the analyses and the tripartite typology in others, depending on the issue addressed.

Organizational Context Variables

Data were collected on a number of characteristics of organizational context in order to test the hypothesis that they affect the impact of intervention programs. Sufficient data for three such variables were obtainable: organization size, organization type, and type of worker. Organization size was recorded as small (100 or fewer employees), medium (101 to 1,000 employees) or large (over 1,000 employees). Organization type was recorded as private (referring to firms organized for profit), government (including the military), or other (a miscellany of not-for-profit, educational, or health service organizations). Type of worker was classified as managerial/professional, blue-collar labor, sales, or clerical/office.

Research Design Variables

In order to examine how the effects of intervention programs vary according to aspects of research design employed, the following design characteristics were noted: (1) the number of weeks elapsing between the initiation of an intervention and the measurement of a dependent variable and (2) the use of comparison groups. The comparison groups were categorized as true control groups, nonequivalent comparison groups, groups subject to treatments other than that of the experimental group, or self-controls employing time-series designs.

Calculation of Effect Sizes

The effect-size measured used in this analysis is the d-statistic, which has its origins in the work of Cohen (1969). It was calculated using the following formula:

$$d = (\bar{X}_E - \bar{X}_C)/s$$

where $\bar{X}_E$ and $\bar{X}_C$ are, respectively, the means of the experimental and comparison/control groups on a given productivity measure, and s is the pooled within-groups standard deviation.[1] Effects calculated in this manner are standardized mean differences that index the magnitude of effects on productivity, irrespective of the particular measure of productivity.

Though an attempt was made to calculate a d-statistic for every meaningful effect, it was often impossible to do so directly because of the absence of necessary information in original research reports. In these instances, methods were adopted for deriving d indirectly (Glass et al., 1981). The analysis was additionally influenced in specific ways by the work of Hedges (1981) and Hunter et al. (1982).

Hedges (1981) presented the distribution theory underlying Cohen's d, demonstrating that it is distributed as a non-central t variate and that it is a biased estimator of the population effect size. He derived equations to correct d for this bias before the cumulation of effects, and those corrections were used in this study.[2]

Hunter et al. (1982) have pointed out that effect-size estimates should be corrected for artifactual error variance. The major source of artifactual variance is usually sampling error, although error may also arise from other sources such as unreliability of measurement and range restriction. In the present study, estimates of effect size were corrected for sampling error according to their specifications. Corrections for other potential sources of error were impossible because the necessary information was absent from the original publications.

Cumulation of Effect Sizes

Controversy exists regarding which of two methods for cumulating effects for analysis is preferable. In one method a single, composite effect-size estimate is calculated for each study. Here, the sample of effects equals the number of studies in the analysis. In the other method, effect-size estimates are calculated for each dependent variable in each study, and the sample of effects equals the number of dependent variables.

In the present study, effect-size estimates were calculated for each dependent variable. This approach enhances statistical power and permits the examination of effects on different aspects of productivity. A potential problem with this approach, however, concerns possible nonindependence of measures, which can lead to overestimates of the significance of effects. Hunter et al. (1982) asserted that this problem is not severe if the number of calculated effect sizes is not large relative to the number of studies. Further, Landman and Dawes (1982) found no substantial difference in results when effect sizes were cumulated by each of the two methods. Those considerations led to the decision here to calculate effect sizes for each productivity variable. However, to minimize possible distortion due to nonindependence, multiple productivity measures within a study were used only if their independence was supported conceptually and by previous research.

Most authorities recommend caution in the interpretation of statistical tests of effect sizes because of the lack of adequate sampling distribution theory. Thus, Landman and Dawes (1982) limit themselves to the presentation of descriptive statistics for effect sizes. Hunter et al. (1982) advocate only the calculation of confidence intervals for mean effect sizes — which was done in the present study. This is a more conservative approach than the calculation of t-ratios between the means.

RESULTS

First we will describe the collective impact of the various intervention programs both on overall productivity and on the three components of productivity: output, withdrawal, and disruptions. Next, evidence concerning effect differences among programs will be presented, again both for overall productivity and for its three components. Data concerning the effects of multiple simultaneous interventions will then be reported, followed by evidence on how intervention programs differ in their effects contingent on contextual factors. Last, we will examine how effects vary with methodological features of the studies. Throughout, the key dependent variables are effect-size estimates. Tables 1 and 2 report observed variance in effect-size estimates, variance attributable to sampling error, and variance estimates when corrected for sampling error. It is noteworthy that corrections for sampling error did not appreciably reduce the variance in effect-size estimates for most programs.

TABLE 1
Effect Sizes and Intervention Programs

Type of Program	$\bar{X}$	N	95% Confidence Interval		Variance		
			Lower Bound	Upper Bound	Observed	Due to Sampling Error	Corrected
All Programs Combined	.44	330	.38	.50	.36	.04	.32
Selection/Placement	−.03	14	−.08	.02	.09	.05	.04
Training	.78	72	.56	1.00	.89	.06	.83
Appraisal and Feedback	.35	26	.08	.62	.62	.12	.50
Management by Objectives	.12	32	.10	.14	.24	.11	.13
Goal Setting	.75	96	.57	.93	.91	.11	.80
Financial Incentives	.57	13	−.10	1.24	1.65	.19	1.46
Work Redesign	.42	18	.28	.56	.21	.13	.08
Decision-Making Strategies	.70	2	—	—	—	—	—
Supervisory Methods	.13	18	.05	.21	.04	.01	.03
Work Rescheduling	.21	27	.09	.33	.12	.02	.10
Socio-Technical	.62	12	.54	.70	.03	.01	.02

Overall Effect

To what extent is worker productivity, defined in any of the ways previously noted, affected by intervention programs based on behavioral science research and theory? The data show the collective effect of all programs on productivity to be substantial. The average effect size for such interventions was .44, a figure significantly different from zero ($p <$ .05). The top row of Table 1 presents this mean overall effect-size estimate and its 95% confidence interval. An effect size of .44 indicates that the average level of productivity among workers exposed to the experimental interventions exceeded the average productivity of workers not experiencing those interventions by nearly one-half standard deviation.

Differences Among Programs

Do intervention programs differ in their impact on worker productivity? Relevant data appear in Table 1, showing distinct differences among programs in their effects on overall productivity. The intervention programs with the most powerful effects on worker productivity were those involving training and goal setting. Large scale socio-technical interventions also showed greater than average

TABLE 2
Effect Sizes and Productivity Criteria

Type of Program	$\bar{X}$	N	95% Confidence Interval		Variance		
			Lower Bound	Upper Bound	Observed	Due to Sampling Error	Corrected
Combined	.44	330	.38	.50	.36	.04	.32
Output	.63	218	.55	.71	.38	.04	.34
Withdrawal	.13	77	.07	.19	.07	.02	.05
Disruptions	.82	35	.45	1.19	1.34	.10	1.24

impact. Programs of work redesign and of appraisal and feedback had the next most powerful effects, followed by interventions involving schedules of work, supervisory methods, and management by objectives. However, even those weakest treatments had effects that were appreciable and statistically significant. The limited evidence on the effect of decision-making interventions also shows them to have had a positive impact, but because only two observations existed for this type of intervention, no confidence interval was computed.

The 95 percent confidence intervals for two of the intervention programs, job-previews and financial incentives, included zero, indicating that the average impact of these types of programs is not statistically significant. The failure to find a statistically significant impact of financial incentives on productivity is surprising. It should be noted, however, that the variance in the effects of financial compensation was the greatest among all the programs. In some applications, financial incentives had very powerful effects on productivity, but there were other instances of negligible effects. Apparently the effects of incentive programs depend heavily on the circumstances and methods of applying them and, as we will soon see, on the criterion of productivity.

Differences Among Criteria

Although the mean effect of intervention programs was significantly positive on each of the three components of worker productivity, the three means were not equal (see Table 2). Effects were strongest on disruptions and weakest on withdrawal, with output in between. The confidence interval for the mean effect on output showed no overlap with the lower mean effect on withdrawal, indicating a significant difference between them. However, the variability of the effect sizes on the disruption criterion was large, and this, together with the small N, leads to skepticism about whether disruption truly is most strongly affected by the interventions.

Differences Among Programs by Criteria

The manner in which the various intervention programs differentially affect

TABLE 3

Productivity Effects According to Program and Criterion Types

	Productivity Criterion					
	Output		Withdrawal		Disruption	
Program Type	$\bar{X}$	N	$\bar{X}$	N	$\bar{X}$	N
Selection and Placement	—	—	−.03	14		
Training	.85*	57	.63	7	.56	8
Appraisal and Feedback	.41*	16	.18	8	1.43	2
Management by Objectives	.45	15	−.01	8	−.31	9
Goal Setting	.65*	74	.10	6	1.68*	16
Financial Compensation	2.12*	8	.34	5	—	—
Work Redesign	.52*	11	.28	7	—	—
Decision Making Strategies	.70	2	—	—	—	—
Supervisory Methods	.51*	9	.11*	9	—	—
Work Rescheduling	.30*	19	.10*	8	—	—
Socio-Technical	.66*	7	.19	5	—	—

Note: Asterisk (*) indicates that 95% confidence interval for the average effect-size estimate does not include zero, indicating that the effect is statistically significant. Dashes are used to show the absence of data.

components of productivity is shown in Table 3. Although the sample of effect-size estimates was quite small for many cells of the table and missing for others, interesting findings emerge nevertheless.

Interventions involving changes in supervisory methods and work schedules had significantly positive effects on withdrawal, whereas other programs did not. The only program with a statistically significant effect on disruptions was goal setting. Several of the programs having a statistically significant effect on output failed to have one on withdrawal — especially noteworthy here is the case of financial compensation. Considering only those intervention programs for which enough data were available to estimate their impact on both output and withdrawal, the effects on output were greater than on withdrawal; that, of course, is consistent with the data of Table 2.

Combinations of Programs

Interventions to improve productivity may involve more than one change. For example, a change in the design of jobs may be accompanied or followed by a change in financial compensation. A question of interest is how much effect the secondary program has beyond that of the primary one.

To examine this, those studies in which a primary and secondary intervention existed were analyzed to compare the combined effects of the two interventions to the sum of the separate effects. Although too few such studies existed for reliable analysis, they suggest that the effects of intervention programs in

TABLE 4
Productivity Effects According to Organizational Factors

Organizational Factors	$\bar{X}$	N	95% Confidence Interval	
			Lower Bound	Upper Bound
Organization Size				
Small (100 members)	.63	34	.53	.73
Medium (100 to 1000 members)	.49	78	.33	.65
Large (1000 members)	.42	218	.34	.50
Organization Type				
For-profit	.38	251	.30	.46
Government	.54	42	.44	.62
Non-profit	.38	37	.30	.46
Type of Worker				
Managerial/Professional	.68	74	.46	.90
Blue Collar Labor	.27	167	.19	.35
Sales	.62	29	.27	.97
Clerical	.22	31	.14	.30

Note: Of the 330 effect-size estimates in the sample, 301 were classifiable according to type of worker.

combination are neither additive nor synergistic, for the total effects were generally less than the sum of the separate effects. However, the effects of combined programs were generally larger than any of the separate effects.

Organizational Context

The hypothesis that the effects of intervention programs are moderated by organizational context factors was tested for three such factors: organization size, organization type, and type of worker. Table 4 displays relevant data about the interventions' effects for the levels of each of the three contextual factors.

Table 4 shows, with regard to organizational size, that the impact of intervention programs was greater in small than in large organizations. In fact, the confidence interval surrounding the mean effect size of interventions in small organizations does not overlap with that of large organizations, indicating a substantial difference in the effectiveness of interventions depending on organization size. The magnitude of effects in medium-sized organizations fell between those in small and large organizations.

With regard to type of organization, the average effect of intervention programs in private for-profit firms was identical to that in nonprofit organizations such as those engaged in education or health service. The impact of interventions in government, however, was substantially greater than that in the other types of organizations, as indicated by the means and confidence intervals contained in Table 4.

As for type of worker, the productivity effects were markedly smaller for blue-collar and clerical workers than for sales

TABLE 5
Effect Size Estimates and Research Designs

			95% Confidence Interval	
Type of Control/Comparison Group	$\bar{X}$	N	Lower Bound	Upper Bound
True Control	.23	54	.15	.31
Nonequivalent Comparison	.37	77	.21	.53
Contrasting Treatments	.72	24	.43	1.01
Baseline/Time Series	.49	185	.39	.59

and managerial/professional workers. It should be noted that training was a particularly popular intervention for use with managerial/professional workers. Thus, the comparatively large effect size for these workers is consistent with the large effect size for training reported in Table 1. In contrast, a wider variety of intervention programs was employed for blue-collar and clerical workers, including some that had weaker impact; even here, however, the average effect was statistically significant.

Overall, the hypothesis that intervention effects are moderated by organizational context was supported for each of the three contextual factors examined. Because of small sample sizes, however, it was not possible to evaluate possible interactions between specific intervention programs and contextual factors.

Research Designs and Effect Sizes

The studies included in this meta-analysis employed a variety of research designs, as might be expected when considering the constraints and opportunities of field research. The possibility that estimates of the impact of intervention programs varied according to research design was examined according to two research design factors: type of control/comparison group and length of time between intervention and measures of dependent variables.

Table 5 shows that, on average, the effect of an intervention was smaller when the design included a true (randomized) control group than it was when it involved some other form of comparison. These findings concerning the presence of true control groups are consistent with those of Foulds (1958) and Mansfield and Busse (1977) but inconsistent with those of Bergin and Lambert (1978). Also of interest is the finding that designs involving two or more contrasting interventions resulted in the largest differences between the groups.

The relationship between the length of time between the initiation of an intervention and measurement of its productivity effects was small but statistically significant ($r = -.10, p < .05$), indicating that weaker effects are registered as the measurement interval increases. No nonlinear component to this relationship was detected.

DISCUSSION

What have we learned that bears on the hypotheses and research questions raised at the outset?

1. Taken as a whole, the 98 experiments significantly improved a concrete aspect of productivity by nearly one-half of a standard deviation. Effects of the magnitude reported here are conventionally regarded as "medium" and are not common in field studies; Cohen (1969) characterizes this as an effect "large enough to be visible to the naked eye" (p. 24). This is a rather impressive result that could have profound economic and social benefits if the treatments were to be widely applied. Since productivity is usually an additive function of both work behavior and other factors (e.g., technology), the improvement of .44 SD may underestimate the behavior changes in situations where behavior was improved by the intervention but the other factors remained unchanged. One caution, noted earlier, is that unsuccessful experiments may be underrepresented in the published literature.

2. Effects vary with the aspect of productivity that is targeted. The quantity and/or quality of worker output generally are more amenable to improvement than are aspects of withdrawal, such as turnover and absenteeism. This may be due to the nature of the programs rather than to any intrinsic resistance to improvement, or it may suggest that withdrawal is more strongly determined by factors beyond an organization's control.

3. Programs differ in their effectiveness in improving productivity. Of the 11 types tabulated, those involving training, goal setting, and socio-technical systems design are the most powerful, on average, with job previews having a negligible effect. In the case of financial incentives, a substantially positive mean effect turns out not to be statistically significant because of enormous variations in results of studies, thus sounding a warning that incentive schemes have traps for the unwary or unsophisticated — a conclusion that has been reached by others (e.g., Hatry, Greiner, & Gollub, 1981; Whyte, 1955). On the other hand, when applied in the right way and in the right situations, they can have strongly positive effects on productivity, especially on output. Our conclusion about money is thus more equivocal than the strongly favorable one reached by Locke et al. (1980) based on a narrower definition of productivity and on a smaller and generally older sample of studies.

4. Another type of contingency is the kind of organization and worker population within which productivity improvement is sought. Generally, these programs seem to work better in smaller organizations, those of a governmental nature, and those with managerial/professional personnel. However, some programs may work better in certain situations than in others.

5. Conclusions 2, 3, and 4, taken together, imply that properly targeted intervention programs can have a considerably greater impact than the average effect size of .44 noted in conclusion 1. Conversely, productivity could be hurt if the right medicine were used for the wrong disease.

6. When two or more programs are applied at the same time, their combined effect is not as great as the simple sum of their separate effects. However, that is by no means an argument against multiple interventions, as the combined im-

pact is nevertheless greater than the impact of the individual programs. The high level of effectiveness of broad sociotechnical systems interventions lends further support to the application of integrated multiple programs.

7. The better controlled the research design, the less impressive are the average results of the intervention, although they are positive even with the most stringent controls. That relationship has been noted in meta-analyses of research on other topics. It remains unclear whether the results of looser designs are spuriously optimistic or whether the imposition of rigorous controls somehow interferes with the experimental programs.

8. On another methodological level, we can ask how the results of meta-analysis differ from those of the more traditional reviews that had been performed of the same literature base by Katzell et al. (1977) and Guzzo and Bondy (1983). One difference that is immediately apparent is the shrinkage of the data base: the 207 studies covered by the earlier reviews had to be reduced to 98 because published reports often omitted data needed for meta-analysis. It is possible that the decrease in quantity may be accompanied by an increase in the quality of the literature, but that is conjectural. The more exact and quantitative nature of meta-analysis did enable us to sort out some of the finer points in our data. Differences in effectiveness among the eleven types of intervention became more apparent, as did interactions between interventions and situational characteristics. Also, since meta-analysis couches results in the form of effect sizes, it provides a quantitative estimate of the magnitude of impact.

Overall, the two strategies of review did not produce conflicting results. The crucial general conclusion is the same for both: *Behavioral science techniques for increasing worker productivity are, on the whole, effective.*

For industrial and organizational psychologists, that should be great news!

NOTES

1. This effect size statistic is similar to the one, g, advocated by Glass, McGaw, and Smith (1981), but they use the standard deviation of the control group in the denominator of the equation. Cohen (1969), Hedges (1981), and Hunter, Schmidt, and Jackson (1983) favor the statistic we employed as the better estimate of the population parameter.
2. Hedges' (1981) correction for bias makes use of the sample size with which an effect size is calculated. When no control group was employed in a study (such as in a time-series research design), Hedges' procedures were adapted to use the single group sample size.

REFERENCES

Bergin, A. E., Lambert, M. J. (1978). The evaluation of therapeutic outcomes. In Garfield, S. L., Bergin, A. E. (Eds.), *Handbook of Psychotherapy and Behavior Change: An Empirical Analysis*. New York: Wiley.

Cohen, J. (1969). *Statistical power analysis for the behavioral sciences*. New York: Academic Press.

Foulds, G. (1958). Clinical research in psychiatry. *Journal of Mental Science, 104,* 259–265.

Glass, G. V., McGaw, B., Smith, M. L. (1981). *Meta-analysis in social research*. Beverly Hills, CA: Sage Publications.

Guzzo, R. A., Bondy, J. S. (1983). *A guide to worker productivity experiments in the United States 1976–81*. New York: Pergamon.

Hatry, H. P., Greiner, J. M., Gollub, R. J. (1981). *An assessment of local government motivational programs: Performance targeting with and without monetary incentives.* Washington: The Urban Institute.

Hedges, L. V. (1981). Distribution theory for Glass's estimator of effect size and related estimators. *Journal of Educational Statistics, 6,* 107–128.

Hunter, J. E., Schmidt, F. L., Jackson, G. B. (1982). *Meta-analysis: Cumulating research findings across studies.* Beverly Hills, CA: Sage Publications.

Katzell, R. A. (1962). Contrasting systems of work organization. *American Psychologist, 17,* 102–108.

Katzell, R. A., Bienstock, P., Faerstein, P. H. (1977). *A guide to worker productivity experiments in the United States 1971–75.* New York: New York University Press.

Katzell, R. A., Guzzo, R. A. (1983). Psychological approaches to productivity improvement. *American Psychologist, 38,* 468–472.

Kondrausk, J. N. (1981). Studies in MBO effectiveness. *Academy of Management Review, 6,* 419–430.

Landman, J. T., Dawes, R. M. (1982). Psychotherapy outcome: Smith and Glass' conclusions stand up under scrutiny. *American Psychologist, 37,* 504–516.

Locke, E. A., Feren, D. B., McCaleb, V. M., Shaw, K. N., Denny, A. T. (1980). The relative effectiveness of four methods of motivating employee performance. In Duncan, K. D., Gruneberg, M. M., Wallis, D. (Eds.), *Changes in Working Life.* New York: Wiley.

Mansfield, R. S., Busse, T. V. (1977). Meta-analysis of research: A rejoinder to Glass. *Educational Research, 6,* 3.

Nicholas, J. M. (1982). The comparative impact of organization development interventions on hard criteria measures. *Academy of Management Review, 7,* 531–542.

Nollen, S. D. (1982). *New work schedules in practice.* New York: Van Nostrand Reinhold.

Ronen, S. (1981). *Flexible working hours.* New York: McGraw-Hill.

White, J. K. (1979). The Scanlon Plan: Causes and correlates of success. *Academy of Management Journal, 22,* 292–312.

Whyte, W. F. (1955). *Money and motivation.* New York: Harper.

Richard A. Guzzo, Richard D. Jette, and Raymond A. Katzell are affiliated with New York University.

Cases

TRW — Oilwell Cable Division
Michael G. Kolchin / Thomas J. Hyclak / Sheree Demming

It was July 5, 1983, and Bill Russell had been expecting the phone call naming him general manager he had just received from the corporate office of TRW in Cleveland. Bill had been the acting general manager of the Oilwell Cable Division in Lawrence, Kansas, since January when Gino Strippoli left the division for another assignment. He had expected to be named general manager, but the second part of the call informing him that he must lay off 20 people or achieve an equivalent reduction in labor costs was greatly disturbing to him. It was now 8:00 A.M. and at 8:15 A.M. Bill had called a meeting of all plant personnel to announce his appointment and, now, to also announce the impending layoffs. He was wondering in his own mind how to handle the tough decisions that lay before him.

TRW

TRW is a diversified, multinational manufacturing firm that in 1983 had sales approaching $5.5 billion (see Table 1). Its roots can be found in the Cleveland Cap Screw Company, which was founded in 1901 with a total investment of $2,500 and employment of 29. Today, through a growth strategy of acquisition and diversification, the company employs 88,000 employees at over 300 locations in 17 countries. The original shareholders investment of $2,500 in 1901 has grown to over $1.6 billion in 1983. As quoted from the company's 1983 Data Book, "This growth reflects the company's ability to anticipate promising new fields and to pioneer in their development — automotive, industrial, aircraft, aerospace, systems, electronics, and energy. We grew with these markets and helped create them." (*TRW 1983 Data Book*).

The organization chart depicting TRW as it existed in 1983 is contained in Figure 1.

OILWELL CABLE DIVISION, LAWRENCE, KANSAS

The Oilwell Cable Division is part of the Industrial and Energy Segment of TRW. In 1983, this segment of TRW's business represented 24% of its sales and 23% of its operating profits. The pumps, valves, and energy-services group, of which the Oilwell Cable Division is a part, accounted for 30% of the Industrial and Energy Segments net sales. The financial data for TRW by industry segment are contained in Tables 2 and 3.

Source: Reprinted by permission of the publisher from "TRW — Oilwell Cable Division" Michael G. Kolchin, Thomas J. Hyclak, and Sheree Demming, *Journal of Management Case Studies,* Vol. No. 3, pp. 170–181. Copyright 1987 by Elsevier Science Publishing Co., Inc.

TABLE 1
TRW Financial Data for 1979–1983

Statement of Consolidated Earnings
($ millions except per share data)

	1983	1982	1981	1980	1979
Net sales	$5,493.0	$5,131.9	$5,285.1	$4,983.9	$4,560.3
Other income	64.6	69.1	52.9	42.4	45.3
	5,557.6	5,201.0	5,338.0	5,026.3	4,605.6
Cost of sales	4,285.1	4,011.0	4,116.4	3,876.3	3,534.6
Administrative and selling expenses	840.6	791.0	734.9	693.1	631.6
Interest expense	29.7	51.2	65.9	66.5	52.3
Other expenses	37.3	7.8	34.8	27.0	32.2
	5,192.7	4,861.0	4,952.0	4,662.9	4,250.7
Earnings before income taxes	364.9	340.0	386.0	363.4	354.9
Income taxes	159.7	143.7	157.2	158.9	166.4
Net earnings	205.2	196.3	228.8	204.5	188.5
Preference dividends	3.5	5.7	8.5	11.6	15.9
Earnings applicable to common stock	$ 201.7	$ 190.6	$ 220.3	$ 192.9	$ 172.6
Fully diluted earnings per share	$ 5.36	$ 5.20	$ 6.13	$ 5.49	$ 5.11
Primary earnings per share	5.53	5.49	6.60	6.15	5.86
Cash dividends paid per share	2.65	2.55	2.35	2.15	1.95
Fully diluted shares (millions)	38.3	37.8	37.3	37.3	36.9
Primary shares (millions)	36.5	34.7	33.4	31.4	29.5
Percent of sales					
Net sales	100.0%	100.0%	100.0%	100.0%	100.0%
Other income	1.2	1.3	1.0	0.8	1.0
	101.2	101.3	101.0	100.8	101.0
Cost of sales	78.0	78.2	77.9	77.8	77.5
Administrative and selling expenses	15.3	15.4	13.9	13.9	13.9
Interest expenses	0.6	1.0	1.2	1.3	1.1
Other expenses	0.7	0.1	0.7	0.5	0.7
	94.6	94.7	93.7	93.5	93.2
Earnings before income taxes	6.6	6.6	7.3	7.3	7.8
Income taxes	2.9	2.8	3.0	3.2	3.7
Net earnings	3.7	3.8	4.3	4.1	4.1
Preference dividends	0.0	0.1	0.1	0.2	0.3
Earnings applicable to common stock	3.7%	3.7%	4.2%	3.9%	3.8%

Sources: TRW 1983 Data Book. Reprinted by permission.

FIGURE 1
Organizational Structure at TRW

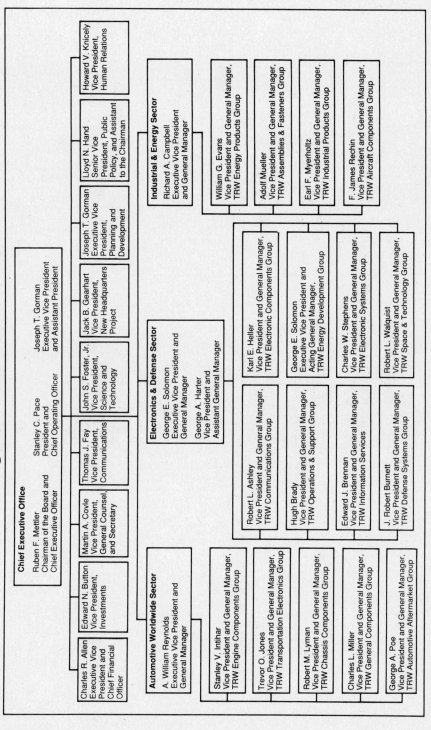

Source: *TRW 1983 Data Book.*

TABLE 2
Financial Data for TRW

Segments of Business by Industry
($ millions)

	1983		1982		1981		1980		1979	
Net sales										
Car and truck										
Original equipment	$1,123		$1,052		$1,200		$1,291		$1,367	
Replacement equipment	472		483		490		461		432	
	1,595	29%	1,535	30%	1,690	32%	1,752	35%	1,799	39%
Electronics and space systems										
Electronic components	396		406		437		419		363	
Computer-based and analytical services	729		546		393		377		284	
Electronic systems, equipment, and services	851		787		772		648		552	
Spacecraft	628		486		430		355		302	
	2,604	47%	2,205	43%	2,032	38%	1,799	36%	1,501	33%
Industrial and energy										
Fasteners, tools, and bearings	486		496		596		562		558	
Pumps, valves, and energy services	394		471		506		436		380	
Aircraft components	414		425		461		435		322	
	1,294	24%	1,392	27%	1,563	30%	1,433	29%	1,260	28%
Net sales	$5,493	100%	$5,132	100%	$5,285	100%	$4,984	100%	$4,560	100%

(Table 2 continued on following page.)

(Table 2, continued)

	$	%	$	%	$	%	$	%	$	%
Operating profits										
Car and truck	$ 116.8	27%	$ 129.2	30%	$ 146.0	30%	$ 149.4	30%	$ 192.7	44%
Electronics and space systems	214.2	50	170.0	40	123.3	25	133.3	28	88.9	20
Industrial and energy	98.2	23	126.9	30	219.9	45	193.9	41	156.8	36
Operating profit	429.2	100%	426.1	100%	489.2	100%	476.6	100%	438.4	100%
Company staff expense	(56.0)		(53.9)		(48.5)		(49.4)		(43.3)	
Interest income	15.1		15.4		12.6		1.4		3.1	
Interest expense	(29.7)		(51.2)		(65.9)		(66.5)		(52.3)	
Equity in affiliates	6.3		(14.0)		(1.4)		1.3		9.0	
Gain on debt exchange	—		17.6		—		—		—	
Earnings before income taxes	$ 364.9		$ 340.0		$ 386.0		$ 363.4		$ 354.9	
Segment assets										
Car and truck	$ 968.6	33%	$1,029.7	35%	$1,101.3	38%	$1,148.1	40%	$1,157.2	43%
Electronics and space systems	1,113.7	37	1,000.6	34	888.3	31	865.1	31	779.9	29
Industrial and energy	886.2	30	921.6	31	915.0	31	808.2	29	752.4	28
Segment assets	2,968.5	100%	2,951.9	100%	2,904.6	100%	2,821.4	100%	2,689.5	100%
Eliminations	(102.0)		(83.2)		(61.7)		(77.9)		(72.2)	
Company staff assets	381.3		176.3		211.9		68.0		79.6	
Investment in affiliates	73.6		79.8		71.8		74.3		52.2	
Total assets	$3,321.4		$3,124.8		$3,126.6		$2,885.8		$2,749.1	
Operating margin										
Car and truck	7.3%		8.4%		8.6%		8.5%		10.7%	
Electronics and space systems	8.2		7.7		6.1		7.4		5.9	
Industrial and energy	7.6		9.1		14.1		13.5		12.4	
TRW segments	7.8		8.3		9.3		9.6		9.6	
Operating return on segment assets										
Car and truck	12.1%		12.5%		13.3%		13.0%		16.7%	
Electronics and space systems	19.2		17.0		13.9		15.4		11.4	
Industrial and energy	11.1		13.8		24.0		24.0		20.8	
TRW segments	14.5		14.4		16.8		16.9		16.3	

Sources: TRW 1983 Data Book. Reprinted by permission.

TABLE 3
Financial Data for TRW

Quarterly date
($ millions except per share total)

	1983				1982			
	Q4	Q3	Q2	Q1	Q4	Q3	Q2	Q1
Net sales								
Car and truck								
Original equipment	$ 288.9	$ 256.9	$ 298.4	$ 278.7	$ 226.5	$ 226.8	$ 300.0	$ 299.0
Replacement equipment	110.1	119.5	127.2	115.5	110.2	116.8	132.5	123.3
	399.0	376.4	425.6	394.2	336.7	343.6	432.5	422.3
Electronics and space systems								
Electronic components	104.2	102.5	98.2	90.9	84.4	101.7	112.3	107.0
Computer-based and analytical services	187.3	184.0	190.1	167.6	178.8	158.1	110.0	98.7
Electronic systems, equipment, and services	213.8	195.9	201.9	239.7	205.5	193.3	187.7	180.8
Spacecraft	143.9	148.2	162.2	173.8	93.6	123.8	149.8	119.1
	649.2	630.6	652.4	672.0	562.3	576.9	559.8	505.6
Industrial and energy								
Fasteners, tools, and bearings	127.1	117.9	122.5	118.4	104.9	113.1	132.8	145.2
Pumps, valves, and energy services	106.9	93.6	96.1	97.0	106.3	114.0	118.3	132.0
Aircraft components	99.2	100.4	108.7	105.8	97.9	94.6	113.1	120.0
	333.2	311.9	327.3	321.2	309.1	321.7	364.2	397.2
Net sales	$1,381.4	$1,318.9	$1,405.3	$1,387.4	$1,208.1	$1,242.2	$1,356.5	$1,325.1
Operating profits								
Car and truck	$ 27.2	$ 30.2	$ 34.2	$ 25.2	$ 20.7	$ 28.4	$ 49.4	$ 30.7
Electronics and space systems	50.1	56.5	54.2	53.4	46.1	47.4	44.3	32.2
Industrial and energy	30.2	24.4	25.7	17.9	24.9	22.7	34.6	44.7
Operating profit	107.5	111.1	114.1	96.5	91.7	98.5	128.3	107.6
Company staff expense	(15.0)	(13.5)	(14.2)	(13.3)	(12.2)	(14.5)	(13.7)	(13.5)
Interest income	5.5	3.9	3.5	2.2	3.2	4.5	3.8	3.9
Interest expense	(5.0)	(7.3)	(8.4)	(9.0)	(17.1)	(10.0)	(10.7)	(13.4)
Equity in affiliates	.4	3.3	4.1	(1.5)	(1.9)	(5.7)	(.3)	(6.1)
Gain on debt exchange	—	—	—	—	—	17.6	—	—
Earnings before income taxes	93.4	97.5	99.1	74.9	63.7	90.4	107.4	78.5
Income taxes	40.8	38.7	45.9	34.3	32.2	31.4	45.7	34.4
Net earnings	$ 52.6	$ 58.8	$ 53.2	$ 40.6	$ 31.5	$ 59.0	$ 61.7	$ 44.1
Earnings per common share								
Fully diluted	$ 1.37	$ 1.54	$ 1.39	$ 1.06	$ .81	$ 1.55	$ 1.66	$ 1.18
Primary	1.41	1.59	1.44	1.09	.83	1.65	1.76	1.25
Common dividends paid	.70	.65	.65	.65	.65	.65	.65	.60
Operating margin								
Car and truck	6.8%	8.0%	8.0%	6.4%	6.1%	8.3%	11.4%	7.3%
Electronics and space systems	7.7	9.0	8.3	7.9	8.2	8.2	7.9	6.4
Industrial and energy	9.1	7.8	7.9	5.6	8.1	7.1	9.5	11.3
TRW segments	7.8	8.4	8.1	7.0	7.6	7.9	9.5	8.1
Effective income tax rate	43.7	39.7	46.3	45.8	50.6	34.7	42.6	43.8

Sources: TRW 1983 Data Book. Reprinted by permission.

TABLE 3
(Continued)

Quarterly data
($ millions except per share total)

	1981				1980				1979		
Q4	Q3	Q2	Q1	Q4	Q3	Q2	Q1	Q4	Q3	Q2	Q1
$ 275.6	$ 273.3	$ 321.7	$ 328.7	$ 337.0	$ 279.4	$ 329.2	$ 345.7	$ 341.1	$ 315.9	$356.9	$ 352.7
108.5	123.8	130.4	127.6	115.2	110.4	125.4	109.7	108.5	112.2	118.9	92.5
384.1	397.1	452.1	456.3	452.2	389.8	454.6	455.4	449.6	428.1	475.8	445.2
107.5	113.2	107.3	108.8	99.9	106.2	105.7	107.1	94.9	91.7	97.1	79.6
104.3	85.0	98.5	105.4	99.5	101.5	97.0	78.8	79.4	72.3	71.9	60.4
185.5	203.0	201.3	182.7	178.0	156.2	162.5	151.3	155.9	131.6	143.2	121.0
109.7	110.7	103.6	105.8	100.4	88.8	83.6	82.0	83.9	78.4	72.9	67.0
507.0	511.9	510.7	502	477.8	452.7	448.8	419.2	414.1	374.0	385.1	328.0
139.4	143.9	156.6	156.0	137.9	131.4	146.3	146.3	142.3	135.4	144.3	136.6
122.9	127.6	132.2	123.0	114.8	116.0	106.6	98.6	101.5	95.9	100.5	82.1
118.4	110.2	113.5	119.5	117.6	103.6	110.4	104.0	87.6	78.2	83.2	72.9
380.7	381.7	402.3	398.5	370.3	351.0	363.3	348.9	331.4	309.5	328.0	291.6
$1,271.8	$1,290.7	$1,365.1	$1,357.5	$1,300.3	$1,193.5	$1,266.7	$1,223.5	$1,195.1	$1,111.6	$1,188.9	$1,064.8
$ 29.9	$ 34.8	$ 44.6	$ 36.7	$ 34.1	$ 33.6	$ 41.0	$ 40.7	$ 40.2	$ 42.2	$ 56.5	$ 53.8
(21.4)	73.1	38.4	33.2	33.5	33.7	35.5	30.6	24.9	22.5	25.3	16.2
45.6	54.6	62.8	56.9	50.0	50.4	50.1	43.4	41.7	38.4	46.4	30.3
54.1	162.5	145.8	126.8	117.6	117.7	126.6	114.7	106.8	103.1	128.2	100.3
(10.5)	(12.8)	(12.5)	(12.7)	(12.8)	(13.8)	(11.5)	(11.3)	(11.4)	(12.5)	(10.9)	(8.5)
5.6	5.4	1.2	.4	.6	.3	.2	.3	1.2	.2	.2	1.5
(14.0)	(16.3)	(18.4)	(17.2)	(17.7)	(17.3)	(17.3)	(14.2)	(14.4)	(13.4)	(12.6)	(11.9)
(1.9)	(1.9)	1.1	1.3	(3.0)	1.1	2.0	1.2	3.0	2.3	1.1	2.6
33.3	136.9	117.2	98.6	—	—	—	—		17.6		
6.4	53.9	53.3	43.6	84.7	88.0	100.0	90.7	85.2	79.7	106.0	84.0
6.4	53.9	53.3	43.6	34.9	39.1	42.1	42.8	41.0	33.4	51.8	40.2
$ 26.9	$ 83.0	$ 63.9	$ 55.0	$ 49.8	$ 48.9	$ 57.9	$ 47.9	$ 44.2	$ 46.3	$ 54.2	$ 43.8
$ .72	$ 2.22	1.72	1.47	$ 1.32	$ 1.30	$ 1.57	$ 1.30	$ 1.20	$ 1.25	$ 1.47	$ 1.19
.72	2.42	1.86	1.60	1.45	1.45	1.78	1.47	1.35	1.44	1.71	1.36
.60	.60	.60	.55	.55	.55	.55	.50	.50	.50	.50	.45
7.8%	8.8%	9.9%	8.0%	7.5%	8.6%	9.0%	8.9%	8.9%	9.9%	11.9%	12.1%
(4.2)	14.3	7.5	6.6	7.0	7.4	7.9	7.3	6.0	6.0	6.6	4.9
12.0	14.3	15.6	14.3	13.5	14.4	13.8	12.4	12.6	12.4	14.1	10.4
4.3	12.6	10.7	9.3	9.0	9.9	10.0	9.4	8.9	9.3	10.8	9.4
19.2	39.4	45.5	44.2	41.2	44.5	42.1	47.2	48.1	41.9	48.9	47.8

The Oilwell Cable Division had its beginning as the Crescent Wire and Cable Company of Trenton, New Jersey. When TRW acquired Crescent, the company was losing money, occupied an outmoded plant, and had significant labor problems. In order to improve the profitability of the Crescent division. TRW decided to move its operations out of Trenton. The first decision was to move oilwell cable production to Lawrence, Kansas in 1976. The line was moved into a new building and all new equipment was purchased. Only Gino Strippoli, the plant manager, and three other employees made the move from Trenton to Lawrence.

The reason for choosing Lawrence as the new site for Crescent division was fourfold. Most importantly, Lawrence was considerably closer to the customer base of the division, which was in northeast Oklahoma. Second, Kansas was a right-to-work state and, given the labor problems of the Trenton plant, TRW was looking for a more supportive labor environment for its new operations. Third, the wage rates for the Lawrence area were very reasonable compared to Trenton. Finally, there was an already existing building that could house the oilwell cable production line in an industrial park in North Lawrence. In addition to the building, there was considerable acreage next to the building that would allow for future expansion.

By just moving the oilwell cable line to Lawrence, TRW hoped to be able to focus in on this product and make it more profitable before moving the other products from the Crescent plant in Trenton. By 1978, when the Oilwell Cable plant had reached division status, no further consideration was given to moving the rest of the Trenton plant. The remaining operations in Trenton were sold.

Team Management at Lawrence

When Gino Strippoli was given the task of starting up operations in Lawrence, he saw a great opportunity to establish a new management system. With a new plant, new equipment, and almost all new employees, the time seemed perfect to test the value of team management. Gino has long been a supporter of team management, and now a golden opportunity was being presented to him to set up an experiment to test his ideas.

Team management is a form of worker participation whereby team members are responsible for task-related decisions concerning their areas of responsibility. Teams are formed along functional lines. In the case of the TRW-Lawrence plant, 11 teams exist ranging in membership from four to 17. The title of the teams and brief descriptions of their make-up are shown in Table 4. Figure 2 depicts the current organization of the Oilwell Cable Division.

The five production teams listed in Table 4 are formed around the production process in use at TRW-Lawrence. Each of the teams meets on a weekly basis or as needed with exception of the resource team, which meets every two weeks. The typical meeting lasts an hour and a half to two hours. There is no formal structure for the team meeting, but most meetings would adhere to an agenda similar to the one described below:

1. scheduling man hours and overtime;
2. round-robin discussion/reporting from various plant committees (e.g., safety, gain-sharing, etc.);

TABLE 4
Team Structure

Team	Number of teams	Composition
Management	1	Members of management
Resource	1	Management information systems, design engineering, process engineering, employment, accounting, chemists, etc.
Technical	1	Nonexempt laboratory personnel
Administration	1	
Maintenance	1	Boiler, electrical, mechanical
Shipping and receiving	1	
Production	5	Extruding, armoring, braiding

3. area manager's comments regarding scrap, labor efficiency, and any new information since the last meeting.

Other decisions made by the team are listed in Figure 3, which illustrates the roles of the various levels of management at the Oilwell Cable Division. Figure 3 also shows the relationships between levels. For instance, management has the responsibility for setting overall divisional goals and objectives and providing the resources necessary to the teams in order to attain these targets.

The role of the area manager is that of an intermediary. They are present at most team meetings to act as facilitators and to provide the teams with information necessary to carry out their scheduling functions. In addition, the area managers fill a coordination function by meeting twice a week to discuss mutual problems and to discuss other items that should be presented at the weekly team meetings.

As can be seen in Figure 3, the teams are filling managerial roles, and the decisions they make are more typical of those made by supervisory levels in more traditional plants. In essence, they, the team members, are given control over their work areas.

For decisions that affect the entire plant, a task force or a division-wide committee is established that includes representatives from all of the teams. Examples of some of these division-wide committees include safety, gainsharing, and benefits.

Results from Team Management

After some initial start-up problems with the team management concept, the experiment started by Gino Strippoli in 1976 seems to be a success. In an article in *Fortune* (Burck, 1981) titled, "What Happens When Workers Manage Themselves," Gino is quoted as saying: "In the beginning we considered it (team management) an experiment, but somewhere along the way we said. 'This is no longer an experiment; this is how we operate.'"

The success of the experiment was not only written up in *Fortune* but also was the subject of several case studies (Verma, 1985; Downs and Hummert, 1984). But this success was not achieved easily. In the beginning, there was a

FIGURE 2
Organizational Structure at the Oilwell Cable Division

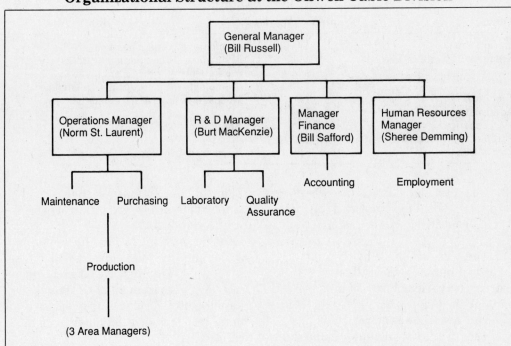

Note: An organizational chart for the Oilwell Cable Division does not exist, and the chart presented here represents the casewriters' depiction of the structure existing at TRW-Lawrence based on discussions with division personnel.

good deal of mistrust among employees regarding management's motives. Also, when first starting up the Lawrence facility, there was only one union employee brought from Trenton. The rest of the people hired had little experience with the production process involved in making wire cable. As a result, there was a lot of frustration with a high level of turnover. The turnover rate of 12% in the first two years of operations compared to a national average of 3.8% at this time (U.S. Department of Labor, 1983, p. 180).

But Gino was not to be deterred from seeing his experiment succeed. He realized that he was concentrating too heavily on team involvement concepts and not paying enough attention to technical concerns. A compensation scheme was developed that encouraged employees to master the various pieces of equipment in the plant. This action seemed to have the desired effect, for the division became profitable for the first time in January 1978.

In 1978, employment had dropped from a high of 132 to what seemed to be a more optimal level of 125. Turnover dropped from an excess of 12% to a range of 2–4%, which was more in line with the national average for manufacturing

FIGURE 3
Relationships Between the Various Levels in the Team Management Concept

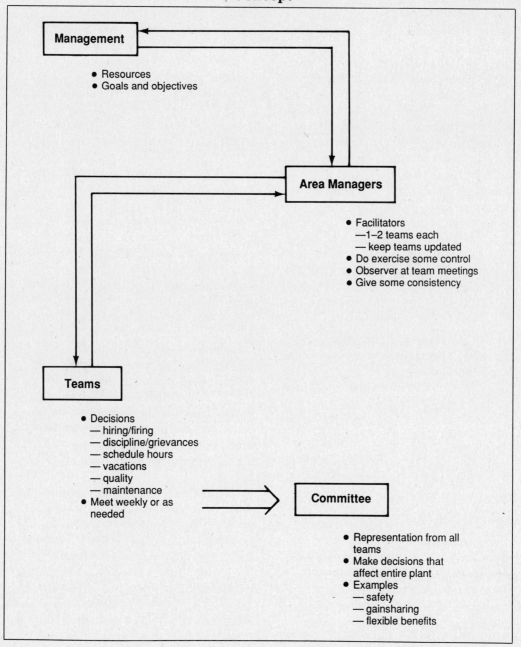

firms. More impressive was the absentee rate, which hovered in the range of 2.5–3% during the period 1978–1982. The national average during this period was closer to 6.5% (U.S. Department of Labor, 1983, p. 136). Productivity was improving steadily as well. The Oilwell Cable Division now enjoyed the highest productivity of any plant in the oilwell cable industry.

It was not only the objective data that indicated that team management was succeeding but comments from employees at the Oilwell Cable Division seemed to confirm this as well. By and large, all employees rated TRW-Lawrence as a good company and preferred the team-management concept to more traditional methods of management.

Some sample comments from the various levels of "management" verify this conclusion.

Team Members
". . . an excellent place to work."
"Team management gives employees a good deal of responsibility."
"Now at least we have some control over scheduling."
"The company gains as much as the employee because of the flexibility. Now there is little idle time."
"Team management gives the employee a feeling of equality."
"Systems allows for the maximum contribution of each member of the team."

Area Managers
"The plant is not a Utopia but I do feel better at the end of the day."
"Decision making is more difficult but team management results in easier implementation and better understanding by team members."

Management
"System allows for crossing over lines of responsibility. There is not the turf issue that exists in traditionally structured plants."
"Team management concept has resulted in an excellent labor climate. TRW-Lawrence is a good place to work and the workers here are receptive to change."
"The major benefit of the team management concept is flexibility while maintaining goal orientation."

This last statement is one of the real keys to team management — flexibility. Under such a management system idle time is greatly reduced, as is the involvement of the plant manager in day-to-day operating problems. As noted by Strippoli, "I really feel for the first time that I am managing rather than putting out fires. The teams are putting out the fires way down in the organization" (Burck, 1981, p. 69).

From the worker's point of view, the major benefit of team management is their ability to control their job. This control has resulted in a high level of commitment by the employees, as evidenced by the numerous suggestions made by the teams that have resulted in significant improvement in quality and productivity.

Of course, the team-management concept is not without its difficulties. As noted earlier, there are numerous problems with start up. It takes a while for participants to become comfortable with the system and to accept the responsibility of managing themselves. In this case, this was a period of two years. However, after the settling-in period, productivity improved dramatically and has been

FIGURE 4
Productivity at TRW-Lawrence, 1978–1983

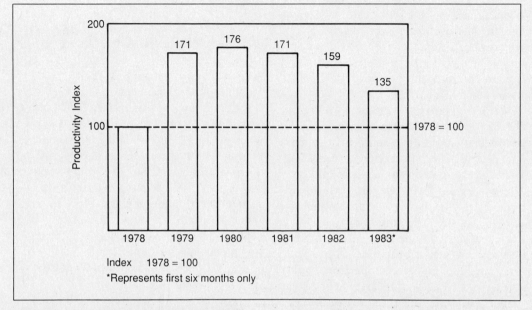

maintained at that level through 1982. This achievement is illustrated in Figure 4.

In addition to start-up problems, the people who filled middle-management positions had great difficulty in adjusting to their new roles as facilitators as opposed to being bosses in the traditional sense. This is an area that is often overlooked in implementing participation schemes in factories. In the case of the Oilwell Cable Division, this inability to adapt to a new system resulted in four area managers leaving their positions. Plant management tried to deal with this problem by providing facilitator training for area managers. Although the current area managers still express some frustration at not being able to simply "tell" workers what to do, they do feel the team-management concept is a much more effective system than traditional supervisory systems and they would not want to go back to a traditional system.

All in all, Gino was very pleased with the experiment. At the end of 1982, he left the Lawrence facility for another assignment and Bill Russell, who had been Gino's operations manager, replaced him as the acting general manager.

THE OILWELL CABLE DIVISION'S MARKET

The basic product produced by the Oilwell Cable Division is wire that provides power to submersible pumps used in oil drilling. As a result, the demand for its product is directly dependent on the demand for submersible pumps, a demand that is a function of the price of crude oil. As the price of oil increases, the demand for pumps increases as it became economically feasible to drill deeper wells.

Drilling deeper wells also produces a need for cables that are able to withstand the harsher environments found in such wells. For example, these wells often require the use of lead jackets to protect the cables from the corrosive effects of hydrogen sulfide.

With the Iranian oil crisis of 1979 and the resultant increase in oil prices, cable producers were able to sell pretty much all they were able to produce. Prices were determined on the basis of quality and delivery. Now, however, with the advent of an oil glut, demand for submersible pumps was dropping and the competitive factors in the market were determined more on the basis of price.

In all, TRW had ten competitors in the cable market. TRW was the market leader with a significant share of the market but, in 1982 and 1983, it was facing strong competition from both domestic and foreign producers. Foreign competition was becoming stronger because of the strength of the U.S. dollar.

Location was also a competitive factor that foreign competitors enjoyed, especially with regard to oil and gas drilling in Southeast Asia and the Middle East. As the production of cable was basically a semicontinuous process, economies of scale were important. With this in mind, it was infeasible to build smaller plants nearer to a customer base that was widely dispersed. As noted earlier, one of the reasons for moving to Lawrence was so that TRW could be closer to its primary customers in Oklahoma.

By the end of June 1983 the market for cable had fallen off dramatically. As Bill Russell reviewed the quarterly financial data (see Table 3) and he observed the idle equipment and employees in the plant, he knew he had to do something soon if he were to maintain market share and profitability.

THE LAYOFF DECISION

As Bill Russell prepared to meet with all personnel at the Lawrence facility, he wondered how he would handle the process of laying off 16% of the current work force of 125. Two things particularly troubled him. First, his predecessor, Gino Strippoli, had implied that there would never be a layoff at the Oilwell Cable Division. Second, and perhaps more importantly, he had to decide whether the decision as to how to reduce labor costs was a decision he should make alone or one that the teams should undertake as their responsibility.

It was now 8:15 A.M. and Bill headed out to meet his employees.

REFERENCES

Burck, Charles G. (1981) "What happens when workers manage themselves," *Fortune,* Jul. 27, pp. 62–69.

Downs, Cal W., and Hummert, Mary Lee (1984) *Case History of TRW Oilwell Cable Division Team Management* (unpublished manuscript), University of Kansas, Lawrence.

TRW 1983 Data Book, TRW Inc., Cleveland, OH.

U.S. Department of Labor (1983) *Handbook of Labor Statistics,* Washington, D.C.: Bureau of Labor Statistics.

Verma, Anil (1985) Electrical cable plant. In Kochan, Thomas A., and Barocci, Thomas A. (Eds.), *Human Resource Management and Industrial Relations,* Boston: Little, Brown and Company, pp. 425–435.

The authors gratefully acknowledge the financial support of the NET Ben Franklin Technology Center and the assistance of Mary Harhigh, our graduate research assistant.

A Change for the Better?
Mary K. Bargielski

The Caven Corporation manufactures motors for different sizes of machines. Most of its customers are also industrial manufacturers who use the motors to power the machines which they make, some for industry (e.g., power saws) and some for consumer goods (e.g., lawn mowers). The company has been very profitable for the last ten years and sales have been steadily increasing.

The manufacturing system is currently using approaches which are similar to the Japanese Kanban. There is a large, movable bulletin board on which there are three columns. They are marked "DO", "DOING", "DONE". Index cards citing manufacturing activities are moved across the board to keep track of the three categories. This allows workers to know exactly where they are in the manufacturing process and how they can divert resources to cover the critical parts of the process. They are also using a Just In Time inventory approach, where suppliers send materials "just in time" for them to be used in the manufacturing process, which helps to keep inventory costs down. Both of these systems are working very well and have helped to create some of the profit the firm now enjoys.

In its effort to stay a jump ahead of its competitors and use profit in a manner which stakeholders will accept, Caven executives have decided to institute a Computer Integrated Manufacturing (CIM) system marketed by IBM. The system is capable of doing bills of material, routing, drawings through CAD (Computer Aided Design), order tracking, materials requirements planning, inventory control, and several engineering functions, among other things. The cost is about $250,000, including hardware and software. Caven plans to integrate the CIM system with robotics which will add to the costs and mean a loss of many production jobs. When the system is put in place, employees will be given a manual from which they can learn to use all the functions available through the CIM program. All of this information is released to employees during a meeting on Friday afternoon called by the CEO, Mr. Fredrick Caven.

After having the weekend to think about this information, a group of six employees from production decide to meet after work for a beer. Selected portions of their conversation at the Iron Duke follow:

DAVID: "Why would they want to change a system that works? What happened to 'if it ain't broke, don't fix it'?"

HEIDI: "Why wouldn't they ask us about CIM first? After all, we are the ones doing these jobs."

MICKY: "Who is going to lose what jobs? Now we have to sit around and quake in our boots until we find out."

"A Change for the Better?" by Mary K. Bargielski is reprinted by permission of the author.

JASON: "How can those left ever learn to use a computer and that crazy CIM program from a manual? Don't they have any sympathy for our positions?"

KATHY: "If they were wondering what to do with profit, why didn't they give some of us a reward for the jobs we've done in creating the profit?"

BRIAN: "So far, all we have are questions. What we really need are answers."

Mary K. Bargielski is an assistant professor at Gannon University.

Readings for Professional Growth and Enrichment

Arvey, R. D., and A. P. Jones (1985). "The Use of Discipline in Organizational Settings: A Framework for Future Research." In L. L. Cummings and B. M. Staw (eds.), *Research in Organizational Behavior*, Vol. 7. Greenwich, Conn.: JAI Press.

Boas, S., and I. Salomon (1985). "Work-at-Home and the Quality of Work Life." *The Academy of Management Review* 10 (July): 455–464.

Brousseau, K. R. (1984). "Job-Person Dynamics and Career Development." In K. M. Rowland and G. R. Ferris (eds.), *Research in Personnel and Human Resources Management*, Vol. 2. Greenwich, Conn.: JAI Press.

Dickman, F., and W. G. Emener (1982). "Employee Assistance Programs: Basic Concepts, Attributes, and an Evaluation." *Personnel Administrator* 27: 55–62.

Donahue, T. J., and M. A. Donahue (1983). "Understanding Interactive Video." *Training and Development Journal* 37 (December): 27–33.

Feldman, J. M. (1983). "Problems and Prospects of Organizational Interventions." In K. M. Rowland and G. R. Ferris (eds.), *Research in Personnel and Human Resources Management*, Vol. 1. Greenwich, Conn.: JAI Press.

Galosy, J. R. (1983). "Curriculum Design for Management Training." *Training and Development Journal* 37 (January): 48–51.

Goldstein, I. (1980). "Training in Work Organization." *Annual Review of Psychology* 31: 229–272.

Gooding, C., and T. W. Zimmerer (1980). "The Use of Specific Industry Gaming in the Selection, Orientation and Training of Managers." *Human Resource Management* 19 (Spring): 19–23.

Griffin, R. W., and T. S. Bateman (1986). "Job Satisfaction and Organizational Commitment." In C. L. Cooper and I. T. Robertson (eds.), *International Review of Industrial and Organizational Psychology*. New York: John Wiley & Sons.

Guilmette, H., and C. Reinhart (February 1984). "Competitive Benchmarking: A New Concept for Training." *Training and Development Journal* 38: 70–71.

Harvey, L. J. (1983). "Effective Planning for Human Resource Development." *Personnel Administrator* 28: 45–52, 112.

Hoenigmann-Stovall, N., and D. J. Gallagher (1982). "Complaint Training." *Supervisory Management* 27 (August): 16–20.

Hoy, F., W. W. Buchanan, and B. C. Vaught (1981). "Are Your Management Development Programs Working?" *Personnel Journal* (December): 953–957.

Hunter, J. E., and F. L. Schmidt (1983). "Quantifying the Effects of Psychological Interventions on Employee Job Performance and Work Force Productivity." *American Psychologist* 38: 473–478.

Jackson, S. E., and R. S. Schuler (1983). "Preventing Employee Burnout." *Personnel* 60: 58–68.

Kearney, W. J. (1975). "Management Development Programs Can Pay Off." *Business Horizons* 18: 81–88.

Langer, S. (1983). "Compensation in Training and Development: An Update." *Training and Development Journal* 37 (May): 48–52.

Latham, G. (1983). "The Role of Goal Setting in Human Resources Management." In K. M. Rowland and G. R. Ferris (eds.), *Research in Personnel and Human Resources Management*, Vol. 1. Greenwich, Conn.: JAI Press.

Locke, E. A., K. N. Shaw, L. M. Saari, and G. P. Latham (1981). "Goal Setting and Task Performance: 1969–1980." *Psychological Bulletin* 90: 125–152.

Mitchell, T. R., and C. A. O'Reilly III (1983). "Managing Poor Performance and Productivity in Organizations." In K. M. Rowland and G. R. Ferris (eds.), *Research in Personnel and Human Resources Management*, Vol. 1. Greenwich, Conn.: JAI Press.

Mohram, S. A., and E. E. Lawler III (1984). "Quality of Work Life." In K. M. Rowland and G. R. Ferris (eds.), *Research in Personnel and Human Resources Management*, Vol. 2. Greenwich, Conn.: JAI Press.

Mohram, S. A., G. E. Ledford, Jr., E. E. Lawler III, and A. M. Mohrman, Jr. (1986). "Quality of Worklife and Employee Involvement." In C. L. Cooper and I. T. Robertson (eds.), *International Review of Industrial and Organizational Psychology*. New York: John Wiley & Sons.

Pinder, C. C., and G. A. Walter (1984). "Personnel Transfers and Employee Development." In K. M. Rowland and G. R. Ferris (eds.), *Research in Personnel and Human Resources Management*, Vol. 2. Greenwich, Conn.: JAI Press.

Porras, J. I., and B. Anderson (1981). "Improving Managerial Effectiveness Through Modeling-Based Training." *Organizational Dynamics* 9: 60–77.

Pritchard, Robert D., Steven D. Jones, Philip L. Roth, K. K. Stuebing, and S. E. Ekeberg (1989). "The Evaluation of an Integrated Approach to Measuring Organizational Productivity." *Personnel Psychology* 42: 69–115.

Scherer, J. J. (1984). "How People Learn: Assumptions for Design." *Training and Development Journal* 38 (January): 64–65.

Scott, R. K. (1982). "GM and the Videodisc: Partners in Training." *Training and Development Journal* 36 (November): 109–110.

Steer, R. M., and R. T. Mowday (1981). "Employee Turnover and Post-Decision Accommodation Processes." In L. L. Cummings and B. M. Staw (eds.), *Research in Organizational Behavior*, Vol. 3. Greenwich, Conn.: JAI Press.

Ward, L. D. (1983). "Warm Fuzzies vs. Hard Facts: Four Styles of Adult Learning." *Training* 20 (November): 31–32.

Wexley, K. N. (1984). "Training Human Resources in Organizations." *Annual Review in Psychology*.

Winstanley, N. B. (1980). "Legal and Ethical Issues in Performance Appraisal." *Harvard Business Review* 58: 186–192.

Zedeck, S. (1984). "A Process Analysis of the Assessment Center Method." In B. M. Staw and L. L. Cummings (eds.), *Research in Personnel and Human Resources Management*, Vol. 2. Greenwich, Conn.: JAI Press.

V

PERFORMANCE APPRAISAL AND REWARD SYSTEMS

Readings

Measure for Measure in Performance Appraisal
Jeffrey S. Kane

Most of what human resource departments do is, in theory, linked to employees' performance (e.g., selection, pay-for-performance, and training). Although the consequent need to measure job performance has spawned a variety of so-called performance appraisal methods, the field's current ability to measure performance is generally recognized to be inadequate. Even the appraisal methods considered most useful — MBO systems, behaviorally anchored rating scales, and behavioral observation scales — are seriously flawed by documented deficiencies. (See the recommended reading section at the end of this article for several critiques of these methods.)

ComPAS (Computerized Performance Appraisal System) was developed by the author not only to overcome the principal deficiencies of existing performance appraisal methods, but to help manage performance. This software, which runs on IBM PCs and PC-compatible hardware, offers a number of performance appraisal capabilities that constitute what can be called a performance appraisal wish list.

WISH LIST

Practitioners and academics generally agree that existing appraisal methods lack at least five significant capabilities:

- Control of rating errors.
- Comparability of performance scores across jobs.
- Limited accountability for the range of feasible performance.
- Consideration of all differences between performances.
- Minimization of paperwork.

Control of rating errors Rating errors occur in two forms: intentional and unintentional. Intentional rating errors are a rater's deliberate distortions to make ratings conform to a preconceived notion about the rated employee's performance. Unintentional rating errors are inaccuracies that result from such unconscious biases as leniency-severity error, central tendency error, and halo error.

Comparability of performance scores across jobs Performance appraisal

---

Source: Jeffrey S. Kane, "Measure for Measure in Performance Appraisal." Reprinted from *Computers in Personnel* (New York: Auerbach Publishers). © 1987 Warren, Gorham & Lamont Inc. Used with permission.

rating scales conventionally take one of two inadequate forms: job-specific scales, which increase accuracy through their specificity but lack comparable scores across jobs, and universal scales, which minimize accuracy and increase comparability. Needed is a methodology that can simultaneously assess performance on a job's specific aspects and produce scores on global features of performance that are universally comparable across jobs, departments, and organizations.

Limited accountability for the range of feasible performance Employees at all organizational levels complain that appraisal systems fail to account for restrictions on performance caused by circumstances beyond their control. An appraisal method is needed to adjust scores to reflect the restrictive influences on performance that occur during each appraisal period.

Consideration of all differences between performances Existing appraisal methods measure only one parameter of employee performance on each aspect of a job — the average level achieved over all the times the employee performed a job aspect. Consideration of how consistently an employee performed a job aspect and of the employee's success at avoiding harmful, costly outcomes are ignored. Consider, for example, a surgeon who, on the average, washes his hands before operations. Would you be willing to be operated on by such a surgeon without knowing how the surgeon rated on consistency of hand washing? A comprehensive performance appraisal method is needed that measures these lost parameters in addition to average performance.

Minimization of paperwork Performance appraisal has always been an exercise in paper shuffling, with forms to complete, copies to distribute, and files to maintain. A computerized appraisal process would not only provide more control over the completeness and logic of rater responses but would also improve the efficiency of scoring, record maintenance, and retrieval of appraisals. Perhaps most important, computerized appraisal data would be more readily accessible for use in HR decision making.

THE COMPAS THEORY

This section describes three concepts that are essential to understanding how ComPAS works:

- Job functions.
- Performance dimensions.
- Performance graphs.

Job Functions

Any job can be broken down into successively narrower components. Performing this kind of breakdown within a job enables us to recombine measurements to express performance on broader job segments. We can also determine the minimum number of observable components on which performance must be appraised to get an adequate representation of overall job performance. The individual job components are called job functions.

Performance Dimensions

Most conventional appraisal methods attempt to directly measure overall performance on each of the job functions included in the system, an approach that fails to recognize the complexity of such a judgment. Performance of any given job function varies along two or more of the following six aspects of value (AOV):

- Quality.
- Quantity.
- Timeliness.
- Cost-effectiveness.
- Need for supervision.
- Effect on other people.

To judge an employee's overall job function performance, a rater must mentally juggle how well the employee did on all of the relevant AOVs, teach an overall judgment, and express it in the form demanded by the rating scale. This task is far too complex for an unaided human mind to perform in a reliable and bias-free manner.

ComPAS addresses this problem by defining each thing to be rated, not as a whole job function, but as only one of the six AOVs of a job function. Each combination of an AOV and a job function is called a performance dimension. For example, when appraising a manager's job performance, planning might be included as one of the job functions. We might determine that three aspects of value are relevant for judging performance on planning: quality, timeliness, and need for supervision. This would result in the formation of three performance dimensions on which each manager would be appraised:

- Quality of planning.
- Timeliness of planning.
- Need for supervision in planning.

EXHIBIT 1
Performance Graph

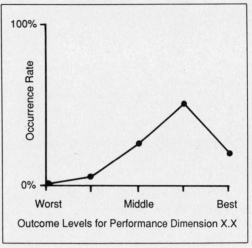

Performance Graphs

An employee's performance on a performance dimension during a specified period of time can be represented on a performance graph, as shown in Exhibit 1.

The outcome levels axis of the performance graph consists of the range of outcomes achievable on some specified AOV whenever the job function is performed. The occurrence rate axis is a range of percentages, from 0% to 100%, of the total number of times that a job function was performed during the appraisal period. Each point on the graph represents the percentage of times on which the corresponding outcome level was produced. A performance graph therefore depicts an employee's complete performance on a performance dimension during a specified period of time.

The primary task of all methods of performance appraisal is to capture and quantify the information contained in performance graphs. Different methods can be used to accomplish this task. ComPAS differs from all other methods in its approach to this task in three ways:

- Its strategy for capturing the rater's image of the performance graph.
- Its choice of performance graph parameters that it seeks to quantify.
- Its approach to accounting for situational constraints on performance.

The Rater's Image of the Performance Graph

ComPAS rejects the traditional belief that people can make reliable, unbiased judgments about something as complex as records of performance. Research over the past 15 years has shown that people are unable to use recollected data to estimate the behavior of people or the outcome of events. ComPAS accepts these findings and refrains from the usual practice of asking the rater to report an overall judgment of how effectively an employee performed on a performance dimension. Instead, ComPAS asks the rater to report the occurrence-rate percentages that form a performance graph. The ComPAS scoring program then takes these percentages and computes all the needed information about the performance graph, free from any further human bias. This approach avoids the opportunities allowed by other methods for human judgment to distort ratings.

Salient parameters   Other appraisal methods consider the average outcome level to be the only meaningful parameter of performance graphs. These methods assume that variation in the outcome levels an employee achieves is simply random noise and should be ignored. ComPAS considers both the consistency of employees' performance and their success at avoiding negative outcomes on an equal footing with their average outcome level.

Constraints on performance   Other appraisal methods that try to express performance levels produce scores that represent how well an employee's performance compared to an ideal performance. Ideal performance consists of achieving the best conceivable outcome level 100% of the time that the employee performs on each performance dimension. But factors beyond the performer's control often make it impossible to achieve such a record on most, if not all, of the performance dimensions in most jobs. Here are some examples of performance-limiting factors beyond the control of job incumbents:

- Failure to receive raw materials needed to meet production quotas.
- Increases or decreases in product demand because of unforeseeable market conditions.
- Computer breakdowns that throw software projects off schedule.

Other appraisal methods fail to express how an employee's actual performance record compares to the best record that was feasible in the employee's situation rather than to the ideal record. Expressing an employee's actual record in relation to the best feasible record offers two advantages:

- Employees are released from accountability for achieving levels of performance made impossible by factors beyond

their control, improving both raters' and rated employees' perceptions of the system's fairness.
- Actual performances in every facet of every job would be compared to an identically defined upper limit or the best record of outcomes that was feasible to achieve. Using a universal upper limit produces scores that are directly comparable across all positions within a job and on common elements — the six AOVs and overall performance — across all jobs, departments, and organizations. For example, the overall job performance scores for all employees would represent how close (as a percentage) the employees came to achieving the best records feasible in all of their job functions. Such percentage scores can be compared directly between any two employees regardless of the differences in their jobs.

For ComPAS to assess an employees' actual performance record against the best feasible record, the rater's report must include two sets of percentages for each performance dimension. Besides reporting the percentages that form a rated employee's actual performance graph for each performance dimension, the rater also reports the percentages that would form the employee's best achievable performance graph on the respective performance dimension.

HOW COMPAS WORKS

ComPAS has two basic components: a rating module and a scoring module.

The rating module All of the rater's interactions with the appraisal system are accomplished through the rating module disk. The rater uses it first to carry out the rating process, which involves responding to questions concerning the best feasible and actual performance records on each of a job's performance dimensions. These raw data entries are stored on a data disk; when the rating is completed, the disk is submitted for scoring. The scoring results are output onto a results disk and returned to the rater. The rater can then select options from the rating module menu to display the appraisal results on the computer screen and to print selected portions of the results.

During the rating process, the rater responds to two sets of four questions for each performance dimension. These questions refer to descriptions of what it looks like to perform at low, middle, and high outcome levels on each performance dimension. These descriptions, called performance level descriptors (PLDs), are generated for each job during the system installation process. The first set of four questions concerns the feasibility of performing at each outcome level. For example, the rater can consider all the times during the appraisal period when the rated employee performed a job function, such as "organized subordinates to carry out a production process." The rater can determine what percentage of these times it was possible:

- To do better than this (description of low PLD).
- To do better than this (description of middle PLD).
- To do as well as this (description of high PLD).
- To do only this well and no better (description of middle PLD).

The second set of four questions concerns the rated employee's actual record of performance. For example, the rater can think back over the times that the rated employee performed a job function, such as "organized subordinates to carry out a production process." The rater can answer what percentage of these times the ratee actually performed:

- More or less like this (description of low PLD).
- More or less like this (description of middle PLD).
- This well or better (description of high PLD).
- Better than this (description of middle PLD).

Each of these questions is displayed in succession on the screen. The minimum and maximum percentages that may be reported for each rating question, based on the answers to all the previous questions for the dimension, are also displayed. Answers violating these limits are disallowed, thereby preventing illogical responses resulting from either confusion or attempts to manipulate ratings.

After completing each dimension's eight questions, the program stores the responses on the data disk. Rating each dimension requires about three minutes of a rater's time.

After all of the dimensions have been rated, the data disk is submitted for scoring. The rater has no further role in generating appraisal scores.

The scoring module This module contains the program for computing the scores and scoring weights from the raw data on the data disk. Running the scoring program on the contents of each data disk should be conducted by clerical personnel specially assigned and trained to do it. Raters should not be allowed to do the scoring or even to possess copies of the score module. This precaution prevents raters from doing ratings by trial and error until they get the results they want.

The scoring procedure consists of raters physically or electronically transferring the file containing their raw rating responses to the appraisal scoring center, along with their copies of the results disks. Each results disk contains the records of up to six sets of appraisal results for an employee.

The appraisal scoring center runs each data disk through the scoring program (about 20 seconds), transfers the results to the results disk for the rated employee, and returns the results disk to the supervisor along with any printed copies of the results that may have been requested.

One or more copies of each ratee's updated results disk should be archived at the scoring center. Most organizations will also want the program to generate a file of the appraisal results in a form that can be added to the orgranzation's HR data base, to a separate performance appraisal data base, or to both.

Scoring Results

The scoring produces four types of reports, each of which presents a progressively more detailed look at a rated employee's performance. Before describing them, here is a brief explanation of the meaning of the numbers contained in the reports.

Scores and weights All four reports express the results using two types of numbers: percentage scores and decimal proportions. The three percentage scores to the right on any given line of any of the reports represent the percentages of best possible performance that the ratee achieved on the three parameters for average outcome level, consistency, and negative range avoidance. The overall scores in the left-hand column are the weighted averages of the parameter scores in the three columns to the right. Appearing under each percentage score is a decimal number between .00 and 1.00. Each of these numbers is a weight representing the proportion of the overall job performance score contributed by the particular aspect of performance to which the weight refers. The three weights to the right always add up to the weight on the left.

The weights are developed during system installation to reflect the difference between the values of the high and low outcome levels on each performance dimension. These differences are used to determine the weights, on the premise that those dimensions for which differences in performance produce a greater difference in value to the organization should be weighted proportionately higher.

When circumstances restrict performance on a dimension, however, the original difference for the dimension is reduced. The operative difference is no longer between the values of always producing the lowest outcome and always producing the highest outcome, because the highest outcome isn't always attainable. Because the upper limit is reduced, achieving a higher percentage score on the dimension becomes correspondingly easier.

Overall performance This report is the most global of the four, addressing both overall performance on the job and on the most universal facets of each job — the six AOVs. This one-page report is shown in Exhibit 2. The scores in this report are reported for all jobs wherever ComPAS is used.

Job function performance A sample first page of this report is shown in Exhibit 3. This report presents the employee's performance from a contrasting perspective; an employee's performance on each job function, averaged across all relevant AOVs instead of performance on each AOV averaged across all job functions as in the previous report. This reporting perspective enables supervisors to identify which job functions and which parameters — average outcome level, consistency, or negative range avoidance — of particular job functions are particularly strong and weak in an employee's performance.

Performance dimension This report, shown in Exhibit 4, enables performance problems to be monitored in detail. This report helps determine the particular AOVs that were problems for an employee on specific job functions. The problem performance parameters on those AOVs can also be identified. This detail permits specific diagnoses of performance problems. Specific diagnoses, in turn, permit specific remedies that can help improve performance.

Performance distributions As shown by the example in Exhibit 5, this is the most detailed of the four reports, presenting the best feasible and actual performance records generated from a rater's responses on each performance dimension.

EXHIBIT 2
Overall Performance Report

Employee Name: Inn O. Vator
ID No: 123-45-6789   Dept No: 11-035
Job Title: Manager of Product Development

Rater Name: Buster Butz
Rater ID No: 987-65-4321   Rater Dept No: 11-035
Rater Job Title: VP for Research and Development

Period Covered by This Appraisal: FROM: 03/01/86   TO: 03/01/87

Date of Rating: 03/07/87

Overall Performance Report

	Effectiveness Scores			
	Overall	Mean Level	Consistency	Negative Range Avoidance
Overall Performance	83%	91% (Wt = 0.79)	58% (Wt = 0.10)	45% (Wt = 0.11)
Overall Quality	64% (Wt = 0.35)	81% (Wt = 0.24)	41% (Wt = 0.04)	20% (Wt = 0.07)
Overall Quantity	88% (Wt = 0.05)	87% (Wt = 0.04)	90% (Wt = 0.01)	— (Wt = 0.00)
Overall Timeliness	89% (Wt = 0.26)	94% (Wt = 0.20)	60% (Wt = 0.03)	79% (Wt = 0.03)
Overall Cost Effectiveness	96% (Wt = 0.04)	95% (Wt = 0.04)	— (Wt = 0.00)	— (Wt = 0.00)
Overall Need for Supervision	98% (Wt = 0.13)	97% (Wt = 0.11)	100% (Wt = 0.01)	100% (Wt = 0.01)
Overall Effect on Other People	96% (Wt = 0.18)	98% (Wt = 0.17)	31% (Wt = 0.01)	— (Wt = 0.00)

EXHIBIT 3
Job Function Performance Report

Employee Name: Inn O. Vator
ID No: 123-45-6789   Dept No: 11-035
Date of Rating: 03/07/87

Effectiveness Scores

Job Function	Overall	Mean Level	Consistency	Negative Range Avoidance
1. Communicating	65% (Wt = 0.34)	83% (Wt = 0.24)	31% (Wt = 0.04)	19% (Wt = 0.06)
2. Organizing and Coordinating	85% (Wt = 0.10)	90% (Wt = 0.08)	67% (Wt = 0.01)	75% (Wt = 0.01)
3. Training or Developing Subordinates	96% (Wt = 0.26)	98% (Wt = 0.23)	66% (Wt = 0.01)	100% (Wt = 0.01)
4. Planning	88% (Wt = 0.17)	94% (Wt = 0.13)	69% (Wt = 0.02)	68% (Wt = 0.02)
5. Allocating Resources	93% (Wt = 0.13)	92% (Wt = 0.11)	93% (Wt = 0.02)	100% (Wt = 0.01)

EXHIBIT 4
Performance Dimension Score Report

Employee Name: Inn O. Vator
ID No: 123-45-6789   Dept No: 11-035
Date of Rating: 03/07/87

Job Function 1: Communicating

Effectiveness Scores

Aspects of Value	Overall	Mean Level	Consistency	Negative Range Avoidance
1.1 Quality	52% (Wt = 0.224)	75% (Wt = 0.148)	17% (Wt = 0.024)	0% (Wt = 0.052)
1.3 Timeliness	91% (Wt = 0.117)	95% (Wt = 0.091)	56% (Wt = 0.014)	100% (Wt = 0.012)

EXHIBIT 5

Performance Distributions Report Details

Employee Name: Inn O. Vator
ID No: 123-45-6789　　　Dept No: 11-035
Date of Rating: 03/07/87

Job Function 1: Communicating

Aspects of Value	Percentage of Best Record Feasible to Exhibit	Percentage of Actual Record That the Ratee Exhibited	Scale Values
1.1 Quality:			
Level 5: Highest Outcome	90	90	125
Level 4: Less than Level 5 but better than Level 3	0	0	−81
Level 3: Intermediate Outcome	10	0	−288
Level 2: Less than Level 3 but better than Level 1	0	10	−494
Level 1: Lowest Outcome	0	0	−700
1.3 Timeliness:			
Level 5: Highest Outcome	80	75	325
Level 4: Less than Level 5 but better than Level 3	5	10	194
Level 3: Intermediate Outcome	15	10	63
Level 2: Less than Level 3 but better than Level 1	0	5	−69
Level 1: Lowest Outcome	0	0	−200

With this information, employees can be shown exactly how much more or less frequently they should produce specific outcomes to raise their scores on each performance dimension.

INSTALLATION

Installation of ComPAS for all or some of an organization's jobs requires five steps:

- Develop job-specific content.
- Establish an appraisal scoring center.
- Adapt software to hardware.
- Train raters and rated employees.
- Provide follow-up consultation.

Job-specific content　Prospective raters and rated employees help develop this material for each job. The material thus produced is used by the system installation team to prepare a set of disk files for the job specifics that ComPAS has focused on.

Appraisal scoring center　This involves assigning and training a clerical staff to process the ratings through ComPAS's scoring software, establish procedures through which the staff can have raters submit their raw ratings to the center, return scoring results to the raters, update the organization's HR data base, and archive appraisal results.

Software to fit hardware Minor software modifications may be necessary to ensure conformity with the user's hardware and to maximize the system's ease of use.

Raters and rated employees Because ComPAS differs so greatly from traditional appraisal methods, training is critical to successfully implementing the system. Training should gradually proceed from conveying the system's capabilities and purposes to hands-on practice in using the system and interpreting its results.

Follow-up consultation ComPAS experts should work with the organization following implementation to iron out any human or administrative problems as well as to advise on the use of the appraisal results for personnel decision making and administrative analyses.

Depending on the number of employees subsumed under a job title, 6 to 10 days are required to complete the first four steps for each job. Installation can proceed simultaneously for two or more jobs if the same supervisors are not involved in developing the job-specific content for more than one job. The number of installation teams available from the consulting organization contracted for the installation will also limit the speed of installation.

The costs of implementing ComPAS should be about the same as those for implementing a Behaviorally Anchored Rating System (BARS) and certainly less than those for any MBO system.

Applications of ComPAS Scores

Most of ComPAS's capabilities derive from the comparability of the percentage scores the system produces on overall performance and on the six AOVs. All percentages have exactly the same meaning across all jobs, departments, organizational levels, and organizations (i.e., the percentage of best feasible performance that an employee achieved).

Comparison and tracking ComPAS's scores on overall performance can be averaged across all members of work units, departments, and whole organizations. The resulting average performance scores can be used for dividing up bonus and merit pay pools and identifying units in which performance is notably low. Scores can be averaged for the organization so that companies can compare their human productivity with other firms in their industry, region, and economic sector.

Companies can also compare the performance they're getting from particular occupations and occupational levels with their own past experience and with the experiences of other firms, their industry, as well as the national economy. Human productivity, defined as an organization's aggregate human performance, can be tracked over time and related to other measures (e.g., financial) of organizational success.

Employee selection Other appraisal methods fail to compare internal candidates for a job opening according to their past performance when all candidates previously held different jobs. ComPAS can be used to appraise performance in all jobs; it not only compares past performances in different jobs but produces directly comparable scores for all candidates on the six AOVs.

Knowing the relative weights of the six AOVs in the vacant job, we could apply those weights to the six AOV scores that the candidates achieved in their current jobs, averaged over as many years as desired. The resulting weighted totals provide a good estimate of how well the candidates would have performed in the job for which they're being considered.

The feasibility ratings generated by ComPAS can be used to identify jobs, work units, departments, and organizational functions in which performance is most seriously restricted by situational constraints. These sites of higher constraint levels are bottlenecks that hinder the whole organization. Identifying them as prime targets for special intervention could prove to be an effective strategy for improving organizational performance.

RECOMMENDED READING

Bernardin, H.J., and Beatty, R. W. *Performance Appraisal: Assessing Human Behavior at Work.* Boston: Kent Publishing Co., 1984.

Bernardin, H. J., and Kane, J. S. "A Closer Look at Behavioral Observation Scales." *Personnel Psychology* 33 (1980), pp. 809–814.

Dunnette, M. D., and Borman, W. C. "Personnel Selection and Classification Systems." *Annual Review of Psychology* 30 (1979), pp. 477–525.

Kane, J. S., and Bernardin, H. J. "Behavioral Observation Scales and the Evaluation of Performance Appraisal Effectiveness." *Personnel Psychology* 35 (1982), pp. 635–642.

Kane, J. S., and Freeman, K. A. "MBO and Performance Appraisal: A Mixture That's Not a Solution, Part 1." *Personnel* 63 (1986), pp. 26–36.

Kane, J. S., and Freeman, K. A. "MBO and Performance Appraisal: A Mixture That's Not a Solution, Part 2." *Personnel* 64 (1987), pp. 26–32.

Landy, F. J., and Farr, J. "Performance Rating." *Psychological Bulletin* 67 (1980), pp. 78–102.

Jeffrey S. Kane is an associate professor of management at the University of Massachusetts at Amherst.

Behind the Mask: The Politics of Employee Appraisal
Clinton O. Longenecker / Henry P. Sims, Jr. / Dennis A. Gioia

There is really no getting around the fact that whenever I evaluate one of my people, I stop and think about the impact — the ramifications of my decisions on my relationship with the guy and his future here. I'd be stupid not to. Call it being politically minded, or using managerial discretion, or fine tuning the guy's ratings, but in the end I've got to live with him, and I'm not going to rate a guy without thinking about the fallout. There are a lot of games played in the rating process and whether we [managers] admit it or not we are all guilty of playing them at our discretion.

According to management books and manuals, employee appraisal is an objective, rational and, we hope, accurate process. The idea that executives might deliberately distort and manipulate appraisals for political purposes seems unspeakable. Yet we found extensive evidence to indicate that, behind a mask of objectivity and rationality, executives

Source: Clinton O. Longenecker, Henry P. Sims, Jr., and Dennis A. Gioia, "Behind the Mask: The Politics of Employee Appraisal," *Academy of Management Executive,* 1987, pp. 183–193. Reprinted by permission.

engage in such manipulation in an intentional and systematic manner. In performance appraisal, it appears that some of the Machiavellian spirit still lives.

Our original goal was to conduct a scholarly investigation of the cognitive processes executives typically use in appraising subordinates. We held in-depth interviews with 60 upper-level executives who had extensive experience in formally evaluating their subordinates on a periodic basis. During these interviews, we heard many frank admissions of deliberate manipulation of formal appraisals for political purposes. In this article we'll discuss the "why and the how" of such politically motivated manipulation.

ON THE APPRAISAL PROCESS

Almost every executive has dreaded performance appraisals at some time or other. They hate to give them and they hate to receive them. Yet, like them or not, every executive recognizes that appraisals are a fact of organizational life. In terms of time, a formal appraisal of a subordinate takes perhaps three or four hours out of the working year; in terms of impact on the lives of executives and their employees, appraisals have significance that reaches far beyond the few hours it takes to conduct them.

Because of the important role appraisals play in individual careers and corporate performance, a great deal of attention has been given to trying to understand the process. Special attention has been directed toward the issue of accuracy in appraisals.[1] Academicians in particular have expended (some might say wasted) substantial energy trying to design the perfect instrument that would yield an accurate appraisal. That effort now appears to be a hopeless, even impossible, task.

More recently, a flurry of activity has centered on the arcane mental processes of the manager who gives the appraisal. It is an intriguing approach because it involves a kind of vicarious attempt to climb inside an executive's head to see how he or she works. Predictably, however, this approach has confirmed the elusiveness of deciphering managerial thought processes. Moreover, it has not yet resulted in appraisals that are any more accurate than existing appraisals.[2]

Even more recently, some effort has been directed toward demonstrating that appraisal is, in addition to everything else, a highly emotional process as well. When emotional variability gets dragged into the process, any hope of obtaining objectivity and accuracy in appraisal waltzes right out the office door.[3]

Taken together, all these approaches apparently lead to the depressing conclusion that accuracy in appraisals might be an unattainable objective.[4] More realistically, perhaps accuracy is simply a wrong goal to pursue. Even if we have a perfect understanding of instruments and mental and emotional processes, would that result in accurate appraisals? Our research indicates that it would not. All of these avenues to understanding appraisal tend to ignore an important point: Appraisals take place in an organizational environment that is anything but completely rational, straightforward, or dispassionate. In this environment, accuracy does not seem to matter to managers quite so much as discretion, effectiveness or,

METHOD

Our research approach involved in-depth, semistructured interviews with 60 executives. The participants in the study came from seven large organizations and represented 11 functional areas. As a group, they averaged more than 20 years of work experience and more than 13 years of managerial experience. Collectively, they had performance appraisal experience in 197 organizations. Conclusions reported here, then, are derived from a diversity of executives.

Each tape-recorded interview was designed to tap the executive's perception of his or her own performance appraisal processes. The interviews averaged more than one and one-half hours in length. Although the interview used some *a priori* "probes," the interviewing strategy mainly encouraged the subject to respond freely and subjectively.

The data collection yielded more than 100 hours of tape-recorded verbal data. All data from each interview were transcribed onto five-by-eight cards that mainly consisted of executives' directly quoted statements, with each card containing one statement, thought, or observation by an executive on a given topic. The transcription process yielded 1,400 cards, which were then classified according to various political issues that emerged during the interviews.

For a classification group to qualify as a potential "finding," a minimum of 72% of the respondents had to have brought up that issue. A research assistant then read each group of cards and assigned a label that captured the "essence" of the executives' views on a particular aspect of the appraisal process. The outcomes from this process were the designated findings of the study. To further enhance the reliability and validity of the research, two research assistants then independently developed frequency counts for each finding. They tallied the number of cards in each classification group that supported the finding that had been identified in the second step of the analysis. The frequencies tabulated by each judge ranged from a low of 43 responses (72%) to a high of 57 (95%). A correlation analysis of the frequencies revealed an $r = .94$ as a measure of inter-rater reliability in identifying the findings.

more importantly, survival. Earlier research has either missed or glossed over the fact that executives giving appraisals have ulterior motives and purposes that supersede the mundane concern with rating accuracy.

ON POLITICS IN PERFORMANCE APPRAISAL

Any realistic discussion of performance appraisal must recognize that organizations are political entities and that few, if any, important decisions are made without key parties acting to protect their own interests.[5] As such, executives are political actors in an organization, and they often attempt to control their destinies and gain influence through internal political actions.

Thus, it is likely that political considerations influence executives when they appraise subordinates.[6] *Politics* in this sense refers to deliberate attempts by individuals to enhance or protect their self-interests when conflicting courses of action are possible. Political action therefore represents a source of bias or inaccuracy in employee appraisal. To understand the appraisal process thoroughly, thus, we must recognize and account for the political aspects of the process.

POLITICS IN APPRAISAL: FINDINGS FROM THE STUDY

The political perspective emerged as a surprisingly important and pervasive issue affecting the way executives appraise their employees. Conclusions derived from our interviews are summarized in Exhibits 1 through 4. Because a strong attempt was made to allow executives to speak for themselves in describing the politics of performance appraisals, direct quotations from the interviews have been included in our analysis, where appropriate. Our findings are discussed below.

Politics as a Reality of Organizational Life

The most fundamental survey finding was an open recognition and admission that politics were a reality in the appraisal process. In fact, executives admitted that political considerations *nearly always* were part of their evaluation process. One vice president summarized the view these executives shared regarding the politics of appraisal:

> As a manager, I will use the review process to do what is best for my people and the division. . . . I've got a lot of leeway — call it discretion — to use this process in that manner. . . . I've used it to get my people better raises in lean years, to kick a guy in the pants if he really needed it, to pick up a guy when he was down or even to tell him that he was no longer welcome here. It is a tool that the manager should use to help him do what it takes to get the job done. I believe most of us here at — — — — operate this way regarding appraisals. . . . Accurately describing an employee's performance is really not as important as generating ratings that keep things cooking.

Executives suggested several reasons why politics were so pervasive and why accuracy was not their primary concern.

First, executives realized that they must live with subordinates in a day-to-day relationship. Second, they were also very cognizant of the permanence of the written document:

> The mere fact that you have to write out your assessment and create a permanent record will cause people not to be as honest or as accurate as they should be.... We soften the language because our ratings go in the guy's file downstairs [the Personnel Department] and it will follow him around his whole career.

Perhaps the most widespread reason why executives considered political action in the appraisal process was that the formal appraisal was linked to compensation, career, and advancement in the organization. The issue of money was continually cited as a major cause of intentional distortions in ratings.

> I know that it sounds funny, but the fact that the process is ultimately tied to money influences the ratings a person receives.... Whenever a decision involves money things can get very emotional and ticklish.

Although the logic of tying pay to the outcome of performance ratings is sound, pay linkages increase the likelihood that ratings will be manipulated. Both managers and the organization as a whole are guilty of using the rating process as an opportunity to reach salary objectives regarding employee compensation that have little, if any, relationship to pay for performance. A director of research and development very candidly described the predicament from the rater's perspective:

> Since the pay raise my people get is tied to the ratings I give them, there is a strong incentive to inflate ratings at times to maximize their pay increases to help keep them happy and motivated, especially in lean years when the merit ceiling is low. ... Conversely, you can also send a very strong message to a nonperformer that low ratings will hit him in the wallet.... There is no doubt that a lot of us manipulate ratings at times to deal with the money issue.

At times, an organization uses the appraisal process as an instrument to control merit increase expenditures. The manipulative process can be summarized as follows:

> This thing [the appraisal process] can really turn into an interesting game when the HR [Human Resources] people come out with a blanket statement like, "Money for raises is tight this year and since superior performers get 7% to 10% raises there will be no superior performers this year." Talk about making things rough for us [raters]! ... They try and force you to make the ratings fit the merit allowances instead of vice versa.

EXHIBIT 1

Politics as a Reality of Organizational Life

Political considerations were nearly always part of executive evaluative processes.

Politics played a role in the evaluation process because:
— executives took into consideration the daily interpersonal dynamics between them and their subordinates;
— the formal appraisal process results in a permanent written document;
— the formal appraisal can have considerable impact on the subordinate's career and advancement.

Influences on Political Culture

Executives made it clear that if an organization was political, the appraisal process would reflect these politics:

> Some organizations are more aggressive and political than others, so it just makes sense that those things carry over into the rating process as well. . . . The organization's climate will determine, to a great extent, how successful any rating system will be, and it follows that if any organization is very political, the rating system will be political. . . .

Several factors were identified by the executives as having a strong influence on the political culture in which the performance appraisal process operates. Perhaps the strongest was the extent to which the formal appraisal process was "taken seriously" by the organization. A plant manager in this study describes what it means for an organization to "take the process seriously":

> At some places the PA [performance appraisal] process is a joke — just a bureaucratic thing that the manager does to keep the IR [industrial relations] people off his back. At the last couple of places I've worked, the formal review process is taken really seriously; they train you how to conduct a good interview, how to handle problems, how to coach and counsel. . . . You see the things [appraisals] reviewed by your boss, and he's serious about reviewing your performance in a thorough manner. . . . I guess the biggest thing is that people are led to believe that it is a management tool that works; it's got to start at the top!

This quote suggests another important factor that turns the appraisal process into a political process: the extent to which higher level executives in the same company use political factors in rating subordinates. A "modeling" effect seems to take place, with managers telling themselves, "If it's okay for the guys upstairs to do it, then we can do it, too."

According to one executive we interviewed,

> I've learned how *not* to conduct the review from the bosses . . . but you do learn from your boss how much slack or what you can get away with in rating your people. . . . It seems that if the manager's boss takes it [the appraisal] seriously, the subordinate [manager] is more likely to follow. If the boss plays games with the review, it seems like the subordinate [manager] is more likely to do so.

The economic health and growth potential of the organization appeared as important factors influencing the organization's culture and, consequently, the appraisal event. Similarly, the executive's own personal belief system — his or her perception of the value of the appraisal process — also seemed to have an impact. Generally, executives who honestly believed the process contributed to the motivation of their subordinates were less likely to allow political factors to affect the appraisal. Conversely, executives who saw the appraisal as a useless bureaucratic exercise were more likely to manipulate the appraisal.

Moreover, if executives believed the appraisals would be seriously scrutinized, reviewed, and evaluated by their superiors, then the influence of political factors was likely to be reduced.

> If somebody is carefully reviewing the marks you give your people, then the game playing is reduced. . . [but] as you rise in the organization, your boss has less

direct knowledge of your people and is less likely to question your judgment, so the door is open for more discretion.

The degree of open communication and trust between executives and subordinates seemed to have some influence on the impact of political factors. The more open the communication, the less likely that politics would play a role:

> If the manager and employee have a trusting and open relationship and shoot straight with each other, then the manager is less likely to play games with ratings.

Last, but not least, the appraiser's level in the organization's hierarchy also seemed to have an influence. Executives generally believed the appraisal process became more political and subjective as one moved up the organizational ladder:

> The higher you rise in this organization the more weird things get with regard to how they evaluate you. . . . The process becomes more political and less objective and it seems like the rating process focuses on who you are as opposed to what you've actually accomplished. . . . As the stakes get higher, things get more and more political.

Inflating the Appraisal

Although academicians have been preoccupied with the goal of accuracy in appraisal, executives reported that accuracy was not their primary concern. Rather, they were much more interested in whether their ratings would be effective in maintaining or increasing the subordinate's future level of performance. In fact, many reported they would deliberately misstate the reported per-

EXHIBIT 2
Factors Influencing the Political Culture of the Organization

The economic health and growth potential of the organization

The extent to which top management supported and, more importantly, did or did not practice political tactics when appraising their own subordinates

The extent to which executives sincerely believed that appraisal was a necessary and worthwhile management practice or just a bureaucratic exercise

The extent to which executives believed that their written assessment of their subordinates would be evaluated and scrutinized by their superiors

The extent to which an organization was willing to train and coach its managers to use and maintain the performance appraisal system

The degree to which the appraisal process was openly discussed among both executives and subordinates

The extent to which executives believed the appraisal process became more political at higher levels of the organizational hierachy

formance level if they felt performance could be improved as a result:

> When I rate my people it doesn't take place in a vacuum . . . so you have to ask yourself what the purpose of the process is. . . . I use this thing to my advantage and I know my people and what it takes to keep them going and that is what this is all about.

Overall, executives reported that deliberate distortions of the appraisal tended to be biased in the subordinate's favor:

Let's just say that there are a lot of factors that tug at you and play on your mind that cause you to tend to soften the ratings you give. It may not have a great impact all the time but when you know a "5" will piss a man off and "6" will make him happy.... You tell me which one you'd choose.... Plus, you don't want to be the bad guy, the bearer of gloom. It seems like ratings are almost always a little inflated at a minimum because of people aspects in the evaluation process.

Typically, executives tended to inflate the overall rating rather than the individual appraisal items. Interestingly, although the overall rating was generally the last item on the appraisal form, this overall rating was determined first; then the executive went back and completed the individual items.

Most of us try to be fairly accurate in assessing the individual's performance in different categories.... If you are going to pump up a person's ratings, for whatever reason, it's done on the subordinate's overall evaluation category. That's all they really care about, anyway.... The problem is these things have to match up, so if you know what the guy's overall rating is in the first place it will probably color the rest of the appraisal.

Of course, this backward procedure is usually contrary to the recommended procedure and is also inconsistent with the typical assumptions about how decisions are supposed to be made "objectively." Executives articulated several reasons as justification for consciously inflating subordinate ratings. The most frequently given reason was to maximize the merit increases that a subordinate would be eligible to receive. This reason was more likely to be given by executives in organizations that closely linked the numerical score on the formal appraisal and the subsequent merit raise.

Sometimes executives wanted to protect or encourage a subordinate whose performance was temporarily suffering because of personal problems. In a similar vein, executives would sometimes inflate a rating simply because they felt sorry for a subordinate. They wanted to avoid short-term "punishment" in the hope that the subordinate would recover and perform once again at an accepable level.

It may sound kind of funny to say this, but sometimes there is a tendency to give subordinates ratings a little higher than they deserve because you feel sorry for them. ... I just had a guy go through a divorce and I'm not going to kick him when he's down, even if his performance drops off. ... If anything, you might use the review to help pick him up and get him back on his feet.

If the appraisal was reviewed by people outside the department, executives sometimes inflated ratings to avoid "hanging dirty laundry out in public." Clearly, many executives preferred to keep knowledge of problems contained within the department.

There are two reviews at times, the written one and the spoken one. The spoken review is the real one, especially if there are things of a sensitive nature. ... I generally don't put those things down on paper in the review for the whole world to read because it is generally none of their damn business. ... I could make all of us look bad or worse than we really are.

Executives also admitted to inflating a rating to avoid a confrontation with a subordinate with whom the executive had recently had difficulties. They took this action mainly to avert an unpleasant incident or sometimes to avoid a confrontation that they believed would not lead to an effective outcome.

On occasion, an executive might inflate the rating because the subordinate's performance had improved during the latter part of the performance period, even though the overall performance did not merit such a rating. Again, the motivation for this higher-than-deserved rating was a desire to encourage the subordinate toward better performance in the next period:

> Many of us have trouble rating for the entire year. If one of my people has a stellar three months prior to the review . . . you don't want to do anything that impedes that person's momentum and progress.

Executives also recognized effort, even though the effort might not pay off in actual performance:

> If a man broke his back trying to do the best job humanly possible, his ratings will generally reflect this if his boss understands people. Take two people with the same performance, but one tried much harder — their ratings will show it in my department. Low ratings might trample that person's desire to put forth effort in the future.

Last, although not frequently reported, a few executives admitted to giving a higher rating to a problem employee to get the employee promoted "up and out" of the department. Although executives only occasionally admitted to this, the

EXHIBIT 3
Inflating the Appraisal

Executives inflated the appraisal to provide ratings that would effectively maintain or increase the subordinate's level of performance (the primary concern was not the accuracy of the ratings).

Inflated ratings occur primarily on the overall performance rating, as opposed to the individual appraisal items

Executive justification for inflating the appraisal:
— to maximize the merit increases a subordinate would be eligible to receive, especially when the merit ceiling was considered low;
— to protect or encourage a subordinate whose performance was suffering because of personal problems (feeling sorry for a subordinate also resulted in an inflated appraisal);
— to avoid hanging dirty laundry out in public if the performance appraisal would be reviewed by people outside the organization;
— to avoid creating a written record of poor performance that would become a permanent part of a subordinate's personnel file;
— to avoid a confrontation with a subordinate with whom the manager had recently had difficulties;
— to give a break to a subordinate who had improved during the latter part of the performance period;
— to promote a subordinate "up and out" when the subordinate was performing poorly or did not fit in the department.

"up and out" rating process was almost universally discussed as something *other* managers actually do. One plant manager candidly remarked:

> I've seen it happen, especially when you get a young guy in here who thinks he's only going to be here a short while before

he gets promoted. People like that become a real pain in the ass.... If you want to get rid of them quick, a year and a half of good ratings should do it.... A lot of people inflate ratings of people they can't stand, or who think they are God's gift to the department, just to get rid of them. Amen.

Of course, this practice helps an executive avoid dealing with performance problems and passes the problem along to someone else. Mainly, this tactic was employed when an executive felt unable or unwilling to deal with a performance problem or, especially, when the source of the problem seemed to be based on "personality" or "style" conflicts.

Deflating the Appraisal

For the most part, executives indicated that they were very hesitant to deflate a subordinate's rating because such a tactic would lead to subsequent problems:

> I won't say I've never given a subordinate lower ratings than he or she deserves because there's a time and place for that type of thing, but let's just say I hesitate to do that sort of thing unless I'm very sure of what the outcome will be and that it won't backfire.

Nevertheless, negative distortions did occur. Executives gave several reasons for using this tactic. First, an overly negative rating was sometimes used to jolt a subordinate to rise to his or her expected performance level:

> I've used the appraisal to shock an employee.... If you've tried to coach a guy to get him back on track and it doesn't work, a low rating will more often than not slap him in the face and tell him you mean business.... I've dropped a few ratings way down to accomplish this because the alternative outcome could be termination down the road, which isn't pretty.

Also, a deliberately deflated rating was sometimes used to teach a rebellious subordinate a lesson:

> Occasionally an employee comes along who needs to be reminded who the boss is, and the appraisal is a real tangible and appropriate place for such a reminder....

Deflated ratings were also used as part of a termination procedure. First, a strongly negative rating could be used to send an indirect message to a subordinate that he or she should consider quitting:

> If a person has had a questionable period of performance, a strong written appraisal can really send the message that they aren't welcome any longer and should think about leaving.... The written review sends a clear message if the person has any doubt.

Second, once the decision has been made that the situation was unsalvageable, negative ratings could then be used to build a strongly documented case against the marginal or poor performer:

> You'll find that once a manager has made up his or her mind that an employee isn't going to make it, the review [the written document] will take on an overly negative tone.... Managers are attempting to protect themselves.... The appraisal process becomes downwardly biased because they [the managers] fear that discussing and

EXHIBIT 4

Deflating the Appraisal

Executives indicated that they were very hesitant consciously to deflate a subordinate's ratings because of potential problems associated with such a tactic.

Nevertheless, they sometimes deflated appraisals:
- to shock a subordinate back on to a higher performance track;
- to teach a rebellious subordinate a lesson about who is in charge;
- to send a message to a subordinate that he or she should consider leaving the organization;
- to build a strongly documented record of poor performance that could speed up the termination process.

---

documenting any positives of the employee's performance might be used against them at a later point in time.

Of course, this tactic has recently become more common because of lawsuits challenging the traditional "employment at will" concept. The courts have clearly stated that terminations must not be frivolous; they must be justified by economic constraints or documentation of poor performance. In these cases managers will use the process to protect themselves from litigation associated with an unlawful termination lawsuit.[7]

SUMMARY

Our research clearly showed that executives believed there was usually a justifiable reason for generating appraisal ratings that were less than accurate. Overall, they felt it was within their managerial discretion to do so. Thus our findings strongly suggest that the formal appraisal process is indeed a political process, and that few ratings are determined without some political consideration. Although research on rater "error" has traditionally suggested that raters can and do inflate ratings (leniency errors) and deflate ratings (stringency errors), researchers have typically not accounted for the realities of the appraisal context to explain why these errors occur.

In the minds of the managers we interviewed, these thoughts and behaviors are not errors but, rather, discretionary actions that help them manage people more effectively. Executives considered many factors beyond the subordinate's actual performance in their ratings. Thus, organizational politics was a major factor in the intentional manipulation of subordinate ratings.

Our findings provide support for the following political realities of organizational life: (1) executives in large organizations are political actors who attempt to avoid unnecessary conflict; (2) they attempt to use the organization's bureaucratic processes to their own advantage; and (3) they try to minimize the extent to which administrative responsibilities create barriers between them and their subordinates.

We also conclude that the organizational culture in which the appraisal event occurs significantly influenced the extent to which political activity would both develop and operate. Of course, organizationwide patterns are also strongly influenced by the support and practice of top management. Indeed, we know that lower-level managers tend to emulate high-status executives, and the way they use the appraisal process is no exception. Thus, if top managers prepare ratings poorly or deliberately distort them, this behavior will tend to cascade down the organization.

Given these findings, what informative observations or constructive recommendations might we make to minimize, or at least manage, the detrimental effects of politics in employee appraisal? In fact, we have several for both the individual manager and the organization as a whole.

The Individual Manager

1. Quite frankly, our data suggest there are times in organizational life when political necessity supersedes the usually desirable goals of accuracy and honesty in appraisal. The executives interviewed suggested several compelling reasons for exercising managerial discretion contrary to traditional appraisal research recommendations. Clearly, there are times when individual employees and the organization as a whole can benefit as a consequence. The caveat, of course, is that the occasions when politics and discretion necessarily intrude on the appraisal process should be chosen judiciously. The overall effect on the organization should be given due consideration.

2. Performance appraisal is perhaps most usefully viewed as a high-potential vehicle for motivating and rewarding employees, rather than as a mandatory, bureaucratic exercise used only for judgmental or manipulative purposes. Ideally, it should be treated as an opportunity to communicate formally with employees about their performance, their strengths and weaknesses, and their developmental possibilities.

3. Executives should bear in mind that appraisal-related actions, like many other organizational activities, serve as guides for subordinates. Employees who must conduct appraisals often learn appraisal attitudes and behaviors from their bosses. Thus if appraisals are to be effective, high-ranking executives must treat the process as significant so that political manipulation is discouraged.

4. In addition, openness and trust between managers and subordinates seems to be associated with a lower level of detrimental political activity. Cultivating understanding seems to reduce the perceived need for resorting to interpersonal politics.

5. Finally, inflating or deflating appraisal ratings for political ends might serve temporarily to help executives avoid a problem with certain employees or to accomplish some specific purpose. However, such intentional manipulation may eventually come back to haunt the perpetrating executive and, ultimately, the organization as a whole. This is especially likely if the company comes to accept political manipulation of appraisals as part of the norm.

The Organization as a Whole

1. The appraisal process should operate in a supportive organizational culture. Effective appraisal systems are characterized by the support of top managers (who conduct appraisals themselves), training, open discussions of the appraisal process on an annual basis (perhaps a quality circle approach to appraisals), and rewarding the efforts of managers who do top-notch appraisals.

2. Systematic, regular, and formal appraisals should start at the top of the organization. We found that top executives want formal appraisals and rarely get them. If appraisals are not done at the top, the message sent to the rest of the organization is, "They aren't very important and thus shouldn't be taken seriously." As a result, the door to more political activity is opened wider.

3. Further, although training on *how* to do effective appraisals is important, managers also need to be trained on *why* they need to be done. Understanding the rationale for appraisals is important in building the perception that the appraisal process is an effective managerial tool and not merely a required bureaucratic procedure.

4. Open discussion of the political aspects of the appraisal process (and their legal ramifications) should be included in appraisal training programs. Although managers made it clear that political manipulation of ratings is commonplace, political issues were *never* openly discussed in either training programs or in management development efforts.

5. When money is tied to the rating process, politically oriented ratings tend to increase. This creates a dilemma: A "pay for performance" management philosophy depends on the "objective" measurement of performance. Yet the realities of politics in the measurement process often mean that measurement will not be objective. Should we therefore divorce appraisal ratings from salary decisions? We think not. Pay for performance is still a good concept in our view, even in light of our findings. Attention to the recommendations we present in this section should minimize the impact of manipulative politics in appraisal ratings.

6. In addition, the number of people who have access to the written appraisal should be minimized. The more people who have access to the appraisal, the greater the temptation for the rater to "impression manage" it. Remember, the fact that the appraisal is written down often means that it is less than completely accurate, simply because it is publicly available.

7. The findings of this study have legal implications as well. Organizations are more susceptible to litigation involving charges of unlawful discharge or discrimination than ever before. Accurate, valid appraisals can help an organization defend itself; inaccurate, invalid appraisals can put the organization at risk. Of course, the relatively recent practice of extensive documentation of poor performance has been in part a response to the modern legal climate. Paradoxically, that climate has arguably *increased* the role of politics in formal appraisal, as organizations try to maintain legal grounds for termination decisions. Still, the often politically motivated practice of building a case for dismissal via documentation of poor performance has come under closer scrutiny as trends in employee appraisal are given closer examination. The best advice here is to stress honesty in appraisal as a "default option" policy. Credible and consistent appraisal practices are the best defense against ligitation. Thus some counseling in the legal ramifications of appraisal should become part of executive training.

CONCLUSION

Perhaps the most interesting finding from our study (because it debunks a popular mythology) is that accuracy is *not* the primary concern of the practicing executive in appraising subordinates. The main concern is how best to use the appraisal process to motivate and reward subordinates. Hence, managerial discretion and effectiveness, not accuracy, are the real watchwords. Managers made it clear that they would not allow excessively accurate ratings to cause problems for themselves, and that they attempted to use the appraisal process to their own advantage.

The astute manager recognizes that politics in employee appraisal will never be entirely squelched. More candidly, most of us also recognize that there is some place for politics in the appraisal process to facilitate necessary executive discretion. The goal, then, is not to arbitrarily and ruthlessly try to eliminate politics but, instead, to effectively manage the role politics plays in employee appraisal.

NOTES

1. For an extensive discussion of this point, see F. J. Landy and J. L. Farr's "Performance Rating," *Psychological Bulletin*, 1980, *87*, 72–107. This issue is further developed in Landy and Farr's book, *The Measurement of Work Performance*, New York: Academic Press, 1983. It is clear that the psychometric aspects of the appraisal process are only one part of understanding and improving appraisals.
2. DeNisi, Cafferty, and Meglino have recently discussed the key issues and complications associated with understanding the psychology of managerial decision making in the appraisal process in their recent article, "A Cognitive View of the Performance Appraisal Process: A Model and Research Prospective," *Organizational Behavior and Human Performance*, 1984, *33*, 360–396. For a discussion of further cognitive complications in the appraisal process as a result of unconscious information processing, refer to D. A. Gioia and P. P. Poole, "Scripts in Organizational Behavior," *Academy of Management Review*, 1984, *9*, 449–459.
3. For an exploration of some of the emotional and affective factors that might bear on appraisal processes, see O. S. Park, H. Sims, Jr., and S. J. Motowidlo's "Affect in Organizations: How Feelings and Emotions Influence Managerial Judgment," in H. P. Sims and D. A. Gioia and Associates (Eds.), *The Thinking Organization*.
4. Jack Feldman suggests in his article, "Beyond Attribution Theory: Cognitive Processes in Performance Evaluation," *Journal of Applied Psychology*, 1981, *66*, 127–148, that raters have certain cognitive flaws in information processing that make complete objectivity and validity in rating unobtainable. Also see W. C. Borman's "Explaining the Upper Limits of Reliability and Validity in Performance Ratings," *Journal of Applied Psychology*, 1978, *63*, 135–144.
5. Jeffrey Pfeffer, in his book *Power in Organizations*, Marshfield, MA: Pittman Publishing Co., 1981, makes a strong case that political gamesmanship and the use of power in organizations surround almost every important decision in organizational life. The implications of the appraisal process (e.g., pay raises, promotions, terminations) make the appraisal of performance an important decision-making enterprise.
6. Bernardin and Beatty, in their book *Performance Appraisal: Assessing Human Behavior at Work*, Boston, MA: Kent, 1984, suggest that extraneous variables that are not performance related have an effect on the rater's decision processes and that this influence is in fact a primary source of bias and inaccuracy in performance ratings.
7. For an in-depth treatment of the legal issues concerning performance appraisal, see P. S. Greenlaw and J. P. Kohl's *Personnel Management*, New York: Harper & Row, 1986, 171–173. See also W. F. Cascio and H. J. Bernardin's "Implications of Performance Litigation for Personnel Decisions," *Personnel Psychology*, Summer 1981, 217.

Clinton O. Longenecker is affiliated with the University of Toledo. Henry P. Sims, Jr., is affiliated with George Mason University and with the Pennsylvania State University. Dennis A. Gioia is affiliated with the Pennsylvania State University.

Some Neglected Variables in Research on Discrimination in Appraisals
Robert L. Dipboye

Any discussion of discrimination should begin with the reality that major segments of American society are economically disadvantaged. Women occupy lower status jobs than men and are paid less than men occupying similar jobs. Also, black, Hispanic, physically handicapped, and older persons must contend with discrimination that places them at an economic disadvantage. There are several factors that contribute to this problem. The present paper is concerned with one potential barrier to the upward mobility of women and minorities, unfair discrimination in performance appraisals.

Recent analyses of court cases indicate that courts are carefully scrutinizing the appraisal systems of organizations as sources of unfair discrimination (Cascio & Bernardin, 1981; Feild & Holley, 1982). Furthermore, field research on discrimination in appraisals has shown that performance appraisal systems are vulnerable to claims of unfair discrimination. Kraiger and Ford (1983), in a meta-analysis of 49 published and unpublished field studies with a cumulated N of 13,706, found a correlation between race of the employee and performance ratings of .192. Their findings indicate a small but consistent tendency for white employees to receive higher ratings than black employees. Cleveland and Landy (1981) found that older employees received lower ratings than young employees on appraisals of self-development and interpersonal skills. In contrast to the research on race and age, the published field research on sex bias has shown that female employees are rated the same (Cascio & Phillips, 1979; Dreher, 1981; Elmore & LaPointe, 1974, 1975; Harris, 1975; Moses & Boehm, 1975; Pulakos & Wexley, 1983; Wexley & Pulakos, 1982) or higher (Mobley, 1982) than male employees. Nevertheless, Fernandez (1981) recently found in a national survey that female managers tend to believe that they are discriminated against in the appraisal of their performance.

The findings of field research show that unfair discrimination is at least a potential problem in the appraisal systems of many organizations. It is impossible, however, to determine from the findings of the typical field study whether differences (or lack of differences) in the appraisals of blacks and whites, men and women, and the young and old reflect the biases (or lack of biases) of the rater or a myriad of factors that are confounded with sex, race, and age. Because of the difficulties involved in interpreting field data, some researchers have taken the phenomenon of unfair discrimination into the laboratory. Much of this research is guided by a cognitive framework, which here is called the stereotype-fit model of discrimination. The essential aspect of this model is that appraisals reflect the rater's perceptions of the fit of the ratee to the perceived requirements or stereotype of the job. Re-

Source: Robert L. Dipboye, "Some Neglected Variables in Research on Discrimination in Appraisals," *Academy of Management Review*, 1985, pp. 116–127. Reprinted by permission.

flecting the idea that discrimination is primarily a cognitive bias, the typical experiment places the rater in the role of a passive-observer who evaluates the ratee solely on the basis of information provided by the experimenter.

The many laboratory experiments on the topic appear not to have contributed significantly to the understanding and elimination of unfair discrimination in performance appraisals. This author's thesis is that this research is limited by an overdependence on the stereotype-fit model and passive-observer research methods.

THE STEREOTYPE-FIT MODEL

Raters possess a variety of cognitive structures, including implicit theories, schemata, and prototypes. A stereotype is a particular type of implicit theory consisting of the characteristics that raters attribute to a category of persons. According to the stereotype-fit model, which is depicted in Figure 1, raters tend to attribute to an individual ratee characteristics consistent with their stereotype of persons similar to the ratee. In like manner, raters tend to attribute to a particular position requirements that are consistent with their stereotype of successful occupants of the position. For instance, some jobs are considered "man's work" requiring masculine characteristics whereas other jobs are considered "woman's" work requiring feminine characteristics (Krefting & Berger, 1979). The current incumbents in the job and other characteristics of the context make salient particular stereotypes of the ratee (1 in Figure 1) and the job (2 in Figure 1). For example, there is some evidence that raters are more likely to describe female ratees with stereotypic female traits when there are more female ratees in a situation than when there is an equal number of male and female ratees (Heilman, 1980). Similarly, raters may be more likely to stereotype a job as a man's job or a woman's job depending on the proportion of men and women currently in the job. The expectations that raters hold for the ratee's performance in a job depend on the extent to which the stereotype of persons similar to the ratee is perceived to fit the stereotype of the ideal job incumbent (3 and 4 in Figure 1). Furthermore, the stereotypes of the ratee guide the raters' encoding and retrieval of information on the ratee's performance (7 in Figure 1) so that information consistent with these stereotypes is more likely to be noticed and recalled than information that is inconsistent with these expectations (Feldman, 1981). Raters then compare the behavior and accomplishments of the ratee to the stereotype of the ideal incumbent and form an opinion of that ratee's fit to the job (8 in Figure 1). The stereotype-fit model predicts that raters evaluate a ratee's performance favorably to the extent that their perceptions of the individual ratee fit their stereotype of the job (9 in Figure 1). Thus, raters who discriminate unfairly against a ratee do so for what they believe to be rational reasons, that is, the ratee lacks the requisite characteristics.

PREVIOUS LABORATORY RESEARCH

The Passive Observer Procedure

Underlying the stereotype-fit model is the assumption that unfair discrimination results primarily from biases in the

FIGURE 1
A Holistic Model of Unfair Discrimination in Performance Appraisals

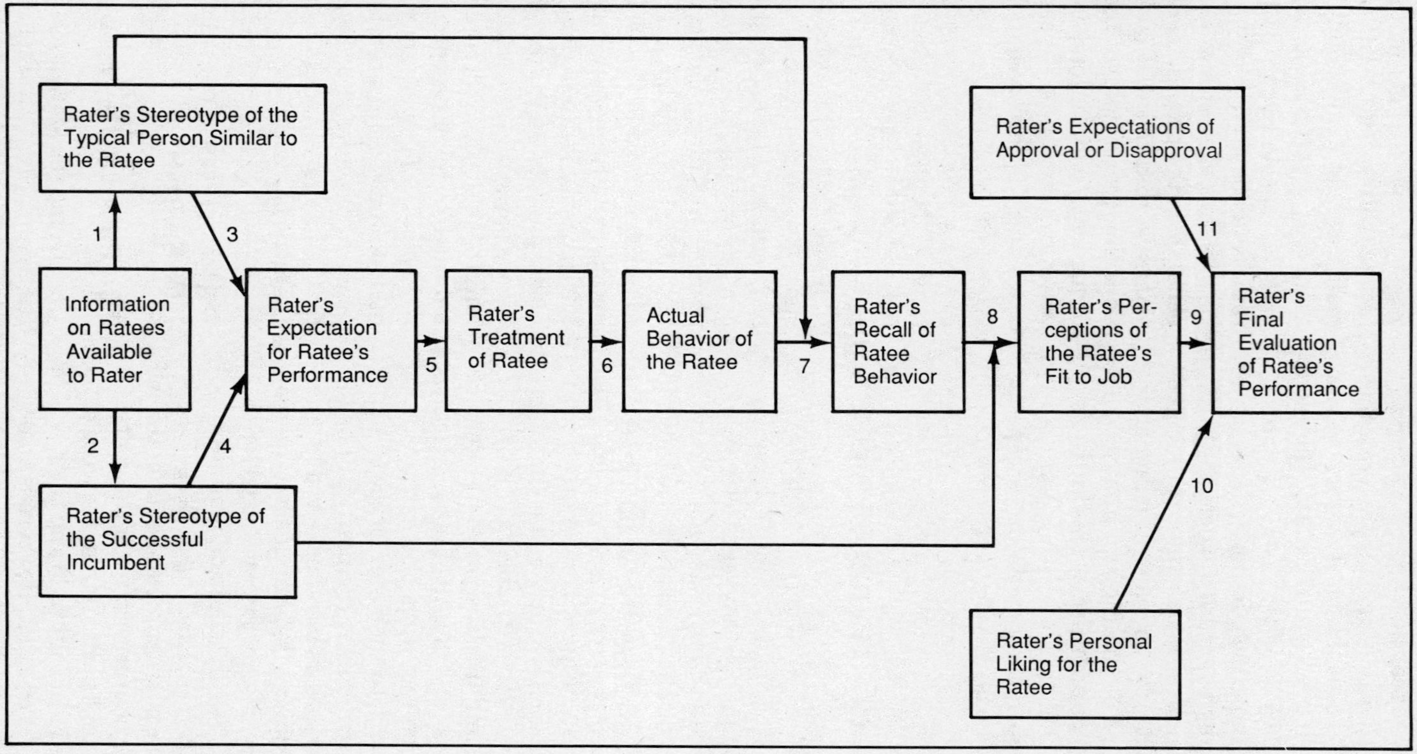

individual rater's processing of information on the ratee. Consistent with this assumption, a typical passive observer study presents a hypothetical ratee in the form of paper credentials or a videotaped performance to raters under instructions to assume the role of evaluator of the ratee. The effects of variations in the characteristics of the ratee such as age, sex and race, on appraisals of the ratee's performance are assessed, either holding constant or independently varying objective performance. Unfair discrimination is operationally defined as different evaluations given to ratees with the same objective performance.

Passive-Observer Research on Ratee Race, Sex, and Age

The few experiments examining race effects have yielded inconsistent findings, with some studies showing bias against blacks (Hamner, Kim, Baird, & Bigoness, 1974), others reporting slight biases in favor of blacks (Bigoness, 1976), and still other studies showing no differences in the ratings as a function of race (Hall & Hall, 1976; Maruyama & Miller, 1980). Yarkin, Town, and Wallston (1982) found that college students rated successful black performers as less able and more motivated than successful white performers. Brugnoli, Campion, and Basen (1979) found that black performers were rated lower than white performers on global performance scales but the same as whites on specific behavioral dimensions. In their meta-analysis of the research on race effects, Kraiger and Ford (1983) found a mean correlation of .032 between race of the ratee and appraisal in an analysis of 10 laboratory studies containing a total N of 992. There was a large amount of variation around this mean, however, with the 95 percent confidence interval ranging from −.25 to .32.

The research on ratee sex has yielded findings as mixed as the race research (Nieva & Gutek, 1980). Bias against female ratees has been found in ratings of the quality of their essays (Cline, Holmes, & Werner, 1977; Goldberg, 1968; Isaacs, 1981; Toder, 1980), how well they relate to customers and other employees (Cohen & Leavengood, 1978; Rosen & Jerdee, 1974), the skill with which they shelve library books (Schmitt & Lappin, 1980), and their contributions to a group discussion (Taylor & Falcone, 1982). Bias against females also has been shown in causal attributions of their performance (Deaux & Emswiller, 1974; Garland & Price, 1977). Finally, several studies have found bias against women who act "out of role" by being directive (Haccoun, Haccoun, & Sallay, 1978; Rosen & Jerdee, 1973; Wiley & Eskilson, 1982) or aggressive (Costrich, Feinstein, Kidder, Maracek, & Pascale, 1975).

Despite the evidence of bias against women, a substantial number of investigators have found no differences in the ratings of men and women (Frank & Drucker, 1977; Hall & Hall, 1976; Heilman & Guzzo, 1978; London & Stumpf, 1983; Penley & Hawkins, 1980; Rose & Stone, 1978; Stumpf & London, 1981) or have found that higher evaluations are given to women (Bigoness, 1976; Hamner et al., 1974; Norton, Gustafson, & Foster, 1977). To complicate the picture further, several studies have found that women are rated as highly as, or higher than, men when they both exhibit high levels of performance and less favorably than men when they both exhibit mediocre or poor levels of performance (Abramson, Goldberg, Greenberg, & Abramson,

1978; Jacobson & Effertz, 1974; Madden & Martin, 1979; Pheterson, Kiesler, & Goldberg, 1971). Also, Rosen and Jerdee (1975) and Mai-Dalton, Feldman-Summers, and Mitchell (1979) have found that females who act "out of role" by behaving aggressively are evaluated more favorably than those who comply with conventional sex role stereotypes.

The few laboratory experiments on age have yielded more consistent findings than either the research on sex or race bias. These studies have found that older ratees are typically rated less favorably than younger employees (Rosen & Jerdee, 1976, 1979; Rosen, Jerdee, & Lunn, 1981). Schwab and Heneman (1978) have found that bias against older raters is more likely to occur among older than among younger raters.

Limitations of Passive-Observer Research

In summary, the laboratory research on race and sex bias is quite inconsistent in showing bias against blacks and women, and even when bias is found, the effects typically are small. Indeed, if one accepts the findings of laboratory research as accurate estimates of the extent of the problem, a logical conclusion is that there is little reason for concern that women, minorities, and the older employee are unfairly discriminated against in performance appraisals. Such a conclusion is unwarranted. Not only is the laboratory an inappropriate setting for determining the prevalence and strength with which a phenomenon occurs in the field, but some doubts exist as to the internal and external validity of this research.

The most frequently mentioned problem is that the findings of laboratory research using college students are not generalizable to experienced raters. Even those laboratory experiments using experienced raters, however, often rely on too few stimuli to allow generalization of findings, and they inappropriately treat stimuli as a fixed effect rather than as a random effect in statistical analyses (Fontenelle, Peek, & Lane, 1983). Past research has given little attention to the possible moderating effects of the task on evaluations of performance, despite the findings of several studies that task type is an important moderator of the effects of ratee sex on appraisals (Cohen, Bunker & Burton, 1978; Deaux & Emswiller, 1974; Isaacs, 1981). Another problem is that investigators continue to use analysis of variance to make group comparisons and ignore the considerable differences that exist among raters in their attitudes and stereotypes (Madden, 1981). Finally, many laboratory experiments on unfair discrimination appear transparent and laden with demand characteristics (Newman & Krzystofiak, 1979).

The aforementioned problems are potentially serious flaws that researchers should take into account in future laboratory experiments. More fundamental than these methodological frailties, however, is the rather limited conceptualization of unfair discrimination underlying laboratory research. Although there is little reason to doubt that stereotypes are important determinants of unfair discrimination, there are behavioral, affective, and social determinants of discrimination as well (Allport, 1954; Fromkin & Sherwood, 1974). For research on unfair discrimination in appraisals to yield findings that are both theoretically important and useful, researchers must take a more holistic view of the determinants of discrimination.

TOWARD A HOLISTIC MODEL

The holistic model of discrimination presented in Figure 1 represents an initial attempt to broaden the view of discrimination in appraisals by incorporating the behavioral, affective, and social determinants of discrimination within the stereotype-fit model. According to the model, the rater's personal feelings enter into the appraisal process and influence evaluations independently of perceived fit to the job requirements (10 in Figure 1). Also, raters are not passive observers but interact with the ratee and influence the performance of the ratee (5 and 6 in Figure 1). Finally, raters in organizations occupy social roles, and their evaluations reflect a compliance to expectations communicated by other persons in the organization as much, if not more, than they reflect the private beliefs of the rater (11 in Figure 1). Corresponding to the emotional, behavioral, and social determinants of appraisals, respectively, bias in the appraisal of employees occurs in the form of personal disliking for the ratee, self-fulfilling prophecies, and conformity to social pressures. Moreover, raters experience ambivalence in their evaluations of ratees to the extent that there are inconsistencies among the affective, cognitive, behavioral, and social components.

Biased Appraisal as Personal Disliking

As indicated earlier, underlying passive-observer research and the stereotype-fit model are the implicit assumptions that discrimination in appraisals is relatively free of affect and has the semblance of rationality. In contrast to this view of the appraisal situation, rater and ratee typically interact face-to-face, and in the process of interacting they form relationships that vary in intimacy and attachment. As stated in Figure 1 (10), raters can be biased in their appraisals of a ratee simply because they dislike the ratee, independent of more objective information on the ratee's performance (Cardy, 1982; Dobbins, 1982; Keenan, 1977; Smith, Meadows, & Sisk, 1970). A face-to-face interaction seems likely to evoke stronger liking or disliking for a ratee, however, than is likely to occur in passive-observer research because of the larger number of auditory and visual cues (Shapiro, 1966; Washburn & Hakel, 1973) and the greater motivational pressures on raters in realistic appraisal situations. For example, raters can find their self-esteem threatened by a high performing female (Grube, Kleinhesselink, & Kearney, 1982), can feel embarrassed and tense in the presence of a physically handicapped person (Kleck, 1966), can fear and distrust ratees of different nationalities and skin color (Allport, 1954), and can feel angered and frustrated over the anticipated failure of a minority ratee (Kipnis, Silverman, & Copeland, 1973).

In contrast to the wide range of emotions that raters experience in face-to-face interactions, raters are unlikely to react with much emotion to the pale and bloodless evaluation tasks performed in most passive observer studies. Consequently, biases emerge in face-to-face interactions that remain dormant when raters are relegated to the role of passive observers. Some evidence of this was reported by Hagen and Kahn (1975), who found that male subjects were more attracted to a competent female than to an incompetent female when they merely observed her performance than when they interacted with her. Also, they were more attracted to both competent and incompetent females when they observed them than when they competed against them.

Biased Appraisal as Self-fulfilling Prophecy

The stereotype-fit model and passive observer research is well described by Neisser who, in criticizing social cognition research, noted that it deals with "an essentially passive onlooker, who sees someone do something (or sees two people do something) and then makes a judgment about it. He (this is the generic passive he) doesn't do anything — doesn't mix it up with the folks he's watching, never tests his judgments in action or in interaction. He just watches and makes judgments" (1980, p. 602). Raters in most realistic appraisal situations obviously interact with those they evaluate, and biases against a minority, female, older, or handicapped ratee often are manifested in the behavior of the rater toward that ratee. Consequently, unlike the passive-observer situation, the rater is a potential cause of the ratee's performance in most organizational appraisals. In some cases, the appraisals of a ratee are the consequence of self-fulfilling prophecies. For example, raters expect a ratee to perform poorly; this expectation leads them to treat the ratee in a biased manner (5 in Figure 1); this biased treatment evokes ratee performances confirming the original expectations of the rater (6 in Figure 1). Thus, unfair discrimination in appraisals in this case results largely from unfair treatment of the ratee.

There are several ways in which rater treatment of the ratee can mediate self-fulfilling prophecies in the appraisal process. Raters typically gather information rather than simply receive information, and previous research has shown that information gathering often is biased in the direction of confirming the information gatherer's expectations (Snyder, 1981). Additionally, most raters supervise the ratee, and biases in supervision have been shown to mediate self-fulfilling prophecies (Eden & Ravid, 1982; Eden & Shani, 1982). The extent to which such self-fulfilling prophecies occur in the supervision of black, female, handicapped, or older employees has not been fully documented. Nevertheless, white male managers have been found to treat white male subordinates as the "in-group" (Fernandez, 1981) and to employ referent and expert power more frequently in managing them (Ayers-Nachamkin, Cann, Reed, & Horne, 1982; Kipnis et al., 1973; Richards & Jaffee, 1972; Rosen & Jerdee, 1977) than they do with black and female subordinates. Furthermore, Eden and Shani (1982) and Eden and Ravid (1982) found that military trainees who were falsely described to their instructors as highly competent actually performed better than trainees in a control group for whom there was no information. Apparently mediating the effects of instructor expectations and trainee performance, instructors treated the "competent" trainees with more support and consideration (Eden & Shani, 1982), and the "competent" trainees felt more self-confident and "overrewarded"

(Eden & Ravid, 1982). A logical extension from these findings is that low expectations for minority, women, handicapped, and older subordinates lead to inconsiderate supervision from the rater and, consequently, to low self-esteem, feelings of underreward inequity, and poor performance in the ratee.

A third category of behavior mediating self-fulfilling prophecies is the nonverbal, paralinguistic, and verbal behavior that accompanies a particular style of supervision and may unintentionally "leak" the attitudes of the supervisor. Kleck and his associates (Kleck, Ono, & Hastorf, 1966) have shown that subjects exhibit more motoric inhibitions and terminate interactions sooner with persons confined to a wheelchair than they do with physically normal persons. Both Word, Zanna, and Cooper (1974) and Weitz (1972) found that white interviewers displayed more negative nonverbal behavior with black interviewees than with white interviewees. Word et al. (1974) also found that the negative nonverbal behaviors exhibited by the white interviewers (low eye contact, backward lean, physical distance) appeared to have a detrimental effect on the interview performance of the black interviewees. Although they suggest possible mediators of self-fulfilling prophecies, the interpretation of these effects and the extent to which they generalize to appraisal contexts are still undetermined.

Biased Appraisal as Conformity to Social Pressures

Another assumption that seems to underlie the stereotype-fit model and passive observer research is that unfair discrimination is based on the private beliefs of the individual decision maker. With the possible exception of experimental demand characteristics, social pressures are given little opportunity to influence appraisals in the typical passive observer study. In organizational appraisals, however, evaluations are conducted by occupants of organizational roles. The frequency and severity with which raters discriminate unfairly are influenced by a variety of social pressures, including the formal policies of the organization and the expectations of subordinates, clients, and managers.

Past research has shown that the evaluations of individual ratees are influenced by the sex and race of the other ratees (Schmitt & Hill, 1977; Toder, 1980). Kraiger and Ford (1983) found in a meta-analysis of field research that bias against blacks declined as the percentage of black employees in the work group increased. A cognitive interpretation of these context effects is that the sex and race composition of a group of ratees serves as informational cues that make salient stereotypes, which, in turn, bias the evaluation of particular ratees (1 and 2 in Figure 1). The social context in a realistic appraisal situation, however, consists of more than informational cues. It also consists of interacting persons, who are actively communicating their expectations to the rater and reinforcing and punishing the rater for complying or failing to comply with these expectations. Moreover, raters in organizations usually are sensitive to the expectations of others and the disapproval that violations of these expectations incur. Consequently, biased appraisals often reflect the conformity of raters to organizational norms in addition to, or instead of, the personal prejudices of raters (10 in Figure 1).

Quinn, Tabor, and Gordon (1968) provided some evidence of the powerful influence of social pressures on discrimination in appraisals in a 1968 study of anti-Semitism. They found that social pressures to discriminate against Jewish employees could lead even those managers who were relatively egalitarian in their private views to discriminate against Jewish employees in evaluations of promotability. Of those managers in their sample who expressed a low level of anti-Semitism and who believed that no third parties would be upset by the hiring or promotion of a Jew, 15 percent were inclined to discriminate against Jews in promotion decisions. Of those managers who believed that two or more third parties would feel uncomfortable with the hiring or promotion of a Jew, 56 percent said they would discriminate against Jews in promotions. Perceived pressures from third parties also appeared to amplify the bias of those who were already anti-Semitic in their private beliefs. Of the anti-Semitic managers, 53 percent said they would discriminate against Jews if they believed that no third party would feel uncomfortable, but 77 percent were inclined to discriminate if they believed two or more third parties would feel uncomfortable. Similarly, Bowman, Worthy, and Greyson (1965) found that the reluctance of managers to promote women to supervisory roles was largely the result of anticipated resistance by co-workers.

The Ambivalent Rater

Unfair discrimination in appraisals is manifested in more ways in realistic appraisals than in the artificial circumstances of most passive observer studies. This is not to suggest, however, that rampant prejudice is the typical state of affairs and that the primary problem with passive observer research is that it has failed to capture this bias. With increasing legal and social prescriptions against unfair discrimination, raging bigotry probably is far less common among raters in organizations today than is ambivalence. A primary problem with passive observer research is that it fails to capture this ambivalence.

Katz and Glass (1979) use the term ambivalence in its psychodynamic sense to refer to conflicts between a person's self-image as fair and unprejudiced and feelings of aversion for a disadvantaged person that threaten this self-conception. Ambivalence is used more broadly here to refer to instability in the behavior and attitudes of raters resulting from inconsistencies among the cognitive, behavioral, social, and affective determinants of their appraisals. For instance, the personal feelings of raters regarding the ratee can conflict with their cognitive appraisals of the ratee's qualifications, as is the case in male supervisors who recognize that a female employee's assertiveness meets the requirements of the job but, nevertheless, personally dislike her for her assertiveness. Ambivalence also might result when the stereotypes and feelings of raters conflict with the policies of the organization, as happens in managers who are convinced that women are unqualified for managerial jobs but who must comply with the formal equal opportunity policy of the organization.

According to Katz and Glass's theory of ambivalence, subjects evaluate a good performance more favorably and a poor performance less favorably to the extent that they are ambivalent in their feelings for the ratee. The effects of rater ambivalence appear moderated by the extent to which there are socially desirable excuses available to raters for their actions. Several experiments have shown that subjects are biased in favor of minority persons when actions against them are likely to appear prejudiced. When there are socially desirable excuses for discriminating against them, however, subjects openly discriminated against these minority persons (Gaertner & Dovidio, 1977; Katz & Glass, 1979; Rogers & Prentice-Dunn, 1981; Snyder, Kleck, Strenta, & Mentzer, 1979). In addition to showing instability in their ratings and treatment of a minority person, raters who are ambivalent toward minority persons may find it particularly difficult to give them negative feedback on their performance. For instance, Feild and Holley (1977) found that the poorer the performance rating given by white supervisors to black subordinates, the less likely the supervisors were to tell them about this appraisal. On the other hand, the poorer the performance of white subordinates, the more likely they were to give them the feedback. Similarly, Hastorf, Northcraft, and Picciotto (1979) found in a laboratory simulation that supervisors were more likely to give unrealistically favorable performance feedback to handicapped subordinates than to normal subordinates. At this time one can only speculate as to the antecedents and consequences of rater ambivalence in organizational contexts, but enough evidence exists to suggest that unfair discrimination in performance appraisals is more complex and subtle than is indicated by the stereotype-fit model and passive observer research.

IMPLICATIONS FOR PRACTICE AND RESEARCH

One obvious implication of the holistic model is that field research is needed that goes beyond the simple group comparisons dominating past field studies and explores the behavioral, cognitive, social, and emotional factors in Figure 1. Although the focus of attention in this paper is on the frailties of laboratory research, it is not the laboratory per se that is the problem but the passive nature of the procedures used in this research. Passive observer research appears poorly suited for capturing the affective, behavioral, and social components of unfair discrimination and the ambivalence associated with these components. Rather than simply replacing "paper-people" with videotaped stimuli, laboratory researchers must end their dependence on passive observer procedures and investigate face-to-face interactions between raters and ratees.

A practical implication of the model is that the particular intervention one chooses to eliminate unfair discrimination in a situation should depend on the relative influence of the affective, social, behavioral, and cognitive factors in that situation. If faulty stereotypes are indeed the cause, then one might train raters to think with more complexity about ratees (Gardiner, 1972) or provide relevant information on the ratee to counteract these stereotypes (Locksley, Borgida, Brekke, & Hepburn, 1980). One also might focus the attention of raters on job relevant information through the use of behaviorally based rating scales (Brugnoli & Campion, 1979) and instructions to avoid biases in using these scales (Latham & Wexley, 1981), although these two approaches appear somewhat ineffective in improving the accuracy of ratings (Bernardin & Buckley, 1981; Schwab, Heneman, & DeCotiis, 1975). If discrimination is rooted in the personal needs and feelings of raters, then "cognitive approaches" such as these may be ineffective, and one may need to make raters aware of their own prejudice (Bass, Cascio, McPherson, & Tragash, 1976; Rokeach, 1971) and provide them with self-insight into its causes (Katz, McClintock, & Sarnoff, 1957).

Biases in the evaluations of performance resulting from biased treatment of the ratee may require training to improve the skill and sensitivity with which raters communicate verbally and nonverbally with female, minority, handicapped, and older employees. Such social skills training appears effective in clinical (Waxer, 1979) and classroom (Wolfgang, 1979) settings and may prove useful as a component of supervisory training. Intercultural training, in which the supervisor is instructed in the norms of the subordinate group (Mitchell & Foa, 1969), also may prove effective in eliminating biases in the supervision of subordinates. Finally, to the extent that unfair discrimination results from social pressures, management needs to counteract these pressures by clearly communicating equal opportunity policies and by rewarding raters for compliance. Quinn et al. (1968) found that even managers with strongly anti-Semitic views were unlikely to discriminate against Jews if they believed that higher management supported equal opportunity.

In conclusion, appraisals in organizations have multiple determinants, and the most effective attempts to understand and reduce unfair discrimination are likely to be holistic. Laboratory research on unfair discrimination in appraisals is likely to make a much more significant theoretical and practical contribution if raters are viewed not only as information processors but as occupants of social roles, whose feelings and behaviors influence the appraisal process.

REFERENCES

Abramson, P. E., Goldberg, P. A., Greenberg, J. H., & Abramson, U. M. The talking platypus phenomenon: Competency ratings as a function of sex and professional status. *Psychology of Women Quarterly,* 1978, 2, 114–124.

Allport, G. W. *The nature of prejudice.* Reading, MA: Addison-Wesley, 1954.

Ayers-Nachamkin, B., Cann, C. H., Reed, R., & Horne, A. Sex and ethnic differences in the use of power. *Journal of Applied Psychology,* 1982, 67, 464–472.

Bass, B. M., Cascio, W. F., McPherson, J. W., & Tragash, H. J. Prosper-training and research for increasing management awareness of affirmative action in race relations. *Academy of Management Journal,* 1976, 19, 353–369.

Bernardin, H. J., & Buckley, M. R. Strategies in rater training. *Academy of Management Review,* 1981, 6, 205–212.

Bigoness, W. J. Effect of applicant's sex, race, and performance on employers' performance ratings: Some additional findings. *Journal of Applied Psychology,* 1976, 61, 80–84.

Bowman, G. W., Worthy, N. B., & Greyson, S. A. Problems in review: Are women executives people? *Harvard Business Review,* 1965, 43(4), 52–67.

Brugnoli, G. A., Campion, J. E., & Basen, J. A. Racial bias in the use of work samples for personnel selection. *Journal of Applied Psychology,* 1979, 64, 119–123.

Cardy, R. L. *The effect of affect in performance appraisal.* Unpublished doctoral dissertation, Virginia Polytechnic Institute and State University, 1982.

Cascio, W. F., & Bernardin, H. J. Implications of performance appraisal litigation for personnel decisions. *Personnel Psychology,* 1981, 34, 211–226.

Cascio, W. F., & Phillips, N. F. Performance testing: A rose among thorns? *Personnel Psychology,* 1979, 32, 751–766.

Cleveland, J. N., & Landy, F. J. The influence of rater and ratee age on two performance judgments. *Personnel Psychology,* 1981, 34, 19–29.

Cline, M. E., Holmes, D. S., & Werner, J. C. Evaluations of the work of men and women as a function of the sex of the judge and type of work. *Journal of Applied Social Psychology,* 1977, 7, 89–93.

Cohen, S. L., & Leavengood, S. The utility of the WAMS: Shouldn't it relate to discriminatory behavior? *Academy of Management Journal,* 1978, 21, 742–748.

Cohen, S. L., Bunker, K. A., Burton, A. L., & McManus, P. O. Reactions of male subordinates to the sex-role congruency of immediate supervision. *Sex Roles,* 1978, 4, 297–311.

Costrich, N., Feinstein, J., Kidder, L., Maracek, J., & Pascale, L. When stereotypes hurt: Three studies of penalties for sex-role reversals. *Journal of Experimental Social Psychology,* 1975, 11, 520–530.

Deaux, K., & Emswiller, T. Explanations of successful performance on sex linked tasks: What is skill for the male is luck for the female. *Journal of Personality & Social Psychology,* 1974, 29, 80–85.

Dobbins, G. H. *The effect of leader performance and leader likableness upon ratings of leader behavior.* Unpublished master's thesis, Virginia Polytechnic Institute and State University, 1982.

Dreher, G. F. Predicting the salary satisfaction of exempt employees. *Personnel Psychology,* 1981, 34, 579–589.

Eden, D., & Ravid, G. Pygmalion versus self-expectancy. Effects of instructor- and self-expectancy on trainee performance. *Organizational Behavior and Human Performance,* 1982, 30, 351–364.

Eden, D., & Shani, A. Pygmalion goes to boot camp: Expectancy, leadership, and trainee performance. *Journal of Applied Psychology,* 1982, 67, 194–199.

Elmore, P. B., & LaPointe, K. A. Effects of teacher sex and student sex on the evaluation of college instructors. *Journal of Educational Psychology,* 1974, 66, 386–389.

Elmore, P. B., & LaPointe, K. A. Effect of teacher sex, student sex, and teacher warmth on the evaluation of college instructors. *Journal of Educational Psychology,* 1975, 67, 368–374.

Feild, H. S., & Holley, W. H. Subordinates' characteristics, supervisors' ratings, and decisions to discuss appraisal results. *Academy of Management Journal,* 1977, 20, 315–321.

Feild, H. S., & Holley, W. H. The relationship of performance appraisal system characteristics to verdicts in selected employment discrimination cases. *Academy of Management Journal,* 1982, 25, 392–406.

Feldman, J. M. Beyond attribution theory: Cognitive processes in performance appraisal. *Journal of Applied Psychology,* 1981, 66, 127–148.

Fernandez, J. P. *Racism and sexism in corporations.* Lexington, KY: Toronto, 1981.

Fontenelle, G., Peek, A., & Lane, D. Generalizing across stimuli as well as subjects. Unpublished manuscript, Rice University, 1983.

Frank, F. D., & Drucker, J. The influence of evaluatee's sex on evaluations of a response on a managerial selection instrument. *Sex Roles,* 1977, 3, 59–64.

Fromkin, H. L., & Sherwood, J. (Eds.). *Integrating the Organization.* New York: Free Press, 1974.

Gaertner, S. L., & Dovidio, J. R. The subtlety of white racism, arousal, and helping behavior. *Journal of Personality and Social Psychology,* 1977, 35, 691–707.

Gardiner, G. S. Complexity training and prejudice reduction. *Journal of Applied Social Psychology,* 1972, 2, 326–342.

Garland, H., & Price, K. H. Attitudes toward women in management and attributions for their success and failure in managerial positions. *Journal of Applied Psychology,* 1977, 62, 29–33.

Goldberg, P. A. Are women prejudiced against women? *Trans-Action,* 1968, 5(5), 28–30.

Grube, J. W., Kleinhesselink, R. R., & Kearney, K. A. Male self-acceptance and attraction toward women. *Personality and Social Psychology Bulletin,* 1982, 8, 107–112.

Haccoun, D. M., Haccoun, R. R., & Sallay, G. Sex differences in the appropriateness of supervisory styles: A nonmanagement view. *Journal of Applied Psychology,* 1978, 63, 124–127.

Hagen, R. L., & Kahn, A. Discrimination against competent women. *Journal of Applied Social Psychology,* 1975, 5, 362–376.

Hall, F. S., & Hall, D. T. Effects of job incumbents' race and sex on evaluations of managerial performance. *Academy of Management Journal,* 1976, 19, 476–481.

Hamner, W. C., Kim, J. S., Baird, L., & Bigoness, W. J. Race and sex as determinants of ratings by potential employers in a simulated work sampling task. *Journal of Applied Psychology,* 1974, 59, 705–711.

Harris, M. Sex role stereotypes and teacher evaluations. *Journal of Educational Psychology,* 1975, 67, 751–756.

Hastorf, A. H., Northcraft, G. B., & Picciotto, S. R. Helping the handicapped: How realistic is the performance feedback received by the physically handicapped? *Personality and Social Psychology Bulletin,* 1979, 5, 373–376.

Heilman, M. E. The impact of situational factors on personnel decisions concerning women: Varying the sex composition of the applicant pool. *Organizational Behavior and Human Performance,* 1980, 26, 386–395.

Heilman, M. E., & Guzzo, R. A. The perceived cause of work success as a mediator of sex discrimination in organizations. *Organizational Behavior and Human Performance,* 1978, 21, 346–357.

Isaacs, M. B. Sex role stereotyping and the evaluation of the performance of women: Changing trends. *Psychology of Women Quarterly,* 1981, 6, 187–195.

Jacobson, M. B., & Effertz, J. Sex roles and leadership perceptions of the leaders and the led. *Organizational Behavior and Human Performance,* 1974, 12, 383–396.

Katz, I., & Glass, D. C. An ambivalence-amplification theory of behavior toward the stigmatized. In W. G. Austin & S. Worchel (Eds.), *The social psychology of intergroup relations.* Monterey, CA: Brooks/Cole, 1979, 55–70.

Katz, D., McClintock, C., & Sarnoff, D. The measurement of ego defense as related to attitude change. *Journal of Personality,* 1957, 25, 465–474.

Keenan, A. Some relationships between interviewers' personal feelings about candidates and their general evaluations of them. *Journal of Occupational Psychology,* 1977, 50, 275–283.

Kipnis, D., Silverman, A., & Copeland, C. Effects of emotional arousal on the use of supervised coercion with black union employees. *Journal of Applied Psychology,* 1973, 57, 38–44.

Kleck, R. E. Emotional arousal in interactions with stigmatized persons. *Psychological Reports,* 1966, 19, 12–26.

Kleck, R., Ono, H., & Hastorf, A. H. The effects of physical deviance upon face-to-face interaction. *Human Relations,* 1966, 19, 425–436.

Kraiger, K., & Ford, J. K. A meta-analysis of ratee race effects in performance ratings. Paper presented at the American Psychological Association, Anaheim, California, 1983.

Krefting, L. A., & Berger, P. K. Masculinity-feminine perceptions of job requirements and their relationships to job-sex stereotypes. *Journal of Vocational Behavior,* 1979, 15, 164–174.

Latham, G. P., & Wexley, K. N. *Increasing productivity through performance appraisal.* Reading, MA: Addison-Wesley, 1981.

Locksley, A., Borgida, E., Brekke, N., & Hepburn, C. Sex stereotypes and social judgments. *Journal of Personality and Social Psychology,* 1980, 39, 821–831.

London, M., & Stumpf, S. A. Effects of candidate characteristics on management promotion decisions: An experimental study, *Personnel Psychology,* 1983, 36, 241–259.

Madden, J. M. Using policy-capturing to measure attitudes in organizational diagnosis. *Personnel Psychology,* 1981, 34, 341–350.

Madden, J. M., & Martin, E. An indirect method of attitude measurement. *Bulletin of the Psychonomic Society,* 1979, 13, 170–172.

Mai-Dalton, R. R., Feldman-Summers, S., & Mitchell, T. R. Effects of employee gender and behavioral style on the evaluations of male and female banking executives. *Journal of Applied Psychology,* 1979, 64, 221–226.

Maruyama, G., & Miller, N. Physical attractiveness, race, and essay evaluation. *Personality and Social Psychology Bulletin,* 1980, 6, 384–390.

Mitchell, T. R., & Foa, U. G. Diffusion of the effect of cultural training of the leader in the structure of heterocultural task groups. *Australian Journal of Psychology,* 1969, 21(1), 31–43.

Mobley, W. H. Supervisor and employee race and sex effects on performance appraisals: A field study of adverse impact and generalizability. *Academy of Management Journal,* 1982, 25, 598–606.

Moses, J. L., & Boehm, V. Relationship of assessment center performance to management progress of women. *Journal of Applied Psychology,* 1975, 60, 527–529.

Neisser, V. On "social knowing." *Personality and Social Psychology Bulletin.* 1980, 6, 601–605.

Newman, J., & Krzystofiak, F. Self-reports versus unobtrusive measures: Balancing method variance and ethical concerns in employment discrimination research. *Journal of Applied Psychology,* 1979, 64, 82–85.

Nieva, V. F., & Gutek, B. A. Sex effects on evaluation. *Academy of Management Review,* 1980, 5, 267–276.

Norton, S. D., Gustafson, D. P., & Foster, C. E. Assessment for management potential: Scale design and development, training effects and rater/ratee sex effects. *Academy of Management Journal,* 1977, 20, 117–131.

Penley, L. E., & Hawkins, B. L. Organizational communication, peformance, and job satisfaction as a function of ethnicity and sex. *Journal of Vocational Behavior,* 1980, 16, 368–384.

Pheterson, G. T., Kiesler, S. B., & Goldberg, P. A. Evaluation of the performance of women as a function of their sex, achievement, and personal history. *Journal of Personality and Social Psychology,* 1971, 19, 110–114.

Pulakos, E. D., & Wexley, K. N. The relationship among perceptual similarity, sex, and performance ratings in manager-subordinate dyads. *Academy of Management Journal,* 1983, 26, 129–139.

Quinn, R. P., Tabor, J. M., & Gordon, L. K. *The decision to discriminate: A study of executive selection.* Ann Arbor, MI: Institute of Survey Research, 1968.

Richards, S. A., & Jaffee, C. L. Blacks supervising whites: A study of interracial difficulties in working together in a simulated organization. *Journal of Applied Psychology,* 1972, 56, 234–241.

Rogers, R. W., & Prentice-Dunn, S. Deindividuation and anger-mediated interracial aggression: Unmasking regressive racism. *Journal of Personality and Social Psychology,* 1981, 41, 63–73.

Rokeach, M. Long-range experimental modification of values, attitudes, and behavior. *American Psychologist,* 1971, 26, 453–455.

Rose, G. L., & Stone, T. H. Why good performance may (not) be rewarded: Sex factors and career development. *Journal of Vocational Behavior,* 1978, 12, 197–207.

Rosen, B., & Jerdee, T. H. The influence of sex role stereotypes on evaluations of male and female supervisory behavior. *Journal of Applied Psychology,* 1973, 57, 44–48.

Rosen, B., & Jerdee, T. H. Influence of sex-role stereotypes on personnel decisions. *Journal of Applied Psychology,* 1974, 59, 9–14.

Rosen, B., & Jerdee, T. H. Effects of employee's sex and threatening versus pleading appeals on managerial evaluations of grievances. *Journal of Applied Psychology,* 1975, 60, 442–445.

Rosen, B., & Jerdee, T. H. The nature of job-related age stereotypes. *Journal of Applied Psychology,* 1976, 61, 180–183.

Rosen, B., & Jerdee, T. H. Influence of subordinate characteristics on trust and use of participative decision strategies in a management simulation. *Journal of Applied Psychology,* 1977, 62, 628–631.

Rosen, B., & Jerdee, T. H. Influence of employee age, sex, and job status on managerial recommendations for retirement. *Academy of Management Journal,* 1979, 22, 169–173.

Rosen, B., Jerdee, T. H., & Lunn, R. O. Effects of performance appraisal format, age, and performance level on retirement decisions. *Journal of Applied Psychology,* 1981, 66, 515–519.

Schmitt, N., & Hill, T. E. Sex and race composition of assessment center groups as a determinant of peer and assessor ratings. *Journal of Applied Psychology,* 1977, 62, 261–264.

Schmitt, N., & Lappin, M. Race and sex as determinants of the mean and variance of performance ratings. *Journal of Applied Psychology,* 1980, 65, 428–435.

Schwab, D. P., & Heneman, H. G., III. Age stereotyping in performance appraisal. *Journal of Applied Psychology,* 1978, 63, 573–578.

Schwab, D. P., Heneman, H. G., III, & De Cotiis, J. D. Behaviorally anchored rating scales: A review of the literature. *Personnel Psychology,* 1975, 28, 549–562.

Shapiro, J. G. Agreement between channels of communication in interviews. *Journal of Consulting Psychology,* 1966, 30, 535–538.

Smith, R. E., Meadows, B. L., & Sisk, T. K. Attitude similarity, interpersonal attraction, and evaluative social perception. *Psychonomic Science,* 1970, 18, 226–227.

Snyder, M. Seek and ye shall find: Testing hypotheses about other people. In E. T. Higgins, C. P. Herman, & M. P. Zanna (Eds.), *Social cognition: The Ontario symposium on personality and social psychology.* Hillsdale, NJ: Erlbaum, 1981.

Snyder, M. L., Kleck, R. E., Strenta, A., & Mentzer, S. J. Avoidance of the handicapped: An attributional ambiguity analysis. *Journal of Personality and Social Psychology,* 1979, 37, 2297–2306.

Stumpf, S. A., & London, M. Capturing rater policies in evaluating candidates for promotion. *Academy of Management Journal,* 1981, 24, 752–766.

Taylor, S. E., & Falcone, H. T. Cognitive bases of stereotyping: The relationship between categorization and prejudice. *Personality and Social Psychology Bulletin,* 1982, 8, 426–432.

Toder, N. L. The effect of the sexual composition of a group on discrimination against women and sex-role attitudes. *Psychology of Women Quarterly,* 1980, 5, 292–310.

Washburn, P. V., & Hakel, M. Visual cues and verbal content as influences on impressions formed after simulated employment interviews. *Journal of Applied Psychology,* 1973, 58, 137–141.

Waxer, P. Therapist training in nonverbal behavior: Toward a curriculum. In A. Wolfgang (Ed.), *Nonverbal behavior: Applications and cultural implications.* Orlando, FL: Academic Press, 1979.

Weitz, S. Attitude, voice, and behavior: A repressed affect model of interracial interaction. *Journal of Personality and Social Psychology,* 1972, 24, 14–21.

Wexley, K. N., & Pulakos, E. D. Sex effects on performance ratings on manager-subordinate dyads: A field study. *Journal of Applied Psychology,* 1982, 67, 433–439.

Wiley, M. G., & Eskilson, A. The interaction of sex and power base on perceptions of managerial effectiveness. *Academy of Management Journal,* 1982, 25, 671–677.

Wolfgang, A. The teacher and nonverbal behavior in the multicultural classroom. In A. Wolfgang (Ed.), *Nonverbal behavior: Applications and cultural implications.* New York: Academic Press, 1979.

Word, C. O., Zanna, M. P., & Cooper, J. The nonverbal mediation of self-fulfilling prophecies in interracial interaction. *Journal of Experimental Social Psychology,* 1974, 10, 109–120.

Yarkin, K. L., Town, J. P., & Wallston, B. S. Blacks and women must try harder: Stimulus persons' race and sex attributions of causality. *Personality and Social Psychology Bulletin,* 1982, 8, 21–24.

Robert L. Dipboye is Professor of Psychology and Administrative Sciences in the Department of Psychology, Rice University.

Training Programs for Performance Appraisal: A Review
David E. Smith

Most performance appraisal systems depend heavily on subjective ratings of performance provided by supervisors, peers, subordinates, and job incumbents. For example, Landy and Farr (1976) have reported that 89 percent of 196 police departments in major metropolitan areas use supervisor ratings as the primary form of performance measurement. In a recent review of the literature in applied psychology, Landy and Trumbo (1980) determined that 72 percent of the validation studies published in the *Journal of Applied Psychology* between 1965 and 1975 used ratings as the primary criterion.

Despite a heavy reliance on performance ratings, it is generally acknowledged that they are too often contaminated by systematic errors (leniency, central tendency, halo, and contrast errors). For many years researchers have faced the shortcomings of performance ratings and have attempted to reduce these errors. The early focus was on developing a better measuring instrument. Unfortunately, little progress has been made in this respect, even after 30 years of effort (Landy & Farr, 1980).

Rater training is an area which has recently shown some promise in improving the effectiveness of performance ratings.

Source: David E. Smith, "Training Programs for Performance Appraisal: A Review," *Academy of Management Review,* 1986, pp. 22–40. Reprinted by permission.

Although its utility was recognized as early as 1948 (Bittner, 1948), only during the last several years have researchers begun to take a serious look at this approach. A number of studies have been completed that evaluate the effects of rater training programs on the psychometric quality of performance ratings. The purposes of this review are to assess the findings of these studies and to identify common aspects of training methods which appear to underlie the success of rater training. Before doing so, it is helpful to consider a model of the performance appraisal process offered by Borman (1978).

THE PERFORMANCE APPRAISAL PROCESS

Borman's model attempts to explain the cognitive processes involved in the establishment of performance ratings. It is a prescriptive model, representing the ideal rating process. Borman suggests that performance appraisal judgments should follow three distinct steps:

1. The rater observes behaviors that are relevant to the job;
2. The rater makes an evaluation of each behavior; and
3. Each evaluation is weighted to arrive at a single rating for a performance dimension.

The first step of the performance appraisal process requires that the rater be given the opportunity to observe a representative sample of a ratee's work behavior. The rater must be able to identify and attend to those behaviors that are relevant to the ratee's performance effectiveness. The focus of the second step of the process is the evaluation of each behavior, independent of other behaviors. According to the model, the evaluation of each behavior should not be influenced by a global impression about the ratee's overall effectiveness. It is only in the final step of the rating process that broader ratings should be established. At this point, the evaluation of each behavior is weighted to arrive at a single rating for either a performance dimension or for a rating of overall performance effectiveness.

Borman suggests that, if raters deal effectively with each of these steps, performance appraisals should be reliable and accurate. It is pointed out, however, that this is typically not done (Borman, 1978). In most instances, the rater does not have the opportunity to observe all of the behaviors that are relevant to the job performance. Also, raters often lack the observation skills necessary to attain observation accuracy.

While step two of the rating process calls for a systematic evaluation of independent behaviors, it is more likely that the rater forms a global impression of ratee effectiveness which influences the ratings of specific behaviors. Forming global impressions allows the rater to simplify and reduce information which can be potentially overwhelming in a work environment. Feldman (1981) has suggested that this "cognitive categorization" is more the rule than the exception in performance appraisal ratings.

In the final step of Borman's model the rater is asked to combine the evaluations of individual behaviors into a single rating on a performance dimension. As Borman has pointed out, raters are likely to differ in the way that they weight behaviors. A particular performance may be judged as effective by one rater and ineffective by another. As a result, interrater reliability often is limited.

Borman's model provides a framework on which one can begin to understand the effects of rater training. It describes the demands that are placed upon raters of performance and identifies the potential for rater training directed at various stages of the rating process.

This review covers research studies that have evaluated the effects of rater training on the psychometric quality of performance ratings. The criteria for inclusion in the review are: (a) The experimental design used in the study must have provided a comparison of training results with other training methods, a control group, or pretest measures; and (b) The dependent variable used in the study must have been some form of performance rating. The rating may be of actual job performance, simulated job performance, or potential job performance (job interview evaluations).

managers of various manufacturing plants, and army officers. Subject samples ranged in size from 6 to 603 raters. The median sample size was 90 raters. The most frequently used stimulus was the performance of college instructors. Eleven of the studies required students to rate the performance of either their actual instructor or a simulated performance by a hypothetical instructor. Other stimuli included performances by army personnel, manufacturing plant workers, supermarket checkers and others. Training programs ranged in length from one 5-minute session to several sessions totaling 14 hours. The median length of training was 83 minutes. The most frequently reported dependent variables were leniency error, halo error, and rating accuracy; they are used in the review to make comparisons across studies. While the definition of each of these variables differs somewhat across studies, they are, for the most part, conceptually similar.

RESULTS OF THE LITERATURE REVIEW

Twenty-four studies met the stated criteria; these are summarized in Table 1. Raters, ratees, and the rating situation are described for each of the studies and annotation of the training methods is provided. If available, the amount of time spent training raters is indicated and for comparison, the results of each study are summarized.

Students were used as raters in the majority of studies (16 out of 24). Other raters included nursing supervisors, engineering supervisors, supervisors and

CATEGORIZATION OF TRAINING METHODS

The majority of studies compared two or more training methods. These methods, summarized in Table 2, are categorized by the *content* of the training and the *method of presentation*.

Method of Presentation

The methods used by researchers to present training are labeled lecture, group discussion, and practice and feedback. Lecture presentations include the tradi-

TABLE 1
Summary of Rater Training Research

Author	Rating Situation	Description of Training	Results
1. Athey (1983)	99 college students rated videotaped lectures of supposedly real college instructors	**METHOD 1** — (30 min) Rating scale was presented to Ss; Ss practiced rating videotaped lecture, Expert ratings were given as feedback along with behavior rationales for each rating **METHOD 2** — (30 min) Ss were given a lecture on the general uses and problems of instructor evaluations **CONTROL** — No training	METHOD 1 produced greater accuracy than METHOD 2; METHOD 2 produced less central tendency than METHOD 1; No training effect on leniency or halo
2. Bernardin (1978)	80 students rated the performance of their college instructors	**METHOD 1** — (1 hr) Definitions, illustrations and examples of common rating errors (e.g., halo, leniency & central tendency) were presented and discussed **METHOD 2** — (5 min) Ss were given an abbreviated presentation of METHOD 1 without discussion **CONTROL** — No training	12 weeks after training, METHOD 1 produced less halo and leniency than METHOD 2 or CONTROL; METHOD 2 produced less halo than CONTROL; No difference between groups 5 months after training
3. Bernardin & Pence (1980)	72 college students rated vignettes of hypothetical instructors	**METHOD 1** — (45 min) Definitions, graphic illustrations and examples of rating errors were presented and discussed **METHOD 2** — (45 min) Ss were lectured on the need to distinguish between dimensions when rating performances; Ss generated dimensions of teacher performance and discussed stereotypes of effective and ineffective performance **CONTROL** — No training	METHOD 1 produced less leniency, halo and less accuracy than METHOD 2 and CONTROL

(continued on next page)

TABLE 1
Continued

Author	Rating Situation	Description of Training	Results
4. Bernardin & Walter (1977)	156 students rated their instructors during the last week of a ten week course	**METHOD 1** — (1 hr) 10 weeks before rating, Ss were presented with definitions, graphic illustrations, and examples of rating errors; 7 dimensions of teacher performance were discussed **METHOD 2** — (1 hr) 10 weeks before rating, Ss received METHOD 1 + copies of the rating scale; They were also asked to keep a diary of critical incidents **METHOD 3** — (1 hr) Immediately before rating, Ss received METHOD 1 training **CONTROL** — No training	METHOD 2 produced less leniency and halo than all other groups; METHOD 1 produced less halo and leniency than CONTROL and less halo than METHOD 3; METHOD 2 produced higher interrater reliability than METHOD 1; All training groups produced less halo than CONTROL
5. Bittner (1948)	603 army officers rated the performance of 2,401 men	**METHOD 1** — (2 hrs) Ss were given instructions on principles of accurate ratings, rating scale traits, and how to use the rating scale **CONTROL** — No training	METHOD 1 produced less leniency than CONTROL and an increase in rating accuracy
6. Borman (1975)	90 managers rated vignettes of hypothetical 1st-line supervisors	**METHOD 1** — (6 min) Descriptions and examples of halo were presented; Raters were warned not to rate all dimensions at the same level No **CONTROL**	Pretest-posttest measures indicated a decrease in halo; No effect on rating accuracy; Interrater reliability decreased
7. Borman (1979)	123 college students rated videotaped actors performing as recruitment interviewers and managers	**METHOD 1** — (3 hrs) Ss practiced rating videotapes, received feedback and discussed ways to reduce rating errors **CONTROL** — No training	METHOD 1 produced less halo than CONTROL on 3 out of 5 rating formats (for recruiting job only); No effect on rating accuracy

(continued on next page)

TABLE 1

Continued

Author	Rating Situation	Description of Training	Results
8. Edwards (1982)	229 college students rated the performance of their psychology instructor	**METHOD 1** — (10 min) Definitions and examples of rating errors were presented; Ss were encouraged to discriminate between performance dimensions **CONTROL** — No training	No training effect was found for halo or leniency
9. Fay & Latham (1982)	90 business students rated videotaped performances of hypothetical applicants in job interviews	**METHOD 1** — (4 hrs) Ss received a list of job qualifications to discuss; Ss practiced rating videotapes of applicants being interviewed; Ss received feedback and discussed ways to reduce rating errors **CONTROL** — No training	METHOD 1 produced less halo, contrast error and 1st-impression error than CONTROL; METHOD 1 increased rating accuracy
10. Ivancevich (1979)	66 supervisory engineers rated the performance of 273 engineers	**METHOD 1** — (14 hrs) Definitions of rating errors were presented and discussed; Ss analyzed the rating scale in detail **METHOD 2** — (14 hrs) Ss received METHOD 1 and Ss practiced rating videotapes of engineers performing their job; Ratings were discussed and compared with expert ratings to identify examples of leniency and halo errors **CONTROL** — No training	6 months after training, pretest-posttest measures showed that METHOD 2 reduced more halo and leniency than METHOD 1 or CONTROL; METHOD 1 reduced more halo than CONTROL; Halo error improvements dissipated 12 months after training

(continued on next page)

TABLE 1
Continued

Author	Rating Situation	Description of Training	Results
11. Latham, Wexley & Pursell (1975)	60 managers rated videotaped interviews of hypothetical job candidates	**METHOD 1** — (9 hrs) Ss received a list of job qualifications to discuss; Ss viewed videotapes of managers making rating errors (contrast, halo, 1st-impressions, and similar-to-me); Ss practiced rating videotapes; Ss discussed their ratings along with ways to reduce rating errors **METHOD 2** — (6 hrs) Definitions and examples of rating errors were presented and discussed; Ss generated and discussed solutions to reduce rating errors **CONTROL** — No training	6 months after training, METHOD 1 Ss made no rating errors; METHOD 2 Ss made impression errors; CONTROL Ss made similarity, halo and contrast errors
12. Levine & Butler (1952)	29 supervisors rated the performance of 395 manufacturing plant workers including unskilled to highly skilled positions	**METHOD 1** — (90 min) Ss were presented with a graph of previous performance evaluations, showing consistently higher ratings for highly skilled workers; They discussed solutions to avoid the rating error **METHOD 2** — (90 min) Ss were given a lecture on technique and theory of performance ratings; They were presented with the same graph used with METHOD 1; They were presented with solutions for avoiding the rating error **CONTROL** — No training	Pretest-posttest measures showed a reduction in halo error for METHOD 1 only

(continued on next page)

TABLE 1
Continued

Author	Rating Situation	Description of Training	Results
13. McIntyre, Smith & Hassett (1984)	164 college students rated videotaped lectures of supposedly real college instructors and candidates applying for the instructor position	**METHOD 1** — (15 min) Definitions and graphic illustrations of rating errors were presented; Ss were warned to avoid the rating errors **METHOD 2** — (30 min) Ss were presented with the rating scale; Ss practiced rating a videotaped lecture; Expert ratings were given as feedback along with behavior rationale for each rating **METHOD 3** — (45 min) Ss received both METHOD 1 and METHOD 2 training **CONTROL** — No training	METHOD 2 produced variance in ratings across dimensions (halo) closer to the variance in expert ratings (true halo) than did METHOD 1 or METHOD 3; CONTROL produced halo closer to true halo than did METHOD 1; METHOD 1 produced greater variance in ratings across dimensions than any other group; Both METHOD 2 and METHOD 3 produced greater rating accuracy than METHOD 1 or CONTROL; No training effect on leniency
14. Pulakos (1984)	108 college students rated videotaped performances of managers talking with problem subordinates	**METHOD 1** — (90 min) Ss practiced rating videotaped performances; Rating errors (halo, leniency, contrast) were identified; Solutions for avoiding errors were discussed **METHOD 2** — (90 min) Ss received lecture on multidimensionality of jobs; Rating scale was presented; Behavior, indicative of effectiveness levels for each dimension, was discussed; Ss practiced rating videotapes; Expert ratings were provided as feedback **METHOD 3** — (90 min) Ss received an abbreviated version of METHOD 1 + METHOD 2 **CONTROL** — No training	METHOD 1 & METHOD 2 produced less halo than METHOD 3 or CONTROL; METHOD 2 & METHOD 3 produced less leniency than CONTROL & METHOD 1; METHOD 2 produced greater accuracy than all others; METHOD 1 & METHOD 3 were more accurate than CONTROL; Training by dimension interaction

(continued on next page)

TABLE 1

Continued

Author	Rating Situation	Description of Training	Results
15. Pursell, Dossett & Latham (1980)	6 supervisors from a pulp and paper plant evaluated the performance of 47 journeyman electricians	**METHOD 1** — (8 hrs) Ss were presented with job descriptions to discuss; Ss viewed videotapes of managers making rating errors; Ss practiced rating videotapes, received feedback and discussed ways to reduce rating errors No **CONTROL**	1 month after training, pretest-posttest measures showed that METHOD 1 produced less leniency error and increased the distribution of ratings
16. Sauser & Pond (1981)	96 college students rated narrated descriptions of 5 hypothetical professors	**METHOD 1** — (6 hrs) Ss participated in the construction of a BARS used in the study **METHOD 2** — (2 hrs) Ss received a lecture on trait differentiation; Ss practiced using the rating scale; Ss discussed rating errors **METHOD 3** — (8 hrs) Ss received METHOD 1 + METHOD 2 training **CONTROL** — No training	Training had no effect on halo or leniency errors
17. Smith (1984)	50 college students rated videotaped lectures of supposedly real college instructors	**METHOD 1** — (30 min) Ss were lectured on principles of observation; A list of behaviors to observe was presented; Ss practiced observing a videotape and received feedback on observations **METHOD 2** — (45 min) Ss received METHOD 1 + the rating scale; Rating dimensions were described; Ss were shown how behavior listed in METHOD 1 related to each dimension; Ss practiced rating videotape **METHOD 3** — (1 hr) Ss received METHOD 1 + METHOD 2 + they were given expert ratings as feedback **CONTROL** — No training	METHOD 1, METHOD 2 & METHOD 3 produced greater rating accuracy than CONTROL; METHOD 3 produced less leniency than CONTROL; No effect on halo

(continued on next page)

TABLE 1
Continued

Author	Rating Situation	Description of Training	Results
18. Smith, Hassett & McIntyre (1982)	124 college students rated videotaped lectures of supposedly real college instructors and candidates applying for the instructor position	**METHOD 1** — (5 min) Ss were presented with the rating scale prior to viewing the videotapes **METHOD 2** — (10 min) Ss were presented with the rating scale; Definitions and graphic illustrations of halo error were presented **CONTROL** — No training	METHOD 2 produced less halo than METHOD 1 or CONTROL; No differences were found in rating accuracy or leniency
19. Spool (1979)	168 college students rated their psychology instructor	**METHOD 1** — (75 min) Ss were presented with a procedure for rating general behavior based on observation of specific behaviors; The rating scale was presented; Ss practiced rating videotaped classroom lectures; Expert ratings were provided as feedback **METHOD 2** — (60 min) Definitions and examples of rating errors were presented; Ss practiced recognizing rating errors; The rating scale was presented; Ss practiced rating videotaped classroom lectures; Expert ratings were provided as feedback; Ss compared the distribution of their ratings to expert ratings **CONTROL** — No training	METHOD 2 produced greater interrater agreement than METHOD 1 or CONTROL when rating abstract dimensions; No training effect on leniency

(continued on next page)

TABLE 1

Continued

Author	Rating Situation	Description of Training	Results
20. Stockford & Bissell (1949)	77 first-line supervisors rated the performance of 1,928 hourly-paid workers	**METHOD 1** — (6 hrs) Trainees received instructions on the principles of rating, including leniency error, halo error and reliability; They received feedback on their performance as raters; Trainees participated in the construction of the rating scale **CONTROL** — No training	METHOD 1 produced less halo and higher test-retest reliability in ratings than CONTROL; No training effect on leniency
21. Vance, Kuhnert & Farr (1978)	112 college students rated audiotaped interviews of 5 hypothetical candidates for the job of resident assistant in a college dormitory	**METHOD 1** — Ss were presented with descriptions and examples of rating errors; They were told to use the entire rating scale and to rate each performance dimension independently **CONTROL** — No training	No training effect was found for halo, leniency or rating accuracy
22. Warmke & Billings (1979)	52 nursing supervisors rated the performance of their staff nurses	**METHOD 1** — (2 hrs) Trainees were presented with definitions, graphic illustrations and examples of rating errors; Suggestions for avoiding the rating errors were presented **METHOD 2** — (2 hrs) Definitions of rating errors were written on the blackboard; Trainees participated in a group discussion, generating examples of rating errors and solutions for avoiding them **METHOD 3** — (2 hrs) Trainees participated in the development of the graphic rating scale used in the study **CONTROL** — No training	1 and 2 weeks after training, METHOD 3 produced less halo and variability (standard deviation within dimensions) than CONTROL; METHOD 1 produced less variability than CONTROL; METHOD 2 produced more variability than CONTROL; No training effects on leniency; 2 months after training, ratings obtained from personnel files showed no positive effects on any rating error

(continued on next page)

TABLE 1
Continued

Author	Rating Situation	Description of Training	Results
23. Wexley, Sanders & Yukl (1973)	20 college students viewed videotapes of hypothetical job applicants and rated their qualifications for a sales position	**METHOD 1** — Ss were warned of contrast errors and urged not to make them **METHOD 2** — Ss were presented with examples of high and low qualified applicants to serve as rating anchors **METHOD 3** — Ss received METHOD 1 and METHOD 2 (strengthened) **METHOD 4** — (2 hrs) Ss received a list of job qualifications to discuss; Ss practiced rating applicants being interviewed; Ss received feedback and discussed ways to reduce rating errors	METHOD 4 was the only training method successful in eliminating contrast effects
24. Zedeck & Cascio (1982)	130 college students rated 33 paragraphs describing the performance of supermarket checkers	**METHOD 1** — (5 hrs) Ss were presented with descriptions and examples of rating errors; Ss practiced rating with the use of role playing; They discussed their ratings and received feedback; Ss were assigned 2–3 hours of outside reading **CONTROL** — No training	3 weeks after training, no difference was found between groups in discriminability (standard deviation of ratings across paragraphs)

tional classroom-type monologue (requiring little or no participation from the trainees in discussing the material being presented). Training approaches that present information through written materials, with no provisions for discussion, also are included in this category.

Group discussion training includes approaches which use participation by the group to ensure that the content of the training is fully understood by each trainee. This approach may require the discussion group to either generate solutions to specific rating errors or to define performance dimensions for the job being evaluated.

Practice and feedback training provide raters with an opportunity to practice evaluating job performance. The rater is allowed to compare his/her ratings with

TABLE 2
Summary of Rater Training Studies Broken Down by Training Content and Training Method[a,b]

Method of Presentation	Content of Training		
	Rater Error Training	Performance Dimension Training	Performance Standards Training
Lecture	1, 2, 3, 4, 6, 8, 12, 13, 18, 19, 20, 21, 22, 23, 24	4, 5, 14, 17, 18, 19	23
Group discussion	2, 3, 7, 9, 10, 11, 12, 14, 15, 16, 22, 23	1, 3, 4, 9, 10, 11, 15, 16, 20, 22, 23	14
Practice and feedback	7, 9, 10, 11, 14, 15, 19, 20, 23, 24	1, 7, 9, 10, 11, 13, 15, 16, 17, 19, 23	1, 9, 10, 11, 13, 14, 15, 17, 19, 23

a. Studies are identified by the order in which they appear in Table 1.

b. Studies appear in more than one cell if they investigated two or more training programs or if the training program combined two or more content areas or methods of presentation.

ratings given by "experts" or predetermined "true scores." Feedback also can include the trainer pointing out specific rating errors (for example, leniency or halo) that were made by the rater.

Content of Training

The content of training falls into three categories: Rater Error Training (RET); Performance Dimension Training (PDimT); and Performance Standards Training (PStandT). Rater error training attempts to directly reduce rating errors, typically by presenting raters with examples of common rating errors such as leniency, halo, central tendency, and contrast errors. After raters are familiar with these errors, they are encouraged to avoid them.

Studies categorized as PDimT attempt to improve the effectiveness of ratings by familiarizing raters with the dimensions by which the performance is rated. This is done by providing descriptions of job qualifications, reviewing the rating scale used in the evaluations, or having raters participate in the actual development of the rating scale.

Training in performance standards (PStandT) attempts to provide raters with a frame of reference for making evaluations of the ratees' performance. The goal is to get raters to share common perceptions of performance standards. A frame of reference is achieved by presenting samples of job performance to trainees along with the appropriate or "true" ratings assigned to the performance by trained experts.

EVALUATION OF TRAINING METHODS

Training studies that reported either a reduction in leniency or halo errors, or an increase in rating accuracy are listed in Table 3. The training methods are categorized by the content of the training, the method used to present the training, and the dependent measure affected.

Method of Presentation

Leniency error Discussion was the most successful method of presenting training to reduce leniency error in performance ratings. The success rate across studies was not substantial, however. Only one-half of the ten studies that used the discussion method and measured its effects on leniency were able to reduce the rating error (Bernardin, 1978; Bernardin & Pence, 1980; Bernardin & Walter, 1977; Pulakos, 1984; Pursell, Dossett, & Latham, 1980). Training content from each of the three categores (RET, PDimT and PStandT) can be found in both the successful and unsuccessful studies. The use of students and nonstudents (for example, supervisors in real ongoing organizations) as raters also can be found in both groups of studies. One might speculate that the length of the training program (eight hours) offered by Pursell et al. (1980) may account for success in their study. However, Stockford and Bissell (1949) reported a failure to reduce leniency error with six hours of training and Ivancevich (1979) failed to reduce leniency with fourteen hours of training.

Evidence favors the side of training hours when practice and feedback is the considered method for reducing leniency. Four studies out of nine reduced leniency with this method (Ivancevich, 1979; Pulakos, 1984; Pursell et al., 1980; Smith, 1984). Again, the studies by Ivancevich and Pursell et al. provided lengthy training programs. Most of the training programs that failed to reduce leniency were considerably shorter, ranging from 30 minutes to two hours (Athey, 1983; McIntyre, Smith, & Hassett, 1984; Sauser & Pond, 1981; Spool, 1979). Smith (1984) and Pulakos (1984) reduced leniency with less than two hours of training; however, both of these studies limited the number of rating dimensions in the rating task.

Lecture was the least successful method for reducing leniency error. Only four studies out of fourteen reported positive results with this method (Bernardin & Pence, 1980; Bernadin & Walter, 1977; Bittner, 1948; Pulakos, 1984). Lecture was generally ineffective in reducing leniency with student raters (Vance, Kuhnert, & Farr, 1978), first-line supervisors (Stockford & Bissell, 1949), and nursing supervisors (Warmke & Billings, 1979). Whether the length of training was five minutes (Bernardin, 1978), or six hours (Stockford & Bissell, 1949), the results were discouraging.

Halo error All of the methods for presenting training were generally effective in reducing halo error. Again, the most successful method was discussion. Practice and feedback and lecture were equal in success rate. Eleven out of the thirteen studies that employed the discussion method and measured its effect on halo successfully reduced the rating error. Discussion was effective in reducing halo error in the ratings of students (Bernardin, 1978), managers (Latham,

TABLE 3

Rater Training Studies Reporting Improvements in Leniency Error, Halo Error or Rating Accuracy, Broken Down by Training Content and Training Method[a]

	Content of Training											
Method of Presentation	Rater Error Training (RET)			Performance Dimension Training (PDimT)			Performance Standards Training (PStandT)		
	Leniency	Halo	Accuracy	Leniency	Halo	Accuracy	Leniency	Halo	Accuracy
Lecture	3 4	2 3 4 6 10 13 18 20		4 5 14	4 14	5 14 17			
Group discussion	2 3 15	2 3 7 9 10 11 12 14	9 14	4 15	4 9 10 11 20 22	1 9	14	14	14
Practice and feedback	10 15	7 9 10 11 14 20	9 14	15	7 9 11 13	1 9 13 17	10 14 15 17	9 10 11 13 14	1 9 13 14 17

a. Studies are identified by the order in which they appear in Table 1.

Wexley, & Pursell, 1975), supervisors of manufacturing plant managers (Levine & Butler, 1952), first-line supervisors (Stockford & Bissell, 1949), nursing supervisors (Warmke & Billings, 1979), and supervisory engineers (Ivancevich, 1979). In most cases, discussion in the training programs focused on descriptions of rating errors and solutions for avoiding them.

The use of practice and feedback to reduce halo error appears to be effective as well. Seven of the ten studies that used this method and reported its effects on halo error were successful in reducing the error (Borman, 1979; Fay & Latham, 1982; Ivancevich, 1979; Latham et al., 1975; McIntyre et al., 1984; Pulakos, 1984; Stockford & Bissell, 1949). The length of the training program may be an important factor here as well. Training programs that were unsuccessful at reducing halo error ranged from thirty minutes to two hours (Athey, 1983; McIntyre et al., 1984; Sauser & Pond, 1981), while all but two of the successful programs (Pulakos, 1984; McIntyre et al., 1984) provided a minimum of three hours and as much as fourteen hours of training for raters.

Nine out of fifteen studies employing the lecture method to reduce halo error reported positive results (Bernardin, 1978; Bernardin & Pence, 1980; Bernardin & Walter, 1977; Borman, 1975; Ivancevich, 1979; McIntyre et al., 1984; Pulakos, 1984; Smith, Hassett, & McIntyre, 1982; Stockford & Bissell, 1949). In most cases, the lecture consisted of definitions and examples of rating errors. It is unclear as to what distinguishes successful training lectures from those that failed to reduce halo. In both categories, the length of training was relatively short and the content of training most often focused on the avoidance of rating errors. Training effectiveness does not appear to be unique to rater characteristics. Both student and nonstudent samples can be found in both the successful and the unsucccessful studies.

Rating accuracy Less than half (eleven) of the studies provided a measure of rating accuracy in their design; all but two of these (Bittner, 1948; Borman, 1975) used college students as raters, making it difficult to draw more than tentative conclusions about training effects on rating accuracy. It appears, however, that the lecture method is ineffective at increasing rating accuracy. Five out of eight studies failed with this method (Athey, 1983; Borman, 1975; McIntyre et al., 1984; Smith et al., 1982; Vance et al., 1978). Two studies that reported an increase in rating accuracy either combined lecture with practice and feedback (Smith, 1984) or combined lecture with discussion and practice and feedback (Pulakos, 1984). The only study that claimed to increase rating accuracy with nothing more than a lecture (Bittner, 1948) did not define how rating accuracy was measured.

Preliminary findings suggest that practice and feedback is an important ingredient for improving the accuracy of ratings. Five out of six studies that included practice and feedback in their training program reported an increase in rating accuracy (Athey, 1983; Fay & Latham, 1982; McIntyre et al., 1984; Pulakos, 1984; Smith, 1984). A study by Borman (1979) employed the same training program (adapted from Latham et al., 1975) used by Fay and Latham but was unable to increase rating accuracy.

Fay and Latham have suggested that the difference in conclusions may be due to the motivation level of the subjects. While subjects in Fay and Latham's study consisted of upper level business students, Borman's subjects were primarily students from a liberal arts college. Fay and Latham suggest that Borman's subjects may not have seen the training programs as personally relevant.

Three studies which used discussion as part of their training program increased rating accuracy (Athey, 1983; Fay & Latham, 1982; Pulakos, 1984). Unfortunately, each of these studies combined discussion with a practice and feedback exercise, making it difficult to isolate the effects of discussion on accuracy. Only one study (Bernardin & Pence, 1980) employed discussion by itself in an attempt to increase rating accuracy. Conclusions from Bernardin and Pence's study suggest that rating accuracy cannot be increased simply by having raters discuss stereotypes of effective and ineffective performance.

Content of Training

Leniency error Bernardin and his colleagues (Bernardin, 1978; Bernardin & Pence, 1980; Bernardin & Walter, 1977) have been the most successful in dealing with leniency error through the use of RET. In these studies, students were asked to rate either the actual performance of their instructor or vignettes of hypothetical instructors. Before doing so, they were presented with definitions, examples, and graphic illustrations of common rating errors. In each of these studies, Bernardin and his colleagues were able to reduce leniency error in ratings.

Unfortunately, except for Ivancevich (1979) and Pursell et al. (1980), all other attempts to replicate Bernardin's findings have failed (Athey, 1983; Edwards, 1982; McIntyre et al., 1984; Pulakos, 1984; Sauser & Pond, 1981; Smith et al., 1982; Spool, 1979; Stockford & Bissell, 1949; Vance et al., 1978; Warmke & Billings, 1979) with both student and nonstudent raters. The training programs offered by Ivancevich (1979) and Pursell et al. (1980) were considerably more extensive than others. Both studies gave trainees the opportunity to practice rating videotaped performances and provided them with feedback, allowing them to identify their rating errors. Pursell et al. also provided a discussion in which trainees brainstormed ways to reduce various rating errors.

Training raters in the dimensions of performance has also been less than effective. Only one study (Bittner, 1948) successfully used PDimT to reduce leniency error without combining the training with other content areas. Bittner provided instructions on rating scale traits and the use of the rating scale to reduce leniency in army officers' ratings of their men's performance. Bernardin and Walter (1980) reduced leniency error by having students discuss various dimensions of teacher performance prior to evaluating their instructors. However, in addition to discussing performance dimensions, the students were presented with definitions, examples, and graphic illustrations of rating errors (RET). Training in performance dimensions was also combined with PStandT to reduce leniency in Pulakos' (1984) study and with PStandT and RET in Pursell et al.'s (1980) study.

Using PStandT to reduce leniency error in ratings appears to be effective. Four out of seven studies using PStandT reported positive results (Ivancevich, 1979; Pulakos, 1984; Pursell et al., 1980; Smith, 1984). The motivation level of trainees may play an important role in this approach — since raters are asked to adopt performance standards that may differ from their own, a commitment on their part to the outcome of training is required. Each of the studies that failed to reduce leniency with PStandT utilized college students as raters (Athey, 1983; McIntyre et al., 1984; Spool, 1979), while Ivancevich (1979) and Pursell et al. (1980) employed supervisors. It is possible that students were less motivated to adopt performance standards dictated to them by others, since they had no vested interest in the outcome of the training program. Smith (1984) may have overcome this by incorporating a contest into the study which monetarily rewarded student raters for adopting the rating standards that were presented to them.

Halo error In contrast to the limited success that rater training has had in reducing leniency error, it is highly successful at reducing halo error. Fifteen out of nineteen studies decreased halo with rater training. The most effective methods is to include RET in the training program (Bernardin, 1978; Bernardin & Pence, 1980; Bernardin & Walter, 1977; Borman, 1975, 1979; Fay & Latham, 1982; Ivancevich, 1979; Latham et al., 1975; Levine & Butler, 1952; McIntyre et al., 1984; Pulakos, 1984; Smith et al., 1982; Stockford & Bissell, 1949). It appears that training raters to recognize halo error is all that is necessary to obtain a reduction in the error (either to increase the variance in ratings across dimensions or to decrease intercorrelations among rating dimensions). In fact, four different studies showed that this can be done with as little as five to fifteen minutes of training (Bernardin, 1978; Borman, 1975; McIntyre et al., 1984; Smith et al., 1982).

Only two studies successfully used PDimT to reduce halo error without including RET. Warmke and Billings (1979) reduced halo by arranging for nursing supervisors to participate in the development of a graphic rating scale used to evaluate the performance of staff nurses. Pulakos (1984) also reduced halo error by presenting college students with a behaviorally anchored rating scale and a lecture on the multidimensionality of jobs, prior to rating videotaped performances of managers dealing with problem subordinates. Students discussed the types of behavior indicative of various effectiveness levels within each rating dimension. They practiced rating videotapes of managers and received feedback in terms of expert ratings, thus obtaining training in performance standards as well as PDimT.

Seven studies attempted to use PStandT to improve halo error (Athey, 1983; Fay & Latham, 1982; Ivancevich, 1979; Latham et al., 1975; McIntyre et al., 1984; Pulakos, 1984; Smith, 1984). McIntyre et al. measured the effects of PStandT, using two different definitions of halo. Training raters in the standards of performance did not reduce halo error measured in the traditional manner (it did not increase the variance of ratings across rating dimensions). However, training did reduce what Cooper (1981) refers to as illusory halo. Training produced variance in ratings across dimensions closer to the variance in ratings provided by experts. Pulakos (1984) also reduced illusory halo by providing raters with PStandT. A reduction in the traditional measure of halo through PStandT was reported by Ivancevich (1979). Fay and Latham (1982) also claimed a reduction in halo error due to PStandT; however, they did not reveal how halo was defined. Finally, Latham et al. (1975) demonstrated a reduction in halo with PStandT in a procedure where job-relevant information was manipulated to influence the evaluation of a rating dimension in which no information was made available.

Rating accuracy Traditionally, it has been presumed that rating accuracy can be improved by reducing common rating errors such as leniency and halo. In summarizing the results of past studies, it is clear, however, that simply reducing rating errors is not the proper goal for performance appraisal training. Rater training (that is, RET) has been particularly successful at reducing halo error in ratings but not at increasing rating accuracy. In most studies where an accuracy measure was provided, RET had no effect on the measure (Athey, 1983; Borman, 1975, 1979; McIntyre et al., 1984; Smith et al., 1982; Vance et al., 1978), and on two occasions RET had negative effects on either the accuracy (Bernardin & Pence, 1980) or the reliability (Borman, 1975) of ratings.

Only two studies employed RET and reported an increase in rating accuracy (Fay & Latham, 1982; Pulakos, 1984). In Pulakos' study, raters in the RET group practiced rating videotaped performances of managers talking with problem subordinates. These ratings were discussed to identify rating errors, and solutions were generated for avoiding them. The design of Pulakos' study closely resembles that of Borman's (1979). Both studies asked students to rate videotaped performance of individuals in a business setting. Both provided a training program that limited its content to rating errors. Unlike other RET studies, both Borman and Pulakos provided trainees with practice and feedback exercises. Finally, both studies estimated rating accuracy, using Cronbach's (1955) measure of differential accuracy. However, unlike Pulakos, Borman did not find an increase in rating accuracy through RET.

Fay and Latham (1982) also reported an increase in rating accuracy while using RET. However, RET was only one of two content areas presented to raters. The training also focused on performance dimensions, which makes it unclear as to whether RET or PDimT was responsible for the increase in accuracy. Fay and Latham's study is one of six studies that successfully trained raters to increase rating accuracy. Most of these studies did not use RET. They employed PDimT (Bittner, 1948; Smith, 1984) and more often PDimT combined with PStandT (Athey, 1983; McIntyre et al., 1984; Smith, 1984). In a direct comparison of RET with a training approach that combined PDimT and PStandT, McIntyre et al. (1984) found that RET had no effect on rating accuracy, while combination training did increase accuracy. A training method that combined all three content areas — RET, PDimT and PStandT — showed no benefit to rating accuracy resulting from including RET in the training design.

The evidence suggests that the best way to increase rating accuracy is to combine PDimT with PStandT. This approach has been more successful than using PDimT alone. Each of three studies that combined these content areas increased the accuracy of ratings (Athey, 1983; McIntyre et al., 1984; Smith, 1984) while two attempts to use PDimT alone (Bernardin & Pence, 1980; Smith et al., 1982), failed.

RATER TRAINING WITHIN BORMAN'S MODEL

One of the major criticisms of rater training research has been the lack of any underlying theoretical structure. Borman's model of the performance appraisal process is one attempt at bringing structure to the field. The ultimate goal of rater training is to bring about performance ratings that are valid (accurate) and reliable. Borman's model identifies specific stages at which training might intervene in the rating process to improve the accuracy and reliability of ratings. It is helpful to view training programs in terms of their impact on each of these stages in order to understand how they affect the outcome of the rating process.

The majority of rater training studies have focused on the second step of Borman's model: the (independent) evaluation of job-relevant behaviors. Both RET and PDimT attempt to train raters to evaluate specific behaviors (independent of each other) and to avoid global judgments of ratee effectiveness. Rater error training does this by adopting what seems to be an oversimplified approach to the problem. Rather than providing raters with instructions on what they should do to improve the rating process, RET limits itself to telling the rater what *not* to do. Raters are simply admonished not to allow global impressions to affect ratings of performance dimensions.

Rater error training has, in many cases, been successful in persuading raters to provide ratings on behaviors that have low interitem correlations (or large variance across rating dimensions). These same ratings have not proven to be any more reliable or accurate than ratings with higher interitem correlations.

Performance dimension training, however, does appear to affect the accuracy of ratings, particularly when combined with PStandT. This is accomplished by familiarizing raters with the specific behaviors that make up each performance dimension. By defining these behaviors early in the rating process, ratees are able to attend to them and to make independent evaluations without relying on global impressions. In contrast to RET, PDimT provides direction to raters for the independent evaluation of specific behaviors.

Much less attention has been given to the first and last steps of Borman's model. Only three of the studies addressed the demands placed on raters during the observation of job-relevant behavior. Bernardin and Walter (1977) required students to maintain a diary of critical incidents performed by the instructor over a ten week period. Students who maintained a diary achieved a higher degree of interrater agreement in their ratings of the instructor. Smith (1984) reported an increase in rating accuracy through observation training. Raters were warned to avoid systematic errors typically made by observers (Campbell, 1958). Specific behaviors to which they should attend were discussed and demonstrated. They also practiced observing ratee performance and received feedback about the accuracy of their observations. A similar training program was researched by Spool (1979).

Although the author did not provide a measure of rating accuracy, Spool did report that observation training failed to increase interrater agreement.

The third step of Borman's model is perhaps the most complex. When raters are asked to combine observations of specific behaviors into a single composite judgment, they must rely on their own individual standards of performance and weight each behavior accordingly. Studies employing PStandT have attempted to provide raters with some direction about how behaviors should be weighted in performance appraisal (Athey, 1983; Fay & Latham, 1982; Ivancevich, 1979; McIntyre et al., 1984; Pulakos, 1984; Pursell et al., 1980; Smith, 1984; Spool, 1979; Wexley, Sanders, & Yukl, 1973). Presenting performance standards to raters prior to the rating process allows them to establish a common frame of reference on which to base their evaluations. The majority of studies have done this by allowing raters to compare their own ratings of sample performance to expert ratings or "true scores." In three of the studies, training also included a detailed description of behavior rationales justifying the expert ratings (Athey, 1983; McIntyre et al., 1984; Smith, 1984). Most of the training programs that employed PStandT also included other training content, making it difficult to assess the unique contribution of PStandT to rating effectiveness. In addition, approximately one-half of the studies did not provide a measure of rating accuracy. It does appear, however, that performance ratings benefit from PStandT. Each of the five PStandT studies that provided accuracy measures in their design reported increases in rating accuracy (Athey, 1983; Fay & Latham, 1982; McIntyre et al., 1984; Pulakos, 1984; Smith, 1984).

SUMMARY AND CONCLUSIONS

Generally speaking, the more actively involved raters become in the training process, the greater the outcome. Providing raters with the opportunity to participate in a group discussion along with practice and feedback exercises produces better results than presenting the training material to them through a lecture. This is particularly true when dealing with leniency error and when the accuracy of ratings is considered. Practice and feedback exercises appear to be a necessary ingredient for increasing accuracy in ratings. Five out of six studies increased rating accuracy with this method. The evidence suggests, however, that discussion without practice and feedback will not be effective.

Participation appears to be less important in dealing with halo error. Halo is more easily dealt with in performance ratings. All three methods of presenting training to raters effectively reduced the rating error. The most popular approach is the use of lecture, since it is the most time-efficient method.

The content of training is more often the important aspect to consider when comparing the effectiveness of training programs. Each of the three content areas reviewed here differs in its ability to deal with leniency error, halo error, and rating accuracy: rater error training offers a dependable, although expedient, method for reducing halo error; training in performance dimensions appears to contribute to the accuracy of ratings;

while PStandT has had, at the very least, moderate success with leniency error, halo error, and rating accuracy.

Rater error training is the most widely used technique for dealing with halo error in performance ratings. Halo has been reduced in over a dozen studies using this approach. Its popularity most likely stems not only from its track record, but also from the fact that RET is very time efficient. Unfortunately, reducing halo error in this way does not guarantee an improvement in the accuracy of ratings.

Rating accuracy can be improved with PDimT or PStandT. It is suggested that training raters on the dimensions of performance promotes accurate ratings by helping raters to deal effectively with the second step of the rating process described in Borman's performance appraisal model. Through training, raters are better able to make independent evaluations of ratee behaviors, avoiding a global assessment of ratee effectiveness early in the rating process. Providing raters with PStandT aids them in the final step of the rating process. Training helps to clarify the weight that should be given each behavior when combining them to determine a final evaluation. The evidence suggests that the best way to increase accuracy is to combine the two training approaches. Before raters are asked to observe and evaluate the performance of others, they should be allowed to discuss the performance dimensions on which they will be rating. They should also be given the opportunity to practice rating sample performance. Finally, they should be provided with "true" or expert ratings to which they can compare their own ratings.

In addition to increasing rating accuracy, PStandT shows some promise in reducing leniency error in performance ratings. This is of particular value since leniency seems to be recalcitrant to other training methods. By providing raters with standards of performance they are able to develop a frame of reference with which to calibrate their evaluations of performance effectiveness. Training in performance standards is also the only method that affects halo error while improving the accuracy of ratings. While RET appears to promote a sometimes meaningless redistribution of ratings, PStandT results in a distribution of ratings that more closely reflects the actual performance.

LIMITATIONS TO CONSIDER

Several limitations need to be considered along with the conclusions offered here. The most immediate limitation lies in the procedure used to compare the various training programs. Comparisons were made using a classification system developed by the author. Training programs were categorized by the content of the training and the method used to present the training. As would be expected, not all training programs fell neatly into one category. Quite often, training programs either combined two or more content areas or used more than one method to present the training. As a result, the unique contribution of each training approach could not always be clearly isolated. Nevertheless, the overall pattern of results appears to be meaningful.

An additional concern is the generalizability of the conclusions to actual performance appraisal settings, since the majority of training studies used students as raters and the most frequently used stimulus was the performance of college instructors. Some indication of generalizability is available by comparing the findings of studies that used students as raters to those that used supervisors and managers in real ongoing organizations. For the most part, training effects for nonstudent raters parallel those of student raters. The more actively involved supervisors and managers become in the training program, the better the outcome. The most efficient way to reduce halo error in nonstudent ratings is through RET and the most effective way to reduce leniency error is through PStandT.

Perhaps the greatest limitation to this review is that information regarding training effects on rating accuracy is almost nonexistent for nonstudents. Only two studies using nonstudents as raters provided an index of rating accuracy (Bittner, 1948; Borman, 1975) and only one of these (Borman) described how accuracy was measured in the study. Borman found no effect on rating accuracy from RET. Clearly, future studies are needed to investigate the effects of rater training on the accuracy of performance ratings offered by individuals in real ongoing organizations.

Future studies should also look at what effects training has over a period of time. In a typical performance appraisal setting, supervisors are required to make evaluations of performance occurring over long periods of time. While a few studies looked at the longevity of training effects, the majority of them did not. Future studies should also address the problem of differences in the skills of trainers. Only one study (Latham et al., 1975) described the training that trainers received before instructing raters. Differences in trainer skills may very well account for some of the conflicting results of past studies. In addition, researchers need to agree upon a standard measure (or set of measures) that describe the psychometric quality of performance ratings so that more precise comparisons can be made across studies. Cronbach's (1955) four components of rating accuracy — elevation, differential elevation, stereotype accuracy, and differential accuracy — provide highly useful descriptions of performance ratings and hopefully will be found in future studies. Finally, there is a need to bring theoretical structure to rater training research. This review has attempted to explain the results of past training studies in terms of Borman's (1978) model of the performance appraisal process. Future studies should benefit from using Borman's model or other cognitive processing models (Feldman, 1981; Cooper, 1981) to guide their research.

REFERENCES

Athey, T. R. (1983) *The effect of group size on rater training and rating accuracy*. Unpublished manuscript, Colorado State University, Fort Collins.

Bernardin, H. J. (1978) Effects of rater training on leniency and halo errors in student ratings of instructors. *Journal of Applied Psychology, 63,* 301–308.

Bernardin, H. J., & Pence, E. C. (1980) The effects of rater training: Creating new response sets and decreasing accuracy. *Journal of Applied Psychology, 65,* 60–66.

Bernardin, H. J., & Walter, C. S. (1977) Effects of rater training and diary-keeping on psychometric error in ratings. *Journal of Applied Psychology, 62,* 64–69.

Bittner, R. H. (1948) Developing an industrial

merit rating procedure. *Personnel Psychology, 1,* 403–432.

Borman, W. C. (1975) Effects of instructions to avoid halo error on reliability and validity of performance evaluation ratings. *Journal of Applied Psychology, 60,* 556–560.

Borman, W. C. (1978) Exploring upper limits of reliability and validity in job performance ratings. *Journal of Applied Psychology, 63,* 135–144.

Borman, W. C. (1979) Format and training effects on rating accuracy and rater errors. *Journal of Applied Psychology, 64,* 410–421.

Campbell, D. T. (1958) Systematic error on the part of links in communication systems. *Information and Control, 1,* 334–369.

Cooper, W. H. (1981) Ubiquitous halo. *Psychological Bulletin, 90,* 218–244.

Cronbach, L. J. (1955) Processes affecting scores on "understanding of others" and "assumed similarity." *Psychological Bulletin, 52,* 177–193.

Edwards, J. E. (1982) *Formats and training effects in the control of halo and leniency.* Paper presented at the meeting of the Academy of Management, New York, NY.

Fay, C. H., & Latham, G. P. (1982) Effects of training and rating scales on rating errors. *Personnel Psychology, 35,* 105–116.

Feldman, J. M. (1981) Beyond attribution theory: Cognitive processes in performance appraisal. *Journal of Applied Psychology, 6,* 127–148.

Ivancevich, J. M. (1979) Longitudinal study of the effects of rater training on psychometric error in ratings. *Journal of Applied Psychology, 64,* 502–508.

Landy, F. J., & Farr, J. L. (1976) Police performance appraisal. *JSAS Catalog of Selected Documents in Psychology, 6,* 83. (Ms. No. 1315)

Landy, F. J., & Farr, J. L. (1980) Performance ratings. *Psychological Bulletin, 87,* 72–107.

Landy, F. J., & Trumbo, D. A. (1980) *The psychology of work behavior* (rev. ed.), Homewood, IL: Dorsey.

Latham, G. P., Wexley, K. N., & Pursell, E. D. (1975) Training managers to minimize rating errors in the observation of behavior. *Journal of Applied Psychology, 60,* 550–555.

Levine, J., & Butler, J. (1952) Lecture versus group discussion in changing behavior. *Journal of Applied Psychology, 36,* 29–33.

McIntyre, R. M., Smith, D. E., & Hassett, C. E. (1984) Accuracy of performance ratings as affected by rater training and purpose of rating. *Journal of Applied Psychology, 69,* 147–156.

Pulakos, E. D. (1984) A comparison of training programs: Error training and accuracy training. *Journal of Applied Psychology, 69,* 581–588.

Pursell, E. D., Dossett, D. L., & Latham, G. P. (1980) Obtaining valid predictors by minimizing rating errors in the criteria. *Personnel Psychology, 33,* 91–96.

Sauser, W. I., Jr., & Pond, B. S. III (1981) Effects of rater training and participation on cognitive complexity: An exploration of Schneier's cognitive reinterpretation. *Personnel Psychology, 34,* 563–577.

Smith, D. E. (1984) Increasing rating accuracy through rater training: A look at the performance appraisal process. (Doctoral dissertation, Colorado State University). *Dissertation Abstracts International, 45,* 1614-B.

Smith, D. E., Hassett, C. E., & McIntyre, R. M. (1982) *Using student ratings for administrative decisions: Are ratings contaminated by perceived uses of the information?* Paper presented at the meeting of the Western Academy of Management, Colorado Springs, CO.

Spool, M. D. (1979) *The effects of rater training and type of item on interrater agreement and leniency error in performance ratings.* Unpublished manuscript.

Stockford, L., & Bissell, H. W. (1949) Factors involved in establishing a merit-rating scale. *Personnel, 26,* 94–116.

Vance, R. J., Kuhnert, K. W., & Farr, J. L. (1978) Interview judgments: Using external criteria to compare behavioral and graphic scale ratings. *Organizational Behavior and Human Performance, 22,* 279–294.

Warmke, D. L., & Billings, R. S. (1979) A comparison of training methods for improving the psychometric quality of experimental and administrative performance ratings. *Journal of Applied Psychology, 64,* 124–131.

Wexley, K. N., Sanders, R. E., & Yukl, G. A. (1973) Training interviewers to eliminate contrast effects in employment interviews. *Journal of Applied Psychology, 57,* 233–236.

Zedeck, S., & Cascio, W. (1982) Performance decision as a function of purpose of rating and training. *Journal of Applied Psychology, 67,* 752–758.

David E. Smith is a Selection Specialist in the Staffing and Organization Development Department of the Anheuser-Busch Companies. The author wishes to thank George C. Thornton III for his critique of an earlier version of this paper.

The Cost of Alternative Comparable Worth Strategies
Richard D. Arvey / Katherine Holt

The State of Minnesota passed legislation during the 1984 biennium requiring all political subdivisions of the state (cities, counties, school districts, etc.) to pay employees on the basis of *comparable work value*. If female-dominated job classes are paid less than similarly evaluated male-dominated job classes, municipalities are required to increase the wages of the first group. Pay equity increases can be costly. Not only are millions of dollars spent in initial salary upgrades, but these base salary increases will also result in higher cost-of-living raises and higher costs for benefits tied to base salaries in future years.

Many articles have been written to address the technical, legal, political, and social aspects of job evaluation and comparable worth, but little has been said about the kinds of strategies organizations should or can use to achieve pay equity. Indeed, several pay strategies may fit the intent and letter of the law, but they have drastically different cost burdens on different municipalities. In this article we outline a variety of strategies that may satisfy pay equity requirements. We then estimate the cost burdens of these strategies on two organizations and discuss further implications.

We have chosen not to address explicitly the legal or political issues associated with comparable worth, or the potential problems of job evaluation methods. Instead, we focus here on implementation issues, given that comparable worth adjustments are already mandated in several states.

ALTERNATIVE PAY EQUITY STRATEGIES

Assume that an organization conducts a comparable worth analysis, finds that the regression line for female-dominated jobs differs significantly from the male-dominated regression line (where the male line is above the female line), and decides to grant pay equity increases. What are some alternative ways to achieve pay equity?

An organization usually first chooses which regression line to use as an adjustment target. The combined regression line for all jobs may reflect the internal pricing policy of the organization as well as some external market rates; female-dominated jobs, however, typically receive a lower rate of return on job evaluation points than male-dominated jobs do. The inclusion of female data in the computation of the combined regression line makes the adjustment target vulnerable to charges of bias and inequity. The male trend line is often recommended as the adjustment target as a

Source: Reprinted, by permission of the publisher, from *Compensation and Benefits Review,* September/October 1988, © 1988. American Management Association, New York. All rights reserved. Parts of this article were presented at the Annual Convention of the American Psychological Association, Washington, D.C., August 1986.

way to avoid this problem. After choosing a target regression line, an organization then must select a strategy for implementing pay equity increases. Several strategies are discussed below.

Strategy 1. Raise female wages to the male trend line Some policy analysts believe that wage levels for only the female-dominated jobs should be raised to the male trend line. It is argued that this approach best demonstrates the principle of comparable worth. This strategy is likely to have a considerable cost impact: Many of the jobs for which pay equity increases are proposed are high-density jobs (where many incumbents hold a single title). Furthermore, adoption of this strategy may result in a considerable compression of wages. No female jobs below the male line and, therefore, less variation among wages would exist.

Strategy 2. Raise all wages to male trend line This means the company would raise the wage levels of *all* jobs (female-dominated, male-dominated, and balanced jobs) that are currently below the male trend line. This strategy is entertained to insure that the pay equity method does not appear discriminatory by dealing only with female jobs (disparate treatment). This strategy has a potentially greater cost burden than others because it involves raising wages for a greater number of job incumbents.

Strategy 3. Eliminate statistically significant sex differences In this case, the company raises the wage level for female-dominated jobs, but only to the point at which there is no significant difference between the male and female regression lines. This presumably would offer a lower cost burden than raising female wages to the male trend line.

Strategy 4. Preserve distribution by giving constant wage increases Another interpretation of the law suggests that the average wage level for male- and female-dominated jobs should be the same at any given point value. That is, the distributional properties of the male- and female-dominated jobs around the wage trend line should be similar. This objective could be met by giving a constant wage increase to all female-dominated jobs so that the entire distribution of these jobs is "pushed up."

Strategy 5. Raise or lower all wages to male trend line The company in this case would raise the wage levels of all jobs below the male trend line while reducing the wage levels of all jobs above the line. In practice this is very difficult to achieve. Organizations typically encounter great resistance when they attempt to freeze wages, much less reduce them. One alternative is to negotiate or mandate smaller increases for jobs above the line until jobs below the line catch up.

What are the actual cost burdens associated with each of these five strategies? To investigate this issue, we conducted cost estimation procedures using data from two organizations.

METHOD

Job evaluation and salary data were obtained from a metropolitan city and a medical center. Both data sets included a full range of positions (343 city classifications and 131 hospital classifications) representing diverse occupational families. The number of incumbent employees in each classification varied widely, from zero to 673. Compensation and job evaluation policies were well established in each organization.

The personnel department in each organization furnished the following information for each classification: (1) the midpoint of the current salary range, (2) the number of full-time equivalent employees, and (3) the total points, based on the organization-wide job evaluation system. The sex assignment of classifications followed the formula used in the Minnesota comparable worth legislation: classifications were *male dominated* if women held less than 20% of the jobs; *female dominated* if women held 70% or more of the jobs; and *balanced* if women held between 20% and 70% of the jobs.

The data for each organization were analyzed using SPSS (the Statistical Package for the Social Sciences) on the Cyber computer at the University of Minnesota. The salary midpoints were regressed on the total points to estimate an overall regression equation as well as separate regression lines for male-dominated, female-dominated, and balanced classifications. Male and female job data were combined for an additional regression that included a dummy variable to represent the predominant sex of each job. The regression lines for each organization appear in Exhibit 1.

Each regression line shows a different intercept and coefficient for total points. From a comparable worth perspective, it would appear that each organization tended to "undervalue" female-dominated jobs: The female regression line for each organization has a lower slope and intercept than most of the other regression lines. The significant coefficient for the sex dummy variable shows that when job evaluation points are held constant, male-dominated jobs were paid more than female-dominated jobs in each organization. On average, females in the medical center were "underpaid" by $231 per month; those who worked for the city, by $366 per month ($169 on a biweekly schedule).

The proportion of salary variance explained by each regression line in our study ranged from .85 to .90 for the medical center and from .78 to .94 for the city. The low value of .78 for the city's male-dominated regression line indicates a potential lack of fit. The rate of increase in the slope coefficient over the range of job evaluation points was investigated by adding a squared term for job evaluation points to the regression; the statistical significance of this term ($p = .0301$) in the city's male regression line confirmed that job evaluation points are an imperfect linear predictor of male salaries in this organization.

When jobs and pricing strategies are compared to determine whether pay equity adjustments may be necessary, the first step often involves identifying a target pricing line. We used the male regression line as the pay equity target for each organization. All female-dominated jobs in the city and 70% of the female-dominated jobs in the medical center fell below the male line. Some balanced and male-dominated jobs in each organization also fell below the male line. The issue of pay equity adjustment involves consideration of *which* classifications to adjust, as well as of *how much* to adjust and *when*.

Five pay equity adjustment strategies,

EXHIBIT 1
Regressions of Salary Midpoints on Job Evaluation (JE) Points*

Regression Lines	Sample Size	R^2	F	Constant	Total JE Points Point Coefficient	Sex Point Coefficient
Medical center classifications						
Male-dominated	21	.90	178.1	1,026.08 (115.63)	193.69 (14.51)	—
Female-dominated	91	.85	506.8	995.51 (50.71)	165.66 (7.36)	—
Balanced	19	.90	148.0	795.25 (113.41)	221.95 (18.24)	—
Male- and female-dominated	112	.87	369.7	961.96 (46.64)	171.05 (6.63)	231.22 (50.86)
Combined	131	.85	720.1	955.34	180.62	—
Metropolitan city classifications						
Male-dominated	244	.78	841.2	395.88 (25.67)	1.96 (0.06)	—
Female-dominated	67	.92	726.6	181.25 (22.95)	2.11 (0.08)	—
Balanced	32	.94	451.8	194.64 (31.13)	2.21 (0.10)	—
Male- and female-dominated	311	.85	884.2	218.93 (20.33)	1.98 (0.06)	168.90 (14.88)
Combined	343	.81	1421.4	257.75 (21.15)	2.23 (0.06)	—

Note: R^2 is the proportion of salary variance explained by the regression. The F column reports values from the authors' statistical test for the significance of the regression. All probability levels are $p < .0000$ for the tests of significance. Numbers in parentheses are standard errors.

*Salary midpoints for medical center classifications were based on monthly rates, while midpoints for city classifications were based on biweekly rates. Each organization used a different job evaluation point system. Dummy variable is equal to 1 if male-dominated, 0 if female-dominated.

discussed in detail earlier, were developed for organizations to consider in light of comparable worth legislation. These are summarized below. Although conditions of "overpayment" as well as "underpayment" obviously may exist in organizations, we concentrated on strategies for the underpayment condition. Again, the strategies are as follows: (1) Use the male regression formula to raise only those female jobs below the male line up to the line; (2) use the male regression formula to raise all jobs (male, female, and balanced) that are currently below the male line up to the male line; (3) give all female jobs below the male line a constant amount that would render the sex dummy variable for the male/female regression no longer statistically significant (p-value at least .0501); (4) compute the average underpayment and give all female jobs a constant amount. (The amount we used as a constant came from the value of the sex dummy

EXHIBIT 2
Organizational Costs of Implementing Pay Equity Strategies

	Organization	
	Medical Center	Metropolitan City
Number of full-time equivalent employees	2,207	2,329
Number of male-dominated classifications	21	244
Number of female-dominated classifications	91	67
Number of balanced classifications	19	32
Number of total classifications	131	343
Current Annual Cost	$51,632,389	$51,489,542
Annual cost increase		
Strategy 1	$7,217,275	$2,863,503
Strategy 2	7,936,521	4,442,247
Strategy 3	3,506,635	2,257,935
Strategy 4	5,095,696	2,731,451
Strategy 5	7,446,737	2,536,281

Note that salary costs were estimated using the midpoint of each salary range. The actual cost to the organization will depend on where employees currently are in their salary ranges and how adjustments are made within salary ranges.

variable from a separate male/female regression); and (5) use the male regression formula to estimate salaries for all jobs, so that all jobs below the male line would be raised to the line, and all jobs above the male line would be lowered to the line.

We costed these five strategies for each organization by computing the wage change for each job and multiplying this amount by the number of incumbents in each job. The costs (and also the "savings" that resulted from using strategy 5) were summed over jobs to calculate a total annual cost for each type of pay equity adjustment, by organization. The results are shown in Exhibit 2.

The two organizations employed approximately the same number of workers (2,207 and 2,329) and had similar annual cost budgets (approximately $51 million). The annual cost to implement comparable worth ranged from 5% to 15% of payroll. The different mix of male- and female-dominated jobs in each organization, however, produces very different pay equity adjustment burdens. The pay equity adjustments are approximately twice as costly for the medical center, where 70% of the jobs are female-dominated; in comparison, only 20% of the city jobs are female-dominated.

Strategy 2 (raising all jobs below the male line to the line) is the most costly strategy for each organization. This strategy may avoid a problem with Strategy 1 — the appearance of reverse discrimination — but it will not result in pay equity by eliminating sex differences in pay. The sex dummy variable continued to be statistically significant when the adjusted salaries resulting from Strategy 2 were regressed on male and female data.

Strategy 5 demonstrates that the costs of Strategy 2 could be partially offset by lowering all jobs above the male regression line to the line. The cost reduction is more dramatic for the city (Strategy 5 saves $1.9 million from the cost of Strategy 2) than for the medical center (where only $0.5 million was saved).

The least costly approach for each organization is Strategy 3. However, this approach may not fully comply with the intent of comparable worth legislation. Because it is based on a statistical premise, the approach is also very susceptible to slight changes in the data. Changes in the composition (such as the predominant sex) of particular jobs or minor salary changes are likely to render Strategy 3 a short-term solution at best.

Adding a constant to *all* female jobs (Strategy 4) is less costly than bringing female jobs below the male line to the line. This strategy preserves the distributional properties of the data, but companies that use it may be particularly vulnerable to charges of reverse discrimination.

SUMMARY AND CONCLUSIONS

Our comparable worth strategies produced dramatic differences in cost burdens. The most costly strategy for each organization was two or three times as expensive as the least costly strategy. Yet any of these strategies could meet the requirements of particular comparable worth legislation. The implications of adopting a particular strategy are complex and may include a variety of outcomes beyond the dollar costs we have summarized. We suggest that organization decision makers discuss the issues spelled out below when formulating pay equity adjustment strategies.

What Target Regression Line Should Be Used?

A specific adjustment target, such as the male regression line, may not be mandated by comparable worth legislators. Inasmuch as the cost burdens may differ greatly between adjustment targets, at least one other target (the common regression line) should be investigated and evaluated. The male regression line is likely to have a higher slope than the female or combined regression lines; adjustments to a higher line are likely to be more costly. The extent to which one or both adjustment targets is likely to become a "moving" target over time may also be assessed. The male regression line may be less stable, as it is based on fewer data points. The common line, however, may move more if many female-dominated jobs are adjusted. Continual adjustments could be required in any regression scenario to maintain equitable pay relationships. The need for continual finetuning represents an additional long-term cost for the organization.

The question of which jobs to include in computing the target regression line is also an important one. Organizations in the comparable worth arena probably tend to include as many jobs as possible, even when their inclusion results in greater lack-of-fit for the regression line. Some organizations have chosen to exclude high-level jobs from their combined regression line to obtain a better fitting line for the majority of jobs. Other commonly excluded jobs include classifications without any (or with only a single) incumbent employee or classifications with anomalous characteristics (like data processing or highly specialized technical jobs that have experienced persistent labor supply shortages).

A related question involves the role of external market comparisons. Some organizations may choose to compute an internal policy line only, realizing that their internal rates undoubtedly have been influenced by market rates, particularly for entry-level positions. Other organizations prefer to include only "key" jobs (with identifiable counterparts in other organizations) in computing their pay policy line. Some organizations can base their pay policy exclusively on external salary data that has been pooled from a variety of organizations using a common job evaluation system. The interplay between internal and external equity considerations and the perceived importance of external market data clearly vary among organizations.

Most pay policy lines are based on relationships among classifications. The number of job incumbents in particular classes is not usually considered in the determination of a pay policy line. Pay adjustments, however, vary in direct proportion to the number of incumbents in the affected classifications. Organizations may wish to consider adopting some sort of weighted regression strategy to reflect the true nature of the underlying distribution of incumbents. Jobs with more incumbents can be weighted more heavily, and a common regression line can be drawn more closely to such classifications.

Another regression issue is whether or not the slope represents a constant (linear) relationship between market value and job evaluation points. A consistent relationship along the entire job evaluation scale may be desirable from an equity perspective. However, a curvilinear pattern has been found in many studies, including our own. Some jobs are compensated at a higher rate than their job evaluation ratings would warrant. This may be caused by historical overvaluing and bias. Alternatively, this could also mean that a company lacks sufficient job evaluation factors to account for their added value. Finally, there may be different functional relationships (for example, some linear and some curvilinear) between job evaluation points and market value at different points along the scale. These individual relationships could be analyzed to determine the best fitting equation for each segment, but this approach does not appear to have much acceptance.

We reiterate that the regression slope is subject to change over time. The pay/point relationship is likely to be affected by changes in the sex composition of particular jobs as well as by changes in market conditions and the mix of organization jobs. If pay equity adjustments increase salaries for some classes and not others, the common regression slope is likely to change. Thus the relationship between salaries and job evaluation points is not really constant. It changes to reflect the market value fluctuations (external and internal) of an organization's job valuation policy.

How and When Should Classifications Be Adjusted, and Which Ones?

The mix of jobs above and below the target line has important cost implications. Although adjusting only female jobs below the male line might be least costly, such a strategy could lead to charges of reverse discrimination. If all jobs below the male line are adjusted, however, we have found that significant differences will remain between the salaries of male- and female-dominated jobs. Adjusting only the jobs below the line without adjusting the higher-paid jobs is likely to produce a "moving target" scenario. The male regression line is likely to remain above the female-dominated or common regression lines as successive pay equity adjustments are made.

As noted before, the number of incumbents in the affected classifications will determine the actual cost burden of the pay adjustments. It may be desirable to implement the adjustments over a period of time, or implement them more slowly for the most populous classification to reduce short-term costs. Collective bargaining agreements are sometimes "backloaded" like this to delay the full impact of wage increases.

The question of how adjustments should be made involves philosophical as well as practical considerations. For example, how much variation in a common regression line should an organization tolerate? The cost burden may be reduced by establishing a "corridor" (such as $+10\%$ to -10%) around the male trend line, to raise wages up to the bottom of the corridor rather than to the line itself. Partial adjustment strategies, such as adding a constant, also produce greater variance than adjusting all jobs to the male regression line. This variance may be welcome if it results in a lower cost burden.

Structural relationships between related occupations are likely to be upset when pay adjustments are made only to certain classifications. Adjustments, such as an additional supervisory differential, may be needed to recruit and retain qualified and motivated individuals. Pay adjustments may also produce dysfunctional consequences. Employees who are negatively affected by the changes may become dissatisfied and quit or request reclassification. Outside of the organization, the cost burden might contribute to a reduction in the long-term demand for labor if employers look for cheaper substitutes. On the other hand, organizations may also be able to attract better qualified applicants for jobs that have received pay increases.

The "comparable worth" idea of valuing all jobs using a common metric may be conceptually simple; some complex philosophical and operational questions should be addressed, however, before pay equity adjustments are made. We have shown that various strategies can produce dramatically different cost burdens and may have very different long-term implications for an organization. We believe that organizations should attempt to identify and evaluate all potential strategies and ramifications for pay equity adjustments before implementing any single approach.

Richard D. Arvey is a professor in the Industrial Relations Center at the University of Minnesota. Katherine Holt is a consultant for Personnel Decisions, Inc. Funding for this research came from the University of Minnesota School of Management Dean's Innovation Fund. The authors wish to thank Dean Preston Townley for his ongoing support and commitment to projects that foster a closer working relationship between the School of Management and the management community. They would also like to thank the personnel department heads who furnished the data for their study.

Pay Concepts for the 1990s, Part 1
James L. Whitney

In fourteen years of dealing with exempt salary administration in a large corporation, I have often been troubled by apparent inconsistencies in the unwritten "rules" that govern how companies pay people. In discussions with other compensation specialists in other large companies, I have found that most have been operating in much the same way; we do, after all, attend the same seminars, read the same literature, and hire the same consultants.

In this article, I have tried to set down some of these unwritten rules, speculate about where they come from, and offer some guidelines that are more appropriate for the environment of the decades ahead. Although these issues are addressed from the perspective of a manager who dealt with exempt employees in a large company, many of the ideas are just as valid for smaller firms and nonexempt employees.

WHERE WE ARE TODAY

A major impediment to developing exempt employee salary programs that work today and will work in the future is that many of those who are developing and approving such plans are unwittingly burdened by the baggage of salary traditions developed in a radically different environment. This baggage, consisting of unexamined and unquestioned axioms about salary administration, is responsible for a number of the inconsistencies, inequities, and motivational weaknesses of current salary programs.

For example, most companies profess to believe in pay for performance, yet many continue practices that result in major differences in compensation among employees who make equal contributions to the organization. In a bygone era, this was not only acceptable, but probably good business practice. Today, however, such behavior stands squarely in the way of the motivational potential of compensation.

To root out the hidden axioms that lie behind some of these compensation problems, we must look at them rationally. Toward that end, let's examine the environment that spawned them.

THE PAST

Thirty-five years ago inflation was negligible, most companies had little in the way of formal compensation programs, and exempt employees could be fired for exchanging salary information with other employees. Starting salaries were usually set at the very minimum required to capture a suitable applicant. The operative principle was, "Get the best you can for the least you can." Adversarial relationships with strong labor unions undoubtedly contributed to that particular mind set.

Employees, for the most part, were

Source: Reprinted, by permission of the publisher, from *Compensation and Benefits Review*, March/April 1988, © 1988. American Management Association, New York. All rights reserved.

largely driven by the Protestant work ethic. With memories of the Great Depression still lingering, jobs were a precious commodity well worth any sacrifice of personal dignity they might entail. There was no expectation of intrinsic job satisfaction. The typical worker was male and the sole provider for his family. The typical employer was either exploitative or paternalistic or both.

Without a salary administration system, the "job rate" for exempt workers was commonly the same as the starting rate. Pay progression through a range, if it existed at all, was often no more than a one-step movement from a probationary starting pay to the job rate. A typical recruiting promise was, "Come to work for us, and if you work out okay, we'll give you a raise in six months." Beyond that, the only real hope of increased earnings lay in the possibility of a promotion. Widespread adoption of the concept of an annual increase came later with the onset of inflation rates that clearly and painfully eroded the buying power of constant wages. Promotions were usually accompanied by a pay raise simply in recognition of the fact that the rate for the new job should be higher than that of the old job, even though formal "rates" often did not exist. It was also an accepted view that a manager should rightfully expect to make more than those who worked for him (rarely her).

THE OLD AXIOMS

The beliefs behind the pay practices that prevailed during this period were not often articulated. After all, pay was a highly confidential subject. For the most part, personal values and tenets about pay were inferred or deduced from observed behavior. Thus without the benefit of dialogue or open questioning, many of the beliefs about pay were unconsciously absorbed by or passed along to many of us who are responsible for developing appropriate pay practices for today's work force. Here are some of the old axioms that should be reexamined.

Old Axiom 1: Starting pay should be no more than necessary to induce a particular candidate to accept the job. ("Get 'em as cheap as you can.") In spite of equal opportunity and affirmative action activities, this axiom is hard to kill. It is logical to question why we should hire someone at $40,000 when we know she or he would accept an offer of $35,000. In the days when all salaries were secret and the job rate was synonymous with the starting rate, $35,000 might have been an appropriate offer. Today, however, there are other issues to consider. If we are to extend equal pay treatment to all employees, how can we continue to base starting salaries on a rate established by another employer? If, for example, the openly published midpoint of a salary range is $50,000 and the professed minimum is $40,000, it is difficult to make a defensible case for a job offer of $35,000 to someone who meets the job's qualifications.

On the other hand, it is equally difficult to deny that the true value of any job is determined by the marketplace — that is, by what a qualified candidate is willing to accept as determined by what competitors are willing to pay. Many have used this argument, apparently successfully, to discredit the concept of comparable worth. Often overlooked in addressing this issue, however, is that, after employment, the candidate will have access to additional information that could well change her perception of the value of the accepted offer. By that time, the "system" often won't allow an increase to bring the salary to what it should have been in the first place.

Given an opening for a $50,000 midpoint job, how should we deal with the external candidate who is currently earning $50,000 and will not accept an offer of less than $55,000? Assuming there is sufficient evidence that the candidate will be able to perform the job adequately and that the company cannot find an acceptable candidate willing to accept less, at least two options are available to the company:

1. Offer a salary of $50,000 (the "job rate") plus an employment bonus of sufficient size to get the candidate to accept the job, or
2. Offer $55,000 but explain that the salary is at 110% of the range midpoint and future increases will be granted in accordance with then-current salary increase guidelines.

One disadvantage of the second approach is that, in the absence of outstanding individual performance or inflationary increases in the salary range, the effect is an extended annuity of $5,000. Another problem relates to how current employees will react to the new employee's higher salary. By and large, employees can better understand and accept the company's paying an employment bonus than they can accept a new employee's receiving a higher salary than theirs; the implication in the latter case is that the new employee is more valuable to the organization than current employees are. (It is important that whichever option is chosen, the candidate be clearly told how the salary offer fits into the company's salary structure.)

With the above considerations in mind, perhaps a better principle for salary offers would be, *"Starting salaries should achieve an acceptable balance between the reality of the marketplace and pay equity for employees, including the candidate."* ("Pay what it takes to be fair.")

Old Axiom 2: The relative value of an employee's contribution should be reflected by the size and frequency of pay raises. (The better you do, the bigger the raise.) When there were no formal appraisal systems, no precise job rates, and no formally established maximum salary limits, the most significant performance feedback available to an employee was the size and frequency of pay raises. Today, however, with openly communicated salary ranges and salary maximums based on individual performance, this axiom must be modified. In a formalized salary system each job has a defined salary range and a maximum value based on the quality of individual performance. (See Exhibit 1.) Once an individual's pay reaches that maximum, the salary system seldom allows any further increases until the salary range itself is increased. Thus, an outstanding performer whose pay is at or near his or her performance ceiling cannot receive, and should not expect, a larger pay raise than an average performer at the minimum of the pay range. Pay equity, that is, equal pay for equal performance, simply cannot be achieved unless those who are low in the range receive larger increases than those who are at their performance ceiling, *regardless of performance.* Yet, for many managers and employees it remains

EXHIBIT 1
Salary Increase Guide

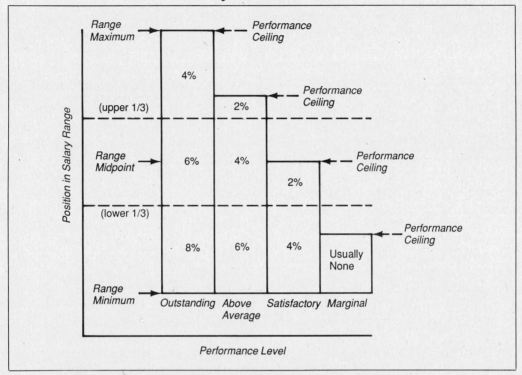

Note: This example of a typical increase guide matrix specifies the size of annual pay increases in accordance with level of individual performance and present position in the salary range. Applying the increase percentages shown, and assuming no increase in the range itself, it would take eight years for the salary of a satisfactory performer starting at the minimum to reach the salary range midpoint. If the salary range is increased without increasing the matrix percentages, the time would be even longer.

difficult to accept that an outstanding employee at the performance ceiling should receive only a 2% salary increase while a mediocre performer who is low in the salary range should receive a 4% or 5% increase. A more appropriate principle in today's environment might be the following: *The relative value of an employee's contribution to the organization should be reflected by the employee's total compensation.* ("The better you do, the more you make.")

To activate this somewhat subtle shift in axiom we must find a way to bring pay to the performance ceiling as quickly as possible. How long can we continue to say to an employee, "Yes, I agree that your performance is better than Harry's, and by giving you larger increases, *someday* you will make more money than Harry."?

Salary increase guidelines that clearly and openly prescribe larger increases for better performance perpetuate the focus on size of increase rather than total pay. Usually these guides take the form of a matrix (see Exhibit 1), with current position in the range on one axis and performance rating on the other. The matrix is usually designed to provide larger increases to those low in the range and those who have higher performance ratings. If an organization insists on using base salary to provide differential rewards based on individual performance, there is another way to prescribe and express increase guidelines. Construct a table that sizes increases on the basis of position in the salary range relative to the individual's performance ceiling, or maximum allowable salary. For example,

Current Salary as a Percentage of Performance Ceiling	Normal Increase
<70%	8%
70–75%	7%
76–80%	6%
81–85%	5%
86–90%	4%
91–95%	3%
96–100%	2%

Assuming there are different salary maximums for different levels of performance, the above table will generate essentially the same results as the more commonly used matrix table — the size of increases declines as salary approaches the allowable maximum, and better performers receive larger increases than others at the same salary level (because they are at a lower percent of their maximum). The advantage: The same table applies to everyone, regardless of performance level, which subtly disassociates size of increase from performance. (It's also an easier table to computerize.)

Old Axiom 3. Good performance should be rewarded by an increase in salary
This axiom trips over the fact that there is a maximum reasonable rate of pay for every job and every individual in an organization. It implies unlimited increases for the duration of "good" performance. It survives because in most current salary systems the number of increases possible for an employee does indeed appear to be almost unlimited. For example, when the economy and other forces are driving salary range midpoints up by 5% per year, good employees can typically expect annual increases of about 7%; thus their pay is creeping up on the job rate at the leisurely pace of 2% per year. Simple mathematics shows that if the employee started at the minimum rate for the job, say 80% of the job rate, it would take eleven years to reach job rate. Slip in a couple of promotions along the way, even with promotional increases, and annual pay raises seem to go on forever.

Further, to maintain a clear connection between pay and performance, this axiom, to be valid, would need to be accompanied by the corollary, *"Poor performance will be punished by a decrease in salary."* Few companies and cultures would accept this corollary. As a result, we continue to reward last year's performance with an increase in this year's salary, even though this year's performance may ultimately be judged significantly better or worse. If it's worse, the best we can do to get salary back in line with performance is to deny or reduce next year's increase. There is an understandable reluctance to impose such pen-ance on an employee whose performance has slipped from very good to merely good or from good to average. Also, few salary systems will allow an extra increase this year to make up for one withheld for performance reasons last year. As a consequence, pay raises tend to become annuities, with salaries reflecting the accumulation of performance ratings over a number of years. Thus the relationship of recent performance to base salary often remains quite foggy.

There is a far better way to reward individual performance. Simply provide a base salary that has the same maximum compa-ratio for everyone and recognize differences in performance levels by means of a periodic bonus. For example, if maximum salary were set at 90% of the job rate or range midpoint, the following annual bonuses could be used to reward performance:

Performance	Bonus as Percentage of Midpoint
Marginal	none
Satisfactory	10%
Above average	20%
Outstanding	30%

In a company with a typical 50% pay range, maximum salary is 120% of midpoint, and minimum salary is 80% of midpoint (maximum is 150% of minimum). The above approach would increase minimum total compensation for a satisfactory performance to 90% of midpoint, since such a performer at 80% of midpoint could expect a performance bonus of 10% of midpoint. Increasing the minimum in this fashion would obviously result in increased compensation costs. In exchange, however, the company could expect greater productivity as employees seek to maximize bonus, and there is less likelihood of paying for performance that isn't there. There would also be a slight cash flow improvement derived from paying bonuses at the end of the year instead of incorporating performance pay into monthly base salary.

If indeed it is desirable to vary pay with performance, a system like this makes the point far more clearly than most. It would not, of course, supplant those bonuses paid to middle managers to reflect business performance and to compensate for base salaries that by themselves are less than competitive.

Perhaps a more appropriate principle here, if pay for performance is to have a significant motivational impact is, *"Good performance should be rewarded by a significant sum, clearly related to that performance and clearly differentiated from normal pay."*

While we're about the business of exposing hidden axioms, let's not forget the one that says, *"The reason we want to pay for performance is that people generally do what they are rewarded for doing."* There are, of course, rewards other than money, but this axiom is probably well worth keeping.

Old Axiom 4: Promotions warrant an increase in pay Like thunder and lightning, promotions and pay raises seem irrefutably linked in the minds of employees and employers alike. Again, the logic seems obvious: If the new job is worth more to the company than the old job, there should be a concurrent increase in pay. This one, too, originated long ago, before salary ranges, midpoints, and performance ceilings. When the "job rate" was the current salary, it was natural to provide immediate reward for increased responsibility. Even then, however, promotional increases were not universal. There was always a body of belief that an employee given a bigger job should prove competence in the new job before getting a raise.

If, as many suggest, pay for performance is one of the keys to business survival in the 1980s and 1990s, this axiom may well be counterproductive. When measured against the expectations of the new job, the performance of a new promotee is very likely to be, at least initially, quite low. A concurrent promotional increase, in effect, rewards poorer, or at least unproven, performance. At best it rewards prospective performance, and at worst it serves as a bribe to induce the employee to accept the job. It might be more consistent with the concept of pay for performance to view the principal reward for promotion as an opportunity for the employee to demonstrate greater value to the organization, with the prospect of higher pay. (An exception may be warranted in those rare cases where current salary is below the established minimum of the new job.)

This is not to say that the next increase for the promoted individual should not be significantly greater than it would have been if that individual had not been promoted. Given reasonably successful adaptation to the new job, it should be. The situation that should be questioned is when the promotion and increase occur concurrently.

Where the concept of promotional increases is deeply imbedded in the organization's culture, it will not be easy to change. This is particularly true where promotional increases are used to offset the higher costs encountered by an employee whose promotion involves geographical relocation. Even if such costs are real or if a financial incentive is needed to induce an employee to accept reassignment, it is inappropriate to address these issues through base pay. A one-time lump sum or fixed installment bonus should serve the purpose equally well without clouding the pay-for-performance aspect of base salary.

Old Axiom 5: The best judge of an employee's performance is his or her manager This axiom is well served in a highly structured, hierarchical system where managers are expected to be more skilled than those who work for them and where lateral communication is minimal. In today's more informal organizational environments, however, this axiom has begun to lose its relevance. It is becoming more and more difficult for supervisors or managers to exceed or even match the technical skills of those who work for them. All employees are expected to interact directly with others inside and outside the organization. As a result, employees' peers and clients are often better able to judge technical competence and effectiveness than managers. A better rule for these times might be, *"Judgments of individual performance must include the perceptions of an individual's manager, subordinates, clients, and peers."* Where such judgments can affect salary or promotion, evaluations should also include input from the individual affected.

The principal role of the manager in performance appraisal should be to lead the process of determining, with the individual, the specific attributes to be rated by the individual's various constituencies, and defining those constituencies. The manager should work with the employee to set performance standards, and the assessment by the constituencies of how well the employee performed against those standards should be the measure of performance. The manager should consolidate the various inputs to arrive at an overall rating and help the employee analyze the results. This presumes, of course, that there is some significant use for such ratings, such as determining readiness for promotion or the size of the individual's increase or bonus. Otherwise, the rating process is not likely to draw much attention or energy from those involved, nor will it be worth that attention or energy.

An added benefit to including peer review as part of the evaluation process is that it helps to counter another flaw prevalent in many compensation systems. To merit an above-average salary or increase, most systems require the employee to demonstrate above-average performance. This often means that the employee must be seen as performing better than his or her peers — an effective disincentive to cooperation and collaboration among peer groups if those groups have no input into the judgment.

Old Axiom 6: Discussions of performance and individual development should be separated from discussions about pay
The supporting theory for this axiom holds that when these subjects are discussed at the same time, the employee tends to focus on the pay issue to the exclusion of meaningful dialogue on performance and development. There is now, however, a body of research suggesting that this is not necessarily true — that employees are more satisfied with pay decisions when such decisions are directly linked to discussions of performance and development. Moreover, if pay for performance is an organizational objective, the logic of separating discussions of the two issues simply collapses. An alternative for the 1990s could be, *"Performance discussions should be held immediately before any planned salary action and should always include an explanation of how the pending pay action will be related to the employee's performance."*

If performance discussions are held immediately before a salary action and the performance rating is clearly communicated, the action itself should hold no surprise for the employee. This also gives the employee the opportunity to have an input into the rating process.

Old Axiom 7: Managers should be paid more than those who work for them.
This axiom stems from a number of assumptions that are no longer universally true. One such assumption is the organizational philosophy that, to be successful, in addition to having managerial or supervisory skills, managers should be technically or professionally superior to those who work for them. In organizations driven by this philosophy, managers are usually selected primarily for superior technical skills and are expected to train those who work for them. By any of the usual job evaluation techniques, this arrangement assures that the manager's job will be valued more highly or judged worth more than the employee's.

Another assumption is that the manager's role is to plan, organize, direct, and control the work of those who work for him or her. Clearly, this longstanding, textbook definition of a manager's job warrants higher pay than the jobs of those who work for him or her.

Today, however, the role and the selection process for managers is often quite different, especially in companies whose business is based on creative efforts in areas of high technology. The leader on any project is often the one with the greatest expertise, regardless of position. Managers are selected primarily for leadership skills, and their job is to create and communicate to their work unit a vision of what the output of that unit should be and to find ways to align the ambitions of its members with the goals of the business. Accountability for the quality of technical output rests primarily with the technologists themselves. The manager is a facilitator and a resource for those who plan, direct, and control their own work. The technologist may quite justifiably earn more than his or her manager.

Companies who use the "high-tech" organizational principles can generally be expected to generate higher quality technical output than those who adhere to traditional structures. Because traditional structures reward hierarchy, individual success — as measured by compensation, power, and prestige — generally accrues to the "management" class. Pursuit of technical excellence is socially neither as acceptable nor as rewarding in traditional organizations as it is in high-tech organizations. To attain higher pay in traditional organizations, therefore, technologists must aspire to management jobs that, if attained, often transform good technicians into mediocre managers. Technologists whose management ambitions are thwarted by the decreasing number of available management positions often seek to satisfy their innate desire for growth and development through activities outside the workplace.

So while "Old Axion #7" may be quite appropriate in a traditional organizational setting, it should not be allowed to prevent our consideration of different organizational structures with appropriate differences in pay relationships.

Old Axiom 8: Nontaxable perquisites are effective rewards for managers Because of the widespread use of perquisites (such as company cars, club memberships, and plush offices) for executives, such perquisites are often seen as essential to attracting and keeping managers. Their use is often rationalized as a cost-effective substitute for cash because they are deductible by the company as a business expense and nontaxable or only partly taxable to the manager. In reality, they become highly visible emblems of distinction that set the managers apart from the rest of the organization.

This poses no particular problem where all of the critical information and decision making resides within the management "club." Visible perquisites can, however, seriously inhibit efforts to generate teamwork that involves both managers and nonmanagers. Management perquisites also reinforce the value system that drives good technologists to become so-so managers.

There is a tendency to view high-tech firms that have deemphasized perquisites as merely trendy or different, but the quantity and quality of their technical output should not be dismissed lightly. The success of a company's efforts to achieve greater employee involvement in running the business will be affected by the company's ability to eliminate class distinctions. A better view of perquisites might be, *"Differences in treatment among employees should be, so far as possible, based on the functional needs of the* job." A salesman, for example, may need a club membership to maintain important contacts while the president may not, or a designer may need a larger office than a department manager needs.

Quite apart from business considerations, the search for equality has become a very real social issue in Western societies. Egalitarianism may not yet have reached the level of fervor of the French Revolution, but it is growing. Legislation and regulation to eliminate discrimination against women, minorities, veterans, handicapped, and others offer incontrovertible evidence of this movement. Companies that ignore this issue do so at their peril.

Old Axiom 9: A discretionary bonus for middle management employees is a useful device to ensure the competitive level of total compensation and to reward individual performance A discretionary bonus that can be used to bolster otherwise low compensation and that can be used to shrink compensation expense in less profitable years is very much in keeping with the autocratic philosophies of yesteryear. By definition, the amount of a discretionary bonus cannot be predicted by the employee. And because it is often used to compensate for deficiencies in the basic salary program, employees may see little correlation between the amount of the bonus and individual or company performance. As a result, it has little motivational value and may instead even create suspicion.

In light of the inevitable movement toward openly communicated compensation systems, there must be a better instrument. One alternative is to introduce a profit-based bonus with a clearly communicated formula. If desired, the formula could include factors based on individual or work unit performance. The important principle here is, *"There is no place for a discretionary bonus in a well-designed compensation system."*

Old Axiom 10: Company management and benefit specialists are the best qualified people to determine the most appropriate kind and level of benefits for employees Fortunately, many companies have already recognized the fallacy of this one. It derives from the days of homogeneous work forces and union-negotiated benefits that were the same for all employees. In some companies it is sustained today by the ancient belief that given a choice among a number of pay and benefit options, employees would be incapable of wise selection. Such companies often treat compensation and benefits as separate systems.

Given the wide disparity of age, family status, and personal values among today's employees, it's difficult to imagine an undifferentiated pay and benefit system suitable for all. To provide the optimal number of options for employees requires that pay and benefits be viewed as interchangeable elements of a single reward system. Implementation of such a system, usually under the label of flexible benefits, does entail increased administrative effort, but nothing beyond the scope of a number of available computer software packages.

Companies who have installed flexible benefits, even as cost-reduction or cost-containment measures, have generally observed increased levels of employee job satisfaction. There is also evidence that employees are quite capable of selecting the options best suited for their individual needs, provided they receive adequate information.

There are well-established employee survey techniques for determining the relative value of various benefits to a particular work group. It is reasonable to assume that benefits chosen as a result of such a survey, coupled with employee options to trade pay for benefits or one benefit for another, would greatly increase the effectiveness of company money previously spent on like-it-or-lump-it benefit programs. The driving principle here should be, *"Pay and benefits should be administered as a single system with maximum possible trade-offs available to employees."*

James L. Whitney is president of the consulting firm Compensation Strategies.

Pay Concepts for the 1990s, Part 2
James L. Whitney

Having examined, in part 1 of this article, some of the old axioms behind today's pay practices, it would now be useful to take a look at some popular concepts prevalent in the compensation field today and evaluate them for future use. Most of these concepts are not really new, but they reflect a changing emphasis as companies struggle to come to grips with doing business in the coming decades.

Pay for Performance

Companies have been trying to pay for performance all along, but they've had varying degrees of success. The concept's emergence as a major issue today reflects a growing awareness that U.S. companies must make some major changes in how they operate if they are to remain competitive in the world marketplace. Facing foreign competitors who have lower wage rates, different profit objectives, and equal or superior products, U.S. companies realize that business as usual is the road to oblivion. No longer can U.S. companies simply bump their prices up to pass along the cost of increased wages. In fact, many companies have discovered they can't successfully maintain the labor costs they already have.

Companies are desperately searching for ways to reduce labor costs and increase productivity at the same time. They are looking for ways to be sure they get what they pay for with labor dollars. This translates into pay for performance. On the basis of the old saying that people generally do what they are rewarded for doing, companies are reexamining pay practices to be sure that they are indeed rewarding the right people for the right things. They are rediscovering these old principles of motivational theory: To motivate, (1) a reward must be perceived as worth working for, (2) the reward must have a clearly perceived connection with the work results, and (3) work goals must be seen as achievable.

At the level of individual performance, traditional pay schemes rarely meet the above criteria. Structures that rely on

Source: Reprinted, by permission of the publisher, from *Compensation and Benefits Review,* May/June 1988, © 1988. American Management Association, New York. All rights reserved.

base salary to differentially reward performance are hard pressed to make a convincing connection between performance and reward. Performance may fluctuate, but salaries rarely do. The real difference in base pay between a good performer and an outstanding one often is not evident until both have reached that part of the salary range that represents the ceiling for their respective performances. As explained earlier, this could take a number of years. In the meantime, the outstanding performer is likely to receive annual increases of only 2% to 3% more than the average performer — hardly a significant motivator.

Among equal performers doing the same job, at any point in time there may be significant differences in annual salaries, depending on the work and salary history of the incumbents. This is probably unavoidable as long as we try to deal realistically with the conflict between the forces of internal equity and those of the job marketplace. The problem is not so much that such differences exist; it is that they tend to exist for so long. In a typical salary system there may be a 50% difference between minimum and maximum for a given job. The minimum is typically 80% of the range midpoint. Assuming that the midpoint is the appropriate salary for a competent performer, someone starting at the minimum needs a 25% increase in salary to reach the midpoint. Assuming that the midpoint climbs in reaction to such economic forces as inflation, in most systems this would be metered out over seven years or more. Few jobs require anything near that long for the incumbent to achieve a competent level of performance. No wonder employees have difficulty making the connection between pay and performance!

One possible answer to the problem of connection lies in the use of performance bonuses for all levels of the exempt work force as suggested in the discussion of Old Axiom #3. Limiting all base salaries to a maximum of something like 90% of the job rate, or range midpoint, and paying the balance of compensation in bonuses would accomplish two things. First, it would abbreviate the base salary range to only 12.5% (80% × 1.125 = 90%). Thus, differences in base pay for comparable performers in the same job could be eliminated over a much shorter period of time. Second, significant bonuses that are based on performance and that must be reearned every year should provide a clear and worthwhile connection between pay and individual performance.

A word of caution about individual performance bonuses: Unless employees have a high level of trust in the appraisal system, such bonuses can backfire. If, in the absence of an ongoing and reliable appraisal process, most employees are led to believe they are above-average performers, bonus time will generate a lot of disappointment and demotivation. Also, if the bonus primarily rewards individual achievement, it may be very difficult to achieve the desired levels of cooperation and collaboration within work groups.

Affordable Pay

The concept of affordable pay means that companies can no longer afford to set pay levels on the basis of what everyone else is doing. The idea is that there is a maximum that a specific company can invest in pay and benefits and remain in business. That amount may be considerably less for some companies and some industries than for others. Ideally, pay should go up when business is good and down when it isn't. This kind of reassessment of pay levels is indeed warranted. However, there is an inescapable rule that cannot be violated without risk of calamity: *"Regardless of how poorly the business may do, the minimum level of compensation must not fall below the level needed to attract and retain competent employees."* Generally, this means that pay levels must compare favorably with those of other employers competing for the same work force. The Japanese scheme of allowing employee compensation to fall drastically (through a bonus plan) when times are bad is not applicable absent the Japanese value system and concept of lifetime employment. Ways in which companies can tie compensation to the fate of the company are through such stock-based plans as stock options and stock appreciation rights or through some type of gainsharing or profit sharing plan as discussed in the next section.

Gainsharing

The quest for greater productivity has led to a resurgence of interest in various gainsharing plans, such as Rucker®, Scanlon®, Impro-share®, and others. Each of these has been demonstrated to help boost productivity in certain environments. Generally, however, such plans seem to be of primary value and impact at the shop floor level, leaving open the questions of who should participate and what plan, if any, is appropriate for other organization members.

For some organizations, profit sharing would be a more appropriate mechanism for varying employee reward with the fortunes of the business. There is probably no better way to instill a sense of partnership and responsibility among employees than for them to share the profits of the business. Making profit sharing work, however, takes a serious commitment by the employer to ongoing employee communication to help employees see the connection between what they do and company profits. Caution: For maximum effectiveness, employees should have the option of taking the profit-sharing payout in cash or readily convertible securities, such as company stock or savings bonds. Deferred forms of profit sharing or plans that require an employee contribution to be matched in a savings program will have significantly less motivational effect on many employees because of the delayed nature of the reward.

Skill-Based Pay

The idea behind skill-based pay is that with proper incentive employees will learn a wide variety of skills, creating a more flexible work force. While today skill-based pay is generally limited to lower-level jobs, primarily in manufacturing, this concept has been given impetus by the movement toward self-managing work teams. In theory, skill-based pay rewards people for what they know rather than for what they do. So far, it has not been applied extensively to exempt jobs, and, in the opinion of many, its long-term value is still in question.

Lump-Sum Increases

Lump-sum increases were first used as a means of emphasizing the value of a pay raise by offering part or all of the annual increase in a lump sum. Such increases have been well received in a number of companies, especially when employees have been given the option of how and when to take the increase. In recent years the lump-sum idea has received greater attention as a cost-containment mechanism. It is a way to increase employee pay without rolling up the cost of pay-dependent benefits. When they are used as an option to give an employee greater control over how and when total compensation is received, lump-sum increases can be an effective adjunct to the total reward system.

WHERE TO NOW?

Unfortunately, recognizing the obsolescence of some of the old axioms will not automatically guarantee a successful rewards system for the 1990s. Nor is copying all or parts of another organization's program likely to produce the desired results. Too much depends on the culture, objectives, and life cycle of the particular organization in question. The following highly recommended steps will help you arrive at a sound compensation program:

1. Determine the role compensation should play in meeting the strategic objectives of the business. Should compensation be used to motivate certain behaviors or should it merely enable the company to attract and retain people with adequate skills to run the business?

2. Determine what the organization policy makers really believe about compensation — reexaminee the old axioms. The results will be greatly influenced by what the policy makers believe about people. Should employees know the details of how their compensation is determined? Should they have an opportunity to participate in those determinations? Is pay for performance really what is wanted; if so, what level of performance should be paid for? Individual? Team? Work unit? Company? All of these?

3. Establish and reduce to writing the company's guiding philosophy regarding compensation.

4. Articulate the principles that will guide the development and administration of compensation programs, and turn them over to a compensation professional to design the system.

An essential key to successful compensation design is to have the right people working on the right components. Policy makers should determine the objectives, the philosophy, and the guiding principles behind the compensation system; then compensation professionals should design it. It is probably best to avoid having the policy makers involved in designing the system. When that happens, the policy makers, who are usually high-level, action-oriented executives, tend to dive right into the design phase, bypassing the critical but tedious and sometimes gut-wrenching process of developing a workable philosophical consensus.

There are no shortcuts. The most successful compensation systems in the 1990s will be those that have been developed through well-reasoned deductive thought processes that take none of the old axioms for granted.

James L. Whitney is president of the consulting firm Compensation Strategies.

Managing Corporate Culture Through Reward Systems
Jeffrey Kerr / John W. Slocum, Jr.

The concept of corporate culture has captured the imagination of executives and researchers alike.[1] For executives struggling to manage organizational change, corporate culture has become an important tool. They realize that significant strategic or structural realignment cannot occur if it is not supported by the organization's values and behavioral norms.[2] Yet, culture has proved to be a subtle, intangible phenomenon — pervasive but difficult to manage or influence. Many managers have found that culture cannot be manipulated directly.[3]

Most have an intuitive understanding of culture. Anthropologist Clyde Kluckhohn has defined culture as "the set of habitual and traditional ways of thinking, feeling and reacting that are characteristic of the way a particular society meets its problems at a particular point in time." (p. 86)[4] A corporation's culture simultaneously determines and reflects the values, beliefs, and attitudes of its members. These values and beliefs foster norms that influence employees' behavior. While most managers are aware of their companies' cultures, they are unsure about how it is maintained, transmitted, or influenced.

We believe that the reward system represents a particularly powerful means for influencing an organization's culture. Much of the substance of culture is concerned with controlling the behaviors and attitudes of organization members, and the reward system is a primary method of achieving control. The reward system defines the relationship between the organization and the individual member by specifying the terms of exchange: It specifies the contributions expected from members and expresses values and norms to which those in the organization must conform, as well as the response individuals can expect to receive as a result of their performance.

The reward system — who gets rewarded and why — is an unequivocal statement of the corporation's values and beliefs. As such, the reward system is the key to understanding culture. An analysis of reward systems can provide executives with a basis for effectively managing long-term cultural change. In this article, we will describe the reward systems operating in a sample of firms and show how these systems reinforced and influenced cultural values and norms. We will then link reward systems and culture to the corporate strategies pursued by top managers in these firms.[5]

EXAMINING REWARD SYSTEMS

Reward systems are concerned with two major issues: performance and rewards. Performance includes defining and evaluating performance and providing

Source: From "Managing Corporate Culture Through Reward Systems" by Jeffrey Kerr and John W. Slocum, Jr., *The Academy of Management Executive,* 1987, Vol. 1, No. 2, pp. 99–108. Reprinted by permission.

employees with feedback. Rewards include bonus, salary increases, promotions, stock awards, and perquisites.

Of course, large corporations with several different businesses may have multiple reward systems. And while they may share some fundamental philosophies and values, they may differ according to the particular business setting, competitive situation, and product life cycle. Thus multiple reward systems can support multiple cultures (or subcultures) within one organization.

Subcultures are a natural by-product of the tendency of organizations to differentiate. As organizations grow with respect to the number of products, services, and divisions, subcultures may reflect a number of distinct work and social environments. Through increasing differentiation, opportunity for the emergence of countercultures is also increased. Countercultures are shared values and beliefs that are in direct opposition to the patterns of the dominant culture. To the extent that divisional reward systems reinforce these distinct behavioral norms and belief systems, subcultures and countercultures are likely to be articulated and even reinforced.

TWO KINDS OF REWARD SYSTEMS

From these interviews, we identified two distinct reward systems: the hierarchy-based system and the performance-based system. Eight firms were classified as hierarchy-based and six as performance-based. Of course, the descriptions of reward systems and cultures that follow are composites representing "pure" types. Actual reward systems and cultures showed some variation but conformed to these general types.

The Corporate Hierarchy

In the hierarchy, superiors defined and evaluated the performance of subordinates. Performance was defined qualitatively as well as quantitatively. Nonquantifiable aspects of the subordinate's role were sometimes considered to be more important than quantifiable ones. Superiors were free to define those aspects of a manager's role that would be considered important. Thus, performance criteria could vary according to who one was working for.

Managers' jobs were broadly and subtly defined. Managers were accountable for how they conducted their interpersonal relationships, as well as the consequences of their actions. Numbers (for example, return on investment) did not tell the whole story, and more subtle aspects of performance were sometimes viewed as more important. Superiors played a critical role in career mobility and success with the firm. They were the source of training, socialization, feedback, and rewards and were to be studied, emulated, and satisfied if subordinates expected to succeed.

Superiors interpreted the performance of subordinates according to subjective criteria. Even in quantified areas, superiors did not hesitate to interpret numerical outcomes in the context of their own knowledge of the situation. Factors such as interdivisional cooperation, long-term relations with customers, leadership style, and development of junior managers were evaluated, despite obvious difficulties in quantifying them. Such

DATA-COLLECTION METHODS

We studied the reward systems of 14 companies in the northeast and midwest regions of the United States. All but one of the companies were included in *Fortune*'s listing of the top 500 corporations. Sales ranged from $125 million to over $8 billion. The companies ranged from single-product industrial firms to multidivisional conglomerates.

Initial contact in each firm was made with the top human resources (HR) manager. HR managers were key informants and provided the names and titles of other managers in their firms who might be willing to participate in the study. To ensure the selection of knowledgeable managers, we asked that only those who had been with the company for at least five years and had received significant rewards (for example, salary increases, bonuses, perquisites) be included. In addition, at least one manager interviewed in each firm was responsible for authorizing rewards for subordinates. Thus, both sides of the reward relationship — allocating and receiving — were represented in the sample.

In all, 75 interviews were conducted. Interview time per manager ranged from one hour to five or six hours. The average interview took 90 minutes and was conducted in the manager's office. We interviewed, on average, 5 managers from each firm, with as many as 10 managers interviewed in one firm. The interviewee group included 5 chief executive officers, 7 group-level executives, 5 line vice-presidents (manufacturing, production), 6 staff vice-presidents, 25 division general managers, and 27 director-level managers.

Initial interviews in each firm concentrated on gathering objective data on the managerial reward system. These focused on performance definition and evaluation, feedback processes, and the administration of rewards (bonus, salary, stock, perquisites, and promotion). The first interviews were structured so that comparable data would be obtained. Subsequent interviews gathered subjective data on the firm's history, founders or dominant leaders, traditions, values, and norms. These interviews were necessarily open-ended and exploratory.

In addition to interview data, company documents such as annual reports, 10-K reports and company histories (when available) were also examined. Some firms provided documentation on the reward system itself. The 10-K and annual reports gave an overview of the firm's products, corporate and business strategy, and past economic performance. The company histories provided insight into the origins of the firm, which included their stated values and traditions. Data from these sources served as a check on the information gathered through the interviews.

evaluation communicated the importance of the hierarchy and the subordinates' dependence on superiors. The subjective nature of evaluation allowed for the inclusion of qualitative performance criteria and reinforced the message that managers had to be concerned with more than the numbers. Subjective evaluation permitted consideration of the long-term consequences of managerial action. This implied an ongoing commitment to the activity or business in questions.

In this system, formal performance appraisals took place once a year. Informal feedback, however, was quite frequent. A high level of interaction existed between superiors and subordinates. Feedback occurred on the job, in the dining room, during executive retreats, or at the country club, and was oriented more toward employee development than toward evaluation. Since performance definition and evaluation were subjective, the quality of performance could be known only through superiors. The high level of interaction coupled with a developmental approach communicated the organization's commitment to the individual manager's success and future. This was conducive to the development of mentoring relationships and to extensive socialization of younger managers. The sense of dependency and vulnerability was balanced by a message of concern for the individual as a valued resource whose development was important to the organization.

Bonuses were based on corporate performance. The system rewarded the team, not individuals. This provided a basic rationale for cooperative rather than competitive behavior. The fact that potential bonus payouts increased by level emphasized the importance of long-term commitment to the organization (tenure was a precondition for promotion) and conformity to its norms. Bonus was a relatively small proportion of total compensation, ranging from 20% to 30%, while salary was the largest part of compensation. By severely limiting bonus for the individual star, the system removed the incentive for behaviors that benefited single managers rather than the entire organization. The bonus system also reinforced the subordinate's dependence on superiors' judgment, because they determined bonus amounts.

Salary increases generally were determined through a formal salary plan, such as the Hay system. Two major factors in the size of a salary increase were tenure (time in grade) and performance (subjective evaluation by superiors). The tenure component gave structure to salary decisions. Policies specified the range of possible increases within job classifications.

Perquisites were even more constrained by policy than were raises and were carefully monitored. Status symbols, such as locations of offices, furniture, club memberships, first-class travel, and so forth, were considered important symbols of rank. Superiors sometimes insisted that managers use them, even if they did not want them. Perquisites communicated the importance of rank, tenure, and commitment, as well as a sense of ritual and tradition. Receiving a particular type of desk upon promotion, being told (not asked) to join a prestigious men's club because everyone of a given rank had always done so, being met at airports by local managers, attending specific executive development programs, were all rituals symbolizing a unique and shared tradition and history. Even for those not eligible for such perquisites, the fact that they existed provided a feeling of belonging not simply to an economic entity but to a social system.

In contrast to perquisites, stock awards were not structured in any obvious way. Managers had little knowledge about how and why awards were made. Awards were not directly related to individual or even corporate performance. Generally, the higher the managerial rank, the greater the eligibility for stock awards. The lack of information about stock awards meant that subordinates could not influence their distribution in any way. This lack of clarity imparted a sense of mysterious ritual to the reward. The message was that subordinates must trust superiors to do the right thing for them. Receiving stock awards symbolized acceptance into the inner circle. Therefore, managers had to be well aware of the total set of company values and norms and how to conform to them. Any deviation might be serious enough to reduce or temporarily eliminate a manager's stock awards.

Promotion from within was the standard policy in hierarchical firms. Promotions were relatively frequent (every two to four years) and were often motivated more by the individual's need for development (that is, exposure to new functional areas) than by the organization's need to fill a slot. Many promotions did not entail significant increases in authority, responsibility, or salary. Commitment to employee development and cross-fertilization often resulted in lateral or diagonal movement rather than vertical movement. Managers were transferred on a regular basis across divisions or functional boundaries, in keeping with the emphasis on developing general managers with strong internal networks throughout the company. Promotion practices expressed concern for the lifetime career of employees. They contributed to a tight, homogeneous organization with common language, experience, and values. Lack of movement signaled a disinvestment in the individual and a loss of interest on the part of the organization.

Clan culture We can characterize the kind of culture that emerged from the hierarchy-based reward system as a clan William Ouchi has used the term *clan* to describe a control system based on socialization and internalized values and norms. Exhibit 1 summarizes the major features of the clan culture. In this culture, individuals in the organization are like a fraternal group. Everyone recognizes an obligation that goes beyond the simple exchange of labor for salary. It is tacitly understood that required contributions to the organization may exceed any contractual agreements. The individual's long-term commitment to the organization (loyalty) is exchanged for the organization's long-term commitment to the individual (security). This relationship is predicated on mutual interests.

The clan culture accomplishes this unity through a long and thorough socialization process. Members progress through the ranks by pursuing traditional career paths in the company. Older members of the clan serve as mentors and role models for younger members. It is through these relationships that the values and norms of the firm are maintained over successive generations of managers. The clan is aware of its

EXHIBIT 1

Characteristics of a Clan Culture

The relationship between individual and organization:
Fraternal relationship
Mutual long-term commitment
Rests on mutual interests, a shared fate
Sense of tradition, history, company, style
Hierarchy structures relationship

The relationship among organization members:
Pride in membership
Sense of interdependence, identification with peers
Extensive collegial network
Pressure from peers to conform
Stresses collective rather than individual initiative, ownership

The process of acculturation:
Long, thorough socialization
Superiors are mentors, role models, agents of socialization
"Rich" normative structure governs wide range of behaviors

---

unique history and often documents its origins and celebrates its traditions in various ceremonies. Statements of its credo or publicly held values are reinforced. Members have a shared image of the organization's "style" and manner of conduct.

In the clan culture, members share a sense of pride in fraternity and in membership. The socialization process results in strong identification among members and a strong sense of interdependence. The up-through-the-ranks career pattern results in an extensive network of colleagues whose paths have crossed and who have shared similar experiences. Communication, coordination, and integration are facilitated by shared goals, perceptions, and behavioral tendencies.

In addition, pressure to conform is considerable. The very richness of the culture creates an environment in which few areas are left totally free from normative pressures. The culture does not usually generate risk taking or behavior or innovation, nor does it generate in members feelings of personal ownership for a division, product, or ideas. Not surprisingly, the culture is not conducive to entrepreneurial activity.

The Performance-Based Reward System

In contrast to the hierarchy, the performance-based system objectively defined and measured performance and explicitly linked rewards to performance — which was almost completely defined quantitatively. Qualitative aspects of performance were generally ignored. Specific rewards or proportions of rewards were directly related to specific performance criteria (for example, bonus based partly on return on assets, and partly on pretax profits, and so forth). In this way, managers exerted influence by objectively weighting the various components of the subordinate's job.

This reward system sent the message that the manager's job was specifically defined. Performance in divergent roles was assessed by a few basic financial outcomes. Accountability was primarily for results and not for the methods by which results were achieved. The message was that the numbers were paramount. Evaluations frequently were based on a formula in which the manager's financial results served as inputs. Nonquantifiable aspects of performance were generally not evaluated. Because of the quantitative emphasis, performance evaluation necessarily focused on the immediate time frame with little consideration of long-term consequences.

This type of evaluation communicated to managers their independence from subjective judgments of superiors, since manager results could be understood by examining financial outcome. Superiors had few channels through which to express concern for stylistic aspects of a subordinate's performance. The system clearly told managers to focus on those performance elements that could be quantified. Because activities that might contribute to long-term competitiveness were sometimes hard to quantify, such activities were not formally incorporated into the reward system.

Performance feedback under this system was erratic. Some companies held one or more formal performance appraisal sessions while others held none. Informal interactions between superior and subordinate were infrequent. Feedback was oriented more toward evaluation than toward employee development. Because performance was defined and measured quantitatively, the subordinate manager was not dependent on the superior for interpretation.

The low level of superior-subordinate interaction and the evaluative, as opposed to developmental, approach to feedback served to emphasize autonomy. Concern was not expressed for subordinate development or long-term career progress. The reward system was not conducive to a mentoring relationship, nor was it likely to contribute to the transference of subtle norms and values. Socialization was not an important function of this system.

Bonuses were a very significant part of compensation. Bonus maximums ranged from 40% of salary to "no limit." In some firms, there was no cap on what a manager could earn in bonus if the financial criteria were met. Bonus was based almost exclusively on the performance of the division over which the manager had authority; the performance of other divisions or the entire corporation, whether better or worse, had almost no effect on the individual's bonus. Each division was a profit center and generated its own bonus pool. Actual bonus payment was determined by formula, and the resulting figure was rarely altered by superiors.

The bonus system communicated that the manager was an independent operator whose fate was somewhat independent of superiors and other divisions as well. No economic rationale for cooperative behavior between or among divisions existed. The potentially large size of bonuses communicated the value placed on the "star" performer rather than the team player. The bonus system also deemphasized rank as an important source of rewards.

Salary increases and stock rewards were indirectly based on managerial performance. Salary increases were affected by the external labor market, the cost of living, and the manager's overall performance. Stock arrangements were frequently negotiated when a manager joined the firm. These rewards were loosely related to performance, and actual amounts were subjectively determined by superiors. This practice opposed the overall emphasis on objectivity, but stock awards and salary increases had a relatively lower value in the reward systems of these organizations. Significant performance feedback was conveyed in a manager's bonus. Perhaps superiors operating under this system needed to have some mechanisms available to them to express subjective perceptions of subordinate performance. The flexibility of salary increases and stock awards, relative to the bonus formula, may have satisfied that need.

Perquisites were almost nonexistent in the performance-based system. Symbols of rank and status were not emphasized, because the manager's level was not emphasized. While this communicated a sense of egalitarianism, it also lessened the sense of community and singularity. If reward rituals (predicted on tenure and hierarchical position) convey the existence of an in-group, then the absence of such rituals weakens the feeling of participation in a tradition and membership in a special group.

Promoting from within was not a norm in this system. It was common to find high-ranking managers brought in from the outside. Many had been with their companies only a few years. Promotions were generally motivated by the organization's need to fill a vacancy rather than the individual's need for exposure. Relative to the hierarchy-based system, promotion occurred infrequently and was usually vertical (and within the same division or function).

The practice of hiring from outside conveyed to members that the organization's commitment to them was not necessarily long-term. Individuals repeatedly could be passed over for promotion when more attractive candidates from other firms or industries were identified. These organizations were indicating that they did not necessarily value tenure or the socialized individual and did not expect a long-term commitment from members. Under such conditions, we found a mutually exploitative relationship. The individual was utilized to fill a role or perform a particular function until he or she was needed elsewhere or was replaced by a more qualified person. This relationship engendered a similar response from individuals, who exploited the organization until better rewards could be gotten elsewhere.

The performance-based system provided few mechanisms for integration between divisions. Vertical promotions rather than cross-divisional movement tended to facilitate specialization. A wide network of managers who had worked together, known each other, and understood each other's responsibilities was not fostered, and promotional practices encouraged divisional independence and uniqueness. These organizations did not seek an integrated system based on shared language, norms, and goals.

Market culture William Ouchi has used the term *market* to describe a system of control in which behaviors are constrained by negotiated terms of exchange. Exhibit 2 lists the major characteristics of the market culture. In this culture, the relationship between individual and organization is contractual. Obligations of each party are specified in advance. The individual is responsible for some level of performance, and the organization promises a given level of rewards in return. Increased levels of performance are exchanged for increased rewards as specified in a negotiated schedule. Neither party recognizes the right of the other to demand more than was originally specified. The organization does not promise (or imply) security; the individual does not promise (or imply) loyalty. The contract, renewed annually if each party

> **EXHIBIT 2**
>
> **Characteristics of a Market Culture**
>
> *The relationship between individual and organization:*
> Contractual relationship
> Mutual short-term commitment
> Rests on self-interest, utilitarianism
> Terms of exchange structure relationship
>
> *The relationship among organization members:*
> Independence from peers
> Limited interaction
> Little pressure from peers to conform
> Stresses individual initiative, ownership
>
> *The process of acculturation:*
> Little socialization
> Superiors are distant; are negotiators, resource allocators
> "Lean" normative structure governing few behaviors

adequately performs its obligations, is utilitarian, since each party uses the other as a means of furthering its own goals. Rather than promoting a feeling of membership in a social system, the market culture encourages a strong sense of independence and individuality in which everyone pursues his or her own interests.

The market culture does not exert a great deal of normative pressure on its members. Members do not share a common set of expectations regarding management style or philosophy. There is little pressure from peers to conform to specific behavior or attitudes. Much of superiors' interactions with subordinates consist of negotiating performance-reward agreements and/or evaluating requests for resource allocations. A superior's influence on subordinate rewards is limited. Superiors are less effective as role models or mentors, and the absence of long-term commitment by both parties weakens the acculturation process.

Relations among peers are also distant. Little evidence of economic independence gives little rationale for cooperating with peers. Managers do not interact frequently with counterparts in other divisions, nor do they develop an extensive network of colleagues in the company. Vertical career paths result in little understanding of or identification with other divisions.

The market culture is not designed to generate loyalty, cooperation, or a sense of belonging to a social system. Members do not feel constrained by norms, values, or allegiance to an accepted way of doing and thinking. But the market culture does generate personal initiative, a strong sense of ownership and responsibility for operations and decisions, and an entrepreneurial approach to management. The individual is free to pursue goals with a minimum of organizational constraints.

REWARD SYSTEMS, CULTURE, AND STRATEGY

It is important to recognize that a given culture and its associated reward system is neither good nor bad, effective nor ineffective, except in terms of its support for the total organizational system of which it is part. The hierarchy-based and the performance-based systems each identify and reward a set of complex behaviors. The difference lies in the cultural values that are expressed through the reward system. To the extent that it is congruent with organizational strategy, structure, and process, the reward system will effectively contribute to organizational goals. Thus the clan culture may be ineffective in an environment that requires innovation, aggressiveness, and a strong desire for individual achievement. Similarly, the entrepreneurship, autonomy, and short-term focus of the market culture may be dysfunctional in mature, capital-intensive industries, where systemwide integration is critical.

Matching Organization Strategy with Reward Systems

We analyzed our sample of firms according to two environmental factors: type of industry and growth strategy. To analyze the corporate growth strategies of our firms, we used Milton Leontiades's steady state-evolutionary distinction.[6] Steady state firms grow through internally generated diversification or through increased penetration of existing markets. They are internally focused and concerned with the development of new products and technologies and with integration across business units. Evolutionary firms grow primarily through acquisitive diversification. They actively pursue new markets and industries and are receptive to mergers and joint ventures.

Each firm's history was examined to ascertain the extent of its external activity (acquisitions, mergers, joint ventures, divestitures). If, within the previous three years, a firm engaged in no external activities that resulted in entering a previously unoccupied industry, it was classified as steady state. In addition, we looked at each firm's 20-year history to determine the consistency of its strategy.

Exhibit 3 shows each firm's industry, growth strategy, and reward system. First, we looked at the relationship between growth strategy and reward systems. All but one firm pursuing a steady state strategy utilized a hierarchy-based reward system. Every firm pursuing an evolutionary strategy utilized a performance-based system.

It is also clear that evolutionary firms are more diverse enterprises than steady state firms. In fact, except for the food products company, the firms pursuing an evolutionary strategy were generally

EXHIBIT 3
Type of Industry and Growth Strategy of 14 Firms

Steady State Strategy	Evolutionary Strategy
Aluminum (H)	Diversified foods products and restaurants (P)
Forest products (H)	
Power generation (utility) (H)	Diversified consumer and industrial products
Integrated chemicals producer (H)	Diversified consumer and industrial products (P)
Mining and related machinery (P)	Diversified consumer products and services (P)
Machine tools (H)	Diversified consumer products and services (P)
Building and home improvement products (H)	Diversified industrial services (P)
Pharmaceuticals (H)	

(H) indicates a hierarchy-based reward system.
(P) indicates a performance-based reward system.

considered to be conglomerates. In contrast, the firms in this steady state group tend to be focused on particular industries or technologies. Most are capital-intensive industries that require long-term commitment and a high degree of vertical integration. Forest products, aluminum, power generation, pharmaceuticals, and machine tools are all mature businesses that, to be effective, require massive investment in plant and equipment, research and development, and distribution systems.

Successfully competing in a mature industry requires long-term commitment to the business and a highly integrated organization. The steady state strategy, with its internal market focus, concern for integration, and growth through market penetration, fits the demand of a mature business. The strategy does not rely on acquisitions or divestitures, and companies survive by committing substantial physical, financial, and managerial resources to a stable set of businesses.

The steady state strategy requires a reward system that encourages stability, cooperation, and a long-term systemwide perspective from its managers. Coordination and control are more important than aggressiveness and entrepreneurship. The hierarchy-based reward system provides this kind of support. Its subjective, qualitative character allows for the inclusion of long-term performance criteria that would be difficult to quantify. Frequent contact between superiors and subordinates encourages the transference of subtle values to a younger generation of managers. Cross-divisional promotions foster integration and understanding of the total system. Promotion from within and bonus based on corporate performance reinforce long-term commitment and a sense of community.

How does corporate culture fit with strategy and reward systems design? A clan culture comprises a set of values and norms that are highly consistent with the demands of a steady state strategy. The need for integration and a systemwide perspective is addressed by the fraternal values, the sense of mutual interest, pride in membership, and an extensive collegial network. Long-term commitment is supported by a sense of history and tradition. The role of superiors as models and mentors emphasizes the importance of continuity and experience. Peer pressure and the rich normative structure underscore the need to perform in ways that are consistent and widely shared among members. The star is not valued as highly as the team player. In other words, the clan culture provides a foundation of values, norms, and attitudes that encourage behaviors consistent with the steady state strategy. Corporate culture and reward system design function as complementary elements in directing members toward achieving the strategic goals of the firm.

The demands of the evolutionary strategy are quite different. The effectiveness of this strategy depends on corporate managers choosing acquisitions carefully and knowing when to divert businesses from the portfolio. It frequently requires that management make business decisions in areas that are partially or even completely unfamiliar to them. Because the strategy hinges on changes in the portfolio of businesses, commitment to a particular business or technology is not as highly valued as it is in firms that have chosen a steady state strategy.

The evolutionary strategy requires a reward system that permits managers to make evaluations and reward decisions that are equitable and defensible to division managers despite their lack of familiarity with these divisions. The reward system should allow corporate managers to make comparisons across unrelated businesses. The large bonus component, based on divisional results, creates a sense of ownership in division management. The autonomy inherent in this system encourages an entrepreneurial orientation. The system tends not to foster cooperation among divisions. Such cooperation is not critical when divestment of divisions occurs with some regularity. In short, the performance-based system rewards independence and entrepreneurship, the star performer versus the team player, and does not require extensive involvement from corporate-level managers in the reward process.

Exhibit 2 shows that the values of the market culture fit closely with both the evolutionary strategy and the performance-based reward systems. The relatively low level of commitment to businesses is reflected in the contractual relationship between organization and individual. The need for autonomous, entrepreneurial relation between divisions is reflected in limited peer interaction, weak peer pressure, and a lean normative structure. We would not expect conformity to be highly valued in an organization that pursued diversity. We would not expect loyalty and commitment to be highly valued in an environment where divestment of divisions and/or their managements was a distinct possibility and part of overall corporate strategy. The performance-based reward system clearly expresses and reinforces a market culture. Clearly, corporate culture is the foundation for normative behaviors that support the overall corporate strategy.

ENGINEERING CULTURAL CHANGE

Reward systems express and reinforce the values and norms that comprise corporate culture. A careful consideration of reward system design can help decision makers successfully modify the organization's culture. Reward systems are, in effect, powerful mechanisms that can be used by managers to communicate desired attitudes and behaviors to organization members. We believe that, over time, cultures are amenable to change through the clear communication of performance criteria and the consistent application of rewards.

At the same time, we hope some sense of the complexity of culture has come through, along with a healthy respect for the difficulty of the task of changing a company's values, norms, and attitudes. Large organizations are like societies; their cultures are reinforced and modified over years. Culture itself is rooted in the countless details of organization life. How decisions are made, how conflict is resolved, how careers are managed — each small incident serves to convey some aspect of the organization's culture to those involved. Given the pervasiveness of culture, it is not surprising that managers are frequently frustrated in their attempts to change it.

There is some basis for optimism, however. Culture does not develop in a vacuum. It is an integral part of the company's fabric. Even with little or no attention paid to it, an organization's culture is likely to evolve in conjunction with the day-to-day activities of the company. Thus, except in unusual circumstances, the manager's task usually is not to create a basic congruence among rewards, culture, and business strategy, but to focus and fine-tune the natural interaction of these elements.

ACKNOWLEDGMENTS

Portions of this article were presented at the American Institute for Decision Sciences meeting in Toronto, November 1984. The authors acknowledge contributions on earlier drafts of this manuscript made by Michael Beer, Bill Joyce, Lynn Isabella, Ralph Kilmann, Edward Lawler, and Randy Schuler.

Support for this project was given through a research grant to the authors from the Center for Enterprising, Cox School of Business, Southern Methodist University.

NOTES

1. Several major popular books about culture have been written in the past five years. Some of the most recent include Edgar Schein's *Organizational Culture and Leadership* and Ralph Kilmann et al.'s *Gaining Control of the Corporate Culture* (both published by Jossey-Bass, San Francisco, 1985). Recent academic reviews of this literature include "Concepts of Culture and Organizational Analysis," by Linda Smircich, *Administrative Science Quarterly,* 1983, 28, 339–358; "The Uniqueness Paradox in Organizational Stories," by Joann Martin et al., *Administrative Science Quarterly,* 1983, 28, 438–453; and "On Studying Organizational Cultures," by Andrew Pettigrew, *Administrative Science Quarterly,* 1979, 24, 570–581.

2. The difficulty of changing an organization's culture so that it is more closely aligned with the firm's strategy has been explored by Howard Schwartz and Stanley Davis in "Matching Corporate Culture and Business Strategy," *Organizational Dynamics,* Summer 1981, 30–48; by Paul Shrivastava in "Integrating Strategy Formulation with Organizational Culture," *Journal of Business Strategy,* Winter 1984, 103–110; and by Jay Barney in "Organizational Culture: Can It Be a Source of Sustained Competitive Advantage?" *Academy of Management Review,* 1986, 11, 656–665.

3. For examples of how culture either facilitated or impeded change, see Thomas Moore's "Culture Shock Rattles the TV Networks," *Fortune,* April 14, 1986; Harold Seneker's "Why CEOs Pop Pills (and Sometimes Quit)," *Fortune,* July 12, 1978; John Main's "Waking Up AT&T: There's Life After Culture Shock," *Fortune,* December 24, 1984; and John Solomon and J. Bussey's "Cultural Change: Pressed by Rivals, Procter & Gamble Company Is Altering Its Ways," the *Wall Street Journal,* May 20, 1985.

4. Anthropologist Clyde Klukhohn's work cited in the text is titled "The Study of Culture," in D. Lerner and H. Lasswell (eds.) *The Policy Sciences,* Stanford, Cal.: Stanford University Press, 1951.

5. For an excellent description of how diversification strategies affect managerial behavior, see Jeffrey Kerr's "Diversification Strategies and Managerial Rewards: An Empirical Study," *Academy of Management Journal,* 1985, 28, 155–179.

6. See Milton Leontiades's *Strategies for Diversification and Change,* Boston, Mass.: Little, Brown, 1980.

Jeffrey Kerr is assistant professor of organizational behavior and business policy at the Edwin L. Cox School of Business, Southern Methodist University. John W. Slocum, Jr., holds the O. Paul Corley Professorship in organizational behavior at the Edwin L. Cox School of Business, Southern Methodist University.

Cases

Chancellor State University
Thomas R. Miller

THE SETTING

Chancellor State University is a large, urban university in the Midwest. Although the University experienced rapid growth in the 1960s and 1970s, overall enrollment had stabilized. The School of Business Administration, however, had continued to grow, drawing students away from programs in the School of Education and the College of Arts and Sciences as well as attracting new students concerned with future vocational opportunities. The faculty and administration of the business school were pleased to see the enrollment growth as it signaled acceptance of their degree programs, but the enrollment expansion also created strong pressure to expand the business faculty.

Under normal circumstances, faculty expansion would simply have meant an active recruitment effort by school administrators. But the situation at Chancellor State was representative of a national phenomenon of enrollment growth in business schools that had resulted in a strong demand for doctorally qualified faculty in the face of a relatively short supply. Thus, faculty recruitment at many business schools had become a priority activity, rather than merely one of the many administrative responsibilities of deans and department heads.

At Chancellor, Fred Kennedy, Chairman of the Management Department, had been actively seeking new faculty members for his staff, which had the heaviest course load in the school. As is often customary in academia, the faculty in the Department of Management participated in recruitment, spending considerable time meeting with the faculty candidates in an effort to evaluate their candidacy for a faculty position. Faculty members could then make recommendations as to whether or not the prospect should be tendered an offer to join the staff.

THE CONFERENCE

It was late in February, and several prospective faculty members had visited Chancellor State for campus job

Source: From "Chancellor State University" by Thomas R. Miller, *Journal of Management Case Studies.* Copyright T. R. Miller, 1985. Reprinted by permission of the author.

This case is based on a real situation but all names are disguised.

interviews. Early one Friday morning, Kennedy was in his office reviewing the job files of prospective faculty members. He looked up as he heard the voice of Larry Gordon, an assistant professor of management who was now in his third year at Chancellor State.

"Good morning, Fred," said Larry, as he walked into the Department office. "Do you have a couple minutes? I want to talk with you about something."

Fred gestured to him to come into his office.

"Sure, Larry, what's on your mind?"

After entering Fred's office, Larry closed the door, indicating to Fred that this was not to be just a casual, friendly conversation.

"Fred," Larry began, "I was wondering what you thought about the prospective faculty member we had in here for an interview last week. I've been talking with a couple other faculty members about him, and they're not really all that impressed. He seems to be OK, I guess, but we may be able to do better. Are we going to make him an offer? If we do, he's sure not worth top dollar in my opinion."

"Well, I've received some of the written evaluations back from the faculty, and they seem to be fairly positive," replied Fred. "They're not as favorable as they could be, but the other faculty seem to think that he would be acceptable and that he could work out pretty well on our staff. His academic credentials are not bad, and he has had some good experience. Given the state of the market for business faculty in his specialty, I expect that we'll extend an offer to him. By the way, I know that he already has a couple of offers in hand from our competition."

Fred could readily see that Larry was not pleased to hear all of this. From their earlier conversations, Fred could anticipate Larry's next comment.

"Yeah, O.K., I can see that we could use him, but what kind of money are we offering in these new positions?" questioned Larry. "I don't mean to pry into somebody else's business, but what sort of salary is the department offering our new faculty?"

Fred winced at this question. He had in the past made no secret about general salary ranges for new faculty members. In fact, this information was generally known throughout the school. But this had become a very sensitive issue in the last few years, given the rapid increases in starting salaries for new business faculty members.

"Well, Larry, I guess you know that we're paying competitively for our new faculty. With our enrollment increase we've got to increase our teaching staff, and to do that we're probably going to have to meet the market," Fred responded.

Larry was obviously not satisfied with this response and was becoming irritated with the conversation. "Fred, I assume that by 'meeting the market' you mean that we're going to offer this guy two to three thousand dollars more than some of us who have been here for several years are now making. This new guy has not yet finished his doctorate, has very little teaching experience, has no publications, and, in my opinion, is not as good as a lot of our current faculty. How much can you justify paying for an unknown quantity? I think it's just unfair to the present faculty to offer him more money than many of us are making. When is somebody going to do something for us? Fred, I'm not unhappy here in this department, but I'm sure going to keep my eyes open for other opportunities. I feel sure that I could move to another school at a higher rank and increase my salary significantly. You may think I'm wrong and maybe I shouldn't feel this way, but this situation is just not fair!"

Fred sighed and tried to calm Larry down. "Larry, I know what you're concerned about, and I'm certainly sympathetic to the problem. After all, this salary compression issue affects me in the same way it does you. I can assure you that I have reservations about paying the kind of money we are for new faculty in light of our existing faculty salaries, but I don't believe that we can attract the kind of faculty we want by paying less than competitive rates. Although this seems to create some internal inequities, I hope that we'll have sufficient salary increase money to make some adjustments to reduce these discrepancies. Certainly I want to be able to reward and retain our productive people . . ."

Larry, feeling a little embarrassed by his earlier emotional statement, interjected: "I know you've got other problems, Fred, and I didn't mean to lash out at you. I know it's not really your fault, but a lot of the other faculty are talking about this salary issue. It surely doesn't help morale any when a new, inexperienced assistant professor is hired for more than some of the associate professors are making."

"Yes, I'm well aware of this, Larry, and I'm making the Dean aware of it as well. We're certainly going to do what we can to try to resolve this salary compression problem," Fred responded.

As Larry moved toward the door, he continued to make his point: "Well, I hope you can do something soon because it's most inequitable at the present time. People are pretty upset about it, and it's likely to cause the department some turnover problems in the future. No one likes to be treated unfairly. I'll see you later, Fred. I've got to run to class. Maybe we can talk about it again later."

As Larry walked out of his office Fred reflected on their conversation. It reminded him of other discussions he had had previously with several other faculty members. In fact, Larry had hinted at his dissatisfaction before, but had not been so outspoken about it. Yes, the salary compression problem was reaching a crisis. No longer was it a matter of the "new hires" nearing the salaries of some present faculty; it was a matter of their exceeding them. Never in his experience had Fred recalled a labor market for faculty that was this chaotic.

Fred had puzzled over this dilemma before, but he had not been able to come up with a solution for the problem. He wondered if, in fact, there was a solution that would enable him to hire the new personnel he wanted without offending some of the present staff. Maybe it's just one of those "no win" administrative situations, he mused. Perhaps this was something that could be discussed with the other department chairmen and the Dean as some of them had basically the same problem. Maybe then, he would have a better idea of how to deal with the situation. He certainly hoped so!

Thomas R. Miller is in the Department of Management, The Fogelman College of Business and Economics, Memphis State University.

Redesigning Performance Appraisal at Citizens Bank
J. Gregory Chachere

Susan Toeffler was the newly promoted Assistant Personnel Director at the Citizens Bank. She had been employed by the bank for fourteen years, during which she had worked as mail room clerk, proof operator, keypunch operator, teller, and — most recently — secretary in the personnel department. While working at the bank, Susan attended the local university part-time and earned first a bachelor's degree in business administration and then an MBA.

Susan's first major assignment as Assistant Personnel Director was to develop and implement a new performance evaluation system for all employees and officers. Not only did she have to develop a good, sound system, but she also had to see to it that the managers throughout the bank used the system. This was no easy task.

The bank had used one performance evaluation form and system for about as long as anyone could remember. The form was a graphic rating scale assessing performance on eight specific dimensions, with one overall assessment of performance at the end. On the anniversary of each employee's date of hire, his or her immediate supervisor was to fill out the form, give feedback to the employee, have the employee sign the form, and then send it to the personnel department, where it was kept in the employee's file.

The system had several major problems. First, once the appraisal form was filed, it was never used again. No one ever even referred to it. Second, the bank did not enforce the performance appraisal procedures. Most of the time, managers did not complete the forms at all. If they did, they did not give feedback to the employees, as evidenced by the number of appraisal forms sent to the personnel department without the employee's signature.

It was obvious that Susan had her work cut out for her. From the materials she had read in the library and obtained from the Society of Human Resource Management (SHRM), she learned that there were a multitude of different performance appraisal forms and approaches — many more than she had realized. How would she ever decide which one to select?

J. Gregory Chachere is a graduate student at Northeast Louisiana University.

"Redesigning Performance Appraisal at Citizens Bank" by J. Gregory Chachere is reprinted by permission of the author.

Readings for Professional Growth and Enrichment

Cascio, W. F., and H. J. Bernardin (1981). "Implications of Performance Appraisal Litigation for Personnel Decision." *Personnel Psychology* 34: 211–226.

Cederblom, D. (1982). "The Performance Appraisal Interview: A Review, Implications, and Suggestions." *Academy of Management Review,* 7: 219–227.

Chonko, L. B., and R. W. Griffin (1983). "Trade-off Analysis Finds the Best Reward Combinations." *Personnel Administrator* 45 (May): 47, 49.

Cockrum, R. B. (1982). "Has the Time Come for Employee Cafeteria Plans?" *Personnel Administrator* (July): 66–72.

Cole, A. (1983). "Flexible Benefits Are a Key to Better Employee Relations." *Personnel Journal* 62: 49–53.

Delaney, W. A. (1983). "Making Fringe Benefits Pay." *Supervisory Management* (May): 36–39.

Ellig, B. R. (1983). "What's Ahead in Compensation and Benefits." *Management Review* (August): 56–61.

Foegen, J. H. (1982). "The Creative Flowering of Employee Benefits." *Business Horizons* 25: 9–13.

Gifford, D. (1984). "The Status of Flexible Compensation and Benefits." *Personnel Administrator* (May): 19–21, 23–25.

Henderson, R. I. (1982). "Designing a Reward System for Today's Employee." *Business* 1 (July–September): 425–478.

Heneman, H. G. III (1985). "Pay Satisfaction." In K. M. Rowland and G. R. Ferris (eds.), *Research in Personnel and Human Resources Management,* Vol. 3. Greenwich, Conn.: JAI Press.

Ilgen, D. R., and J. M. Feldman (1983). "Performance Appraisal: A Process Focus." In L. L. Cummings and B. M. Staw (eds.), *Research in Organizational Behavior,* Vol. 5. Greenwich, Conn.: JAI Press.

Kane, J. S., and E. E. Lawler III (1979). "Performance Appraisal Effectiveness: Its Assessment and Determinants." In B. M. Staw (ed.)., *Research in Organizational Behavior,* Vol. 1. Greenwich, Conn.: JAI Press.

Kovach, K. A. (1983). "New Directions in Fringe Benefits." *Advanced Management Journal* (Summer): 55–63.

Latham, G. P. (1986). "Job Performance and Appraisal." In C. L. Cooper and I. T. Robertson (eds.), *International Review of Industrial and Organizational Psychology*. New York: John Wiley and Sons.

Meyer, P. (1983). "Executive Compensation Must Promote Long-Term Commitment." *Personnel Administrator* (May): 37–42.

Morrison, A. M., and M. E. Kranz (1981). "The Shape of Performance Appraisal in the Coming Decade." *Personnel* (July–August): 12–22.

Rynes, S. L., and G. T. Milkovich (1986). "Wage Surveys: Dispelling Some Myths about the 'Market Wage.'" *Personnel Psychology* 39: 71–90.

Sashkin, M. (1981). "Appraising Appraisal: Ten Lessons from Research for

Practice." *Organizational Dynamics* 9: 37–50.

Taylor, M. S., C. D. Fisher, and D. R. Ilgen (1984). "Individuals' Reactions to Performance Feedback in Organizations: A Control Theory Perspective." In K. M. Rowland and G. R. Ferris (eds.), *Research in Personnel and Human Resources Management,* Vol. 2. Greenwich, Conn.: JAI Press.

Wagner, J. A. III, P. A. Rubin, and T. J. Callahan (1988). "Incentive Payment and Nonmanagerial Productivity: An Interrupted Time Series Analysis of Magnitude and Trend." *Organizational Behavior and Human Decision Processes* 42: 47–74.

Wexley, K. N., and R. Klimoski (1984). "Performance Appraisal: An Update." In K. M. Rowland and G. R. Ferris (eds.), *Research in Personnel and Human Resources Management,* Vol. 2. Greenwich, Conn.: JAI Press.

VI

MAINTAINING HUMAN RESOURCES

Readings

Labor Relations: Research and Practice in Transition
John A. Fossum

The 1980s follows 50 years after the Great Depression, during which public policy enabled industrial unionization through the Wagner Act. This law declared collective bargaining to be the preferred method for resolving employment conflicts, defined employee rights and employer obligations, and established the National Labor Relations Board (NLRB) to settle questions of representation and the conduct of collective bargaining.

In the 1940s the focus of union-management relations shifted from organizing to conflict resolution. Although wartime legislation prohibited strikes and the National War Labor Board had implemented dispute resolution procedures, substantial time was lost to strikes. Fears that the readjustment to a peacetime economy would be plagued with strikes were realized in late 1945 and 1946. In reaction, Congress passed the Taft-Hartley Act to reduce union bargaining power and provide conflict resolution mechanisms through the establishment of the Federal Mediation and Conciliation Service (FMCS).

The AFL and CIO merged in 1955. Union membership, as a percentage of the labor force, peaked at 33% in 1956. In 1959, after congressional hearings into corruption in union-management relations, legislation to regulate union finances and protect the rights of individual members was passed.

Both productivity and wages increased rapidly during the early 1960s. As the Vietnam War increased in intensity, so did inflation. Cost-of-living allowances (COLAs) were included in an increasing number of contracts. In the 1960s and 1970s organizing, bargaining, and dispute resolution procedures for public sector employees were subjects of state and federal legislation.

The 1980s have been as turbulent as the 1930s, but without strikes. Union membership, in both absolute and relative terms, has fallen sharply. Nonunion companies have been increasingly successful in remaining unorganized. Offshore competitors with low labor costs are taking increasingly large shares of markets served by traditionally unionized producers. High unemployment has emboldened management in replacing employees if strikes occur.

The relationship between the federal government and organized labor has also changed as the result of several actions, including President Reagan's firing of striking air traffic controllers in 1981, his appointments to the NLRB, reduced

Source: John A. Fossum, "Labor Relations: Research and Practice in Transition," *Journal of Management,* 1987, pp. 281–299. Reprinted by permission.

funding for the Department of Labor, and unfilled vacancies in other labor agencies, all of which signalled that his administration did not view the interests of organized labor as a high priority in its agenda.

EVOLUTION IN THEORY AND METHOD

Early students of labor relations (Commons, 1934) applied an institutional perspective focusing on rules, transactions, and collective actions rather than individual exchange. In the 1930s, a new discipline, industrial relations, was begun with its domain centered on the employment relationship (Heneman, 1969). Although early theory and research in industrial relations was developed primarily by institutional economists, numerous psychologists, sociologists, and political scientists also contributed to its focus and methods. (See Kochan, 1980, for a summary of the development of industrial relations as a discipline.) Systems of industrial relations were defined by either identifying a "web of rules" that bound the actors in employment together (Dunlop, 1958) or by operationally defining and measuring the direction and magnitude of relationships between employment variables (Heneman, 1969).

In 1978, Strauss and Feuille lamented a malaise in labor relations research, but saw hope in emerging work by economists, psychologists, and a new generation of industrial relations scholars. Their prescience was accurate. An explosion of research has extended knowledge on individuals and union membership, and the effects of unions on productivity, profitability, and the economy. The new research reflects a diversity of approaches. Several efforts seem to have led the way in stimulating labor relations research. In roughly chronological order, these are

1. Getman, Goldberg, and Herman's (1976), *Union Representation Elections: Law and Reality,* which used the Freedom of Information Act to gain access to voters in union representation elections, both praised and harshly criticized, was largely responsible for the NLRB abandoning its policy of requiring election reruns where untruthful campaign materials had been used.[1]
2. The *Journal of Labor Research,* begun in 1980, has provided a forum for an eclectic set of papers in which labor relations is the common theme.
3. Richard Freeman and others at the National Bureau of Economic Research have studied the effects of unions on employee and employer outcomes and identified variations in personnel policies attributable to collective bargaining. *What Do Unions Do?* (Freeman & Medoff, 1984) is one of the few scholarly books that has

---

1. The string of cases in which truth in campaign issues would be a factor in certifying the results of an election began with *General Shoe Corp.*, 77 NLRB 127 (1948) and was reiterated in *Hollywood Ceramics Co.*, 140 NLRB 221 (1962). These precedents were abandoned in *Shopping Kart Food Markets, Inc.*, 228 NLRB 190 (1977), reinstated by *General Knit of California, Inc.*, 239 NLRB 101 (1978), and most recently abandoned again in *Midland National Life,* 263 NLRB No. 24 (1982).

TABLE 1
Units of Analysis-Process Matrix

Unit of Analysis	Organizing	Negotiating	Impasse Resolution	Contract
Administration				
Societal	X	X		
Industrial	X	X	X	
Firm	X	X	X	X
Individual	X	X	X	X

had a recent impact on the popular press.

4. The longitudinal and cross-sectional studies of the effects of changes in industrial relations practices on organizational outcomes reported by a group of MIT scholars culminating in the publication of *The Transformation of American Industrial Relations* (Kochan, Katz, & McKersie, 1986).

Four major processes are involved in collective bargaining (i.e., organizing, negotiating, resolving impasses, and administering contracts) and the study of each may use multiple units of analysis (i.e., societal, industrial-national union, firm-local union, or individual). At the individual level both behaviors and attitudes can be measured. This review focuses on research by unit of analysis within processes. Table 1 shows a matrix of the processes and units of analysis and indicates the cells in which contemporary empirical research has been reported (subject to the constraints listed above). It also focuses on individual attitudes toward unions and briefly examines unions and politics. In doing so, the review is limited. First, only selected research and theory published since 1980 is covered. Second, only research explicitly involving employment or the actual actors in labor relations is reviewed. Experimental studies of negotiation and arbitration are *not* covered in this review *unless* they involve actual negotiators or arbitrators. Third, only theory development and empirical research is reported. Reviews of research or descriptive papers are omitted.

ORGANIZING AND REPRESENTATION

Union membership does not ensure coverage under a collective bargaining agreement, nor does nonmembership confer an exemption. Representation for collective bargaining requires that a majority of employees want a union to be its representative. Representation by a union occurs through unions winning elections, by accepting employment in a represented unit, or by an employer agreeing that a new facility will be added to an established bargaining unit. Joining a union is voluntary except where a collective bargaining agreement specifies that membership is a condition of continued employment. These are prohibited in states having so-called "right-to-work" (RTW) laws.

Societal Level Research

Union membership depends on employment levels in unionized establishments and on organizing nonunion employers (Heneman & Sandver, 1981). Membership has decreased since 1979 (Kokkelenberg & Sockell, 1985). Since 1950, changing organizing rates, decreased union success in representation elections, and declining employment in heavily unionized industries combined to explain the dropping percentage and absolute number of the unionized work force, with economic factors contributing most to this decline (Dickens & Leonard, 1985).

Decertification elections, in which employees vote on whether or not to oust their representative, have increased recently, and unions are losing more often. Ahlburg and Dworkin (1984) found several macroeconomic factors including inflation, strike frequency, low union density in the industry, and small bargaining unit size to predict the decertification of existing unions.

Industrial-National Union Level Research

In the 1960s and 1970s, laws and regulations were enacted by many jurisdictions to specify representation rights for public sector employees. Saltzman (1985) found that state laws which required bargaining with an elected representative were the most important cause of increased representation among teachers. Other factors positively associated were more male teachers, larger schools, reduced teacher employment, higher real per capita income in the area, and the extent of bargaining in earlier periods. Attitudes favoring public employee unions in the state and those contiguous to it predicted laws that encouraged organizing.

Past success in organizing by national unions leads to an increasing proportion of resources being devoted to representation activities (Block, 1980). This reallocation is to the economic benefit of the present membership (Voos, 1983). Where union representation in an industry is low, organizing rather than representation activities produce greater gains for present members because higher unionized percentages reduce wage competition within the industry. Since 1950 real expenditures on organizing activity have increased, but are a smaller proportion of national expenditures (Voos, 1984).

Firm-Local Union Research

Employers with unionized facilities have increasingly adopted goals to reduce or eliminate represented units (Kochan, Katz, & McKersie, 1986). Some abandon or replace antiquated plants that were unionized and others eliminate expansion or further capital investment in organized plants.

Employers with unionized facilities have been able increasingly to resist organizing in new plants (Kochan, McKersie, & Chalykoff, 1986). Where unions have collective bargaining rights in a significant proportion of the company's other plants, resistance has not been as successful. However, union avoidance strategies and workplace participation innovations were associated with reduced organizing success in even heavily unionized firms.

Several contextual factors are related to unions losing representation elections. These include units larger than 50 employees, industries not traditionally represented by the union, location in a southern RTW-law state, low unemployment, low unionization in the industry, and delays in conducting the election (Cooke, 1983). Locating plants in rural areas having low union representation may not enhance union avoidance since evidence at the SMSA level suggests that these are positively related to union success in representation elections (Hunt & White, 1985). Regional effects (Cooke, 1983) may result from the larger size of recent election units in the South and the greater likelihood of procedural delays there (Sandver, 1982).

Substantial research on the effects of representation election tactics on election outcomes has been reported since the Getman, Goldberg, and Herman (1976) study. They concluded that voters remembered few campaign issues and few votes were swayed by the campaign. Corroborating evidence from an election to choose between two unions to represent faculty members suggested that voters were relatively unswayed by campaign material (Walker & Lawler, 1986).

Dickens (1983) simulated election outcomes using the Getman et al. (1976) data and their associated NLRB decisions. Unions had won 36% of them. In the simulations, "light" legal company campaign yielded a union win rate of 63%. An intense legal campaign reduced union wins to 22%, whereas a campaign combining legal and unfair tactics reduced union wins to 4%.

Smaller employers in highly competitive and unionized markets often retain consultants to help them plan and execute active election campaigns (Lawler, 1984). Consultants often recommend covert information gathering, restricting opportunities to solicit employees, demanding that the NLRB determine the appropriate unit in which to conduct the election, and waging an intense campaign (Lawler, 1981; Murrmann & Porter, 1982). Consultant activities may make a difference in close elections, but unit size and local labor market conditions have been found to be more important (Lawler, 1984).

Employers more frequently violate employee rights to engage in union activities when employment levels are decreasing, where unionization is more pervasive, and the employer had previous violations (indicating that there might be little to lose from repeated violations) (Kleiner, 1984).

Individual Level Research

Individual level research on organizing poses some problems unless the study is done within the election unit because representation is a unit-level, not an individual phenomenon. However, studies that examine predictors of either a willingness to or an actual vote for a union increase our understanding of variables that may make a difference in voting in actual bargaining units.

A decreasing proportion of the labor force is represented by unions, but proportional representation of blacks, women, and more educated employees has increased (Kokkelenberg & Sockell, 1985). Several characteristics predict pro-union attitudes. Using 1980 NLS data for 28–38-year-old males, Hills (1985) found that 87% of union and 27% of nonunion employees would vote for a union if an election were held. Among unorganized employees, blacks and government and construction workers were more likely to voice pro-union sentiments. Fiorito and Greer (1986) found that women who were minority group members, non-metropolitan residents, government employees, workers perceived as having greater job mobility, and workers perceiving unions as instrumental were less likely to be pro-union than similar men.

Studies within individual units are difficult to conduct because it is hard to determine when organizing begins and to gain cooperation to encourage responses. Three faculty union campaigns are exceptions. In two studies, demographic variables were unrelated to intentions to vote for a union, but distrust of management, dissatisfaction with work content, current salary, perceived inequity, and union instrumentality beliefs were (Allen & Keaveny, 1981; Hammer & Berman, 1981). In the third study, Zalesny (1985 found attitudes were stronger predictors than economic factors and attitudes toward the union predicted voting intent more strongly than the reported vote. Studying 11 nearly contemporaneous elections in small units, Rosse, Keaveny, and Fossum (1986) found that perceptions of noneconomic issues, union instrumentality beliefs, and co-worker voting preferences predicted reported union votes.

COLLECTIVE BARGAINING PRACTICES AND OUTCOMES

The structure, subjects, and outcomes of negotiations have been strongly influenced by economic changes in the 1980s: foreign competition; deregulation in trucking and airlines; very low inflation; the firing of the striking air traffic controllers; persistent unemployment; and bankruptcies, restructurings, and mergers. Concurrent with these have been the economic concessions made by unions. Leap and Grigsby (1986) proposed a theory of bargaining power that helps to place concessions in perspective. Extending the work of Bacharach and Lawler (1981), they argue that one's bargaining power is directly related to the opponent's dependence on bargaining. With deregulation, foreign competition, alternative investment opportunities, and employer options involving reductions in employment; union bargaining power is substantially decreased because of the employers' decreased dependence on employment.

Societal Level Research

Union wage concessions involve a reduction in either real wages or wage premiums. Union wage premiums rose from 19 to 23% between 1973 and 1978, dropped to 18% in 1979, and returned to 22% in 1984 (Freeman, 1986). Relative wage levels have fallen in only a few industries. Holding economic conditions constant, recent settlements have been no more or less concessionary than at other times over the last 30 years.

Several differences characterize the pay programs of unionized employers. Freeman (1981, 1982) found that the effect of unions is 17% greater for fringe benefits than other forms of pay. Further, unions tend to flatten pay structures since dispersion is 22% less in unionized settings. Lower dispersion reduces differences between lower and top-level employees in a unit, whereas greater fringes (particularly health and pension benefits) reward long tenure. The indexation of wages to changes in the cost-of-living is also more frequent in union contracts, but evidence suggests that its effect in total wage changes has not been large (Kaufman & Woglom, 1986; Vroman, 1985).

Two-tier pay systems may predict future conflict because new employees hired to perform similar work are paid less than present employees. Jacoby and Mitchell (1986) found two-tier systems much more prevalent among unionized firms, and were installed usually on a temporary basis without requiring significant management concessions. Managers expected that two-tier plans will be associated with decreased morale and productivity and more difficult union-management relations, but were evenly divided on whether or not they expected to be able to maintain them in the longer run.

Jacoby and Mitchell (1984) found that employers believe 1-year contracts lead to more strikes, more contract administration problems, lower morale, higher and more unpredictable labor costs. Unions have often demanded some type of wage indexation in return for multiyear agreements. Recently, however, managements have obtained multiyear contracts by offering upfront bonuses. Longer term contracts may be difficult to negotiate where the parties are involved in an uncertain environment. Cousineau and Lacroix (1986) found that agreement was more difficult where a long-term contract was expiring; foreign competition was great; capacity utilization, selling prices, and vacancy rates varied substantially during the contract period; buyer or seller concentration in the industry was high; employers were larger; and inflation rates were high.

A great deal of research has been completed recently detailing the effects of unions on the economic performance of employers. Freeman and Medoff (1984) concluded that blue-collar union workers were substantially more productive than their nonunion counterparts, but white-collar union workers were somewhat less productive than nonunion employees.

Greater capital intensity is used in production in unionized situations because substitution of capital for labor occurs as relative wages increase. Ironically, unions increase their bargaining power as a result because relatively higher fixed costs would result from a shutdown (Kahn, 1984).

Industry-National Union Level Research

About one-third of the 1981 contracts in meatpacking and tires included concessions (Capelli, 1985). Union concessions were influenced by plant age and size, relative wage level within the industry, and nature of the product; all were potentially associated with job security. In beef packing, concessions occurred most often in high wage, low capacity plants. In pork processing, expiring contracts had more uniform wages and, as a result, rollbacks were agreed to in 10 percent of contracts, compared to 40 percent in beef packing. Concessions in rubber occurred more frequently in older, smaller plants producing bias ply tires. Plant level concessions pose difficult problems for the national union: wage variation between plants is associated with future concession demands because wages are no longer out of competition.

Unionization has a variety of effects within industries. Research on construction industry productivity found that unionized workers on private sector projects are up to 30 percent more productive than their nonunion counterparts. The differentials decreased markedly in public sector construction projects, however (Allen, 1986a, 1986b). In education, student achievement is negatively affected by unionization among public school teachers through increased use of administrators and reductions in instruction time; but positively influenced through increased preparation time, teacher experience, and smaller student/teacher ratios (Eberts, 1984).

The extent of unionization increases wages within industries, but not across occupations (Moore, Newman, & Cunningham, 1985). Extent effects are moderated by firm size, however. Podgursky (1986) found that union wages are matched by large employers regardless of the extent of unionization in the industry, medium-sized employers are sensitive to wage increases where unionization is significant, and small employers are essentially insensitive.

Norsworthy and Zabala (1985) examined measures of worker behavior and productivity in automobile manufacturing between 1959 and 1976 and found that grievances, quits, and unauthorized strikes all increase costs. Worker attitude and behavior problems were highest during peak output periods. They concluded that a 10 percent improvement in worker behavior indices was associated with about a 3 to 5 percent decrease in unit production costs.

Firm-Local Union Level Research

Industrial relations activities are part of a firm's production function. But little research has assessed the effect of industrial relations practices on profitability. In General Motors, Katz, Kochan, and Gobeille (1983) found that grievance and discipline rates, absenteeism, the number of local contract demands, and negotiating time were all significantly related. These may be underlying measures of an employee relations construct. Supporting Norsworthy and Zabala (1985), they found grievances and absenteeism rose during periods of high production. Product quality and productivity measures were negatively related to industrial relations problems. Managerial attitudes were positively related to both labor relations and productivity improvement programs. Quality of work life (QWL) programs were associated with higher quality and lower grievance rates, but not with productivity.

Negotiations after first gaining representation are difficult with only 77% resulting in an agreement (Cooke, 1984). Contracting success was retarded by NLRB election certification delays and all types of ULPs, but was facilitated by large cohesive units, the participation of a national union representative in the negotiations, and high pay in the industry. Objections to elections required a median of 209 days for the NLRB to process, reducing probabilities of agreement by 27%. Employer bargaining ULPs reduced the probability by 25%, whereas discrimination ULPs reduced it by 44%.

Individual Level Research

Within bargaining units, the willingness to concede probably increases when nonconcession would be seen as detrimental by a majority of the bargaining unit. To achieve a contract, a bargain must be ultimately acceptable to the "median voter" in the unit (White, 1982). If job security is an issue, wage concessions would be likely when the alternative is a layoff that includes the person with the median seniority level in the unit.

Unionization affects the demographic composition of the firm's work force. Beginning a union job becomes less attractive with age since many rewards are tied to seniority (Abowd & Farber, 1983). Abraham and Medoff (1984) estimated that 97% of union workers are significantly protected from layoff by seniority provisions as opposed to 86% of unorganized workers. Minority employment is also influenced by unions. Leonard (1985) sampled over 1200 California manufacturers and found that between 1974 and 1980, except for Hispanic females, unions generally facilitated the employment of minorities. In fact, the effect of unions on minority employment among federal contractors has been greater than Affirmative Action Program audits.

Turnover is lower and internal transfer and promotion rates are higher in unionized settings (Olson & Berger, 1983; Freeman, 1980). Some of this may be due to seniority-based "bumping" during layoffs, whereas low turnover may be tied to the predictability of promotions. More highly educated employees were more likely to be transferred out of the bargaining unit and, unlike nonunion situations, men and women were promoted at similar rates. Wage premiums for taking a unionized job are about 3 to 8%, but losses from leaving them are 7 to 11% (Cunningham & Donovan, 1986).

Union workers are absent about 29% more frequently than nonunion workers, other things being equal (Allen, 1984). If satisfaction is associated with attendance, this relationship should not be surprising because studies indicate that union workers are less satisfied. Olson and Berger (1983) found that job satisfaction increased for union members whose jobs changed as a result of a transfer or promotion, but not as a result of quitting. For nonunion employees, satisfaction increased with turnover, but not internal transfer. The change in satisfaction following transfer may reflect the instrumentality of unions for wage gains through promotions or job retention through "bumping," whereas quitters run a relatively large risk of wage losses (Cunningham & Donovan, 1986). Berger, Olson, and Boudreau (1983) reported lower job satisfaction among unionized employees in a national cross-section. More revealing, however, they found higher levels of satisfaction with pay (which respondents reported valuing more and receiving more of) and promotions. Union employees were less satisfied with supervisors and co-workers and their jobs (which had narrower scopes than nonunion jobs).

IMPASSES AND THEIR RESOLUTION

A great deal of research on interest arbitration[2] followed the enactment of laws governing impasse resolution in the

---

2. Third party determination of the terms of an agreement within limits specified by the parties.

public sector. Research on impasses has shifted away from processes, toward predictors and outcomes, and away from arbitration and toward strikes. The theory of industrial conflict has also been advanced through Wheeler's (1985) multidisciplinary integration.

Industrial-National Union Level Research

Stability in employers, unions, and their environments are associated with fewer strikes (Cousineau & Lacroix, 1986; Kaufman, 1983). Strikes occur more frequently in hazardous industries (Leigh, 1984). If employees there are risk-takers, then strikes may be a manifestation of risk-taking behavior. Strikes occur more often where the strike costs are lower for both employers and employees (Maki, 1986).

Work stoppages during a contract (wildcat strikes) most frequently involve plant administration issues and generally last 3 days or less (Byrne & King, 1986). Wildcats were predicted by union penetration in the industry, unsafe working conditions, high shipment to inventory rates, a liberal political environment, and a moderate degree of bargaining experience. Factors negatively related to wildcat strike incidence include filing ULP charges, unemployment, real wages in the industry, percent of women in the bargaining unit, location in the South, and a long-term bargaining relationship.

Firm-Local Union Level Research

Strikes occur more frequently where they are not punished. Teacher strikes in Pennsylvania were more frequent in districts where instructional days lost to strikes were made up and paid (Olson, 1984). Well-enforced penalties or threats of firings reduced public sector strikes (Olson, 1986). Poorly enforced laws had no effect, whereas permitting strikes appeared to increase them. Strikes were reduced where interest arbitration was available.

Gramm (1986) analyzed 1050 negotiations between 1971 and 1980 and found the incidence, duration, and maintenance of intensity of strikes were related to several demographic, economic, union, and firm factors. Larger, labor intensive units with higher proportions of males, stable product demand, decreasing real wage levels, and a RTW-law state location had higher strike rates. Duration was associated with these factors and high income-to-debt ratio of strikers and low regional union penetration. Maintenance of intensity, as measured by proportion of possible worker days lost, was predicted by essentially the same factors as incidence.

Strike and other impasse resolution outcomes can be considered from the perspective of the striker or the owner (shareholder). If the public sector, Feuille & Delaney (1986) found that wages were positively influenced by the availability of collective bargaining, interest arbitration, and the past use of arbitration, but negatively by present use. However, market factors accounted for more variance in wages than collective bargaining factors.

Immediate economic effects of strikes appear to be quite small, with struck firms drawing down inventory and competitors' increased production (Neumann & Reder, 1984). Managers believe costs related to fluctuations in capacity utilization are relatively small. Management chief negotiators felt that firms gain more from strikes than a union if they have the ability to remain in operation and/or if a large proportion of the employees would require strike benefits from the union (Shirom, 1982).

Stock prices decline before a strike is accounced (Neumann, 1980). However, between 1962 and 1982, of an average decrease of 4.1% in share price for firms with strikes involving 1000 or more workers (Becker & Olson, 1986) only about one third occurred before a strike was announced.

During the 1970s, increased use of interest arbitration in the public sector led to the conclusion that it had a "narcotic effect," that users were "hooked," and had abandoned bargaining. Variations such as "final offer arbitration"[3] were introduced to make arbitration less "addictive." Recent evidence suggests rather that the parties apparently sampled arbitration, found they didn't like the results and reverted to conventional bargaining. (Butler & Ehrenberg, 1981; Champlin & Bognanno, 1985).

Individual Level Research

Martin (1986) found nonprofessional public school employee union members could be divided into "militant" and "faithful union participant" groups on the basis of potential strike issues. Significantly greater willingness to strike for high (24%) wage increases was found among younger racial minority members. Striking for a 10% wage increase would be supported by those with positive attitudes toward the union and a propensity for endorsing violence and be negatively predicted by personal hardship. Strikes to support the union were related positively to present hourly pay, support from other community sectors, attitude toward the union, and perceptions of internal pay inequity.

A major difficulty in identifying arbitrator decision-making criteria is that the economic and legal situations in which they are involved vary substantially. Bazerman and Farber (1985; Bazerman, 1985) sent 25 simulated final offer arbitration cases to members of the National Academy of Arbitrators to make awards. Results indicated that they seldom "split the difference." Arbitrators weighed facts more heavily than positions of the parties, paying more attention to management "facts" as awards were closer to management offers. Most arbitrators displayed high internal consistency in their decision criteria, but differences emerged between them. The most common norm appeared to be one of "anchored equity" in which wages were adjusted by the average negotiated increase in the industry as presented in the cases.

CONTRACT ADMINISTRATION

Previous research has concentrated on rights arbitration[4] issues and procedures. Studies of intracontract disputes have tended to be descriptive; however, process models have been proposed and tested recently.

---

3. A variation of interest arbitration in which the third party *must* select one of the parties' offers on either an issue-by-issue or total contract basis.

4. Third party determination regarding whether an action was permitted by the negotiated contract.

Firm-Local Union Level Research

It has been argued that the parties' approach to arbitration has become excessively formal, inhibiting the parties in arriving at their own solutions. Deitsch and Dilts (1986) found that pre-arbitral settlements occur more often for cases scheduled for arbitration when the parties are not represented by outside attorneys, even when case complexity is held constant.

Ichniowski (1986) examined grievance rate histories in several mills of paper manufacturer and found that productivity and profitability were negatively related to grievances. Their deleteriousness increases markedly in low profit margin operations.

Individual Level Research

Labig and Helburn (1986) developed and tested a model to identify union and management policy influences on initiating formal grievances. Using a sample of management and union representatives from 60 Texas public sector bargaining units, they found that performance and disciplinary standards indirectly encouraged the union to grieve and directly influenced formal grievances. Interunion rivalry increased grievance rates. Positive management attitudes and willingness to compromise during the process were both negatively related to formal grievances; however, management consultation with the union increased rates. Economic conditions had no effect.

Knight (1986) proposed a model of the effects of grievance processing over time. Outputs include withdrawals, settlements, and arbitral decisions. Feedback through settlements and decisions is presumed to assist subsequent resolution through its value as a precedent. Results suggested that only management uses feedback to assist in subsequent positions and that more formal dispositions are used as precedents the higher the level of settlement. References to earlier decisions were made most often in discipline and work assignment cases, which were also the most frequent types of grievances.

LABOR ORGANIZATIONS AND THEIR ENVIRONMENT

The AFL-CIO has recently undertaken a thorough reexamination of its goals and methods (Medoff, 1985). Several mergers have occurred among national unions as the industries in which they were powers have shrunk. Recent research has focused on how unions attempt to influence the political environment. Masters and Delaney (1984, 1985) found that the size of political action committee (PAC) allocations by national unions to federal candidates between 1978 and 1982 was higher among medium-sized unions with a propensity to strike in the primary industry they organized; and inversely related to heterogeneity in representation; PAC contributions made by employers in the industry; and primary representation in mining, construction, agriculture, manufacturing, service, or the public sector. The number of lobbyists employed is related to the degree of democracy within the union.

At the federal level, political and lobbying activity by unions has been only moderately successful. Federal employee unions have not coordinated their activities well, and their wage demands have uniformly been denied as Congress has deferred to administration recommendations (Masters, 1985).

MEMBER ATTITUDES AND PARTICIPATION IN UNION ACTIVITIES

Earlier surveys generally found low participation by most members and concluded that they were disinterested as long as the union fulfilled its instrumental role in gaining better employment conditions. Recent research suggests dissatisfaction with the union was related in some circumstances with decreased participation. Chacko (1985) found that voting for or election to union office was predicted by dissatisfaction with the union, perceived responsiveness of the union to member concerns, perceived performance of the union in obtaining intrinsic benefits, and youth. Attendance at meetings was predicted by dissatisfaction, perceived union responsiveness, perceived union power, and member education level. Grievance filters were predicted by perceived nonresponsiveness of the union to its members.

McShane (1986) found the perceived value of a union local to its members was predicted by seniority and lower education. Willingness to participate in union activities was predicted by low job involvement, high perceived value of the union, and interest in union business. Actual participation was predicted by permanent employment status, higher education levels, higher seniority, and willingness to participate.

Commitment to the union and the employer has been demonstrated to be independent. Variation in dual commitment has been found to be related to both unit-level and individual differences (Angle & Perry, 1986; Fukami & Larson, 1984). Martin, Magenau, and Peterson (1986) examined commitment among a group of stewards and found dual commitment, but higher commitment to the union than the employer. Commitment to the employer was predicted by tenure; perceptions of immobility, supervisor support, promotion opportunities, and influence on the employer; and employment in smaller establishments. Union commitment was related to perceived immobility, belief that the union should use grievances to punish the employer, involvement in union activities and decision making, and larger establishments. High dual commitment was predicted by involvement in union decision making, perceived immobility and influence on the employer, being a woman, and being unskilled. Unilateral commitment to the union was predicted by low economic outcomes, perceived involvement in the union, and lack of support from the employer.

THE EFFECTS OF LAWS AND REGULATIONS

Under federal labor law, the NLRB investigates and rules on ULP charges raised by employers, employees, and unions in most private sector industries. Recently, some union leaders have called for the abolition of the labor acts and a return to an unregulated labor-management relations environment, charging that the NLRB's current approach to their enforcement favors management.

Societal Level Research

NLRB members appointed by a president of the same political party were 20% less likely than members of a different political party to decide in favor of unions if the members were Republicans and 12 percent more likely if they were Democrats (Cooke & Gautschi, 1982). The Taft-Hartley Act's paradoxical emphasis on both collective bargaining and individual rights allows liberal and conservative boards to construe the act in contrary fashions (Gross, 1985).

SUMMARY AND IMPLICATIONS

Industrial relations have changed profoundly in this decade (cf. Kochan, Katz, & McKersie, 1986). Although this review focused on unionized employees, corollary changes have taken place in nonunion employment. For practitioners, some important conclusions can be drawn from this review.

Employers have adapted in the short run to changing competitive conditions through lower wages and fewer permanent employees. Labor has countered by attempting to enhance employment security. Vehicles to achieve this have included restrictions on subcontracting, between-facility transfer rights, and retraining programs. Firms appear to treat unionized plants as cancers. Investment in new equipment is restricted or ended. New facilities are established where unions are believed to be abhorred.

Changes in employment structure in the U.S. have profound implications for future labor relations. Although manufacturing is shrinking, the service sector is growing rapidly. Service jobs differ from manufacturing occupations in that work cannot be separated presently from the worker. Ultimately, advice, care, and delivery functions must be performed by individuals. Services are not patentable, and their production processes are transferrable across firms. Thus, future competitiveness will require more attention to "voice" as compared to "exit" programs. Primary investments will shift from physical to human capital as service industries increase in importance and more attention in both union and nonunion situations will be paid to training and development.

Locational factors that employers use to avoid unions account for relatively little variation in organizing outcomes at the election unit level. Wage differences between employers is not the primary pre-organizing concern of employees. Rather, they are impelled to organize by a perception that a union is required to improve employment conditions. Groups traditionally less likely to organize have increased recently their relative organizing activity.

Although the costs of organizing service employees have been great relative to unit size, new initiatives such as associate membership, and the vulnerability of service employers to employee turnover where proprietary services are vended, increase the attention that will be paid to employee relations through earlier collective bargaining or personnel management initiatives.

Implications for Research

This review has adopted a process approach in which organizing precedes negotiation, impasse resolution, and contract administration. It examined research in which the dependent variable was measured at the societal, industrial, employing organizational, or individual level. Not all processes are covered at each unit of analysis level. Table 1 shows the coverage.

In the U.S., the representation of employees by labor unions as a proportion of the labor force reached its high point in 1956. At that point, the CIO was just over 20 years old. Many industries were highly organized. The greater the degree of organization and the more concentrated the industry, the easier the economic costs of collective bargaining gains could be externalized to consumers. Employers might be expected to prefer bargaining relationships which decreased the effects of competition and unions would prefer situations in which employers had a lower motivation to resist wage and benefit increases. Over this period a number of devices to reduce competition were introduced, including multiemployer bargaining, industry-wide bargaining, and coordinated bargaining.

Ross (1948) suggested that bargaining outcomes are influenced by "orbits of coercive comparison" in which subsequent settlements are influenced by an earlier pattern-setter. For example, the steel or auto settlements would strongly influence those organizations that supply or distribute to these industries. Unions might be expected to choose favorable settlements as those they wish to emulate in their contract demands and negotiations. Their ability to gain these settlements depends on their bargaining power vis-à-vis the employer. Kochan, Katz, and McKersie (1986) indicate that pattern settlements are a thing of the past, however, with concessions and local level contracts increasingly negotiated.

Researchers may want to examine bargaining outcomes more closely though. It may be possible that we are simply moving from a period in which union-preferred patterns were negotiated, externalizing costs to consumers, and into a period in which employers are externalizing cost differences to the employees. One might study bargaining to determine the economic events and/or seminal bargains around which other bargains tend to revolve. One might apply catastrophe modeling, time series, and/or cluster analytic techniques in this exploration.

Substantially more research on the role of information and public policy on unionization and bargaining outcomes is necessary. Literature on bluffing in negotiations suggests that asymmetric demands result from greater management economic information (Bowlby & Schriver, 1979). The implementation of public policy clearly influences both management and union behavior in the organizing and negotiating arenas. Simulations could be run to estimate the effects of various detection/penalty levels for rule violations on collective bargaining outcomes.

Necessary are longitudinal studies of how employee groups that are soon to be organized or already are organized coalesce around a position on an issue or contract. How, except by measuring demographic variables, can the "median voter" be determined? This type of research may be very helpful in aggregating results from individual level studies because particular difficulties exist in arguing the external validity of individual level results, especially as collective bargaining outcomes are determined at a bargaining level unit of analysis. Similarities or differences between median voters could be used to predict conflict in national level bargaining and/or national union elections. At the industrial and societal level, differences in between-unit and industry variation should lead to more conflicts in collective bargaining situations, whereas differences in within-unit variation should increase conflict in nonunion organizations because the implicit contract will fit the noncollective needs of individuals less well.

Finally, research to examine the effects of negotiation processes and outcomes on subsequent contract administration is needed. Some research has been done linking the two with contract administration as the independent variable (Meyer, 1986), but little has examined it as a dependent variable. More time series research needs to be done to identify the thresholds of conflict in negotiations resulting from the past relationships between the parties.

REFERENCES

Abowd, J. S., & Farber, H. S. (1983). Job queues and the union status of workers. *Industrial and Labor Relations Review, 36,* 354–367.

Abraham, K. G., & Medoff, J. L. (1984). Length of service and layoffs in union and nonunion work groups. *Industrial and Labor Relations Review, 38,* 87–97.

Ahlburg, D. A., & Dworkin, J. B. (1984). The influence of macroeconomic variables on the probability of union decertification. *Journal of Labor Research, 5,* 13–28.

Allen, R. E., & Keaveny, T. J. (1981). Correlates of university faculty interest in unionization: A replication and extension. *Journal of Applied Psychology, 66,* 582–588.

Allen, S. G. (1984). Trade unions, absenteeism, and exit-voice. *Industrial and Labor Relations Review, 37,* 331–345.

Allen, S. G. (1986a). The effect of unionism on productivity in privately and publicly owned hospitals and nursing homes. *Journal of Labor Research, 7,* 59–68.

Allen, S. G. (1986b). Unionization and productivity in office building and school construction. *Industrial and Labor Relations Review, 39,* 187–201.

Angle, H. L., & Perry, J. L. (1986). Dual commitment and labor-management climates. *Academy of Management Journal, 29,* 31–50.

Bacharach, S. B., & Lawler, E. J. (1981). *Bargaining: Power, tactics, and outcomes.* San Francisco: Jossey-Bass.

Bazerman, M. H. (1985). Norms of distributive justice in interest arbitration. *Industrial and Labor Relations Review, 38,* 558–570.

Bazerman, M. H., & Farber, H. S. (1985). Arbitrator decision making: When are final offers important? *Industrial and Labor Relations Review, 39,* 76–89.

Becker, B. E., & Olson, C. A. (1986). The impact of strikes on shareholder equity. *Industrial and Labor Relations Review, 39,* 425–438.

Berger, C. J., Olson, C. A., & Boudreau. J. W. (1983). Effects of unions on job satisfaction: The role of work related values and perceived rewards. *Organizational Behavior and Human Performance, 31,* 289–324.

Block, R. N. (1980). Union organizing and the allocation of union resources. *Industrial and Labor Relations Review, 33,* 110–130.

Bowlby, R. C., & Schriver, W. R. (1979). Bluffing and the 'split-the-difference' theory of wage bargaining. *Industrial & Labor Relations Review, 32,* 161–171.

Butler, R. J., & Ehrenberg, R. G. (1981). Estimating the narcotic effect of public sector impasse procedures. *Industrial & Labor Relations Review, 35,* 3–20.

Byrne, D. M., & King, R. H. (1986). Wildcat strikes in U.S. manufacturing, 1960–1977. *Journal of Labor Research, 7,* 387–401.

Capelli, P. (1985). Plant-level concession bargaining. *Industrial and Labor Relations Review, 39,* 90–104.

Chacko, T. I. (1985). Member participation in union activities: Perceptions of union priorities, performance, and satisfaction. *Journal of Labor Research, 6,* 363–373.

Champlin, F. C., & Bognanno, M. F. (1985). "Chilling" under arbitration and mixed strike-arbitration regimes. *Journal of Labor Research, 6,* 375–387.

Commons, J. R. (1934). *Institutional Economics: Its*

Place in the Political Economy. New York: Macmillan.

Cooke, W. N. (1983). Determinants of the outcomes of union certification elections. *Industrial and Labor Relations Review, 37,* 402–414.

Cooke, W. N. (1984). The failure to negotiate first contracts: Determinants and policy implications. *Industrial and Labor Relations Review, 38,* 163–178.

Cooke, W. N., & Gautschi, F. H. III (1982). Political bias in NLRB unfair labor practices decisions. *Industrial and Labor Relations Review, 36,* 539–549.

Cousineau, J.-M., & Lacroix, R. (1986). Imperfect information and strikes: An analysis of Canadian experience, 1967–82. *Industrial and Labor Relations Review, 39,* 377–387.

Cunningham, J. S., & Donovan, E. (1986). Patterns of union membership and relative wages. *Journal of Labor Research, 7,* 127–144.

Deitsch, C. R., & Dilts, D. A. (1986). Factors affecting pre-arbitral settlement of rights disputes: Predicting the methods of rights dispute resolution. *Journal of Labor Research, 7,* 69–78.

Dickens, W. T. (1983). The effect of company campaigns on certification elections: *Law and Reality* once again. *Industrial and Labor Relations Review, 36,* 560–575.

Dickens, W. T., & Leonard, J. S. (1985). Accounting for the decline in union membership, 1950–1980. *Industrial and Labor Relations Review, 38,* 323–334.

Dunlop, J. T. (1958). *Industrial Relations Systems*. New York: Holt, Rinehart & Winston.

Eberts, R. W. (1984). Union effects on teacher productivity. *Industrial and Labor Relations Review, 37,* 346–358.

Feuille, P., & Delaney, J. T. (1986). Collective bargaining, interest arbitration, and police salaries. *Industrial and Labor Relations Review, 39,* 228–240.

Fiorito, J., & Greer, C. R. (1986). Gender differences in union membership, preferences, and beliefs. *Journal of Labor Research, 7,* 145–164.

Freeman, R. B. (1980). The effect of unionism on worker attachment to firms. *Journal of Labor Research, 1,* 29–61.

Freeman, R. B. (1981). The effect of unionism on fringe benefits. *Industrial and Labor Relations Review, 34,* 489–509.

Freeman, R. B. (1982). Union wage practices and wage dispersion within establishments. *Industrial and Labor Relations Review, 36,* 3–21.

Freeman, R. B. (1986). In search of union wage concessions in standard data sets. *Industrial Relations, 25,* 131–145.

Freeman, R. B., & Medoff, J. L. (1984). *What Do Unions Do?* New York: Basic Books.

Fukami, C. V., & Larson, E. W. (1984). Commitment to company and union: Parallel models. *Journal of Applied Psychology, 69,* 367–371.

Getman, J. G., Goldberg, S. B., & Herman, J. B. (1976). *Union Representation Elections: Law and Reality*. New York: Russell Sage Foundation.

Gramm, C. L. (1986). The determinants of strike incidence and severity: A micro-level study. *Industrial and Labor Relations Review, 39,* 361–376.

Gross, J. A. (1985). Conflicting statutory purposes: Another look at fifty years of NLRB law making. *Industrial and Labor Relations Review, 39,* 7–18.

Hammer, T. H., & Berman, M. (1981). The role of noneconomic factors in faculty union voting. *Journal of Applied Psychology, 66,* 415–421.

Heneman, H. G., Jr. (1969). Toward a general conceptual system of industrial relations. In G. Somers (Ed.). *Essays in industrial relations theory* (pp. 1–25). Ames, IA: Iowa State University Press.

Heneman, H. G. III, & Sandver, M. H. (1981). Union growth through the election process. *Industrial Relations, 20,* 109–116.

Hills, S. M. (1985). The attitudes of union and nonunion male workers toward union representation. *Industrial and Labor Relations Review, 38,* 179–194.

Hunt, J. C., & White, R. A. (1985). The effects of management practices on union election returns. *Journal of Labor Research, 6,* 389–403.

Ichniowski, C. (1986). The effects of grievance activity on productivity. *Industrial and Labor Relations Review, 40,* 75–89.

Jacoby, S. M., & Mitchell, D. J. B. (1984). Employer preferences for long-term union contracts. *Journal of Labor Research, 5,* 215–228.

Jacoby, S. M., & Mitchell, D. J. B. (1986). Management attitudes toward two-tier pay plans. *Journal of Labor Research, 7,* 221–237.

Kahn, L. M. (1984). The effect of collective bargaining on production technique: A theoretical analysis. *Journal of Labor Research, 5,* 1–12.

Katz, H. C., Kochan, T. A., & Gobeille, K. R. (1983). Industrial relations performance, economic performance, and QWL programs: An interplant analysis. *Industrial & Labor Relations Review, 37,* 3–17.

Kaufman, B. E. (1983). The determinants of strikes

over time and across industries. *Journal of Labor Research, 3,* 159–175.

Kaufman, R. T., & Woglom, G. (1986). The degree of indexation in major U.S. union contracts. *Industrial and Labor Relations Review, 39,* 439–448.

Kleiner, M. M. (1984). Unionism and employer discrimination: Analysis of 8(a)(3) violations. *Industrial Relations, 23,* 234–243.

Knight, T. R. (1986). Feedback and grievance resolution. *Industrial and Labor Relations Review, 39,* 585–598.

Kochan, T. A. (1980). *Collective bargaining and industrial relations.* Homewood, IL: Irwin.

Kochan, T. A., Katz, H. C., & McKersie, R. B. (1986). *The transformation of American industrial relations.* New York: Basic Books.

Kochan, T. A., McKersie, R. B., & Chalykoff, J. (1986). The effects of corporate strategy and workplace innovations on union representation. *Industrial and Labor Relations Review, 39,* 487–501.

Kokkelenberg, E. C., & Sockell, D. R. (1985). Union membership in the United States, 1973–1981. *Industrial and Labor Relations Review, 38,* 497–543.

Labig, C. E., Jr., & Helburn, I. B. (1986). Union and management policy influences on grievance initiation. *Journal of Labor Research, 7,* 269–284.

Lawler, J. J. (1981). Labor-management consultants in union organizing campaigns: Do they make a difference? *Proceedings of the Industrial Relations Research Association, 34,* 374–380.

Lawler, J. J. (1984). The influence of management consultants on the outcome of union certification elections. *Industrial and Labor Relations Review, 38,* 38–51.

Leap, T. L., & Grigsby, D. W. (1986). A conceptualization of collective bargaining power. *Industrial and Labor Relations Review, 39,* 202–213.

Leigh, J. P. (1984). A bargaining model and empirical analysis of strike activity across industries. *Journal of Labor Research, 5,* 127–137.

Leonard, J. S. (1985). The effect of unions on the employment of blacks, Hispanics, and women. *Industrial and Labor Relations Review, 39,* 115–132.

Maki, D. R. (1986). The effect of the cost of strikes on the volume of strike activity. *Industrial and Labor Relations Review, 39,* 552–563.

Martin, J. E. (1986). Predictors of individual propensity to strike. *Industrial and Labor Relations Review, 39,* 214–227.

Martin, J. E., Magenau, J. M., & Peterson, M. F. (1986). Variables related to patterns of union stewards' commitment. *Journal of Labor Research, 7,* 323–336.

Masters, M. F. (1985). Federal employee unions and political action. *Industrial and Labor Relations Review, 38,* 612–628.

Masters, M. F., & Delaney, J. T. (1984). Interunion variation in congressional campaign support. *Industrial Relations, 23,* 410–416.

Masters, M. F., & Delaney, J. T. (1985). The causes of union political involvement: A longitudinal analysis. *Journal of Labor Research, 6,* 341–362.

McShane, S. L. (1986). A path analysis of participation in union administration. *Industrial Relations, 25,* 72–80.

Medoff, J. L. (1985). *The public image of American labor.* Washington: AFL-CIO.

Meyer, D. G. (1986). *An expanded study of the grievance procedure: Problem creation, channeling, and resolution in a unionized workplace.* Unpublished doctoral dissertation, University of Michigan, Ann Arbor.

Moore, W. J., Newman, R. J., & Cunningham, J. (1985). The effect of the extent of unionism on union and nonunion wages. *Journal of Labor Research, 6,* 21–44.

Murrmann, K. F., & Porter, A. A. (1982). Employer campaign tactics and NLRB election outcomes: Some preliminary evidence. *Proceedings of the Industrial Relations Research Association, 35,* 67–72.

Neumann, G. R. (1980). The predictability of strikes: Evidence from the stockmarket. *Industrial & Labor Relations Review, 33,* 525–535.

Neumann, G. R., & Reder, M. W. (1984). Output and strike activity in U.S. manufacturing: How large are the losses? *Industrial and Labor Relations Review, 37,* 197–211.

Norsworthy, J. R., & Zabala, C. A. (1985). Worker attitudes, worker behavior, and productivity in the U.S. automobile industry, 1959–1976. *Industrial and Labor Relations Review, 38,* 544–557.

Olson, C. A. (1984). The role of rescheduled school days in teacher strikes. *Industrial and Labor Relations Review, 37,* 515–528.

Olson, C. A. (1986). Strikes, strike penalties, and arbitration in six states. *Industrial and Labor Relations Review, 39,* 539–551.

Olson, C. A., & Berger, C. J. (1983). The relationship between seniority, ability, and the promotion of union and nonunion workers. In D. B. Lipsky, & J. M. Douglas (Eds.). *Advances in Industrial and Labor Relations* (pp. 91–129). Greenwich, CT: JAI Press.

Podgursky, M. (1986). Unions, establishment size, and intra-industry threat effects. *Industrial and Labor Relations Review, 39,* 277–284.

Ross, A. M. (1948). *Trade union wage policy.* Berkeley, CA: Institute of Industrial Relations, University of California.

Rosse, J. G., Keaveny, T. A., & Fossum, J. A. (1986). *Predicting union election outcomes: The role of job attitudes, union attitudes, and coworker preferences.* Unpublished manuscript, College of Business and Administration, University of Colorado, Boulder.

Saltzman, G. M. (1985). Bargaining laws as a cause and consequence of the growth of teacher unionism. *Industrial and Labor Relations Review, 38,* 335–351.

Sandver, M. H. (1982). South-nonsouth differentials in National Labor Relations Board certification election outcomes. *Journal of Labor Research, 3,* 13–30.

Shirom, A. (1982). Strike characteristics as determinants of strike settlements: A chief negotiator's viewpoint. *Journal of Applied Psychology, 67,* 42–52.

Strauss, G., & Feuille, P. (1978). IR research: A critical analysis. *Industrial Relations, 17,* 259–277.

Voos, P. B. (1983). Union organizing: Costs and benefits. *Industrial and Labor Relations Review, 36,* 576–591.

Voos, P. B. (1984). Trends in union organizing expenditures, 1953–1977. *Industrial and Labor Relations Review, 38,* 52–63.

Vroman, W. (1985). Cost-of-living escalators and price-wage linkages in the U.S. economy. *Industrial and Labor Relations Review, 38,* 225–235.

Walker, J. M., & Lawler, J. J. (1986). Union campaign activities and voter preferences. *Journal of Labor Research, 7,* 19–40.

Wheeler, H. N. (1985). *Industrial conflict: An integrative theory.* Columbia, SC: University of South Carolina Press.

White, M. D. (1982). The intra-unit wage structure and unions: A median voter model. *Industrial and Labor Relations Review, 35,* 565–577.

Zalesny, M. D. (1985). Comparison of economic and noneconomic factors in predicting faculty vote preference in a union presentation election. *Journal of Applied Psychology, 70,* 243–256.

John A. Fossum is in the Industrial Relations Center, University of Minnesota, Minneapolis. The author wishes to thank Alison Barber for her research assistance and three referees for their helpful comments.

Employee Fitness Programs: Their Impact on the Employee and the Organization
Loren E. Falkenberg

More and more companies either are planning or have developed physical fitness programs for their employees. In Canada approximately 1,000 companies are involved in employee fitness, and in the U.S. it is estimated that 50,000 business firms promote physical activity (Cox, 1984; Driver & Ratliff, 1982). The scope of employee fitness programs ranges from company-paid memberships at private fitness clubs to complete on-site facilities; these programs cost from two thousand dollars to millions. Organizations that support these programs consider them an inexpensive benefit that produces the following returns: (a) increased ability to attract competent employees; (b) improved attitudes and loyalty; (c) a reflection of the firm's concern for the nonwork aspects of the employees' lives; and (d) indirectly, increased productivity (Howard and Mikalachki, 1979).

Three lines of reasoning underlie these

Source: Loren E. Falkenberg, "Employee Fitness Programs: Their Impact on the Employee and the Organization," *Academy of Management Review,* 1987, pp. 511–522. Reprinted by permission.

beliefs. First is the assumption that fitness centers are attractive to employees. It is estimated that 20 percent of the North American population exercises intensely and regularly enough to produce cardiovascular fitness, while another 40 percent exercises enough to receive at least some benefit (Stephens, Jacobs, & White, 1985). As more individuals recognize the benefits of exercise, the ability to do so during the work day will become more important; thus, employee fitness centers will reflect the concern an organization has for its employees. Employee fitness programs also are viewed as a mechanism for recruiting and retaining employees (Debats, 1981). The major increase in participation in fitness programs has occurred among young, well-educated members of the higher socioeconomic groups (Dishman, Sallis, & Orenstein, 1985; Stephens et al., 1985); thus, fitness programs may be important in hiring and retaining those individuals companies find most desirable.

A second rationale is that employee fitness programs may reduce the impact of stress. Corporations are becoming more concerned with stress since it has been perceived that high stress levels result in poorer work performance, lower productivity, higher turnover, absenteeism, and accidents (Galt, 1985). Employee fitness programs are thought to reduce the impact of stress by improving the health of the employees through higher fitness levels (Driver & Ratliff, 1982), and improved health from fewer stress symptoms has been assumed to reduce absenteeism (Perks, 1985).

The third line of reasoning is indirectly related to the first two; that is, increasing the fitness level of employees should improve productivity. The latter is achieved in part through reduced absenteeism and turnover. Also, it is assumed that the increased capacity for physical work from improved fitness levels will transfer to an ability to work harder and longer in the office. This transfer from physical to mental capacity is expected to improve an individual's ability to maintain higher levels of concentration and mental effort.

Since the value of implementing fitness programs has not yet been established, these large investments are being made on the basis of limited research. The experimental and applied research on physical exercise and work-related variables suffers from poor design and methodology; therefore, results are inconclusive (Howard & Mikalachki, 1979; Hughes, 1984). The research used to support the models primarily has been taken from physical fitness research; no attempts have been made to integrate related variables from the stress, cognitive processes, and organizational behavior research domains. This lack of appropriately designed research has limited the development of scientifically based models upon which a focused research pattern can proceed: Without reliable results, many fitness programs may be based on erroneous assumptions, leading to poorly designed programs and undesired outcomes.

EXERCISE AND THE INDIVIDUAL

Relationship Between Stress and Exercise

Exercise has been viewed as a coping mechanism which may be employed prior to or during a stressful situation (Gal & Lazarus, 1975; Mobily, 1982). As a coping mechanism it is theorized to reduce the physiological consequences of stressful situations through one of three actions. The first action is that long-term aerobic exercise may decrease the level of physiological arousal that normally occurs during stressful situations. The physiological response to stressful situations involves increased muscle tension, increased respiration rate, sympathetic stimulation of sweating, increased heart rate, dilation of blood vessels and coronaries of the heart, and release of glucose by the liver. The physiological changes that develop with long-term aerobic exercise occur in the same systems that are activated during a physiological/psychological stressful situation. For any given physical workload, more physically fit individuals demonstrate less muscular activity, slower respiration, a lower resting heart rate, and less accumulation of the acid by-products of exercise (Ledwidge, 1980). Thus, physical training may help to reduce extreme activation both during physical activity and stressful situations (Michael, 1957; Selye, 1975; Terjung, 1979).

Both exercise and reactions to physiological/psychological stressors also involve increased secretion of catecholamines. Edington and Edgerton (1976) hypothesized that extending the capacity of the adrenal medulla to generate catecholamines through exercise may help to reduce the experience of stress. Specifically, it appears that an increased hormonal response capacity is associated with a calmer, more stress tolerant human temperament (Dienstbier et al., 1981). In support of this hypothesis, Frankenhaeuser (1979) found that more emotionally stable and conservative school children demonstrated higher levels of catecholamines in response to classroom challenges than less emotionally stable classmates.

The second action is that aerobic or anaerobic exercise during a stressful event may reduce the physiological severity of the immediate stress response. Both during or immediately after stress, exercise will metabolize the fatty acids released into the blood stream; in general, it will discharge the physical excitation built up in a reaction to a stressor (Everly & Rosenfield, 1981). Although this potential action has not received as much attention as the first, it may play a more critical role in reducing the negative consequences of stress. The physiological changes that occur during stressful situations bring about a rapid mobilization of energy, that in previous time periods would have allowed an individual to respond to the threat physically. Today, however, most stressful situations do not involve a physical response; thus, an individual under stress mobilizes his/her system for physical effort, but does not expend the built-up energy. Physical exercise may be a vehicle by which the mobilized energy either can be discharged or, at least, can be more evenly dispersed among body systems (Selye, 1975).

The third action is that either after or during a stressful experience, exercise (aerobic or anaerobic) may bring about a state of relaxation. This hypothesis is based on a study by deVries and Adams (1972) which compared the effects tranquilizers and exercise had on anxiety. They found that if an individual engaged in 15 minutes of walking, at a heart rate of 100 beats per minute, there was a significant decrease in the electromyographic activity in the muscles (their measure of anxiety) while tranquilizers did not appear to have an effect on anxiety/tension.

Relationship Between Mental Health and Exercise

It appears that the effects of physical exercise on mental health are dependent on the duration of participation. Long-term participation has been found to change personality traits, while short-term participation affects mood states (Folkins, Lynch, & Gardner, 1972; Lichtman & Poser, 1983; Young & Ismail, 1977). Much of the research, though, has been limited by poorly designed methodologies. In their review, Folkins and Sime (1981) found that only 15 percent of the studies qualified as true experiments, and most were on clinical populations.

The impact that long-term exercise has on personality traits was examined by Young and Ismail, who tested subjects during a four-year period (Ismail & Young, 1973, 1976; Young & Ismail, 1976a, 1976b, 1977). Their subjects were classified according to exercise converts (those who did not exercise prior to the formal program, but continued after the program), and long-term exercisers (those who regularly exercised prior to the formal program). In the initial testing, prior to the formal exercise program, the exercise converts demonstrated a more conservative temperament than the long-term exercisers; however, this difference ceased after four years, with the exercise converts demonstrating a less extreme score. In addition, those who were more physically fit demonstrated greater emotional stability and security than those who were less physically fit.

Also, long-term exercise has been found to be associated with decreases in trait (general disposition across situations) depression and anxiety. Kavanagh and Shephard (1973) found significant decreases in depression in subjects who continued to exercise four years after completing a formal exercise program. In another study, highly trained (physically fit) individuals had significantly lower levels of anxiety and depression than nontrained subjects (Tharp & Schlegelmich, 1977). Testing on a short-term orientation of five or six months, however, did not produce differences in anxiety levels (Morgan & Pollock, 1978; Stern & Cleary, 1982).

Studies examining state (situational experiences) depression and anxiety levels before and after exercise have produced equivocal results, both within studies as well as across studies. In two of the studies, subjects reported the exercise sessions to be exhilarating; however, the state depression and anxiety measures did not differ prior to or after the exercise sessions (Bahkre & Morgan, 1978; Morgan, Roberts, & Feinerman, 1971). Part of the inconsistency in results between studies may be related to the type of exercise used in the studies. After reviewing a series of studies, Dishman (1982) concluded that reductions in state anxiety are associated most consistently with jogging and/or vigorous exercise.

When highly trained subjects were tested, levels of anxiety and depression were found to be lower after exercise periods (Greenberg, cited in Lichtman & Poser, 1983; Dienstbier et al., 1981). In particular, Dienstbier et al. compared highly trained subjects' reactions to stressors on exercise and nonexercise days; they found subjects demonstrated lower anxiety scores on exercise days. These results indicated that even when subjects are highly trained, physical exercise can further reduce anxiety levels.

It has been noted that the level of fitness, at least in short-term measures of mood, may not be as important as engaging in the physical activity itself (Dishman, 1982; Heaps, 1978; Killip, 1985). Killip (1985) observed that engaging in physical exercise (aerobic or anaerobic) may be perceived as a fitness endeavor and it may stimulate positive feelings about one's self: Movement may bring about feelings of muscular endurance and increased physiological arousal. In support of this premise, Killip found a stronger relationship between physical activity level, rather than cardiovascular fitness, and psychological variables. Lichtman and Poser's (1983) results also support this premise: Subjects who had engaged in physical activity, regardless of their fitness level, felt more exhilarated and relaxed than subjects who participated in a hobby class.

Relationships Among Exercise, Cognitive Functioning, and Performance

Generally, it is assumed that productivity will increase when individuals are involved in fitness programs, because more physically fit individuals are capable of working harder on cognitive tasks. However, the research that has examined the potential improvements of cognitive functioning through exercise has produced mixed results. This inconsistency may be related to at least three factors: (a) many experiments were poorly designed; (b) different definitions of fitness were employed, for example, physiological measures of fitness versus activity inventories; and (c) different dependent variables were used, such as the impact of long-term physical exercise versus activity immediately prior to or during a cognitive task.

Impact of fitness on performance The rationale for fitness affecting performance stems from the interaction between the state of the physiological system and the specific task requirements. Specifically, the physiological arousal of a more fit individual is substantially less, for a given physical workload, than that of a less fit individual. Transferring this to mental work, the physiological arousal of a more fit individual should be substantially less for a given cognitive load. It is generally accepted that complex motor and/or cognitive tasks are best performed under low arousal levels. Thus, a more physically fit person should be able to perform better on complex mental tasks, particularly when working under stressful conditions (Weingarten, 1973).

This theory has been investigated through two different research designs. One design tested subjects prior to and immediately after physical exercise under the assumption that short-term physical activity should improve an individual's arousal levels in relation to the work being performed. Zuercher (1965) examined performance on a vigilance task after subjects engaged in either stretching exercises or a conversation, during a five-minute break: He found that either exercise or conversation improved performance. Lichtman and Poser (1983) required subjects to complete a demanding cognitive task prior to and after either vigorous exercise or a hobby class. These researchers found that only exercise produced a significant improvement in the performance on the cognitive task.

A variation of the above methodology has been to manipulate both the fitness level of the subject and the activity (rest or varying intensities of exercise) performed prior to the criterion task. The rationale behind this variation is that exercise prior to the task acts as a stressor, and the more physically fit individual should be better able to perform a cognitive task after a stressor. Butler (1969) and Gutin (1966) found a positive relationship between the degree of improvement in physical fitness and the degree of improvement in ability to perform complex mental tasks. However, neither investigator found a difference in performance between subjects who had rested and those who had engaged in physical exercise prior to the mental task. Weingarten (1973), and Gutin and DiGennaro (1968) found that differences between trained (fit) and untrained groups occurred after vigorous exercise but did not appear under more relaxed conditions. The combined results of these studies suggest that physical fitness becomes a factor only under "more stressful" conditions, with more physically fit individuals performing better after a stressful condition (vigorous exercise).

Impact of fitness on cognitive functioning
Studies designed to test the effects of physical fitness on cognitive functioning manipulated fitness levels but not activity prior to the test periods. The rationale for this design is that more physically fit individuals should perform better on demanding cognitive tasks (Cox, Evans, & Jamieson, 1979; Hollander & Seraganian, 1984; Keller & Seraganian, 1984; Sinyor, Schwartz, Peronnet, Brisson, & Seraganian, 1983). Although these studies did not find a difference in cognitive performance between fit and less fit subjects, they did indicate that the fit subjects recovered faster from cognitive work. Specifically, Keller and Seraganian (1984) found that as fitness level improved there was a corresponding faster recovery period.

One criticism of the reviewed studies is that the experimental conditions involved expending cognitive effort over a short time period, twenty minutes to one hour. Since during a normal workday individuals may be involved in demanding cognitive tasks for eight to ten hours, these experimental situations may not represent the typical cognitive workload. Two studies have examined the cost of doing mental work over a minimum eight-hour period. Frankenhaeuser and Johansson (1982) found that women who were engaged in attention-demanding but boring tasks (data entry) demonstrated more signs of psychological stress than women whose jobs required a variety of tasks. Rissler (cited in Frankenhaeuser & Johansson, 1982) found that a group of women who worked overtime for an extended period of time had higher adrenaline levels and heart rates in the evenings and expressed feelings of irritability and fatigue. Thus, there appears to be a gap in the literature, since many jobs require mental effort over eight-hour periods, but no research has analyzed the impact of physical exercise on cognitive effort extended over this type of time period.

EMPLOYEE FITNESS PROGRAMS AND WORK-RELATED FACTORS

Productivity

In all of the studies reviewed, subjects claimed they could work harder mentally and their work performance improved after participating in an employee fitness program (Durbeck et al., 1972; Heinzelman & Bagley, 1970; Rhodes & Dunwoody, 1980; Rossman, 1983; Yarvote, McDonagh, Goldman, & Zuckerman, 1974). Unfortunately, the majority of these studies used subjective comments, rather than objective measures, to determine improvements in productivity. In a more controlled study, Bernacki and Baun (1984) found a strong association ($Z = 2.47$, $p < .01$) between the proportion of individuals with above average performance and adherence to a fitness program.

Absenteeism

The only reviewed study to measure absenteeism objectively found that high level participants in a fitness program had a significantly lower rate of absenteeism (22 percent less) than either low level participants or nonparticipants (Cox, Shephard, & Corey, 1981; Shepard, Cox, and Corey, 1981). No explanation for the reduced absenteeism rate was provided.

It generally is assumed that absenteeism rates will drop with increased physical fitness levels because: (a) increased fitness levels lead to improved health, and (b) healthier employees are less likely to be absent. This assumption, however, only relates to absences due to medical reasons: yet, employees stay away from work for more reasons than simply health problems. Johns and Nicholson (1982) hypothesized that absence is a dynamic temporal behavior through which organizational members attempt to derive the most benefit from their allocation of work and nonwork time. Youngblood (1984) expanded this premise by suggesting that the degree of attachment to work and nonwork will affect the allocation of time to each. Given this hypothesis, employee fitness programs should reduce absences for individuals who: (a) place a higher value on participating in physical exercise (nonwork) than work, and (b) highly value both work and exercise. Those employees who place a higher value on physical exercise than on work derive more benefit by going to work because they also can exercise while there. Those employees who hold similar values for work and exercise would have more flexibility in allocating their time between two valued activities, thus deriving a higher benefit by going to work.

Another consequence of increased flexibility in scheduling may be a reduction in lateness. Although this potential outcome was not reviewed in the literature, there is an inherent logic to it. Employees who exercise before work, at lunch, or at sites other than the workplace, need extra travel time which either extends into their exercise time or their work time. By reducing travel time, it is more likely that employees will be punctual for work since they have more time to exercise.

This relationship between employee fitness programs and absenteeism is one of the more tenuous hypotheses. An alternative outcome to this relationship is that employees who place a higher value on exercise than work may choose not to come to work because of limited facilities and/or lack of adequate time to get a good workout. The presence of an exercise facility at the workplace may tempt the individual to spend more of the workday in the gym than desired.

Commitment and Turnover

Very little attention has been given to what impact employee fitness programs have on commitment and turnover. A negative relationship between commitment and turnover (high levels of commitment are associated with lower rates of turnover) has occurred consistently (Clegg, 1983; Michaels & Spector, 1982; Porter, Steers, Mowday, & Boulian, 1974; Steers, 1977). One factor which has been identified as influencing commitment is the extent to which an organization is seen as dependable in carrying out its commitment to employees. It is more likely that an organization will be perceived as concerned about employees' welfare if the organization supports an identifiable activity that is related more directly to employee goals rather than company goals. As noted in the introduction, given the rising participation in physical activity, employee exercise programs address the personal needs of many employees. Thus by supporting an employee fitness program, a company can demonstrate concern for employees' health and nonwork needs.

Employee fitness programs also may have a direct impact on turnover. Mobley, Griffeth, Hand, and Meglino (1979) suggested that it is not merely the visibility of alternatives that increases the intent to leave, but also it is the attraction of the alternatives. If there are similar opportunities in other companies, the differentiating factors in the decision process will not be the job characteristics, but the attractiveness of the working conditions. Individuals who participate in employee fitness programs may realize there are similar opportunities, but may be motivated to stay with their current company because of the attractiveness of the fitness program/facilities.

Only one study analyzed employee turnover (Cox, Shephard, & Corey, 1981). When comparisons were made between groups, both low and high adherents to fitness had significantly less turnover than nonparticipants; the participant turnover rate was 1.5 percent while the nonparticipant turnover rate was 15 percent. This finding is limited because Cox, Shephard, and Corey did not adequately control for long-term employees versus short-term employees.

Limitations of the Studies

With the exception of the Cox, Shephard, and Corey (1981) study, the major methodological weakness was the measurement of the psychological/emotional factors. The questionnaires employed did not control for reliability and validity. Single questions, rather than scales, were used in the analysis, preventing reliability analysis. The majority of the conclusions were based on comments by participants with little reference to comments by control subjects.

The problems associated with a lack of control for reliability and validity are highlighted in the Cox, Shephard, and Corey (1981) study. Job satisfaction was measured with a previously published scale (Job Description Index, Smith, Kendall, & Hulin, 1969), and it was found that this index did not differ before and after the program. After the program, however, the participants stated that they experienced greater feelings of satisfaction with work. The inconsistency of these results, even with the use of a published scale, demonstrates the problems involved in accurately interpreting responses to questionnaire items. Complicating this issue is the probability of a halo effect since the majority of the questionnaires were administered either during the program or immediately after it. Participants may have felt positively about the program and the attention they received from the researchers, and may have transferred these feelings to their comments.

Other limitations of these studies were the lack of control groups and the nonrandom assignment of subjects to control and experimental groups. Unfortunately, the lack of appropriate control groups, with the exception of the Cox, Shephard, and Corey study (1981), precludes the use of regression or analysis of variance techniques. Correlations and t-tests, which do not allow any inferences about cause and effect, were the only statistical techniques employed.

Although most of the identified studies were constrained by methodological limitations, they have produced similar results, giving some validity to their findings. It appears that participants of employee fitness programs felt these programs had a positive impact on their attitudes and work behaviors. Also, the results of the most controlled study indicate that an employee fitness program does reduce turnover and absenteeism.

A MODEL

On the basis of the reviewed literature, the following model of the relationships among physical fitness, physical activity, and employee fitness programs including work and individual variables was developed (see Figure 1). A critical feature of this model is the separate delineation of the benefits of exercise at the individual employee level and the advantages for the organization of supporting employee fitness programs. If an employee exercises on his/her own (outside any organization facility or without financial assistance), both the individual and the organization derive the benefits of the first component of the model. The benefits delineated in the second part of the model are additional to those that develop from having physically fit employees. That is, an organization supporting employee fitness programs receives the advantages of having physically fit employees, as well as the short-term consequences arising from exercise and the long-term benefits arising from greater commitment and increased flexibility in scheduling activities. Thus, to maximize benefits in-house programs should be initiated.

The first component of this model outlines the short- and long-term consequences of individuals engaging in physical activity. The immediate consequences of participation in physical activity are an improved mobilization of fatty acids generated during demanding cognitive work, enhanced relaxation, and lower levels of anxiety and depression, which should lead to a reduction in the stress symptoms experienced. Another consequence of engaging in physical activity during a work period is that it may produce more appropriate arousal levels for cognitive work, thus improving short-term productivity.

In terms of long-term participation in physical exercise, individuals have demonstrated: (a) greater emotional stability, (b) enhanced feelings of security,

FIGURE 1

Model of the Relationships Among Physical Fitness, Physical Activity, and Employee Fitness Programs Including Individual and Organizational Factors

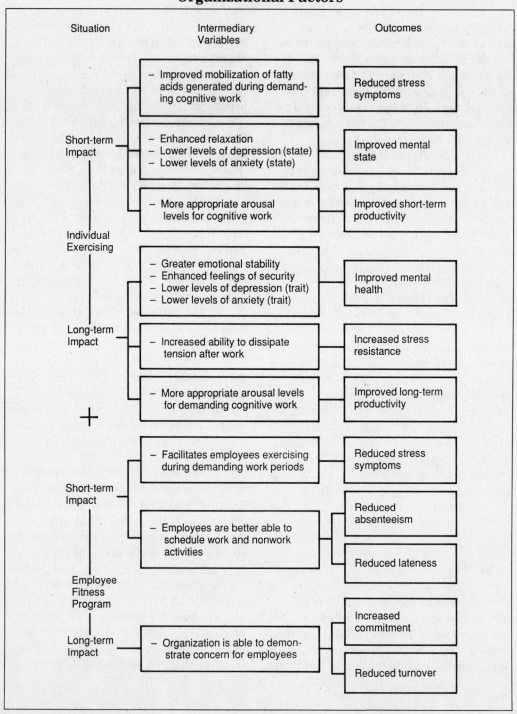

(c) lower levels of depression, and (d) lower levels of anxiety. These consequences lead to conditions of positive mental health. Also, physically fit individuals have demonstrated a more rapid dissipation of the physiological indices of tension after demanding cognitive work, and they may have more appropriate arousal levels (lower than the less fit individual) for complex cognitive tasks. These conditions should lead to increased stress resistance and improved productivity.

Within the model, the only intermediary variables which would require long-term aerobic, as opposed to anaerobic exercise, are an increased ability to dissipate tension after work and more appropriate arousal levels for demanding cognitive work. Both of these changes involve a more efficient cardiovascular system which is best developed through aerobic exercise. Currently, there is not a sufficient research base to distinguish whether the other intermediary variables would occur with only aerobic or anaerobic exercise.

The second component of this model delineates the intermediary consequences and final outcomes that may occur with employee fitness programs. The availability of fitness facilities at work provides the opportunity for employees to take an exercise break during periods of demanding cognitive work. This exercise break would produce the short-term effects of physical activity leading to reduced stress symptoms and greater productivity. Employees who want to exercise also will have greater flexibility in scheduling work and nonwork activities, leading to reduced absenteeism and lateness.

In relation to long-term outcomes, employee fitness programs provide an opportunity for organizations to demonstrate concern for employees. If employees perceive the organization is concerned about their welfare, they may develop more loyalty to the company, indirectly leading to reduced turnover.

DISCUSSION

The model presented here provides a framework upon which to generate future research. In particular, more experimental research is needed on the relationship between physical fitness and the ability to maintain high levels of cognitive functioning during an eight-hour day. Also, the immediate effects of physical exercise on mood, attitudes, and the ability to relax, particularly after cognitive work, should be examined. Applied research should be directed at analyzing differences in stress symptoms, absenteeism, and productivity between fit and nonfit individuals, and the impact employee fitness programs have on commitment, turnover, and absenteeism should be examined, specifically.

It is suggested that future research should integrate the following criteria: (a) using standardized measures of psychological constructs, or reporting the reliability analysis of questionnaire data; (b) using a within subject design that tests psychological constructs prior to and after the exercise period to analyze short-term consequences; (c) gathering subjective data two to three months after a fitness program in order to reduce the possibility of a halo effect; and (d) designing studies to test specifically for the short- and/or long-term impact of exercise. Although it is difficult to overcome the nonrandomization of subjects given the limitations associated with human rights and the assumption that employee fitness programs are for all employees, perhaps potential changes may be better measured through a within subject design.

Organizations generally are concerned with identifiable returns such as lower absenteeism and turnover when they support employee fitness programs. There is relatively little information available as to whether employee fitness programs produce these returns although more substantial, though not conclusive information, in support of exercise and the returns for individual employees (i.e., better mental health, improved stress resistance) is available. It is the author's view that if organizations and researchers want to improve the quality of work life, these returns should be expected. The returns of increased productivity and commitment, and decreased absenteeism and turnover should be "additional icing on the cake."

REFERENCES

Bahkre, M. S., & Morgan, W. P. (1978). Anxiety reduction following exercise and meditation. *Cognitive Therapy and Research, 2,* 323–333.

Bernacki, E. J., & Baun, W. B. (1984). The relationship of job performance to exercise adherence in a corporate fitness program. *Journal of Occupational Medicine, 26,* 529–531.

Butler, K. N. (1969). The effect of physical conditioning and exertion on the performance of a simple mental task. *Journal of Sports Medicine and Physical Fitness, 9,* 236–240.

Clegg, C. W. (1983). Psychology of employee lateness, absence and turnover: A methodological critique and an empirical study. *Journal of Applied Psychology, 68,* 88–101.

Cox, M. H. (1984). Fitness and lifestyle programs for business and industry: Problems in recruitment and retention. *Journal of Cardiac Rehabilitation, 4,* 136–142.

Cox, T. P., Evans, J. F., & Jamieson, J. L. (1979). Aerobic power and tonic heart rate responses to psychosocial stressors. *Personality and Social Psychology Bulletin, 5(2),* 160–163.

Cox, M., Shephard, R., & Corey, P. (1981). Influence of an employee fitness programme upon fitness, productivity and absenteeism. *Ergonomics, 24,* 795–806.

Debats, K. (1981). Industrial recreation programs: A new look at an old benefit. *Personnel Journal, 60,* 620–627.

deVries, H. G., & Adams, G. M. (1972). Electromyographic comparison of single doses of exercise and meprobamate as to effects on muscular relaxation. *American Journal of Physical Medicine, 51,* 130–141.

Dienstbier, R. A., Crabbe, J., Johnson, G. O., Thorland, W., Jorgensen, J. A., Sadar, M. M., & Lavells, D. C. (1981). Exercise and stress tolerance. In M. H. Sacks & M. L. Sachs (Eds.). *Psychology of running* (pp. 192–210). Champaign, IL: Human Kinetics.

Dishman, R. K. (1982). Contemporary sport psychology. In R. L. Terjung (Ed.), *Exercise and sport sciences reviews* (Vol. 10, pp. 120–159). New York: Franklin Institute Press.

Dishman, R. K., Salis, J. F., & Orenstein, D. R. (1985). The determinants of physical activity and exercise. *Public Health Reports, 100,* 158–171.

Driver, R. W., & Ratliff, R. A. (1982). Employers' perceptions of benefits accrued from physical fitness programs. *Personnel Administrator, 27(8),* 21–26.

Durbeck, D. C., Heinzelmann, F., Schacter, J., Haskell, W. L., Payne, G. H., Moxley, R. T., Nemiroff, J., Limoncelli, D. D., Arnold., L. B., & Fox, S. M. (1972). The national aeronautics and space administration — US public health service health evaluation and enhancement program. *American Journal of Cardiology, 30,* 784–790.

Edington, D. W., & Edgerton, V. R. (1976). *The biology of physical activity.* Boston: Houghton Mifflin.

Everly, B. S., Jr., & Rosenfeld, R. (1981). *The nature and treatment of the stress response: A practical guide for clinicians.* New York: Plenum Press.

Folkins, C. H., Lynch, S., & Gardner, M. M. (1972). Psychological fitness as a function of physical fitness. *Archives of Physical Medicine and Rehabilitation, 53,* 503–508.

Folkins, C. H., & Sime, W. E. (1981). Physical

fitness training and mental health. *American Psychologist, 36,* 373–389.

Frankenhaeuser, M. (1979). Psychoneuroendocrine approaches to a study of emotions as related to stress and coping. In H. E. Howe, Jr. & R. A. Dienstbier (Eds.), *Nebraska symposium on motivation* (Vol. 27, pp. 123–161). Lincoln: University of Nebraska Press.

Frankenhaeuser, M., & Johansson, G. (1982, July). *Stress at work: Psychobiological and psychological aspects.* Paper presented at the 20th International Congress of Applied Psychology, Edinburgh.

Gal, R., & Lazarus, R. S. (1975). The role of activity in anticipating and confronting stressful situations. *Journal of Human Stress, 1,* 4–20.

Galt, V. (1985, August 16). Employee fitness programs are among innovative health benefits. *The Globe and Mail,* p. B15.

Gutin, B. (1966). Effect of increase in physical fitness on mental ability following physical and mental stress. *Research Quarterly, 37,* 211–220.

Gutin, B., & DiGennaro, J. (1968). Effect of one-minute and five-minute step-ups on performance of simple addition. *Research Quarterly, 39,* 81–85.

Heaps, R. A. (1978). Relating physical and psychological fitness: A psychological point of view. *Journal of Sports Medicine and Physical Fitness, 18,* 399–408.

Heinzelman, F., & Bagley, R. W. (1970). Response to physical activity programs and their effects on health behavior. *Public Health Reports, 85,* 905–911.

Hollander, B. J., & Seraganian, P. (1984). Aerobic fitness and psychophysiological reactivity. *Canadian Journal of Behavioral Science, 16,* 257–261.

Howard, J., & Mikalachki, A. (1979). Fitness and employee productivity. *Canadian Journal of Applied Sport Sciences, 4,* 191–198.

Hughes, J. R. (1984). Psychological effects of habitual aerobic exercise: A critical review. *Preventive Medicine, 13,* 66–78.

Ismail, A. H., & Young, R. J. (1973). The effect of chronic exercise on the personality of middle-aged men by univariate and multivariate approaches. *Journal of Human Ergology, 2,* 45–54.

Ismail, A. H., & Young, R. J. (1976). Influence of physical fitness on second and third order personality factors using orthogonal and oblique rotations. *Journal of Clinical Psychology, 32,* 268–272.

Johns, G., & Nicholson, N. (1982). The meaning of absence: New strategies for theory and research. In L. L. Cummings & B. M. Staw (Eds.), *Research in organizational behavior* (Vol. 4, pp. 127–172). Greenwich, CT: JAI Press.

Kavanagh, T., & Shephard, R. J. (1973). The immediate antecedents of myocardial infarction in active men. *Canadian Medical Association Journal, 109,* 19–22.

Keller, S., & Seraganian, P. (1984). Physical fitness level and autonomic reactivity to psychosocial stress. *Journal of Psychosomatic Research, 28,* 279–287.

Killip, S. M. (1985). *Aerobic fitness: Effects on stress and psychological well-being.* Unpublished doctoral dissertation, University of Calgary, Calgary, Canada.

Ledwidge, R. (1980). Run for your mind: Aerobic exercise as a means of alleviating anxiety and depression. *Canadian Journal of Behavioral Science, 12(2),* 126–140.

Lichtman, S., & Poser, E. G. (1983). The effects of exercises on mood and cognitive functioning. *Journal of Psychosomatic Research, 27,* 43–52.

Michael, E. D. (1957). Stress adaptation through exercise. *Research Quarterly, 28,* 51–54.

Michaels, C. E., & Spector, P. E. (1982). Causes of employee turnovers: A test of the Mobley, Griffeth, Hand and Meglino model. *Journal and Applied Psychology, 67,* 53–59.

Mobily, K. (1982). Using physical activity and recreation to cope with stress and anxiety: A review. *American Corrective Journal, 36(3),* 77–81.

Mobley, W. H., Griffeth, R. W., Hand, H. H., & Meglino, B. M. (1979). Review and conceptual analysis of the employee turnover process. *Psychological Bulletin, 86,* 493–522.

Morgan, W. P., & Pollock, M. L. (1978). Physical activity and cardiovascular health: Psychological aspects. In F. Landry & W. A. R. Orban (Eds.), *Physical activity and human well-being* (Vol. 1, pp. 163–181). Miami, FL: Symposia Specialist.

Morgan, W. P., Roberts, J. A., & Feinerman, A. D. (1971). Psychological effect of acute physical activity. *Archives of Physical Medicine and Rehabilitation, 52,* 422–425.

Perks, M. (1985, February 9). Happier workers: Extra payoff for employers in many ways. *The Financial Post,* pp. 33, 35.

Porter, L. W., Steers, R. M., Mowday, R. T., & Boulian, P. V. (1974). Organizational commitment, job satisfaction, and turnover among psychiatric technicians. *Journal of Applied Psychology, 59,* 603–609.

Rhodes, E. C., & Dunwoody, D. (1980). Physiological and attitudinal changes in those involved in an employee fitness program. *Canadian Journal of Public Health, 71,* 331–336.

Rossman, R. J. (1983, October). Participant satisfaction with employee recreation. *Journal of Physical Education, Recreation and Dance, 62,* 30–32.

Selye, H. (1975). *Stress without distress.* New York: Signet.

Shephard, R. J., Cox, M., & Corey, P. (1981). Fitness program participation: Its effect on workers' performance. *Journal of Occupational Medicine, 23,* 359–363.

Sinyor, D., Schwartz, S. G., Peronnet, F., Brisson, G., & Seraganian, P. (1983). Aerobic fitness level and reactivity to psychosocial stress: Physiological, biochemical and subjective measures. *Psychosomatic Medicine, 45,* 205–217.

Smith, P., Kendall, L., & Hulin, C. (1969). *The measurement of satisfaction in work and retirement.* Chicago: Rand McNally.

Steers, R. M. (1977). Antecedents and outcomes of organizational commitment. *Administrative Science Quarterly, 22,* 46–56.

Stephens, T., Jacobs, D. R., & White, C. C. (1985). A descriptive epidemiology of leisure-time physical activity. *Public Health Reports, 100,* 147–158.

Stern, M. J., & Cleary, P. (1982). The national exercise and heart disease project: Long-term psychosocial outcome. *Archives of Internal Medicine, 42,* 1093–1097.

Terjung, R. (1979). Endocrine response to exercise. *Exercise and Sport Science Reviews, 7,* 153–180.

Tharp, G. D., & Schlegelmich, R. P. (1977). Personality characteristics of trained versus untrained individuals. [Abstract]. *Medicine and Science in Sports, 9,* 55.

Weingarten, G. (1973). Mental performance during physical exertion: The benefit of being physically fit. *International Journal of Sport Psychology, 4,* 16–26.

Yarvote, P. M., McDonagh, T. J. Goldman, M. E., & Zuckerman, J. (1974). Organization and evaluation of a physical fitness program in industry. *Journal of Occupational Medicine, 16,* 589–598.

Young, R. J., & Ismail, A. H. (1976a). Personality differences of adult men before and after a physical fitness program. *Research Quarterly, 47,* 513–519.

Young, R. J., & Ismail, A. H. (1976b). Relationship between anthropometric physiological, biochemical and personality variables before and after a four-month conditioning program for middle-aged men. *Journal of Sports Medicine and Physical Fitness, 16,* 267–276.

Young, R. J., & Ismail, A. H. (1977). Comparison of selected physiological and personality variables in regular and nonregular adult male exercisers. *Research Quarterly, 48,* 617–622.

Youngblood, S. A. (1984). Work, nonwork and withdrawal. *Journal of Applied Psychology, 69,* 106–117.

Zuercher, J. D. (1965). The effects of extraneous stimulation of vigilance. *Human Factors, 7,* 101–105.

Loren E. Falkenberg is an assistant professor in the Department of Management in Organization and Human Resources, University of Calgary.

The Nature of Collective Bargaining
Betty W. Justice

Collective bargaining is the process by which workers participate in making the decisions that affect their work lives. Through collective bargaining, workers, represented by their union, are able to impose restraints upon the otherwise largely unrestrained authority of management to make decisions regarding conditions of work. The very obligation to recognize a union and to bargain is in

Source: From Betty W. Justice, "The Nature of Collective Bargaining," reprinted by permission from *Unions, Workers, and the Law* by Betty W. Justice, pp. 69–87, copyright © 1983 by the Bureau of National Affairs, Inc., Washington, D.C.

an absolute sense a restriction on the employer's "management rights." Public law has imposed this limitation. Furthermore, the heart of collective bargaining is that management must share some of its previously exclusive decision-making authority and must participate in a joint determination of "wages, hours, and other conditions" of employment.

The collective bargaining process typically results in a collective bargaining agreement, generally referred to as a "contract." The contract, almost always a written document, binds both parties to specified rules on which they have mutually agreed for a set period of time. These rules cover a wide variety of issues, such as rates of pay, pension benefits, procedures for layoffs, rights of the union and management, and methods for resolving disputes over the meaning of contract language. In a sense, collective bargaining is a form of lawmaking, wherein the rules embodied in the contract are the laws that govern the workplace.

Prior to the Wagner Act, workers could participate in this decision making concerning their work lives only through the threat or the use of economic actions, such as a strike, against an employer. The Wagner Act imposed a legal obligation to bargain on the employer and thereby substituted, or at least added, legal compulsion to the resources of workers seeking to bargain with their employer. The bargaining duty of employers and unions is described in Section 8(d) of the Labor Management Relations Act (LMRA):

> ... to bargain collectively is the performance of the mutual obligation of the employer and the representatives of the employees to meet at reasonable times and *confer in good faith* with respect to wages, hours and other terms and conditions of employment, on the negotiation of an agreement, on any question arising thereunder, ... but such obligation *does not compel either party to agree to a proposal or to require the making of a concession* ... (Emphasis added.)

In addition to defining the duty to bargain, Section 8(d) also contains detailed procedural notice requirements that must be met when a party seeks to "terminate or modify" a contract. Failure to abide by these requirements is not a basis for a refusal-to-bargain charge, but employees who engage in a strike in violation of these requirements lose their status as employees under the law and therefore all of their protection and rights under the LMRA.

One of the employer practices defined as an unfair labor practice by the Wagner Act in Section 8(a)(5) was "to refuse to bargain collectively with the representatives of his employees with respect to rates of pay, wages, hours of employment or other conditions of employment." This provision imposed upon an employer the obligation to bargain and made failure to do so a violation of the law. It did not, however, impose a reciprocal obligation on unions. The Taft-Hartley Act shifted the emphasis of federal labor policy from one of protecting the rights of employees to organize unions to one of umpiring disputes between two competing forces assumed to be of relatively stable and equal strength. Consequently, it imposed upon a union an obligation to bargain collectively with an employer whose employees it represents. The failure to do so was defined as a union unfair labor practice in Section 8(b)(3): "It shall be an unfair labor practice for a union ... to refuse to bargain collectively with an employer, provided it is the representative of his employees subject to the provisions of section 9(a)...."

The duty to bargain applies to every decision that affects "wages, hours, [and] terms and conditions" of employment. This means that the duty to bargain applies not just to negotiations for a contract but continues throughout the term of the contract. For example, if an employer wants to change the work schedule during the term of a contract, then the duty to bargain applies. If the employer makes a unilateral decision — a decision made without bargaining — in changing the schedule, the union can file an unfair labor practice charge. Such a change would ordinarily be a violation of a substantive contract provision as well as of the procedural right to bargain. A union would typically seek correction of the violation through the contract procedure instead of going to the National Labor Relations Board (NLRB) with an unfair labor practice charge. This course would be followed because the NLRB does not as a rule have the authority to condemn the substantive decision of the employer, whereas the decisionmaker under the contract does have such power. The duty to bargain also requires compliance with the grievance/arbitration procedure or any contractually established method for dispute settlement.

In enacting the Wagner and Taft-Hartley acts, Congress did no more than erect a skeleton — a bare framework of the manner in which it believed collective bargaining ought to take place. During the more than 45 years since collective bargaining became subject to governmental regulation, there have been thousands of NLRB and court decisions which have spelled out just what the duty of collective bargaining entails.

THE UNION AS EXCLUSIVE REPRESENTATIVE

A primary feature of U.S. labor law as it applies to collective bargaining is the principle of exclusive representation by a majority union. This principle is specifically declared in Section 9 of the LMRA:

> Representatives designated or selected for the purposes of collective bargaining by the majority of the employees in a unit appropriate for such purposes, shall be the exclusive representative of all the employees in the unit for the purpose of collective bargaining in respect to rates of pay, wages, hours of employment, or other conditions of employment....

The provision means that once a union is selected as the collective bargaining representative, by law it acquires the right and the responsibility to deal with the employer on behalf of all employees in the unit. Philosophically, this derives from the notion of "one for all, all for one" that historically underpins organized labor. Practically, it recognizes that the individual worker possesses little meaningful power to deal with an employer. The union which holds bargaining rights for a unit of employees is entitled to represent all of the employees in that unit regardless of the desires of individual employees to represent themselves and regardless of whether or not employees are union members.

The LMRA makes it an unfair labor

practice for an employer to refuse to bargain collectively with the representative of his employees. An employer is obligated to deal with a designated majority union and is forbidden to deal individually with employees or with a competing organization about any matter subject to collective bargaining. In *J. I. Case v. NLRB* (1944), a case which involved the impact of a collective agreement on existing individual contracts, the Supreme Court stated:

> The practice and philosophy of collective bargaining looks with suspicion on such individual advantages. . . . They are a fruitful way of interfering with organization and choice of representatives . . . often earned at the cost of breaking down some other standard thought to be for the welfare of the group and . . . paid at the long-range expense of the group as a whole.

The basis for exclusive representation is a belief that any form of plural representation would permit an employer to grant favor to certain individuals or groups and thereby foster rivalries that would erode the strength of the union, ultimately resulting in disadvantages for all.

In *Emporium Capwell v. WACO* (1975), the Supreme Court clarified the extent to which public policy exalts the principle of exclusive representation by a majority union under the LMRA. Through contractually specified procedures, a union was pursuing charges of racial discrimination against an employer, a department store, which was forbidden by contract to engage in racial discrimination. Several employees felt that the contract grievance procedure focusing on individual grievances was inadequate to correct a problem as deep-rooted and widespread as racial discrimination. These employees unsuccessfully urged direct economic action by the union against the employer and refused to participate in meetings concerning the grievance.

After failing in their attempts to meet with company officials to discuss the problem as they saw it (companywide, or systematic, discrimination), the dissident employees themselves instituted the direct action which the union had refused to take. They held a press conference, denounced the store's policy as racist, reiterated their desire to deal directly with top management over minority employment, and subsequently on their own time picketed the store, urging customers not to patronize it.

Two of the dissident employees, after being warned by the employer that a repetition of the picketing would subject them to discharge, were fired following a second day of picketing. The General Counsel of the NLRB charged the employer with an unfair labor practice, maintaining that the discharges violated the right of employees to engage in concerted activity under Section 7 of the LMRA. The NLRB dismissed the complaint, however, concluding that protection of such activity would undermine the principle of exclusive representation mandated by the statute. To permit workers to make direct demands on the employer would diminish the effectiveness of the union's efforts. The Board believed that an employer would be unreasonably burdened if legally required to bargain with the union but economically forced to deal with a competing group concerning issues lawfully subject to bargaining.

An appeals court reversed the NLRB

decision, holding that the principle of exclusive representation must be subordinated to the strong national policy requiring the elimination of racial discrimination in employment. The Supreme Court reversed the court of appeals, however, and adopted the NLRB's reasoning that the right and responsibility to bargain belong exclusively to the majority union. In rejecting the premise that the employees' efforts complemented rather than clashed with those of the union, the Supreme Court declared:

> This argument confuses the employees' substantive right to be free of racial discrimination with the procedures available under the NLRA for securing these rights. Whether they are thought to depend upon Title VII [of the Civil Rights Act of 1964] or have an independent source in the NLRA, they cannot be pursued at the expense of the orderly collective bargaining process contemplated by the NLRA. The elimination of discrimination and its vestiges is an appropriate subject for bargaining, and an employer may have no objection to incorporating into a collective agreement the substance of his obligation not to discriminate in personnel decisions. . . . But that does not mean that he may not have strong and legitimate objections to bargaining on several fronts over the implementation of the right to be free of discrimination. . . . Similarly, while a union cannot lawfully bargain for the establishment or continuation of discriminatory practices, it has a legitimate interest in presenting a united front on this and on other issues and in not seeing its strength dissipated and its stature denigrated by subgroups within the unit separately pursuing what they see as separate interests.

The reaffirmation of the primacy of the exclusion representation principles rejects any form of plural representation — either by individuals or by organizations. It clears the way for a union to speak with a united voice in asserting workers' interests. However, another aspect of exclusive representation is the channeling of all disputes into narrowly defined procedures, thereby insulating the employer from more basic challenges to its authority. This relieves the employer of the burden of dealing with individual employees who are sometimes more militant in their demands than their union — often severely constrained both by the law and by the contract in its ability to assert employee interests.

THE ROLE OF THE GOVERNMENT IN COLLECTIVE BARGAINING

An oft repeated description of industrial relations in the United States is that "free" collective bargaining is the basic feature of the country's labor policy. A fundamental policy articulated in the LMRA is to promote private bargaining without governmental interference into the substantive terms of collective bargaining agreements. (One of the provisions contained in the proposed Labor Law Reform Act of 1977 would have granted the NLRB some of the authority it lacks under the present system. In cases where the parties are negotiating their first contract and where an employer was found by the NLRB to have unlawfully refused to bargain, the provision would have authorized the NLRB to order compensation lost because of the delay. In essence, it would have permitted the NLRB to write the economic terms of a contract to cover the period of time between the time the bargaining obligation arose and the time the employer actually began to bargain in good faith. The current trend for many employers to invest substantial effort and resources into resisting unionization, including systematic violations of the law, means that this issue is likely to emerge in the future.)

However, both in statutory language and in decisions by the NLRB and the courts, the government has carved out a significant role for itself in shaping collective bargaining. Some types of contract provisions are forbidden by statute as contrary to public policy without regard to the willingness or desire of the parties to collective bargaining to bind themselves to such provisions. Two examples of these forbidden practices are closed shops, and hot cargo agreements. The NLRB, with the statutory authority to decide "appropriateness" of bargaining units and a court-approved arrogation of the power to decide what subjects are covered by collective bargaining, also exercises substantial control on the structure of collective bargaining.

Despite these intrusions by government into collective bargaining, the clearest statement in the LMRA concerning the role of the government in labor-management relations is the declaration that the law does not "compel either party to agree to a proposal or require the making of a concession." A significant exception to this concept of "free" collective bargaining is government-imposed wage ceilings, a subject of great controversy during the 1970s.

The high regard for this view of collective bargaining free of governmental interference into the actual outcome is demonstrated by Supreme Court decisions rebuking intrusions by the NLRB into this forbidden territory of the substantive terms of a contract. The NLRB cannot force the making of a concession; the right to use economic weapons allows either party to attempt to force concessions that the opposing party is otherwise unwilling to make.

In *H. K. Porter Co. v. NLRB* (1970), a major case on the issue, the Supreme Court was asked to decide whether the NLRB might require the inclusion of a checkoff provision in a contract as a remedy for the employer's unlawful refusal to bargain in good faith on that subject. A checkoff clause requires the employer, upon authorization from the employee, to automatically deduct union dues from the employee's paycheck and transmit them to the union. Finding that the policy of neutrality expressed in Section 8(d) applied to Section 10(c), which describes the Board's remedial powers, the Supreme Court declared:

> ... allowing the Board to compel agreement when the parties themselves are unable to do so would violate the fundamental premise on which the Act is based — private bargaining under governmental supervision of the procedure alone, without any official compulsion over the actual terms of the contract.

BARGAINING IN GOOD FAITH

To promote collective bargaining, Section 8(d) requires a standard of conduct demonstrating good faith — an open mind and a willingness to try to find common ground. Good faith is the standard of conduct which a party must bring to bargaining in order to protect itself against a charge of refusal to bargain by the other party to the negotiations.

However, some kinds of conduct are considered to be so destructive of bargaining that the NLRB has decided that such conduct is a *per se violation* of the duty to bargain. The Supreme Court expressed approval of the Board's position in *NLRB v. Katz* (1962). "Per se" literally means "in and of itself." If a party engages in this kind of conduct, it is subject to a refusal-to-bargain charge regardless of its intent and regardless of the good faith its other conduct may have shown. Only a few types of conduct are grounds for a *per se* bargaining charge. Some of these are (1) a refusal to meet for the purposes of collective bargaining, (2) a refusal to execute a written agreement, (3) a refusal to discuss mandatory subjects (discussed at length in the next chapter), and (4) a change in a condition subject to bargaining without consulting the union. Despite what appears to be a clear-cut rule, its application is sometimes fuzzy. Cases may have elements of objectionable conduct of the *per se* variety and other conduct tending to show bad faith.

Measuring Good Faith

Other than *per se* cases in which the conduct alone is sufficient to support a refusal-to-bargain charge, the question is whether a party has shown good faith in its bargaining conduct. Since good faith describes a party's state of mind, it cannot be precisely measured. The NLRB, in considering charges of bad-faith bargaining, has adopted a case-by-case approach. In making a determination, the Board looks at the *totality* or the *entire course of that party's bargaining conduct. (NLRB v. Virginia Electric & Power Co.* (1941) and *General Electric Co.* (1964). The NLRB attempts to deduce the state of mind or attitudes that the party has brought to the bargaining process from a party's actual behavior. While no single element of a party's behavior may be sufficient to constitute a breach of good faith, its overall conduct may be such as to support a charge of refusing to bargain in good faith.

The NLRB utilizes several tests in determining a party's good faith. Even though the law does not compel agreement, it does require that parties meet and sincerely attempt to reach agreement. Meeting together for the purpose of bargaining contemplates more than merely "going through the motions." Consequently, many bad-faith bargaining cases involve types of conduct that the NLRB has concluded demonstrate an absence of any sincere desire to reach agreement. The NLRB has identified several of these types of conduct that may but do not necessarily support a charge of bad-faith bargaining. *Surface Bargaining* is one type: Even though a party is willing to meet, inflexible adherence to its own demands and the total rejection of those of the other party are considered an indication of a "closed mind." Surface bargaining refers to the nature or the quality of bargaining, and not to the frequency of bargaining.

The law clearly states that bargaining does not require the making of a concession. However, the *willingness of a party to compromise* — to engage in give-and-take — is frequently looked to as evidence of a party's good faith. The NLRB found in *NLRB v. Reed & Prince Mfg. Co.* (1953) that while the Board itself cannot require specific concessions, the Board can look at the making of some concessions in the overall context of bargaining as highly relevant to a determination of a party's desire to reach agreement. The *willingness of a party to make proposals, demands, and counterproposals* is also a measure of its good faith. Withdrawal of proposals after their prior acceptance has been considered evidence of bad faith, as has the introduction of new issues after an agreement has been substantially concluded. Proposals that are so unreasonable that their predictable effect would be to frustrate further negotiations and agreement may also be considered evidence of bad faith.

An outright refusal to meet at all is a *per se* bargaining violation. Lesser forms of similar conduct, such as repeated *delays* in scheduling or other evasions of the responsibility to meet and seek agreement, are indications of a party's bad faith. For instance, failure to invest the bargaining representative with any significant authority to conclude an agreement is a sign that a party is not taking negotiations seriously.

Stipulating that an agreement must include acceptance of prescribed conditions may be considered to show a closed mind. The *preconditions* may relate to matters subject to bargaining, such as the settling of certain contract terms before negotiating on others. Such barriers are thought to interfere with a give-and-take atmosphere. Or preconditions may relate to external issues, such as an insistence on bargaining about voluntary subjects (discussed in the next chapter) or the relinquishment of certain rights, like the dropping of pending unfair labor practice charges. A refusal to negotiate for the duration of a legal economic strike is an unacceptable condition that could predictably frustrate agreement and is generally the basis for a refusal-to-bargain charge.

Employer conduct occurring contemporaneously to bargaining that discriminates against union members, or undermines the union, or promotes the decertification of the union as bargaining representative raises questions as to the employer's sincerity and genuine participation in the bargaining process. Such conduct then — in addition to being independent unfair labor practices — may also be considered as evidence of bad-faith bargaining.

Boulwarism "Boulwarism" is the popular name of a bargaining technique pioneered by the General Electric Company and named after the GE vice president who developed the strategy in the 1950s. Based on its own research of the employees' needs, the company formulated a set of proposals. It presented this package as a "firm and fair offer" with nothing held back for later trading and subject to change only if new facts were shown to require it. The company then conducted an extensive advertising campaign designed to convince both its employees and the public that it was doing the best possible for its employees. It asserted that it was doing so voluntarily, without the need for any union pressure or a strike.

Along with several specific refusal-to-bargain findings, the NLRB found GE guilty of refusing to bargain based on the totality of its conduct. In affirming this NLRB finding, the U.S. Court of Appeals emphasized in *NLRB v. General Electric Co.* (1969) that

> . . . an employer may not so combine "take-it-or-leave-it" bargaining methods with a widely publicized stance of

unbending firmness that he is himself unable to alter a position once taken.

In effect, the employer had attempted by its action to preempt entirely the bilateral decision making which the LMRA requires. Central to the court's condemnation of GE's approach was the company's attempt to deal directly with employees. Through the use of the publicity campaign and direct communications, the employer sought to bypass the union altogether and convince employees that the company could be relied on to look after their best interest without any need for the union. According to the court, the company desired "to deal with the union through the employees, rather than with the employees through the union," as the law requires.

Boulwarism, as revealed in later cases, exists *only* if it features a combination of "firm offers" and communication of this to employees. The law does not prohibit either hard bargaining or all communications to employees. At some point in the negotiations, an employer may make a firm and final offer. The NLRB in *Philip Carey Mfg. Co.* (1963) held that an employer did not violate Section 8(a)(5) when it made a final offer in the eleventh session of a series of "give-and-take" sessions.

Unilateral Actions

The essence of collective bargaining is the mutual obligation of an employer and a union to "bargain" concerning the wages, hours, terms, and conditions of employment of those employees whom the union represents. Bargaining implies that joint determination or bilateral decision making is to be substituted for unilateral, or one-sided, decisions by an employer regarding those matters subject to bargaining. For example, during the term of an existing contract, an employer that unilaterally granted merit increases, changed the sick leave policy, and instituted a new system of automatic wage increases was subsequently charged with a refusal to bargain. The employer contended that unilateral actions alone were insufficient to support a refusal-to-bargain charge. It argued that the NLRB must make a finding of bad faith — of which unilateral changes might be evidence — in order to find it guilty of refusing to bargain. The Supreme Court noted in *NLRB v. Katz* (1962) that when a party has refused to negotiate or has circumvented negotiations by instituting changes, then the opportunity to consider the issue of good faith is foreclosed. Bargaining is preempted by the actual making of changes and in effect bypasses the union. In finding that unilateral action by an employer obstructs bargaining, the Supreme Court approved the use of the *per se* refusal-to-bargain concept with respect to this type of conduct but declined to announce an absolute rule pertaining to such changes. Thus, the NLRB may occasionally consider a unilateral change merely as evidence of bad faith rather than as an outright violation of the duty to bargain.

In thinking about unilateral changes, it should be remembered that what the law requires is bargaining. If bargaining possibilities have been exhausted so that an impasse exists, then an employer is free to make changes. A unilateral action consistent with past practice, or which maintains the status quo, is lawful despite the fact that a union is not afforded an opportunity to bargain. However, any past practice can be made the subject of future contract negotiations, and contract language can change the application of the practice.

USE OF ECONOMIC WEAPONS DURING BARGAINING

A major case on the issue of good faith involved bargaining in which the union, during contract negotiations, simultaneously engaged in economic activity designed to further its position. The question for the NLRB was whether economic pressure used to support union demands during negotiations with an employer was equivalent to an unlawful refusal to bargain. The NLRB ruled that the union's reliance upon harassing tactics during the course of negotiations, for the avowed purpose of compelling the company to capitulate, was the antithesis of reasoned discussion which the nation was dutybound to follow. In *NLRB v. Insurance Agents International Union* (1960), the Supreme Court disagreed, finding that apart from a requirement that parties confer in good health, "Congress intended that the parties should have wide latitude in their negotiations, unrestricted by any governmental power to regulate the substantive solution of their differences." The Supreme Court condemned what it perceived as NLRB intrusion into the substantive aspects of bargaining and discussed at length the concept of collective bargaining premised on government neutrality. The Supreme Court declared:

> It must be realized that collective bargaining, under a system where the government does not attempt to control the results of negotiations, cannot be equated with an academic collective search for truth — or even what might be thought to be the ideal of one. The parties — even granting the modification of views that may come from a realization of economic interdependence — still proceed from contrary and, to an extent, antagonistic viewpoints and concepts of self-interest. The system has not reached the ideal of the philosophic notion that perfect understanding among people would lead to perfect agreement among them on values. The presence of economic weapons in reserve, and their actual exercise on occasion by the parties, is part and parcel of the system that the Wagner and Taft-Hartley acts have recognized. . . . At the present statutory stage of our national labor relations policy, the two factors — necessity for good faith bargaining between parties and the availability of economic pressure devices to each to make the other party incline to agree on one's terms — exist side by side.

Employers too are permitted to use economic weapons, such as a lockout, in furtherance of a bargaining position.

Since the right to use economic weapons is independent of the duty to bargain, their use does not suspend the duty to bargain. An employer still has a duty to bargain even when the union is engaged in a lawful economic strike, and the employer cannot in any way make cessation of the strike a condition for further bargaining. The employer is free to use certain countermeasures to employees' concerted activity without consulting the union. For instance, the employer is not required to subsidize a strike and can therefore terminate wages and economic benefits, such as payment of insurance premiums, to striking employees. An employer is also free to replace strikers and to temporarily subcontract out the struck work in order to maintain business operations. However, an employer has no obligation to bargain with a union engaging in unlawful strike activity, such as strikes characterized by violence and strikes in violation of the union's contract obligations.

IMPASSE

The duty to bargain does not require the parties to actually conclude an agreement. After good-faith bargaining possibilities have been exhausted and there remain irreconcilable differences in the parties' positions, the law recognizes an impasse. An impasse may occur either in negotiations for a new contract or during the term of an agreement when an employer proposes to make a change in a condition of employment subject to bargaining. There is, however, no litmus test to distinguish between a legal impasse and a stalemate caused by unlawful bargaining conduct. Whether the NLRB will find that a legal impasse has occurred depends on all of the facts in each case. If a party takes an action based on a belief that a lawful impasse exists, it risks the NLRB later finding that no "legal" impasse existed.

Generally an impasse occurs at that point when further discussions would be fruitless. This determination, like that relative to other aspects of collective bargaining, depends upon all of the circumstances peculiar to each situation. In *Taft Broadcasting Co.* (1967), the Board described it in the following manner:

> Whether a bargaining impasse exists is a matter of judgment. The bargaining history, the good faith of the parties in negotiations, the length of the negotiations, the importance of the issue or issues as to which there is disagreement, the contemporaneous understanding of the parties as to the state of negotiations, are all relevant factors to be considered in deciding whether an impasse in bargaining existed.

During the period of an impasse, the duty to bargain on those subjects on which impasse has been reached is suspended. Typically, an impasse applies to all bargaining and not to particular subjects, since bargaining is usually aimed at securing a total "package" or contract. Once impasse is reached, an employer is free to make unilateral changes in wages and conditions consistent with but no more favorable than those which have been rejected by the union. However, an employer may not take any action on any other matter subject to bargaining that is not covered by the impasse.

The end of an impasse is as imprecise as its beginning. Any circumstance which changes the relative bargaining position of the parties will terminate an impasse. Examples of such changes are strikes, lockouts, changes in the business environment, or any development which indicates that a party might now be willing to depart from its previous position and that bargaining would no longer be futile.

WAIVER OF BARGAINING RIGHTS

A frequent employer defense to a refusal-to-bargain charge is that the union has waived its right to bargain on the matter in dispute. The waiver argument often arises out of a unilateral action taken by an employer during the term of an agreement.

Several types of waivers are recognized by the NLRB. Since the obligation to bargain arises only when bargaining is requested, the failure to ask for bargaining, acquiescence, is a basis for assuming that a party is waiving its bargaining rights with respect to a particular change. A waiver of the right to bargain over certain issues may also be expressed in the contract. However, the NLRB is reluctant to recognize such waivers and will usually do so only when a waiver is supported by "clear and unmistakable" language in the contract. A broadly stated management rights clause is, as a rule, not sufficient reason to infer that a union has waived its right to bargain on changes in working conditions during the term of the contract. But management rights clauses with specific reservations of authority to management do permit an employer to make unilateral decisions with regard to the matters such reservations cover. For instance, a clause reserving to the employer the sole right to determine employee qualifications was found by the NLRB in *Le Roy Machine Co.* (1964) to constitute a waiver by the union of its right to bargain over the use of physical examinations. The Supreme Court in *NLRB v. C&C Plywood* (1967) upheld the authority of the NLRB to review and construe contract language for the purpose of determining whether a union has by contract waived its statutory right to bargain. However, the NLRB cannot determine the extent of contract rights but only whether the union by agreement has ceded its right to bargain.

Waivers can also be based on the bargaining history of a subject if the issue was fully discussed and if the union consciously yielded its position. The mere discussion and discarding of a demand does not constitute a waiver. To find that all issues put on the table and then abandoned constitute a waiver would discourage the give-and-take that is integral to collective bargaining. When a contract is in effect, it usually contains language that binds both parties on all subjects covered in the agreement. Neither side can compel bargaining on the subjects covered in the contract during the term of the agreement, although the two parties may voluntarily reconsider and amend contract language.

THE RIGHT TO INFORMATION

The LMRA does not specifically establish a right of access to information for unions nor does it create an obligation for the employer to supply requested information. However, the right of the union to relevant information within the possession of the employer has become firmly grafted onto the law as a corollary of the duty to bargain. The failure to supply requested information is an unlawful refusal to bargain. A contract may also create a union's right to information. This right is independent of the statutory right.

The Supreme Court first had occasion to review this concept in *NLRB v. Truitt Manufacturing Co.* (1956) when the NLRB upheld a charge of refusal to bargain against an employer claiming that it could not afford the wage level the union demanded while at the same time refusing to supply any information to substantiate its claim. In upholding the NLRB, the Supreme Court noted:

> Good faith bargaining necessarily requires that claims made by either bargainer should be honest claims. . . . If an argument is important enough to present in the give and take of bargaining, it is important enough to require some sort of proof of its accuracy.

Subsequent cases have made it clear that this right to information applies to all aspects of collective bargaining performed by a union on behalf of its members. The justification is that the lack of adequate and accurate information prevents the occurrence of effective bargaining and denies the union the opportunity to properly perform its bargaining responsibilities. The right to information pertains to contract negotiations, grievance adjustments, the policing of a contract, and preparing for future bargaining. It is not clear under what circumstances a union might be required to supply information to an employer.

Examples of information which the NLRB has required an employer to share with the union are wages paid to individual employees and groups of employees, compensation of employees outside the bargaining unit, wage rates paid at other plants of the employer, costs of an insurance plan, information on job classifications, time study materials, employees' ages, and productivity information. This list illustrates but does not exhaust the types of information covered.

A union is entitled to information only if it requests it. A request must be fairly specific about what information the union requires. The information a union can obtain must pertain to matters of negotiation with the employer. Both the NLRB and the courts use a liberal definition in deciding "relevance," saying that information is relevant if it is reasonably necessary for the union to perform its bargaining representative function. Some categories of information are presumed relevant, which means that the union does not have to show why it desires or needs the information. For instance, in connection with wage negotiations, an employer is required to supply wage data upon request in a form that allows the union to determine exactly what each person is being paid. Financial information on the employer's operation is relevant any time an employer asserts that it cannot afford to meet a union's demand for wages or benefits. This requirement is based on the notion that parties to negotiations should make "honest" claims which they should be willing to prove. An employer's claim that it is financially unable to meet a union's demand is usually called a "plea of poverty." It includes not only outright inability to pay but also includes claims that meeting the union's demands would make it uncompetitive or erode its profit margin.

The NLRB and the courts must evaluate the confidentiality of requested information before requiring an employer to disclose such information to a union. Recently, the Supreme Court concluded in *Detroit Edison v. NLRB* (1979) that an employer lawfully refused to disclose aptitude test scores of individual employees who had not consented to disclosure even though the scores might have been relevant to the processing of promotion grievances. The Board had ordered the release of both the test itself and the individual answer sheets to the union. The employer had offered to submit the test and the answer sheets to an industrial psychologist selected by the union and to disclose to the union the score of any employee who consented thereto. The Supreme Court held the "arguably relevant" nature of information does not always predominate over all other interests. In this case, the employer's interest in protecting the integrity of the test for future use plus the privacy of the tested employees were sufficient to offset even the legitimate interest the union had in the information.

The Board has subsequently ruled in *Minnesota Mining and Manufacturing Co.* (1982) that employers must give unions access to worker health and safety records with names and identifiers deleted. The Board also ordered the employers — three chemical companies — to provide a listing of substances used and produced at the plants in question. As to substances on which the employers claimed a trade secret, the Board suggested that the parties negotiate a method under which the unions could receive the information while maintaining safeguards for the employers' interests. If such efforts fail to reach a mutually satisfactory result, then the Board will engage in a balancing of the competing rights of the unions and the employers.

BARGAINING WITH SUCCESSOR EMPLOYERS

With the current growth in the number of mergers, sales, and consolidations of business operations, the effect of a change in the employer on collective bargaining agreements is a concern for unionized workers. The LMRA does not require an employer to assume the preceding employer's collective bargaining agreement, since to do so would compel the employer to accept the previous employer's concessions and would therefore conflict with Section 8(d). Nor does a succeeding employer have to hire the predecessor's employees. Contracts generally provide greater protection in this area.

The Supreme Court ruled in *NLRB v. Burns International Security Services* (1972) that a successor employer does have an obligation to recognize and bargain with the union which represented its predecessor's employees if it retains those employees. But not every employer that takes over another employer's operations is a "successor" employer within the meaning of the law, which involves several inquiries, all focusing on the continuity between the old and new employer's enterprise. Some of these are:

- Is there continuity in the work force?
- Is there continuity in the employing industry? (Does it produce the same product or service?)
- Is the bargaining unit still an appropriate one?
- What was the impact of any shutdown before the new employer began operations?

If it is clear that the new employer intends to retain the employees in the unit with no indication that they are expected to work under new or different terms, then the obligation to bargain arises. But if the offer to hire is conditioned upon acceptance of different terms of employment, then the new employer is not required to consult with the union over those changes. NLRB policy generally favors allowing the new employer to establish its own initial terms and conditions of employment on the theory that to do otherwise would discourage new employers from even considering the continued employment of original employees.

However, the Board determined in *Mason City Dressed Beef, Inc.* (1977) that an employer cannot intentionally refuse to hire employees of the former employer simply as a way to avoid dealing with the union. The NLRB soundly condemned such discrimination in *Potter's Drug Enterprises* (1977) by finding an employer to be a successor even though holdover employees were not a majority of the new work force.

Where a successor employer not only applies the substantive terms of a predecessor's agreement but consults and negotiates with the union as well, the NLRB has held that the employer has by its actions assumed the contract. But the continuation of economic benefits provided in the contract is not considered sufficient evidence to support a charge that the new employer had adopted the contract. The Supreme Court held in *Golden State Bottling Co. v. NLRB* (1973) that a purchaser of a business with notice of pending unfair labor practice proceedings against the predecessor may have a duty to remedy those practices including reinstatement and back pay. However, this rule applies only if there is continued operation of the business without interruption or changes in method of operation or personnel.

A Systems Model for Labor-Management Cooperation: Organizing a Program to Achieve Cooperation and Trust
David P. Swinehart / Mitchell A. Sherr

Labor-management cooperation frequently suffers due to a failure to adequately establish the proper groundwork. Preliminary steps leading to cooperation must be taken, and essential contributory behaviors must be assessed — and in some instances, changed — before proceeding. Implementation steps should be planned in the same manner in which one would plan a production process. Often, the difference between a well-thought-out management approach and a fad lies in the degree of attention that is paid to preliminary questions and necessary developmental activities, and in the systematic organization of the relevant steps.

Labor-management cooperative programs such as in-plant committees, quality-of-worklife (QWL), quality circles (QC) or Scanlon-type group input gain-sharing plans assume that both management and labor are ready to at least suspend the mutual distrust and adversarial position that have developed over many years. The innocent — and perhaps well-meaning — plea to "trust me" frequently leads only to skepticism or

Source: David P. Swinehart and Mitchell A. Sherr, "A Systems Model for Labor-Management Cooperation," *Personnel Administrator,* 1986. Reprinted by permission.

fears of exploitation. Failure of either side to recognize and understand these viewpoints and values (which differ on many significant issues) often leads to frustration and overall failure, even in a good-faith attempt to establish a program that is beneficial to both sides or that may even be a necessity for organizational survival.

There are a number of ways to approach this problem. However, the one which offers the greatest flexibility and a realistic chance for success appears to be the systems approach. In analyzing surveys and studies from researchers such as Schuster (1982, 1983, 1984) and Leone (Leone, 1982a, 1982b; Leone and Eleey, 1982) along with data compiled by the U.S. Department of Labor (1982, 1984), certain key elements become apparent. First, a preliminary analysis is essential in order to establish goals and needs, as well as to identify the current positions of management and union leadership. Some preliminary steps may be necessary in order to begin shaping attitudes and gaining insight into the values of the other participants. Cooperation and trust cannot be gained by playing one element against the other. Understanding and communication are critical from the very beginning of the process.

After the preliminary steps have been taken, it is necessary to develop programs in a way that avoids creating new problems while solving old ones. It is merely common sense to begin with simple programs and, as they succeed, to move on to more complicated ones. It also is necessary to evaluate all critical elements of a successful program as comprehensively as possible, and to organize them in a logical sequence similar to a critical path method (Moder & Phillips, 1970). Failure to consider necessary elements and their proper order can lead to delays and retracing steps to correct deficiencies, or to the total abandonment of a program that cannot succeed because of a missing element.

Often, one finds that cooperative programs from a participative, progressive management may be accompanied by a reluctance to negotiate contracts with the proper language of cooperation for fear of giving up management rights. A good QWL program cannot be a substitute for an effective grievance procedure. Ill will resulting from aggressive collective bargaining or contract administration disputes may create a negative environment that can cloud union leaders' or workers' perceptions of management's commitment to a positive cooperative program (Kochan and Dyer, 1976).

Finally, many change programs suffer from a loss of confidence and commitment, as early stages of adaptation require unlearning as well as relearning (Margulies and Wallace, 1973). The process drags on through confrontation after confrontation. When the end seems to be lost in a myriad of details, it is beneficial to have adopted a systematic approach that measures success in terms of questions resolved and steps accomplished rather than strictly in terms of bottom-line results.

For these reasons, we have developed a systems model that is designed to provide a starting point and frame of reference for organizations that are considering a cooperative program, trying to analyze why one has failed, or attempting to revive an ailing one. The model is not intended to be comprehensive in scope, but rather is intended to be adapted to some extent on an individual basis. However, it does provide a logical pattern and a model checklist.

PHASE 1 — THE PRELIMINARY QUESTIONS

In considering the preliminary steps (see Figure 1), the first question which management must answer is one of philosophy. Is cooperation between labor and management really a goal? If a general shift is planned from authoritarian leadership to more team-oriented approaches or participative management, then cooperation is a legitimate implied goal. However, if management's primary objective is to get rid of the union or exert as much unilateral power as possible over it, an adversarial relationship is implied.

Assuming that cooperation, not continuation of adversarial roles, is the goal, the first place where management must look for change is within its own ranks. It is not enough that the organization's CEO and top advisors agree that labor and management must cooperate. This philosophy must be defined, communicated to all levels, and practiced. Affirmative steps need to be taken to ensure that resistance to change is eliminated at all levels of management (Luthans and Kreitner, 1975). This process begins with an assessment of the current management philosophy as it is being translated into action on a day-to-day basis. The degree to which managers are *willing* to change — to see the need for it and desire it — can be analyzed through questionnaires, surveys or meetings.

When the current acceptance level for managerial cooperation is ascertained, a coherent philosophy and strategy for change must be developed utilizing input from all levels. In turn, this leads to the development of a plan for training managers, not only for behavioral change, but also for acquiring the skills that are necessary to implement a cooperative program (Schuster, 1984). Naturally, development of communications and human relations skills is important, but managers also must develop technical skills that will assist in communicating the economic status of the company to employees. Such skills include the areas of accounting and finance, simple statistical analysis and the company's short- and long-range plans. Also, managers must be taught to avoid the danger of committing an unfair labor practice while dealing directly with employees instead of the union leadership on issues that properly fall within the domain of collective bargaining (*Safeway,* 1977; Labor Management Relations Act of 1947).

Finally, a reward system must be established to reinforce desired behaviors in management. This may be difficult because in the early stages, the manager who does not change may be able to deliver better bottom-line results than the more participative manager. Top management must take steps to place the emphasis on rewarding managers based upon how they get the job done, not strictly on their results. Changing evaluation criteria and formats to reflect the new philosophy and predicating financial rewards on team results (modified group gain-sharing or profit-sharing plans) is necessary to make rewards coincide with the new philosophy (Hoyer, 1979).

After management is well on its way

FIGURE 1
Integrated Cooperative Labor-Management Relations Model — Preliminary Steps

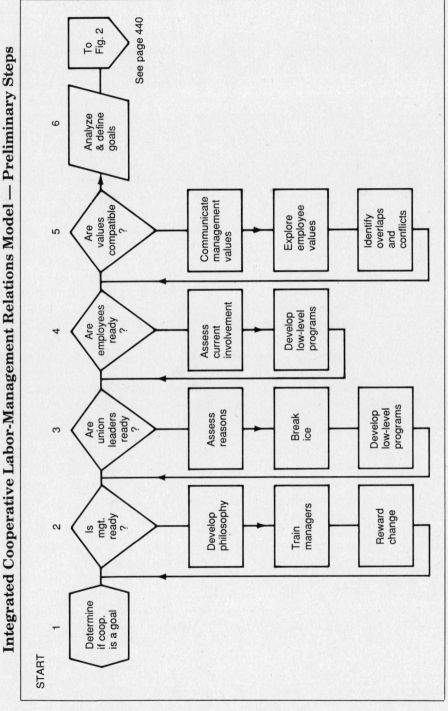

toward a cooperative philosophy, the position of union leadership must be assessed. Separating the bargaining unit into leaders and members for analysis purposes, the first concern for change will be with the leadership. Although many cooperative interventions such as QWL or QC programs have been instituted successfully without active involvement by union leadership, it is clear that opposition by union leaders will be fatal to any hopes for change (Schuster, 1982). Progress in this area may be measured in inches at first, but overcoming union leaders' resistance to change is a necessary preliminary to any change in the work force.

The first step that is needed for effective change is to assess the reasons for resistance. Has management's behavior in recent years been aggressively hostile to union leadership? Are labor and management currently in an adversarial posture? Even if union leaders appear to be docile due to a temporary economic advantage by management, there will be a latent mistrust of sharp changes in position.

If management is in the process of change, meetings can be scheduled with union leaders to inform them of the need for change and to seek their input to and acceptance of proposed changes. Asking for their input only as a formality, however, is counter-productive. Willingness to adapt plans based on constructive input is necessary in building trust between management and union leadership. On an interactive level, early programs of cooperation should be kept low-key. Safety concerns and greater cooperation in resolving minor grievances *are* likely areas for cooperation in the early stages; major economic shifts are *not* (Schuster, 1984). Top management also must be vigilant to avoid inadvertent destruction of progress by the actions of lower-level managers, who may continue resisting change.

Presuming at least passive cooperation from union leadership, the next question which must be asked is whether or not the work force is ready for change, including both union and nonunion employees. Are employees even interested in participation and the resulting higher levels of involvement? Do they trust management? Union leadership? Employee attitudes and opinions should be explored in depth before initiating any major programs or changes leading toward cooperation (Schuster, 1982).

Development of low-level test programs is another way to assess readiness — for example, voluntary unit informational meetings in which supervisors meet with employees to answer questions and inform them of unit progress. In this manner, simple problems can be discussed and solved, gradually encouraging involvement in areas where employees previously have not contributed.

A corollary to the question of employee readiness is the compatibility of management and employee value systems. The first step in this process is for management to isolate and define those values which are critical to the success or failure of a cooperative program (Schuster, 1982). Value assessment should go beyond global statements such as, "we believe in a strong work ethic," or, "successful organizations demand the involvement of all members." Instead, concentration should be on the specific value statements that relate to the corporate goals and organizational population —

for example, "being concerned with your job and the jobs of those you work with is critical to your unit's success," or, "if you want job security and growth potential, you must learn to operate effectively as a team member."

After a comprehensive list of critical value statements has been compiled, it should be communicated positively and gradually to employees, allowing for testing against the employees' beliefs and value systems. Any conflicts will soon become apparent, and corrective measures should be taken. Here is where the old adage, "build on your strengths and work on your weaknesses," can guide management's behavior. If there are substantial areas of *overlap*, implementation of programs should be relatively simple; if there are substantial areas of *conflict*, implementation should be delayed until values have been reconciled. Value changes can be achieved by training and development efforts, behavior modification or a careful selection process that considers values as an element in selection criteria (Ondrack, 1973).

Once all parties are properly informed, motivated and ready to accept changes that will lead to cooperation, specific programs can be explored and implemented. Progressing to this second phase of the model without successfully completing the first virtually assures failure in the more complicated second stage activities.

PHASE 2 — INTERACTIVE STEPS

Phase Two programs involve the negotiation and administration of the labor contract and the integration of some key management processes (compensation, communications and evaluation) into the traditional labor-management relationship.

The sequencing of the many activities in the interactive steps (see Figure 2) are not as critical as the steps in the preliminary phase. Each major operation or step consists of a number of secondary activities that may be approached concurrently with substeps from any other part of Phase Two, with the exception of the final evaluation phase.

Collective bargaining is one activity in which cooperation can be accomplished with a minimum of external change. Although most organizations bargain from the distributive model (as adversaries) on most issues, especially on economics, the integrative (cooperative) model often is employed when the issues lend themselves to mutually beneficial goals and adversarial roles may be destructive (McKersie and Hunter, 1973). Employee safety and health and dispute-resolution processes (grievance procedures and arbitration) are examples of naturally integrative issues.

Thus, the framework for cooperation exists and only needs to be broadened to encompass more issues. The first activity for collective bargaining is attitude structuring — letting the other side know what to expect (McKersie and Hunter, 1973). Much of this has been the subject of the preliminary steps, especially the value structuring. If employees and their labor leaders know that the company is sincere and willing to move on issues relating to cooperation, there will be pressure on the labor negotiating committee to move in the direction of cooperation, especially when all parties

FIGURE 2
Integrated Cooperative Labor-Management Relations Model — Interactive Steps

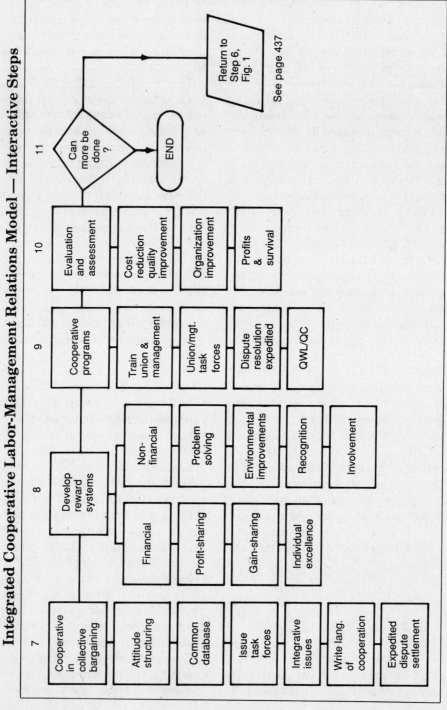

recognize the potential for mutual benefit. Management must promote this change of direction.

One key item for developing integrative bargaining is the use of a common database. One way to gain trust is for management to open up information sources to the union leadership (Jick, McKersie and Greenhalgh, 1982). This already may be happening as a result of some of the preliminary steps, but it should be formalized as part of collective bargaining exchanges. If a company makes claims of economic difficulty in seeking wage concessions or productivity improvement, they should be prepared and, in some situations, have a legal obligation to explain their position in clear and convincing terms, utilizing raw financial and economic data. Doctoring data or using processed wage surveys to prove a point at the expense of accuracy or distortion may lead to distrust, and prevent meaningful dialogue in areas of cooperation both now and in the future. Early agreement on the database for economics will strengthen the credibility of management claims (*NLRB v. Truitt Mfg.*, 1956).

Another useful tool in developing integrative bargaining is the use of task forces in addition to the main bargaining committee. A joint labor-management task force can reach agreements or define complicated issues without much of the traditional posturing and game-playing that are common to the collective bargaining process (Walton and McKersie, 1965; Jick, McKersie and Greenhalgh, 1982). Wherever possible, task forces should be used during the term of an existing collective bargaining agreement or prior to the beginning of "meaningful bargaining" to reduce the adversarial positions of the parties and replace them with problem-solving positions.

Naturally, some issues do not lend themselves to this more informal approach, but careful selection of integrative, "win-win" issues will help build confidence in the sincerity of both sides to cooperate, and will reduce the number of adversarial encounters (Walton and McKersie, 1965; Jick, McKersie and Greenhalgh, 1982). Whether or not an issue is integrative is often situational. Normally, wages are not, but in some situations, management and union may agree that wages should be raised to meet labor market pressures to attract and maintain skilled personnel, or that wages must be adjusted to help keep labor costs competitive so that they do not threaten job security or organizational survival. When these situations arise, they can and should be treated integratively.

A seemingly minor step in the collective bargaining process with potential major overtones is writing into the contract the language of cooperation. Replacing terms and clauses that emphasize the adversarial nature of the process with "friendlier" terms or clauses may not magically change the reality of workplace conflicts, but it can lead to actual reductions in tension and help change attitudes and behaviors. One such example of this type of change is the addition of a voluntary expedited dispute settlement or arbitration process. This will not replace the traditional formal arbitration step, but instead may permit resolution of many minor workplace disputes. Traditionally, arbitration has been costly and drawn out. Employees and labor leaders were not given a way to discuss legitimate problems or vent frustrations short of arbitration. Low-cost, speedy techniques which are not precedent-setting may offer one answer. Union leaders may find this a helpful way of discharging their duty to "fair representation" on noncritical cases, and management may find it a low-cost and low-risk means of resolving minor workplace problems before they blossom into more serious ones that may threaten positive relations (Jacobs, 1977; Fossum, 1982).

Another major step in the process of building cooperation is the development of reward systems. Rewards can be classified as either financial or nonfinancial (Fossum, 1982; Schuster, 1984). Most financial reward systems must be bargained with the union, either in the contract itself or as a modification to it. The types of rewards that support cooperation in the workplace are team-related or organizational in nature. Profit-sharing plans or group gain- sharing programs (such as Scanlon plans) are gaining acceptance by workers and management.

Generally speaking, individual productivity incentives such as piece work or measured day work plans have a divisive, rather than a positive team-building, effect (Schuster, 1984). However, some systems which reward individual excellence can be beneficial as long as they do not encourage intragroup competition or arbitrary treatment by management. Special care must be taken in initiating a cooperative program where individual incentive programs exist.

Nonfinancial rewards may be initiated with or without actual negotiations, depending upon the nature of the existing contract language and the type of incentive. Simple steps to initiate workplace problem-solving groups (embryonic QCs) to identify and deal with problems within the group can provide both a training ground for more sophisticated approaches and a means for positively reinforcing cooperative or participative behavior. Complaints about an uncomfortably hot or cold workplace, annoying fumes, unnecessary work steps, etc., can lead to immediate action and, in turn, result in a more pleasant and productive workplace, a more productive group, and satisfaction and recognition for the employee or team that came up with the idea.

The process of idea, suggestion, change and recognition leads to further involvement and reward for the kind of behaviors the organization needs to develop. (Special recognition programs may or may not require approval by the bargaining committees.) Any special perquisites given as a result of a reward system should either be discussed or negotiated with the union before their implementation (*Safeway,* 1977).

The more sophisticated programs of training and development, joint committees and QWL or QC programs are one of the final stages of the development of a cooperative workplace environment. Such institutionalized programs will be the natural outgrowth of all of the preliminary steps and some of the preliminary implementation ones. One of the reasons that many QWL or QC programs do not meet expectations or other cooperative programs fail is not the fault of the programs themselves, but of the failure of the organization to properly set the stage for the changes (Ephlin, 1974; Kochan and Dyer, 1976). The results do not occur instantly. Many failures accompany success in "debugging" a program. Parties must remain committed, and not abandon a well-thought-out program prematurely. Initially, many programs see a decline or decrease in production while employees are adjusting to the new program. Often, positive results cannot be expected for a period of six months to a year (Schuster, 1983).

In addition to the positive programs of cooperation, all labor-management situations should include some means of constructively addressing the inevitable workplace conflicts that will arise. Setting up a cooperative type of program will not eliminate disputes. However, the new philosophy makes the resolution of such grievances the most important issue. In a cooperative environment, dispute resolution must be quick, certain and friendly. The parties may be more willing to bend and compromise in order to resolve the problem. This does not mean that either side must "cave in" or compromise with important principles. However, the development of some expedited approach to handle the bulk of non-precedent-setting disputes that arise is a necessity. In-plant hearing panels, mini-arb panels such as those in the steel industry or expedited rules for tripartite panels are examples that have been tried successfully in many organizations (Hoyer, 1979; Elkouri and Elkouri, 1973). The formal programs on cooperation and dispute resolution are the payoff rather than the starting point, as many organizations erroneously believe.

As with most human resource programs, the final and perhaps most important stage of a cooperation program involves evaluating and auditing. Many changes are intangible, and are difficult to measure objectively. They are often difficult to separate from other internal and external changes that affect the objective outcomes. Of course, programs which are experimental in nature can be observed by using experimental control systems such as control groups, statistical evaluation and validation techniques, but most organizations wishing to install cooperation programs are anxious to get to the payoff and are hesitant or simply unwilling to enter a program if the return on investment is five to 10 years away (as is the case with many experimental design changes).

Therefore, many of the most useful measurements for success or failure remain the less sophisticated but more relevant financial and accounting indexes and measurements (Cascio, 1982). R.O.I. measures, unit cost of labor, cost-benefit analysis and P&L statements, as the common language of business, remain the quantitative approaches that are used most widely to measure the success or failure of cooperation programs. Economic measures such as productivity improvement or qualitative measures such as quality improvement, either direct (e.g., reduction of scrap costs) or indirect (customer satisfaction measures), also are important.

The final step in the process is to evaluate whether or not the changes have brought about the desired results. If they have, the programs need to be institutionalized and fine-tuned periodically to ensure that they continue to produce. If they have not, the programs need to be reevaluated and new goals defined.

Although no two organizations will follow the same pattern — nor will they achieve the same results from the same actions — the use of a systems approach will at least guarantee that important preliminary steps are not bypassed, that a logical sequence is followed, and that programs will have greater potential for success.

REFERENCES

W. F. Cascio, *Costing Human Resources: The Financial Impact of Behavior in Organizations*. Boston: Kent Publishing Co., 1982.

F. Elkouri and E. A. Elkouri, *How Arbitration Works*, 3rd ed. Washington, DC: The Bureau of National Affairs, Inc., 1973.

D. Ephlin, "The union's role in job enrichment programs," *Industrial Relations Research Association*, 1974, pp. 219–223.

J. A. Fossum, *Labor Relations: Development, Structures, Process*. Dallas, TX: Business Publications, Inc., 1982.

D. Hoyer, "A program of conflict management: An exploratory approach," *Industrial Relations Research Association*, 1979, pp. 334–335.

M. S. Jacobs, "Fair representation and binding arbitration," *Labor Law Journal 28(6)*, 1977, pp. 369–379.

T. D. Jick, R. McKersie and L. Greenhalgh, "A process analysis of labor-management committee problem-solving," *Industrial Relations Research Association Series, Proceedings of the Thirty-Fifth Annual Meeting*, 1982, pp. 182–188.

T. A. Kochan and L. Dyer, "Model of organizational change in the context of union-management relations," *Journal of Applied Behavioral Sciences 12(1)*, 1976, pp. 59–78.

Labor Management Relations Act of 1947, 29 U.S.C. Sections 151–168 (1984).

R. D. Leone (1982a), "Area-wide labor management committees: Where do we go from here?" *Industrial Relations Research Association Series, Proceedings of the Thirty-Fifth Annual Meeting*, 1982, pp. 173–181.

R. D. Leone (1982b), *The Operation of Area Labor-Management Committees*. Washington, DC: U.S. Government Printing Office (1982-O-389-997/54), 1982.

R. D. Leone and M. Eleey, *The Origins and Operations of Area Labor-Management Committees*. Unpublished manuscript. Temple University Center for Labor and Human Resources Studies, 1982.

F. Luthans and R. Kreitner, *Organizational Behavior Modifications*. Glenview, IL: Scott, Foresman & Co., 1975.

N. Margulies and J. Wallace, *Organizational Change: Techniques and Applications*. Glenview, IL: Scott, Foresman & Co., 1976.

R. B. McKersie and L. Hunter, *Pay, Productivity and Collective Bargaining*. London: Martins Press, 1973.

J. J. Moder and C. R. Phillips, *Project Management with CPM and PERT*, 2nd ed. New York: Van Nostrand Reinhold Co., 1970.

NLRB v. Truitt Manufacturing Co., 351 v.s. 149. 38 LRRM 2042 (1956).

D. A. Ondrack, "Emerging occupational values: A review and some findings," *Academy of Management Journal 16(3)*, 1973, pp. 423–432.

Safeway Trials, Inc., 233 NLRB 171, 96 LRRM 1614 (1977).

M. Schuster, "Problems and opportunities in implementing cooperative union management programs," *Industrial Relations Research Association Series, Proceedings of the Thirty-Fifth Annual Meeting*, 1982, pp. 189–197.

M. Schuster, "The impact of union-management cooperation on productivity and employment," *Industrial and Labor Relations Review 36(3)*, 1983, pp. 415–430.

M. Schuster, *Union-Management Cooperation: Structure, Process and Implementation*. Kalamazoo, MI: E. R. Upjohn Institute for Employment Research, 1984.

U.S. Department of Labor, *Resource Guide to Labor Management Cooperation*. Washington, DC: U.S. Government Printing Office (1982-O-361-270/4957), 1982.

U.S. Department of Labor, *Perspectives on Labor-Management Cooperation*. Washington, DC: U.S. Government Printing Office (1984-421-608/4681), 1984.

R. E. Walton and R. B. McKersie, *A Behavioral Theory of Labor Management*. New York: McGraw-Hill, 1965.

David P. Swinehart is an associate professor of personnel and industrial relations and director of the Labor Management Institute at Indiana University–Purdue University at Fort Wayne. Mitchell A. Sherr is an assistant professor in the supervision department and codirector of the Labor Management Institute at Indiana University–Purdue University at Fort Wayne.

The Process of Retirement: A Review and Recommendations for Future Investigation
Terry A. Beehr

It has been recognized explicitly in recent years that retirement is a process that starts with planning and decision making some time before the actual end of one's working life and is not completed for years after the point of retirement (e.g., Atchley, 1971; Kasl, 1980; Minkler, 1981). Therefore, if one is to study it, longitudinal designs must be employed so that events of some duration can be assessed. Only then can the retirement decision and events or states caused by retirement be understood fully.

Employee retirement has been an important element in political, economic, and human issues in recent years. It is practically an irreversible fact of life that the American population is aging due to changes in the birth and death rates over the past several decades, yet in recent years the work force participation rates of elderly male workers, aged 60–69, are declining. Apparently, therefore, early retirement has been increasing (O'Meara, 1977; Sheppard, 1976). There are, however, factors that may work to offset this trend. Rulings under the Age Discrimination in Employment Act of 1967 and its amendment in 1978 have tended toward the elimination of mandatory retirement based slowly upon age (e.g., King, 1982). Thus, older workers may be better able to maintain their working status if they so desire, and it would be valuable to know what influences employees in making this retirement decision. In addition to legal actions that may tend to reverse the early retirement trend, Clark and Spengler (1980) note that demographic factors may also soon become conducive to later retirement; for example, after the postwar baby boomers pass through their employing organizations, there will be fewer new people coming into organizations to take up positions and to pressure oldsters for their jobs.

Despite the obvious importance of retirement to individuals, their employing organizations, and the larger society, industrial/organizational psychology has shown little interest in the topic. Although Smith, Kendall, and Hulin's (1960) Job Descriptive Index is probably the most frequently used measure of job satisfaction, its companion instrument, the Retirement Descriptive Index, is by comparison unused by I/O psychologists. Another indication of the paucity of interest in retirement shown by I/O researchers can be observed by perusing the references at the end of this article — few are from traditional I/O journals.

Two major psychological events or states are the foci of this review: (1) the effects of retirement on the individual and the organization and (2) the individual and environment factors leading to retirement. Before these issues can be discussed, however, a clearer definition

Source: Terry A. Beehr, "The Process of Retirement: A Review and Recommendations for Future Investigation," *Personnel Psychology*, 1986, pp. 31–56. Reprinted by permission.

of retirement is necessary. Palmore, George, and Fillenbaum (1982), reporting data from seven longitudinal studies, argued that the relationships of other variables to retirement vary according to how retirement is assessed, for example, being employed less than full time and receiving a pension, being retired "early" (e.g., before the age of 65), age at retirement or the amount of employment (e.g., the number of hours worked per week) after retirement. The definition of retirement is more complex than one might expect, and one of the needs of retirement research is the development of definitions of different types of retirement in order to investigate the different factors predicting and predicted by each. A single, narrow definition of retirement would probably not serve well in all research projects; instead, it makes more sense to delineate various types of retirement, which may be related differentially to other psychological variables. There are different styles of retirement, and there is no reason to expect them to be equivalent in their causes or consequences.

Typical thinking about styles of retirement classifies retirees dichotomously on one or more criteria. Figure 1 includes three of the most common dichotomies for illustration: voluntary versus involuntary retirement, early versus on-time retirement, and partial versus complete retirement. These are more accurately conceived as continuous rather than dichotomous variables, and a common situation (complete, on-time, involuntary retirement) appears in one corner (shaded) of the figure, leaving "room" for more than one other level of each dimension.

Each of the three dimensions is quite general and is therefore made more operational by the accompanying phrase in parentheses in the figure. Thus age at the point of official retirement is a more researchable variance than early versus on-time retirement, and the number of hours that the retiree works per week is a more accurate representation of this continuous variable than partial versus complete retirement is. More research needs to be done to determine who has "free choice" in retiring (Kingson, 1982). Regarding this variable, the retiree's perception of the degree to which he or she retired voluntarily is continuous and captures the psychological nature of voluntary versus involuntary retirement — terms that have been weakly defined at best in the literature (Sheppard, 1976). While those more operational specifications of the three types of retirement are recommended as more useful than the more generally phrased dichotomous labels, other operationalizations are possible, for example, the difference between retirees' retirement ages and "typical" retirement ages in the profession, the company, or the nation as a measure of early versus on-time retirement; the current earned income of the retiree as a measure of partial versus complete retirement; and the health and physical (or mental) capacity of the retiree to continue working as a measure of voluntary versus involuntary retirement. The three specifications in the figure are recommended as consistent with typical thinking about the three variables, but there are obviously other possibilities. The point is that different types of retirement need to be considered in designing retirement research, since they may have different psychological meanings and may be related to other variables differently.

FIGURE 1

Forms of Retirement: Voluntary vs. Involuntary, On-time vs. Early, and Part-time vs. Full-time

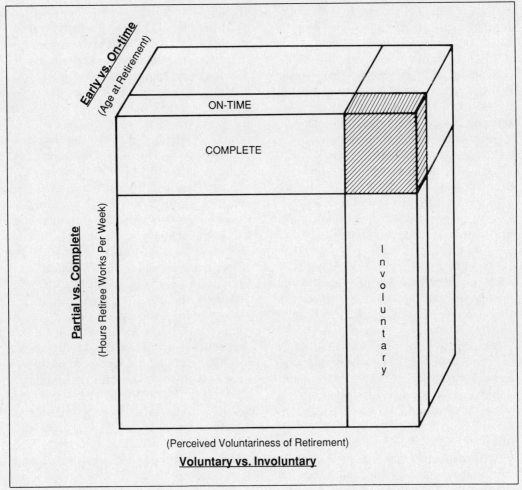

THE EFFECTS OF RETIREMENT

Most of the behavioral science approaches to retirement come from the fields of gerontology, from subspecialties within social, clinical, and developmental psychology that focus on adult development and aging, and from sociologists interested in aging. Perhaps as a result, general theories of aging have been applied directly to and have become the dominant theories of retirement. These theories have focused on the effects of retirement on retirees' quality of life, for example, on physical and mental health, on satisfaction with life and retirement, and even on mortality. These typical criterion variables focus on the individual, as opposed to the organizational outcomes of retirement. Missing from the published research are estimates of the psychological effects — such as changes in organizational climate — of retirement on organizations. This focus is probably a natural consequence of the domination of the literature by fields tending to focus on personal outcomes.

Although employee retirement and employee turnover both involve the withdrawal of employees from the work organization, the effects of retirement are likely to be different from the effects of typical turnover situations because of the differences in the types of employees who are withdrawing. Turnover tends to be more common among younger employees, while retirement is more common among older employees. Retirees are less likely to return to the work force than are employees who quit their jobs. Age differences in health and activities are also likely to lead to different individual outcomes for retirement than for turnover.

Age and experience differences also account for expected differences in organizational outcomes for retirement and turnover. All of the proposed organizational outcomes of retirement (Figure 2) are based specifically on the assumption that retirees tend to be older, more experienced, and at higher levels in the organization's hierarchy than is the average employee.

Effects of Retirement on Individuals

There is no want of propositions and theories about the effects of retirement on individuals. There are theories proposing that retirement has little effect on the quality of life, that it has a large effect, and that its effect depends on some moderating factors.

Examples include continuity theory (Atchley, 1971, 1977), which proposes that, with the obvious exception that people do not spend as much time at work, activities and attitudes do not change dramatically after retirement. At times, however, this has appeared to be a fallback or default theory when researchers failed to find strong effects of retirement. Another "little effect" approach, activity theory (e.g., Havighurst, 1963) proposes that retirees strive to maintain the activities they enjoyed in middle age. On the other hand, crisis theory (Bell, 1978–79), a "large effect" theory, assumes that retirement has a negative effect on the quality of life in retirement. Similarly, one of the earliest theories, disengagement theory (e.g., described by Atchley, 1977; Tissue, 1968), maintains that retirees withdraw from their roles as active members of society and that society aids this withdrawal. Consistency theory (e.g., Bell, 1978–79), taken from cognitive consistency theories, holds that the effects of retirement are moderated by the extent to which the person's expectations are met. When a retiree's expectations are disconfirmed (by his or her experiences in retirement), dissatisfaction with retired life will result.

While these theories have shaped thinking and research about retirement, none of them were developed as theories of retirement specifically. Instead, most are theories about the more general process of aging. In retirement research, one is more specifically interested in the effects of the retirement process on retirees

FIGURE 2
Proposed Individual and Organizational Outcomes of Retirement

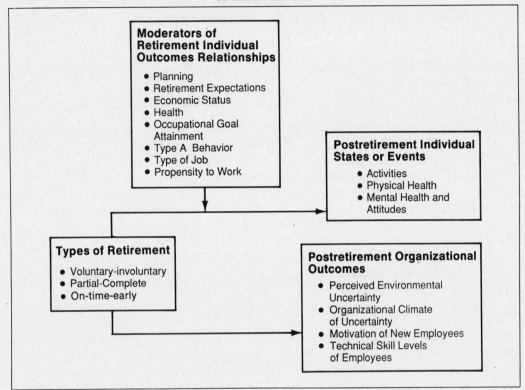

compared with people of the same generation who have not retired. If a theory describes the processes through which people of an older generation pass regardless of their working/retirement status, it is not a true theory of retirement. As Kasl (1980) has concluded, "there is no single well-articulated, logically organized, comprehensive theory of retirement which is sufficiently compelling to force an organization and interpretation of the evidence in relation to it" (p. 148). Instead of following one theory, therefore, this paper offers research propositions developed using variables that have been suggested in the literature as being effects of retirement and/or as moderating the relationship between retirement and its hypothesized effects. Propositions in this section focus on specific postretirement states/events and potential moderating variables. The types of retirement are not given separate attention in the propositions; instead, it is advocated here that research be designed that can determine the validity of each proposition for each type of retirement.

The top half of Figure 2 contains variables that are proposed in the literature as representing the effects of retirement on individuals or as moderating these retirement-effects relationships. Thus, disengagement theory, for example, maintains that the activities of retirees are changed by a withdrawal from previous activities, while continuity theory maintains that this withdrawal does not occur. Regarding individual's activities, the following proposition is offered:

Proposition I. Individuals' activities after retirement tend to be consistent with their leisure-time activities before retirement.

This proposition is consistent with the spirit of continuity theory. It assumes that most people continue to do in retirement what they found rewarding or necessary in their nonworking lives before retirement.

Logically, retirees may even increase their participation in these activities because of the increase in their leisure time. This is expected to be true for most points on the voluntary-involuntary and on the on-time-early retirement continua. It may not be as true for all points on the partial-complete retirement continuum, however, since less complete retirements allow less leisure time for the retiree.

This proposition must be tempered by some corollaries regarding hypothesized moderator variables. In response to inconsistent results, several authors have argued for the need for research on potential moderator variables in the retirement-outcome relationship (e.g., Atchley, 1979; Bell, 1978–79; Kasl, 1980). To be true moderators, these variables would interact with retirement; that is, their effects on the activities of retirees would be different from their effects on a cohort of nonretirees. Proposition IA identifies potential moderator variables for Proposition I.

Proposition IA. The degree of consistency between individuals' pre- and postretirement activities is affected by their formal and informal planning, economic status, health, and occupational goal attainment.

Perhaps because planning for retirement makes so much intuitive sense, little rigorous research has been undertaken to determine whether it is effective or the degree to which it is effective. Although there are many reports of preretirement programs that claim success (e.g., Fitzpatrick, 1979; Manion, 1976; Ullmann, 1976), Glamser (1981) has made one of the few solid assessments of such programs. Comparing a comprehensive group discussion program, an individual briefing program, and a control group, he found no evidence that the preretirement programs had any long-term value. Since there are apparently a large number of preretirement programs used in the United States (Siegel & Rives, 1978, 1980), it would be valuable to know which types of programs, if any, are especially effective.

While economic status and health have been popular variables in attempts to predict employees' decisions to retire (e.g., Kimmel, Price, & Walker, 1978; Kingson, 1982; McCune & Schmitt, 1981; Palmore, George, & Fillenbaum, 1982) and in predicting postretirement quality of life (e.g., Beck, 1982; Glamser, 1981; Kimmel, Price, & Walker, 1978; Price, Walker, & Kimmel, 1979), they have not been tested as potential moderators of retirement-outcome relationships.

Occupational goal attainment has often been assumed to be part of job satisfaction measures in the retirement literature, but it has not usually been assessed directly in retirement studies (Kasl, 1980). It is proposed here as a potential moderator on the grounds that people who are confident that they have reached their life's work-related goals are less likely than other retirees to miss work and to regret not having continued to work longer.

Proposition II. Individuals' age-adjusted health after retirement will be better than their health before retirement.

Contrary to predictions of crisis theory, Kasl's (1980) review of the literature on the stressful effects of retirement concluded that there is little evidence that retirement is a stressful event in the lives of most people. The popular perception that retirement is stressful and causes poor health probably comes in part from the well-publicized stressful life events scales (e.g., Holmes & Rahe, 1967), which list retirement as a stressful event. These studies do not isolate retirement as a separate variable, however, making it difficult to determine whether there is evidence for retirement in particular as a stressor. No sophisticated, accepted life-events scale has been developed specifically for the elderly (Minkler, 1981), and any relationship between retirement and the later incidence of ill health may be due to age rather than to the event of retirement itself. Although the results regarding the retirement-health relationship have been inconsistent, it has been suggested that poor health may more likely be a cause than an effect of retirement (e.g., MacBride, 1976) and that people have tended to report that the frequency and severity of their illness *drop* immediately after retirement (e.g., Minkler, 1981).

Methodological problems have made this research difficult to interpret, however. For example, since people who retire may no longer have as many demands (e.g., demands to work) on them, mild ill health can be ignored — it has less functional effect on their lives and therefore seems less serious. A longitudinal study (Ekerdt, Bosse, & LoCastro, 1983) supports this interpretation. As with the first proposition, Proposition II also must be tempered by the following proposition regarding potential moderator variables.

Proposition IIA. The relationship between retirement and subsequent health is affected by retirees' economic status, types of preretirement jobs, preretirement health, and Type A behavior.

The inconsistent results regarding the relationship between retirement and retirees' health suggests a need for research on potential moderating variables in the relationship (Kasl, 1980). Along these lines, Minkler (1981) has noted that an unanswered question regarding the potential stressfulness of retirement is whether blue- or white-collar employees experience more stress due to retirement. Economic status has been suggested as a situational detail in need of research (MacBride, 1976), and it is suggested as a moderator here because of its general relationship with health. Upper classes in society and people occupying higher levels of organizational hierarchies tend to have better health than people at lower levels, somewhat contrary to the popular conception that stress is particularly acute among executives (Payne, 1980). Furthermore, one study (Haynes, McMichael, & Tyroler, 1978) found that low status workers retiring "on time" were likely to die within three years of retirement, while high status workers were more likely to die between four and five years after retirement. If death can be taken as a partial indicator of health, this suggests that hierarchical status may somehow be linked to postretirement health.

Hierarchical status is also relevant regarding the nature of preretirement job as a potential moderator. In addition, it is possible that jobs on the same hierarchical level may vary in ways that are important in determining retirees' health. More physically demanding jobs may have effects on individuals' physical conditioning that are different from the effects of more sedentary jobs, for example; or jobs that are more stressful may result in retiree health status that is different from the health status of retirees from less stressful jobs. The experience of stressful jobs may leave people "weak" when they retire and in poorer health; alternatively, employees who have of necessity found ways to overcome stress in the workplace might become hardy enough to stay healthy in retirement. There is no solid evidence that bears precisely on this issue, but it is worth investigating.

Preretirement health is an obvious choice as a variable influencing postretirement health. It has been found to predict survival for early retirement (Haynes, McMichael, & Tyroler, 1978), and it has been recommended for use in research into postretirement health (e.g., MacBride, 1976).

There has been a need for more study of the potential role of individual differences in the retirement process (Bell, 1978–79). One such variable, Type A behavior (Friedman & Rosenman, 1974), has long been thought associated with the incidence of coronary heart disease but has not been tested as a potential moderator of the retirement-health relationship. Atchley (1979) has suggested that Type A behavior be investigated for the part it may play in the retirement process.

Proposition III. Individuals' mental health after retirement will be similar to their mental health prior to retirement.

Retirees' mental health is thought to be a separate issue from their physical health, and more research on it has been advocated (MacBride, 1976; Minkler, 1981). Figure 2 combines mental health and attitudes on the assumption that some mild mental health symptoms such as depressed mood or low self-esteem are measured similarly to and blend conceptually with certain attitudes such as life satisfaction and satisfaction with retirement.

It is possible that the proposition is less correct for involuntary than for voluntary retirement, for two reasons. First, involuntary retirement might be planned less intensively than voluntary retirement is, leading to poorer adjustment to retirement. Second, the individual may have less sense of control during involuntary retirement, a feeling that is often considered to be linked to poor mental health.

Contrary to crisis theory, there is little solid evidence that retirement is stressful for the typical retiree (Kasl, 1980). Therefore, no main effects of retirement on mental health are proposed. Instead, the following corollary proposition is offered as the focus on retirement-mental health research.

Proposition IIIA. The relationship between retirement and individuals' mental health is affected by their propensity to work, formal and informal planning, occupational goal attainment, and expectations about retirement.

Stagner (1979) has proposed the propensity to work, an individual difference variable, as an important variable in retiree behavior. Although his own data and reading of the literature lead to the conclusion that only a minority of retirees would rather work, it is proposed here that for this minority retirement is likely to have a negative effect on their mental health and attitudes — simply because such people are in a situation they do not like. A similar variable, commitment to work, has been found related negatively to life satisfaction in retirement (Glamser, 1981).

Planning for retirement is also proposed as a moderator of the relationship between retirement and the retiree's mental health and attitudes. This proposal is primarily based on the rationale that planning helps individuals to have more predictability and control over their retired lives. Such control, in turn, should lead people to feel better about themselves and their lives. Since planning can refer to almost anything, different researchers investigating "its" effects have often investigated very different types of planning. In formal retirement planning programs, the most frequently included characteristic is financial planning, followed by psychologically related counseling (Siegel & Rives, 1980).

Counseling, of course, can take a wide variety of forms, including group discussion or individual briefings (Glamser, 1981), and may focus on obtaining and working at jobs after "retirement" (e.g., programs for military retirees; Schlenoff, 1977). Following the reasoning for proposing planning as a moderating variable, researchers would expect to find that preretirement planning, whether formal or informal, would moderate the retirement-mental health relationship to the extent that it enhances the individual's feeling of control over retirement events.

Occupational goal attainment is proposed as a moderator of the retirement-mental health relationship because it might engender positive attitudes toward one's self and lend a sense of worth to the retiree's life.

The experience of unmet expectations has been proposed as a potentially upsetting experience in several facets of life, including work-related life (e.g., in the lack of realistic job previews; Colarelli, 1984; Wanous, 1977). It would also be worthwhile to test its potential moderating effects on the retirement process. Such effects might lend support to consistency theory.

The most important propositions offered about the effects of retirement on individuals have been those regarding moderator effects. As argued earlier, the research regarding the simpler main effects has resulted in inconsistent evidence, leading to this focus on moderator effects for future research.

Effects of Retirement on Organizations

Compared to the effects of retirement on individuals, the psychological literature contains little reference to the effects of retirement on employing organizations. Presumably, if substantial proportions of employees retire in a short period of time, their organization has the potential for rapid organizational change, however. Since this is a newer, less explored topic, Figure 2 and the propositions offered here focus on simple, main effects rather than the more complicated moderating effects — on the grounds that it would be wiser and more parsimonious initially to start with tests of simple explanations.

Proposition IV. Organizations with high rates of retirement will have more unstable, uncertain perceived environments than organizations with lower rates of retirement.

The word perceived in the proposition is very important, since it is not assumed that the environments of organizations with high retirement rates change or become less certain in any objective manner just because of high retirement rate. Instead, organizational knowledge about the environment decreases as those members who have spent years dealing with the people and organizations comprising the environment retire. This is expected to be less of a problem for partial than for complete retirement (if the individual's part-time work is in the organization for which he or she formerly worked full-time), because the retirees' skills are not entirely lost to the organization.

Control over some elements of the environment decreases both because of this erosion of knowledge and because of the simultaneous erosion of the personal influence some of the retirees had acquired over sectors of the environment relevant to their jobs. Studies attempting to measure such environmental uncertainty have usually relied entirely upon subjective data obtained from members of the organization (Starbuck, 1976), and these perceptions are the focus of the proposition. These perceptions are assumed to change as a function of the people in the organization. As the more experienced and knowledgeable people retire, the environment appears more uncertain.

Proposition V. Organizations with high rates of retirement will have more unstable, uncertain organizational climates than organizations with lower rates of retirement.

While instability and uncertainty have been used frequently to describe the environments surrounding organizations, they are used here to describe psychological (perceived) properties of the organizations themselves. This is consistent with Schneider's (1975) conclusion that climate refers to an area of research instead of being a concept limited to a particular set of dimensions. Thus, organizations may be perceived by their members as being unstable and uncertain. This is more likely to happen when people are leaving the organization, especially people who are experienced enough to know who has special expertise, who is willing to help in a pinch, who has informal influence, and so on. Since many retirees know these "nooks and crannies" of the organization through long years of experience, they take with them sources of knowledge about the organization. As Payne and Pugh (1976) argued, individual differences affect organizational climates, and this proposition maintains that seniority (an individual difference) in a system tends to lead to more knowledge about the system. As with the previous proposition, this should be a less serious problem with partial than with complete retirement.

> *Proposition VI.* Organizations with high rates of retirement will have new employees who are more motivated than organizations with lower rates of retirement will.

Newly hired, younger employees often start their careers with enthusiasm and high achievement needs (Hall & Mansfield, 1975; Porter, 1961), but they often become frustrated, in part because of their low statuses and positions of relatively low power. In organizations with high rates of retirement, however, these employees should be better able to fulfill some of their achievement needs because of the potential for more rapid advancement than they might encounter in organizations with lower retirement rates. This proposition may be especially true of professional and managerial personnel, groups upon which previous research on these needs has focused.

> *Proposition VII.* Organizations with high rates of retirement will have personnel whose knowledge about rapidly changing technical areas is more current than personnel in organizations with lower rates of retirement.

Organizations with high rates of retirement, if they are remaining the same size, must replace the retired personnel with new and probably more recently trained people. In rapidly changing technological areas, this may lead to a more up-to-date, skilled work force for the employer. In professional/technical areas for which people are often trained outside the organization before they are hired (e.g., areas in which higher education provides training), the new people may be more up-to-date than those who retired. High rates of retirement would therefore give the organization a net gain in current expertise in a few areas. This proposition assumes that the training agencies (e.g., higher education) do indeed produce graduates who are well-versed in the most modern technologies and that training programs in the employing organization itself lag behind those in the outside agencies. This assumption needs verification, however.

CAUSES OF EMPLOYEES' RETIREMENT DECISIONS

The research on the causes of employees' decisions to retire necessarily focuses on retirement that is to some degree voluntary, since there is no decision for the employee to make if the retirement is entirely involuntary. The potential causes of the retirement decision do not divide easily into individual and organizational causes. This is because individuals' decisions are often based on inseparable combinations of personal preferences and the environment's potential for matching these preferences, and the organization is part of this environment. For example, an employee might prefer to retire if he or she expected to have a certain amount of money after retirement, and the employing organization might offer a large cash incentive to early retirees. In this case, it is not clear that the retirement decision would be caused by either personal or organizational factors separately.

Some research and opinion suggests that employees retire voluntarily because of declining health, adequate projected financial resources after retirement, and attitudes toward work or toward a specific job (e.g., reviews by MacBride, 1976; Morrison, 1982; Sheppard, 1976). Recent research continues to use these labels for variables explaining retirement decisions, but the use of a label does not necessarily communicate what has been measured in a study — especially in the case of job-related attitudes.

McCune and Schmitt (1981), for example, found that job-related attitudes and financial variables predicted the employees' decisions to retire even when the predictive power of job level and employee education were removed. One of the predictive "attitude" measures, however, was the Job Diagnostic Survey, which asks people to describe rather than to evaluate their jobs. The apparent intent of the survey's authors (Hackman & Oldham, 1975, 1980) and its face validity suggests that it may measure job descriptions rather than attitudes toward jobs. McCune and Schmitt also used the Minnesota Satisfaction Questionnaire (Weiss, Dawis, England, & Lofquist, 1967), one of the most frequently employed job attitude/satisfaction questionnaires, but it did not predict the retirement decision. One of the problems with retirement research has been its use of different operationalizations of attitudes/satisfaction, some of which are dubious as indicators of job satisfaction. Kasl (1980) has noted, for example, that Palmore's (1971) well-known finding that work satisfaction is a strong predictor of longevity of life was based upon a measure of job satisfaction that included a majority of items reflecting the ability of employees to carry out work rather than satisfaction with work. The finding may be more appropriately interpreted as meaning that physical functioning (health?) is predictive of mortality. Stated thusly, the result has a very different meaning from the statement that job satisfaction predicts longevity.

As noted earlier, predictors of retirement may vary according to the form of retirement (Palmore, George, & Fillenbaum, 1982). One of the needs of retirement research is the development of definitions of different "types" of retirement. This is especially true in the case of research on the causes of retirement decisions. Palmore et al. have made a good beginning at this process in their study using sets of existing data. Studies are needed that are designed to do this from the outset, however, since that study (Palmore et al., 1982) had to investigate whatever forms of retirement were available in the data already collected rather than choosing the most important forms prior to collecting the data.

A final note on previous research into the causes of the retirement decision is that the data do not justify the use of the word "causes." This is because of the use of nonexperimental designs to study retirement decisions, designs that do not readily lend themselves to strong inferences regarding causation. The use of such designs is likely to continue, however, due to the difficulty and even potentially unethical nature of many straightforward "ideal" experimental designs for use in studying retirement decisions. Experimental manipulations designed to induce people to retire or not retire would have to be strong and would intrude into the lives of private individuals and employing organizations. Since national and organizational policies on

FIGURE 3
Proposed Individual and Environmental Causes in the Process of Retirement

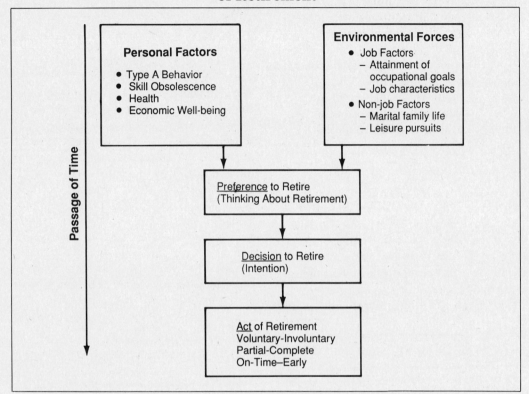

retirement do change from time to time, however, serendipitous research employing quasi-experimental designs may be executed. Until then, our knowledge about "causes" of retirement decisions is more correctly labeled knowledge about "predictors" of retirement decisions.

Figure 3 illustrates potential processes and key variables that might be involved in the decision to retire. It suggests that retirement is a process that occurs over time rather than a single, one-time event. Employees prefer to and then decide to retire before they actually do it, and this may take some time. Therefore, the figure suggests that researchers should try to measure and understand some of the employees' psychological processes that precede the act of retirement if they want to understand the whole process. It proposes, for example, that the typical predictors of retirement might have greater power in explaining the preference to retire than in explaining the actual act of retirement.

Many of the factors in the retirement decision proposed in the figure could also be proposed as factors in employee turnover. This is to be expected, since retirement and turnover can both be conceived as forms of withdrawal from the workplace. These factors are more likely to lead to retirement than to turnover, however, because the older employee has retirement as a readily available, socially acceptable role. Unemployment or locating a new job, alternatives for younger employees, are less socially acceptable or less readily available.

Of primary interest in this section are the personal and environmental factors that lead to older employees' preferences to retire. The following propositions, therefore, focus on these variables.

Personal Factors Leading to Retirement Decisions

As illustrated by the figure, four characteristics of the person are proposed as likely causes of employees' decisions to retire: Type A behavior, skill obsolescence, health, and economic well-being.

> *Proposition VIII.* Employees with Type A behaviors are less likely to decide to retire than Type B employees are.

Type A behavior, characterized by hard-driving, aggressive, impatient activity, has been proposed as an indicator of coronary-prone individuals (e.g., Friedman & Rosenman, 1974). It has also been suggested as a variable that ought to be investigated for its part in the retirement process (Atchley, 1979), although it is not entirely clear just how it might play a part. It is proposed here that Type A people are less likely to prefer to retire than others are, because the Type A's are more likely to miss the chance to compete and to work at a fast pace. There is at least the common belief in our culture that retirees' lives are slower moving, and if Type A's believe this, they may not prefer to retire.

> *Proposition IX.* Employees are more likely to decide to retire to the extent that their job skills are obsolete.

When employees' job skills become obsolete, they are more likely to retire for two reasons. First, they may feel unhappy doing work for which they are ill-prepared and at which they probably perform poorly. If such workers are older, they may exercise their option of retiring to escape this unhappy situation. Second, if organizations believe workers' skills are obsolete, the organizations' decision makers might offer particularly attractive retirement incentives to such employees to entice them to retire, replacing them with more skilled, younger employees. Minkler (1981) has also noted that organizations in such situations may try to get people to retire in order to reduce labor costs by getting rid of "expensive" senior people.

> *Proposition X.* Employees are more likely to decide to retire to the extent that they have chronically poor health.

Most reviews have concluded that health is one of the more consistent predictors of the retirement decision (e.g., reviews by Kasl, 1980; Minkler, 1981). It is possible, however, that health affects decisions to retire early less than it affects on-time (later) retirement decisions if health tends to vary inversely with age.

A recent study found no incremental relationship between health and retirement after the effects of demographic variables had been controlled (e.g., McCune & Schmitt, 1981). Health is such an intuitively obvious predictor that it bears further study; future studies of its effects would benefit from the control of demographics, however. If the no-relationship finding is replicated, this would be an important piece of new information about the retirement process.

Proposition XI. Employees are more likely to decide to retire to the extent that they expect to be well-off financially in retirement.

Personal financial states appear to be important in the retirement decisions of many people (e.g., studies by McCune & Schmitt, 1981; Palmore, George, & Fillenbaum, 1982). This is probably not the only important factor, however, as results from a national sample of workers suggested that employees' desires to quit their jobs (as opposed to retiring) varied according to the type of work the employees were doing. Blue-collar workers were almost twice as likely to report that they would quit if they could make it financially than white-collar workers were (Sheppard, 1976). Also, it is expected that finances have a greater impact on early retirement than on on-time (later) retirement decisions, because people retiring early usually lose more years of high-paying employment and receive lower annual retirement pay than people retiring later. This would make finances a more important consideration for early than for later retirement decisions.

Environmental Factors Leading to Retirement Decisions

Some job and some nonjob environmental factors are likely to lead employees to decide to retire. These are the attainment of occupational goals, job characteristics, marital and family situations, and leisure pursuits.

Proposition XII. Employees' decisions to retire are related to their attainment of their own occupational goals.

No direction for this potential relationship is proposed here, since either a positive or negative relationship between these two variables seems logically possible. An employee may feel that he or she has accomplished all that is desired and have no further achievement-related reason to work, or he or she may become so frustrated at a failure to achieve these goals that the only course of action is to give up and retire. Either possibility is interesting, but there is currently no solid research on the topic.

Proposition XIII. Employees are more likely to decide to retire to the extent that their jobs have "undesirable" characteristics.

In the presumed pull-of-nonwork factors and push-of-work factors in a retirement decision, undesirable job characteristics are seen as a push to get out of the job. The presumably intrinsically motivating job characteristics measured by the Job Diagnostic Survey (Hackman & Oldham, 1980) have been found related to retirement decisions (McCune & Schmitt, 1981), but not much other work has been done in this area. There are a great many other job characteristics that could be related to decisions to retire, including the degree of required travel, physical labor, outdoor work, the nature of the physical working conditions, supervisory styles, and so forth. Some job characteristics may exaggerate other potential causes of retirement; for example, jobs characterized by rapid technological change might lead to employees' skills becoming obsolete, which in turn might make retirement more attractive.

Proposition XIV. Employees' decisions to retire are related to their marital and family situations.

There is little in the empirical research on retirement to indicate the potential influences of family situations on retirement decisions. It is proposed here that these forces can influence employees' retirement decisions, but specific family situations and directions of their influence are not included in the proposition. A few examples will be used to illustrate the bounty of potential influential variables, however.

First, since home life may be seen as an alternative to work life in the sense that people probably expect to spend more time at home with their families after retirement than before it, the attractiveness of the employee's family situation might influence his or her willingness to retire and spend more time in that setting.

Second, family situations may increase or decrease the employee's perceived financial obligations. The need to finance children in college, for example, may make employees less likely to retire; children's college graduations may make retirement financially easier. In this instance, family situations have some of their effect by influencing one of the personal factors discussed earlier (economic well-being).

Third, widowhood (a marital/family situation) of employees might make an employee either more or less likely to retire. Some recently widowed employees might become depressed and withdraw from social activities, including withdrawing from the workplace in the form of retirement. Interpreting "health" broadly, this means the family situation influences the retirement decision through its effect on health (depression). Alternatively, the death of a spouse who has been chronically ill and in need of care for a long period of time might make the employee feel a new sense of vigor and freedom to work harder — or to quit work and to engage in favored leisure activities. There are many possible influences of family and marital situations on employees' decisions to retire, and most of them are in need of solid research.

Proposition XV. Employees are more likely to decide to retire to the extent that they have attractive alternative (leisure) activities.

Seldom studied by psychologists — and especially by I/O psychologists interested in retirement decisions — is the pull of nonwork activities on the employee. Although a retiree's frequency of participation in particular leisure activities may not increase after retirement (Bosse & Ekerdt, 1981), it is the employee's expectation of such an increase that might act as a "pull" toward retirement. Thus, for example, employees who like to travel may see retirement as a way to enjoy more of this attractive activity.

SUMMARY AND RECOMMENDATIONS

Retirement is a process that occurs over a period of time and includes making decisions, acting on those decisions, and experiencing their consequences. Both individual characteristics and factors in the individual's environment influence the decision to retire, and both the individual and the employing organization experience outcomes due to retirements. Although the decision to retire and the act of retirement are amenable to study in I/O psychology, neither has caught the attention of the field very strongly in the past. The study of retirement has until now been dominated by fields whose major interest is the welfare of the individual. I/O psychologists, with their dual interest in both the individual and the organization, are likely to add substantially to knowledge about retirement if they study it from their viewpoints.

Each study of retirement needs first to define the topic of inquiry. Retirement comes in several forms, and these forms may be preceded by different causes and may predict different outcomes. Exactly what the different studies are investigating will be made more evident by clearly defining retirement and its operationalizations. When more information has been gathered about retirement, it may become obvious that each type fits a theoretical model that is slightly different from the models that the other types fit.

Methodological improvements over previous studies could help the field advance significantly. This is especially obvious in regard to much of the research on the effects of retirement on individuals. A single improvement, the use of longitudinal designs, is a major need at present (Schmitt, Coyle, Rauschenberger, & White, 1979). Since retirement is a process that occurs over time, cross-sectional data cannot capture the process very well. A few recent studies covering periods of time are strong arguments for longitudinal studies since some of their results from a single point in time did not match their results over time (e.g., Bosse & Ekerdt, 1981; George & Maddox, 1977; Glamser, 1981; Goudy, 1981). Assuming that retirees' activities are the same as what employees say they will do after retirement, assuming that retirees' descriptions of their former jobs are accurate, and believing retirees when they report the reasons for their retirement decisions, are but a few reasonable-sounding tactics used in past research. It would be much better, however, to assess employees' jobs while they are still employees, retirees' activities after they retire, and so forth. In order to measure characteristics of the employee and his or her environment and characteristics of the same person after he or she has retired, longitudinal studies are necessary.

The exact starting point of such studies is impossible to determine, since the point at which employees begin to plan for retirement is unknown and probably variable. A workable strategy that would result in useful information at the present state of retirement research is to study a large number of employees in a sequential developmental design (Friedrich & Van Horn, 1976). The sample size would be determined by retirement rates of employees at various ages among the population to be sampled, and measures would be taken of older employees as they think about retirement, decide to retire, and actually retire. This would require contacting employees periodically (say, every six months) to determine whether they have yet begun thinking seriously about retirement or have actually decided to do it.

The relevant variables (i.e., those in the propositions) would be measured upon initial contact with the employees, and again whenever their retirement "phase" changes (e.g., when they decide to retire and again after they retire). The process of periodic contact and measurement would continue until large enough numbers of people have passed through each retirement phase to allow statistical analysis — and long enough beyond retirement (at least one year) to allow the retirees' lives to stabilize. The required time for such a study is impossible to specify and would depend on the size of the initial sample, but three years is probably a rough minimum for samples of several hundred to a thousand. Much of the measurement could be done via survey techniques and inspection of personnel records.

Regarding professional practice in the area of retirement, I/O psychologists apparently should not recommend and offer retirement planning or workshops aimed at alleviating the stress of retirement for all older employees or retirees. These practices should focus selectively on the minority that need it, since it is apparent that most people adjust to their retirement without major psychological crisis. Health and finances are major concerns of retirees and those contemplating retirement, and planning efforts should be directed at those parts of retirees' lives. Those companies that provide programs for their own older employees and/or retirees often do include financial planning as a topic, but health is apparently not a major focus (e.g., Siegel & Rives, 1978, 1980).

In organizations whose effectiveness is highly dependent upon personal contacts of organizational members with people in the environment, high rates of retirement are proposed as potential problems. Such organizations, therefore, should not offer especially attractive early retirement packages or should encourage partial retirement, in which experienced employees with valuable personal contacts continue working part-time for as long as is necessary. Conversely, in industries with rapid technological changes with which formal education and training institutes keep pace, high rates of retirement (and replacement by newly trained employees) may make the organization more effective. Such organizations, therefore, might do well to offer especially attractive early retirement packages.

Finally, it should be noted that the propositions were developed after, and no doubt influenced by, reading previously published research and theorizing about retirement. The domain of research outlined here has expanded upon the list of variables apparent in previous publications, especially in the discussion of the effects of retirement on the organization. If one considers retirement an area of research that concerns all the processes through which an older generation of employees passes, however, still other heretofore unexplored parts of the domain might become apparent. I/O psychologists may even be able to generate especially creative research because they are not "contaminated" with the same preconceptions as researchers in fields with long histories of work with retirees.

REFERENCES

Atchley R. C. (1971). Disengagement among professors. *Journal of Gerontology, 26,* 476–480.

Atchley R. C. (1977). *The social forces in later life* (2nd ed.). Belmont, CA: Wadsworth.

Atchley R. C. (1979). Issues in retirement research. *The Gerontologist, 19,* 44–54.

Beck S. H. (1982). Adjustment to and satisfaction with retirement. *Journal of Gerontology, 37,* 616–624.

Bell B. D. (1978–79). Life satisfaction and occupational retirement beyond the impact year. *International Journal of Aging and Human Development, 9,* 31–50.

Bosse R., Ekerdt J. J. (1981). Change in self-perception of leisure activities with retirement. *The Gerontologist, 21,* 650–654.

Clark R. L., Spengler J. (1980). Economic response to population aging with special emphasis on retirement policy. In Clark R. L. (Ed.), *Retirement policy in an aging society* (pp. 156–166). Durham, NC: Duke University Press.

Colarelli S. M. (1984). Methods of communication and mediating processes in realistic job previews. *Journal of Applied Psychology, 69,* 633–642.

Ekerdt D. J., Bosse R., LoCastro J. S. (1983). Claims that retirement improves health. *Journal of Gerontology, 38,* 231–236.

Fitzpatrick E. W. (1979). Evaluating a new retirement planning program — results with hourly workers. *Aging and Work, 2,* 87–94.

Friedrich D. D., Van Horn R. D. (1976). *Developmental methodology: A revised primer.* Minneapolis, MN: Burgess Publishing Company.

Friedman M., Rosenman R. H. (1974). *Type A behavior and your heart.* New York: Alfred A. Knopf.

George L. K., Maddox G. L. (1977). Subjective adaptation to loss of the work role: A longitudinal study. *Journal of Gerontology, 32,* 456–462.

Glamser F. D. (1981). Predictors of retirement attitudes. *Aging and Work, 4,* 23–29.

Goudy W. J. (1981). Changing work expectations: Findings from the Retirement History Study. *The Gerontologist, 21,* 644–649.

Hackman J. R., Oldham G. R. (1975). Development of the Job Diagnostic Survey. *Journal of Applied Psychology, 60,* 159–170.

Hackman J. R., Oldham G. R. (1980). *Work redesign.* Reading, MA: Addison-Wesley Publishing Company.

Hall T. D., Mansfield R. (1975). Relationships of age and seniority with career variables of engineers and scientists. *Journal of Applied Psychology, 60,* 201–210.

Havighurst R. J. (1963). In Williams R. H., Tibbits C., Donahue W. (Eds.), *Process of aging* (Vol. 1). New York: Atherton Press.

Haynes S. G., McMichael A. J., Tyroler H. A. (1978). Survival after early and normal retirement. *Journal of Gerontology, 33,* 269–278.

Holmes T. H., Rahe R. H. (1967). The Social Readjustment Rating Scale. *Journal of Psychosomatic Research, 11,* 213–218.

Kasl S. V. (1980). The impact of retirement. In Cooper C. L., Payne R. (Eds.), *Current concerns in occupational stress* (pp. 137–186). Chichester, England: Wiley.

Kimmel D. C., Price K. R., Walker J. W. (1978). Retirement choice and retirement satisfaction. *Journal of Gerontology, 33,* 575–585.

King F. P. (1982). Benefits and costs of continuing pension accruals past normal retirement age. *Aging and Work, 5,* 31–36.

Kingson E. R. (1982). Current retirement trends. In Morrison M. H. (Ed.), *Economics of aging: The future of retirement* (pp. 98–135). New York: Van Nostrand Reinhold Co.

MacBride A. (1976). Retirement as a life crisis: Myth or reality? *Canadian Psychiatric Association, 21,* 547–556.

Manion U. V. (1976). Preretirement counseling: The need for a new approach. *Personnel and Guidance Journal, 55,* 119–121.

McCune J. T., Schmitt N. (1981). The relationship between job attitudes and the decision to retire. *Academy of Management Journal, 24,* 795–802.

Minkler M. (1981). Research on the health effects of retirement: An uncertain legacy. *Journal of Health and Social Behavior, 22,* 117–130.

Morrison M. H. (Ed.). (1982). *Economics of aging: The future of retirement.* New York: Van Nostrand Reinhold Co.

O'Meara R. (1977). *Retirement: Reward or rejection?* The Conference Board.

Palmore E. (1971). The relative importance of social factors in predicting longevity. In Palmore E., Jeffers F. C. (Eds.), *Prediction of life span* (pp. 237–247). Lexington, MA: Heath Lexington Books.

Palmore E. B., George L. K., Fillenbaum G. G. (1982). Predictors of retirement. *Journal of Gerontology, 37,* 733–742.

Payne R. (1980). Occupational stress: Is it really a problem? [Abstract.] *Proceedings of the Seventeenth Annual Conference of the Eastern Academy of Management,* p. 168.

Payne R., Pugh D. S. (1976). Organizational structure and climate. In Dunnette M. D. (Ed.), *Handbook of industrial and organizational psychology* (pp. 1125–1173). Chicago: Rand McNally.

Porter L. W. (1961). A study of perceived need satisfaction in bottom and middle management jobs. *Journal of Applied Psychology, 45,* 1–10.

Price K. F., Walker J. W., Kimmel D. C. (1979). Retirement timing and retirement satisfaction. *Aging and Work, 2,* 235–245.

Schlenoff D. (1977). Considerations in counseling the retired career officer. *Journal of Employment Counseling, 14,* 131–135.

Schmitt N., Coyle B. W., Rauschenberger J., White J. K. (1979). Comparison of early retirees and non-retirees. PERSONNEL PSYCHOLOGY, *32,* 327–340.

Schneider B. (1975). Organizational climates: An essay. PERSONNEL PSYCHOLOGY, *28,* 447–479.

Sheppard H. L. (1976). Work and retirement. In Binstock R. H., Shanas E. (Eds.), *Handbook of aging and the social sciences* (pp. 286–309). New York: Van Nostrand Reinhold Co.

Siegel S. R., Rives J. M. (1978). Characteristics of existing and planned retirement programs. *Aging and Work, 1,* 93–99.

Siegel S. R., Rives J. M. (1980). Preretirement programs within service firms: Existing and planned programs. *Aging and Work, 3,* 183–191.

Smith P. C., Kendall L. M., Hulin C. L. (1969). *The measurement of satisfaction in work and retirement.* Chicago: Rand McNally.

Stagner R. (1979). Propensity to work: An important variable in retiree behavior. *Aging and Work, 2,* 161–172.

Starbuck W. H. (1976). Organizations and their environments. In Dunnette M. D. (Ed.), *Handbook of industrial and organizational psychology* (pp. 1069–1123). Chicago: Rand McNally.

Tissue T. L. (1968). A Guttman scale of disengagement potential. *Journal of Gerontology, 23,* 513–516.

Ullmann C. A. (1976). Preretirement planning: Does it prevent postretirement shock? *Personnel and Guidance Journal, 55,* 115–118.

Wanous J. P. (1977). Organizational entry: Newcomers moving from outside to inside. *Psychological Bulletin, 84,* 601–618.

Weiss D. J., Dawis R. V., England G. W., Lofquist L. H. (1967). *Manual for the Minnesota Satisfaction Questionnaire: Minnesota studies in vocation rehabilitation.* Minneapolis, MN: Vocational Psychology Research, University of Minnesota.

Terry A. Beehr is director of the doctoral program in Industrial/Organizational Psychology at Central Michigan University.

How to Avoid Grievance Arbitration
Rebecca Ballard / Michael D. Crino

In January 1978, Nettle Creek Corp. of Richmond, IN, participated in arbitration proceedings after it discharged an employee for theft. Interpretation of the employee's polygraph test suggested she intended to steal thread from the company. The discharge was upheld.

In August 1985, an arbitrator found that Avis Inc., headquartered in Garden City, NY, was not justified in discharging an employee for theft, although the employee's polygraph found that he was deceptive in his answers.

These two similar grievance cases resulted in opposite arbitrated outcomes. Both companies invested much time and money preparing and presenting their cases, and both believed they had compelling evidence to support their termination decisions. Yet management's decision was still rejected on one case. We believe that a properly designed expert system would have enabled the overruled company to more accurately predict the outcome of its case.

The rule generation process generally used to support expert system develop-

Source: Rebecca Ballard and Michael D. Crino, "How to Avoid Grievance Arbitration." Reprinted from *Computers in Personnel* (New York: Auerbach Publishers). © 1989 Warren, Gorham & Lamont Inc. Used with permission.

EXHIBIT 1

Arbitration Cases Used to Derive Rules for an Arbitration Expert System

American Maize-Products Co v. Oil, Chemical and Atomic Workers International Union, 56 LA 421 (1971).

Avis Rent a Car System Inc v. General Teamsters, 85 LA 435 (1985).

Bethlehem Steel Corp v. United Steelworkers of America, 68 LA 581 (1977).

Bisbee Hospital Association v. United Food and Commercial Workers' Union, 79 LA 977 (1982).

Bowman Transportation Co Inc v. International Union of District 50, 59 LA 283 (1972).

Bowman Transportation Co Inc v. United Steelworkers of America, 60 LA 8 (1973).

Bowman Transportation Co Inc v. United Steelworkers of America, 64 LA 453 (1975).

Braniff Airways Inc v. Association of Flight Attendants, 73 LA 304 (1979).

Brink's Inc v. Teamsters, Chauffeurs, Warehousemen and Helpers, 70 LA 909 (1978).

Cardinal Services Inc v. Bartenders, Motel, Hotel and Restaurant Workers, 77 LA 213 (1981).

Chapman Harbor Convalescent Hospital v. Hospital and Service Employees Union, 64 LA 27 (1975).

Daystrom Furniture Co v. United Paperworkers International Union, 65 LA 1157 (1975).

General Portland Inc v. United Cement, Lime, Gypsum and Allied Workers International, 81 LA 230 (1983).

Golden Pride Inc v. Chauffeurs, Warehousemen and Helpers, 68 LA 1232 (1977).

Grocers Supply Co v. International Brotherhood of Teamsters, General Drivers, Warehousemen and Helpers, 59 LA 1280 (1972).

Mount Sinai Hospital Medical Center v. Hospital Employees Labor Program, 73 LA 297 (1979).

Nettle Creek Industries Inc v. Upholsterers' International Union, 70 LA 100 (1978).

Ralston Purina Co v. American Federation of Grain Millers, 75 LA 313 (1980).

---

ment can be applied to published grievance arbitration cases. A system built from these rules can help HR departments make employment decisions and predict probable outcomes of grievance cases should they result in arbitration. We use as an example rules derived from 18 published arbitration cases (listed in Exhibit 1), to demonstrate the logic of rule generation. These cases all involve employees discharged in connection with polygraph examinations.

FEASIBILITY FIRST

An expert system best supports a problem of HR management that doesn't necessarily require common sense for its solution, according to Donald A. Waterman, author of *A Guide to Expert Systems* (Addison-Wesley Publishing Co, 1986), but does require cognitive skills and must be clearly understood. In addition, human experts practiced at solving that problem must be available, agree on solutions to the problem, and be able to articulate their methods. Also, according to Waterman, any problem that can be supported by an expert system requires a heuristic solution (i.e., uses self-education), can't be solved with algorithms, has practical value, is of manageable size, is not easy to solve, and requires symbol manipulation (i.e., is not solved readily through mathematics).

Arbitration and HR-related court cases meet these criteria. For example, an arbitrator's work (i.e., determining the merits of a grievance) requires interpretation of data according to certain standards (e.g., contractual provisions), not common sense. Interpretation requires cognitive skills and no physical effort. The task is not too difficult, requiring only a limited amount of time and material. Although a case's circumstances may seem confusing, arbitration is both understood and highly structured. Furthermore, human experts (i.e., arbitrators and justices) are available, and their decisions and the factors on which their decisions are based are available in published accounts of the cases.

A critical criterion for defining rules is agreement between the experts on a solution (i.e., case outcome). Although an arbitrator or judge may occasionally take a unique path to reach a decision, a predictable set of circumstances supports the majority of case outcomes.

Costs, Geography, Consistency

Three criteria help determine the justifiability of an expert system for employee actions. The first, suggested by Waterman, is that the problem has a high payoff. The costs of legal representation, expert testimony, witness time spent away from the job, adverse judgments, and arbitrators' fees underscore the negative financial consequences of inappropriate employment decisions. For example, there are now 25,000 wrongful discharge cases pending in state courts. Ford Motor Co.'s aerospace subsidiary recently paid $107,000 in a wrongful discharge case. Similar cases cost IBM $300,000, TRW $700,000, and Exxon $10.1 million. These awards were in addition to often substantial court expenses. (Expert systems can also provide relatively inexpensive training for supervisors with HR responsibilities, minimizing the possibility that they might handle a problem inappropriately so it winds up in arbitration.)

The second criterion (also from Waterman) is that supervisors are often geographically dispersed, operating independently from the HR department, so that expertise is needed in scattered locations as an employee management situation unfolds.

The third, which seems special to HR problems, is that the collective expertise contained in published decisions exceeds the grasp of individual human experts. Use of an expert system (depending on the situation) may be superior to the personal wisdom of human experts.

RULE DEVIATION

One of the most important elements in building an expert system is its rule derivation process. The rules an expert system depends on must accurately reflect the decision-making behavior of the arbitrators. To demonstrate, we organized this process as three steps (see inset for illustration).

Case Groups

Before actually building a system, system developers must determine the subgrouping of cases from which rules can be derived. It is impossible to simultaneously derive rules from hundreds of divergent cases. The case should first be subdivided into groups reflecting or dealing with particular HR issues. Cases that might fall into more than one group should be reviewed case by case, and if appropriate, added to more than one group. The number of cases in each group should be small enough to be manageable yet large enough so that a meaningful set of rules can be derived from them. Sometimes, older cases may be excluded if they are inconsistent with new legislation, court rulings, or current thinking. And on a rare occasion, an arbitrator can make a decision that is inconsistent with the majority for similar cases. We recommend that these exceptions to the mainstream be excluded from the rule derivation process.

Isolating Decision Factors

Rule development requires that parameters (i.e., decision factors defining the important elements of cases) be isolated from the cases. In cases we selected for illustration, the nature of the offense and length of employee service were decision factors mentioned by arbitrators, and thus are parameters, which are defined by various values. For example, the length of service parameter can have values corresponding either to actual years of service (e.g., 1,2,3) or categories representing ranges of service years (e.g., 0, 1–5).

Goals are a special type of parameter; their values are the arbitration case outcomes users want their system to help them predict. Goals generally fit one of two models: employee grievance is sustained (and management's action is overruled) or employee grievance is not sustained (and management action is upheld). The goal may even follow a third model: grievance is sustained and penalty modified if the arbitrator agrees that management had sufficient reason to discipline its employee, but considers the punishment too harsh.

In determining relevant parameters, system developers should note those factors arbitrators cited as important to their decisions. Although some of these factors might seem to provide only minimally useful or redundant information, developers should resist the temptation to eliminate them; all potentially useful factors should be retained.

Isolating parameters may require detective work because arbitrators do not always explain all the factors that influenced their decisions. Every detail of a case that seems intuitively important should be included; the rule derivation process identifies the useful information.

After system developers determine a preliminary set of parameters, they must identify the range of relevant values for each one. There are two types of parameter values: numerical (e.g., 1,2,3) and categorical (e.g., yes, no). Numerical data can be classified in either category depending on how arbitrators treat them. For example, if the specific number of years an employee has been with a company affects the ultimate decision, those specific values might need to be retained. If the important factor is, however, only whether an employee has worked for a company a short time (e.g., 0 to 5 years) or long time (e.g., more than 5 years), the ranges of numerical data should be treated as the values for the parameter called length of service. For nonnumerical data (i.e., categorical), all available values should be retained in this initial stage.

HOW TO DERIVE EXPERT SYSTEM RULES

The following three-step method enables system developers to refine the arbitration case data needed to establish the rules an arbitration expert system refers to when helping users make employment decisions and plan arbitration strategy in court.

Organize cases into groups We chose 18 grievance arbitration cases from the 1970s and 1980s in which employees were discharged due in part to the results of their polygraph exams.

Isolate relevant parameters Although a number of parameters were defined in the selected cases, we chose four to simplify this example:

- The case result was either *discharged for refusing to take a polygraph exam* or *discharged in connection with the results of a polygraph exam.*
- The question of whether the employee had committed a previous offense had three possible answers: *yes, no,* and *not mentioned* (in the published case summary) — It is possible that *not mentioned* meant that the employee was neither an exemplary nor a troublesome

(Continued on next page)

EXHIBIT A

Arbitration Case Records Sorted by Goal and Parameter Values

Goal: Grievance Sustained?	Case Type: Discharge for...	Previous Offense	Corroborating Evidence	Severity of Offense
Yes	Refusing to take	Not mentioned	—	—
Yes	Refusing to take	Not mentioned	—	—
Yes	Refusing to take	No	—	—
Yes	Refusing to take	Not mentioned	—	—
Yes	Refusing to take	Not mentioned	—	—
Yes	Results	Not mentioned	No	Severe
Yes	Results	Not mentioned	No	Severe
Yes	Results	Not mentioned	No	Moderate
Yes	Results	No	No	Severe
Yes	Results	Yes	No	Severe
Yes	Results	No	No	Moderate
No	Results	No	Yes	Severe
No	Results	Not mentioned	Yes	Severe
No	Results	Not mentioned	Yes	Severe
No	Results	Not mentioned	Yes	Severe
No	Results	Not mentioned	Yes	Moderate
No	Results	No	Yes	Severe
No	Results	No	Yes	Severe

HOW TO DERIVE EXPERT SYSTEM RULES (cont.)

EXHIBIT B
Consultation with an Arbitration Expert System

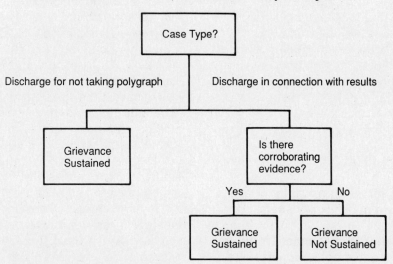

employee or that a provision in the contract prevented the arbitrator from divulging that information.
- Corroborating evidence was either available or not available to corroborate the results of the polygraph exam.
- Because all of these cases were filed to appeal discharges, only two values could describe the severity of the offense: *moderate* and *severe.*

Use parameters to develop rules
Entropy is a measure of the certainty with which a goal or the value of a specific parameter can be predicted. The formula for entropy's mathematical calculation as well as an explanation is in Thompson and Thompson.[1] Our method, which follows, is a more intuitive way to achieve the same results:

- Type goal values and other parameter values into a spreadsheet or data base.
- Sort case records by goal value to help identify relationships between parameter values and goal values (see Exhibit A) — Each parameter can be used as a secondary sort key, one at a time, to help determine which is most strongly related to the case outcomes (i.e., goal values). Because only two of the parameters are relevant to all cases, our analysis begins with those two. (Note that in Exhibit A, only *Case Type* and *Previous Offense* have values for all cases.) In this example, *Case Type*

(*Continued on next page*)

> **HOW TO DERIVE EXPERT SYSTEM RULES (cont.)**
>
> offers the most predictive power. The value of *Previous Offense* cannot predict the case outcomes with any certainty. The goal values, by *Previous Offense,* are:
> — *Not mentioned* (grievance sustained in 7 cases, grievance not sustained in 4 cases).
> — *No* (sustained in 3 cases, not sustained in 3 cases).
> — *Yes* (sustained in 1 case, not sustained in 0 cases).
>
> Case Type predicts the outcome of 5 cases:
> — Discharge for refusing to take (sustained in 5, not sustained in 0).
> — Discharge in connection with results of the polygraph exam (sustained in 5, not sustained in 7).
>
> - The cases whose values are predicted by *Case Type* are removed (i.e., those in which the value for *Case Type* is *Refusing to Take*). The rule is: If *Case Type* is *discharged for refusing to take a polygraph exam,* the grievance is sustained.
> - All remaining cases are discharged in connection with the results of a polygraph exam, but more information is needed to predict their outcomes because they are split between grievance sustained (in 5 cases) and grievance not sustained (in 7 cases). Normally, they would be sorted again, using each of the other three parameters as a tertiary sort key, to support the analysis. But because the format of these cases makes the relationship clear, corroborating evidence is the determining parameter for the remainder of the cases.
>
> Also if the *Case Type* is discharged in connection with the results of a polygraph exam, and *Corroborating Evidence* is *yes,* the grievance is *not sustained.* And if *Case Type* is discharged in connection with the results of the polygraph exam, and *Corroborating Evidence* is *no,* the grievance is *sustained.*
>
> The system follows the dialogue outlined in Exhibit B's schematic when consulting with users.
>
> **Note**
>
> 1. B. Thompson and W. Thompson, "Finding Rules in Data," *Byte* (November 1986), pp. 149–158.

Rule derivation isolates the parameters that most influenced human arbitrators in their decisions, and can help establish a set of decision rules. In our example, we use entropy to determine the important parameters. Entropy is a measure of the knowledge about a case outcome that a particular fact or set of facts helps provide.

The fewest parameters possible should be used to predict a case's outcome because, the fewer parameters used, the smaller or more parsimonious the resulting rule set can be. Deriving rules with a measure of entropy enables system developers to use a minimal amount of information for each rule, and to derive the fewest possible number of rules.

RULES AND SHELLS

After rules are derived from data, they must be entered into an expert system shell. A very flexible and powerful shell is IBM's Expert Systems Environment (ESE), a VM-compatible package for IBM mainframes. Numerous personal computer packages are also available, but their capabilities are limited.

Combined rules and shell form a system that interacts (or consults) with HR professionals. It asks users questions about the current employee action or grievance to yield both the parameter's current values as derived from past cases and the system's rule set. As important values are determined, the system can, depending on its design, recommend actions or predict the probable result if the employee action would be brought to arbitration.

Users must remember that, like human experts, HR expert systems are fallible, and that decisions should be based on the same factors that influenced past decision makers. Even so, conclusions can still be inaccurate. An expert system's expertise is only as expert as the human experts from whom its rules were derived and works best when used to supplement, not replace, HR managers' decision making.

RECOMMENDED READING

Krebs, V. "Can Expert Systems Make HR Decisions?" *Computers in Personnel* (Winter 1988), pp. 4–8.

Rebecca Ballard is pursuing a Ph.D. in management at Clemson University. Michael D. Crino is a professor of management at Clemson University. Funding for the authors' research was provided by the Center for Industrial Management at Clemson University.

Modeling the Skills Obsolescence Process: A Psychological/Economic Integration
John A. Fossum / Richard D. Arvey / Carol A. Paradise / Nancy E. Robbins

Technological or skills obsolescence has been a recurring theme over the past 30 years, often achieving prominence in reaction to a major change in the environment such as the advent of astronautics, the energy crisis, and sophisticated foreign competition. Potential organizational and personal factors contributing to skills obsolescence have been examined by Dubin (1973) and Kaufman (1975). Methods for counteracting skills obsolescence such as retraining (Miller, 1979), job redesign (Crystal & Deems, 1983), and continuing education (Renck,

Source: John A. Fossum, Richard D. Arvey, Carol A. Paradise, and Nancy E. Robbins, "Modeling the Skills Obsolescence Process: A Psychological/Economic Integration," *Academy of Management Review,* 1986, pp. 362–374. Reprinted by permission.

Kahn, & Gardner, 1969) have been suggested. However, the conclusions regarding the etiology and definition of obsolescence have seldom been theoretically or empirically based.

Three major deficiencies exist in the study of skills obsolescence: (a) imprecision in its definition, (b) no guiding model to suggest important variables and potential processes in its development, and (c) a failure to use a multidisciplinary approach in explaining its development. The present authors believe that skills obsolescence is determined by interactions involving the individual, the employer, and the external market; that it is manifested in a failure to accomplish responsibilities required of position holders in evolving jobs; and, thus, research would benefit from an integration of psychological and economic perspectives.

The purposes of this paper are threefold. First, a summary of how the skills obsolescence process has developed is presented and a definition is provided. Second, a model of the skills obsolescence process is proposed. Third, the available direct and indirect literatures which support some of the linkages in this proposed model are reviewed. In the development of this model, expectancy and human capital theories are highlighted and integrated to account for the development of skills obsolescence.

DEFINING OBSOLESCENCE

Previous Definitions

Shearer and Steger (1975) defined professional obsolescence from a between-person within-occupation perspective:

> A person is obsolescent to the degree that, relative to other members of his profession, he is not familiar with, or is otherwise unfitted to apply, the knowledge, methods, and technologies that generally are considered to be important by members of his profession (p. 265).

Obsolescence was defined in "deficiency" terms by Kaufman (1974):

> Obsolescence is the degree to which organizational professionals lack up-to-date knowledge or skills necessary to maintain effective performance in either their current or future work roles (p. 23).

Obsolescence should be contrasted from other forms of unsatisfactory performance through the "up-to-date" characterization given above by Kaufman (1974). This definition recognizes an inequality between how quickly job requirements change and rates of acquiring knowledge and skills. It is a longitudinal process through which the capabilities of a means of production (i.e., capital, materials, or labor) become less effective than available substitutes as the demand for products and services in the market changes. Finding the causes of obsolescence involves either identifying changes in job requirements or changes in talents, capacities for change, or motives of the jobholder. Both psychological and economic theories lend themselves to examining obsolescence from this person/job perspective.

Psychological/Economic Definitions of Personal Inputs

In staffing and selection models, jobs require particular knowledge, skills, and abilities (KSAs) which are necessary for effective performance of tasks and duties. Knowledge refers to the content or technical information needed to perform adequately in a job and is typically obtained through formal education, on-the-job experience, and information media (cf. McCormick, 1976). "Knowledge" requirements represent cognitive structures which are necessary, but not sufficient, conditions to perform.

Skills are the specific psychomotor processes necessary to perform the job's present requirements and are displayed through behaviors (e.g., writing Fortran programs, developing budget plans, etc.). Skills also include the facility to select from among a repertoire of possible behaviors those which are most appropriate for the particular situation in which the overall job duties are being applied. The present authors' definition of skills would include interpersonally-oriented behaviors which influence others to behave in ways that facilitate the accomplishment of a person's individual job requirements.

Abilities refer to cognitive factors which represent present capabilities or achievement levels (Dunnette, 1976). Abilities should be distinguished from aptitudes which are broad *capacities to learn* the KSAs needed to perform a job. Individuals' aptitude levels impose limitations on their potential for acquiring new KSAs. Unlike KSAs, aptitudes are not susceptible to much change. Individual aptitude levels influence the breadth of job duties that can be accomplished (Schwab & Cummings, 1976) and the rate at which new KSAs may be added.

Economic theory identifies three major means of production: capital, raw materials, and labor. These are presumed to be combined in proportions leading to the most efficient production of an organization's products and/or services. The productive potential of labor varies among individuals through differences in types and levels of acquired KSAs. The potential residing within a given individual is called "human capital." Individuals differentially possess aptitudes which enable them to improve their human capital. Persons with greater aptitude levels are more "economically able" in a human capital sense since the speed, depth, and breadth of acquiring KSAs are influenced by aptitude levels.

Human capital (Becker, 1975; Schultz, 1961; Thurow, 1970) is divided into two categories: general human capital (GHC) and specific human capital (SHC). GHC consists of knowledge, skills, and abilities (KSAs) which are of equivalent value for performing jobs common to many employers. For example, the skill "writing Fortran programs" would be equally useful to a set of employers who hire scientific applications programmers. SHC consists of KSAs which are of value to a single employer and involve the particular manner in which work is performed in that organization. The skill "running programs on the local computer installation" would be an example of SHC.

Psychological/Economic Definitions of Job Requirements

Jobs have also been defined in terms of tasks, duties, elements, responsibilities, or behaviors which are necessary to attain an organization's goals (McCormick, 1976). While jobs have most often been described by the tasks and behaviors necessary to perform them, they may also be characterized by the KSAs inferred as necessary to perform required behaviors (Dunnette, Hough, & Rosse, 1979).

Job requirements may also be viewed as derived from the demand for the organization's services and products. A job's configuration may change as the derived demand for skills associated with an organization's outputs changes or when the cost of capital, labor, or raw materials, relative to the others, changes. Thus, job requirements are a function of both the cost of KSAs and other factors in the market and the demand for goods and services these KSAs will produce.

Defining Obsolescence

Given the prior discussion, we define obsolescence as follows:

> Obsolescence occurs when the person requirements of a job which are demanded by its tasks, duties, and responsibilities become incongruent with the stock of knowledge, skills, and abilities currently possessed by the individual; given that the knowledge, skills, and abilities were previously congruent with job demands.

Obsolescence is a function of two major elements: the job and the person. For obsolescence to occur, person and job requirements which were congruent at one time must no longer fit due to job changes or individual changes or both. Job requirements may increase, stay the same, or decrease in comparison to the need for specific KSAs over time. Similarly, employees may develop certain talents, maintain them, or allow them to deteriorate. Any efforts to remedy obsolescence must attend to both the nature and degree of changes in jobs and the rate of growth, decline, or change in employees' KSAs.

MODEL OF SKILLS OBSOLESCENCE

What are the elements which contribute to changes in job requirements, and what are the variables which contribute to changes in employee talents? The model shown in Figure 1 suggests that obsolescence is a function of incongruence between person and job factors manifested in a longitudinal process. New technologies, materials, organizational goals, and organizational structures which are responses to a change in the external environment are the driving forces behind changing job requirements. The individual is the other element involved in the obsolescence process. Over time, individuals make decisions and behave in ways which maintain, improve, or allow their KSAs to deteriorate as job requirements evolve. Several factors affect potential changes in a person's KSAs. These include organizational rewards, aptitudes, individual differences, and motivational levels, as well as nonwork aspects unique to the individual. Obsolescence can occur as the result of job requirements which expand more rapidly than KSAs or job requirements which change in a direction different from the types of KSAs previously acquired.

Factors Contributing to Job Changes

Job changes appear to be due to several influences:

1. Changing goals   New products require different KSAs than those previously necessary. The new products could either be initiated by the organization or they could be in response to competition. As a result, the demand for positions

FIGURE 1
Factors Involved in Skills Obsolescence

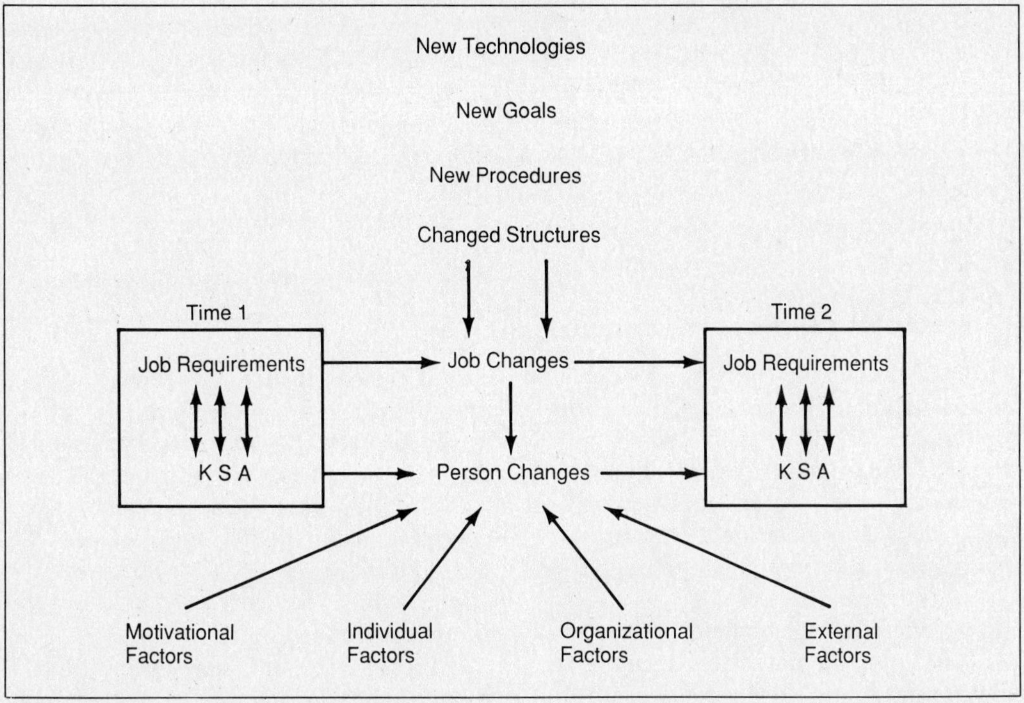

New Technologies

New Goals

New Procedures

Changed Structures

Time 1: Job Requirements ↔ K S A

Job Changes

Time 2: Job Requirements ↔ K S A

Person Changes

Motivational Factors, Individual Factors, Organizational Factors, External Factors

---

within a job or the numbers and requirements of jobs may expand, contract, or be eliminated.

2. Changing technologies or materials Although the type and level of products and services may remain relatively constant, the technology or materials used to produce them may change radically. Job requirements and the skills associated with these requirements have changed markedly in the U.S. economy over relatively short periods (Rumberger, 1981). For example, Buchanan and Boddy (1982) found that the KSAs required of typists were substantially altered by the introduction of word processing technology even though output remained similar.

3. Changing structures Organization redesign necessitates a new mixture of job requirements. The changes in the responsibilities of supervisors accountable for types (and numbers) of personnel, products, and services, alter job requirements.

While the literature is replete with references to job change, little has been done from the perspective of the firm to measure these changes. If an organization wishes to diagnose where obsolescence is most likely to occur, it makes sense to identify the jobs in which change is most rapid. But how is this measurement done? One avenue is to compare job description information across time periods. Precision depends heavily on the job analysis method used and the type of information collected (e.g., tasks, behaviors, KSAs required, etc.). Increased attention should be focused on the *rate* as well as the dimensionality of job changes. Other things being equal, increases in either the scope of the job or the rate of change in the job, require more able employees.

Motivational Factors Contributing to Person Changes

Motivational factors have been suggested as important influences on skill acquisition. Kaufman (1973) collected critical incident behaviors indicative of engineers who were considered either up-to-date or obsolete. Positive motivational factors were mentioned as the most frequent characteristics of engineers who stayed current in their fields. Although this indicates the potential influence that motivation plays, no theory was suggested to define its role. Expectancy theory and human capital theory both incorporate information relating to individual choices in skill acquisition.

Expectancy theory The theory (Campbell & Pritchard, 1976; Vroom, 1964) predicts that behaviors result from choices individuals make based on the kinds and levels of rewards they expect to accrue and the ways rewards can be obtained. The theory has been applied to professional updating and obsolescence by Arvey (1973), Harel and Conen (1982), and Porter (1971). Expectancy theory first predicts that individuals will learn and apply relevant KSAs if they believe that they are capable of acquiring them. Second, individuals will acquire the KSAs they believe will be instrumental in attaining valued rewards. Individuals might decide to acquire certain sets of KSAs over others, or they might decide *not* to acquire any new KSAs based on expected relative costs and benefits. Individuals will be "motivated" to acquire KSAs if: (a) they believe they can acquire them, (b) they perceive that acquiring KSAs will lead to certain outcomes, and (c) they value these outcomes. These propositions lead to the following implications for the suggested model:

1. If preferred outcomes change, individuals may not wish to acquire new KSAs because they are not instrumental for attaining these new outcomes.

2. Individuals must have positive expectations that the KSAs can be acquired under present job/organizational circumstances before an effort to develop them is expended.

3. Individuals' aptitude levels may represent limitations on the scope and level of KSAs they can acquire.

4. If no rewards are available for acquiring KSAs, there will be little incentive to acquire them. In order to "motivate" individuals to acquire and maintain KSAs, organizations will need to reinforce and reward job-related acquisition behaviors. If expectancy theory is applicable, beliefs in long-run rewards are part of the incentive assessment.

5. If individuals perceive that benefits are greater from expending effort in their present jobs than in preparing for future job and work roles, few new KSAs will be learned.

There have been many studies of expectancy theory predictions in general, but none have investigated the propositions directly within the context of acquiring KSAs. Porter (1971) and Arvey (1973) suggested that expectancy theory could be applied within the obsolescence context, but did not test the theory directly. Arvey and Neel (1976) conducted a cross-sectional study of expectancy theory propositions among a group of older nonsupervisory engineers and found that the three most valued outcomes for this group were: making use of abilities, accomplishment, and security (measured on an ipsative scale). Following earlier research studies on expectancies and valences, Kopelman (1977) constructed a measure which combined both job-related expectancies and outcome valences and found it to be negatively related to age among engineers. If either updating related outcomes which become important to aging employees, or the expectation of obtaining them are perceived to decrease with age, then obsolescence would be predicted to be related to age. Kopelman's results support such a proposition. However, none of the studies have made longitudinal assessments of job or person changes which might influence expectancy theory component perceptions.

Most of the expectancy theory propositions and empirical tests of the theory in employment settings have studied jobholders (the labor suppliers). However, it is important to recognize that the propositions also apply to managers (the labor demanders). Managers may configure job requirements in ways which they believe will be most instrumental for their own outcomes. Employees may be one of the instruments for obtaining valent managerial outcomes. Thus, in their efforts to maximize their own outcomes, managers may neglect or avoid to develop employees' KSAs if it will not yield a return while they still hold the management job.

Human capital theory This economically based theory suggests that persons will invest in acquiring KSAs by purchasing or participating in training and foregoing earnings if the stream of future benefits (earnings) exceeds the costs necessary to enter or move up in an occupation. As in expectancy theory, the investment decision to engage in a particular type of training is made in the *belief* that it will yield maximum future earnings over other alternatives. To the degree that there is a perceived risk associated with obtaining outcomes from training, the perceived benefits must be *discounted* by the degree of risk. Interest rates may also be included to discount future returns. The higher the interest (discount) rate people perceive, the lower their motivation to engage in training. The theory has several important implications for the study of skills obsolescence.

1. Individuals may differ in their willingness to invest in training and acquiring KSAs as a function of age. Older individuals may be less willing to invest in updating because of a shorter stream of payoffs. There should be little difference, however, among persons of different ages if the payoff period associated with the training is fully realized within their anticipated remaining work lives and expected acquisition risks are similar across age groups. Persons will more likely choose training to acquire "durable" rather than rapidly changing KSAs if they expect that they will have career patterns which will include significant periods of nonuse (McDowell, 1982).

2. The model is useful for examining the potential narrowing of benefits accruing to individuals as they gain tenure or move toward the top of a job ladder. For example, if technical occupations peak out at a certain salary level and managerial progressions begin around that level, persons nearing the top of the technical hierarchy are unlikely to invest in additional technical training but would obtain managerial training since they have nearly achieved their maximum occupational earnings from their technical human capital.

3. From a managerial standpoint, organizations must decide which employees will receive SHC investments. These judgments consider the rate of return expected on the investments. One of the factors associated with decisions about who and what to train revolves around anticipated turnover. Because of the risk of turnover, organizations avoid investing in GHC because of the applicability of these KSAs across employers. Places in a training queue are assumed to be allocated given the organization's assessment of employees' "economic ability," where economic ability is the net expected benefit accruing to the organization from the additional human capital as compared to its acquisition costs (which include foregone productivity during training, higher future wages, and replacement costs associated with potentially higher risk levels of turnover). Managers would be expected to invest resources in training, to the degree that training present employees will enhance departmental performance more than investments in alternative factors. Managers might be unwilling to invest in training using resources from *their* budgets when training enhances promotion and transfer opportunities and employees are expected to move before increased performance in the unit recoups the costs.

Combining Expectancy and Human Capital Theories

Both theories share some obvious common elements. First, they emphasize a rational decision heuristic where outcomes perceived to have the greatest return are chosen. Second, both are concerned with beliefs that individuals have about the future rewards and costs associated with alternative courses of action. Third, both attend to a variety of possible outcomes associated with each individual. However, human capital theory adds to the understanding of the acquisition of KSAs by more specifically attending to the organizational factors involved in investment in human capital. It helps to explain why the costs of acquiring certain types of KSAs must be assumed by the individual while other costs must be assumed by the organization. Finally, the theory explains why relatively large future rewards may be necessary to "motivate" people to acquire KSAs even where the risk factor is relatively small, if present rewards are foregone during the training period.

PERSON CHANGES AND OBSOLESCENCE

Recently, theories related to career development and life stages which may influence the onset of obsolescence have been articulated (cf. Hedaa & Joynt, 1981; Levinson, Darrow, Klein, Levinson, & McKee, 1978; London, 1983).

Levinson et al. (1978) called attention to different developmental stages in adult life and suggested that there are career "peaks" and "maintenance" periods for individuals. There may be developmental changes in what individuals desire for job outcomes and the believed "stream" of costs and rewards for updating. Hill and Miller (1981) used a life-stage approach to examine career events and found that interest in improving KSAs seemed either high or increased through the thirties and subsequently declined through the remaining years in a career. Shearer and Steger (1975) found that "obsolescence decreased until the mid-thirties and increased thereafter" (p. 268). Ference, Stoner, and Warren (1977) made a distinction between individuals who have career "plateaus" due to organizational factors (lack of promotional opportunities) as compared to personal factors (lack of ability or desire to achieve higher level jobs). Near (1985) has found that plateauing may also be a function of boss-subordinate conflicts unrelated to the absence of job-related KSAs. It is possible that attributions regarding life stages are the result of aggregating individual outcomes. "Maintenance" periods may be more prevalent later in life because opportunities associated with continued development decline.

While the term "plateau" typically means lack of upward mobility, KSA plateaus may reflect the tendency of some individuals to maintain relatively fixed KSAs. If they are nearing retirement, they may believe the future stream of rewards is not worth the costs of achieving new KSAs. These beliefs are probably realistic. Studies in intraorganizational mobility (Rosenbaum, 1979a, 1979b) suggest that promotional potential decreases with time spent in a position.

Effects of Individual Differences on Skills Obsolescence

Age It is frequently speculated that older individuals are more prone to obsolescence due to: (a) the longer time period during which their KSAs could erode, or the potentially lower quality of their initially obtained KSAs; (b) the assumption that aptitudes decrease with age; and (c) the possibility that older employees see a weaker relationship between acquiring KSAs and obtaining valued rewards than younger individuals. But, obsolescence explanations often involve the substitution of age as a proxy for other variables, such as tenure, motivation, etc., while obsolescence may actually be more closely related to these unmeasured variables.

Shearer and Steger (1975) found a significant curvilinear (U-shaped) relationship between age and obsolescence among managers and officers working in the military. Dalton and Thompson (1971) presented evidence that age was associated with accelerating obsolescence. Several studies (cf. Lehman, 1963; Mali, 1969) have also reported lower productivity associated with older workers. Doering, Rhodes, and Schuster (1983) recently reviewed 28 studies of the age-performance relationship conducted during the last 30 years. Age-performance decrements were found in 15 studies, increases were found in 4 studies, and no significant relationship was found in 9. They conclude that "The . . . studies . . . revealed essentially an inverted U-relationship between age and performance for scholars, engineers, and scientists" (p. 63). These were studies of the age-performance and *not* the age-obsolescence relationship of direct interest here.

One needs to be very careful about drawing any immediate conclusion that older workers are prone to obsolescence. Rosen and Jerdee (1976) found that older workers were less likely to receive support for retraining compared to equally qualified younger individuals. The relationship between age and obsolescence may not be caused by age but may result from employers withholding developmental resources from older employees.

Although tenure might likely be associated with the erosion of applicability in KSAs, there is little evidence to suggest there are significant decrements in broad general abilities as a function of the aging process (cf. Baltes & Schaie, 1974). With regard to specific abilities, there seems to be a rather broad consensus that intellectual performance which requires speed usually declines with age (Birren, Cunningham, & Yamamoto, 1983). If there is any relationship between age and obsolescence it probably depends on the particular KSAs involved. More research is needed to establish any such linkages.

Education Both Dalton and Thompson (1971) and Shearer and Steger (1975) found that a person's educational level was negatively related to obsolescence. It is possible that educational level and achievements represent indirect measures of individuals' aptitudes and subsequently, their capabilities to acquire KSAs. When educational level is examined at particular job levels, lower education might also be associated with fewer KSA acquisition skills.

Breadth of interests Arvey (1973) hypothesized that individuals who are interested in a wide variety of activities and events may be more likely to keep updated. Kaufman (1972) found that an interest inventory was predictive of relatively creative efforts (measured by a patent criterion) for engineers. Pelz and Andrews (1966) found that scientists and engineers with several areas of specialization tended to exhibit higher levels of performance. Dunnette and Kirchner (1958) found that sales managers who displayed a relatively "broad" interest pattern were more effective in their jobs than managers who displayed more "narrow" interest patterns. From an ecological standpoint, the breadth of interest-obsolescence results may reflect the greater adaptability of these individuals to job requirement changes.

Personality variables Kaufman (1974) noted that personality dimensions such as self-reliance, need for achievement, autonomy, locus of control, etc., have been suggested as being linked to the avoidance of obsolescence. He suggested that flexibility of styles is particularly important in responding to change. Individuals who are relatively rigid, not open to new ideas, and low risk takers may be more prone to obsolescence. Unfortunately, there is essentially no empirical literature that tests these hypothesized relationships.

Aptitudes Kaufman (1974) suggested that "an important psychological quality that facilitates or inhibits obsolescence among professionals is capacity for knowledge acquisition" (p. 51). Aptitudes probably establish the upper limits for individual KSA acquisition. Thus, negative relationships might be expected between well-established aptitude measures and measures of obsolescence when motivation is held constant. In studying the effects of aptitudes on (voluntary) skill acquisition, the motivation levels of a set of individuals being trained may be relatively equal since they have all selected the same training program to obtain more valued outcomes. The study of obsolescence, however, is more difficult and would require knowledge of individuals' levels of a "force to adapt or change" which might be gathered using expectancy theory measures to statistically control for motivational differences.

Specific aptitudes may be differently related to particular kinds of KSA incongruencies. Mathematical proficiency may be associated with the avoidance of obsolescence among professionals in engineering and computer systems, while general problem-solving aptitudes may be more important for keeping managers current (Kaufman, 1974).

JOB AND ORGANIZATIONAL INFLUENCES ON OBSOLESCENCE

Job reward magnitude and allocation mechanisms (represented by motivational and organizational factors in Figure 1) are expected to influence updating, skill acquisition, or obsolescence. Following expectancy and human capital theories, decision makers may feel it is more instrumental to simply utilize the current KSA base of their employees in order to achieve immediate goals and objectives, rather than to invest in providing opportunities for skill acquisition to accomplish future goals or to reward acquisition behavior.

Job influences

Challenging job performance levels within jobs can contribute to the acquisition of KSAs. By presenting employees with new tasks, duties, and responsibilities within the context of the present job, they will acquire needed KSAs through experience. Shearer and Steger (1975) found that the more varied job assignments individuals had, the less obsolete they were. Kaufman (1978) found that the degree of technical challenge experienced by engineers early in their careers related positively to their professional competence in subsequent years. Dubin (1973) suggested that "the exploration of new tasks enables the scientist and engineer to assess his own knowledge and fill in gaps and deficiencies" (p. 8). Other studies (e.g., Berlew & Hall, 1966) have shown that early challenge is important in the future retention and performance of employees. Early career challenges and events have been found to influence the organizational success of employees in nontechnical areas as well as engineering and scientific occupations (cf. Hall, 1976; Schein, 1978).

Skill acquisition may also be enhanced in jobs involving contact with other organizational members, colleagues in other organizations, and the news media. There may be greater pressure on individuals in these kinds of positions to keep updated in order to share information when asked and to present information to outside sources. Dubin (1973) indicated that an organizational environment, which provides opportunities for peers to interact promotes learning, innovation, and the development of ideas. "Such experiences come from interchanges with colleagues, discussions with managers and experts, talking with colleagues in other disciplines, or participating on panels and committees" (p. 9). Ebadi and Utterback (1984) have found that communication with others is related to innovation in organizations.

Effect of Organizational Influences on Skills Obsolescence

It is also important to identify the impetus for job changes. If it is external to the organization, then necessary KSAs might be gained most rapidly through hiring. If the organization is creating the change, changing employees' KSAs to fit new requirements must be undertaken by the employer. It should also be recognized that some individuals have the aptitudes to rapidly acquire KSAs while others do not. From an organizational perspective matching individuals who can accommodate (and perhaps enjoy) high rates of change with dynamic jobs will be beneficial (cf. Staw, Sandelands, & Dutton, 1981). If the scope or rate of change in a job is relatively large, however, it might be impossible for an individual to acquire the necessary KSAs with the job configured the way it is.

Several general organizational variables potentially influence updating and skill acquisition. If the organization or department focuses on immediate outcomes and neglects long-term perspectives, individuals are not likely to engage in updating behaviors (because of either time demands or the lack of opportunities). Managers might perceive an insufficient period to justify a payoff from development. The relative emphasis that organizations place in rewarding goal accomplishment would influence updating behavior and resources allocated to it by managers.

Organizations also differ in the degree to which updating is directly and overtly rewarded. This might take the form of raises, promotions, etc. There are also potential hidden costs for individuals who engage in updating efforts; these should be recognized by organizations interested in increasing updating behaviors. For example, when individuals participate in training workshops (2–3 days), a good deal of work may accumulate during this absence. It may actually be *punishing* for individuals to update due to the increased workload.

A related issue concerns the consequences for individuals who do not update. If individuals are rewarded, or if there is a current stream of positive outcomes for simply maintaining a current talent base of KSAs, little updating can be expected.

Recent research on organizational stress has examined some of the same factors attributed to the causation of skills obsolescence. For example, Schuler (1984) listed organizational change, work pace, and work overload as elements contributing to stress. The available literature indicates that stress can have considerable impact on individuals across a wide range of organizational variables (Brief, Schuler, & Van Sell, 1980). It is also likely that stress will have some impact on KSA acquisition. There is essentially no literature in the obsolescence area which provides evidence of this hypothesis, but it is suspected that updating and KSA acquisition will more likely take place under low stress organizational conditions.

IMPLICATIONS FOR RESEARCH AND PRACTICE

The model depicted in Figure 1 suggests that obsolescence results from changes over time in either jobs or individuals which create mismatches between individual KSAs and job requirements. Changes in production technology, organizational goals, and policies and procedures were seen as an exogenous (but possibly related) set of variables determining job requirements. Motivation, aptitude level, personal situation factors, and organizational position factors were exogenous variables influencing the composition of the stock of an employee's KSAs over time.

This review suggests that most cognitive aptitudes do not decline to any great extent during the normal working lives of most adults. Similarly, measures of individual differences reflected in personality and interest measures are relatively reliable over time (cf., Birren et al., 1983; Cronbach, 1970). If the collection of tasks and duties included in an evolving job are still within the aptitude levels of the employee, then skills obsolescence is probably a function of motivational and external factors, and could be avoided by modifying job rewards to make them congruent with valent individual outcomes. However, when motivational and external factors are not barriers to updating, aptitude levels dictate the scope and depth of future job designs if obsolescence is to be avoided.

Expanding job requirements may interact with personality and interest variables as they influence updating activity. Persons with broad interests, who see themselves as controlling their environments, might be expected to react more quickly to external changes or to take an active hand in shaping the environments (and hence, job designs) in which they work. This implies that organizations need to communicate information on anticipated future environments to enable employees to exert control in more likely job requirement areas.

RESEARCH ISSUES IN OBSOLESCENCE

Obsolescence can occur in both general and specific KSAs. General KSA obsolescence is associated with changes external to the organization and would be concentrated in areas related to technology, materials, and product demand which influence organizational goals. From an organizational structure perspective, it is expected that skills obsolescence in general KSAs will be greater among those positions that do not have significant contact with the external environment. Specific KSA obsolescence could be expected in certain positions. For example, if a job offers little exposure to internal information sources (which might alert the jobholder to likely changes in KSAs which will be required in the future), then obsolescence might occur. To assess the degree to which structural isolation might be related to obsolescence, job analysis, job attitude, and organizational network data could be gathered to measure social, technical, and physical isolation. Expert judges within an organization could rate a sample of jobs (regarding their perceived obsolescence, or their measures of performance against a changing external market) and business entities and their job configurations could be identified which appear to lack the ability to lead or compete. If isolation were related to perceived obsolescence or measured inadequate performance, then this component of organizational structure would be a correlate.

Our model suggests that job rewards influence the acquisition and maintenance of KSAs. Several research directions are suggested by this linkage. First, if individuals have some knowledge of their aptitudes to acquire KSAs and believe that these aptitudes are valued by organizations, they have some economic power in the hiring process. If organizations also have knowledge about the potential of applicants, they would be willing to pay more for employees with high potential. Other things being equal, higher paying organizations (at entry) should be able to acquire work forces that will be more resistant to obsolescence because they possess higher levels of aptitudes for acquiring new KSAs. Second, employees are likely to acquire and maintain those KSAs which have the highest perceived future rewards. The structure and system of pay in an organization signals opportunities to individuals. Where technical obsolescence is a concern, it would be expected that those organizations which have shorter job ladders for technical occupations and in which relative increase magnitudes are greater for nontechnical occupations, will find technical employees disinterested in upholding their skills.

When individual difference measures suggest that employees are not likely to develop their own KSAs, or where organizational structure creates barriers to the acquisition of externally initiated general KSAs, organizations are primarily responsible for informing and providing training to employees. An examination of the relative efficacy of formal training to reduce or eliminate skills obsolescence among employees with different personality factors (e.g., locus of control) or in different levels of organizational isolation would be revealing.

Practice Issues

The research issues cited above obviously have implications for practice. Many of them relate to the personnel analog of the "build or buy" decision. For organizations that espouse "lifetime" career values, "build" approaches are necessary. This means that employees must be considered as fixed assets and a corporate resource. Managers will have to be evaluated not only on accomplishing output criteria but also on their stewardship regarding the enhancement of the human capital assigned to them. Organizations would need to routinely do massive KSA retooling at the conclusion of various projects, and when there are changes in production or organizational structure.

Programs (of payment) need to be constructed that reward behavior and the acquisition of KSAs that will be most necessary for the organization to accomplish its future goals. If job requirement changes will be rapid, and if selection procedures are valid, higher pay levels should attract employees with greater capabilities for adaptation to change. Pay differentials between jobs must be examined periodically and adjusted in a manner which clearly offers increased returns for employees who continue to acquire and use KSAs that are closely aligned with the needs of the organization, given its current external and internal environment.

REFERENCES

Arvey, R. D. (1973). Motivational models and professional updating. In S. S. Dubin, H. Sheldon, & J. McConnell, (Eds.), *Maintaining professional and technical competence of the older worker* (pp. 142–166). Washington: American Society of Engineering Education.

Arvey, R. D., & Neel, C. W. (1976). Motivation and obsolescence in engineers. *Industrial Gerontology, 3,* 113–120.

Baltes, P. B., & Schaie, K. W. (1974). Aging and IQ: The myth of the twilight years. *Psychology Today, 7(10),* 35–38.

Becker, G. S. (1975). *Human capital* (2nd ed.). New York: National Bureau of Economic Research.

Berlew, D. E., & Hall, D. T. (1966). The socialization of managers: Effects of expectations on performance. *Administrative Science Quarterly, 11,* 207–223.

Birren, J. E., Cunningham, W. R., & Yamamoto, M. (1983). Psychology of adult development and aging. In M. R. Rosenzweig, & L. W. Porter (Eds.), *Annual review of psychology* (pp. 543–575). Palo Alto, CA: Annual Reviews.

Brief, A. P., Schuler, R. S., & Van Sell, M. (1980). *Managing job stress.* Boston: Little, Brown.

Buchanan, D. A., & Boddy, D. (1982). Advanced technology and the quality of working life: The effects of word processing on video typists. *Journal of Occupational Psychology, 55,* 1–11.

Campbell, J. P., & Pritchard, R. D. (1976). Motivation theory in industrial and organizational psychology. In M. D. Dunnette (Ed.), *Handbook of industrial and organizational psychology* (pp. 63–130). Chicago: Rand McNally.

Cronbach, L. J. (1970). *Essentials of psychological testing* (3rd ed.). New York: Harper & Row.

Crystal, J. C., & Deems, R. S. (1983). Redesigning jobs. *Training and Development Journal, 37(2),* 44–46.

Dalton, G. W., & Thompson, P. H. (1971). Accelerating obsolescence of older engineers. *Harvard Business Review, 49(5),* 57–67.

Doering, M., Rhodes, S. R., & Schuster, M. (1983). *The aging worker: Research and recommendations.* Beverly Hills, CA: Sage.

Dubin, S. S. (1973). Defining obsolescence and updating. In S. S. Dubin, H. Sheldon, & J. McConnell (Eds.), *Maintaining professional and technical competence of the older worker* (pp. 1–12). Washington: American Society of Engineering Education.

Dunnette, M. D. (1976). Aptitudes, abilities, and skills. In M. D. Dunnette (Ed.), *Handbook of industrial and organizational psychology* (pp. 473–520). Chicago: Rand McNally.

Dunnette, M. D., Hough, L. M., & Rosse, R. L. (1979). Task and job taxonomies as a basis of identifying labor supply sources and evaluating employment qualifications. *Human Resource Planning, 2,* 37–51.

Dunnette, M. D., & Kirchner, W. K. (1958). Validation of psychological tests in industry. *Personnel Administration, 21(3),* 20–27.

Ebadi, Y. M., & Utterback, J. M. (1984). The effects of communication on technological innovation. *Management Science, 30,* 572–585.

Ference, T. P., Stoner, J. A., & Warren, E. K. (1977). Managing the career plateau. *Academy of Management Review, 2,* 602–612.

Hall, D. T. (1976). *Careers in organizations.* Pacific Palisades, CA: Goodyear.

Harel, G. H., & Conen, L. K. (1982). Expectancy theory applied to the process of professional obsolescence. *Public Personnel Management, 11,* 13–21.

Hedaa, L., & Joynt, P. (1981). Managerial obsolescence: The forgotten human resource function. *Human Resource Planning, 4,* 139–149.

Hill, R. E., & Miller, E. L. (1981). Job change and the middle seasons of a man's life. *Academy of Management Journal, 24,* 114–127.

Kaufman, H. G. (1971). Relations of ability and interest to currency of professional knowledge among engineers. *Journal of Applied Psychology, 56,* 495–499.

Kaufman, H. G. (1973). A critical incident study of personal characteristics associated with technical obsolescence among engineers. *Studies in Personnel Psychology, 5,* 63–67.

Kaufman, H. G. (1974). *Obsolescence and professional career development.* New York: AMACOM.

Kaufman, H. G. (Ed.). (1975). *Career management: A guide to combatting obsolescence.* New York: IEEE Press.

Kaufman, H. G. (1978). Continuing education and job performance: A longitudinal study. *Journal of Applied Psychology, 63,* 248–251.

Kopelman, R. E. (1977). Psychological stages of careers in engineering: An expectancy theory taxonomy. *Journal of Vocational Behavior, 10,* 270–286.

Lehman, H. C. (1963). *Age and achievement.* Princeton, NJ: Princeton University Press.

Levinson, D. J., Darrow, C., Klein, E., Levinson,

M., & McKee, B. (1978). *The seasons of a man's life*. New York: Knopf.

London, M. (1983). Toward a theory of career motivation. *Academy of Management Review, 8*, 620–630.

Mali, P. (1969). Measurement of obsolescence in engineering practitioners. *Manage, 21*, 48–52.

McCormick, E. J. (1976). Job and task analysis. In M. D. Dunnette (Ed.), *Handbook of industrial and organizational psychology* (pp. 651–696). Chicago: Rand McNally.

McDowell, J. M. (1982). Obsolescence of knowledge and career publication profiles: Some evidence of differences among fields in costs of interrupted careers. *American Economic Review, 72*, 752–768.

Miller, D. (1979). Counteracting obsolescence in employees and organizations. *Training/HRD, 16*, 80–82.

Near, J. P. (1985). A discriminant analysis of plateaued versus nonplateaued managers. *Journal of Vocational Behavior, 26*, 177–188.

Pelz, D. C., & Andrews, F. M. (1966). *Scientists and organizations*. New York: Wiley.

Porter, L. W. (1971). *A motivational theory for updating*. Paper presented at XVII International Congress of Applied Psychology, Liege, Belgium.

Renck, R., Kahn, E. L., & Gardner, B. B. (1969). *Continuing education in R & D careers*. NSF Report #69-20, prepared by Social Research, Inc. Washington: Government Printing Office.

Rosen, B., & Jerdee, T. H. (1976). The influence of age stereotypes on managerial decisions. *Journal of Applied Psychology, 61*, 428–432.

Rosenbaum, J. E. (1979a). Tournament mobility: Career patterns in a corporation. *Administrative Science Quarterly, 24*, 220–241.

Rosenbaum, J. E. (1979b). Organizational career mobility: Promotion chances in a corporation during periods of growth and contraction. *American Journal of Sociology, 85*, 21–48.

Rumberger, R. W. (1981). The changing skill requirements of jobs in the U.S. economy. *Industrial and Labor Relations Review, 34*, 578–590.

Schein, E. H. (1978). *Career dynamics: Matching individual and organizational needs*. Reading, MA: Addison-Wesley.

Schuler, R. S. (1984). *Personnel and human resource management* (2nd ed.). St. Paul: West.

Schultz, T. W. (1961). Investment in human capital. *American Economic Review, 51*, 1–17.

Schwab, D. P., & Cummings, L. L. (1976). A theoretical analysis of the impact of task scope on employee performance. *Academy of Management Review, 1*, 23–35.

Shearer, R. L., & Steger, J. A. (1975). Manpower obsolescence: A new definition and empirical investigation of personal variables. *Academy of Management Journal, 18*, 263–275.

Staw, B. M., Sandelands, L. E., & Dutton, J. E. (1981). Threat-rigidity effects in organizational behavior: A multilevel analysis. *Administrative Science Quarterly, 26*, 501–520.

Thurow, L. C. (1970). *Investment in human capital*. Belmont, CA: Wadsworth.

Vroom, V. H. (1964). Work and motivation. New York: Wiley.

John A. Fossum and Richard D. Arvey are affiliated with the University of Minnesota. Carol A. Paradise and Nancy E. Robbins are affiliated with Control Data Corporation.

After the Ax Falls: Job Loss as a Career Transition
Janina C. Latack / Janelle B. Dozier

Although career transitions involving entry of managers and professionals into the organization have received considerable attention (Wanous, 1980), organizations have become increasingly concerned about exit transitions brought about by termination of employment (e.g., Hymowitz, 1985; Langley, 1984a, 1984b; O'Boyle, 1985; Symonds, Kaufman, Guyer, & Frank, 1985). In 1984,

Source: Janina C. Latack and Janelle B. Dozier, "After the Ax Falls: Job Loss as a Career Transition," *Academy of Management Review,* 1986, pp. 375–392. Reprinted with permission.

the number of articles and books on termination in the management literature was more than four times what it was in 1981. This concern stems from economic pressures, the bottom-line payoffs to smoothing the termination decision, and broad-based approaches to career development.

First, economic pressures, particularly the recent recession, have generated unprecedented publicity about managers and professionals who lose their jobs. Even as the economy improves, many firms continue to consolidate and reduce staff. It has been estimated that this retrenchment has resulted in a reduction of nearly 500,000 managerial and professional jobs since 1979 (O'Boyle, 1985). Furthermore, economic projections indicate that turbulence and slow growth along with an oversupply of educated workers will force periodic employment shifts among white collar groups for some time to come (Crowley, 1972; Jahoda, 1981; Kaufman, 1982; Kelvin, 1980; Maurer, 1979). As public concern about terminated managers and professionals escalates, organizations will be pressed to manage terminations effectively.

Second, as the "employment-at-will" doctrine erodes and threats of litigation for unjust discharge and age discrimination increase, organizations recognize the bottom-line payoff for smoothing the exit transition for terminated employees. In addition to avoiding lawsuits, other potential organizational payoffs include maintenance of a positive public image and the continued commitment and loyalty of remaining employees.

Finally, many progressive organizations are taking a broad approach to employee career development, recognizing that career development must occur through avenues other than upward promotions that may have been more available in the past. This broad approach to career development has been spurred by demographic changes in the work force: the baby boom has entered middle management; the retirement age, now 70, may be abolished entirely; and people are living healthier lives, longer. In short, many employees expect to maintain career involvement over a longer time span than earlier cohorts, but moving up within the organization may not be an option. For some, moving out of the organization will be required. In light of this, many organizations have broadened their approach to career development by assuming increased responsibility for smoothing exit transitions, including outplacement assistance. Therefore, helping employees find growth opportunities within the job loss transition has become one feature of progressive career development programs.

This paper discusses how career growth may be generated from the job loss transition and applies empirical evidence to build a model of career growth factors. The career growth focus is important because, although job loss may be associated with stress and disruption (e.g., Warr, 1984), stressful life events can lead to growth because they spur people to consider new alternatives, to develop new competencies, and to restructure their lives in positive directions (Schlossberg, 1981; Sheehy, 1981). To date, there has been little attention to how job loss might lead to growth. The application of empirical evidence is important because much of the literature beamed at managers and professionals consists of "how-to-fire" articles based largely on anecdotal accounts (e.g., Berack, 1982; Bucallo, 1982). Clearly, organizational responses should be based on empirical evidence and must extend far beyond how the individual termination decision is handled.

Specifically, this paper answers three questions. First, what factors may promote career growth within the job loss transition? Second, how should organizations manage the job loss transition to promote career growth and renewal instead of a downward spiral of bitterness and career withdrawal? Third, how can researchers interested in career management improve understanding of this increasingly common involuntary career transition?

The term job loss is used in this paper rather than unemployment to emphasize job loss as a transition. That is, the transition is set in motion by a "trigger event," job loss, which occurs before the person may be unemployed. In addition, job loss denotes involuntary termination of employment as contrasted with voluntary quitting, and thus focuses our attention on a transition that the individual does not control and does not desire. Evidence is mounting that events viewed as uncontrollable and undesirable are more likely than other life events (Holmes & Rahe, 1967) to be associated with psychological and physical distress (Fontana, Hughes, Marcus, & Dowds, 1979; Husaini & Neff, 1980; Latack, 1984a; McFarlane, Norman, Streiner, Roy, & Scott, 1980; Pearlin, Lieberman, Menaghan, & Mullan, 1981; Suls & McMullen, 1981). Therefore, an understanding of this type of career transition is a critical focus for contemporary career management.

A CAREERS PERSPECTIVE ON JOB LOSS

Definitions of careers emphasize the sequence of work-role related experiences over time, both objectively viewed and subjectively interpreted by the individual (Gutteridge, in press; Hall, 1976). Within this sequence are transition periods, which may involve either an objective change in career role or a change in subjective orientation toward the career role (Louis, 1980). Although it is argued that any career transition is likely to be stressful (Nicholson, 1984; Van Maanen & Schein, 1979), the careers literature has focused on transitions from one role to another rather than loss of the career role. As noted above, job loss is a particularly stressful career transition for many people.

To focus on career growth from job loss, the present authors first relate job loss to the psychological success cycle of careers (Hall, 1976), and then build a model that suggests how job loss may lead to career growth, based on empirical studies available to date. Although this paper emphasizes studies of managers and professionals (see Dooley & Catalano, 1980 for a general review of job loss studies), representative examples of blue collar studies (e.g., Jackson & Warr, 1984; Kasl & Cobb, 1979) are included to highlight factors that may promote career growth.

Job Loss and the Psychological Success Cycle

The psychological success model of careers provides a vehicle for understanding and promoting career growth (Hall,

1976). Individuals who set challenging but attainable job goals and reach these goals within a context of supportive autonomy experience a sense of enhanced competence and self-esteem which in turn contributes to satisfaction, involvement, and setting new goals. Career growth occurs through this cycle of setting new goals so that the person's competence is stretched and career satisfaction and involvement are maintained over time (Howard, 1984).

For managers and professionals, job loss breaks the psychological success cycle. From an objective viewpoint, job loss removes the very arena within which work-role success may be achieved. Interest in the subjective impact of job loss has been spurred by aggregate studies (e.g., Brenner, 1973; Eyer, 1977) suggesting a connection between unemployment and a variety of health and social problems, such as suicides, admissions to prisons and mental hospitals, and even death rates (see Dooley & Catalano, 1980 for a review). Although numerous individual-level studies of blue collar workers have examined the psychological stresses associated with job loss (e.g., Warr, 1984; Jackson & Warr, 1984; Kasl & Cobb, 1979), studies focusing on managers and professionals point to a heightened concern about the stress effects of job loss (see Fineman, 1983, and Kaufman, 1982 for reviews).

In fact, Kaufman (1982) has argued that the psychological stresses associated with job loss for professionals differ from those of other occupational groups because work provides a larger portion of their ego-identity. Although empirical evidence comparing occupational groups is sparse, data from a recent study supported this notion (Payne, Warr, & Hartley, 1984). Stybel (1981) noted that among managers, termination of employment represents the "ultimate corporal punishment — banishment from the organization with little or no recourse to alter the sentence" (p. 1). The severity of the trauma is reflected in the colloquial terms for firing such as "getting axed" and "walking the plank."

Empirical studies summarized in Table 1 describe the disruption of the psychological success cycle and also suggest factors that may help to reestablish career growth. Job loss, the antithesis of psychological success, is often described in terms of psychological failure and decreased self-esteem: shame, degradation and inferiority (Fineman, 1983); disillusionment, betrayal, impotence (Braginsky & Braginsky, 1975); "a living hell" (Leventman, 1981); "like losing a leg" (Swinburne, 1981); "like being raped" or "like dying professionally" (Latack, 1984b). Empirical comparisons of unemployed and employed managers and professionals support that unemployment is associated with higher levels of psychological stress (Braginsky & Braginsky, 1975; Hepworth, 1980; Swinburne, 1981), anomie (Little, 1976), anxiety and depression (Estes, 1973; Pearlin et al., 1981), lower levels of life satisfaction (Kaufman, 1982) and lower self-esteem (Braginsky & Braginsky, 1975; Kaufman, 1982; Pearlin et al., 1981).

From a career standpoint, job loss can have a "poisoning effect" causing permanent damage to careers. This permanent damage may be reflected in feelings of uncertainty, lower commitment, and cynicism that carry over to the next job (Braginsky & Braginsky, 1975; Fineman,

TABLE 1
Empirical Studies of Job Loss among Managers and Professionals[a]

Author and Date	Purpose of Study	Sample
Braginsky & Braginsky (1975)	Does U cause a change in a person's views of self and society? Are Ud similar to other "surplus populations" (old, handicapped)?	Ud men (n = 46); control group (n = 53). Middle-class 80% Ud for first time in 20 years, recruited through newspaper ad.
Estes & Wilensky (1978)	Can the connection between the family life cycle and level of personal morale be affected by changes in job patterns, income flows and debt loads?	Married professionals under age 30 (n = 230). $\bar{X}$ education = 5.7 years of college. 52% graduate degrees. 68% Ud. 32% EEd. 23% female.
Fineman (1983)	Examine impact of U on white collar workers.	Ud British managers and professionals (n = 100) enrolled in a 1–2 week government career review program.
Goodchilds & Smith (1963)	Does social status mediate connection between stress and unemployment?	Ud males, high and low occupational status. Two samples (n = 72) (n = 99). $\bar{X}$ age = 27. Recruited at state employment office.
Hartley (1980)	Impact of U on self-esteem of managers.	Ud British managers who applied for training class (n = 87). EEd controls (n = 64).
Hepworth (1980)	Examine moderators of the psychological impact of U.	Ud men (n = 78). $\bar{X}$ age = 34.5. U duration ranged from one month to over two years.
Jones (1979)	Analyze stages of psychological reaction to job loss.	Managers and professionals. Clinical assessment interviews.
Kaufman (1982)	Impact of U on professionals.	Ud professionals (n = 51). EEd controls (n = 54). 84% engineers. 94% male. $\bar{X}$ age = 29. $\bar{X}$ duration of U = 25.4 weeks. 82% B.S. degree, 18% graduate degree. Reasons for U: involuntary 67%; voluntary 15%; new graduates 17%.
Leventman (1981)	Impact of U on professionals.	Technical professionals Ud between 1970 and 1972 randomly selected from Rt. 38 in Boston area (n = 50). EEd control group (n = 50). Median education — M.S.

Study	Research Question	Sample[a]
Little (1976)	How do middle-class technical professionals react to U?	U professional men (n = 100). Rt. 128 Professional Service Center, Boston.
Payne, Warr, & Hartley (1984)	Does social loss mediate the effects of U on psychological health?	Ud married men, argued 25 to 39, Ud 6 to 11 months. Middle-class (n = 203). Working class (n = 196).
Pearlin, Lieberman, Menaghan & Mullan (1981)	How do life events, life strains, self-concepts, social resources, and coping behavior influence depression?	Predominantly professional and middle-class heads of household in Chicago (n = 1106). Interviewed twice; 59 lost jobs between first and second interviews. 58% female.
Powell & Driscoll (1972)	Exploratory study of the effects of U on professionals.	Ud scientists and engineers (n = 75). $\bar{X}$ age = 41. $\bar{X}$ U = 9.5 months. $\bar{X}$ education = 16 years.
Ragland-Sullivan & Barglow (1981)	Study process through which loss of job affects Ph.D.'s sense of identity at time of firing and immediate period afterward.	Letters written by fired Ph.D.s (n = 100); professors denied tenure in Chicago-area schools (n = 13).
Schlossberg & Leibowitz (1980)	Pilot study to assess positive and negative effects of job loss and patterns contributing to re-employment.	Laid off male employees of Goddard Space Flight Center, NASA (n = 53).
Stybel (1981)	Analyze stages of psychological reaction to job loss.	Managers and professionals. Clinical outplacement interviews.
Swinburne (1981)	Explore range of individuals' reactions to U.	Ud British managers in training course (n = 20). Age 21–57. 14 involuntarily U. 6 voluntarily U. U ranged from two to over seven months.
Thomas, McCabe, & Berry (1980)	Replication of Cavan and Ranck (1938) depression study. Does U cause family crisis?	Ud male managers, engineers and scientists (n = 90). Age 35–54. 52% upper level managers; 65% college degree; 27% grad degree. Two-thirds had pre-U income of $25,000+ and one-third had pre-U income of $30,000+. U ranged from one month to one year.

a. U = unemployment
Ud = unemployed
EEd = employed

1983). As one individual put it, "I can tell you that from now on, I'll *always* be looking" (Latack, 1984b).

Although research has emphasized the stress and disruption of job loss, like other stressful life events, job loss can precipitate a transition that leads to growth.

CAREER GROWTH FROM JOB LOSS

Researchers have noted that many individuals see positive aspects to job loss (Fineman, 1983; Hartley, 1980; Latack, 1984b; Little, 1976; Swinburne, 1981). It is argued here that one positive aspect of the job loss transition is career growth.

Career Growth Defined

Career growth related to job loss is defined in two ways. First, career growth occurs if the person makes a transition from job loss to a new job that provides new opportunities for psychological success (Hall, 1976). In some cases, the new job provides not only *new* psychological success opportunities but also *more* psychological success opportunities than the previous job. Although it will not be elaborated upon in this paper, it is important to acknowledge that growth from job loss also may take the form of retirement.

A second dimension of career growth from job loss might be explained by the question, "Are you better off now?" In a normative sense, growth has occurred if one can look back on the job loss transition, identify not only the losses but also the gains from that experience, and conclude that, relative to one's career, the gains outweigh the losses. This notion is taken from the literature on adult development (Levinson, Darrow, Klein, Levinson, & McKee, 1978; Sheehy, 1981) and life transitions (Adams, Hayes, & Hopson, 1977; Schlossberg, 1981; Weiss, 1976). A recurring theme in this literature is that one should do more than just survive unexpected life events; one should derive some personal or professional profit from the transition process evoked. In this sense, career growth from job loss peaks with "the best thing that ever happened" and has a minimum anchor point in the proverbial "good learning experience."

Thus, career growth is more than just surviving the loss and finding another job. It means finding another psychological success job and concluding that the career gains of the job loss transition outweigh the losses.

Factors Contributing to Career Growth: A Model

In order to build a model of career growth, empirical evidence is considered which suggests how the job loss transition might lead to growth. To begin with, the stress literature has consistently linked moderate stress levels with growth, arguing that up to a point, stress is associated with motivation and challenge whereas extreme stress brings about performance decrements and psychological debilitation (Lazarus & Folkman, 1984; Schuler, 1980; Selye, 1956). Therefore, in order for job loss to lead to growth, the stress of this event must be maintained at a moderate level. Studies of factors which moderate stress during the job loss transition point the way toward career growth because they suggest

FIGURE 1
Career Growth from Job Loss

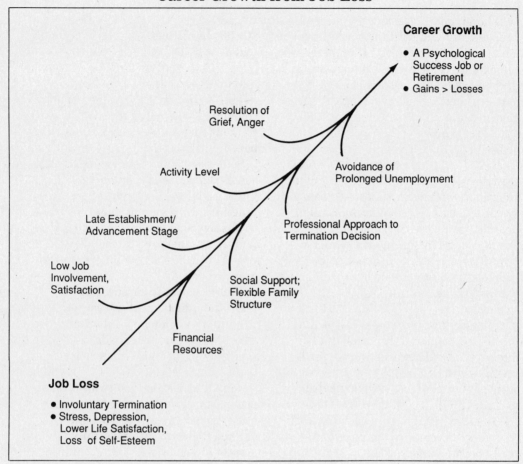

how stress can be maintained at a moderate, growth-producing level.

Keeping stress at a moderate level would enable individuals to search productively for new jobs, to take control, and to focus on the self-assessment and career planning necessary for career growth (Gutteridge, in press; London & Stumpf, 1982). The research on job loss among managers and professionals suggests three categories of factors which moderate the stress of job loss such that career growth could occur; these are shown in Figure 1.

Individual characteristics: Pre-job loss work attitudes, career stage, activity level.

Environmental characteristics: Financial resources, social support, flexible family structure.

Characteristics of the transition process: Professional approach to the termination decision on the part of the organization, resolution of grief and anger, avoidance of prolonged unemployment.

Individual characteristics Concerning pre-job-loss work attitudes, prior level of job involvement and job satisfaction influences career growth from job loss. Individuals who are less involved in their jobs experience less psychological and psychosomatic stress (Fineman, 1983), and those who view their previous job as stressful and dissatisfying are more likely to see positive aspects to job loss (Hartley, 1980; Little, 1976). Therefore, the people who may profit most from job loss are those who were uninvolved in, and dissatisfied with, their jobs. For them, job loss may provide the motivation that gets them out of a bad job that was tolerated previously due to inertia or fear of change.

The timing of job loss relative to career stage is another individual factor that has been considered. It is well-documented that older workers in general are less likely to be reemployed subsequent to job loss (Ferman & Aiken, 1964; Foltman, 1968; Parnes, Gagen, & King, 1981) and when reemployed, they are less likely to move to jobs at a higher skill level (Zahniser, Ashley, & Inks, 1985). Thus, age can be a formidable barrier to career growth. Studies of psychological reactions related to career stage, however, do not suggest a simple linear relationship. In fact, the mental attitude toward job loss can be quite different at various career stages. Among blue collar samples, it has been suggested that early and late career workers are less adversely affected than middle-aged workers (30–49) (Jackson & Warr, 1984). Among professionals, however, conflicting results have been presented, complicated in part by the selection of different age brackets. For example, Little (1976) noted that the most positive attitudes were expressed by those in the 30–50 year range with those under 30 and over 50 being more negative. In contrast, Hepworth (1980) noted that middle-aged workers (35–44) were most negative toward job loss and experienced the most stress while older workers (55–65) tended to be more satisfied and reported lower stress.

Schlossberg and Liebowitz (1980) shed some light on these contradictory findings, noting that the most negative reactions were among those who viewed themselves old enough to have difficulty finding another job but too young to retire. Thus, those in the later phases of mid-career may have the most difficulty turning job loss to career growth.

On the other end of the career continuum, the evidence hints that job loss may also be particularly disruptive to career growth for those in the very early years of a career, as it was for a young woman who lost her job two years after graduation from college. Actively engaged in her first "real" job, she was devastated by termination because it meant a giant step backwards from independence which included moving back home to live (Latack, 1984b). Thus, when job loss occurs in the early establishment stage, it interrupts the process of proving competence and independence in the adult work world (Levinson et al., 1978).

This evidence suggests that individuals may be more likely to reap career growth from job loss in the late establishment/advancement stage of their careers (Hall, 1976; Super, 1957). People in this stage may be peaking in accomplishments and productivity but may be young enough to avoid worries about age discrimination and obsolescence. Similarly, those in the disengagement stage may be contemplating leaving the work role already and view it as appropriate to their career stage.

Another important individual factor is activity level. Hepworth (1980) noted that those who were able to occupy their time productively, in the job search and other activities, experienced the least stress. A structural reanalysis of Hepworth's data (Brenner & Bartell, 1983) suggests a causal connection between activity and psychological stress. Other studies confirm the importance of productive activity (Latack, 1984b; Swinburne, 1981) and proactive job search (Fineman, 1983). Furthermore, among unemployed managers enrolled in a training program, there were no significant self-esteem differences compared to employed managers, nor was there any connection between duration of unemployment and self-esteem (Hartley, 1980).

Maintenance of structured activity may contribute to career growth because it replaces feedback and preserves a sense of identity, competence, and self-esteem needed to reestablish the psychological success cycle. After describing his leadership role in a community Fourth of July celebration, a health care consultant, unemployed for two months, observed "I'm getting a lot of positive feedback from doing that and it really keeps me going. It reassures me that I can still contribute" (Latack, 1984b).

Environmental Characteristics Turning to environmental characteristics, financial resources are a key factor in the career growth framework. For many people, job loss brings economic decline. In fact, studies of blue collar populations argue that the single most critical stress factor is economic deprivation (Ferman & Aiken, 1964; Gore, 1978; Kasl & Cobb, 1979). Among managers and professionals, when economic hardship is not widespread, only a small percentage report deterioration in relations with spouses and children (Thomas, McCabe, & Berry, 1980). Furthermore, there is evidence that substantial numbers of managers and professionals may not be as shielded from economic impacts as has been assumed. For example, Estes and Wilensky (1978) reported that over 40 percent of their sample of unemployed professionals reported heavy financial pressures. In comparing unemployed professionals with employed workers in general, those with financial distress had lower morale while those without financial distress showed no differences in morale from the employed group. Little (1976) noted that those who rated their financial position as excellent or good were more likely to have positive feelings about unemployment.

Obviously, some managers and professionals are not shielded from unemployment and the associated economic deprivation following job loss. Financial resources during this time would be important because people are more likely to focus on how job loss might be turned into career growth, which is essentially a higher-order concern (Maslow, 1965), if they are not worrying about how to survive financially.

Another environmental characteristic is social support. Social support is defined as the feeling of being cared for and esteemed within an interpersonal network of communication and mutual obligation (Cobb, 1976; House, 1980).

Studies suggesting the importance of support networks for blue collar samples (Bakke, 1940; Gore, 1978; Kasl & Cobb, 1979), have been replicated with professionals (Fineman, 1983; Powell & Driscoll, 1973; Ragland-Sullivan & Barglow, 1981). Following job loss, social support could act in much the same way as structured activity, providing a sense of value and self-esteem necessary to pursue career growth (Pearlin et al., 1981).

One key source of social support is the family. Although the literature on careers has argued for studying career events within the context of nonwork (Bailyn & Schein, 1976; Near, Rice, & Hunt, 1980; Rapoport & Rapoport, 1975; Van Maanen, 1977), most of the studies which explore the family and social context of job loss date from the Depression. Several researchers concluded that job loss must be accompanied by a flexible, adaptable family where members assume new roles (Angell, 1936; Bakke, 1940; Cavan & Ranck, 1938; Marsh, 1938). If the family is not "plastic" enough (Angell, 1936) to redefine family roles, then extreme tensions and conflicts, even disintegration of the family unit, could occur. Similar findings have emerged from a contemporary study of technical professional men (Leventman, 1981).

Since one of the key sources of support, the family, may be very much at risk during the job loss transition, particularly if there is financial deprivation and a rigid, traditional family structure (Leventman, 1981), extra-family sources of support may be critical for career growth. Schlossberg and Liebowitz (1980) noted that unemployed professionals in their sample derived more support from co-workers and organizational outplacement programs than from family members. Therefore, although social support may come from a flexible family structure, work-related sources of support could also be important.

Characteristics of the Transition Process
Important characteristics of the transition process are the manner in which the termination decision is communicated, resolution of grief and anger, and length of unemployment. Regarding the termination decision, job loss appears to be less stressful if it is handled with what we refer to as a "professional" approach. That is, organizations view managers and professionals as important human resources, demanding involvement and commitment during the time they are employed. When employment is terminated, however, the decision is often communicated by the organization in a manner that is inconsistent with its professional status, and is downright dehumanizing. The empirical evidence suggests that several actions indicative of a professional approach can moderate stress. These actions include providing advance warning (Fineman, 1983; Swinburne, 1981) as contrasted with terminating the individual on Friday morning and asking him/her to be out of his/her office by Monday. Providing explanations and reasons for the termination decision (Swinburne, 1981) also appears to moderate stress as does communicating the decision through the immediate superior. Feelings of outrage and anger seem more acute and long-lasting for those individuals who learn of the termination of employment through someone other than their immediate superior such as a member of the personnel staff, or the boss's superior. As one individual put it, "My boss didn't even

have the decency to tell me himself; he sent some bozo from personnel who I didn't even know to do the hatchet job" (Latack, 1984b).

A reason why a professional approach to the termination decision may lead to career growth is that it may help the individual to maintain self-esteem and to reestablish a sense of control, both of which are reduced by termination of employment. Advance warning permits time to adjust to the shock and to begin a job search prior to becoming officially unemployed. Being provided an explanation and information helps the individual make sense out of the event, which would contribute to a sense of control over future career direction. Furthermore, if the explanation includes accurate performance feedback, it may lead to either a better person-job match in the next position or to development of new competencies through training. Finally, if the decision is handled professionally by the immediate superior, there may be less anger to resolve before redirecting one's efforts toward career growth.

The importance of resolving grief and anger during the job loss transition has emerged from observations that many individuals who have been terminated pass through stages of reactions (Jones, 1979; Stybel, 1981) parallel to those associated with death and dying (Kübler-Ross, 1969) and other critical life transitions (Adams, Hayes, & Hopson, 1977; Schlossberg, 1981; Weiss, 1976). Data on these stages are important because they suggest how the job loss transition can lead to growth. After the initial shock, people move through stages of disbelief and supreme confidence coupled with denial of the rigors of the job search; anger and blame directed toward self and others; questioning competence and guilt; depression; and finally acceptance and desire to learn from the event and see positive meaning (Jones, 1979; Stybel, 1981). Although it is acknowledged that not all individuals experience every stage, nor do the stages necessarily occur in this order, it is argued that grief and anger must be resolved before positive growth can be achieved (Stybel, 1981). This resolution of negative emotions would be necessary to restore self-esteem and to permit energy to be devoted to self-assessment, career planning, and job search.

The importance of avoiding prolonged unemployment is suggested by studies of what happens as unemployment continues over time. Studies on duration of unemployment have been spurred in part by the popular wisdom that the longer the person is without a job, the more stressful the experience. Evidence suggests this is an oversimplified view (Hepworth, 1980; Goodchilds & Smith, 1963; Fineman, 1983; Hartley, 1980; Little, 1976). In fact, researchers have observed different stages of psychological reactions as unemployment drags on over time (Kaufman, 1982; Little, 1976; Powell & Driscoll, 1973). Kaufman (1982) proposed four stages of unemployment that occur after the initial shock of the termination decision: (a) relaxation and relief (one month) — a release of tension built up as the individual anticipated or suspected the termination, reluctance to take the job loss seriously; (b) concerted effort (three months) — optimistic job search campaign; (c) vacillation and doubt (six weeks) — questioning ability to find a job, anger; (d) resignation and cynicism (final stage) — withdrawal, infrequent job seeking, loss of motivation along with a more stabilized and less anxious mental state.

Thus, reemployment within a relatively short number of months represents a clear "bottom line" relative for career growth. Over time, a downward spiral of career withdrawal occurs and individuals lose the motivation, self-esteem, and capacity for goal-setting needed to reestablish the psychological success cycle.

Summary and Limitations As shown in Figure 1, the empirical evidence discussed here suggests several factors that may promote career growth within the job loss transition. Before composing a list of organizational strategies, however, some limitations should be noted. Few studies specifically focus on managers and professionals; sample sizes are small ($\bar{X}n = 76$), virtually all male; and response rates are low, rarely above 50 percent. In addition, the samples frequently include individuals who have not technically "lost" their jobs but rather have left voluntarily.

Despite the limitations, these findings pave the way for proactive management of the job loss transition and provide a departure point for managerial interventions to be evaluated through organizational research.

ORGANIZATIONAL STRATEGIES

The career growth implications of job loss extend far beyond considerations of how to fire someone: recommendations focus on policies related to termination decisions and severance benefits, the content and structure of outplacement programs, proactive attention to training and career development, as well as performance appraisal.

The Termination Decision and Severance Benefits

To begin with, managers should not be diverted from the psychological trauma that involuntary job loss can inflict. Personnel terminology such as "excessing," "decruiting," "reduction in force," "outplacement," and "career continuation program" stand in stark contrast to the vivid, painful metaphors such as "losing a leg; dying professionally" which denote how individuals experience job loss (Kaufman, 1982; Latack, 1984b; Swinburne, 1981). As organizations take on the responsibility of career growth from job loss, accentuating the positive is appropriate, but this emphasis should coexist with, rather than substitute for, an ongoing awareness of the gravity of the event for some individuals. If job loss is to result in career growth, organizational exit cannot be viewed as merely an antiseptic reversal of organizational entry.

Concerning professional communication of the decision, organizational needs for maintaining employee productivity and involvement conflict with employee needs for advance warning so that the event can be psychologically accepted and so that the search for other jobs can begin. Obviously, if individuals have been terminated or even if they anticipate this termination, their job productivity will decline as they cope with that event. If termination of employment occurs primarily due to organizational cutbacks, advance warning includes providing employees with accurate data on when and where the termination of employment will occur and identifying as early as possible the specific employees affected. This benefits the organization because when rumors of terminations abound, the most productive employees may leave because of greater ease of replacing their current job.

When particular individuals are terminated, advance warning means they stay on the payroll and use an office as they search for another job while they are still employed, albeit on paper only, rather than unemployed. This official connection with the organization may help compensate for loss of self-esteem and stigma that detracts from an effective job search.

The importance of severance benefits is evident from this review. Thus, part of the human resource responsibility for career growth is a financial one. Adequate severance pay and continuation of health and life insurance programs are a requirement. A problem arises, of course, when the terminations are related to financial difficulties; those employees who need economic support do not receive it because the organization lacks sufficient resources. This suggests that in profitable times funds be committed for severance benefits, particularly for volatile sectors of the economy, such as high tech firms, or for cyclical industries such as steel and housing.

Outplacement Programs

Based on this discussion, human resource professionals who are responsible for outplacement programs could use Figure 1 as a needs assessment tool to identify individuals who will need the most assistance following job loss. These individuals would be: those in either the late mid-career or early trial/establishment stages, who receive no advance warning, and whose termination is handled in an unprofessional manner. Additional risk factors would be: high levels of job involvement and satisfaction, lack of a support network of co-workers and friends, a rigid, "traditional" family structure, lack of financial resources, and a projected long period of unemployment (perhaps due to obsolescence or geographic immobility). Outplacement programs should not be limited to these individuals, but they may need particular attention in order to turn job loss toward career growth.

One key component of outplacement programs would be recognition and discussion of the psychological stages of the transition. Many outplacement programs emphasize immediate immersion in the job search and "getting on with it" rather than dwelling on the job loss. Even outplacement consultants may not recognize the importance of resolving the grieving process. As one outplacement counselor said, "I give them a half hour to complain and get rid of all that anger. Then, I say, 'Okay, now let's turn the page on that part of your life and get on with it' and try to get them to use the anger in a positive way" (Latack, 1984b).

Obviously, people must put the past behind if they are to grow professionally from job loss and at some point it becomes unproductive to dwell on anger and outrage. We could legitimately question, however, whether 30 minutes is adequate given the emotional impact and intensity of those reactions for many people. Furthermore, Stybel (1981) observed that the anger stage can pose a particular problem for career growth. Managers who actively job hunt before resolving the anger stage often take jobs exactly like the one they lost in an attempt to "show those SOB's" they made a mistake. Obviously, a job similar to the previous one may not be the best career move.

The data on stages of reactions to job loss also suggest that individuals may benefit from knowing that there is a typical psychological progression. Understanding that one's reactions are typical rather than abnormal can reduce stress. Since grief stage reactions may be common to many, these should be recognized and discussed while keeping in mind that individuals may vary in the order of the stages and length of time needed to progress through a particular stage. People may also be motivated if they realize that, once unemployed, the length of time prior to the withdrawal and resignation stage is thought to be relatively short, perhaps just under six months. This may spur people to work on resolving denial and anger and move toward seeing some positive meaning so that they can take advantage of, and prolong, the "concerted effort" stage in order to move ahead professionally.

In addition to a discussion of stages, people should be given a realistic assessment of their strengths and weaknesses based on the reasons for termination of their employment. Beyond that, using and developing support networks should be covered. People should understand that job loss can put stress on the family and strategies for restructuring family roles should be considered. Furthermore, there may be times when the family is incapable of providing support, so people must know how to use and develop other support sources, including friends, coworkers and community services. The impact of stress on the family due to job loss points out the need to include family members in the outplacement workshop.

In terms of the structure of an outplacement program, the research clearly prescribes more than the two-hour workshop which is typical in many organizations. An integrated, ongoing program is indicated, with formal follow-up to continue as long as the person is unemployed. This follow-up could be regular individual or group meetings with a human resource staff member emphasizing structured activity, support, and goal setting. One unemployed individual indicated that participation in longitudinal research interviews motivated him. He commented, "I figured I'd better get my act together so that I'd have something to tell you" (Latack, 1984b). At the very least, organizational outplacement programs should link individuals with community job clubs or social service agencies. It should be kept in mind, however, that, with the exception of the 40+ Club which focuses on higher level managers and executives, most job clubs and social agencies are not directed toward managers and professionals.

Training and Career Development Programs

Training managers in how to communicate termination decisions is obviously important, but at the present time many "how to fire" articles emphasize avoidance of legal action (Brown, 1983; Buccallo, 1982; Leonard, 1983). The research reviewed here provides another reason why managers should be trained in professional approaches to communicating termination decisions — so that feelings of anger and incompetence are not exacerbated. Not only is this consistent with contemporary human resource development philosophy which advocates that individual needs be accounted for in staffing decisions (Von Glinow, Driver, Brousseau, & Prince, 1983), but it is also in the organization's self-interest because people who feel angry and powerless due to unprofessional treatment could be more likely to sue.

The evidence also underscores the importance of ongoing training and career development. One focus should be mid-career renewal and updating of credentials for mature employees so that they are not obsolete if their employment is terminated. This may also lessen the need for termination of employment in cases where obsolescence would have led to job termination. Career planning and development programs should also incorporate the reality that many managers and professionals could face an involuntary job move at some point in their careers. Like death, job loss is not something that people want to contemplate. Nonetheless, career planning programs should raise the issue, and indicate how people may be able to insulate themselves from some of the disruption through: development of support networks and flexible family roles, participation in community activities, and planning personal finances. In this case, advance warning not only generates coping strategies before the event (Lazarus & Folkman, 1984) but also encourages people to engage in activities that are beneficial for balancing work and nonwork life (Evans & Bartolomé, 1981) even if they never lose their jobs.

Performance Appraisal

Advance warning is important and one source of advance warning is performance appraisal feedback. In many cases, even if terminations are necessitated by organizational cutbacks, mergers, or redirection, the lower performers go first. Part of giving employees advance warning is tied to accurate and ongoing performance appraisal. If those who are below the best have an accurate picture which suggests that they may not be retained in the event of cutbacks, the shock and negative reaction may be less severe.

An important issue, however, is whether or not the advance warning is heeded. In some cases, individuals ignore the "handwriting on the wall" (Burke, 1984; Stybel, 1981). As the grief stage studies suggest, the first stages are characterized by denial. Many individuals who suspect job loss is imminent may enter the denial phase even before the official termination decision is communicated. As one individual admitted, "I saw it coming. I just kept thinking it wouldn't happen" (Latack, 1984b). Since some people may deny the reality because they do not know how to cope, outplacement programs and ongoing career planning and development programs may help these individuals acknowledge the advance warning because they provide coping resources.

Finally, the "poisoning effect" may be one reason for a complete exploration of other alternatives to termination. Clearly, for some individuals, particularly late mid-career employees, job loss represents a permanent career disruption from which they may never recover. One way organizations might turn job loss into career growth is to avoid it altogether by a full examination of alternatives such as reassignment to other jobs and locations, lateral and downward moves, sabbaticals, salary reductions, early retirement incentives, and part-time schedules.

It is clear, however, that organizations can take a variety of policy and program initiatives when terminating managers and professionals, based on empirical data, to turn job loss toward career growth. Although the feasibility and desirability of a particular strategy may vary depending on the reasons for termination (e.g., large-scale business downturn vs. failed performance), it should be noted that these career growth recommendations are based on studies that did not take these contextual distinctions into account. Therefore, the connection between these strategies and career growth may not depend substantially on contextual factors behind the termination. Potential payoffs for the organization include: reduced probability of lawsuits, loyalty and commitment of remaining employees, and a positive public image that may help in recruiting new employees when needed. In order to evaluate the payoff to these career growth strategies, however, additional research studies are needed.

RESEARCH DIRECTIONS

Imbedded in both the findings and limitations of the studies reviewed are two major research directions. First, studies are needed that test the effects of each career growth factor identified in this discussion. To date, no studies have done this. Second, there are important caveats regarding sampling and data collection.

Concerning factors contributing to career growth, the general hypothesis modeled in Figure 1 is that career growth is more likely to accrue to individuals whose job loss transition is characterized by the factors listed. Career growth has been defined as making the transition to a psychological success job and concluding that the gains of the job loss transition outweigh the losses. Data supporting this general hypothesis are a prerequisite for development of more complex models of career growth from the job loss transition. Therefore, the most critical task for future research is to test if those factors are positively related to career growth and to begin to isolate the relative importance of, and the interrelationships between, those factors.

Concerning sampling and data collection, several suggestions will remedy the shortcomings identified in this review. First, the contextual factors behind the job loss should be controlled. This includes comparing those who have been involuntarily terminated with those who leave voluntarily. From the standpoint of career growth, the job loss transition for someone who has been involuntarily terminated will differ from that experienced by someone who is without a job voluntarily. At this point, we can only speculate about these differences. The importance of distinguishing between those who were terminated and those who voluntarily left was noted some time ago (Eisenberg & Lazarsfeld, 1938) and has been reiterated in the turnover literature (Porter & Steers, 1973; Price, 1977).

In addition, reasons for involuntary termination should be specified. Someone who becomes unemployed due to a business downturn and organizational cutbacks or mergers will view job loss differently than someone who was fired for failed performance or political reasons. For example, an individual who was terminated due to a business downturn may insulate his/her self-esteem by statements such as, "I know it's not me; the whole economy is bad" (Latack, 1984b). This individual may experience less anger, and may move through the transition stages relatively quickly but making the transition to career growth may be a challenge nonetheless, based on financial resources and the necessity of geographic relocation. The individual who was fired for failed performance may experience a more severe blow to self-esteem, and may need career counseling and skill updating in order to turn job loss into career growth.

These particular issues are difficult to unravel, however. Many individuals who report they left voluntarily have, in fact, been fired. Moreover, the publicly-stated reason for termination may not be the real reason. Isolating the reasons for turnover has been a longstanding dilemma in the turnover literature (Hinrichs, 1975; Lefkowitz & Katz, 1969). Individuals are frequently allowed to save face by leaving "voluntarily" or by taking early retirement due to "reorganizations" when, in fact, they have been fired for performance reasons. In such cases, the person may not receive the accurate feedback necessary to take appropriate next steps relative to career development. Finally, as previously noted, when organizations cut back, they focus on weeding out the poorer performers. At a minimum, researchers need the cooperation of human resource professionals so pre-job-loss performance data can be collected and the "real" reasons for termination can be discerned.

Second, people participating in outplacement or retraining programs should be compared with those who do not participate in such programs. These programs could provide both the social support and maintenance of structured activity that may contribute to career growth but little hard data on the effects of these programs is available.

Finally, virtually all previous samples have been male. Including women is particularly important since women may be at a disadvantage based on length of service, which often affects termination decisions. Researchers should make special efforts to find research sites that include substantive numbers of women managers and professionals.

In closing, it is interesting to note that the first studies to suggest that higher occupational status workers may experience unique difficulties subsequent to job loss appeared in the 1930s (Eisenberg & Lazarsfeld, 1938). Despite the intervening 50 years, the database accumulated on job loss among managers and professionals remains small. It is clear that we must devote systematic attention not only to managing but also to researching this career transition. This review and the concluding suggestions are aimed at focusing that attention and promoting career growth and renewal from job loss.

REFERENCES

Adams, J., Hayes, J., & Hopson, B. (Eds.) (1977). *Transitions: Understanding and managing personal change*. Montclair, NJ: Allenheld and Osmun.

Angell, R. C. (1965). *The family encounters the Depression*. Gloucester, MA: Peter Smith (originally printed in 1936).

Bailyn, L., & Schein, E. H. (1976). Life/career considerations as indicators of quality of employment. In A. D. Biderman & T. F. Drury (Eds.),

Measuring work quality for social reporting. New York: Wiley.

Bakke, E. W. (1940). *Citizens without work.* New Haven, CT: Yale University Press.

Berack, J. A. (1982, April). Termination made easier: Is outplacement really the answer? *Personnel Administrator, 27,* 63–71.

Braginsky, D. D., & Braginsky, B. M. (1975, August). Surplus people: Their lost faith in self and system. *Psychology Today, 9,* 69–72.

Brenner, M. H. (1973). *Mental health and the economy.* Cambridge, MA: Harvard University Press.

Brenner, S. O., & Bartell, R. (1983). The psychological impact of unemployment: A structural analysis. *Journal of Occupational Psychology, 56,* 129–136.

Brown, F. (1983). Limiting your risks in the new Russian roulette — discharging employees. *Employee Relations Law Journal, 18,* 380–406.

Bucallo, J. P., Jr. (1982, October). Administering a salaried reduction in force effectively. *Personnel Administrator, 27,* 79–89.

Burke, R. J. (1984). Disengagement from organizations: Job loss through termination, permanent lay-off and retirement. In K. Srinvas (Ed.), *Human Resource Management in Canada,* Toronto: McGraw-Hill.

Cavan, R. S., & Ranck, K. H. (1938). *The family and the Depression.* Chicago: The University of Chicago Press.

Cobb, S. (1976). Social support as a moderator of life stress. *Psychosomatic Medicine, 38,* 300–314.

Crowley, M. F. (1972). Professional manpower: The job market turnaround. *Monthly Labor Review, 95,* 9–15.

Dooley, D., & Catalano, R. (1980). Economic change as a cause of behavioral disorder. *Psychological Bulletin, 87,* 450–468.

Eisenberg, P., & Lazarsfeld, P. F. (1938). The psychological effects of unemployment. *Psychological Bulletin, 35,* 450–468.

Estes, R. J. (1973). *Emotional consequences of job loss.* Unpublished doctoral dissertation, University of Pennsylvania.

Estes, R. J., & Wilensky, H. L. (1978). Life cycle squeeze and the morale curve. *Social Problems, 25,* 277–292.

Evans, P., & Bartolomé, F. (1981). *Must success cost so much?* New York: Basic Books.

For, J. (1977). Does unemployment cause the death rate peak in each business cycle? *Journal of Health Services, 7,* 625–662.

Ferman, L. A., & Aiken, M. T. (1964). The adjustment of older workers to job displacement. In A. B. Shostak and W. Gomberg (Eds.), *Blue collar world* (pp. 493–498). Englewood Cliffs, NJ: Prentice-Hall.

Fineman, S. (1983). *White collar unemployment, impact and stress.* Bath, Avon: Pitman Press.

Foltman, F. F. (1968). *White and blue collars in a mill shutdown.* Ithaca, NY: W. F. Humphrey.

Fontana, A., Hughes, L., Marcus, J., & Dowds, B. (1979). Subjective evaluation of life events. *Journal of Consulting and Clinical Psychology, 47,* 906–911.

Goodchilds, J. D., & Smith, E. W. (1963). The effects of unemployment as mediated by social status. *Sociometry, 26,* 287–293.

Gore, S. (1978). The effect of social support in moderating the health consequences of unemployment. *Journal of Health and Social Behavior, 19,* 157–165.

Gutteridge, T. (in press). *Career planning and management.* New York: Little, Brown.

Hall, D. T. (1976). *Careers in organizations.* Pacific Palisades, CA: Goodyear.

Hartley, J. F. (1980). The impact of unemployment upon the self-esteem of managers. *Journal of Occupational Psychology, 53,* 147–155.

Hinrichs, J. R. (1975). Measurement of reasons for resignation of professionals: Questionnaire versus company and consultant exit interviews. *Journal of Applied Psychology, 60,* 530–532.

Hepworth, S. J. (1980). Moderating factors of the psychological impact of unemployment. *Journal of Occupational Psychology, 53,* 139–145.

Holmes, T., & Rahe, R. (1967). The social readjustment rating scale. *The Journal of Psychosomatic Research, 11,* 213–218.

House, J. S. (1980). *Work stress and social support.* Reading MA: Addison-Wesley.

Howard, A. (1984). Cool at the top: Personality characteristics of successful executives. Symposium at the annual meeting of the American Psychological Association, Toronto.

Husaini, B., & Neff, J. A. (1980). Characteristics of life events and psychiatric impairment in rural communities. *Journal of Nervous and Mental Disease, 168,* 155–166.

Hymowitz, C. (1985, February 14). No more meekly shuffling away: Fired workers bargain for benefits. *Wall Street Journal,* p. 33.

Jackson, P. R., & Warr, P. B. (1984). Unemployment and psychological ill-health: The moderating role of duration and age. *Psychological Medicine, 14,* 605–614.

Jahoda, M. (1981). Work, employment and unemployment: Values, theories and approaches in social research. *American Psychologist, 36,* 184–191.

Jahoda, M., Lazarsfeld, P. F., & Zeisel, H. (1933). *Marienthal: The sociography of an unemployed community.* Chicago: Aldine-Atherton. (1971 edition).

Jones, W. H. (1979). Grief and involuntary career change: Its implications for counseling. *Vocational Guidance Quarterly, 31,* 196–200.

Kasl, S. V., & Cobb, S. (1979). Some mental health consequences of plant closing and job loss. In L. Ferman & J. Gordus (Eds.), *Mental health and the economy.* Kalamazoo, MI: W. E. Upjohn Institute for Employment Research.

Kaufman, H. G. (1982). *Professionals in search of work.* New York: Wiley.

Kelvin, P. (1980). Social psychology 2001: The social psychological bases and implications of structural unemployment. In R. Gilmore and S. Duck (Eds.), *The development of social psychology.* London: Academic.

Kübler-Ross, E. (1969). *On death and dying.* New York: Macmillan.

Langley, M. (1984a, November 29). White-collar layoffs: Many middle managers fight back as more firms trim work forces. *Wall Street Journal,* pp. 37, 43.

Langley, M. (1984b, November 29). Some profitting from job loss. *Wall Street Journal,* p. 37.

Latack, J. C. (1984a). Career transitions within organizations: An exploratory study of work, nonwork and coping strategies. *Organizational Behavior and Human Performance, 34,* 296–322.

Latack, J. C. (1984b). *Pilot study of job loss among managers and professionals.* Columbus: Ohio State University, College of Administrative Science.

Lazarus, R. S., & Folkman, S. (1984). *Stress, appraisal and coping.* New York: Behavioral Science Books.

Lefkowitz, J., & Katz, M. L. (1969). Validity of exit interviews. *Personnel Psychology, 22,* 445–455.

Leonard, M. (1983, February). Challenges to the termination-at-will doctrine. *Personnel Administrator,* 49–56.

Leventman, P. G. (1981). *Professionals out of work.* New York: The Free Press.

Levinson, D. J., Darrow, C. N., Klein, E. B., Levinson, M. H., & McKee, B. (1978). *Seasons in a man's life.* New York: Knopf.

Little, C. B. (1976). Technical-professional unemployment: Middle class adaptability to personal crisis. *The Sociological Quarterly, 17,* 262–274.

London, M., & Stumpf, S. (1982). *Managing careers.* Reading, MA: Addison-Wesley.

Louis, M. R. (1980). Career transitions: Varieties and commonalities. *Academy of Management Review, 5,* 329–340.

Marsh, L. C. (1938). *Health and unemployment: Some studies of their relationships.* Toronto, Canada: Oxford University Press.

Martin, R., & Fryer, F. H. (1973). *Redundancy and paternalist capitalism.* London: George Allen and Unwin, Ltd.

Maslow, A. H. (1965). *Eupsychian management: A journal.* Homewood, IL: Irwin-Dorsey.

McFarlane, G. H., Norman, G. R., Streiner, D. L., Roy, R., & Scott, D. J. (1980). A longitudinal study of the influence of the psychological environment on health status: A preliminary report. *Journal of Health and Social Behavior, 21,* 124–133.

Maurer, H. (1979). *Not working: An oral history of the unemployed.* New York: Holt, Rinehart & Winston.

Near, J. P., Rice, R. W., & Hunt, R. G. (1980). The relationship between work and nonwork domains: A review of empirical research. *Academy of Management Review, 5,* 415–429.

Nicholson, N. (1984). A theory of work role transitions. *Administrative Science Quarterly, 29,* 172–191.

O'Boyle, T. F. (1985, July 11). Loyalty ebbs at many companies as employees grow disillusioned, *Wall Street Journal,* p. 27.

Parnes, H. S., Gagen, M. G., & King, R. H. (1981). Job loss among long-service workers. In H. S. Parnes (Ed.), *Work and retirement: A longitudinal study of men* (pp. 65–92). Cambridge, MA: MIT Press.

Payne, R., Warr, P., & Hartley, J. (1984). Social class and psychological ill-health during unemployment. *Sociology of Health and Illness, 6,* 153–174.

Pearlin, L. I., Lieberman, M. A., Menaghan, E. G., & Mullan, J. T. (1981). The stress process. *Journal of Health and Social Behavior, 22,* 337–356.

Porter, L. W., & Steers, R. M. (1973). Organizational, work and personal factors in employee turnover and absenteeism. *Psychological Bulletin,* 151–176.

Powell, D. H., & Driscoll, P. J. (1973). Middle class professionals face unemployment. *Society, 10,* 18–26.

Price, J. L. (1977). *The study of turnover.* Ames, IA: The Iowa State University Press.

Ragland-Sullivan, E., & Barglow, P. (1981). Job loss: Psychological response of university faculty. *Journal of Higher Education, 52,* 45–66.

Rapoport, R., & Rapoport, R. (1975). Work and family in contemporary society. *American Sociological Review, 40,* 381–394.

Schlossberg, N. K. (1981). A model for analyzing human adaptation to transition. *The Counseling Psychologist, 9,* 2–18.

Schlossberg, N. K., & Leibowitz, Z. (1980). Organizational support systems as buffers to job loss. *Journal of Vocational Behavior, 17,* 204–217.

Schuler, R. S. Definition and conceptualization of stress in organizations. *Organizational Behavior and Human Performance, 25,* 184–215.

Selye, H. (1956). *The stress of life.* New York: McGraw-Hill.

Sheehy, G. (1981). *Pathfinders.* New York: Morrow.

Steers, R. M., & Mowday, R. T. (1981). Employee turnover and post-decision accommodation processes. In L. L. Cummings & B. M. Staw (Eds.), *Research in organizational behavior* (Vol. 3, pp. 235–281). Greenwich, CT: JAI Press.

Stybel, L. J. (1981, August). Implications of logotherapy in working with dismissed executives. Paper presented at the annual meeting of the National Academy of Management, San Diego.

Suls, J., & McMullen, B. (1981). Life events, perceived control, and illness: The role of uncertainty. *Journal of Human Stress, 4,* 30–34.

Super, D. S. (1957). *The psychology of careers.* New York: Harper & Row.

Swinburne, P. (1981). The psychological impact of unemployment on managers and professional staff. *Journal of Occupational Psychology, 54,* 47–64.

Symonds, W. C., Kaufman, M., Guyer, L., & Frank, J. (1985, February 4). Suddenly, the world doesn't care if you live or die. *Business Week,* pp. 97–98.

Thomas, L. E., McCabe, E., & Berry, J. E. (1980). Unemployment and family stress: A reassessment. *Family Relations, 29,* 517–524.

Van Maanen, J. (1977). *Organizational careers: Some new perspectives.* London: Wiley.

Van Maanen, J., & Schein, E. H. (1979). Toward a theory of organizational socialization. In B. M. Staw & L. L. Cummings (Eds.), *Research in organizational behavior* (Vol. 1, pp. 209–264). Greenwich, CT: JAI Press.

Von Glinow, M. A., Driver, M. J., Brousseau, K., & Prince, B. (1983). The design of a career-oriented human resource system. *Academy of Management Review, 8,* 23–32.

Wanous, J. P. (1980). *Organizational entry: Recruitment, selection, and socialization of newcomers.* Reading, MA: Addison-Wesley.

Warr, P. (1984). Job loss, unemployment and psychological well-being. In V. L. Allen & E. Van de Vliet (Eds.), *Role transitions: Explorations and explanation.* New York: Plenum Press.

Weiss, R. S. (1976). Transition states and other stressful situations: Their nature, programs, and management. In G. Caplan & M. Killilea (Eds.), *Support systems and mutual help: Multidisciplinary explorations* (pp. 213–232). New York: Grune & Stratton.

Zahniser, G., Ashley, W. L., & Inks, L. (1985). *Helping the dislocated worker: Adjusting to occupational change.* Columbus: Ohio State University, National Center for Research on Vocational Education.

Janina C. Latack is an assistant professor in the Faculty of Management and Human Resources, Ohio State University. Janelle B. Dozier is a doctoral candidate in Management and Human Resources, Ohio State University.

Cases

Southwestern Bell Telephone Company
Chimezie A. B. Osigweh / James Ball

The chill of the late fall was starkly apparent the morning of December 10. The breath of the picketers rose like wispy smoke as they walked around the central telephone exchange in Kirksville, Missouri. The placards that they carried were inscribed "Wilson Construction and Southwestern Bell violate area standards, Local 307 United Iron and Steelworkers of America." The word "strike" was not present on any of the posters. The steelworkers had been displaying their signs since 7:30 A.M., and it was increasingly obvious that they had no intention of removing themselves before 8:00 A.M., at which time the Southwestern Bell employees would normally report for work.

THE INFORMATIONAL PICKET ACTION

As noted by the placards, the picketers were representatives of Local 307 of the United Iron and Steelworkers of America (U.I.S.A.), headquartered in Ottumwa, Iowa. During a meeting held the evening of December the 9th, it was agreed by the rank and file that they would erect an "informational picket" at the telephone office in Kirksville. Presiding at that meeting was William Johnson, president of the U.I.S.A. local, and Ron Mikel, vice president and steward representing the Kirksville membership. The informational picket action was being taken because of the presence of Wilson Constructors, Inc. of Lenexa, Kansas[1] at Southwestern Bell's telephone office on Washington Street in Kirksville. Wilson Constructors was a nonunion general contractor that presented the low bid for the construction of a new microwave tower on top of the existing telephone building. Southwestern Bell Telephone Company had, by law, to consider all bids submitted to it for new construction. The company could not discriminate against bidders on the basis of their union or nonunion status. The local steelworkers carefully had monitored the progress that Wilson made on the tower project for several weeks; all of the prior work performed had been in preparation for the actual handling and erecting of the steel tower.

On December 9, however, preparation work was not the steelworker's concern.

Source: Reprinted by permission of the publisher from "Southwestern Bell Telephone Company" by Chimezie A. B. Osigweh and James Ball, *Journal of Management Case Studies,* Vol. No. 1, pp. 179–184. Copyright 1985 by Elsevier Science Publishing Co., Inc.

This case is based on a real situation, but all names are disguised.

1. The state of Kansas is a right-to-work state.

The first truckload of steel had arrived at the job site, along with a 15-ton crane on December 4. All attempts by Mikel to get Wilson Constructors to hire some of his people had failed. As a result, the union felt that its next course of action was to set up a picket line. The problem was common situs picketing: the operations of a secondary employer were being disrupted.[2] The secondary employer was being picketed.

FROM THE WINDOW PANE

Jim Thompson, Network Service Supervisor, switching (local service) and Jim Ball, Network Service Supervisor, toll (long distance) watched the patrolling picketers through the windows of a large office inside the telephone building.

"Why did the company (Southwestern Bell) wait until it was too late to talk to these people?" Ball asked. Thompson answered with only a shake of the head.

Ball recalled many of the events of the last few weeks that had led up to the current situation. During a preconstruction meeting held in Kansas City on November 10, he and Thompson had stated that once construction on the tower started, some kind of work action from the steelworkers local was almost a hundred percent certain if Wilson did not use some union labor. Ball and Thompson also informed the Legal Department representative that this particular union had a reputation for "busting heads" if anyone tried to cross their picket lines.

"Yes," Ball thought, "we've told them all several times." But given the present situation, that thought alone provided very little consolation.

As 8:00 A.M. approached both supervisors felt crippled. "Is there anything that *we* can do to get these guys away from our employees' entrance?" Thompson asked. "No," replied Ball, "the boss (Wes Storm — Manager) said for us to hang loose until we see what Legal has to say."

"Gee, that will take all day," responded Thompson. "You and I know that our craft people will not cross that picket line!"

About that time the phone rang. Ball put the call on the speaker so that he and Thompson could both hear what Wes had found out from the Legal Department.

"O.K.," Wes began, "Legal is trying to contact the steelworker's local office right now. They will attempt to get the picketers to clear the telephone employees' entrance so that our people can come to work. Heck, their 'grievance' isn't with us anyway. It's with Wilson for refusing to hire some of the union steelworkers."

"Darn it Wes," Ball countered. "Why didn't Legal take Thompson and I seriously three weeks ago in Kansas City when we told them that there would be trouble if Wilson uses strictly nonunion labor in our building?"

After a slight pause Wes replied, "Nobody actually thought there would be any problems. We are building towers in Moberly, Sedalia, Chillicothe, and downtown Kansas City; and to this date we have not had any problems with any of the other local unions."

Just about that time, 7:55 A.M., another one of the office phones began to ring. Jim Thompson answered and talked for several minutes. He then hung up and returned to the speaker phone.

---

2. See Appendix.

"That was one of our repeatermen (telephone craft title)," Thompson stated. "I'm sure it was Eldon Coy. He says that everyone is waiting over at Doughboy's Donut Shop to see what happens." They had contacted Scat Davis, president of their own union, the Communications Workers of America (C.W.A.), local chapter, to see what the union wanted them to do, but at that time they still had not heard from St. Louis headquarters as to the next course of action.

"Eldon maintains," continued Thompson, "that regardless of what the union says, none of the Kirksville craftpeople have any intention of crossing that picket line. They think that someone will get hurt if they try to cross. They're a little scared."

"I understand that," Wes replied. "But they have to come to work nonetheless. Legal says that this is only an informational picket set up against Wilson and that it does not bind our people not to cross."

The legal staff had, indeed, added quick references to a certain NLRB's (National Labor Relation Board's) "Reserved Gate" doctrine, as well as to a Denver case, and to another IUEW (International Union of Electrical Workers) case,[3] but they did not elaborate. The legal staff had some more "checking into" to do before jumping to the conclusion that any of these previous cases applied to Bell's current situation.

THE UNION'S RESPONSIBILITY

Eight o'clock came and went and still no telephone employees had come to work. Shortly after eight, another of the repeatermen called the office and asked if he and the other outside repairmen could report to their company vehicles and drive to their work sites. All company vehicles had been removed from the telephone exchange parking lot several weeks earlier because Wilson was using the company parking lot to store materials for the new tower. Therefore the telephone vehicles were not on Southwestern Bell's property, but instead were parked in the municipal parking lot a few blocks away. This would allow some of the employees to report for work without having to cross the picket line.

John's request was, however, refused by Ball, his immediate supervisor. Wes supported Ball's refusal to grant the request. "The first floor of the telephone building is the reporting location and not the front seat of a company vehicle," Wes stated flatly. "Besides," added Ball, "it is the company's view that we, and not the union, should decide where the craftpeople report for work. We do not alter policy in order to allow union members to circumvent their contract responsibilities. In this case the union is asking us to make an exception for them, which could constitute a dangerous precedent should a situation like this occur again."

---

3. According to the Reserved Gate doctrine, an employer who awards a bid to a subcontractor should reserve an entrance for the subcontractor's employees. Because the subcontractor's employees can only get into the plant through the entrance, strikes against the subcontractor have to be picketed only at the entrance. The work done by the users of the Reserved Gate must be unrelated to the normal activities of the employer. The Denver case probably refers to the Supreme Court ruling in *NLRB v. Denver Building and Construction Trades Council* [341 US 675 (1951), 95 L Ed 1284], while the IUEW case refers to *Local 761, International Union of Electrical Workers v. NLRB* [366 US 667 (1961), 6 L Ed 2d 592].

FIGURE 1

ARTICLE II

Service Interruption

The company and the Union recognize their responsibility in the interests of the public and the employees to avoid interruptions in telephone service. Accordingly, they will process promptly employee complaints and grievances which are subject to handling under the grievance procedures for the purpose of avoiding interruption of telephone service to the public and economic loss to employees from work stoppages.

Any employee complaint or grievance which is subject to handling under the grievance procedures shall be presented and heard promptly in accordance with the provisions of those procedures and the arbitration procedures, where applicable.

As to those employee grievances which are subject to arbitration, the Union, its officers, or representatives will not order or sanction a work stoppage or slowdown at any time.

According to one member of the management staff, the union's responsibility in matters of this nature had been made clear under the "service interruption" provisions of the contract[4] (see Figure 1). Once it was determined that the picket was informational in nature, it was the union's responsibility to ensure that its members reported to work, whether or not picketers were present.

The picketers remained in place at *all* entrances until approximately 10:30 A.M. that morning. At that time, the picketing steelworkers were asked by their union to reposition themselves *only* at the entrances that had been clearly designated as those to be used by contractors only.[5] An agreement had been reached between the steelworkers and the company's attorneys.

THE SETTLEMENT

The agreement was reached between 10:00 A.M. and 10:20 A.M.; by this time all of the damage had already been done. The telephone employees (represented by the C.W.A.) who had refused to cross the picket line were docked for 2½ hours of pay, and the lost time was chaged to their payroll records as unexcused absence. Unexcused absence is one of the criteria that helps to determine whether employees receive a satisfactory or an unsatisfactory appraisal for their yearly performance. Their appraisal, in turn, affects their hopes for transfer or promotion. It was not very surprising, therefore, that the employees involved had no intention of accepting without a fight the unexcused absence charged to their records.

---

4. 1980 Agreement of General Application, *Collective Bargaining Agreement CWA* (Southwestern Bell, Kirksville), p. 195.

5. These entrances had been so designated from the very first day that Wilson Construction arrived at Kirksville.

FIGURE 2

ARTICLE III

Unusual Grievances

Whenever the Vice President of the Union (or in his or her absence, the Assistant to Vice President) informs the Vice President-Personnel of the Company (or in his or her absence, the Assistant Vice President-Labor Relations) that a complaint or grievance exists which in the opinion of the Vice President of the Union involves a condition which constitutes a serious and immediate threat to the health or safety of an employee or group of employees and which in his or her opinion requires prompt handling, and it is mutually agreed that such a question of health or safety is in fact involved, then such complaint or grievance may be presented and heard at such level of the Grievance Procedure as the Vice President of the Union may select. The first meeting with respect to such complaint or grievance shall be held at a time and place to be agreed upon and as promptly as conditions permit; the two-week time limitation set forth in the Grievance Procedure shall be applicable. There shall be no obligation on the part of the Union to appeal such complaint or grievance to any higher level, and the grievance if arbitrable shall then be subject to the provisions of the arbitration procedures of this Agreement.

The first step was taken by Roger Elmore, union steward for the Kirksville telephone employees. Roger promptly informed the local C.W.A. president, Scat Davis, of the situation, and that all of the telephone craftpeople at the Kirksville office wanted the unexcused absence removed from their payroll records. They also wanted to be reimbursed for the 2½ hours of pay that they had lost.

While Roger hoped that Scat would decide on an appropriate line of action, it was Roger's contention that this vexing and dangerous situation should have been averted by the company and the union. The failure of both the company and the union to react to the evidence of an imminent strike action was clearly a case of negligence on both sides. Roger also contended that the failure of both sides to act in the face of this situation was a violation of Article III of the General Application section of the 1980 Collective Bargaining Agreement (see Figure 2). Moreover, he saw the refusal of the Kirksville C.W.A. members to cross the steelworkers' picket line as the culmination of a month-long "ignore-it-and-it-will-go-away" course of action.

At any rate, tempers reached the boiling point and the Kirksville employees demanded that some action be taken. Subsequently, Scat Davis scheduled an emergency union meeting for the evening of December 15th. The major item up for discussion by the membership was whether C.W.A. should reimburse the Kirksville employees for their lost time out of the union's general fund or whether the union would formally grieve the work stoppage and the subsequent withholding of pay.

APPENDIX: SOUTHWESTERN BELL TELEPHONE COMPANY[6]

The State of the Law

Most relevant to this case is the National Labor Relations Act (NLRA), Section 8(b)(4)(A), as amended by the Labor Management Relations Act.

According to Section 8:

(b) It shall be an unfair labor practice for a labor organization or its agents —

(4) (i) to engage in, or to induce or encourage any individual employed by any person engaged in commerce or in an industry affecting commerce to engage in, a strike or a refusal in the course of his employment to use, manufacture, process, transport, or otherwise handle or work on any services; or (ii) to threaten, coerce, or restrain any person engaged in commerce or in industry affecting commerce where in either case an object thereof is — (A) forcing or requiring any employer or self-employed person to join any labor or employer organization or to enter into any agreement which is prohibited by Section 8(e).

Section 8(e) states, in part that

It shall be an unfair labor practice for any organization and any employer to enter into any contract or agreement, express or implied, whereby such employer ceases or refrains or agrees to cease or refrain from handling, using, selling, transporting or otherwise dealing in any of the products of any other employer, or to cease doing business with any other person, and any contract or agreement shall be to such extent unenforceable and void . . .

Common Situs Picketing

The events in this case are similar to those of *NLRB v. Denver Building and Construction Trades Council* [341 US 675 (1951), 95 L Ed 1284]. In this landmark case, the Trades Council struck a construction site in order to force a subcontractor to employ union workers. Workers of other subcontractors observed the picket line established by the striking union. The project was thus disrupted; the general contractor filed unfair labor practice charges with the NLRB on the grounds that the union involved secondary employers or neutrals in the dispute. The NLRB found the union guilty within Section 8(b)(4)(A) of the National Labor Relations Act (NLRA). The Supreme Court upheld the NLRB decision. Employers at the construction site (e.g., the company/general contractor/each subcontractor) were recognized as separate entities and any strikes or picket lines involving neutrals or secondary employers were ruled illegal.

The Reserved Gate Doctrine

Support for the Reserved Gate doctrine was established by the Supreme Court's

---

6. Source: Chimezie A. B. Osigweh, "Teaching Note: Southwestern Bell Telephone Company," 1985, pp. 2–4.

Local 761, International Union of Electrical Workers v. National Labor Relations Board [366 US 667 (1961), 6 L Ed 2d 592]. In this case, General Electric hired a construction company to work at the General Electric plant. One of the five entrances to the plant was specifically designated for use by employees of the independent contractor. The plant had signs that conspicuously identified the gates to be used by General Electric employees, and the one gate to be used by the contractor. When General Electric employees went on strike, however, they picketed all the gates. The NLRB found the picketing illegal; it violated Section 8(b)(4)(A) of the NLRA. The Supreme Court upheld the decision.

Midsouth University
Fraya W. Andrews / Jon W. Beard

Midsouth University was founded in 1931 as a teaching college and has grown into a four-year university with three colleges: Arts and Sciences, Business and Economics, and Education. There are approximately 23,000 students, with enrollment increasing at an average rate of 10 percent over the past five years. The university has 650 full-time and 250 part-time faculty. Sixty-three percent of the faculty are 50 years old or older. The full-time faculty consists of 42 percent full professors, 13 percent associate professors, 27 percent assistant professors, and 18 percent instructors. Over 60 percent of the students are commuters, and the average age of the student body is 23. The university has no doctorate programs, but each college has several master's degree programs.

The financial situation at Midsouth has improved over the difficult times of the last few years. The state has recently approved a 6 percent tuition increase for next year. State appropriations for the university have been increased by 10 percent during the most recent legislative session; they had not grown in the last three years due to revenue problems caused by the sluggish state economy. Yet, even during this period, several new building construction projects were begun and others were finished. These were funded through the Permanent Fund, a trust valued at over $600 million, which was created from revenue generated by the development of natural resources in or under land owned by the university. The money from this trust could be used only to improve the university's physical plant. Even with all the construction, during the past year the faculty has been complaining about the overcrowding of classrooms and the lack of equipment and supplies for certain classes caused by the rapidly increasing enrollment.

The faculty was unionized in 1975. Other than a two-week strike in 1978, the relationship between the union and the university has been relatively cooperative. The current contract, which expires August 30, is a two-year contract. It has specified an average raise of 5 percent for the first and second years. There have been several grievances recently filed regarding salary and overcrowding issues.

Of the 650 full-time faculty, 475 are

"Midsouth University" by Fraya W. Andrews and Jon W. Beard is reprinted by permission of the authors.

members of the union. Because the union has negotiated an agency shop agreement, even faculty members who do not join must pay an agency fee to the union. All dues and agency fees are automatically deducted from faculty paychecks. The union has a bargaining council, with members representing all departments. This council, and its appointed committees, research and approve a recommended list of demands that are forwarded to the union's executive committee. The executive committee selects the negotiating team. The negotiating team members are the vice president of the union (who is also a faculty member) and faculty members from four other departments. The negotiating team for the administration are the director of labor relations, the associate provost, the dean of one of the colleges, a department head, and an associate dean of one of the colleges.

The union has presented the administration with a list of economic and noneconomic demands. The administration has responded in some way to all the demands. Both sides have tentatively agreed to most of the noneconomic and language changes. The main issues remaining are the economic demands. The basic area of disagreement is that faculty members feel they have "done without" during the lean years when the university did not have a lot of resources. Now that the university is in a better financial situation, they want their share of the resources. The university contends that it can't accede to all the faculty's economic demands because it needs to spend money on maintenance of equipment and buildings that have been neglected over the last five years.

The university has already agreed to a 10 percent contribution into the faculty retirement plan (a 1 percent increase over the current contract), and language in the contract has been changed to clarify a faculty member's right to make suggestions regarding issues such as scheduling and appointment of part-time faculty. The remaining issues of concern for the faculty are a salary increase, increases in promotion increments, and benefits for retirees.

The union is now asking for a 10 percent annual salary increase for two years for all ranks. The administration's last offer was a 6.5 percent annual salary increase for three years for all ranks or a 7 percent increase for full professors for two years and a 5 percent increase for all other ranks for two years. Currently Midsouth is slightly above the national average for faculty salaries at the instructor, assistant, and associate level but about 10 percent below the average for full professors. Also, the most recent average salary increases for faculty at three state universities in the surrounding states have been as follows:

University A: 7.5 percent (first year, nothing second year)
University B: 7.0 percent (first year), 6.5 percent (second and third years)
University C: 6.9 percent (first year), 6.1 percent (second and third years)

However, these three universities have not had the same increase in enrollment as Midsouth, and their state allotments were not increased by as much as Midsouth's.

The union is also asking for increases in the promotion increments for faculty. Currently the increments are:

promotion to assistant professor: $800
promotion to associate professor: $900
promotion to full professor: $1,800

The union is asking for the following:

promotion to assistant professor: $1,200
promotion to associate professor: $1,500
promotion to full professor: $1,800

The administration's last offer is

promotion to assistant professor: $1,000
promotion to associate professor: $1,100
promotion to full professor: $1,400

The union is asking for the university to pay the entire cost for medical coverage for retirees that would equal the coverage of full-time faculty, and also to pay for a $25,000 life insurance policy for retirees. (Full-time faculty now receive paid life insurance equal to twice the value of their annual salary.) Currently, retirees are not eligible for any paid medical coverage or life insurance from the university once they retire. The number of faculty members who will actually be retiring is unknown, and so is the exact cost of the medical coverage. (The university's cost for medical coverage for full-time faculty is approximately $350 per month.) The administration's response has been no to this demand due to the uncertain cost involved.

Fraya W. Andrews is an associate professor of business at the University of Eastern Michigan. Jon W. Beard is an assistant professor of management at the University of Richmond.

Readings for Professional Growth and Enrichment

Baysinger, B. D., and W. H. Mobley (1983). "Employee Turnover: Individual and Organizational Analysis." In K. M. Rowland and G. R. Ferris (eds.), *Research in Personnel and Human Resources Management,* Vol. 1. Greenwich, Conn.: JAI Press.

Boudreau, J. W., and C. J. Berger (1985). "Toward a Model of Employee Movement Utility." In K. M. Rowland and G. R. Ferris (eds.), *Research in Personnel and Human Resource Management,* Vol. 3. Greenwich, Conn.: JAI Press.

Brett, J. M. (1984). "Job Transitions and Personal and Role Development." In K. M. Rowland and G. R. Ferris (eds.), *Research in Personnel and Human Resources Management,* Vol. 2. Greenwich, Conn.: JAI Press.

Brett, J. M. (1980). "Behavioral Research on Unions and Union Management Systems." In B. M. Staw and L. L. Cummings (eds.), *Research in Organizational Behavior,* Vol. 2. Greenwich, Conn.: JAI Press.

Brett, J. M. (1980). "Why Employees Want Unions." *Organizational Dynamics* 8 (Spring): 47–59.

Briggs, S. (1981). "The Grievance Procedure and Organizational Health." *Personnel Journal* 60: 471–474.

Drexler, J., and E. Lawler (1981). "A Union-Management Cooperation Project to Improve the Quality of Worklife." *Journal of Applied Behavioral Science* (July–September): 35–36.

Fryer, D., and R. Payne (1986). "Being Unemployed: A Review of the Literature on the Psychological Experience of Unemployment." In C. L. Cooper and I. T. Robertson (eds.), *International Review of Industrial and Organizational Psychology,* New York: John Wiley & Sons.

Fottler, M. D., and D. W. Shuler (1984). "Reducing the Economic and Human Costs of Layoffs." *Business Horizons* 27: 9–16.

Gallagher, D. G. (1983). "Integrating Collective Bargaining and Human Resources Management Research." In K. M. Rowland and G. R. Ferris (eds.), *Research in Personnel and Human Resources Management,* Vol. 1. Greenwich, Conn.: JAI Press.

Hoover, J. J. (1983). "Workers Have New Rights to Health and Safety." *Personnel Administrator,* April.

Imberman, W. (1983). "Who Strikes and Why." *Harvard Business Review* 61 (November–December): 18–29.

Johns, G., and N. Micholson (1982). "The Meanings of Absence: New Strategies for Theory and Research." In B. M. Staw and L. L. Cummings (eds.), *Research in Organizational Behavior,* Vol. 4. Greenwich, Conn.: JAI Press.

Kochan, T. A. (1980). "Collective Bargaining and Organizational Behavior Research." In B. M. Staw and L. L. Cummings (eds.), *Research in Organizational Behavior,* Vol. 2. Greenwich, Conn.: JAI Press.

Martinko, J. J., and W. L. Gardner (1982). "Learned Helplessness: An Alternative Explanation for Performance

Deficits." *Academy of Management Review* 1:195–204.

Mills, D. Q. (1983). "Reforming the U.S. System of Collective Bargaining." *Monthly Labor Review* 106:18–22.

Mills, D. Q. (1983). "When Employees Make Concessions." *Harvard Business Review* 61 (May–June): 103–113.

Mitchell, T. R., S. G. Green, and R. Wood (1981). "An Attributional Model of Leadership and the Poor Performing Subordinate." In L. L. Cummings and B. M. Staw (eds.), *Research in Organizational Behavior,* Vol. 3. Greenwich, Conn.: JAI Press.

Oliver, A. T., Jr. (1982). "The Disappearing Right to Terminate Employees at Will." *Personnel Journal* 61 (December): 910–917.

Peters, L. H., E. J. O'Connor, and J. R. Eulberg (1985). "Situational Constraints: Sources, Consequences, and Future Considerations." In K. M. Rowland and G. R. Ferris (eds.), *Research in Personnel and Human Resources Management,* Vol. 3. Greenwich, Conn.: JAI Press.

Pinder, C. C., and G. A. Walter (1984). "Personnel Transfers and Employee Development." In K. M. Rowland and G. R. Ferris (eds.), *Research in Personnel and Human Resource Management,* Vol. 2. Greenwich, Conn.: JAI Press.

Schrank, R. (1979). "Are Unions an Anachronism?" *Harvard Business Review* 57: 107–115.

Steep, J. R., and R. Baker (1982). "Helping Labor and Management See and Solve Its Problems." *Monthly Labor Review* (September): 40–51.

Tannenbaum, A. S. (1983). "Employee Owned Companies." In L. L. Cummings and B. M. Staw (eds.), *Research in Organizational Behavior,* Vol. 5. Greenwich, Conn.: JAI Press.

Weinberg, E. (1981). "Labor Management Cooperation: A Report on Recent Initiatives." *Monthly Labor Review* (April): 30–39.

Wheeler, H. A. (1985). "Toward an Integrative Theory of Industrial Conflict." In K. M. Rowland and G. R. Ferris (eds.), *Research in Personnel and Human Resources Management,* Vol. 3. Greenwich, Conn.: JAI Press.

Youngblood, S. A., and Bierman (1985). "Due Process and Employment-at-Will: A Legal and Behavioral Analysis." In K. M. Rowland and G. R. Ferris (eds.), *Research in Personnel and Human Resources,* Vol. 3. Greenwich, Conn.: JAI Press.

VII

BEYOND FUNCTIONAL CONCERNS

Readings

The Strategic Implications of HR Planning
Barbara E. Heiken / James W. Randell, Jr.
with Robert N. Lear

At Equitable's Individual Financial Services Management Company, human resource officer Kay Henry is effecting a new merger of human resources (HR), information technology, and the company's strategic business plan; at Chase Manhattan's Metropolitan Community Bank division, regional executive John Mitchell is considering the use of information technology to help identify the talent that Chase needs to expand its entrepreneurial branch system. Both Henry and Mitchell are part of a new cadre of senior line and human resource professionals who, as members of management planning teams, are actively engaged in charting their companies' futures.

As HR consultants and recruiters for Fortune 500 companies and Fortune 50 financial organizations, we have noticed a dramatic change in job specifications for both HR and line professionals during the past five years. Since 1982, one out of three of our searches for such professionals has required that candidates have hands-on experience in integrated planning and in designing or implementing tracking systems (either automated or manual systems). An increasing number of human resource job specifications call for a mixture of human resource credentials and practical business experience; senior line executives are increasingly hired for their ability to effect change through the strategic deployment of people as well as to run the business.

Many of our client companies, facing competitive demands and organizational change, have begun to integrate HR management into overall business planning. They have recognized the important link between performance-based compensation, corporate culture, and work force development and between personnel management and profits. As a result, senior-level human resource professionals and line executives who approach their roles with an open perspective and see the potential in applying human resource information systems (HRISs) to strategic planning are being recruited in unprecedented numbers.

EQUITABLE REORGANIZATION

Equitable Individual Financial Services, which has 6,000 employees and 8,000

Source: Barbara E. Heiken and James W. Randell, Jr., "The Strategic Implications of HR Planning." Reprinted from *Computers in Personnel* (New York: Auerbach Publishers). © 1987 Warren, Gorham & Lamont Inc. Used with permission.

full-time dedicated salespeople, reorganized recently, making Kay Henry the head of a staff division. She works closely with senior managers in the business lines and acts as a sounding board for the chief executive. Her mission is to increase Equitable's share of the individual life, annuity, and financial products market.

Until recently, Individual Financial Services was divided according to function, with the product development and service operations separate from the sales force, which reported directly to the CEO. Under the reorganization, the product development and service operations groups and the service and sales force have been consolidated into a single unit with the same reporting line. To get to the market faster with a wider range of products, the company has supplemented its dedicated sales force with two diversified financial groups; one is responsible for domestic distribution, the other for international distribution.

"Historically, the company manufactured what the sales force sold," Kay Henry says. "Now the company develops new products only if they are profitable."

The human resource implications of this structural reorganization are awesome. According to Henry, Equitable's strategic goals for human resources in 1986 are work force integration and staff development. To meet these goals, the company is installing mechanisms to support integration in the agent organization. Because of the new ventures, markets, and methods, Henry has noticed a shortage of talent. "We need more general managers who can run new ventures and manage projects, more marketing people [i.e., market driven rather than sales driven], more financial types [accounting based rather than actuarial based], and more computer systems people."

To find general managers to run new ventures, Equitable plans to move people across divisional lines. The company is implementing the Executive Continuity/Succession Planning Program, which is currently aimed at the top two levels of the organization. As part of the program, organization heads and their key staff are being asked to identify the organizational structure and support they will need in two years as well as the key positions they will need to fill. They are also being asked to name the top candidates for those positions. Equitable plans to repeat the process with agency heads, then develop the identified candidates and recruit others.

Henry says that Equitable is also undertaking a major job classification effort and has converted a system originally developed for compensation into an expanded job classification, compensation, and evaluation system, which is now being implemented at the officer level. "We are looking to accurately describe 130 positions, rank them internally, price them on the market, and determine eligibility for incentive compensation relative to base pay," Henry explains. "The entire effort is, in turn, plugged into the Executive Continuity Program. By the end of 1986, we will have completed job classification, compensation review, and evaluation for the exempt population. In 1987, we will repeat the process for nonexempts."

A task of this size and complexity cannot be managed manually. Henry lists three steps that Equitable must take to automate this system:

- Computerize the Hay System (now operating for office-level staff), and the

Factors and Executive Continuity programs.
- Continue building a more comprehensive and integrated tracking and recordkeeping system than the computerized personnel planning system that the company developed for Affirmative Action, Equal Employment Opportunity (EEO), and salary forecasting several years ago. Equitable is currently moving to develop such a system internally.
- Develop a system that does not rely exclusively on codes, which cannot quantify the invaluable human data that is obtained in interviews.

"Basically, we would like to capture the two-page form we now use in our Executive Continuity Program," Henry says, "but I suspect that any such program in natural language would be impractical and a bear to search through."

CHASE REASSESSMENT

At Chase, John Mitchell recalls a time when human resource executives were old-line personnel managers. Ten years ago, he says, human resource executives, almost by definition, functioned reactively. The best human resource people were those who could guess what was going to happen tomorrow and make it seem as if they knew about it all along.

Before assuming his current senior line position, Mitchell had been head of human resources for the bank's consumer sector, corporate personnel planning executive, and international HR executive. One reason he was brought into the leadership of a business line, with responsibility for the financial products Chase offers in the boroughs of New York City (other than Manhattan), was his ability to function as both a skilled human resource executive and a pragmatic businessperson. According to Mitchell, it was precisely this combination of strengths in his former boss that helped to change the company's regard for human resources.

"Because he knew the business as well as he knew human resources," Mitchell contends, "he made the line believe that the human resource executive was valuable to this corporation."

Such persuasion was undoubtedly made easier by the fact that, by 1978, Chase, like the rest of the deregulated banking industry, was going through a period of radical change, with unprecedented competition for markets, products, and customers.

Mitchell describes the Chase professional before 1978 as a careful monitor. "Since the process was regulated, business came to you," he says. "All you had to do was be in the right corner of the market. After 1978, we began actively developing our own people and looking for new people who could still handle the fiduciary responsibility but who were also sales-oriented, customer-oriented, aggressive winners. We needed those people first in operations and on the product development side, then in the mortgage business and direct response specialties. By 1981, we began developing the same kind of people for all of our branches."

Mitchell believes that deregulation and the potential for a national market gave human resource executives an opportunity to play key roles in the business.

"Once Chase saw that the consumer market represented one of the best opportunities for profit potential, provided it remained low cost and we could get in early, there was only one piece missing: the right kind of people with the right kind of marketing skills to make it happen," Mitchell says. "We began to realize that our senior-level people were good Chase products but not necessarily good products relative to the rest of the banking community. That's when we began to take a closer look at the staffing issue and the development of people, areas where our view had been a little insular."

This scrutiny has led the bank to redefine its mission, refocus its markets, and institute the organization's first systematic cultural change study. According to Ron Koprowski, vice president for human resources in the Metropolitan Community Bank, the development of staff who can apply a mix of creativity, innovation, and skill has become a critical goal for the division and a key component of the Community Bank's business plan. "It has resulted in a much earlier involvement of HR executives in senior management decisions around new business targets," Koprowski says, "specifically in the development of a distributive strategy. For example, where we are going to have branches now depends upon the availability, training, and skills of people."

Mitchell says that since his early days with the bank, he has maintained that "we can't grow the business without growing the people." He is accountable for an entire business line, with 1,000 employees at several locations, and he estimates that in 1986, HR issues will take up 85 percent of his time. This represents a significant shift in the traditional line manager role. Only 25 to 30 percent of Mitchell's explicit goals are related to human resource issues; however, as much as 85 percent of the time he spends meeting his line's overall business objectives will be devoted to such HR-related issues as making sure that the right people are in the right place at the right time and that they are adequately trained, supported, and compensated. As Mitchell has moved into the business of the line, the line has moved into the business of human resources.

In many ways, Chase is a prototypical company in the application of information technology to human resource planning, given its multiple divisions, growing population, cultural reorientation to the management and movement of people, and clear integration of human resources with business. While Chase uses several, sometimes disparate personnel data bases, it has thus far resisted committing to a fully automated and integrated human resource information system. Part of this hesitancy, which is shared by many corporations otherwise disposed to human resource information technology, stems from a lingering affection for the ability to consider intangible factors when matching people to jobs, an ability that some fear will be denied to human resource executives by a more complete and sophisticated system. This fear is probably a result of oversell by software vendors whose programs have been designed by technicians with little or no human resource experience and whose marketing approach is to sell a system that allegedly replaces rather than supplements management's ability to make informed decisions.

Mitchell feels that a human resource system flexible enough to satisfy the changing demands of Chase's business would be very valuable. He envisions a system with the following interrelated components:

- A factual, sortable demographic data base on individuals that provides such information as personal history, skills, and roles.
- A component that monitors ongoing training and development, so that employees can be tracked and strategically developed for specific jobs in the future.
- A historic profile of functional experience, including the generic skills attendant to previous roles.
- A component that could also be applied to external recruitment, matching skills and individuals to jobs within the company.

HUMAN RESOURCES AND THE PLANNING PROCESS

The issues that Henry and Mitchell are confronting are by no means unique. The 1985 *Work Value Signal: A Study of Changing Work Values and Employee Motivations* (Yankelovich, Skelly & White [YS&W], New York: 1985), a study of the work force in the US, indicates that the human resource departments of major businesses are currently struggling with four major issues: cost control, work force development, productivity, and capturing discretionary effort.

Jeffrey Heilpern, former vice president for human resources at YS&W, says that large organizations are beginning to confront these issues, and many are looking to information technology for help. "The human resource performance equation is critical," Heilpern says. "Career pathing, especially for high potentials, and succession planning are the great drives for large organizations today."

HR executives in many organizations now control assets, resources, and personnel and are trying to develop strategic practices for effective implementation of corporate policies. Heilpern asserts that these executives need to create a mosaic of programs and "develop a marketing orientation toward employees, who are their internal customers for the product called work."

A recent Business Week conference on succession planning, corporate repositioning, cost strategy, and the future painted a similar picture. The copy on the cover of the conference brochure reads as follows:

> CEOs of forward-looking companies recognize that if you want to beat the competition in today's world, the real difference is people. Consequently the top human resource position at the most progressive companies has become a strategic, not an administrative, position. Human resources is becoming more integrated into total corporate operations. The senior human resource executive is a peer member of the top management team.

There are two basic steps that a company can take to integrate HR planning into strategic planning. First, it can institute the kind of human resource leadership that will command the function and steer it in the direction of the business. Second, it can regard the human resource leader as a full member of the senior management team charged with developing and clarifying the business plan.

With the input of a business-oriented

HR professional, management has an understanding of the human factors involved in implementing the business plan. Management must explain in very clear terms what the business is and where it is going before the human resource executive can advise on whether the company's current HRISs, manual or automated, are sufficient.

AUTOMATING HUMAN RESOURCE PLANNING

There is no sense in building a new data base or designing a new system for human resource planning unless the direction and scope of the business plan, the calendar of goals, and the size and structure of the organization demand it. For some, a better method may be to integrate the components of the existing system to make better use of available information to drive the business plan.

In developing HR data base management systems for our consulting business and for clients in a range of industries, we have learned that the following are sound reasons for a company to automate:

- To allow senior management to move quickly and efficiently to lower costs and increase productivity.
- To allow middle management to achieve improved employee performance and provide for timely recruitment and succession.
- To create efficiency: automation lets decision-makers spend more time planning and implementing and less time gathering information. The greater the demand for information in an organization, the faster it must be processed and available.

These reasons are not sufficient to justify moving full throttle into human resource information technology. In addition to gauging the operational benefits of such automation, a company must estimate the strategic benefits and decide how well an automated human resource information system would support the business plan.

F. Warren McFarlan argues convincingly that information technology, when accurately assessed for its potential strategic impact, can change the way a company competes ("Information Technology Changes the Way You Compete," *Harvard Business Review* [May–June 1984]: 98–103). McFarlan, professor of management information systems and information systems administration at the Harvard Business School, did not deal with human resource information technology specifically, but three of the five questions he asks management to consider in evaluating the ultimate impact of information systems technology can be applied.

Question 1. Can information systems technology build barriers to entry? Would your company be better positioned to gain or retain a competitive edge if more of the right people were in the right place today? If the answer is yes, your company probably already considers human resources to be strategic resources.

Question 2. Can information systems change the balance of power in supplier relationships? Would the company find it more efficient and cost-effective to become its own best supplier of talent?

Automating HR information processing can provide an opportunity to integrate and systematize several functions that may not have been correlated before, including replacement and succession planning, performance appraisal, career development, and tracking of high-potential employees. Specifically, automation can enable a multidivisional company to establish a network for tracking talent to fill new jobs and defining (or redefining) positions that have been created or changed by the latest business plan.

Question 3. Can information systems technology generate new products? Assuming that diversification of the product line is part of the business plan, as it is in the highly competitive financial services and electronics industries, is there a competitive advantage in identifying and developing talent today that will be needed to design, manufacture, and market new products in one to three years? Tracking candidates and developing them for future positions is one of the primary reasons for moving to HR information technology.

A strategic business plan can provide the impetus for integrating and automating human resource information; however, the reverse is also often true: a well-conceived human resource information system can shape an organization's strategic opportunities. "The new [information] technology has opened up a singular, one-time opportunity for a company to redeploy its assets and rethink its strategy," McFarlan concludes. "The technology has given the organization the potential for forging sharp new tools that can produce lasting gains in market share."

FLEXIBILITY AND HUMAN RESOURCE TECHNOLOGY

As we have noted in the cases of Chase and Equitable, there is a lingering concern that whatever automated human resource system is adopted or refined may inhibit management's decision-making prerogative. As Kay Henry puts it, "We must protect the role of professional human judgment in making key personnel decisions. We must be able to control the data, not be controlled or limited by the forms."

In 1982, when we at Randell-Heiken were looking for a data base management system (DBMS) for human resource planning and executive recruiting, we were also determined to preserve our ability to make the professional judgments upon which our consulting business is based. At the time, there was no human resource software on the market that satisfied our need for flexibility, so we developed our own series of applications, called OPTEM (Organizational Planning and Tracking for Effective Mobilization).

The recruiting side of our business involves not only personnel tracking but also tracking job movement in client companies, changes in management direction, and adjustments in corporate culture that inevitably affect the compatibility between people and positions. Therefore, we needed a dynamic data base that could respond to frequent organizational change.

As former HR professionals at large corporations, we knew the issues and variables that can affect key decisions on replacement, applicant tracking, or personnel planning. Like Kay Henry, we were looking for a management tool that would help us factor variables but would not wrest control of the process. At the time, we did not realize that the data base we created for our own use could be applied to a range of industries.

ASSESSING HUMAN RESOURCE TECHNOLOGY

The number and diversity of micro-based human resource information systems currently available testifies to the pivotal role human resource professionals now play in corporate strategy. If your company decides to integrate and automate its human resource records, it can choose from a myriad of DBMSs. The following questions should be asked to assess the ability of a DBMS to serve your organization's needs:

- Has the system been designed to provide senior and middle managers with the human resource information they need to support the business plan? That is, is it a problem-solving management tool?
- Can the system adapt to changes in the business, the product line, or the structure of the organization?
- Does it provide a series of modular, integrated, and internally flexible data bases that users with little or no previous knowledge of computer operations can manipulate? Can a line manager with no computer background use the system to get needed information?
- How comprehensive are the modules? How many of the following human resource functions do they include?
  —Employment.
  —External recruiting and personnel selection.
  —Employee tracking.
  —Employee mobility.
  —Human resource planning.
  —Human resource forecasting.
  —Succession planning.
  —Organizational design.
  —Performance management.
  —Executive development planning.
  —EEO tracking.
  —Affirmative action.
  —Compensation planning.
  —Benefits reporting.
- Can the system produce reports in formats that allow management to make informed decisions?
- Is the system easily understood, so that the user has little need to consult a manual?
- Does the DBMS recognize that there is discretionary and subjective information that is intrinsically difficult to capture in code? Does the system have the flexibility to allow entry of this information either in purely narrative form or as easily comparable data?

In the final analysis, decisions on whether to implement an HRIS and on its configuration depend on where the business plans to go and on how committed it is to using and maintaining the data base. Ultimately, the decisions reflect senior management's acceptance of human resources as a strategic element and its resolve to deploy this element creatively and effectively.

Barbara E. Heiken and James W. Randell, Jr., are co-founders of Randell-Heiken, Inc., a New York consulting firm that specializes in human resource planning for Fortune 500 companies, Fortune 50 financial corporations, and major international consulting firms. Mr. Randell is chief executive officer of the firm and Ms. Heiken is the firm's president. Robert N. Lear is a New York-based business writer and a specialist in international training and technology transfer.

Linking Competitive Strategies with Human Resource Management Practices
Randall S. Schuler / Susan E. Jackson

Over the past several years there has been increased recognition that there is a need to match the characteristics of top managers with the nature of the business. According to Reginald H. Jones, former chairman and CEO of the General Electric Company,

> When we classified . . . [our] . . . businesses, and when we realized that they were going to have quite different missions, we also realized we had to have quite different people running them.[1]

Within academia there has been similar growing awareness of this need. Although this awareness is being articulated in several ways, one of the most frequent involves the conceptualization and investigation of the relationship between business strategy and the personal characteristics of top managers.[2] Here, particular manager characteristics such as personality, skills, abilities, values, and perspectives are matched with particular types of business strategies. For example, a recently released study conducted by Hay Group Incorporated, in conjunction with the University of Michigan and the Strategic Planning Institute, reports that when a business is pursuing a growth strategy it needs top managers who are likely to abandon the status quo and adapt their strategies and goals to the marketplace. According to the study, insiders are slow to recognize the onset of decline and tend to persevere in strategies that are no longer effective; so, top managers need to be recruited from the outside.

> Recruiting outsiders as a part of strategy has been successful for Stroh Brewing Co., once a small, family-run brewery in Detroit. Some 20% of its senior management team of 25 executives, including President Roger T. Fridholm, have been brought into Stroh since 1978. They've been instrumental in transforming it into the third-largest U.S. brewer.[3]

The result of such human resource staffing practices has been rather significant:

> Growth companies that staffed 20% of their top three levels with outsiders exceeded their expected return on investment by 10%. Those that relied on inside talent fell short of their goals by 20%. The same holds true for companies in declining industries: companies with outsiders in one out of every five top management jobs exceeded expected returns by 20%; those with a low proportion of outsiders fell 5% short.[4]

Outsiders, of course, are not always helpful. When a business is pursuing a mature strategy, what is needed is a stable group of insiders who know the intricacies of the business.

Source: "Linking Competitive Strategies with Human Resource Management Practices" by Randall S. Schuler and Susan E. Jackson, *The Academy of Management Executive*, 1987, Vol. 1, No. 3. Reprinted by permission of the authors.

The results of the Hay study suggest that the staffing practices of top management be tied to the nature of the business because different aspects of business demand different behaviors from the individuals running them. The implication, then, is that selecting the right top manager is an important staffing decision.

Another perspective holds that top managers are capable of exhibiting a wide range of behavior, and all that is needed is to match compensation and performance appraisal practices with the nature of the business. Peter Drucker, commenting on the relationship between compensation and a strategy of innovation, observed that:

> I myself made this mistake [thinking that you can truly innovate within the existing operating unit] 30 years ago when I was a consultant on the first major organizational change in American history, the General Electric reorganization of the early 1950s. I advised top management, and they accepted it, that the general managers would be responsible for current operations as well as for managing tomorrow. At the same time, we worked out one of the first systematic compensation plans, and the whole idea of paying people on the basis of their performance in the preceding year came out of that.
>
> The result of it was that for ten years General Electric totally lost its capacity to innovate, simply because tomorrow produces costs for ten years and no return. So, the general manager — not only out of concern for himself but also out of concern for his group — postponed spending any money for innovation. It was only when the company dropped this compensation plan and at the same time organized the search for the truly new, not just for improvement outside the existing business, that GE recovered its innovative capacity, and brilliantly. Many companies go after this new and slight today and soon find they have neither.[5]

Similar results illustrating the power of performance appraisal and compensation to affect individual behavior have been reported in the areas of reinforcement, behavior modification, and motivation theories.[6] However, while there has been much written on matching the behavior of top managers with the nature of the business, less attention has been given to the other employees in the organization. Nevertheless, it seemed reasonable to assume that the rest of the work force would also have to be managed differently, depending on the business. This, then, became our focus of attention.

A critical choice we had to make in our study concerned which aspects of the business we were going to use. Consistent with previous studies, we decided to use the general notion of organizational strategy.[7] On the basis of previous studies that looked at strategy and human resource practices, we decided to adapt Porter's framework of competitive strategy.[8] Using the competitive strategy framework, we developed three archetypes of competitive strategy — PHRM practices combinations. These were derived from the literature, secondary sources, and our previous research. We then examined each of the three archetypes in-depth, using additional secondary data and field results, and addressed issues regarding implementation and revision of the archetypes. All are presented in this article.

First, we shall review the nature and importance of competitive strategy, and then we shall describe the concept of needed role behavior that enabled us to link competitive strategies and HRM practices.

COMPETITIVE STRATEGIES

Crucial to a firm's growth and prosperity is the ability to gain and retain competitive advantage. One way to do this is through strategic initiative. MacMillan defines "strategic initiative" as the ability to capture control of strategic behavior in the industries in which a firm competes.[9] To the extent one company gains the initiative, competitors are obliged to respond and thereby play a *reactive* rather than proactive role. MacMillan argues that firms that gain a strategic advantage control their own destinies. To the extent a firm gains an advantage difficult for competitors to remove, it stays in control longer and therefore should be more effective.

The concept of competitive advantage is described by Porter as the essence of competitive strategy.[10] Emerging from his discussion are three competitive strategies that organizations can use to gain competitive advantage: innovation, quality enhancement, and cost reduction. The *innovation strategy* is used to develop products or services different from those of competitors; the primary focus here is on offering something new and different. Enhancing product and/or service quality is the primary focus of the *quality enhancement strategy*. In the *cost reduction strategy,* firms typically attempt to gain competitive advantage by being the lowest cost producer. Although we shall describe these three competitive strategies as pure types applied to single business units or even single plants or functional areas, some overlap can occur. That is, it is plausible to find business units, plants, or functional areas pursuing two or more competitive strategies simultaneously. This, and how to manage it, are discussed later.

COMPETITIVE STRATEGY: NEEDED ROLE BEHAVIORS

Before developing a linkage between competitive strategy and HRM practices, there must be a *rationale* for that linkage. This rationale gives us a basis for predicting, studying, refining, and modifying both strategy and practices in specific circumstances.

Consistent with previous research, the rationale developed is based on what is needed from employees apart from the specific technical skills, knowledges, and abilities (SKAs) required to perform a specific task.[11] Rather than thinking about task-specific SKAs, then, it is more useful to think about what is needed from an employee who works with other employees in a social environment.[12] These needed employee behaviors are actually best thought of as needed role behaviors.[13] The importance of roles and their potential dysfunction in organizations, particularly role conflict and ambiguity, is well documented.[14]

Based on an extensive review of the literature and secondary data, several role behaviors are assumed to be instrumental in the implementation of the competitive strategies. Exhibit 1 shows several dimensions along which employees' role behaviors can vary. The dimensions shown are the ones for which there

EXHIBIT 1

Employee Role Behaviors for Competitive Strategies

1. Highly repetitive, predictable behavior	—Highly creative, innovative behavior
2. Very short-term focus	—Very long-term behavior
3. Highly cooperative, interdependent behavior	—Highly independent, autonomous behavior
4. Very low concern for quality	—Very high concern for quality
5. Very low concern for quantity	—Very high concern for quantity
6. Very low risk taking	—Very high risk taking
7. Very high concern for process	—Very high concern for results
8. High preference to avoid responsibility	—High preference to assume responsibility
9. Very inflexible to change	—Very flexible to change
10. Very comfortable with stability	—Very tolerant of ambiguity and unpredictability
11. Narrow skill application	—Broad skill application
12. Low job (firm) involvement	—High job (firm) involvement

Source: Adapted by permission from *Readings in Personnel and Human Resource Management* by R. S. Schuler, S. A. Youngblood, and V. L. Huber (Eds.). Copyright © 1988 by West Publishing Company. All rights reserved. Page 27.

are likely to be major differences across competitive strategies. This can be illustrated by describing the various competitive strategies and their necessary organizational conditions in more detail, along with the needed role behaviors from the employees.

Innovation Strategy and Needed Role Behaviors

Because the imperative for an organization pursuing an innovation strategy is to be the most unique producer, conditions for innovation must be created. These conditions can be rather varied. They can be created either formally through official corporate policy or more informally. According to Rosabeth Moss Kanter:

> Innovation [and new venture development] may originate as a deliberate and official decision of the highest levels of management or there may be the more-or-less "spontaneous" creation of mid-level people who take the initiative to solve a problem in new ways or to develop a proposal for change. Of course, highly successful companies allow both, and even official top management decisions to undertake a development effort benefit from the spontaneous creativity of those below.[15]

To encourage as many employees as possible to be innovative, 3M has developed an informal doctrine of allowing employees to "bootleg" 15% of their time on their own projects. A less systematic approach to innovation is encouraging employees to offer suggestions for new and improved ways of doing their own job or manufacturing products.

Overall, then, for firms pursuing a competitive strategy of innovation, the profile of employee role behaviors includes (1) a high degree of creative behavior, (2) a longer-term focus, (3) a relatively high level of cooperative, interdependent behavior, (4) a moderate degree of concern for quality, (5) a moderate concern for quantity, (6) an equal degree of concern for process and results, (7) a greater degree of risk taking, and (8) a high tolerance of ambiguity and unpredictability.[16]

The implications of pursuing a competitive strategy of innovation for managing people may include selecting highly skilled individuals, giving employees more discretion, using minimal controls, making a greater investment in human resources, providing more resources for experimentation, allowing and even rewarding occasional failure, and appraising performance for its long-run implications. As a consequence of these conditions, pursuing an innovation strategy may result in feelings of enhanced personal control and morale, and thus a greater commitment to self and profession rather than to the employing organization. Nevertheless, benefits may accrue to the firm as well as the employee, as evidenced by the success of such innovative firms as Hewlett-Packard, the Raytheon Corporation, 3M, Johnson & Johnson, and PepsiCo.

Thus, the innovation strategy has significant implications for human resource management. Rather than emphasizing managing people so they work *harder* (cost-reduction strategy) or *smarter* (quality strategy) on the same products or services, the innovation strategy requires people to work *differently*. This, then, is the necessary ingredient.[17]

Quality-Enhancement Strategy and Needed Role Behaviors

At Xerox, CEO David Kearns defines quality as "being right the first time every time." The implications for managing people are significant. According to James Houghton, chairman of Corning Glass Works, his company's "total quality approach" is about people. At Corning, good ideas for product improvement often come from employees, and in order to carry through on their ideas Corning workers form short-lived "corrective action teams" to solve specific problems.

> Employees [also] give their supervisors written "method improvement requests," which differ from ideas tossed into the traditional suggestion box in that they get a prompt formal review so the employees aren't left wondering about their fate. In the company's Erwin Ceramics plant, a maintenance employee suggested substituting one flexible tin mold for an array of fixed molds that shape the wet ceramic product baked into catalytic converters for auto exhausts.[18]

At Corning, then, quality improvement involves getting employees committed to quality and continual improvement. While policy statements emphasizing the "total quality approach" are valuable, they are also followed up with specific human resources practices: feedback systems are in place, team work is permitted and facilitated, decision making and responsibility are a part of each employee's job description, and job classifications are flexible.

Quality improvement often means changing the processes of production in ways that require workers to be more involved and more flexible. As jobs change, so must job classification systems. At Brunswick's Mercury Marine division, the number of job classifications was reduced from 126 to 12. This has permitted greater flexibility in the use of production processes and employees. Machine operators have gained greater opportunities to learn new skills. They inspect their own work and do preventive maintenance in addition to running the machines.[19] It is because of human resource practices such as these that employees become committed to the firm and, hence, willing to give more. Not only is the level of quality likely to improve under these conditions, but sheer volume of output is likely to increase as well. For example, in pursuing a competitive strategy involving quality improvement, L.L. Bean's sales have increased tenfold while the number of permanent employees has grown only fivefold.[20]

The profile of employee behaviors necessary for firms pursuing a strategy of quality enhancement is (1) relatively repetitive and predictable behaviors, (2) a more long-term or intermediate focus, (3) a modest amount of cooperative, interdependent behavior, (4) a high concern for quality, (5) a modest concern for quantity of output, (6) high concern for process (*how* the goods or services are made or delivered), (7) low risk-taking activity, and (8) commitment to the goals of the organization.

Because quality enhancement typically involves greater employee commitment and utilization, fewer employees are needed to produce the same level of output. As quality rises, so does demand, yet this demand can be met with proportionately fewer employees than previously. Thanks to automation and a cooperative work force, Toyota is producing about 3.5 million vehicles a year with 25,000 production workers — about the same number as in 1966 when it was producing one million vehicles. In addition to having more productive workers, fewer are needed to repair the rejects caused by poor quality. This phenomenon has also occurred at Corning Glass, Honda, and L.L. Bean.

Cost-Reduction Strategy and Needed Role Behaviors

Often, the characteristics of a firm pursuing the cost-reduction strategy are tight controls, overhead minimization, and pursuit of economies of scale. The primary focus of these measures is to increase productivity, that is, output cost per person. This can mean a reduction in the number of employees and/or a reduction in wage levels. Since 1980, the textile industry's labor force decreased by 17%, primary metals, almost 30%, and steel, 40%. The result has been that over the past four years, productivity growth in manufacturing has averaged 4.1% per year, versus 1.2% for the rest of the economy.[21] Similar measures have been taken at Chrysler and Ford and now are being proposed at GM and AT&T. Reflecting on these trends, Federal Reserve Governor Wayne D. Angell states, "We are invigorating the manufacturing sector. The period of adjustment has made us more competitive."[22]

In addition to reducing the number of employees, firms are also reducing wage levels. For example, in the household appliance industry where GE, Whirlpool, Electrolux, and Maytag account for 80% of all production, labor costs have been cut by shifting plants from states where labor is expensive to less costly sites. The result of this is that a new breed of cost-effective firms is putting U.S. manufacturing back on the road to profitability.[23]

Cost reduction can also be pursued through increased use of part-time employees, subcontractors, work simplification and measurement procedures, automation, work rule changes, and job assignment flexibility. Thus, there are several methods for reducing costs. Although the details are vastly different, they all share the goal of reducing output cost per employee.

In summary, the profile of employee role behaviors necessary for firms seeking to gain competitive advantage by pursuing the competitive strategy of cost reduction is as follows: (1) relatively repetitive and predictable behaviors, (2) a rather short-term focus, (3) primarily autonomous or individual activity, (4) modest concern for quality, (5) high concern for quantity of output (goods or services), (6) primary concern for results, (7) low risk-taking activity, and (8) a relatively high degree of comfort with stability.

Given these competitive strategies and the needed role behaviors, what HRM practices need to be linked with each of the three strategies?

TYPOLOGY OF HRM PRACTICES

When deciding what human resource practices to use to link with competitive strategy, organizations can choose from six human resource practice "menus." Each of the six menus concerns a different aspect of human resource management. These aspects are planning, staffing, appraising, compensating, and training and development.

A summary of these menus is shown in Exhibit 2. Notice that each of the choices runs along a continuum. Most of the options are self-explanatory, but a rundown of the staffing menu will illustrate how the process works. A more detailed description of all menus is provided elsewhere.[24]

Recruitment

In each of these areas, a business unit (or a plant) must make a number of decisions; the first choice involving where to recruit employees. Companies can rely on the internal labor market, e.g., other departments in the firm and other levels in the organizational hierarchy, or they can rely on the external labor market exclusively. Although this decision may not be significant for entry-level jobs, it is very important for most other jobs. Recruiting internally essentially means a policy of promotion from within. While this policy can serve as an effective reward, it commits a firm to providing training and career development opportunities if the promoted employees are to perform well.

Career Paths

Here, the company must decide whether to establish broad or narrow career paths for its employees. The broader the paths, the greater the opportunity for employees to acquire skills that are relevant to many functional areas and to gain exposure and visibility within the firm. Either a broad or a narrow career path may enhance an employee's acquisition of skills and opportunities for promotion,

EXHIBIT 2
Human Resource Management Practice Menus

Planning Choices

Informal	——	Formal
Short Term	——	Long Term
Explicit Job Analysis	——	Implicit Job Analysis
Job Simplification	——	Job Enrichment
Low Employee Involvement	——	High Employee Involvement

Staffing Choices

Internal Sources	——	External Sources
Narrow Paths	——	Broad Paths
Single Ladder	——	Multiple Ladders
Explicit Criteria	——	Implicit Criteria
Limited Socialization	——	Extensive Socialization
Closed Procedures	——	Open Procedures

Appraising Choices

Behavioral Criteria	——	Results Criteria
Purposes: Development, Remedial, Maintenance		
Low Employee Participation	——	High Employee Participation
Short-Term Criteria	——	Long-Term Criteria
Individual Criteria	——	Group Criteria

Compensating Choices

Low Base Salaries	——	High Base Salaries
Internal Equity	——	External Equity
Few Perks	——	Many Perks
Standard, Fixed Package	——	Flexible Package
Low Participation	——	High Participation
No Incentives	——	Many Incentives
Short-Term Incentives	——	Long-Term Incentives
No Employment Security	——	High Employment Security
Hierarchical	——	High Participation

Training and Development

Short Term	——	Long Term
Narrow Application	——	Broad Application
Productivity Emphasis	——	Quality of Work Life Emphasis
Spontaneous, Unplanned	——	Planned, Systematic
Individual Orientation	——	Group Orientation
Low Participation	——	High Participation

From R. S. Schuler, "Gaining Competitive Advantage Through Human Resource Management Practices." Reprinted by permission of John Wiley & Sons, Inc.

but the time frame is likely to be much longer for broad skill acquisition than for the acquisition of a more limited skill base. Although promotion may be quicker under a policy of narrow career paths, an employee's career opportunities may be more limited over the long run.

Promotions

Another staffing decision to be made is whether to establish one or several promotion ladders. Establishing several ladders enlarges the opportunities for employees to be promoted and yet stay within a given technical specialty without having to assume managerial responsibilities. Establishing just one promotion ladder enhances the relative value of a promotion and increases the competition for it.

Part and parcel of a promotion system are the criteria used to deciding whom to promote. The criteria can vary from the very explicit to the very implicit. The more explicit the criteria, the less adaptable the promotion system is to exceptions and changing circumstances. What the firm loses in flexibility, the employee may gain in clarity. This clarity, however, may benefit only those who fulfill the criteria exactly. On the other hand, the more implicit the criteria, the greater the flexibility to move employees around to develop them more broadly.

Socialization

After an employee is hired or promoted, he or she is next socialized. With minimal socialization, firms convey few informal rules and establish new procedures to immerse employees in the culture and practices of the organization. Although it is probably easier and cheaper to do this than to provide maximum socialization, the result is likely to be a more restricted psychological attachment and commitment by the employee to the firm, and perhaps less predictable behavior from the employee.

Openness

A final choice to be made in the staffing menu is the degree of openness in the staffing procedures. The more open the procedures, the more likely there is to be job posting for internal recruitment and self-nomination for promotion. To facilitate a policy of openness, firms need to make the relevant information available to employees. Such a policy is worthwhile; since it allows employees to select themselves into jobs, it is a critical aspect of attaining successful job-person fit. The more secret the procedures, the more limited the involvement of employees in selection decisions, but the faster the decision can be made.

A key aspect of the choices within the staffing activity or any other HRM activity is that different choices stimulate and reinforce different role behaviors. Because these have been described in detail elsewhere, their impact is summarized below.

HYPOTHESES OF COMPETITIVE STRATEGY-HRM ARCHETYPES

Based on the above descriptions of competitive strategies and the role behaviors necessary for each, and the brief typology of HRM practices, we offer three summary hypotheses.

Innovation Strategy

Firms pursuing the innovation strategy are likely to have the following characteristics: (1) jobs that require close interaction and coordination among groups of individuals, (2) performance appraisals that are more likely to reflect longer-term and group-based achievements, (3) jobs that allow employees to develop skills that can be used in other positions in the firm, (4) compensation systems that emphasize internal equity rather than external or market-based equity, (5) pay rates that tend to be low, but that allow employees to be stockholders and have more freedom to choose the mix of components (salary, bonus, stock options) that make up their pay package, and (6) broad career paths to reinforce the development of a broad range of skills. These practices facilitate cooperative, interdependent behavior that is oriented toward the longer term, and foster exchange of ideas and risk taking.[25]

Quality-Enhancement Strategy

In an attempt to gain competitive advantage through the quality-enhancement strategy, the key HRM practices include (1) relatively fixed and explicit job descriptions, (2) high levels of employee participation in decisions relevant to immediate work conditions and the job itself, (3) a mix of individual and group criteria for performance appraisal that is mostly short-term and results-oriented, (4) relatively egalitarian treatment of employees and some guarantees of employment security, and (5) extensive and continuous training and development of employees. These practices facilitate quality enhancement by helping to ensure highly reliable behavior from individuals who can identify with the goals of the organization and, when necessary, be flexible and adaptable to new job assignments and technological change.[26]

Cost-Reduction Strategy

In attempting to gain competitive advantage by pursuing a strategy of cost reduction, key human resource practice choices include (1) relatively fixed (stable) and explicit job descriptions that allow little room for ambiguity, (2) narrowly designed jobs and narrowly defined career paths that encourage specialization, expertise, and efficiency, (3) short-term, results-oriented performance appraisals, (4) close monitoring of market pay levels for use in making compensation decisions, and (5) minimal levels of employee training and development. These practices maximize efficiency by providing means for management to monitor and control closely the activities of employees.

AN INNOVATIVE STRATEGY: ONE COMPANY'S EXPERIENCE

Frost, Inc. is one company that has made a conscious effort to match competitive strategy with human resource management practices.[27] Located in Grand Rapids, Michigan, Frost is a manufacturer of overhead conveyor trolleys used primarily in the auto industry, with sales of $20 million.[28] Concerned about depending too heavily on one cyclical industry, President Charles D. "Chad" Frost made several attempts to diversify the business, first into manufacturing lawn mower components and later into material-handling systems, such as floor conveyors and hoists. These attempts failed. The engineers didn't know how to design unfamiliar components, production people didn't know how to make them, and sales people didn't know how to sell them. Chad Frost diagnosed the problem as inflexibility. "We had single-purpose machines and single-purpose people," he said, "including single-purpose managers."

Frost decided that automating production was the key to flexibility. Twenty-six old-fashioned screw machines on the factory floor were replaced with 11 numerical-controlled machines paired within 18 industrial robots. Frost decided to design and build an automated storage-and-retrieval inventory control system, which would later be sold as a proprietary product, and to automate completely the front office to reduce indirect labor costs. The new program was formally launched in late 1983.

What at first glance appeared to be a hardware-oriented strategy turned out to be an exercise in human resource management. "If you're going to reap a real benefit in renovating a small to medium-size company, the machinery is just one part, perhaps the easiest part, of the renovation process," says Robert McIntyre, head of Amprotech, Inc., an affiliated consulting company Frost formed early in the automation project to provide an objective, "outside" view. "The hardest part is getting people to change."

Frost was clearly embarking on a strategy of innovation. As it turns out, many of the choices the company made about human resource practices were intended to support the employee role behaviors identified as being crucial to the success of an innovation strategy.

For example, the company immediately set out to increase employee identification with the company by giving each worker 10 shares of the closely held company and by referring to them henceforth as "shareholder-employees." The share ownership, which employees can increase by making additional purchases through a 401(d) plan, are also intended to give employees a long-term focus, which is another behavior important for an innovation strategy to succeed. Additional long-term incentives consist of a standard corporate profit-sharing plan and a discretionary profit-sharing plan administered by Chad Frost.

Frost's compensation package was also restructured to strike a balance between results (productivity) and process (manufacturing). In Frost's case, the latter is a significant consideration, since the production process is at the heart of the company's innovation strategy. Frost instituted a quarterly bonus that is based on companywide productivity, and established a "celebration fund" that managers can tap at their discretion to reward significant employee contributions. The bonuses serve to foster other needed employee role behaviors. By making the quarterly bonus dependent on companywide productivity, the company is encouraging cooperative, interdependent behavior. The "celebration fund" meanwhile, can be used to reward and reinforce innovative behavior. (Even the form of the celebration can be creative. Rewards can range from dinner with Chad Frost to a weekend for an employee and spouse at a local hotel, to a belly dancing performance in the office.)

Frost encourages cooperative behavior in a number of other ways as well. Most offices (including Chad Frost's) lack doors, which is intended to foster openness of communication. Most executive perks have been eliminated, and all employees have access to the company's mainframe computer (with the exception of payroll information) by way of more than 40 terminals scattered around the front office and factory floor.

In our view, a vital component of any innovation strategy is getting employees to broaden their skills, assume more responsibilities, and take risks. Frost encourages employees to learn new skills by paying for extensive training programs, both at the company and at local colleges. It even goes further, identifying the development of additional skills as a prerequisite for advancement. This is partly out of necessity, since Frost has compressed its 11 previous levels of hierarchy into four. Because this has made it harder to reward employees through traditional methods of promotion, employees are challenged to advance by adding skills, assuming more responsibilities, and taking risks.

Honda's Quality-Enhancement Strategy

We can identify those human resource practices that facilitate product quality by examining Honda of America's Marysville, Ohio plant.[29] With a current work force of approximately 4,500, this plant produces cars of quality comparable to those produced by Honda plants in Japan. Although pay rates (independent of bonuses) may be as much as 30–40% lower than rates at other Midwest auto plants, Honda has fewer layoffs and lower inventory rates of new cars than its competitors. How is this possible?

One possible explanation is that Honda knows that the delivery of quality products depends on predictable and reliable behavior from its employees. In the initial employee orientation session, which may last between 3 and 4 hours, job security is emphasized. Employees' spouses are encouraged to attend these sessions, because Honda believes that spouse awareness of the company and its demands on employees can help minimize absenteeism, tardiness, and turnover. Of course, something so critical to quality as reliable behavior is not stimulated and reinforced by only one human resource practice. For example, associates who have perfect attendance for four straight weeks receive a bonus of $56. Attendance also influences the size of the semiannual bonus (typically paid in spring and autumn). Impressive attendance figures also enhance an employee's chances for promotion. (Honda of America has a policy of promotion from within.)

In addition to getting and reinforcing reliable and predictable behavior, Honda's HRM practices encourage a longer-term employee orientation and a flexibility to change. Employment security, along with constant informal and formal training programs, facilitate these role behaviors. Training programs are tailored to the needs of the associates (employees) through the formal performance appraisal process, which is developmental rather than evaluational. Team leaders (not supervisors) are trained in spotting and removing performance deficiencies as they occur. To help speed communication and remove any organizational sources of performance deficiencies, the structure of the organization is such that there are only four levels between associates and the plant manager.

At Honda, cooperative, interdependent behavior is fostered by egalitarian HRM practices. All associates wear identical uniforms with their first names embossed; parking spaces are unmarked, and there is only one cafeteria. All entry-level associates receive the same rate of pay except for a 60-cents-an-hour shift differential. The modern health center adjacent to the main plant is open to all. These practices, in turn, encourage all associates to regard themselves collectively as "us" rather than "us" versus "them." Without this underlying attitude, the flexible work rules, air-conditioned plant, and automation wouldn't be enough to sustain associate commitment and identification with the organization's goal of high quality.

The success of Honda's quality enhancement strategy goes beyond concern for its own HRM practices. It is also concerned with the human resource practices of other organizations, such as its suppliers. For example, Delco-Remy's practice of participative management style, as well as its reputation for producing quality products at competitive prices, was the reason why Delco was selected by Honda as its sole supplier of batteries.[30]

A Cost-Reduction Strategy at United Parcel Service

Through meticulous human engineering and close scrutiny of its 152,000 employees, United Parcel Service (UPS) has grown highly profitable despite stiff competition. According to Larry P. Breakiron, the company's senior vice president of engineering, "Our ability to manage labor and hold it accountable is the key to success."[31] In other words, in an industry where "a package is a package," UPS succeeds by its cost-reduction strategy.

Of all paths that can be taken to pursue a cost-reduction strategy, the one taken by UPS is the work standard/simplification method. This method has been the key to gains in efficiency and productivity increases. UPS's founder, James E. Casey, put a premium on efficiency. In the 1920s, Casey hired pioneers of time and motion study such as Frank Gilbreth and Fredrick Taylor to measure the time each UPS driver spent each day on specific tasks. UPS engineers cut away the sides of UPS trucks to study how the drivers performed, and then made changes in techniques to enhance worker effectiveness. The establishment of effective work standards has led not only to enormous gains in efficiency and cost reduction; it actually makes employees less tired at the end of the day. During the day, the employees engage in short-term, highly repetitive role behaviors that involve little risk taking. Because specialists identify the best way to accomplish tasks, employee participation in job decisions is unnecessary.

Through the use of time and motion studies, UPS has established very specific ways for workers to perform their jobs. The company also monitors closely the performance of the workers. More than 1,000 industrial engineers use time and motion study to set standards for a variety of closely supervised tasks. In return, the UPS drivers, all of whom are Teamsters, earn approximately $15 per hour — a dollar or so more than the drivers at other companies. In addition, employees who perform at acceptable levels enjoy job security.

IMPLEMENTATION ISSUES

These descriptions of Frost, Honda, and UPS illustrate how a few organizations systematically match their HRM practices not only with their articulated competitive strategies, but also with their perceptions of needed role behavior from their employees. Although only a beginning, the success of these firms suggests that HRM practices for all levels of employees are affected by strategic considerations. Thus, while it may be important to match the characteristics of top management with the strategy of the organization, it may be *as* important to do this for *all* employees.

Although the results of these examples generally support the three major hypotheses, they also raise several central issues: Which competitive strategy is best? Is it best to have one competitive strategy or several? What are the implications of a change of competitive strategy?

Which Competitive Strategy Is Best?

Of the three competitive strategies described here, deciding which is best depends on several factors. Certainly customer wants and the nature of the competition are key factors. If customers are demanding quality, a cost-reduction strategy may not be as fruitful as a quality improvement strategy. At the Mercury Marine division of Brunswick and at Corning Glass Works, the issues seem to be quality. According to McComas, "Customers, particularly industrial trial buyers, would have been no more inclined to buy their products even if the manufacturer could have passed along savings of, say, 10% or even 20%."[32]

If, however, the product or service is relatively undifferentiated, such as the overnight parcel delivery industry, a cost-reduction strategy may be the best way to gain competitive advantage. Even here, though, there is a choice. United Parcel Service, for example, is pursuing the cost-reduction strategy through work process refinements such as work clarification, standardization, measurement, and feedback. Roadway, in contrast, pursues the same strategy by combining employee independence and ownership (drivers own their own trucks, of various colors; UPS drivers do not own their brown trucks) with as much automation as possible.[33] The advantage of these latter approaches to cost reduction, compared with such approaches as wage concessions or workforce reductions, is the amount of time required to implement them. Cost reduction through wage concessions or work force reductions, is though painful, can be relatively straightforward to implement. As a consequence, it can be duplicated by others, essentially eliminating the competitive advantage gained by being able to offer lower prices. The adoption of two-tiered wage contracts within the airline industry is a good example: Soon after American Airlines installed a two-tier wage system for its pilots, Eastern, United, and Frontier Airlines negotiated similar contracts with their employees.

There may, however, be some external

conditions that might permit the success of a strategy of cost reduction to last. After four straight years of losses and a shrinkage in the number of stores from nearly 3,500 in 1974 to a little more than 1,000 in 1982, the Great Atlantic & Pacific Tea Company (A&P) and the United Food and Commercial Workers (UFCW) saw the handwriting on the wall: Either reduce costs and be competitive, or go out of business. According to a *Business Week* article,

> In an experimental arrangement negotiated with the .... UFCW at 60 stores in the Philadelphia area, workers took a 25% pay cut in exchange for an unusual promise: If a store's employees could keep labor costs at 10% of sales — by working more efficiently or by boosting store traffic — they'd get a cash bonus equal to 1% of the store's sales. They'd get a 0.5% bonus at 11% of sales or 1.5% at 9.5% of sales. It was a gamble in the low-margin supermarket business, but it worked.[34]

The result? An 81% increase in operating profits in 1984 and a doubling of A&P's stock price. Although the UFCW agreed with the incentive compensation scheme at A&P, the union appears unwilling to see this practice spread. Consequently, competitors of A&P, such as Giant Food Inc., would have difficulty implementing the same scheme.[35]

By contrast, a quality improvement strategy, whether by automation or quality teams, is more time consuming and difficult to implement. As the U.S. auto industry has experienced, it is taking a long time to overcome the competitive advantage gained by the Japanese auto industry through quality improvement. The J.D. Powers 1986 Consumer Satisfaction Index of automobiles suggests, however, that Ford's dedicated approach to quality enhancement may be reaping benefits.

One Competitive Strategy or Several?

Although we focused on the pursuit of a common competitive strategy in our examples, this may be oversimplifying reality. For example, at Honda in Marysville, associates are encouraged to be innovative. Each year the group of associates that designs the most unique or unusual transportation vehicle is awarded a trip to Japan. At UPS, teamwork and cooperation are valued and at Frost, Inc., product and service quality are of paramount importance. Lincoln Electric is recognized as one of the lowest cost *and* highest quality producers of arc welders. While these examples indicate that organizations may pursue more than one competitive strategy at a time, it may be that organizations actually need to have multiple and concurrent competitive strategies. Using multiple strategies results in the challenge of stimulating and rewarding different role behaviors while at the same time trying to manage the conflicts and tensions that may arise as a consequence. This may be the very essence of the top manager's job. According to Mitchell Kapor of Lotus Development Corporation:

> To be a successful enterprise, we have to do two apparently contradictory things quite well: We have to stay innovative and creative, but at the same time we have to be tightly controlled about certain aspects of our corporate behavior. But I think that what you have to do about paradox is embrace it. So we have the kind of company

where certain things are very loose and other things are very tight. The whole art of management is sorting things into the loose pile or the tight pile and then watching them carefully.[36]

Perhaps, then, the top manager's job is facilitated by separating business units or functional areas that have different competitive strategies. To the extent that this separation is limited or that a single business unit has multiple strategies, effective means of confrontation and collaboration need to exist. However, even with this issue under control, there is another equally significant challenge.

Change of Competitive Strategies

By implication, changes in strategy should be accompanied by changes in human resources practices. As the products of firms change, as their customers' demands change, and as the competition changes, the competitive strategies of firms will change. Consequently, employees will face an ever-changing employment relationship. A significant implication of this is that employees of a single firm may be exposed to different sets of human resource practices during the course of employment. Thus, employees may be asked to exhibit different role behaviors over time and they may be exposed to several different conditions of employment. Although it remains to be seen whether all employees can adjust to such changes, it appears that many can and have. For those who wish not to, firms may offer outplacement assistance to another firm, or even to another division in the company. For those who have problems changing, firms may offer training programs to facilitate the acquisition of necessary skills and abilities as well as needed role behaviors.

Another implication is that all components of a system of human resource practices need to be changed and implemented simultaneously. The key human resource practices work together to stimulate and reinforce particular needed employee behaviors. Not to invoke a particular practice (e.g., high participation) implies invoking another (e.g., low participation) that is less likely to stimulate and reinforce the necessary employee behaviors. The likely result is that employees will experience conflict, ambiguity, and frustration.

CONCLUSION

The recent attack on U.S. firms for failing to keep costs down, not maintaining quality, and ignoring innovation are misdirected, given what many firms like Frost, Honda-Marysville, UPS, Corning Glass, A&P, 3M, and Brunswick are doing.[37] These firms and others are pursuing competitive strategies aimed at cost reduction, quality improvement, and innovation. The aim in implementing these strategies is to gain competitive advantage and beat the competition — both domestically and internationally. While cost and market conditions tend to constrain somewhat the choice of competitive strategy, the constraint appears to be one of degree rather than of kind. Consequently, we can find firms pursuing these three competitive strategies regardless of industry.

All firms are not seeking to gain competitive strategy. Not doing so, however, is becoming more of a luxury. For those attempting to do so, the experiences of other firms suggest that effectiveness can be increased by systematically melding human resource practices with the selected competitive strategy. Certainly, the success or failure of a firm is not likely to turn entirely on its human resource management practices, but the HRM practices are likely to be critical.[38]

NOTES

1. C. Fombrun, "An Interview with Reginald Jones," *Organizational Dynamics,* Winter 1982, p. 46.
2. D. C. Hambrick and P. A. Mason, "Upper Echelons: The Organization as a Reflection of Its Top Managers," *Academy of Management Review,* 9, 1984, 193–206; A. K. Gupta, "Contingency Linkages Between Strategy and General Manager Characteristics: A Conceptual Examination," *Academy of Management Review,* 9, 1984, 399–412; A. K. Gupta and V. Govindarajan, "Build, Hold, Harvest: Converting Strategic Intentions into Reality," *Journal of Business Strategy,* 4, 1984a, 34–47; A. K. Gupta and V. Govindarajan, "Business Unit Strategy, Managerial Characteristics, and Business Unit Effectiveness at Strategy Implementation," *Academy of Management Journal,* 9, 1984b, 25–41; M. Gerstein and H. Reisman, "Strategic Selection: Matching Executives to Business Conditions," *Sloan Management Review,* Winter 1983, pp. 33–49; D. Miller, M. F. R. Kets de Vries, and J. M. Toulouse, "Top Executives' Locus of Control and Its Relationship to Strategy-Making, Structure, and Environment," *Academy of Management Journal,* 25, 1982, 237–253; A. D. Szilagyi and D. M. Schweiger, "Matching Managers to Strategies: A Review and Suggested Framework," *Academy of Management Review,* 9, 1984, 626–637; and J. D. Olian and S. L. Rynes, "Organizational Staffing: Integrating Practice with Strategy," *Industrial Relations,* 23, 1984, 170–183.
3. Lee J. A. Byrne and A. Leigh Cowan, "Should Companies Groom New Leaders or Buy Them?" *Business Week,* September 22, 94–95.
4. Ibid.
5. A. J. Rutigliano, "Managing the New: An Interview with Peter Drucker," *Management Review,* January 1986, 38–41.
6. D. Q. Mills, *The New Competitors,* New York: The Free Press, 1985; and M. Beer, B. Spector, P. R. Lawrence, D. Q. Mills, and R. E. Walton, *Managing Human Assets,* New York: Macmillan, Inc., 1984; R. M. Kanter, "Change Masters and the Intricate Architecture of Corporate Culture Change," *Management Review,* October 1983, 18–28; and R. M. Kanter, *The Change Masters,* New York: Simon and Schuster, 1983.
7. J. L. Kerr, "Diversification Strategies and Managerial Rewards: An Empirical Study," *Academy of Management Journal,* 28, 1985, 155–179; J. W. Slocum, W. L. Cron, R. W. Hansen, and S. Rawlings, "Business Strategy and the Management of Plateaued Employees," *Academy of Management Journal,* 28, 1985, 133–154; D. C. Hambrick and C. C. Snow, "Strategic Reward Systems," in C. C. Snow (Ed.), *Strategy, Organization Design and Human Resources Management,* Greenwich, CT: JAI Press, 1987.
8. For detailed examples of how firms use their human resource practices to gain competitive advantage, see R. S. Schuler and I. C. MacMillan, "Gaining Competitive Advantage Through Human Resource Management Practices," *Human Resource Management,* Autumn 1984, 241–255; R. S. Schuler, "Fostering and Facilitating Entrepreneurship in Organizations: Implications for Organization Structure and Human Resource Management Practices," *Human Resource Management,* Winter 1986, 607–629; and M. E. Porter, *Competitive Strategy,* New York: The Free Press, 1980; and M. E. Porter, *Competitive Advantage,* New York: The Free Press, 1985.
9. For an extensive discussion of competitive initiative, competitive strategy, and competitive advantage, see I. C. MacMillan's "Seizing Competitive Initiative," *Journal of Business Strategy,* 1983, 43–57.
10. See Endnote 18, Porter, 1980, 1985.
11. B. Schneider, "Organizational Behavior," *Annual Review of Psychology,* 1985, 36, 573–611.
12. D. Katz and R. L. Kahn, *The Social Psychology of Organizations,* 2nd Ed., New York: John Wiley, 1978.
13. J. C. Naylor, R. D. Pritchard, and D. R. Ilgen, *A Theory of Behavior in Organizations,* New

York: Academic Press, 1980; T. W. Dougherty and R. D. Pritchard, "The Measurement of Role Variables: Exploratory Examination of a New Approach," *Organizational Behavior and Human Decision Processes, 35,* 1985, 141–155.
14. J. R. Rizzo, R. J. Hose, and S. I. Lirtzman, "Role Conflict and Ambiguity in Complex Organizations," *Administrative Science Quarterly, 14,* 1970, 150–163; S. E. Jackson and R. S. Schuler, "A Meta-Analysis and Conceptual Critique of Research on Role Ambiguity and Role Conflict in Work Settings," *Organizational Behavior and Human Decision Processes, 36,* 1985, 16–78.
15. R. M. Kanter, "Supporting Innovation and Venture Development in Established Companies," *Journal of Business Venturing,* Winter 1985, 47–60.
16. H. DePree, *Business as Unusual.* Zeeland, MI: Herman Miller, 1986.
17. The following discussion is based on our survey and observations, and findings reported on by others. For a review of what others have reported, see R. S. Schuler's "Human Resource Management Practice Choices," *Human Resource Planning,* March 1987, 1–19.
18. M. McComas, "Cutting Costs Without Killing the Business," *Fortune,* October 13, 1986, p. 76.
19. For a detailed presentation of Marine Mercury's program to improve quality, see Endnote 18 above.
20. S. E. Prokesch, "Bean Meshes Man, Machine," *The New York Times,* December 23, 1985, pp. 19, 21.
21. S. E. Prokesch, "Are America's Manufacturers Finally Back on the Map?" *Business Week,* November 17, 1986, pp. 92, 97.
22. Ibid., p. 92.
23. Ibid., p. 97. For more on Electrolux's human resource practices, see B. J. Feder's "The Man Who Modernized Electrolux," *The New York Times,* December 31, 1986, p. 24.
24. Schuler, 1987.
25. E. E. Lawler III, "The Strategic Design of Reward Systems," in R. S. Schuler and S. A. Youngblood (Eds.), *Readings in Personnel and Human Resource Management,* 2nd Ed., St. Paul, MN: West Publishing, 1984, pp. 253–269; and R. S. Schuler, "Human Resource Management Practice Choices," in R. S. Schuler, S. A. Youngblood, and V. L. Huber (Eds.), *Readings in Personnel and Human Resource Management,* 3rd Ed., St. Paul, MN: West Publishing, 1988. Other factors that can influence the human resource practices are top management, hierarchical considerations, what other firms are doing, what the firm has done in the past, the type of technology, size and age of firm, unionization status, and the legal environment and its structure (see R. K. Kazanjian and R. Drazin, "Implementing Manufacturing Innovations: Critical Choices of Structure and Staffing Roles," *Human Resource Management,* Fall 1986, 385–404).
26. P. F. Drucker, *Innovation and Entrepreneurship,* New York: Harper & Row, 1985; K. Albrecht and S. Albrecht, *The Creative Corporation,* Homewood, IL: Dow Jones-Irwin, 1987.
27. P. F. Drucker, "Quality Means a Whole New Approach to Manufacturing," *Business Week,* June 8, 1987, 131–143; P. F. Drucker, "Puleeze! Will Somebody Help Me?" *Time,* February 2, 1987, 48–57; and R. L. Desatnick, *Managing to Keep the Customer,* San Francisco: Jossey-Bass, 1987.
28. This description is expanded upon in detail by S. Galante, "Frost, Inc.," *Human Resource Planning,* March 1987, 57–67.
29. For additional collaborating information, see J. Merwin, "A Tale of Two Worlds," *Forbes,* June 16, 1986, 101–105; and S. Chira, "At 80, Honda's Founder Is Still a Fiery Maverick," *The New York Times,* January 12, 1987, p. 35.
30. As reported in Schuler and MacMillan, "Gaining Competitive Advantage Through Human Resource Management Practices," *Human Resource Management,* Autumn 1984, 249–250.
31. D. Machalaba, "United Parcel Service Gets Deliveries Done by Driving Its Workers," *Wall Street Journal,* April 22, 1986, pp. 1 and 23.
32. M. McComas, "Cutting Costs Without Killing the Business," *Fortune,* October 13, 1986, p. 77.
33. Ibid.
34. M. McComas, "How A&P Fattens Profits by Sharing Them," *Business Week,* December 22, 1986, p. 44. For an excellent discussion of the difficulties to be overcome in dealing with changing from human resource practices based on hierarchy or status to those based on performance or what's needed, see R. M. Kanter, "The New Workforce Meets the Changing Workplace: Strains, Dilemmas, and Contradictions in Attempts to Implement Participative and Entrepreneurial Management," *Human Resource Management,* Winter 1986, 515–538.

35. For a discussion of relevant issues, see D. Q. Mills, "When Employees Make Concessions," *Harvard Business Review,* May-June 1983, 103–113; and R. R. Rehder and M. M. Smith, "Kaizen and the Art of Labor Relations," *Personnel Journal,* December 1986, 83–94.
36. *The Boston Globe,* January 27, 1985.
37. Recent attacks on public and private firms have been summarized by the use of the word "corpocracy." A description of corpocracy is found in M. Green and J. F. Berry's "Takeovers, a Symptom of Corpocracy," *The New York Times,* December 3, 1986.
38. The application of these human resource practices to strategy can be done by a firm on itself and even upon other firms that may be upstream or downstream of the local firm. For a further description, see Schuler and MacMillan (Endnote 30).

Randall S. Schuler and Susan E. Jackson are affiliated with New York University. The authors wish to thank John W. Slocum, Jr., C. K. Prahalad, and John Dutton for their many helpful suggestions, and the Human Resource Planning Society, the Center for Entrepreneurial Studies, New York University, and the University of Michigan for their financial support of this project.

The Performance Measurement and Reward System: Critical to Strategic Management
Paul J. Stonich

In many companies, considerable emphasis has been put on combining strategy formulation and resource allocation to improve strategic implementation. Unfortunately, such efforts have not been wholly effective because the necessary performance measurement and reward system that completes the cycle is often missing. Although management has traditionally used the measurement and reward process to influence employees' activities, the measurement process rarely reflects the organization's strategic needs. Alfred Rappaport, a professor at Northwestern University's J. L. Kellogg Graduate School of Management, underscored the problem in a recent issue of *Business Week:* "Many executive compensation systems are just pay-delivery systems linked to what executives think are strategic objectives, like earnings-per-share growth and return on investment, but which are not."

What is needed is a mechanism to encourage managers to behave in ways that are truly in the firm's long-term interest. This mechanism should monitor and recognize corporate progress toward strategic objectives and demonstrate senior management's interest and investment in attaining strategic goals that are in the company's best long-term interest. The reward system and the performance measurement on which it is based form that mechanism. Consequently, rewards and the measurement framework should be designed as an integral part of the entire strategic management process.

One company provides a good example of how overlooking the power of measurement and reward systems can hamper

Source: Paul J. Stonich, "The Performance Measurement and Reward System: Critical to Strategic Management." Reprinted, by permission of the publisher, from *Organizational Dynamics,* Winter 1984, © 1984 American Management Association, New York. All rights reserved.

FIGURE 1
Interaction of Key Variables in Strategy

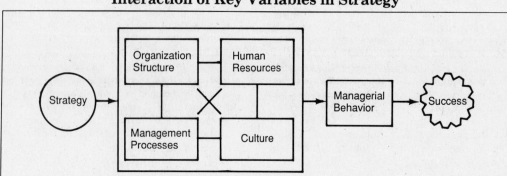

an otherwise sound program. Over the last three years, this multibillion-dollar, diversified manufacturer installed a strategic planning process and training program that succeeded in getting managers to think in more strategic terms. The company also regrouped its business units more logically and became more formal in reallocating its corporate resources. In short, management made excellent progress.

Unfortunately, the results have not yet fully paid off. The sticking point is the short-term orientation of the measurement and reward systems. Because division net profits still serve as the primary measure of performance, it is understandable that managers are reluctant to take strategic actions. Long-term actions will tend to hurt their units' near-term performance and therefore reduce their personal compensation.

Aligning the performance measurement and reward system with a corporation's strategy is not in itself enough, however. The system must also be either consistent with, or specifically designed to help modify, certain of the firm's internal characteristics. While reward systems have long been acknowledged as motivators of managerial performance, they are frequently overlooked as tools to better align strategy with the firm's internal characteristics.

Used alone or out of context, measurement and reward systems cannot influence managerial behavior strongly enough to make strategy happen. The interaction of a number of key variables needs to be carefully orchestrated, along with measurements and rewards to achieve success. Figure 1 shows how these interactions take place. (See box on pages 557–559 for details of basic concepts and a model for implementing strategy.)

Management can and should make careful decisions about all the interrelated variables. For example, a large midwestern bank spent one year — and hundreds of thousands of dollars — developing a strategy based solely on market needs and economic facts. Although the resulting strategy looked good on the surface, the bank's top management was uncomfortable with it. "This strategy simply doesn't fit our culture, our people, or our way of doing things," said the executive vice president.

And he was right. While elegant, the strategy simply could not be implemented in that particular bank without significant behavioral changes. No amount of overhauling measurements and rewards could change that fact. The lesson is simple, yet essential: Measurement and reward processes are only part of the equation. To achieve intended results, the whole set of interrelated variables must be carefully managed by top management to effect changes that work in concert, not in conflict. Sending one message through an explicit strategy statement and a conflicting one through the measurement or reward system can only cause confusion and frustrate positive results. Key questions to keep in mind when examining the effectiveness of a particular approach include the following:

- How does the system fit with strategy, organizational structure, human resources, culture, and other management processes?
- Are performance measurement criteria explicitly tied to the rewards structure?
- Does the system provide incentives to accomplish the organization's long-term strategies and its short-term objectives?

In short, does the approach under consideration encourage or discourage the behavior necessary to successfully execute the corporate strategy?

In the following sections we will consider the three sets of relationships that are particularly important to the design of an effective measurement and reward process. The first relationship is that between measurement and the organization structure. Because structure is typically out of step with strategy, the measurement and reward systems must reflect that gap and close it. Next we will discuss the relationship between measurement on the one hand and the corporate culture and subcultures on the other. A reward process that causes behavior dramatically different from what is "culturally acceptable" may well result in frustrated managers and "climate" problems. Finally, we will look at the explicit links between measurement, rewards, and strategic priorities.

MEASUREMENT LINKED TO ORGANIZATION STRUCTURE

A most important yet frequently overlooked relationship is that between the company's formal organization and the measurement process. The size, nature, and diversity of a corporation's business impact organization structure and, in turn, the performance measurement and reward system. However, executives responsible for compensation programs have been unable or unwilling to recognize these factors in the past because of the technical difficulty of collecting relevant performance data or because of their desire to keep things simple through uniform approaches and procedures. Techniques are now available to tailor the measurement and reward processes to varying organizational forms. Before considering appropriate measurement and reward systems, we should understand the four major types of organization structure: centralized function, division, holding company, and matrix.

The *centralized function* organization is made up of specialized units — marketing, sales, production, engineering, research and development, personnel, finance, and administration — each with a single manager at the top and a single chain of command reporting to each functional head; the specialization that develops in this structure is most effective when the company sells a single product or a very few products. A *division* structure emphasizes a decentralized organization based on product or market groupings; division structure often mirrors the definitions of the business, with each division having its own dedicated functional resources. A *holding company* is a collection of separate businesses — designated as divisions or subsidiaries — held together by a financial control system; corporate staffs are kept small and do not get involved in division operations, with the exception of financial performance decisions. *Matrix* structure is characterized by two types of managers: (1) a matrix manager in charge of either a function or a product and (2) a "two-boss" manager, responsible for a defined work package, who reports both to a functional manager and to a product manager. The matrix structure is generally used by businesses involving multiple products or families of products.

The relation between structures and measurement systems can be explained by placing them on two parallel continuums as shown in Figure 2. At one extreme, companies following a centralized, often functional, organizational philosophy frequently use functional measurements for performance. At the other extreme, decentralized companies such as holding companies frequently use return on equity as the primary method of performance measurement. The use of profit-center measurement is frequently aligned with divisional organization. This alignment is not automatically desirable; too often, companies adopt profit-center measurement even though they are not using a decentralized, divisional type of organizational format. This alignment will be dysfunctional if managers are not given the authority and control needed to influence the parameters being measured. Thus in a functional organization, with its centralized decision making, rewarding managers on the basis of profit measures over which they lack control cannot effectively motivate them.

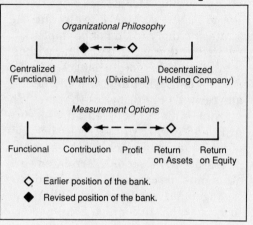

FIGURE 2

Divisional Measurement Options

The diamonds in Figure 2 mark changes in the position of a large money-center bank as it worked to align its organization philosophy, measurement methodology, and business strategy. During the 1970s the bank followed a traditional approach to organization and measurement by using divisions and return on assets as its primary focus. As commercial banking evolved as a result of high inflation rates and increased internationalization of the banking business, the bank introduced a number of changes in its organization and measurement system to improve its alignment with its environment. To recognize the dual nature of many aspects of the banking business, matrix organization was introduced. For example, funds management within branches was placed in a matrix reporting both to the local branch manager and to a centralized funds management organization. International commercial banking was also matrixed, with some loan officers reporting both to the local branch management and to a centralized world corporation management group.

This shift in organization paralleled the bank's strategic decisions to emphasize its services to large global corporations and to improve its control of the funding or treasury side of the bank. The move toward matrix organization was in effect a move toward more centralized control of the bank's activities.

Paralleling this change in organization, the bank changed its measurement system to reduce dependence on return on assets by setting up a contribution form of measurement. The bank also double-counted the contribution coming from those operations operating in a matrix, thereby further reducing the bottom-line orientation previously in use. The purpose of this measurement change was to reinforce the cooperation required by the more centralized form of organization in effect. In this example, measurement philosophy was directly aligned with organization philosophy to implement the strategy intended by the bank.

Measurement philosophy provides a creative opportunity that can be used either to complement or to counterbalance a company's organizational changes to implement strategic direction. Strategy implementation can involve dealing with a misalignment of organizational philosophy and measurement philosophy. For example, a company may be driven toward decentralization by the need to spread its operations across a broad geographical area. The independence created by physical separation frequently creates a drive for decentralized structure and complementary measurement methods. However, if an organization seeks to maintain a firm-wide approach to products or services, striving for overall efficiency and effectiveness as opposed to automatically opting for decentralized responsiveness, a purposeful mismatch of organization and measurement philosophies may accomplish the desired results.

For instance, a large consulting firm operating in over twenty offices around the world chooses to use a single profit center for measuring performance in the firm. In spite of the fact that, in terms of structure, each of its offices is accorded a degree of independence approaching that of divisions, this consulting firm does not measure profit at the office level. Rather, it uses such functional forms of measurement as overhead control, salary control, firmwide utilization and productivity measures, and revenue measures. The firm deliberately does not bring these functional measures together to create a profit calculation for each office in the organization.

This mismatch between organizational and measurement philosophies is explicitly designed to recognize the realities of geography through organization form, and to offset this reality with a measurement philosophy that requires a firm-wide view. In this way, the firm is able to maintain consistency in practice across the firm, to force individual offices to work together toward the common good of the firm, and to strive for firmwide benefits and economies that would inevitably be lost by a measurement system that was as decentralized as the firm's structure.

MEASUREMENT AND THE IMPACT OF CORPORATE CULTURE

Over the long term an organization's culture or guiding beliefs can be shaped by the effective use of measurement and reward. Indeed, much of any organization's current culture can be specifically attributed to past reward policies. Profit-center measurement and the resulting well-known "profit centeritis" may have served a useful purpose at a point in many companies' history, but now such an orientation can form a major roadblock to achieving the cross-organizational cooperation necessary for many contemporary strategies.

However, the more important issue at this point is the impact of inconsistencies between measurement and reward on the one hand and culture on the other during the short term. One multibillion-dollar industrial firm had a history of being a highly political, nondemanding organization. A new chief executive officer was brought in and, within five years, had introduced formal strategic planning, resource allocation at a strategic level, and a sophisticated personal objective-setting process that was linked to the business-planning process and the compensation system. Managers were held accountable for strategic goals that reasonably reflected strategic direction. Still, there was some room for individual negotiation around the measured results that took some of the teeth out of the measurement and reward process. When the budget was tightly integrated into the process, a significant climate problem arose. The disciplined, results-oriented behavior demanded by the management process was at variance with the "way things are done" and managers could not "escape" the system by saying "I don't have enough resources to meet my objectives." In subsequent years the linkages were relaxed, allowing more flexibility in the system. The company has become a premier competitor in its industry and the climate problems have diminished as "the way things are" have approached the way management wanted them eight years ago.

MATCHING MEASUREMENT/REWARD SYSTEMS WITH STRATEGIC GOALS

The previous sections described how the conceptual design of the measurement process can be made consistent with a company's organization structure and culture and yet be supportive of the philosophy and strategy driving the organization. That is not enough, however. It is important to tailor the details of the measurement and reward process to the company's specific strategy and situation.

Toward this end, several approaches are available to help match measurement/rewards with explicit strategic goals and timeframes; these approaches include (1) weighted factor, (2) long-term evaluation, (3) strategic funds, and (4) combined approaches.

The Weighted-Factor Approach

The weighting of performance measurements reflects the generally accepted idea that funds should be invested in strategic business units (SBUs) with high growth opportunity. Conversely, where it has been deemed that there is little opportunity for growth, cash flow and return on assets (ROA) measures are weighted more heavily. This weighted-factor approach can be fine-tuned to reflect each individual strategy by using such additional points as target market share, productivity levels, product quality measures, product development measures, and personnel development measures. These measurements form the basis for determining appropriate rewards.

A large manufacturing company recently completed a rigorous planning process that went far beyond that which most companies attempt. In an effort to tie long-term strategy to operations, an executive committee identified programs having long-term benefits and funded those programs on a priority basis. However, the expected surge of managerial enthusiasm in support of the future-oriented programs failed to appear. The reason for the absence of enthusiasm was ultimately uncovered: The reward system continued to reinforce attainment of short-term goals.

The company's approach for bridging this strategy-results gulf was creative. After categorizing each of its strategic business units as "high growth," "medium growth," or "maintenance," it developed a measurement system unique to the desired strategy and growth for each unit. The new weighted-factor approach measured the performance of each unit against the strategic goals of that unit. High-growth SBUs were measured in terms of market share, sales growth, cash-flow potential, and progress of several future-oriented strategic projects. Low-growth SBUs were measured in terms of their cash-generating ability. Just one year after initiating the new measurement and reward system, management behavior began to change. There was a noticeable increase in enthusiasm for the strategy formulation, planning, and programming processes resulting in better implementation.

The weighted-factor approach used by the manufacturing company described above called for developing a measurement system that fit the behavior required of each SBU to achieve its strategic goals. Table 1 illustrates how performance measurement factors such as ROA, cash flow, strategic-funds programs, and increases in market share were weighted according to the importance of each factor in achieving the SBU's desired performance.

The Long-Term Evaluation Approach

This method explicitly motivates managers toward a future orientation by compensating managers for achieving set goals over a multiyear period. Long-term evaluation usually involves deferred income or incentive compensation, typically deferred stock awarded on the basis of attaining an earnings growth target over an extended period. Alternatively, it can be designed so that bonus payments are reinvested in the business, and growth of the reinvested bonuses is contingent on future corporate and unit performance. Currently about 15 percent

TABLE 1
A Weighted-Factor Approach to Rewarding Achievement of Strategic Goals

Strategic Business Unit Category	Factor	Weight
High growth	Return on Assets	10%
	Cash Flow	0%
	Strategic-Funds Programs	45%
	Market-Share Increase	45%
		100%
Medium growth	Return on Assets	25%
	Cash Flow	25%
	Strategic-Funds Programs	25%
	Market-Share Increase	25%
		100%
Low growth	Return on Assets	50%
	Cash Flow	50%
	Strategic-Funds Programs	0%
	Market-Share Increase	0%
		100%

of companies with sales over $500 million have long-term income programs that compensate managers with some sort of deferred stock to achieve set goals over a multiyear period.

The long-term evaluation approach hopefully ties the interest of the firm's managers to the long-term interests of the firm's shareholders. The approach does, however, pose two problems. First, there is relatively little that any one manager (except for the top officers) can do to affect long-term stock price or earnings growth. Therefore, the approach may not fully take advantage of the motivating potential inherent in measurement systems. Second, unless the long-term measure is aligned with the successful implementation of all aspects of the firm's strategy, the approach can motivate managers to slight those strategy aspects that do not maximize the measure chosen.

The Strategic-Funds Approach

A strategic-funds approach is another way to improve the linkage between short-term and long-term goals. This approach encourages executives to consider certain developmental expenses apart from current operations. Table 2 shows a profit and loss statement that's somewhat different from the type that accountants require for outside reporting purposes. Note that the manager is measured on two bases. The top part of the income statement is familiar in that it shows sales, cost of sales, gross margin, operating general and administrative expenses, and operating return on sales.

TABLE 2
Strategic Business Unit Profit and Loss Statement (*illustrating segregation of strategic funds*)

Sales	$12,300,000
Cost of sales	6,900,000
Gross margin	$ 5,400,000
Operating (general and administrative expense)	−3,700,000
Operating (return) on sales)	$ 1,700,000, or 33%
Strategic funds	−1,000,000
Pre-tax profit	$ 700,000, or 13.6%

The unique aspect of this statement is that strategic funds, conventionally included in the operating and administrative account, are separated out below operating return on sales. These funds are identified during the programming process, and are the resources devoted to future-oriented activities. The manager is given an incentive to invest strategic funds in the future and is able to determine how much is invested in the future of the business. The statement indicates pretax profitability both before and after strategic funds are accounted for.

This approach differentiates between those monies spent on future-oriented activities and those expended on current activities. Managers who follow their natural inclination to manage to the "bottom line" are able to do so if operating ROS is considered the bottom line. This approach provides a practical way for executives to plan, manage, and be evaluated on two important aspects of their jobs: maintaining optimal operating performance during the short term while positioning the business for the future. Thus current company operations need not be short-changed and, more important, future investments through strategic funds are encouraged.

The Combined Approach

An effective way to achieve the desired strategic results through a reward system is to combine the weighted-factor, long-term evaluation, and strategic-funds approaches.

First, segregate future-oriented strategic funds from short-term funds, list them, and report them as in the strategic-funds approach. Second, develop a weighted-factor chart for each strategic business unit, including return on assets, cash flow, strategic-funds programs, market-share increase, and others. (Specific factors taken into account depend on the strategy of the particular business unit.) Third, measure performance on three bases: the bottom-line in the strategic-funds approach, the weighted factors, and long-term evaluation of the corporation's and SBU's performances.

The relative weights that can be assigned to each of these in a combined approach will vary from SBU to SBU and from company to company depending on its business environment and the organization's culture. Progressive corporations made up of highly diverse businesses already structure their measurements this way. General Electric and Westinghouse provide two excellent examples. In these companies mature SBUs are judged on their ability to generate large profits and positive cash flows while maintaining market share. The emphasis is immediate, and financial compensation correspondingly relies on short-term incentives. But in budding, high-growth areas, GE and Westinghouse make their evaluations of SBUs against other, usually nonfinancial criteria. These criteria include effectiveness in research and development as well as success at sniffing out new marketing opportunities. Consequently, compensation for managers of these SBUs is tied to longer-term performance.

VEHICLES FOR REWARDS

As we have seen, the behavior of groups of managers and individual managers can be measured, and such behavior does affect the company's performance. Managers and groups of managers can be rewarded in various ways on the basis of their performance measurement. Compensation is the most obvious and tangible means of reward. It includes salary, bonus, benefit packages, perquisites, insurance, pension plan, stock options and grants, deferred income, and so forth. Obviously, this is a very direct reward and is a very powerful motivator in many cases. However, people's psychological needs often go beyond pure compensation.

Two other important factors need to be considered. The first is power. Power can be granted through promotion, organizational placement, recognition, title, or even simple visibility within the organization. For some individuals this is an extremely powerful motivator. A second factor at the disposal of management is personal development and career pathing. Education and personal growth and development are rewards that can be used to motivate a desired performance. These alternative factors may become more important in the less hierarchical, "atomized" organizations some business observers predict for the future.

For the reward system to work well, it must complement the measurement system and, in turn, be complementary to all of the other elements in the strategic model presented earlier. Thus the reward system must balance the firm's long- and short-term strategies by granting both long-term and short-term behavior incentives to managers.

From an internal point of view, the reward system needs to be consistent within the business environment and within industry standards. Obviously, this means that, to be fair, rewards must be aligned along the continuum from best performance to worst. They must also be aligned within the industry to maintain a competitive position.

A favorite saying of the chief operating officer of a *Fortune* 500 company is, "If you provide appropriate rewards, their hearts and minds will follow." The operative phrases in his philosophy are *appropriate rewards* and *hearts and minds will follow*. We have discussed that rewards must be appropriate in matching the measurement system and the other elements in the model, as well as the realities of the firm. We've also discussed that it's important to achieve a certain set of behaviors to carry out strategy.

MEASUREMENT AND REWARD SYSTEMS: IN PERSPECTIVE

Successful strategy implementation depends, in part, on a well-designed measurement and reward system. A measurement and reward system serves

IMPLEMENTING STRATEGY: THE MODEL

The performance measurement and reward system has sometimes been considered incidental to and separate from a company's business. The system is in reality a basic subelement of an organization's management process. The management process is, in turn, one of the five key elements — strategy formulation, organization structure, human resources, corporate culture, and management processes — that drive an organization's ability to implement strategy. Success — achievement of strategic objectives through implementation of the strategy — is brought about through a complex interaction of all these elements.

Strategy Formulation

Strategy formulation is fundamentally the process of deciding where a company is today and where it should be tomorrow. Its primary focus is external, though it must be balanced by assessment of internal capabilities. Questions that must be considered include these: Can enough of the needed human resources be marshaled to make the strategy work? How will existing planning, budgeting, and reward processes have to be modified to meet the strategy's requirements? Will the strategy require full or partial reorganization? Does the proposed strategy go against the grain of current organizational values and norms of behavior?

Organization Structure and Human Resources

Broadly speaking, structure is the formal authority hierarchy that delineates the various roles, responsibilities, and reporting relationships within a firm. If there is a poor fit between the strategy and the structure in place, managers have two choices: Either they must develop restructuring alternatives, or they must attempt to refocus the chosen strategy to fit the existing structure.

Similarly, trying to implement a strategy without people who have the requisite skills, attitudes, and training will lead to disaster. If human resources are deficient, managers must make difficult choices: Alter the strategy to fit the available human resources, develop the skills of existing staff, or hire the new people needed to bring the strategy to fruition.

Corporate Culture

Culture comprises the unofficial and usually unspoken "rules of the game" in any organization. Culture, more than any other element, subtly dictates what can and will be done. The success of the strategic planner depends on his or her ability to assess the cultural risks inherent in a chosen strategy.

Management Processes

Planning, budgeting, programming, and the measurement/reward compo-
(Continued)

IMPLEMENTING STRATEGY: THE MODEL (cont.)

nent make up the vital "nervous system" that directs and sends signals throughout an organization and stimulates its movement toward the chosen objectives. These major management processes make up the set of tools that management has available to implement strategy. (See Figure 3.)

The *planning* process is closely related to strategy formulation but is different in several ways. First, strategy formulation develops a specific strategy for a firm or business unit while planning describes the current strategy to top management and provides the link to detail programming and budgeting. Where there are several business units, planning pulls together the strategies of those units and allows top management to develop a corporate strategy and to allocate scarce resources.

Second, strategy formulation studies are done periodically when the need arises for a new strategy, while planning is done every year at the same time to communicate all current business unit strategies concurrently to management.

Third, strategy formulation is typically an exhaustive analysis involving top management as well as many line and staff managers. Planning generally involves less effort and fewer people.

Fourth, strategy formulation is done in reaction to and in anticipation of changes in the environment. Planning profiles those changes and their impact on the strategy.

Planning, therefore, can be thought of as the communication of strategy to top management. The strategy may or may not have changed over the previous year, but the periodic nature of the process ensures that the strategy or strategies that are pursued are moving the firm in a rational way toward its overall strategic objectives.

Budgeting is the mechanism used to make operational resource allocation decisions and to record them for subsequent measurement. In the budgeting process, the dollars and the people necessary to carry out all organizational tasks are decided and forecast. This is a key process in implementing strategy because it is very close to the action — the actual carrying out of the critical tasks necessary for the company to meet its strategic objectives. Without an appropriate budget it is unlikely that strategy will be implemented effectively. And budgeting is intricately interrelated to the organization structure (who budgets?), the culture (what kind of process will be accepted?), and human resources (can they prepare good budgets?).

Two allocation periods or timeframes are important to the top management of a firm: the operational, or short-term, and the strategic, or long-term. The emphasis in many companies is focused on both strategy formulation and short-term budgeting. When the budget is not closely linked with strategy, resources can be

(Continued)

> **IMPLEMENTING STRATEGY: THE MODEL (cont.)**
>
> allocated in a manner that stifles rather than promotes a firm's long-range strategy. Thus, although budgeting may be highly developed and although it may provide the information required to reach decisions about day-to-day operations and to set goals that must be achieved by taking specific actions, the resulting resource allocation often is short-term oriented and not designed to explicitly move the firm toward its strategic objectives.
>
> *Programming* is the management process that allocates resources on a multiyear basis toward the fulfillment of strategic goals. Programming requires the identification and analysis of strategic programs, which in turn require managers to pass judgment on the needs for each program, its risks, its fit with criteria, its chance for success, and the costs involved. Once the strategic funds programs have been approved and funded, the next phase is controlling the progress toward the initial strategic goal. This implies that the proposals have already specified a timetable, milestones, and other controllable and measurable activities.
>
> *Measurement/reward sytems,* our interest here, involve considerations well beyond the salary and benefit packages required to attract and keep people of the caliber needed to implement an organization's chosen strategy. Effective rewards also motivate management to take actions that move the firm toward its strategic goals.
>
> All of these elements work together to influence managerial behavior — and managerial behavior makes or breaks successful implementation of strategies.

not only to demonstrate senior management's interest and investment in attaining strategic goals, but also to motivate managers to make strategic business decisions.

Strategy formulation, organization structure, human resources, management process, and culture are the five elements that drive an organization to implement strategy. A performance and reward system is a subelement of an organization's management process. Successful corporate performance occurs when an appropriate strategy is implemented through the rationalization of these five key elements along with the measurement and reward system. The internal consistency of these elements is referred to as "fit."

Measurement and reward systems send powerful signals to a company's people about their performance. Rewards should motivate people to take action that moves the firm toward its strategic goals. By necessity, the size, nature, and diversity of a business impact the type of performance measurement and reward system that should be utilized.

Reward systems can be designed to motivate both short-term and long-term performance. The company that rewards exclusively on the basis of today's bottom-line may well be hindering the achievement of its long-term strategic

FIGURE 3
Tools for Implementing Strategy

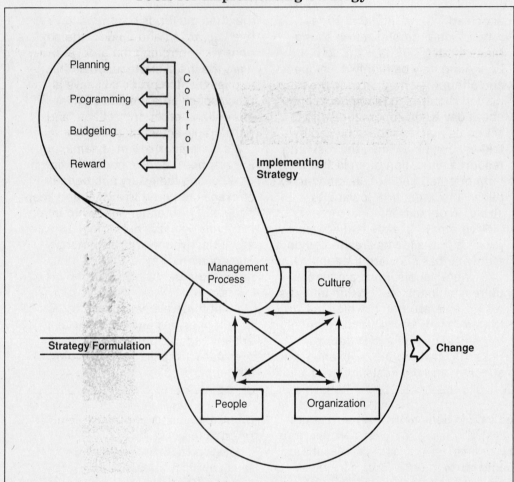

goals. Several approaches to reward systems work to integrate strategy with management incentives without sacrificing short-term performance: weighted factor, long-term evaluation, strategic funds, and a combined approach that utilizes features of the other three.

Some companies do a good job of developing strategy, managing culture, organizing, and developing other management processes, but do not achieve a well-implemented strategy because their measurement and reward system is not in tune. Successful implementation of strategy requires a very carefully designed measurement and reward system. If you measure and reward managers on the appropriate management tasks, their "hearts and minds will follow."

Paul J. Stonich is director of the organizational effectiveness division at Harbridge House, Inc., in Boston.

Human Resources: The Forgotten Factor in Mergers and Acquisitions
Dealing with the Human Side of a Merger
David L. Schweiger / John M. Ivancevich

"Don't go down the cellar," Chris's suicide note warned his family. That's where the 38-year-old economist hanged himself, four days after he lost his $63,000-a-year job, when his company was acquired by another firm.[1]

"I worked for 18 years and gave them everything I had. Look how I end up, just like a run-over flat can in the street. There is no loyalty, no commitment, no feeling. When it got tough, they bailed out and let us sink," stated Tom, a manager for a larger diversified firm that sold controlling interest to a hostile acquiring company.

After four months of rumor, gloom and gossip, Joan, a financial control staff specialist, comments on the recent takeover of her company: "One day we are in business and the next day we disappear from the face of the earth. I'll have to start all over again learning the job, the policies, the people. Is it really worth it?"

These items indicate the growing and critical effect that mergers are having on today's employees. However, they only reflect the tip of the iceberg. Concern with being merged or acquired by another company seems to be on the minds of many American employees these days. If we look at the statistics it becomes evident that many of these concerns are real. During the last decade, for example, 23,000 mergers and acquisitions were consummated, with a total value of approximately $398 billion. Eighty-two of those acquired were *Fortune* 500 companies. The 10 largest mergers in 1984 directly affected the lives of more than 250,000 employees.[2] Every indication suggests that merger and acquisition activity will continue at a significant rate for some time.

Although mergers and acquisitions have long been the subject of debate, especially with respect to their effects on the utilization of capital, the level of competition and society in general, little attention has been given to human resource concerns. These concerns must be dealt with specifically by the managements of both the acquiring and acquired firms if the retention and continued commitment and productivity of valued employees are to be achieved. Top executives, investment bankers and lawyers usually do not give much time, energy or thought to human costs in terms of lost jobs, reduced status and power problems, family conflict, strain, uprooting and shaken self-esteem when concocting the merger deal. In most cases, however, the human element is influential in determining the eventual success of the merger.

Mergers and the rumors associated

Source: David L. Schweiger and John M. Ivancevich, "Human Resources: The Forgotten Factor in Mergers and Acquisitions." Reprinted from the November 1985 issue of *Personnel Administrator,* copyright, 1985, The American Society for Personnel Administration, 606 North Washington Street, Alexandria, VA 22314.

with them often lead to a number of concerns for employees. The major one, however, is how it will affect them in both the short and long term. For most people, it is a period of uncertainty and insecurity, both of which can create considerable stress and a diverse array of consequences associated with stress. The major focus of this paper is to call attention to how mergers can create managerial and employee stress. Also included are some specific guidelines which can be initiated through a team effort by the acquiring and acquired firms that may mitigate the possible negative effects of such stress.

STRESS AND MERGERS

During the past 30 years, research on stress has emerged, stimulated primarily by the desire to understand breakdowns in adaptive behavior observed in extreme situations. Military combat, bereavement, presurgical circumstances, and imprisonment have been classified as extreme and dramatic situations. Currently, researchers of the stress phenomenon have also examined job, occupational, and personal factors such as work overload, responsibility, time pressures, job security, self-esteem, need for personal control, and organizational culture as potential contributors to a stress response and its consequences. However, to date neither researchers nor managers have systematically addressed and examined merger stress and its consequences. Even well-orchestrated mergers can result in change that is threatening, unsettling and stressful for some employees. The void in the literature on merger stress is unexplainable when one realizes that for many people a merger is a very dramatic situation.

By *stress* we mean an imbalance between the requirements to make an adaptive response to some change, event or condition and the repertoire of the individual. The change we are discussing is the merger events and attitudes (e.g., negotiations, rumors, implementation and after-effects) as it is seen and experienced by an individual. The greater the uncertainty surrounding the merger, the greater the perceived discrepancy between the pressure of the merger and the individual's response capacity; additionally, the higher the appraised cost of making such a reaction, the more stress acting on the person. A merger might be perceived more as a threat by an individual who has not developed an adequate coping response than by one who has. In short, merger stress, like other stress, involves transactions that trigger many individualized actions, thoughts and feelings. Unfortunately, merger events and activities can impose an unmanageable burden on an individual's system, if the person does not possess an appropriate repertoire.

Clearly, how an individual responds to merger stress is a personal matter. Responding to stress involves perceptual interpretative behavior and physiological adjustments. Menninger elaborated on a series of stages comprising the stress response that illustrates how individualized adjustments can occur. These stages seem particularly appropriate for better understanding the potential stress caused by mergers.[3] The following is a sketch of the sequence of stages that might occur over the course of a merger.

- *Alarm* — Suppose merger discussions are taking place between top managers of two firms. The merger and its perceived job and personal consequences are perceived by individuals in various ways. For some, there is increased arousal, such as paying attention to the merger discussions, rumors, and gossip, cessation of activities (e.g., motivation to work hard, completing a job on time, being loyal to the organization), and going on with business as usual (e.g., I can't control anything so why worry about it?).

- *Appraisal* — An assessment is made of the nature of the merger — individuals focus on what the merger means to them. Does a merger mean a loss of personal power, restructuring of the job, being terminated, losing retirement and health insurance benefits, etc.? The merger can be accurately appraised, but the merger-associated consequences for the individual can be denied, distorted, minimized or exaggerated. Appraisal entails both identification and recognition of the sources of pressure, uncertainty and anxiety.
- *Coping strategy* — Dysfunctional physical, psychological and behavioral arousal provoked by a merger can be decreased when there is anticipation, control or mastery through the use of a coping strategy. Since merger activities are usually unfamiliar to individuals, no coping strategy exists in the individual's repertoire. Coping strategies can be improvised that deal either directly with the merger or indirectly with the consequences of the merger. Control in the indirect case is gained by dealing with the meaning of the merger and not its direct potential negative impact.
- *Dysfunctional response* — This stage involves acute dysfunctional effect states (e.g., grief, anomie, anxiety, hostility, anger), inadequate ego defenses,

poor cognitive organization and activation of altered physiological patterns. The final segment of this stage for some individuals may be a state of either disorganization or exhaustion.

Because a merger is a dramatic event for many employees, it can initiate the first stage of the stress response, which in turn can lead to the second stage, and so on. Furthermore, each stage has associated psychological, behavioral and physiological components. The final outcome of the stress response can involve mastery, exhaustion or disorganization. Human resource managers should consider initiating a set of merger stress management activities that can improve employees' mastery of the merger activities and situation.

MERGER STRESS PROCESS: A FRAMEWORK

The effect of a merger on employees and the intensity of these effects are a function of several factors. Essentially a merger creates a number of potential and powerful antecedents of stress (stressors). Whether these stressors create stress and its ensuing negative outcomes depends on the characteristics, predisposition and goals of the employees involved, as well as the organization's plan for systematically intervening and helping employees manage merger-induced stress.

A general framework which depicts major relationships involved in the merger stress process is presented in Figure 1. Proceeding from left to right, Figure 1 suggests that merger stressors (e.g., uncertainty, job change) can become stressful (e.g., cognitive) for some employees

FIGURE 1
Merger Stress Process

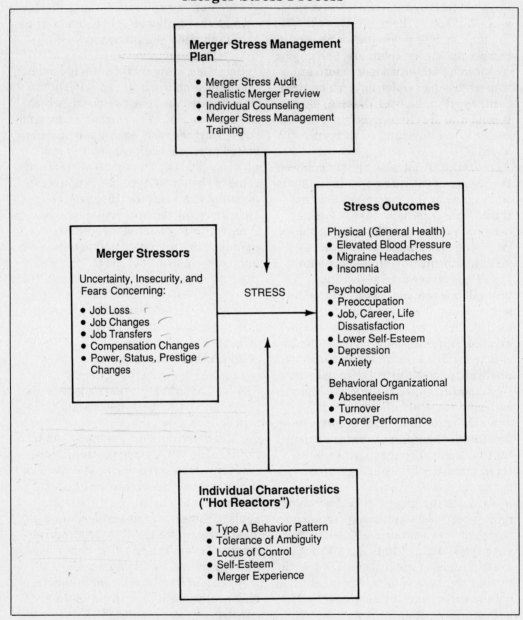

Note: Only a sample of possible factors is presented in each box.

and that the stress may result in various outcomes (e.g., decreased performance, health problems). The framework suggests that human resource managers can develop and implement a program that can influence the stressor-stress and stress-outcome associations. It is also suggested that individual characteristics such as Type A Behavior Pattern, locus of control and previous experience with a merger can influence these associations.

Merger stressors Some employees experience significant psychological reactions when organizations merge. From the point at which a merger is announced publicly, uncertainty and insecurity seem to consume these employees. It is quite natural to experience a significant psychological reaction, especially if the organizations involved have not included consideration of human resources in the merger plan. This uncertainty is often created by people's *perceptions* of how the merger will affect their lives, careers and work. Essential to understanding the merger stress process is the realization that people respond to their perceptions and conceptualizations of the changes rather than to the actual changes themselves. In the initial stages of the merger process these perceptions are probably the least accurate with respect to the actual effects of the merger on them. During this period, information concerning the actual implementation of the merger is scarce. Usually, all that is known is that the two relatively independent entities are going to be brought together.

Typically, there is minimal knowledge about specific integration plans. Because of so much uncertainty, it is doubtful that the degree and depth of job, workflow, policy and design changes have been specified, and if they have, they have not been clearly communicated to either managers or employees. As such, it is likely that employees will develop a number of inaccurate perceptions of the merger's effects — and in many cases will imagine numerous negative outcomes. These anticipated consequences of the merger will tend to increase anxiety levels and exacerbate the stress. It is essential during this period that inaccurate perceptions of the changes that will occur and the stress that they create be dealt with immediately. In addition to uncertainty and insecurity, a sense of loss of control also will tend to increase. Not knowing what changes are going to be made, employees will develop and worry about scenarios concerning job loss, transfers, etc.

To say that mergers and the perceived or actual changes brought by them leads to stress is an understatement. However, how stress manifests itself, how it intensifies and whether it is mastered depends to some extent on how human resource managers handle it. A major stress category to deal with in a merger is change. Change for most employees means a disruption in the life and work patterns to which they have become accustomed and comfortable with over time. Essentially, it means a change in daily habits and job and life roles. At a more concrete level, this may include: (1) job loss; (2) job changes — new role demands, new administrative systems; (3) job transfer; (4) compensation changes; (5) new bosses, colleagues, and/or employees; (6) geographical moves; (7) new career paths; and (8) changes in power, status and prestige.

When the merger is first announced, a primary concern of some employees is job loss. The press has documented in stark numbers the boxscore of job loss in most mergers. For example, in April 1984, Chevron acquired Gulf, and by April 1985 about 20,000 jobs had been lost. The employee roster has shrunk by over 6,000 following Texaco's acquisition of Getty Oil Co. Thus, mergers certainly have a history of threatening the job security of some employees. Mergers may also have damaging psychological effects, such as creating a diminished sense of self-esteem. Furthermore, mergers often bring spouses and other family members into the center of the stress, since it directly affects them as well. Job changes and transfers often mean learning new skills or applying existing ones in new environments. This may lead to changes in work relationships such as new bosses, colleagues or employees, resulting in new social relationships.

Geographical changes such as moving to a new office or factory may involve selling and buying houses, leaving old friends and acquiring new ones, and switching children to new schools, among other issues. Being merged into another company also raises questions concerning pensions, compensation and how career paths in the new company differ from those in the old one. Although these changes might bring improvements in one's work, career and life, it is often the case that the initial shock and disbelief associated with the perceived changes which the merger brings will create negative thoughts and feelings.

Merger stress and its outcomes Merger stress can have a number of negative consequences for both the individual and the organization. Stress researchers have clearly demonstrated that dramatic changes can have a pronounced physiological impact if they are not coped with properly. Physiological responses to a merger may include high blood pressure, migraine headaches, muscle aches, sleeplessness, trembling, muscle tics, etc. Depending upon the duration of the stress, the intensity of these outcomes and possible short- and long-term health problems vary.

From a psychological perspective, one typical merger stress response is preoccupation. In many cases, employees find it quite difficult to concentrate on their work during this period, especially if they do not think that they will be retained in their job long-term. This preoccupation frequently manifests itself in daydreaming and aimless "wandering" about the organization. To help cope with the "uncertainty," employees tend to seek out other employees during work to check the validity of rumors or to get new information. Depression and anxiety are also quite common.

Other psychological outcomes may include lower job, career and life satisfaction and lower self-esteem. Common behavioral outcomes include increased absenteeism, turnover, lower productivity and destructive behavior. Stress may make it difficult for people to face their day-to-day responsibilities. Under some conditions a merger, because of its powerful psychological impact, can result in resentment and hostility toward the acquiring firm and its representatives. Anger directed toward others can show up in terms of covert activities such as sabotaging work performance. Anger can also contribute to slowing down the work pace, interfering with the work of others and not attending to "business as usual." When management ignores or is unaware of the powerful nature of anger, it indirectly reinforces it.

If the labor market is such that jobs are plentiful, key employees may elect to leave and seek employment elsewhere; these might be the employees who were judged to be instrumental to the new organization. Key individuals nearing retirement may also elect to end their careers early to escape an uncertain and changing situation. At an organizational level, stress reactions, if left unmanaged, may mean a reduction in productivity, a loss of key people and a general disruption of the organization.

Individual characteristics How employees respond to a merger, however, is not just a function of the merger itself. Some employees will deal with the changes and ensuing uncertainties and insecurities better than others. However, it is essential that the organization identify what can be called the "hot merger reactors" — employees who are most likely to respond poorly to a merger. These individuals are likely to become highly stressed when faced with uncertainty and change. Characteristics which typify "hot merger reactors" include individuals with: (1) a Type A behavior pattern; (2) low tolerance for ambiguity; (3) an internal locus of control; and (4) low self-esteem. Other factors such as previous experience with mergers, length of employment with the firm being merged, social support, financial security, alternative job opportunities and the presence of other stress factors in one's life may also help determine whether an employee is likely to be a "hot merger reactor."

MANAGING MERGER STRESS: THE CONTROL ELEMENT

As stated earlier, mastery refers to the perception that the events in our personal world may be brought under reasonable control. A sense of mastery is crucial for properly managing the stress created by a merger. The sense of mastery is important not so much because it has direct effects on actions but because a sense of control, or mastery, colors a person's cognitive interpretation of the "real world." It is generally seen as good to be in control of our world; if the world is appraised as good, the emotional tone will be positive. A merger situation and its accompanying series of threatening or frightening events may become manageable — or even amusing or interesting — when we feel a sense of mastery, even though our actual control has not changed. What has changed is our understanding and knowledge of the merger situation or events. It is the subjective sense of control that is important, not the objective control of the situation or event.

A sense of mastery can reduce the deleterious effects of merger stress and alleviate the emotional upheaval. This can happen under two conditions:

- Actions which are directly related to the merger may change its threatening aspect. For example, a managerial intervention which is designed to aid the employees in learning about the acquiring firm's management style, reward system, or plans can change fear, anxiety, or uncertainty to assurance, confidence, or challenge.
- Without any change in its objective features, the merger may be reinterpreted in such a way that it is no longer considered to be threatening or as a harbinger of loss. The overall structure under which the merger is perceived is changed to reinterpret the event in more positive or more beneficial terms.

The important point in both conditions is the value of taking some action. Gal and Lazarus have illustrated how activity on the part of individuals may help lower stress reactions.[4] Taking individual action or participating with others in personally managing and coping with merger stress could lower stress reactions because the involvement and activities tend to increase feelings of control or mastery.

RECOMMENDED MERGER STRESS MANAGEMENT PLAN

Certainly not all employees of an acquired company react to the merger by becoming angry, hostile and depressed. Some employees are likely to view the merger as a new start, a chance to reassess their careers and goals and an opportunity to change their work habits. However, many employees involved in a merger have some anxiety and fear of loss that can be minimized if human resource managers help them develop coping strategies. Four activities which can help minimize the negative fallout of mergers should be enacted just prior to and after the formal announcement of the merger. Depending upon the complexity of the merger and the ensuing stress that it creates for employees, the duration of each activity will vary. The four activities are:

1. Merger stress audit. Talking with and listening to employees are important activities for learning about their attitudes and feelings about the merger and its consequences. Another activity which can provide insightful attitudinal information can be generated by a "merger stress audit." The merger stress audit (MSA) is an attitude survey that provides an assessment of employees' perceptions of the merger and identifies potential "hot merger reactors." The MSA requires careful planning and thorough professional development. Scales to assess employees' collective perception of stress in areas such as compensation, rewards, job duties, job security, and co-workers are included. The results of the MSA can be used for planning a program and sequence of activities to minimize stress and help employees acquire mastery in the merger environment.

The MSA should be administered to all levels of the acquired organization. (It could also be used with modifications in the acquiring firm.) If it is possible and if costs are not prohibitive, all employees should be invited to complete the MSA. By using specific occupational and demographic groupings, it is possible to partition groups (e.g., managers, non-managers) and individuals for appropriate analysis. If it is not feasible to canvass all employees, a representative sample of key employees and those who might be "hot merger reactors" should be selected randomly.

2. A realistic merger preview. In the last decade, the concept of providing "realistic job previews" has drawn considerable attention from researchers and human resource managers concerned with the recruitment and selection of employees.[5] Wanous claims that by providing job applicants with an accurate description of the job, those who accept the job will be more satisfied with it and thus less likely to leave it voluntarily. Receiving a realistic job preview provides individuals with a picture of what to expect; consequently they can cope more realistically with job demands. There is also the development of trust in that the employee communicates with an "air of honesty" to applicants.

Using procedures that are incorporated in providing realistic job previews seems relevant to developing a realistic merger preview (RMP) for the acquired firm's employees. The RMP can be provided through a film, videocassette or booklet, or in large group presentations. A combination of media also may be beneficial. Whichever delivery medium is used, the intent is to improve employees' mastery of the merger events and activities. The employees should be presented with information on what they can realistically expect in terms of:

- Organizational goals, missions, and markets
- Management style and organizational culture
- Work schedules, benefits, and compensation
- Equipment, resources, and information flow
- Job security
- Career paths
- Training and development
- Performance evaluation

The results of the merger stress audit could provide information that is quite instrumental in developing an RMP. Included in any RMP should be an attempt to cover areas identified in the merger stress audit as being especially troublesome. Special attention, comment and discussion of these areas is important in improving employee mastery and reducing anxiety.

Material for the RMP also might be developed by creating a transition task force. This task force, composed of top executives from both the acquiring and acquired companies, would attempt to determine and provide a preview of the future "look" of the new organization.

3. Individual counseling. The merger stress audit and realistic merger preview may not be sufficient to improve a person's mastery, especially in the case of "hot merger reactors." If this is the case it might be beneficial to make a voluntary individual counseling package available.

Individual counseling on the merger can be divided into three categories: Personal adjustment counseling, educational counseling and career counseling. These three types of counseling are not independent of each other. In each type, the counseling involves a one-to-one interaction between a counselor and an employee. The objective of the one-to-one session is to help the employee solve the problem(s) associated with merger stress; recommend, demonstrate and initiate coping with merger stress strategies; or improve the employee's mastery.

Personal adjustment counseling emphasizes individual emotional responses to the merger. The counselor is concerned with helping the individual identify stress responses and behaviors toward the merger. Also, the counselor attempts to spell out a series of coping methods that can improve the emotional distress being experienced.

Educational counseling is concerned with providing the employee with information about the merger. The RMP may not have been sufficient to alleviate some employees' fears and uncertainties, and they may request additional detail. If possible, additional information should be provided on a one-to-one counseling basis.

Career counseling in a merger situation involves issues dealing with choices and opportunities. Making adjustments to an acquiring firm's management system and culture can be a part of the career counseling. The identification of career pathways and objectives in the new organizational arrangement can be important information for employees. A counselor — again on a one-to-one basis — can assist employees in working through career goals, pathways, and opportunities. Of course, it is important to emphasize that only a "realistic" career picture should be provided to individuals.

The counselor in each of these three types of counseling needs to be skillful in listening and communicating as well as understanding. In addition, knowledge about the acquiring firm in the merger is necessary to interpret the information gathered from listening in order to understand the meaning and emotions that are projected in the one-to-one counseling sessions.

4. *Merger stress management training*. Instead of individual counseling (or in addition to it) some employees may prefer or need a training course in merger stress. Any training program should be available on a voluntary basis to employees. It should begin by identifying the kinds of merger-related stress that employees are experiencing, how the stress affects job performance and how thoughts and perceptions may be at the root of the stress.

Two useful methods for identifying merger stress are individual checklists and group sharing. In using a checklist procedure, a list of common and relevant stressor and stress reactions is developed individually. The group sharing method initially isolates several small groups that work without a trainer to develop a list. Each group's list can be presented to the total group and to the trainer for analysis and comparison. Once employees identify the type of merger stressors they perceive and their stress reactions, they can begin steps and procedures necessary to manage the stress.

Next, it is important to present to trainers the stages of the stress response. Explaining and discussing each of these stages improves the trainees' understanding of their cognitions, emotions, and behaviors. An important part of this phase of training is to have each individual discuss and analyze a major stress response in terms of alarm, appraisal, coping, and dysfunctional response. This type of discussion and analysis by each trainee can help identify personal inaccuracies, exaggerations, and commonly shared fears.

At some point in the training, there should be some emphasis that for "hot merger reactors," the stress responses to a merger can be self-generated because of an individual's normal behavioral pattern. Some individuals are typically aggressive and competitive, and store up latent hostility. These individuals are classified as Type A individuals, and they may be extremely susceptible to the inability to control events surrounding a merger. Type A behavior rarely can be changed, only modified or altered. In this module, the Type A behavior pattern, self-generated merger stress and its physical consequences and health are examined.

Next, the trainer should explore with trainees individual coping strategies. The trainer can spell out, demonstrate and discuss briefly coping strategies such as cognitive restructuring, biofeedback, autogenic relaxation, meditation, guided imagery and personal goal-setting. Strange as it may seem, many people need to be taught how to examine their thoughts, relax, and set goals. This module introduces the notion that each of the individual coping strategies requires patience and practice. Proper use of any of these individual strategies will not totally eliminate all of the stress generated by a merger; however, each of the strategies can give individuals the opportunity to gain some portion of control over their lives in the organization.

Finally, each trainee should be encouraged to develop a personalized merger stress management action plan. This part of the training is actually a problem-solving and goal-setting skill development segment. Personal goal contracts should be established to serve as a guide for coping and to evaluate progress in handling merger stress. Goals should be established in no more than the three most stressful merger-initiated areas. The contract then can be taken from the training setting to the work setting and monitored by each individual. At the end of an approximately four-week period, a two-hour group sharing discussion to evaluate progress and problems should be conducted. Finally, a redrawn goal contract should be established for individuals to take out into the organization for their own personal use.

wheeling and dealing and secret backroom deals. However, unless a systematic attempt to deal with the human side of a merger is made, the merger experience is likely to be traumatic, dysfunctional and costly. Proper management of the employees involved has a lot to do with the success or failure of a merger. By and large, organizations fail to seriously consider the fact that a merger involves a form of dramatic stress. The consequences of excessive amounts of merger stress can result in the loss of key personnel, poor performance and deterioration of employees' health and well being.

An acquiring organization with a well-prepared human resource department can act to help employees adjust and cope with inevitable merger stresses. It can work with the acquired firm to develop a merger stress audit, a realistic merger preview program, individual counseling opportunities, or a voluntary merger stress management training program. These programs, if well done, can help employees acquire some mastery over the inevitable series of peaks and valleys that typifies a merger. Also, a systematic set of viable opportunities such as those outlined here can minimize dysfunctional stress responses.

CONCLUSION

There is no single recipe for efficiently managing merger stress. Reports in the press often make mergers sound like high drama replete with corporate

REFERENCES

1. Myron Magnet, "Help! My company has just been taken over," *Fortune,* July 9, 1984, p. 44.
2. Ibid.
3. K. Menninger, "Regulatory devices of the ego under major stress," *International Journal of Psychoanalysis,* Vol. 35 (1954), pp. 412–420.
4. R. Gal and R. S. Lazarus, "The role of activity in anticipating and confronting stressful

situations," *Journal of Human Stress*, Vol. 1 (1975), pp. 4–20.

5. J. P. Wanous, *Organizational Entry: Recruitment, Selection and Socialization of Newcomers.* Reading, MA: Addison-Wesley, 1980.

David L. Schweiger is an assistant professor in the department of systems and strategy at the University of Houston. John M. Ivancevich is a professor in the department of organizational behavior and management at the University of Houston.

Unions in the Next Century: An Exploratory Essay
Joseph Krislov

I. INTRODUCTION

Unionization, as a percentage of nonagricultural employment in the United States, has declined from about one-third in the late 1950s to about one-fifth in the early 1980s. The decline has led to a substantial literature about the future of the American labor movement,[1] but there have been few efforts to discuss the outlook for unionism throughout the world. This essay, therefore, focuses on the question: What are the prospects for unionization throughout the world in the next century?

This inquiry is important for several reasons. First, an inquiry into the prospects for unionism may eventually strengthen democracy, because it may result in an expansion of unionism. Because some form of worker participation is viewed as a feature of democratic societies, it seems likely that union growth will enhance a nation's democratic patterns. Second, studies of prospects for unions abroad should be valuable to American trade unionists who have long supported organizational efforts in developing countries. Such studies may be useful in directing the allocation of American resources; they may also be useful in determining the type of assistance. Third, a comparative study of any institution throughout the world may result in information that can be effectively used in other countries. Several trade union movements in the West are currently having difficulties, and they may profit from a world-wide inquiry into unionism. Fourth, efforts at delineating long-term prospects can often be quite useful for individuals, companies, and governments planning for the future. A well-organized labor movement is likely to have a considerable affect on a nation's public policy, particularly its social welfare expenditures (Stephens, 1980). A poorly organized labor movement is likely to have little influence either on politics or bargaining.

II. BACKGROUND

Unions in the West typically triumphed over employer/governmental hostility and emerged as an independent source of economic and political power. Authoritarian governments in the West gradually became democratic and permitted (often

Source: Joseph Krislov, "Unions in the Next Century: An Exploratory Essay," *Journal of Labor Research,* 1986, pp. 165–174. Reprinted by permission.

encouraged) the development of independent power centers. Thus, unionism in the West is often equated with independence from government.

Nondemocratic countries[2] have seldom permitted workers to have organizations that are not controlled. These units claim to speak for workers but often function only within narrow boundaries established by the government. Worker organizations in nondemocratic countries are often largely controlled by either a political party or government agencies, and members often have little direct influence on the organization.

Should we accept these worker organizations as legitimate spokesmen for employees?[3] There is little doubt that in some countries these organizations have had considerable worker support and have even challenged the government. In other countries, they have had a limited and perhaps meaningless role. Even in countries where unions are basically controlled by governmental authority, the mere existence of workers' organizations suggests some recognition of worker interest (Wiarda, 1975). As a result, these organizations probably have some influence that benefits members. In some countries, the influence may be focused almost entirely in the plant; in others, the organization's influence may be entirely political. In time, these organizations may be assigned additional authority and emerge with some autonomous direction. Thus, this essay assumes that worker organizations (even though basically controlled by party, military, or government authorities) contribute in some way to employees' welfare. Admittedly, however, objective studies of an organization in a particular country may conclude that it does little to promote employee interests.

Having accepted the legitimacy of existing worker organizations, we began our analysis by asking: What will happen to these organizations during the remainder of the twentieth century and the early decades of the twenty-first century? An answer necessitates dividing the world into politically free and non-free countries.

Dahl's landmark 1971 study, *Polyarchy,* identified the characteristics of free societies and then determined which countries met those characteristics. According to Dahl, polyarchies "may be thought of as relatively (but incompletely) democratized regimes, or, to put it in another way, polyarchies are regimes that have been substantially popularized and liberalized, that is, highly inclusive and extensively open to public contestation." Specifically, these countries have a high degree of public contestation and participation. In 1969, about two dozen of the 140 independent nations qualified as polyarchies. As for the future, Dahl argued that it was "unrealistic" to forecast a "dramatic change in the number of polyarchies within a general or two." Moreover, "the safest bet about a country's regime a generation from now is that it will be somewhat different, but not radically different, from that it is today."[4]

For over a decade, Freedom House (a nonprofit, nongovernmental organization) has been conducting a survey of freedom throughout the world. As indicated in its 1984 report, the survey's purpose

> has been to give the educated public a better grasp of the variations in politically relevant freedoms that exist in the world. By limiting the Survey to only this aspect of the subject and by emphasizing its

heuristic purposes, many of the potential problems of the project have been set aside. As the Survey has been repeated over more than a decade, an additional purpose has come to be the provision of a standard by which the educated public can judge trends in these freedoms.

During the last decade, about 35 percent of the world's population lived in politically free countries, about one-fifth in partially free countries, and the remaining 40 to 45 percent in countries that are not free (Gastil, 1984).

As delineated by the survey, freedom is concentrated in North America, Western Europe, India, Oceania, and Japan. Partially free countries predominate in Latin America and exist in Africa and Asia. Non-free countries are concentrated in Asia and Africa. Because worker organizations in partially free countries frequently face extensive controls, our discussion will include these countries with nations that are not free. As a result, we divide the world into the free and partially free/non-free nations (hereafter called "non-free").

III. UNIONISM IN NON-FREE COUNTRIES

The role of unions in non-free countries is not always easily ascertained. Unions are banned in some countries; in others, unions may exist but are tightly controlled by government machinery. The government's attitude toward unions is paramount in establishing unionism and in prescribing its role (Karatnycky et al., 1980).

Unions will undoubtedly expand if non-free countries choose to become free. Following World War II, there was a widespread view that political freedom would spread throughout the world.[5] Much of this optimism was related to the fact that wealthy countries tended to be democratic. Because economic development was inevitable, many countries would become "wealthier." Whatever the specific relationship between wealth and freedom, the forces linking them would eventually manifest themselves. In time, then, the newly emerging wealthy nations would adopt freedom.

In the mid 1980s scholars are not so sanguine. After examining the income levels of countries during the 1980s, Huntington identified twenty-odd countries that were approaching the threshold income level that is presumably necessary to move to democracy. He concluded, however:

> If the wealth theory of democracy were valid, one would predict further movement toward democracy among the twenty-odd states in this group, perhaps particularly on the part of the East Asian NIC's and the B-A states of South America. Experience suggests, however, that what is predictable for these countries in the transition zone is not the advent of democracy but rather the demise of previously existing political forms. Economic development compels the modification or abandonment of traditional political institutions; it does not determine what political system will replace them. That will be shaped by other factors, such as the underlying culture of the society, the values of the elites, and external influences.[6]

Since Huntington's assessment in 1984, it does appear that Brazil/Argentina have moved toward freedom.[7]

Confirming Dahl's 1971 prediction, Freedom House's survey does not suggest any pronounced change of governmental patterns. Predictions regarding sudden shifts of power are quite hazardous, but it hardly seems likely that freedom will be widely adopted. There is little evidence to suggest that Communist nations are likely to adopt freedom, nor is there any indication that non-free African and Asian nations are moving in that direction. In the mid 1980s, Latin American nations seem to be moving toward democracy, but that movement can be viewed as a phase of the traditional cycle of altering civilian, democratic regimes with military and authoritarian ones (Anderson, 1967, Chapter 4).

Without embracing political freedom, it is possible that some non-free countries may adopt policies that will advance unionism. Countries that presently forbid unionism, for example, may permit a very limited form of unionism. China, which curtailed or virtually abolished unionism during the Cultural Revolution, resurrected unions and currently permits them to operate. Similarly, nations that presently permit a very limited unionism may sanction an expanded role for unions. The authority of Russian trade unions was expanded under Khrushchev's leadership during the late 1960s; and while Russian unions are subject to party control, they seem to have more influence today than they did several decades ago (Ruble, 1981). There may be comparable developments in other non-free countries during the next decade, but it is not possible to predict where they may occur.

IV. UNIONISM IN FREE COUNTRIES

The extent of unionism in free countries varies considerably. Nordic countries have the highest percentage of potential membership in unions, and unions have organized well over half of the potential members in each country, with Sweden's unionization well over three-fourths of the potential membership. In contrast, countries such as the United States, France, and Italy have organized approximately one-fourth to one-fifth of the potential membership (Hamermesh and Rees, 1984).

In many free countries, there are several patterns emerging during the 1980s that suggest that unions will encounter difficulties in the future. Unless some of these patterns are reversed, union membership will certainly not grow and may decline.

Stagnation and recession, accompanied by inflation, characterized many of the economies of the free world during the last part of the 1970s. Economic growth in many of these countries was quite modest, and high unemployment rates prevailed. Employers faced keen competition from both domestic and international firms. As a result, management-union relations were strained and unions encountered difficulties in maintaining memberships and bargaining. These difficulties could persist during the 1980 decade and beyond.[8]

During the past decade, many western democracies have experienced a resurgence of conservative ideas, and the victories of Nixon and Reagan may be the result of a return to these views. Michael Hughey has characterized the new conservatism in the United States as centering "on the principles of classical liberalism, emphasizing fiscal austerity, free enterprise, business competition, a minimum of government intervention in the market place, and unification of the public good with the welfare of business."[9] Such an ideology will result in legislation that hinders union organizational effort. Moreover, administrators appointed to enforce laws will hesitate to pursue policies that will aid unions; they may pursue policies that will discourage unions. With both legislative and administrative authorities opposing their programs, unions will have great difficulties.

The changing nature of work in industrially developed countries is a second reason why unions will have difficulties in the future. Unskilled and semi-skilled jobs are gradually being eliminated, with employment growth typically occurring in professional and skilled employment, areas in which unions have not been overly successful. Moreover, work is becoming less central in many countries, as the welfare state provides a bare subsistence to many. Workers who work regularly devote far less time to work during their lifetime; they attend school longer, retire earlier, and enjoy more holidays and longer vacations (IRRA, 1983). The growing participation of women in the labor force also tends to reduce the importance of work as a central concern to a family. With two wage earners, the family will survive even if wages and working conditions at one job are not particularly satisfactory.

Government as an alternative source of benefits has long been apparent in the United States. As early as 1951, Reder (Neumann and Rissman, 1984) pointed out:

> The evolution of society in the past 50 years has transferred many union functions elsewhere. Social Security and educational functions have been largely taken over by the state. The many diversions of urban society have robbed the union of the position it once had as a focus of member social activity. What is left to the union primarily is collective bargaining, and the political activity ancillary to it.

Public provision of union goals is the third reason why unions will have difficulties.

In their study of union membership in the United States during the twentieth century, Neumann and Rissman argued that "both the time-series evidence of social welfare expenditures and the evidence of implicit contract exceptions to employment-at-will doctrine suggest that the public provision of income or employment security competes with the private provision of these services by unions."[10] Of course, no comparable study of trade union membership in other free countries has been made, but it does not appear that union membership in free countries has declined. Kassalow's data for union membership in 1948 and 1979 for nine countries reveal declines for only the U.S. and Japan (Kassalow, 1984). Presumably, social welfare expenditures have increased in many free countries, and perhaps some association between union membership and social welfare expenditures can be discovered. The United Kingdom's unfair dismissal law presents researchers with an unusual opportunity.[11] Presumably, the provision at public expense of a traditional union service suggests that unionism should have declined during the period.

Disadvantaged groups in the American environment (women and minorities) have been organizing and sustaining nonunion groups to secure benefits. Women's groups, for example, have actively pursued efforts to achieve equal pay. Clearly, these groups are alternatives to unionism and may reduce the support for unions.

Management resistance to unionism in the United States hindered unionization during the 1970s. Aware of the growing conservative trend, employers have been able to thwart union organizational efforts. Freeman's summary of studies as to "how company opposition affects union success" and his own analysis strongly support the view that management opposition in the United States has reduced union organizing success and union density (Freeman, 1985). It is difficult to believe that these management efforts will not continue in the United States, but it is not obvious that managements in other countries will increase their opposition (Kassalow, 1984).

V. SUMMARY

We draw three conclusions from this essay. Because independent unionism, as we know it in the West, is tied to a democratic commitment, independent trade unions will prosper only if there is an increase in the number of democratic governments. There is presently a democratic ferment in Latin America, but it is not clear whether it will lead to permanent institutions. Hence, it seems unlikely that there will be a startling expansion in the number of independent trade unions in the world.

It is possible that some non-free countries may relax controls over their internal societies. Employee organizations may be accorded a more important role, and existing governmental or party control may be relaxed. Certainly, there is little evidence to suggest any widespread movement in this direction. Moreover, Poland's recent experience with a surge of worker interest in unionism suggests that Communist societies have difficulties adapting to the growth of independent power centers.

The third conclusion continues to be pessimistic. Trade unions in free countries will be faced with many difficulties, and it is not clear that they will maintain their present strength. Unionism in the United States seems to be particularly vulnerable.

NOTES

1. Edwin White (1958) wrote one of the first articles on the subject. For a more recent view, see Heshizer and Graham (1984). A good summary of the issue can be found in Barbash (1984) and Kassalow (1984).
2. Political scientists make distinctions among nondemocratic countries. One such distinction is between a totalitarian country and an authoritarian one. Linz (1969).
3. A strong case for recognizing the contribution of unions in non-Communist, non-free countries was made by Frederick Harbison (1956). His views are found on pp. 67–70; see Abraham Siegel's remarks (1956) on page 82.
4. See Dahl (1971, pp. 1–16). Polyarchies are defined on page 8.
5. See, for example, Lipset (1959). A critical examination of Lipset's views can be found in Rustow (1970).
6. Huntington (1984). The quotation is on page 201.
7. At roughly the same level of economic development fifteen years earlier, each country moved away from democratic practices. O'Donnell (1972).
8. For more details, see Kassalow (1984).
9. See Hughey (1984). For more specific views of the difficulties encountered by labor with a conservative administration, see Barbash (1985).
10. For a discussion of the employment-at-will doctrine, see Steiber (1984). For a general discussion, see Neumann and Rissman (1984).
11. For a discussion of Britain's unfair dismissal law, see Wedderbern et al. (1983).

REFERENCES

Anderson, Charles W. *Politics and Economic Change in Latin America* (New York: Van Nostrand, 1967), Chapter 4.

Barbash, Jack. "Trade Unionism from Roosevelt to Reagan." *The Annals of the American Academy of Political and Social Science: The Future of American Unionism,* vol. 473 (May 1984).

———. "Trade Unionism." In Richard L. Rowan's *Reading in Labor Economics and Labor Relations* (Homewood, Ill.: Irwin, 1985), pp. 13–16 and 21–22.

Dahl, Robert A. *Polyarchy: Participation and Opposition* (New Haven: Yale University Press, 1971), pp. 1–16.

Freeman, Richard B. "Why Are Unions Fairing Poorly in NLRB Representation Elections?" In Richard L. Rowan's *Readings in Labor Economics and Labor Relations* (Homewood, Ill.: Irwin, 1985), pp. 129–142.

Gastil, Raymond D. "The Comparative Study of Freedom 1984." *Freedom at Issue* (January-February 1984), pp. 3–15, 26–27.

Hamermesh, Daniel S. and Albert Rees. *The Economics of Work and Pay* (New York: Harper & Row, 1984), pp. 205–207.

Harbison, Frederick. "American Labor and the World Crisis." Industrial Relations Research Association, *Papers, 9th Annual Meeting* (1956), pp. 50–82.

Heshizer, Brian and Harry Graham. "Are Unions Facing a Crisis? Labor Officials Are Divided." *Monthly Labor Review* (August 1984), pp. 23–25.

Hughey, Michael W. "The New Conservatism: Political Ideology and Class Structure in America." *Social Research* 49 (1984), p. 791.

Huntington, Samuel P. "Will More Countries Become Democratic?" *Political Science Quarterly* 99 (1984), pp. 193–218.

Industrial Relations Research Association. *The Work Ethic: A Critical Analysis* (Madison, Wisconsin: Pantograph, 1983), Chapters 1, 5, and 7.

Karatnycky, Adrian, Alexander J. Motyl, and Adolph Sturmthal. *Workers Rights, East and West* (New Brunswick, N.J.: Transactions Books, 1980).

Kassalow, Everett M. "The Future of American Unionism: A Comparative Perspective." *The Annals of the American Academy of Political and Social Science: The Future of American Unionism,* vol. 473 (May 1984).

Linz, Juan L. "An Authoritarian Regime: Spain." In Erik Allarot and Yrjo Littonen's, *Cleavages, Ideologies, and Party Systems: Contributions to Comparative Political Sociology,* vol. 10 (Helsinki Academic Bookstore, 1969), pp. 297–299.

Lipset, Seymour M. "Social Requisites of Democracy: Economic Development and Political Legitimacy." *American Political Science Review,* vol. 53 (1959), pp. 69–105.

Neumann, George R. and Ellen R. Rissman. "Where Have All the Union Members Gone?" *Journal of Labor Economics* 2 (1984), p. 175.

O'Donnell, Guillermo. *Modernization and Bureaucratic-Authoritarianism: Studies in South American Politics* (Berkeley: Institute for International Studies, University of California, 1972).

Ruble, Blair A. *Soviet Trade Unions: Their Development in the 1970s* (London: Cambridge University Press, 1981).

Rustow, Dankwart A. "Transitions to Democracy: Toward a Dynamic Model." *Comparative Politics,* vol. 2 (1970).

Siegel, Abraham. "American Labor and the World Crisis." Industrial Relations Research Association, *Papers, 9th Annual Meeting* (1956), pp. 50–82.

Stephens, Joseph. *The Transition from Capitalism to Socialism* (New York: Academic Press, 1980).

Stieber, Jack. "Most US Workers Still May Be Fired Under Employment-at-Will." *Monthly Labor Review* 107 (May 1984), pp. 34–38.

Wedderburn, Lord, Roy Lewis, and Jon Clark. *Labor Law and Industrial Relations: Building on Kahn-Freund* (Oxford: Clarendon Press, 1983), pp. 138–140, 142–143, 175–178, and 207–209.

Wiarda, Howard J. "Corporate Origins of the Iberian and Latin American Labor Relations Systems." *Studies in Comparative International Development* (Spring 1978), pp. 3–37.

Witte, Edwin. "The Crisis in American Unionism." National Academy of Arbitrators, *Proceedings* (1958), pp. 172–187.

Joseph Krislov is affiliated with the University of Kentucky. He is indebted to Kenneth W. Coleman for considerable guidance.

Balancing Work Life and Home Life: What Can Organizations Do to Help?
Douglas T. Hall / Judith Richter

Balancing work life and family life has become a major issue for today's work force. The issue is especially critical for employees who are part of two-career families — a group that now includes approximately 47 million people in the United States.[1] At a time when many companies are streamlining their work force to become "lean and mean," expecting more work from fewer people, it is becoming increasingly difficult for employees to cope with the demands of professional careers, child rearing, home management, job relocation, and other long-term stresses. While this work-home strain is experienced by both female and male employees (as men assume more family-care responsibilities), it is often felt most strongly by women. Work-family strains have become a special concern for organizations with large numbers of professional and managerial women in their mid-thirties who have achieved positions of considerable responsibility and are now considering or just starting a family.

Most of the literature to date on this topic has dealt with theoretical issues.[2] Little has dealt with the practical organizational implications of the strain created by the conflicting demands of work and home. Surprisingly, while many of the remedies touted in the popular press entail greater integration of work and home (such as home-based employment), our findings indicate a greater need for *separation* of the two domains.

The purpose of this article is to discuss what organizations can do to foster more effective management of professional and private lives. We will argue, for example, that organizations need to help employees define the boundaries between home and work, that these boundaries should be more flexible than they currently are, that the value of transition time between home and work should be recognized (as should the differences in employees' styles of making these daily transactions), and that the family should be more consciously integrated into career and human resource management.

First, however, let us look into why so little management attention has been given to this issue.

WHY ORGANIZATIONS AVOID LOOKING AT HOME AND FAMILY LIFE

Rosabeth Kanter has used the term "the myth of separate worlds" to describe a process whereby management acts as if

Source: From "Balancing Work Life and Home Life: What Can Organizations Do to Help?" by Douglas T. Hall and Judith Richter, *The Academy of Management Executive,* 1988, Vol. 11, No. 3, pp. 213–223. Reprinted by permission.

the employee's home world did not exist; that is, as if the work world were everything.³ Many executives perpetuate this myth, even though they know home life has a major impact on work and organizational life, and vice versa.

There are two reasons organizations do little to address the conflicts employees experience between home life and work life. First, while some organizations may be willing to consider work/home issues, they are uncertain about what action would be appropriate and effective. And second, many organizations, for a variety of reasons, are simply unwilling to work on these issues. Let us look at the first group first.

WHY ORGANIZATIONS HAVE DIFFICULTY UNDERSTANDING HOME AND FAMILY LIFE

Many organizations value the importance of work/home balance and have a sincere desire to address it. However, despite their concern, they simply do not know how to approach the question. Let us examine some of the reasons the issue is so difficult.

Lack of Models

Organizations have very little precedent to draw on in the work/family area. There simply are not yet any models of effective response to these issues from which an organization might learn. The primary models that exist are negative ones; for example, the old-fashioned, paternalistic approach in which the company controls the family.⁴

Concerns About Employee Privacy

In our experience, the most frequent executive concern in addressing work/family issues is a sincere question about the ethics of dealing with an employee's family and personal life, a concern about the invasion of privacy. (Indeed, there are laws that protect employees' privacy.) While management knows it is already invading the employee's family life through high job pressure, long work hours, extensive travel and geographic relocation, there is still uncertainty about the possible intrusiveness of raising family problems for explicit discussion.

Lack of Knowledge About Work/Home Dynamics

Most organizations do not know much about the various points of interface between an employee's work life and his or her family and personal life. Management needs to understand this unstructured, largely undefined, and highly charged process by which work and home affect each other on a daily basis before it can begin to solve the problems involved.

WHY SOME ORGANIZATIONS ARE UNWILLING TO ADDRESS WORK/FAMILY ISSUES

Now let us switch gears and examine another group of organizations: those in which management resists the whole idea of addressing work/family issues.

Here the issue is not lack of ability but lack of willingness. Why do some companies resist examining work/family interactions?

Personal Threat to Midlife Executives

Most people are sensitive about their personal lives and the complex feelings, relationships, and problems associated with their family relationship. Fernando Bartoleme has argued that some executives use work as an "alibi" to avoid getting too involved in family life. Since many executives are men in midlife, often involved in some sort of stressful transition (for example, divorce, loss of a parent, children leaving home), there may be a certain amount of pain associated with personal life, pain that they might prefer to avoid. And they may be using work involvement as a way to escape from personal and family problems. As Abraham and Rhoda Korman found, many executives have experienced great success in their career yet feel a sense of failure in their family life. They have made many tradeoffs at the expense of their family to achieve their career success, often in the guise of making these sacrifices "for the family" — when in fact they did it for their own needs for achievement, power, and esteem. Thus, personal life may be the *last* topic many executives might want to see put on the organization's agenda.[5]

Influence of Organizational Culture and Career Paths

A person who values advancement as a sign of career success will usually be motivated toward task (not personal) learning; he (and it usually is he) will not be stimulated to examine issues of personal identity or adult development needs.[6] He will be motivated primarily by the organization's values and needs, accepting geographic relocation cheerfully despite the difficulties created for his children and especially if the potential payoff is a key vice-presidency or the top job itself. Indeed, most executive career development processes reinforce this strong task orientation and low concern for self-reflection in the mobile executive.[7] A rising executive is not forced to examine deeply what he or she values most in life and wants to do with his or her career, whereas a laid-off or plateaued individual has undoubtedly had to face these personal questions. Thus, a high-level executive in his fifties has possibly still not had to confront the midlife transition issues normally faced by people in their early forties.[8]

When such a career-oriented executive looks at an employee who *is* concerned about work/home balance, the executive simply cannot understand the values of that employee. The executive interprets a need for balance as "low motivation" or "weak commitment." And when the employee is a woman, this negative perception is often stronger. Thus, an upward mobility ethic held by senior management leads an organization to view the examination of work/family issues with suspicion.

Work/Family Issue Seen as a "Woman's Problem"

Perhaps because of the complexity of the above issues or perhaps naively, many

male senior executives view the relationship between family and work as an issue of concern primarily for female employees — and therefore not of major importance to the organization and its effective functioning. It is often at best seen as an issue to be dealt with as part of equal employment/affirmative action activities. In many cases, the only time top management deals with the issue is either to avoid problems with female employees or because it is a "good thing to do." This attitude can lead to issues of corporate sexism and the "glass ceiling," which block the progress of women just as they are about to move into key senior-level power positions.[9] Organizations are also concerned with legal issues related to sex discrimination, and this often prevents them from asking job candidates and employees about their marital status and family life.

Avoidance of Complexity: The Lure of the "Quick Fix"

With the great emphasis on short-term performance in contemporary organizations, there is an associated avoidance of complex, longer-term problems such as work/family conflicts. Many executives will simply not deal with an issue if there is not an easy solution handy (which is definitely the case with work/family issues). There is often a reluctance to adopt a total-system perspective for examining the effect of the work/family interaction on productivity, work quality, and employee involvement; or to consider the host of cultural, psychological, sociological, historical, and political factors that contribute to the avoidance of this topic.

Not Seeing the Payoff at Work

Many organizations invest much effort in promoting employee involvement in decision making and problem solving on the job, without considering that family involvement may interfere with an employee's making greater emotional investment in work. Because many executives lack awareness of the link between work involvement and family involvement, they simply do not see the payoff that reducing work/home conflicts would have for organizational effectiveness.

A NEW CONCEPT: DAILY TRANSITIONS

Because a large part of the problem, then, appears to be a lack of top management understanding of the various complex ways in which home life and work life affect each other, our first need in this article is to clarify the impact on home life or work life (and vice versa). We believe that the best way to study the work/home relationship is to look at people's actual behavior as they deal with the conflicts and other effects these two domains have on each other. (We will use the generic term "domain" to describe the areas represented by "home" and "work.")

The method we propose involves looking at the daily transitions that people make as they cross the boundaries between work and home. The idea is that the best way to understand how the two domains affect each other is to look at them in their interface; that is, as they come into contact with one another. The point at which home and work come into contact with one another is when the employee is moving, either physically or psychologically, from one to the other. We propose that the transitions between work and home capture the major issues in the general relationship between the two domains.

Transitions across the boundaries between work and home domains can occur either with the physical move from one domain to the other at the start or the end of the working day, or with the psychological shift that occurs when a person is physically in one domain and becomes mentally concerned with the other. The former are called planned transitions, while the latter are termed interposed transitions.

Interposed transitions can be either self-initiated or imposed by the actions of members of the other domain who intervene in one's current domain.

Domains are separated by boundaries, which are created by both the individual and by the work and home settings. Boundary demarcation may be physical, in which case the markers are time and location, or psychological, in which case what Kurt Lewin called the individual's "life space" (or view of the world) is separated into regions representing different roles or areas of activity.[10]

The boundaries are described by two dimensions: flexibility and permeability. Flexibility describes the extent to which the physical time and location markers, such as working hours and workplace, may be changed. Permeability describes the degree to which a person physically located in one domain may be psychologically concerned with the other.

Transition Styles

The process of crossing physical and psychological boundaries during scheduled transitions defines an individual's transition style. There are three basic styles: *anticipatory, discrete,* and *lagged.* By anticipatory we mean that concern with the domain of destination begins before the person physically leaves the current domain. In the discrete style the individuals' concern with the domain of destination starts upon arrival there. In the lagged style, the person's concern with the newly entered domain does not start until he or she has been physically present for a period of time.

How do people cross the boundaries between work and home? Is the transition from home to work different from that of work to home? How is the transition experienced within the family? Do organizations have rituals or procedures to assist people in crossing these boundaries?

In the following sections we will discuss research findings related to the ways people cross the work/home boundaries on a daily basis and how they attempt to gain balance between the two domains. We will then consider steps that organizations can take to help employees manage work/home boundaries more effectively.

Differences Between Morning and Evening Transitions

We have found that people tend to use an anticipatory transition style in the move from home to work and a discrete transition style in the shift from work to home. In other words, in the morning, people begin thinking about work long before they leave home. In the afternoon, on the other hand, people do not start thinking about home until they leave work. In terms of boundary permeability, this indicates that the morning home boundaries tend to be permeable, while in the evening the work boundaries tend to be impermeable.

Our research also found that as people make daily transitions, they change their concepts of themselves; that is, the way they see themselves. In other words, there is a "work self" and a "home self." The process of changing self-image is asymmetrical, however. In the afternoon, people change to their "home self" only after leaving the office (discrete), while in the morning they change into their work self when they are still at home (anticipatory).

From the family's perspective, morning transitions are not experienced as an issue of conflict within the family, and most people are satisfied with the way they or their spouse leave home in the morning. Conflict is more often associated with the way people reenter their home. Describing the difference, one man said:

> Morning is always so rushed. You have to get up and get to work, you have to get through it, you don't have free time in the morning. When I come [home], I have much more choice of what to do. Whenever there is a chance, there is always a conflict as to what choice should be made (children, wife, personal time). So I'd say the evenings are more difficult than the mornings. The mornings take care of themselves.

None of the organizations involved in our study seems to have any set rituals or procedures regarding entry into the workplace. The predominant organizational culture supports quick entry to work, and morning socializing is limited. This is especially true for younger, more junior employees, who need to be visibly hard-working and motivated. Similarly, in most cases concluding work is not associated with any organizational procedures or rituals. Organizations do, however, clearly convey the message that they expect time boundaries to be followed, and most employers set minimums — expecting workers to be available beyond them as well, at least occasionally. This expectation epitomizes a very clear conflict between the family and the organization, as an expansion of work hours has a direct effect on family time.

Gender Differences in Transition Styles

Evening transitions from work to home are experienced differently by the men and women in our sample. For women, the evening shift was considered highly stressful. The period of reentering their home was most often seen by women as the day's most hectic period, as they had to shift abruptly to their home roles and get immediately involved in their domestic chores. The men tended to leave the office later than the women; they were also more likely than their wives to go through an unwinding period (reading the newspaper, for example) before getting fully involved in their home activities. Thus, men experienced more flexible boundaries than women, both at work and at home. Spouses often seemed out of sync in the evening, as men tended to unwind from work rather slowly at home, while women became immediately involved in home tasks as soon as they arrived.

Interposed Transitions: The Management of Boundary Permeability

The research interviews consistently showed home boundaries to be more permeable than work boundaries, to both externally imposed and self-initiated penetrations. However, different patterns of work and home boundary permeability were found for men and women. Women's home boundaries were cognitively more permeable (that is, they thought about work at home more often than did men) while men's were behaviorally more permeable (that is, men did more actual job-related work in their homes than did women).

Many of the women we interviewed were pioneers in their respective careers and felt that they were "test cases." Their high work involvement might stem in part from strong motivation to establish their positions. A typical remark was:

> It [work] is very much with me all the time. Even on the weekend, dealing with friends. Particularly because many of the men, my friends, think it is probably a bigger deal than it is because it is still relatively unusual for a woman to be at my level in a big company. It does affect everything you do.

While women's level of involvement at work did not differ from men's, they admitted to a certain level of concern with home issues at work. As one of them put it, "There's always a low hum to cope with" — caused by the tendency of children to call their mothers more than their fathers at work, thereby forcing higher permeability of work boundaries on women.

Our findings suggest that different families have different norms about spouses bringing work home. Some encourage it, viewing it as a support for advancing the spouse's career or as a family endeavor ("What he/she does is for us"). Others discourage it, viewing it as a violation of the family's time.

Exterally imposed penetration of work into the home (for example, a telephone call) is often perceived by the spouse as a matter of choice and control by his or her mate, thus potentially becoming an area of disagreement. We found that career stage can affect the way couples deal with such penetration and their adjustment efforts. As one man commented about his wife's attitude toward his being engaged in work at home:

> I think she would say I'm not as preoccupied [with work as I once was], but I allow more interference of work into my private life than she might like, and I think she's tending to recall earlier years, when I had less control. I'm doing a better job now of telling her that I also consider it an interference, and we agree that anyone who calls is going to get put off, whereas when I was a new guy at the company I probably put off my dinner until later, listening to whoever called.

Overall, spouses tend to agree in their attitudes toward boundary permeability. Differences arise in men's greater conflict regarding activity and time-consuming home matters penetrating their work. Our research found that organizations did not have any specific structural regulations regarding this phenomenon.

PERSONAL BOUNDARY MANAGEMENT

Need for Separation of Work/Home Boundaries

On the basis of our findings, two conclusions about boundaries can be drawn: First, that people have a preference for a psychological separation between work and home parallel to the physical separation and, second, interference can more easily be dealt with when home issues come to work than vice versa.

People have greater control over home interference at work and can handle it by simply asking that the interaction be delayed until a more favorable time. People are much less likely to consider making such a request when work penetrates the home, as unconditional availability is highly valued by individuals and their employers (though not always by the spouse). Moreover, people generally trust their relationships with their spouse and believe they can compensate for not being available while at work, but being unavailable to work at home is more risky.

Boundary permeability epitomizes role conflict, as a person engaged in a specific role is called on to operate in another role simultaneously. This might result in "role overload" and conflict between the expectations of the two domains.

Effects of Organizational Level and Career Stage

While organizations often have no official policy regarding the permeability of home boundaries, it seems that the nature of the position one holds clearly relates to the extent of work penetration into the home. People in management positions mentioned that in earlier career stages, when they were more in "individual-contributor" positions (engineers, for example), their work inherently had more emergencies that required rapid action. Thus, junior employees had to be available to a greater extent than their seniors, and home boundaries were more permeable to work penetration, at least in regard to telephone calls. People in advanced career stages often noted that when lower on their career ladder they tended to carry work home more often. One of them, now in charge of his own company, said that once established in his business he tried to stop taking work home but hoped that his subordinates would continue and even commented, "They'd better do it."

On the basis of detailed calculations, Bartoleme has proposed that, in fact, after subtracting actual working hours from the day, managers could still spend more time with their families and that they tend to use their work as an "alibi" for their actual or psychological absence from home.[11] In our research we found home boundaries were frequently violated and were more permeable than work boundaries, as leaving the workplace did not necessarily mean reducing one's psychological work involvement. Participants reported that this continuous concern with work was even stronger early in their career.

WHAT ORGANIZATIONS CAN DO

As recently as five to ten years ago, many senior executives felt that any conflict between an individual's private and professional lives was solely that person's responsibility.[12] Now many companies are looking for ways to help employees manage and reduce these conflicts. We hasten to add, however, that this is still very new territory, and only pioneering organizations have so far initiated systematic efforts in this direction. Thus, we are talking about truly "cutting edge" activities, and there is not a lot of concrete corporate experience to draw upon at this point. It does seem clear, however, that work/home conflicts are an important area and that organizations need to take action to help employees manage work/home boundaries.

Let us consider some specific ideas. We will start with changes aimed at helping the individual employee, and then we will move to changes related to organizational policies and practices.

Helping Individuals Cope: Separating Work and Home

Many of the proposed remedies in the area of work/life conflicts, such as working at home and at-work child care, entail integration of work and home. Our findings, however, indicate a far greater need for separation of the two domains. For example, in a training seminar for district sales managers in a large corporation, an important issue that arose frequently was that of the boundary between work and home. Many managers felt that the boundaries were too "permeable" (as Richter also found was true for many people who work at home).[13] A district sales manager's work/home boundaries are quite permeable in that he or she is always "on call" vis-à-vis sales reps, often works at home, and has to travel to the field during personal time (evenings and weekends).

Legitimizing Boundaries

An important step in managing these work/home boundaries is legitimizing them. This entails a negotiation between the individual and the people involved in each of his or her domains so that they can agree on the limits of where work stops and home begins. For example, if a company has a policy that employees are not to be expected to travel on weekends, it should try to plan distant meetings so that they are not scheduled for Monday mornings or Friday afternoons. Another example of legitimizing boundaries would be a clear statement from top management that work should be conducted during working hours in the office and that employees should not be called at home on business. Or in the case of one organization whose district sales managers need to be available to sales representatives in the field at all times, calling guidelines were set that specified no calls were to be made during dinner (5 p.m.–7 p.m.) or after 10 p.m.

Unfortunately, in many organizations, part of the current effort to enhance productivity — to do more with less staff — means the work day is spilling over into personal time, and work/home boundaries are becoming more blurred, not clarified. As a very concrete example, consider the breakfast meeting and the "power breakfast." As lunch schedules become more crowded, breakfast has become the new "free" time for work. As a recent *Wall Street Journal* column pointed out, breakfast meetings fly in the face of employees' need for transition time:

> Breakfast meetings are wrong because people start their days trying to rescue personal problems. Those first-hour job fogs — which turn off later in the day — include wondering if Polly deposited that check yesterday, if the car will be ready at 5:30 tonight, if we really have to go to her mother's on Sunday. . . . [14]

In short, breakfast meetings should be avoided as a frequent practice, and early morning time should be reserved for personal transitions. Managers should attempt to set priorities and plan work so that if a meeting is necessary it can be held during normal working hours.

Planning Personal Time

Another way to set boundaries is through advance personal planning. In the distict seminars described earlier, there was a long discussion about simple ideas such as marking on one's new office calendar, at the beginning of each year, important family dates (birthdays, anniversaries, etc.), so that no business travel or dinner meetings would be scheduled at those times, and discussing with family members when peak times can be expected so that the family will be prepared for the individual's absence.

The critical point here is to make boundaries clear and discussable. What causes tension is boundaries becoming set through unspoken norms that develop over time and become undiscussable. This is an especially severe problem on the home side, since home life is usually affected more by work life than vice versa. Thus, unless explicit boundaries are set, home life can easily find itself at the mercy of work.

CHANGING ORGANIZATIONS

Most of the suggestions so far have dealt with ways the organization can support individuals in managing work/home transitions. Now let us shift our focus and consider ways the organization itself might be changed to facilitate balance in daily transitions.

Recognizing the Value of the Transition

A critical first step is for organizations to recognize the value of the transition for the employee and the employer. The morning "fog period" mentioned earlier serves the important function of letting the employee disengage from unfinished tasks at home so that he or she can be fully available for work. If the individual's normal way of making the transition is interrupted, those home concerns may remain as unfinished business throughout the day, interfering with involvement in work tasks.

Similarly, the afternoon transition plays an important buffering role, letting the individual unwind from work before getting involved at home. Not only does this time increase the individual's availability to the family (and thus the quality of family life) but it also provides emotional rest from work, which improves the person's effectiveness the next day.

Making Boundaries More Flexible

In addition to flexibility in work arrangements, flexibility can take the form of staying late at work or coming in late. One of the most popular methods of adding flexibility at work is flextime, in which employees choose their own work hours surrounding certain core hours during which all employees work.

Another form of flexibility is flexplace, under which individuals are allowed to do certain work at home. An estimated 1.9 million Americans do paid work in their homes.[15] For example, Control Data has a Home-Work program, in which computer programmers work at home with computer terminals using a centrally located small office when they need meeting space or the use of support services, such as typing or photocopying.

As a bonus, IBM lets strong performers take computer terminals home. This is not a formal Home-Work program like Control Data's, but it does make it possible for employees to do work on personal time or to be "at work" on the home computer during regular working hours. (At IBM all employees are on salary, and there are no rigid boundaries for working hours.) Other examples of work that can be done in the home include counseling, accounting, law, publishing, finance, and garment making.

To make matters more complex, although working at home can be an attractive way to reduce the need for externally provided child care, Alex Kotlowitz reports that many people are finding that working at home makes it virtually impossible to create boundaries between the work and home domains. Brenda Schuldt, a factory worker who tried working at home while caring for her two young children, finally went back to her old job. She put it this way: "I couldn't draw a definite line — I'd drop everything for my children."

As another example, Larry Mortimer and his wife started a planning and architectural business in their home. But after their son was born, they could not maintain work and home in the same place: "Being able to set the child down just to play — that just didn't happen. He was constantly bringing things over, or he would want to be held." The couple finally established boundaries by moving the business out of the home and hiring a baby-sitter.[16]

A study by Honeywell Information Systems, cited by Kotlowitz, asked employees what they would prefer if given a choice between working at the office or at home by telecommunication. The preferences were as follows: continue to go the office every day — 56%; split time between home and office — 36%; work at home — 7%. Kotlowitz reports that results were found in a Wisconsin insurance firm where the majority of home-based clerical workers could not juggle work and child care in the same space and time; many quit within two years.

Kotlowitz reports that it is not impossible to combine work and home. Some people do make it work. It seems to become easier when the work is part-time and the children are past the toddler stage. These conditions make boundary-setting easier, as part-time work is more easily segmented and older children can be more understanding of work boundaries.

However, there are still risks, as the employee may be deprived of office social contact, and work demands might spillover too much into the territory of the home role. Thus, the greater flexibility permitted by arrangements such as flextime and flexplace is often at the expense of the greater permeability of the home domain: Work is literally moving into the home. Unless the employee can set clear boundaries, both physical and psychological, such arrangement can increase rather than decrease work and family stress.

Scheduling for Natural Working Day Rhythms

People develop natural rhythms as they make their daily transitions between work and home.[17] In the morning, some people start off in that "job fog" described earlier, while others arrive at work without any "leftovers" from home. In fact, many people are psychologically involved in work even before leaving home, so that once they enter the office they are already into their "work self" and available for almost any task. People tend to prefer to have that first half-hour or so unstructured to ease into work, go over their day's schedule, and plan the rest of the day.

In light of this, organizations considering flextime should be aware that it means employees may be out of sync with respect to where they are in their daily transitions. We suggest that the scheduling of formal work take into account a boundary zone that allows time for people to adjust to being at work. Specifically, this means that meetings should not be scheduled too close to the beginning or end of the day. We have already warned about breakfast meetings. But many managers also purposely schedule meetings late, so that people will be motivated to finish quickly or, if the meeting goes late, it will not conflict with other organizational activities. However, for many people — especially women — such timing is considered very disadvantageous. The greatest stress is caused by meetings scheduled around 4:00 p.m., as this poses a direct threat to their time boundaries at home. As one woman said, "When I know a meeting is scheduled for 4:30, I get a sense of disaster." Happily, it now seems more socially acceptable for employees to cite child care responsibilities as a reason for leaving work on time.

Understanding Employee Transition Styles

Not only should employees' needs for transition time be taken into account, but managers should be sensitive to individual differences among employees in their ways of making those transitions. Failure to do so could result in unnecessary group conflict and unfair "labeling" of peers. For example, what if one employee in a department tends to make discrete transitions, being immediately ready for work on arrival, while a co-worker makes more lagged transitions, taking more time to settle into work? And what if their manager regularly holds department meetings at the start of the work day? Chances are that those two employees are not going to be able to communicate too well with each other at that time of day. The person who made the transition faster would feel frustrated that the co-worker is not really available in the meeting, and the latter would feel off-balance and pressured to become engaged too abruptly. And the lagged transitioner would probably be perceived as "slow" or "uninvolved," which could be damaging to his or her career.

We have already seen that there are male-female differences in transition styles, especially in the afternoon. Women tend to start thinking about home matters before they leave work, while men stay engaged in work until they arrive home. What if a particular meeting was always held in the afternoon, and one of its attendees was a woman who was perceived as "uninvolved" because she was thinking ahead to picking up her child at school? This would be a case of negative attribution, which could cause career damage, associated with gender, and would be completely unfair because the observed behaviors would be caused by a natural difference in transition style and not by a difference in work performance or dedication.

Managers should be able to construct a profile of the transition styles of their employees (or, better yet, have employees diagnose their own styles). What issues might a particular combination suggest? How should they be dealt with? A self-diagnosis by employees, followed by an open discussion, could be a useful form of team building. Our experience is that people can easily diagnose their own styles and are quite comfortable discussing them. It is a safe and usually lively way to discuss issues of work/home conflicts.

Optimal Commuting and Office Location

The daily commute to and from work plays an important psychological function in that it gives people a chance to get "into" work in the morning and to "unwind" in the afternoon. The commute serves as a buffer, an interface between professional and private life. Living too close shortens this crucial time. Some people who live near work schedule a transition period, such as walking around the block, before going home. According to our findings, a commuting time of about 30 minutes is ideal, as it allows time for gearing up in the morning and winding down in the evening. The use of car pools should be encouraged, not only because of energy conservation, but also because they free people to some extent psychologically from the strain of driving and allow them to put full energy into the transition to or from work.

Child Care at Work

Our study found that living too close to work put women under considerable pressure to be home more frequently, especially when they had young children, and thus increased the permeability of work and home boundaries. Accordingly, we would caution organizations about providing child care in the work setting because of its potential blurring of the work/family boundary. This does not necessarily mean that organizations should not provide child care benefits, but these benefits could be alternatives to on-site child care, such as child care vouchers and information about child care services. If an employer does provide child care, it should be located far enough away from the work setting that employees do not necessarily feel expected to go there during the day. We would caution employers that too permeable a boundary between work setting and a child care facility can lead employees to feel guilty if they are not there at lunch time and to feel not totally separate from their children during work hours. They could possibly feel too accessible, which could interfere with work concentration. We realize that this is a complex and controversial issue, but it does need to be taken into account as part of current policy discussions about on-site, employer-provided child care.

INTEGRATING FAMILY INTO WORK

The Family and Career Discussions

Once the boundaries between work and home are clear, it is possible to cross them at specific times and for specific purposes. One of the most underutilized ways of doing so is involving the family in discussions and decisions regarding the employee's work and career at critical times. For example, when an employee is offered a transfer to a different city, the family certainly has a stake in the decision of whether or not to accept it. And the family will, in all probability, discuss with the employee at home the pros and cons of such a move. Why not do this more formally and bring the family into the work setting to discuss the matter with a manager or human resources professional, both to give the family realistic information about the new location and to help them think it through? Many companies are already doing this for major international transfers, such as to the Middle East, which are very expensive — especially if they don't work out — and which represent major adjustments for the family.

One of the reasons this approach is not taken more often is the concern that employees' spouses may not be open during such discussions out of fear of hurting the employee's career. These discussions would only have value if management were in fact truly open to the family concerns and were prepared to accept the employee's final decision. External third-party facilitators could be helpful in making these meetings problem-solving discussions and not just airings of employees' grievances.

Recruiting and Relocation

Today, more and more companies are offering spouse relocation assistance as an employee benefit. Companies that offer such assistance have found that it is a powerful aid in recruiting.

Recreation

Another way of integrating the family into work is providing company resources for family recreational and education use. Many companies are now offering personal computers at a discount to employees, and these machines can be used both for the job and by the family. Employee country clubs, such as those at IBM and Bethlehem Steel, also foster family/work integration.

Family Days at Work

Other ways of linking work and family at clearly defined times include company "family days" when family members are invited into work, taken on plant or office tours, wined and dined by management, and given a chance to see exactly what Mom or Dad does each day and how it fits into the company's overall activities. These are usually very popular events, cost very little, are a good source of information for family members, and increase the employee's pride in working for the organization.

ONE COMPANY'S EXPERIENCE WITH WORK/FAMILY SEMINARS

To illustrate how difficult and sensitive work/home relationships are for a company, consider the following experience. A leading manufacturing organization, often cited in various lists of "well managed companies," had been offering training seminars to district sales managers on new concepts in human resources management, including career management (for both oneself and one's subordinates). The issue of how the managers' careers affect their family life had often come up as their responsibilities made heavy demands on their personal and family life: round-the-clock calls at home from reps with problems, a requirement of 100 days spent in the field with reps each year, a need for an office in the home, and so on. The suggestion was repeatedly made that the next round of seminars should cover the topic of work/family relationships.

What did this organization do? It presented a two-day seminar on career and family life planning. Participants were asked to discuss the topic with their spouses and families and come prepared to discuss the results of these conversations in the seminar. The focus was on sharing ideas on what the individual and the organization could do to reduce conflicts (for example, eliminating Sunday travel) and facilitate the management of conflicts (e.g., entering family events on one's work calendar far in advance).

At the end of the seminar, a senior executive and the personnel director were available to discuss these boundary management ideas and additional organizational resources that might be available (often participants were unaware of just how many resources were in fact available to them). As a result of the seminar, many managers initiated similar discussions with their sales reps when they returned to their home districts. The topic of work/family relationships has been made part of the agenda in district sales meetings. The issue is now becoming "discussable" in the organization.

Many organizations, from Continental Bank in the United States to Strauss Dairy in Israel, offer similar seminars at the end of the day to any employee who is interested. The sessions are often given half on company time and half after work, on employee time. Not only is this end-of-the-day time the perfect way to split the "cost" of the seminar between the employee and the organization, but it is also transition time, when the employee is most "tuned in" to these work/home issues.

Changing Policies

For the purpose of examining and changing corporate policies, one organization used a problem-solving workshop organized around an instrument developed to help employees examine their ways of dealing with work and home boundaries. The instrument consisted of measures of permeability of work and home boundaries, level of involvement in work and family life, job stress, and so on.

The questionnaires were administered in the workshop, and participants received immediate feedback. Each individual's boundaries could be compared with those of other employees throughout the organization.

On the basis of these results, problem-solving discussions were developed with spouses to find better ways of handling the boundaries between work and home domains. At the same time, explanations of the organization's policies regarding work boundaries took place. Employees and personnel managers compared employee needs and organizational requirements and negotiated changes regarding the setting of boundaries between work time and private time.

More and more companies are using similar workshops to address work/home boundary problems. For example, one organization used the workshop to develop a policy that deals with the flexibility of working hours during the week. It was decided that each person would have one day in the week in which boundaries would be kept rigid — that is, quitting time would be kept fixed at an early hour. However, on the other days of the week, quitting time would be kept more flexible, based largely on the needs of the work setting. Knowing in advance about having one day with a fixed ending time was considered by employees and spouses to be a great contribution to the quality of home life, while the more flexible availability of the employees on other days was highly appreciated by the employer.

The workshop also helped another organization better manage its five-and-a-half-day workweek. Because of its continuous-flow operation of machinery, it was necessary for the company to remain open five and one-half days per week, yet the employees wanted a five-day workweek. In the work/home workshop, workers and managers agreed to an arrangement in which each worker would have this half day off once a month, while co-workers agreed to work harder to cover the time. This arrangement was highly favored by the spouses and workers and was easily accepted by the employer, who was also pleased by the higher level of job satisfaction among the workers.

It is interesting to note two other benefits that senior managers reported from the workshop experience. First, since the managers were also employees of the organization, they realized that they too would benefit personally from the changes that were agreed upon. Second, they had expected employees' spouses to act as adversaries toward the company, but instead the spouses showed a sincere interest in the company and responded positively to the opportunity to work together on these work/family issues. Seeing spouses as allies rather than adversaries represented a new form of relationship between the organization and the families of its employees.

CONCLUSION

The most fruitful way to understand work/family interactions is to examine the transitions between the two domains. People tend to have consistent styles of dealing with home/work transitions, and these styles are affected by factors such

STUDY METHODOLOGY

The transition concepts discussed in this article were developed from a clinical study by Judith Richter on managing home and work boundaries.* Participants were selected according to three criteria: life stage, family structure, and managerial position. Life stage requirements were that the participants be 32–42 years old (an age group strongly concerned with work and family life) with a youngest child of preschool age (a particularly demanding life stage for men as well as women). For family structure, only spouses in dual-career families were studied, since dual-career families have more complex work/home relationships than do single-career families. The job requirement criterion called for participants to be in managerial positions, because of their greater scheduling flexibility and their potentially greater intrusiveness, relative to lower-level jobs. The net result of the criteria was a sample group with high levels of work and family responsibility — and potentially high conflict between the two.

Organizations in both the industrial and service sectors were represented. During individual in-depth interviews, participants answered 60 open-ended questions such as: What do you think about at home in the morning? During your commute? Upon arriving at work? How often do you bring work to be done at home in the evening? During the weekend? In what activities do you engage at your office in the morning and in the evening at home? What are your spouse's reactions to your coming home late from work and/or your working during weekends? What are the norms of entering and leaving the workplace in your organization?

It should be noted that we examined the work/home relationship in the common framework of a working day extending from morning to evening. We believe, however, that most of the findings are applicable to other working schedules as well.

*See Richter, Endnote 13.

---

as gender, type of work, and career stage.[17] As we have seen, organizations are becoming more active in helping employees manage their home and work boundaries more effectively.

In particular we have found that examining the work/home relationship in terms of boundaries and transitions helps generate ideas that often run counter to traditional prescriptions in this area. Many of these current prescriptions entail greater integration of work and home, such as at-work child care and working at home. However, we argue that the employee needs to have clear boundaries between the two domains and some degree of separation. Too much overlap between work and home can cause employee burnout.

A boundary does not necessarily mean a solid wall between the two areas, but something that helps define the separate entities while permitting interchange between them. A split-rail fence does not totally cut off two yards from each other, but it does demarcate private spaces while permitting visual contact and good neighborly conversation. As with fences and neighbors we conclude that good boundaries make for good employment relationships.

NOTES

This is a revised version of a paper, "Managing the Work/Home Interplay in the Organizational Context," presented at the Annual Meeting of the Academy of Management, New Orleans, April 11, 1987. This research was supported in part with funding from the Israel Institute of Business Research of Tel Aviv University's Faculty of Management and from the Human Resources Policy Institute at Boston University. The authors gratefully acknowledge the support of Fred Foulkes and the helpful comments of Kathy Kram on an earlier draft of this article.

1. See the Conference Board Report No. 868, *Corporations and Families: Changing Practices and Perspectives,* New York: The Conference Board, Inc., 1985.
2. For an overview of this literature, see P. A. L. Evans and F. Bartolome, "The Changing Pictures of the Relationship Between Career and Family," *Journal of Occupational Behavior,* 5, 1984, 9–21; P. A. L. Evans and F. Bartoleme, *Must Success Cost So Much?* New York: Basic Books, 1981; J. H. Greenhaus and N. J. Beutell, "Sources of Conflict Between Work and Family Roles," *Academy of Management Review,* 10, 1985, 76–88; B. Schneider, "Organizational Behavior," *Annual Review of Psychology,* 36, 1985, 573–611; J. P. Near, R. H. Rice, and R. G. Hunt, "The Relationship Between Work and Non-Work Domains: A Review of Empirical Research," *Academy of Management Review,* 5, 1980, 415–429; and S. E. Jackson, S. Zedeck, and E. Summers, "Family Life Disruptions: Effects of Job Induced Structural and Emotional Interference," *Academy of Management Review,* 28, 1985, 574–586.
3. Seminal work in this area was reported in R. M. Kanter, *Work and Family in the United States: A Critical Review and Agenda for Research and Policy,* New York: Russell Sage, 1977.
4. See F. S. Hall and D. T. Hall, "Dual Career Couples — How Do Couples and Companies Cope with the Problems?", *Organizational Dynamics,* Spring 1978, 57–77; and D. T. Hall and Associates, *Career Development in Organizations,* San Francisco: Jossey-Bass, 1986.
5. See F. Bartolomè, "The Work Alibi: When It's Harder to Go Home," *Harvard Business Review,* Vol. 61, No. 2, 1982, 66–75; and A. Korman and R. Korman, *Career Success/Personal Failure,* Englewood Cliffs, NJ: Prentice-Hall, 1980. See also D. J. Levinson's "A Conception of Adult Development," *American Psychologist,* 41, 1986, 3–13.
6. See Hall et al., Endnote 4.
7. See Hall et al., Endnote 4.
8. These ideas on the executive's need for personal learning and the dysfunction of many fast-track executive succession systems are elaborated in D. T. Hall's "Dilemmas in Linking Succession Planning to Individual Executive Learning," *Human Resource Management,* 25, 1986, 235–265.
9. For an excellent study of this phenomenon, see A. M. Morrison, R. P. White, and E. Van Velsor's *Breaking the Glass Ceiling: Can Women Make It to the Top in America's Top Corporations?* Reading, MA: Addison-Wesley, 1987.
10. See K. Lewin's *Field Theory in Social Science,* New York: McGraw-Hill, 1951.
11. See Bartolomè, Endnote 6.
12. This point becomes painfully clear in the work of Hall and Hall (Endnote 4) and R. Hertz, *More Equal than Others: Men and Women in Dual Career Marriages,* Berkeley, CA: The University of California Press, 1986.
13. Richter's work is described in more detail in J. Richter's *The Daily Transitions Between Professional and Private Life,* unpublished Ph.D. dissertation, Boston University, 1984.

14. See R. Schaffer, "The Breakfast Meetings," *Wall Street Journal,* December 15, p. 26.
15. See A. Kotlowitz, "Working at Home While Caring for a Child Sounds Fine — in Theory," *Wall Street Journal,* March 30, 1987, p. 21.
16. See Kotlowitz, Endnote 15.
17. This research is reported in Richter (Endnote 13) and in J. Richter and D. T. Hall's "Psychological Availability and Daily Transitions: A New Way to Examine the Relationships Between Work Life and Personal Life," unpublished working paper, School of Management, Boston University, 1987.

Douglas Tim Hall is a professor of organization behavior and a core faculty member of the Human Resources Policy Institute at the School of Management, Boston University. Judith Richter is a member of the faculty of the Graduate School of Business Administration at Tel Aviv University.

A Role Model Approach to Sexual Harassment
Paula M. Popovich / Betty Jo Licata

Sexual harassment, particularly the harassment of women by men, has been gaining greater recognition as an organizational problem. Incidents of sexual harassment may cause a decline in employee morale and productivity and result in sex discrimination lawsuits. This has forced organizations to identify and deal with existing sexual harassment situations and to implement policies and procedures designed to prevent future occurrences. A major impediment to the successful identification and prevention of sexual harassment in organizations has been the confusion and controversy surrounding this issue. The research on sexual harassment has also been limited by such problems and, though becoming more empirical in nature, it is still in need of a common focus.

The literature on sexual harassment may be grouped into three categories: definition, detection, and prevention. The amount of research in these areas, however, has been limited (Almquist, 1971). It has consisted primarily of case studies and surveys that have been used to support various definitions of harassment behavior, illustrate the incidence of sexual harassment in the workplace, and propose preventative interventions. Because of the organizational and methodological difficulties surrounding research on such a sensitive topic, much of this literature has been anecdotal or descriptive in nature. Recent research on sexual harassment, although more empirical, still shows an "absence of any single, agreed-upon conceptual framework or research paradigm" (Brewer, 1982, p. 149).

A new theme in the literature that offers such a theoretical focus is the identification of sexual harassment as a role problem. From her review of survey results, Farley (1978) suggested that sexual harassment on the job occurs when a male "asserts a woman's sex-role over her function as a worker" (p. 33). Recently, Gutek and Morasch (1982) have proposed through their empirical research that the sexual harassment of women on the job is often the result of

Source: Paula M. Popovich and Betty Jo Licata, "A Role Model Approach to Sexual Harassment," *Journal of Management,* 1987, pp. 149–161. Reprinted by permission.

"sex-role spillover." They define this spillover as the "carry-over into the workplace of gender-based expectations for behavior that are irrelevant or inappropriate to work" (p. 55). It is these expectations, inappropriate though they may be, that result in the role behaviors seen on the job.

The purpose of this paper is to review the relevant sexual harassment literature in the areas of definition, detection, and prevention and to propose that the existing literature on role theory and role problems may provide a theoretical framework to guide empirical investigations of the causes and preventions of sexual harassment in organizations.

DEFINING SEXUAL HARASSMENT

There have been many attempts to define what behaviors compose sexual harassment. The majority of these definitions may be categorized as either descriptive or causal.

Descriptive definitions are primarily concerned with those behaviors that are considered to be sexual harassment. The best example of this type of definition is provided by the Equal Employment Opportunity Commission (EEOC), which describes sexual harassment as:

> Unwelcome sexual advances, requests for sexual favors, and other verbal or physical conduct of a sexual nature when submission to such conduct is made either explicitly or implicitly a term or condition of an individual's employment; submission to or rejection of such conduct by an individual is used as the basis of employment decision affecting the individual; or such conduct has the purpose or effect of unreasonably interfering with an individual's work performance or creating an intimidating, hostile, or offensive work environment (1980, p. 74677).

This type of very specific definition provides guidelines as to the identification of harassment behaviors on the job. However, it does not explain why these behaviors occur, nor does it suggest how to predict or prevent the occurrence of sexual harassment.

The second category of definitions deals more directly with the causes of sexual harassment. A major influence on this group of definitions has been the feminist perspective, which views sexual harassment as the result of the unequal distribution of power between the sexes. This inequality is particularly evident in the workplace. According to this perspective, harassment behavior may be seen as part of the "continuum of male-aggressive, female-passive patterns" (Medea & Thompson, 1974, p. 11) that are part of our society. Although this definition is more useful in describing why sexual harassment may occur in an organization, it still does not deal with how to prevent it (short of altering the power distribution of society).

The power differential definition does have a much broader application if it is viewed in the context of role theory. According to this approach, it is the transfer of male-aggressive and female-passive sex-role patterns to the expectations and roles of the workplace that may be the cause of harassment behavior. Conceptualizing sexual harassment as a role problem provides both a descriptive and causal definition of harassment behavior.

Roles and Sex Roles in the Organization

This perspective of sexual harassment as a role problem is also consistent with current views of organizational theory. Katz and Kahn (1978), who emphasize a systems approach to the study of organizations, consider roles to be an integral element of the organizational system. They conceptualize the organization as a system of roles and define a role as the set of behaviors that an individual performs and that are expected of him/her by other members of the organization (Kahn, Wolfe, Quinn, Snoek, & Rosenthal, 1964).

Katz and Kahn also acknowledge that each individual has multiple roles, both within and outside of the organization. An employee may have roles as both a manager and social organizer for his/her department and also have the roles of husband/wife and father/mother at home. The multiple job roles have been recognized as a source of complexity for the focal person (Katz & Kahn, 1978), but with more women entering the work force, the influence of sex roles on the individual's work role is just beginning to be realized.

An individual's sex role becomes a part of every other role that he or she may take, both on and off the job. Schein (1978) has pointed out that a number of empirical studies have shown sex role stereotypes do affect selection decisions as well as both the actual and the perceived performance of women on the job. This indicates that members of an organization do attend to gender on the job.

Cohen (1983) has hypothesized that this recognition of gender differences leads to the conscious and unconscious use of "courting cues" as members of both sexes deal with each other in the work situation. For this reason, sexual attraction between men and women often takes place on the job and the resulting relationships have become a fact of life for the organization. When this attraction is mutual and there is no abuse of power attached to it, the relationship (though it may be distracting in the workplace) is not necessarily a problem (Jamison, 1983). Even when there is an abuse of power, but by mutual agreement (such as in the case of an exchange of sexual favors for a promotion), this becomes "sexual politics" and, although other members of the organization may object, the relationship according to the parties involved is acceptable. The question of when sexual attraction and sexual politics become sexual harassment is difficult to answer, but a useful guideline to follow is that when the attraction is not mutual or there is an abuse of power in the relationship, problems may occur, including sexism and/or sexual harassment.

The distinction between sexism and sexual harassment is sometimes difficult to make. Sexism describes any situation in which there is differential treatment of the sexes, often resulting in the social, political or economic discrimination of women by men. Sexual harassment, on the other hand, refers to a sub-set of sexual discrimination behaviors. As can be seen from the EEOC definition offered earlier, these behaviors describe what can occur when unwelcome sexual attentions are made part of the work role. According to Cohen (1983), these sexual harassment behaviors are the result of a communication problem between men and women on the job, but it is more

FIGURE 1
A Theoretical Model of the Role Episode Process
(Adapted from Kahn et al., 1964, p. 30)

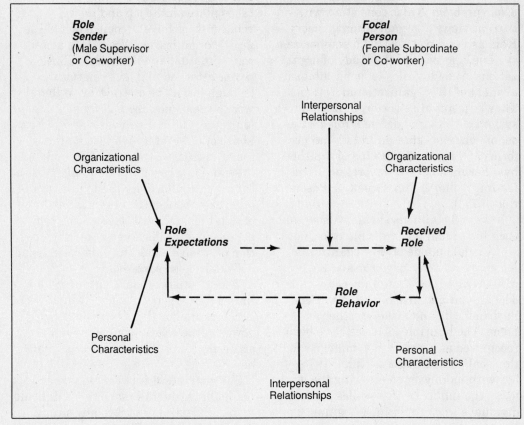

than just misreading courting cues in the office. It occurs when sex roles become part of the communication of work roles in the organization, specifically, when the expectations of the woman's work role include aspects of her sex role.

The communication of these role expectations from the members of an organizational group (i.e., the role senders) to an individual who is involved with that group (i.e., the focal person) is called a role episode. Kahn et al. (1964) have developed a theoretical model of the role episode process, a version of which can be seen in Figure 1. The role episode process may be affected by at least three context factors: the characteristics (or climate) of the organizational situation, the attributes (personal factors) of the individuals involved, and their interpersonal relations (Katz & Kahn, 1978). The role episode process may be seen as a description of the communication of expectations, not only between members of a role group, but also between individuals of two different status or power levels (e.g., Graen, 1976), such as leader/member relations. It may also serve to describe the communication of expectations between a male and a female on the job, including the complexities that arise when the work role includes aspects of the sex role.

The following description of a role episode shows what happens in many sexual harassment situations, with a male supervisor or co-worker as the role sender and the female employee as the focal person. Such a cycle may begin when a male role-sender allows his expectations of a woman's gender-based role to interfere with his expectations of a female focal person's work role. These expectations are then communicated in a way that is direct and verbal (e.g., a demand for sex) or in a more indirect and nonverbal way (e.g., placing his arm around her shoulder). This sent role is received by the focal person and is then translated into a role behavior that completes the cycle. If the female focal person in this example responds in a manner which meets the male role sender's expectations (e.g., by accepting his sexual overtures), the sex-role related expectations will be reinforced and the cycle will continue in this way. If she ignores or overtly resists his expectations, problems may arise.

It is also possible that if the expectations were communicated in an unclear (e.g., indirect, nonverbal) way, the miscommunication of the expectations may become the problem. Although miscommunication may take place at any time in the role episode process, there are two points at which it is most likely. The first of these is between the sent role and the received role. Such a miscommunication may occur in a case of subtle sexual harassment, in which the expectation of the role sender is communicated through a touch or a comment that may or may not be intended as sexual and is misperceived by the focal person. Miscommunication may also occur between the focal person's role behavior and subsequent role expectations of the role sender, such as when a woman's rejection of a man's sexual advances is perceived as coyness on her part. Such a misperception may lead to an increase in sexual advances by the role sender, instead of the decrease expected by the focal person (Crull, 1982).

Because of the role episode is part of an on-going cycle, the conflict between the focal person's behavior and the role sender's expectations may be resolved through the modification of the role sender's expectations so that they are more consistent with the behavior and the expectations of the focal person. If the role sender does not change his expectations, and those expectations continue not to be met by the focal person, a variety of problems may occur. These problems may include charges of sexual harassment and increased stress for the focal person, the role sender, and other members of the work group. In an analysis of the Kahn et al. (1964) role episode, McGrath (1976) compared this four-stage cycle to his own stress cycle. He noted their similarities and pointed out that the role cycle can become a stress cycle when there is a problem in the role episode. The effects of stress have been well documented in organizations and include health problems, reduced job satisfaction, and turnover (Beehr & Newman, 1978). Although there are a number of possible problems that may arise during the role episode, malfunctions in the cycle are generally classified as either role conflict or role ambiguity, both of which are potential causes of stress for the focal person (Quick & Quick, 1984).

Role conflict refers primarily to conflicting expectations between members of the role set and the focal person (Van Sell, Brief, & Schuler, 1981). Conflict may occur when there are inherent conflicts or contradictions in the communicated expectation (or expectations) of a role-sender (*intra-sender conflict*), or discrepancies between the expectations of two or more role-senders (*inter-sender conflict*). *Person-role conflict* may occur when there is a discrepancy between the role expectation and the character or personality of the focal person. *Role overload* describes a situation in which too much is expected of the focal person by the role-sender, and *inter-role conflict* occurs when an individual holds two or more roles that conflict, such as employee role and family role.

This last example of role conflict has been long considered one of the major problems of working women (O'Leary, 1974). Hall (1972) believes that many of the role conflict problems of women come from their multiple roles as employees, wives, and mothers, and not from intra-role conflicts or role ambiguity associated with their gender. A study by Chacko (1982), however, has shown that working women who "perceive that they were selected because of their sex . . . experienced more role conflict and role ambiguity than women who felt that sex was not an important factor in their selection" (1982 p., 119).

Sexual harassment is a prime example of the type of inter-role conflict that may take place for a woman whose sex role is a salient factor on the job. This is the premise behind the concept of sex-role spillover (Gutek & Morasch, 1982; Nieva & Gutek, 1982). Spillover has been hypothesized to occur in situations where the female sex role is most salient, such as traditionally female jobs (in which the position becomes defined in terms of the sex role of its major occupants) and traditionally male jobs (in which a female's gender stands out in the crowd of other, mostly male, employees). Although spillover may not always lead to sexual harassment in an organization (Gutek & Morasch, 1982), it may increase the possibility of problems in the communication of expectations between males and females on the job.

A woman may experience role conflict if she does not want to behave in a sex-stereotyped way, yet that is what the male role sender expects. This conflict would lead to a state of stress, not only for the female focal person, but possibly for the male role sender as well. The reason for this conflict may be unclear to both parties, but the consequences of the problem may be reflected on the job in the attitudes and the performance of the focal person and can lead to voluntary or involuntary turnover.

Role ambiguity arises in more complex organizations or in situations where there is a high rate of change in the organization or environmental system, but it may also result from unclear or inadequate communication between members of the role set and the focal person (Kahn et al. 1964,). Specifically, role ambiguity may occur when there is insufficient or confusing information about the expectations, when there is uncertainty about the behaviors that will meet the expectations, or when the consequences of the role behaviors are unclear (Van Sell et al., 1981). An example of role ambiguity may be seen in a situation in which a male supervisor or co-worker is not sure of how to deal with a woman on the job (intra-sender ambiguity). As a result of his uncertainty, he may send very unclear cues as to the expected role behaviors (Driscoll, 1983). It may also be true that a woman who is not given clear cues as to how to behave in a work situation may interpret the sent role as being a sex-role cue. Or, if she is unsure of how to behave on the job, she may fall back on sex-stereotyped behaviors of which she is more sure, which, in turn, can affect the expectations of role senders in subsequent role cycles. The results of a recent major meta-analysis of the research on role conflict and role ambiguity (Jackson & Schuler, 1985) provide support for a relationship between these role problems and affective reactions, including job dissatisfaction, the tension and anxiety that characterize stress, organizational commitment, and turnover intentions.

According to Jackson and Schuler, many of the relationships between role conflict or role ambiguity and other antecedent and consequent variables may be affected by moderator variables. One of the variables that has been identified as a possible moderator between role problems and consequent stress is the sex (gender) or sex role of the focal person. Jick and Mitz (1985) have pointed out that research has shown women do report a greater incidence of psychological distress than men and that one of the reasons for this difference may be due to the fact that "women face unique sources of job stress" (p. 413), including role overload and role conflict. What the authors do not mention is that sexual harassment is one of the sources of job stress that is unique to women, one that may be explained as a form of the role conflict or role ambiguity that women face on the job. The negative consequences of role problems in the organization are similar to the effects of sexual harassment on the job, in that they also lead to stress for the focal person or victim of the harassment.

A recent survey of over 250 victims of sexual harassment (Crull, 1982) found that "almost all of the women experienced debilitating stress reactions as a result of the harassment" (p. 541). These reactions included physical and psychological symptoms as well as difficulties related to job performance. One of the most frequent complaints of these women was about the role conflict that resulted when they could not concentrate enough to do their work while being subjected to sexual comments. There was also evidence of role ambiguity in the reports of women who felt anger or fear because they did not know what to do or where to go to deal with their sexual harassment problems.

Viewing sexual harassment as a role communication problem may serve to define the process, to determine when sexual attraction becomes sexual harassment, and to prevent or deal with the problems that arise from sexual harassment. A model of sexual harassment as a role communication (see Figure 1) identifies several of the categories of variables that are believed to influence the role communication process, some of which have already been shown to affect sexual harassment in organizations.

The first of these categories includes *organizational characteristics* (or characteristics of the work group). Research by

Gutek and Morasch (1982) has shown that skewed sex ratios in the organization may lead to sex-role spillover and, in turn to sexual harassment. Other characteristics of organizations that have been shown to influence clarity in the role communication process include size (Katz & Kahn, 1978) and degree of formalization, which has been found to influence role ambiguity more than role conflict (Jackson & Schuler, 1985). These should also be variables to consider in research on sexual harassment.

A second source of influence on the communication cycle is the *personal characteristics* of the individuals involved. Powell (1983) has shown that androgyny may be related to perceptions of behaviors as sexual harassment. It is likely that other personality attributes, such as locus of control, which has been linked to perceptions of role conflict and ambiguity on the part of the focal person, may also influence perceptions of certain expectations and behaviors as sexual harassment.

Another personal characteristic which has been shown to be related to role problems is educational level. It has been shown that educational levels of focal persons are positively related to experienced role conflict and role ambiguity in organizations. A similar relationship has also been found in the sexual harassment literature: Those women who have achieved higher educational levels show a higher incidence of reported sexual harassment experiences (U.S. Merit Systems Protection Board, 1981; Terpstra & Cook, 1985).

There has been little research on the personal characteristics of the role sender and their influence on role problems (Jackson & Schuler, 1985). This is an omission that has a parallel in the lack of research on the role sender/harasser in the sexual harassment process.

Finally, the state of the *interpersonal relationships* between the role sender and the focal person may help to determine when an exception or behavior is considered to be harassment. A change in the relationships between those involved in the role communication may alter the focal person's perception of the sent role or the role sender's perception of the resulting role behavior. For example, a change in the position of the role sender with respect to the focal person may influence the perception of a situation as sexual harassment. Popovich, Licata, Nokovich, Martelli, & Zoloty (1986) have shown that certain behaviors were considered to be more definitely sexual harassment when exhibited by a supervisor than those same behaviors exhibited by a co-worker. Other interpersonal relationships' variables that have been shown to affect the role communication are liking, closeness, and trust between members of the role set (Katz & Kahn, 1978) and leader consideration, which has been found to correlate negatively with both role conflict and role ambiguity (Jackson & Schuler, 1985).

It is proposed that confusing a woman's work role with her sex role is a problem which may be explained accurately from a role-theory perspective. It may be hypothesized that sexual harassment occurs more frequently in organizations (or in areas of a single organization) where the work role of the individual is ill-defined or in conflict as a result of the communication of expectations that are related more to a woman's sex role than to her work role. This is not to imply a causal relationship between sexual harassment and role problems, but rather to suggest that both are similar and possibly related. Specifically, it is proposed that

1. Organizations or departments that have higher incidence of role problems will also have higher incidence of sexual harassment behaviors because the climate arising from the increased role problems will allow more confusion between a woman's sex role and her work role.
2. Higher incidence of role problems and sexual harassment will be affected by
   a. the organizational characteristics (with known variables being conditions of sex-role spillover, and possible variables including size of the organization and formalization);
   b. the personal characteristics of the parties involved (with known variables being androgyny and possible variables including locus of control);
   c. the state of the interpersonal relationships between the role sender and the focal person (with known variables being changes in position and possible variables including liking, degree of closeness or trust in the relationship, and leader consideration).

At this point it is difficult to hypothesize about the relationship between sexual harassment and role conflict *or* role ambiguity. Much of the research on role stress has involved investigating both role conflict and role ambiguity in the same studies, and there is reason to believe that they are not unrelated (Van Sell et al., 1981). However, Jackson and Schuler (1985) have cautioned that research on role problems should consider role conflict and role ambiguity as separate constructs. This should also be true for any empirical investigation of sexual harassment.

The use of the role communication episode model to explain sexual harassment may help to define important variables for research, but it can also serve to identify potential problem spots in the organization where sexual harassment behaviors are more likely to occur.

DETECTING THE OCCURRENCE OF SEXUAL HARASSMENT

The problems associated with defining sexual harassment have also affected researchers' abilities to detect sexual harassment behavior in an organization. Major cross-organizational studies (e.g., Collins & Blodgett, 1981; U.S. Merit Systems Protection Board, 1981) have shown large numbers of women who indicate they were harassed on the job. However, attempts to pinpoint trouble spots within a single organization are virtually nonexistent due to the sensitive nature of the topic and the lack of agreement among employees as to what constitutes sexual harassment behavior.

Although it may be difficult to measure the actual occurrence of sexual harassment in an organization, determining the degree to which role problems exist is much more feasible. An organizational climate characterized by role problems may signal existing or potential harassment situations, and detection may be accomplished using already established, empirically supported methods.

The majority of empirical research in the area of role problems has employed the Rizzo, House and Lirtzman (1970) scales to measure role conflict and ambiguity in organizations (Fisher & Gitelson, 1983). Questions about role problems in the organization, such as those contained in the Rizzo et al. instrument, are more innocuous and would be expected to elicit more honest responses than would questions concerning sexual harassment behavior. Organizations should be more open to administering a role problems questionnaire, since it in no way acknowledges an existing sexual harassment problem, nor does it stimulate a potential problem situation.

The scale does have its limitations. There has been some question as to the construct validity of the scales (e.g., Tracy & Johnson, 1981) and Jackson and Schuler (1985) have noted:

> Whereas existing research tools give good assessments of general perceptions, they are not very useful for evaluating specific role relationships (e.g., employee-client; employee co-worker; employee-supervisor; client-supervisor), nor are they useful for assessing the CONTENT of ambiguities or conflicts (p. 48).

New or refined instruments which are designed to address these issues would also improve sexual harassment research in which both the relationship between the role sender and focal person and the content of the problems are important variables.

PREVENTING SEXUAL HARASSMENT IN THE ORGANIZATION

Organizations have focused on trying to prevent future harassment rather than on trying to detect and eliminate present harassment because of the difficulties in identifying an existing harassment situation. Professional personnel journals have responded to this need by providing articles on the prevention of sexual harassment (e.g., Biles, 1981; Peterson & Masengill, 1982; Thurston, 1980; Woodrum, 1981). These articles stress the importance of establishing channels to report such behavior and propose training programs to increase employee awareness of the potential for sexual harassment, especially its legal (and consequently, financial) ramifications for the organization.

Sexual harassment training programs usually focus on how to deal with sexual harassment once it occurs (e.g., grievance procedures, discipline) and what behaviors may be considered harassment. These programs do not address why sexual harassment occurs. Although grievance procedures and discipline may be adequate, albeit temporary measures, the real causes must be determined in order to eliminate sexual harassment in the workplace.

Unfortunately, awareness of what constitutes harassment may not be enough to change a problem situation, and evaluations of these training programs have not been reported. The extensive research on role problems has suggested several well established interventions, or role classification techniques, that may be used to address the potential causes of sexual harassment as well as other organizational problems. An advantage of using role clarification techniques within the context of a sexual harassment training program is that the program's effectiveness is not threatened by the sensitive nature of the topic. The use of role clarification techniques also avoids the designation of *victims* and *perpetrators* of sexual advances, by focusing instead on the work roles of the individuals involved.

A first step in preventing role problems is to insure that the focal person in the role set is aware of the role expectations that the other role-set members have for him/her. This may be done during what Graen (1976) has referred to as the role-defining process. It is at this starting point that potential conflicts and ambiguities, such as those created by confusing a woman's sex role with her work role, may be identified and confronted, and the roles may be defined for both the focal person and the members of the role-set. Nevertheless, in sexual harassment awareness programs, this initial socialization may not always be enough. Specific techniques are needed to help clarify roles in situations in which role conflict and role ambiguity may already exist.

One method which deals with improving role relations is Harrison's (1977) Role Negotiation Technique (RNT), which is a version of the popular Role Analysis Technique (RAT) (Dayal & Thomas, 1968). RNT provides the group with a fair, negotiated settlement to role conflict and is most appropriate for situations in which there is a climate of competitiveness and power problems, as is characteristic of sexual harassment. Each group (or role set) member lists on paper (often anonymously), what he or she feels the other members should do more of or better, what to do less of, and what to change. Negotiations based on these comments are also conducted in writing and a final contract is drawn up after agreement is reached. Once work roles have been clarified, periodic checks may be made on the role-set members through standard organizational channels, such as performance appraisals and attitude or climate surveys.

The use of role clarification techniques may be useful in a potential or existing situation of sexual harassment behavior, especially if the written lists can be kept anonymous and confidential. For example, a female who begins a job in a traditionally male area, such as engineering, may experience sexual harassment as the result of sex-role spillover because her male supervisor or co-workers, who are unsure of how to treat a "female engineer," are responding more to her sex role than her work role. A male supervisor may expect female subordinates to be pleased in the same way as a wife or a girlfriend to his flirtatious behavior and comments on their physical attractiveness. The use of role negotiation may help by identifying the sex-role related expectations (e.g., "My supervisor comments on the physical attractiveness of female employees") in an anonymous way and provide work-role related alternative behaviors (e.g., "I would like my supervisor to limit his comments to business-related issues").

It may not even be necessary to mention actual harassment behaviors in these negotiations, since the emphasis on work-related behavior serves to de-emphasize sex-role behaviors. The use of role negotiation techniques creates an atmosphere in which a woman may feel more comfortable stating exactly what she does and does not find to be acceptable work-related behavior before a serious problem occurs.

Clarifying the work role itself should allow less conflict and ambiguity as well as decrease the opportunity for a person's sex role and work role to become confused. The use of role clarification techniques provides an added dimension to traditional sexual harassment awareness programs by creating a channel to exchange expectations. The greater opportunity for communication and emphasis on specific work-related behaviors should increase the effectiveness of traditional programs in preventing harassment behaviors in the organization.

IMPLICATIONS

It has been proposed that sexual harassment research can benefit by using the models from existing research on role theory. Investigating sexual harassment as a role problem will also contribute to the area of role theory. The characteristics of the harasser/role sender and specific role relationships have received limited attention in the research on role theory, but are essential to any investigation of sexual harassment.

Understanding sexual harassment as a role problem will serve to help resolve some of the confusion and controversy that surround this issue. This will aid practitioners in the identification and prevention of sexual harassment in the workplace through the use of familiar concepts and established methods.

The relationship between sexual harassment and the incidence of role problems in the organization must now be investigated to determine the extent to which sexual harassment can be explained from a role theory perspective. Once this link is established empirically, the existing literature on role problems may be fully used to deal more effectively with defining, detecting and preventing sexual harassment in the organization.

REFERENCES

Almquist, E. M. (1977). Women in the labor force. *Signs: Journal of Women in Culture, 2*, 843–844.

Beehr, T. A., & Newman, J. A. (1978). Job stress, employee health, and organizational effectiveness: A facet analysis, model, and literature review. *Personnel Psychology, 31*, 665–699.

Biles, G. E. (1981). A program guide for preventing sexual harassment in the workplace. *Personnel Administrator, 26*(6), 49–56.

Brewer, M. B. (1981). Further beyond nine to five: An integration and future directions. *Journal of Social Issues, 38*(4), 149–158.

Chacko, T. I. (1982). Women and equal employment opportunity: Some unintended effects. *Journal of Applied Psychology, 67*, 119–123.

Cohen, L. R. (1983). Nonverbal (mis)communication between managerial men and women. *Business Horizons, 26*(1), 13–17.

Collins, E. G. C., & Blodgett, T. B. (1981). Sexual harassment: Some see it . . . some don't. *Harvard Business Review, 59*(2), 77–95.

Crull, P. (1982). Stress effects of sexual harassment on the job: Implications for counseling. *American Journal of Orthopsychiatry, 52*, 539–543.

Dayal, I., & Thomas, J. M. (1968). Operation KPE: Developing a new organization. *Journal of Applied Behavioral Science, 4*, 473–506.

Driscoll, J. B. (1981). Sexual attraction and harassment: Management's new problems. *Personnel Journal, 60*(1), 33–35.

Equal Employment Opportunity Commission (1980). Interpretative guidelines on Sexual Harassment. *Federal Register,* Vol. 45, No. 219, p. 74677.

Farley, L. (1978). *Sexual shakedown: The sexual harassment of women on the job.* New York: Warner Books.

Fisher, C. D., & Gitelson, R. (1983). A meta-analysis of the correlates of role conflict and role ambiguity. *Journal of Applied Psychology, 68,* 320–333.

Graen, G. (1976). Role-making processes within complex organizations. In M. Dunnette (Ed.), *Handbook of industrial and organizational psychology* (pp. 1201–1245). Chicago: Rand McNally.

Gutek, B. A., & Morasch, B. (1982). Sex-ratios, sex-role spillover, and sexual harassment of women at work. *Journal of Social Issues, 38*(4), 55–74.

Hall, D. T. (1972). A model of coping with role conflict: The role behavior of college educated women. *Administrative Science Quarterly, 17,* 471–486.

Harrison, R. (1973). Role negotiation: A tough minded approach to team development. In W. G. Bennis, D. E. Berlew, E. H. Schein, & F. I. Steck (Eds.), *Interpersonal dynamics* (pp. 469–479). Homewood, Illinois: Dorsey Press.

Jackson, S. J., & Schuler, R. S. (1985). A meta-analysis and conceptual critique of research on role ambiguity and role conflict in work settings. *Organizational Behavior and Human Decision Processes, 36,* 16–78.

Jamison, K. (1983). Managing sexual attraction in the workplace. *Personnel Administrator, 28*(8), 45–51.

Jick, T. D., & Mitz, L. F. (1985). Sex differences in work stress. *The Academy of Management Review, 10,* 408–421.

Kahn, R. L., Wolfe, D. M., Quinn, R. P., Snoek, J. D., & Rosenthal, R. A. (1978). *Organizational stress: Studies in role conflict and ambiguity.* New York: Wiley.

Katz, D., & Kahn, R. L. (1978). *The social psychology of organizations.* New York: Wiley.

McGrath, J. E. (1976). Stress and behavior in organizations. In M. Dunnette (Ed.), *Handbook of industrial and organizational psychology* (pp. 1351–1395). Chicago: Rand McNally.

Medea, A., & Thompson, K. (1974). *Against rape.* New York: Farrar, Strauss & Giroux.

Nieva, V. F., & Gutek, B. A. (1982). *Women and work: A psychological perspective.* New York: Praeger.

O'Leary, V. E. (1974). Some attitudinal barriers to occupational aspirations in women. *Psychological Bulletin, 81,* 809–826.

Petersen, D. J., & Masengill, D. (1982). Sexual harassment — A growing problem in the workplace. *Personnel Administrator, 27*(10), 79–88.

Popovich, P. M., Licata, B. J., Nokovich, D., Martelli, T., & Zoloty, S. (1986). Assessing the incidence and perceptions of sexual harassment behaviors. *Journal of Psychology, 120,* 387–396.

Powell, G. N. (1983). *Sex-role identity and definition of sexual harassment: Are they related?* Paper presented at the national meeting of the Academy of Management, Dallas, TX.

Quick, J. C., & Quick, J. D. (1984). *Organizational Stress and Preventative Management.* New York: McGraw-Hill.

Rizzo, J. R., House, R. J., & Lirtzman, S. I. (1970). Role conflict and ambiguity in complex organizations. *Administrative Science Quarterly, 15,* 150–163.

Schein, V. E. (1978). Sex role stereotyping, ability and performance: Prior research and new directions. *Personnel Psychology, 31,* 259–268.

Terpstra, D. A., & Cook, S. E. (1985). Complainant characteristics and reported behaviors and consequences associated with formal sexual harassment charges. *Personnel Psychology, 38,* 559–574.

Thurston, K. (1980). Sexual harassment: An organizational perspective. *Personnel Administrator, 25*(12), 75–80.

Tosi, H., & Tosi, D. (1970). Some correlates of role conflict and role ambiguity among public school teachers. *Journal of Human Relations, 18,* 1068–1075.

Tracy, L., & Johnson, T. W. (1981). What do role conflict and role ambiguity scales measure? *Journal of Applied Psychology, 66,* 464–469.

United States Merit Systems Protection Board. (1981). *Sexual harassment in the federal workplace: Is it a problem?* Washington, D.C.: U.S. Government Printing Office.

Van Sell, M., Brief, A. P., & Schuler, R. S. (1981). Role conflict and role ambiguity: Integration of the literature and directions for future research. *Human Relations, 34*(1), 43–71.

Woodrum, R. L. (1981). Sexual harassment: New concern about an old problem. *S.A.M. Advanced Management Journal, 46*(1), 20–26.

Paul M. Popovich and Betty Jo Licata are affiliated with Ohio University. A previous version of this paper was presented at the meeting of the Academy of Management, Boston, August 1984. The authors wish to thank John Stinson, Larry Waters, and two anonymous reviewers for their helpful comments.

Expatriate Assignments: Enhancing Success and Minimizing Failure
Rosalie L. Tung

A major U.S. food manufacturer was seeking someone from corporate staff to head its Japanese marketing division. Mr. X was selected because he was clearly one of the company's bright young talents; he had also demonstrated superior marketing skills in the home office. Those making the appointment did not assess his ability to relate to and work with Japanese because it was assumed that a good manager in the United States would be a good manager abroad. Prior to his 18-month assignment, Mr. X was given some literature pertaining to Japan's geography, climate, banking, and educational institutions and was asked to share this material with his family.

However, during the initial six months in Japan, Mr. X was unable to devote much time to company activities because he was preoccupied with problems he and his family were having in adapting to the new environmental setting. Similarly, in the last six months, he often worried about his upcoming job change. He heard that a peer and rival at home had just been promoted to a position for which both men had aspirations. What must he do to get back into the race? While he was trying to strategize about this new assignment, his wife continually questioned him about their new West Coast relocation. The result: In the course of Mr. X's 18-month assignment to Japan, his company lost 98% of its existing market share to a major European competitor.

What went wrong? Why was Mr. X, a person with a proven track record in corporate headquarters, such a dismal failure in his assignment to Japan?

Mr. X's experience is not unique. In a questionnaire survey of expatriate assignments within 80 U.S. multinationals, it was found that more than half of the companies had failure rates of 10–20%. Some 7% of the respondent firms had recall rates of 30%.[1] ("Failure" in the survey was defined as the inability of an expatriate to perform effectively in a foreign country and, hence, the need for the employee to be fired or recalled home.) These statistics are consistent with the findings of others that approximately 30% of overseas shipments within U.S. multinationals are mistakes.

These "casualties" not only represent substantial costs to the companies, but also constitute a human resource waste since most of those who failed had a noteworthy track record in the home office prior to overseas assignment. Such failures often constitute a heavy personal blow to the expatriates' self-esteem and ego. Hence, even if they are accepted back by corporate headquarters, it may take some time before they regain confidence in their own abilities. The unsettling experience for the person's family, both emotionally and physically, represents yet another consequence.

Source: "Expatriate Assignments: Enhancing Success and Minimizing Failure" by Rosalie L. Tung, *The Academy of Management Executive,* May 1987, pp. 118–125. Reprinted by permission.

PROBLEMS OF U.S. EXPATRIATES

What are the causes of expatriate failure in U.S. multinationals?

In the survey, the respondents were asked to indicate the most important reasons for expatriate failure. The reasons given, in descending order of importance, were:

1. Inability of the manager's spouse to adjust to a different physical or cultural environment;
2. The manager's inability to adapt to a different physical or cultural environment;
3. Other family-related problems;
4. The manager's personality or emotional immaturity;
5. The manager's inability to cope with the responsibilities posed by overseas work;
6. The manager's lack of technical competence; and
7. The manager's lack of motivation to work overseas.

These findings are consistent with other studies that show that the "family situation" and "relational abilities" factors are usually responsible for failure or poor performance abroad. In the case of Mr. X, we see that the family situation and lack of cultural awareness were largely responsible for his poor performance in Japan. Mr. X's problems were compounded by four other factors: (1) the short duration of his overseas assignment; (2) the expatriate's concern with repatriation; (3) overemphasis on the technical competence criterion to the disregard of other attributes necessary for effective performance abroad; and (4) lack of training for overseas assignment. Each of these compounding factors is discussed briefly below.

Although most overseas assignments of U.S. multinationals are for two or three years, such short stints abroad are not conducive to high performance. The expatriate barely has time to adjust before transfer home or to another overseas location. In the case of Mr. X, there were only six months out of the 18 months in which he was contributing to the subsidiary's operation. Research has shown that when expatriates are exempted from active managerial responsibilities in the first several months of foreign assignment, particularly to countries with great cultural differences, "This will ease their acculturation and help prevent mistakes they tend to make during this period [which are] usually detrimental to both the expatriate and his organization."[2]

However, extending the overseas assignment can lead to the second factor, namely, concern by the employee about repatriation. Since the "plum" positions in U.S. multinationals are back home, expatriates are understandably reluctant to accept extended periods of overseas assignments because of their concerns about being forgotten and hence passed up for promotion. These fears are to a large extent justified, as a result of the revolving door policy at the top management level in U.S. corporations. An expatriate who has been away for a number of years may find himself or herself a stranger to members of the board. This was apparently Mr. X's principal concern — he learned that while he was away from center stage his rival had been promoted over him.

The third compounding factor is overemphasis on the technical competence criterion to the disregard of other important attributes. In the case of Mr. X, technical competence was used as the sole criterion for selection and no assessment was made of his ability to relate to and work with the Japanese. According to E. L. Miller, this practice is fairly common among U.S. multinationals and stems from two primary causes: the difficulty of identifying and measuring attitudes appropriate for cross-cultural interaction and the self-interest of the selectors. Since technical competence almost always prevents immediate failure on the job, particularly in high pressure situations, the selectors play safe by placing a heavy emphasis on technical qualifications and little on the individual's ability to adapt to a foreign environment.[3] There is abundant research to show that while technical competence is an important factor in the overall determination of success, relational abilities appear to increase the probability of successful performance considerably.[4] Lack of relational abilities, i.e., the inability of the individual to deal effectively with one's clients, business associates, superiors, peers, and subordinates was found to be a principal cause of failure. However, the relational skills criterion is seldom emphasized in the selection decision.[5]

The fourth factor that often compounds the problem is inadequate training for overseas assignments. In the case of Mr. X, he was presented with the most basic factual information about Japan. These are commonly referred to as environmental briefing programs. When used alone, the environmental briefing is inadequate in preparing trainees for assignments that require extensive contact with the local community, as was the case with Mr. X as head of marketing in Japan.

One apparent solution to the problem of high expatriate failure is the use of host country nationals, which is already an extensive practice. In the survey, it was found that U.S. multinationals used local nationals more extensively at all levels of management in industrialized countries than in the less developed regions. This is logical, as one would expect the more developed nations to have a larger pool of personnel who possess the necessary manpower and technical skills to staff management-level positions.

This practice of employing local nationals, however, does not resolve all the problems of international human resource management for at least three reasons. First, local nationals may have problems relating to organizational members in the head office because of nonfamiliarity with corporate culture. As such, many multinational companies perceive the need to use expatriates to serve as an interface between corporate head office and the local subsidiary. This was a reason behind IBM's decision in early 1985 to expatriate some 250 American families to Japan as part of their restructuring efforts in checking Fujitsu's growing market share in that country. Second, companies need to send expatriates (or other alternative sources of manpower) to the less developed nations because of the lack of talent in these countries. In most instances, these are the countries that pose the major problems of adjustment for expatriates. Third, given the increasing globalization of industries and business activities, international experience in strategic markets (Japan being one of them) should be considered an integral part of any high flyer's career development program. While Japan is a highly industrialized country, its widely divergent cultural norms and practices are a major source of adjustment problems for Westerners. According to Seward, nine out of ten expatriates were significantly less productive in Japan than they were back home. This was consistent with an earlier finding by Adams and Kobayashi.[6]

Given the continued need to use expatriate staff, what should companies do to redress the situation?

To shed light on the issue, let us examine how the European and Japanese multinationals are faring in this regard. European and Japanese multinationals represent interesting study and comparative analysis cases for several reasons. First, multinationals from these countries assign very high priority to their international market because of the smaller size of their domestic markets. Second, there is a significantly longer history of overseas operations and expatriation among European multinationals. Third, while the Japanese as a result of culture and history do not readily mix with *gaigins* (foreigners), they have performed extremely well in foreign markets within the short span of two or three decades. The Japanese who were sent abroad to establish foreign subsidiaries have succeeded in making Japan a formidable economic power.

A questionnaire survey similar to the one administered to U.S. multinationals was given to 29 West European and 35 Japanese multinationals. For both the Europeans and the Japanese, failure rates were lower than the Americans'. Fifty-nine percent of the West European firms had recall rates of under 5%, 38% had recall rates of 6–10%, and only 3% had failure rates of 11–15%. For the Japanese sample, 76% of the firms had failure rates of below 5%, 10% had recall rates of 6–10%, and 14% had failure rates of 11–19%.[7] A cursory review of these statistics would suggest one of two possible explanations for the lower failure rates among European and Japanese multinationals. West Europeans and Japanese expatriates are by nature, selection, and training more adept at living and working in a foreign environment. Also, European and Japanese multinationals use different criteria for judging whether a person could work effectively in a foreign country. In the case of Japan, this may arise from the more paternalistic role assumed by the firm and the practice of life-time employment among the career staff from which the expatriate population is drawn.

To gain a better understanding of the reasons for the lower expatriate failure rate among European and Japanese firms, in-depth interviews were conducted with another sample of 17 European and Japanese multinationals in diverse industries. On the average, two senior executives responsible for expatriate assignments were interviewed from each of these multinationals. The failure rates for the European and Japanese multinationals interviewed were under 6 and 5%, respectively. These studies provide insights into the human resource management programs in European and Japanese multinationals, particularly as they relate to overseas assignments. The highlights of this study follow.[8]

REASONS FOR LOWER FAILURE RATES AMONG EUROPEAN AND JAPANESE MULTINATIONALS

Based on the interviews, there appear to be several common denominators to successful performance among European and Japanese multinationals. These are:

1. Their long-term orientation regarding overall planning and performance assessment;
2. Use of more rigorous training programs to prepare candidates for overseas assignments, particularly by Japanese multinationals;
3. Provision of a comprehensive expatriate support system;
4. Overall qualification of candidates for overseas assignments; and
5. Restricted job mobility.

In the European multinationals, there are three additional factors that may account for their greater successes with expatriation. These included their

- international orientation,
- longer history of overseas operations, and
- language capability.

In the case of Japanese multinationals, two factors may also account for low rates of expatriate failure: selection for overseas assignments and the role of the family. The common denominators to success in both European and Japanese multinationals will be examined first.

Long-Term Orientation with Regard to Overall Planning and Performance Evaluation

U.S. multinationals generally possess a short-term orientation with regard to planning and assessment of performance. In contrast, European and Japanese multinationals espouse a long-term orientation in their human resource management practices. This is shown in several ways. First, the rate of turnover among managerial personnel is very low. Mid-career changes are rare since most companies espouse a policy of promotion from within. This "cradle to grave" philosophy implies certain obligations and responsibilities on the part of the employer and the employee. In Europe and Japan, employers are generally more tolerant of circumstances that may temporarily affect a person's performance. Consequently, they tend to make allowances for performance that is less than average in the initial period of assignment abroad. Some of the European multinationals interviewed allowed an adjustment period of up to one year. In the case of Japanese multinationals, many indicated they did not expect the expatriate to perform to full capacity until the third year of assignment.

A second implication of this long-term orientation among European and Japanese multinationals is a greater willingness to invest large sums of money in career development programs, particularly in the case of Japanese multinationals. These will be discussed later.

A third way in which this long-term orientation affects international human resource management practices is the extended periods of overseas assignments. Except for overseas postings that are strictly for career development purposes, expatriate assignments in European multinationals average five years or more. Similarly in Japanese multinationals, the average duration of an overseas assignment is five years.[9] This is consistent with a 1982 survey by the *Japan Economic News* on 612 expatriates, which found that the average duration of an overseas assignment was 4.67 years.

This longer duration of overseas assignment is possible because "plum" positions may be abroad rather than at domestic headquarters. Companies also provide a comprehensive support system to allay expatriate concerns about repatriation. The longer durations of overseas assignments allow the individual more time to adjust. In addition, these firms provide greater incentive for the expatriate to learn and adapt to local circumstances.

A fourth implication of the long-term orientation among European and Japanese multinationals is the tendency to place equal, if not heavier, emphasis on a person's potential (as opposed to actual performance) in assessing his or her overall contribution to the organization. Given the practice of life-time employment among most managerial personnel, the company can afford to take such an approach.

Training for Cross-Cultural Encounters

As noted earlier, a principal reason for expatriate failure in U.S. multinationals is a lack of relational abilities. Despite this recognition, most U.S. multinationals do not provide formal training to prepare expatriates for cross-cultural encounters. This reluctance to invest large sums of money in training stems from the fear that employees may leave the company. This fear is justified, to a large extent, because of the high mobility of the U.S. work force.

In comparison, given the very low turnover rates among management personnel in European and Japanese multinationals, these companies feel safe investing in an employee's future by spending large sums of money to develop overall management skills. Since international experience is considered an integral part of one's overall career development, most European companies provide some programs to prepare candidates for assignments to locations outside Western Europe, North America, and Australasia. Similarly, 70% of the 267 largest companies in Japan offer some preparatory courses for their expatriates (1982 survey by *Japan Economic News*). While the programs differ in content and emphasis, they often consist of the following components:

Language training   Most employees of European multinationals have studied a second or third language in school. Consequently, refresher courses like those conducted by Berlitz are often sufficient. While the majority of European multinationals studied did not offer training in exotic languages such as Japanese, Chinese, or Arabic, some did.

Almost all the Japanese companies interviewed sponsored intensive language training programs, ranging from three months to one year in duration. To promote fluency in a foreign language, many Japanese companies invite Caucasians to share the same dormitories to provide their trainees ample opportunity to practice their language skills and to gain a better understanding of the foreign country.

Cross-cultural training   Many of the European multinationals studied used a training facility known as the Center for International Briefing at Farnham Castle in the United Kingdom. The Center offers two types of residential programs: a four-day regional program and a week-long cultural awareness program. These programs are generally attended by both husband and wife. The regional program, as its name suggests, focuses on the specific region or country to which the individual is sent. Over the course of the four-day program, the trainee is exposed to factual information about the historical, political, religious, and economic factors that shape the mentality of the people in a given region, and how these factors differ from those in Western Europe. The objective is "To help the individual adjust, in a very practical way, to the work environment and the personal situation," to quote the Center's director. For example, if the target region is the Middle East, the course will examine "What Islam means in the way that people actually behave, and in their attitudes toward each other, their families, age, education, women and, most important, expatriates or foreigners who come to live among them."

The information is conveyed through a mix of lectures, audiovisual presentations, and discussions with outside speakers. The latter includes returned expatriates and foreign nationals. The Center has recently begun to offer courses to fit the specific needs of a firm.

The second type of residential program, the cultural awareness program, does not focus on a specific region of the world per se. Rather, the purpose is to broaden an individual's understanding of and sensitivity to other countries through lectures and experiential exercises. The Center trains about 1,000 people every year, with slightly more than half the candidates coming from the United Kingdom and the remainder from continental Europe. Virtually all British multinationals interviewed for this study used the Center's facilities, and a number of Swiss and Italian firms currently enroll or propose to enroll their candidates.

Besides Farnham Castle, other cross-cultural training facilities used by the European multinationals studied include the Tropen Institute (the Netherlands), the Carl Duisberg Center, and Evangelische Akademie (both Federal Republic of Germany).

Most European multinationals, in addition, provide ample opportunities for outgoing families to discuss their overseas assignments with expatriates who have returned. Since most of the European multinationals included in the study have a longer history of overseas operations, there is usually a fairly large contingent of resident experts, either located in corporate headquarters or abroad, who can brief expatriates and their spouses about the overseas situation.

Japanese companies typically provide a more comprehensive and rigorous training program to prepare their expatriates for cross-cultural encounters. Besides language training, a typical program would include:

Field experience Many of the Japanese multinationals surveyed select members of their current staff to their overseas offices to serve as trainees for one year. As trainees, their primary mission is to observe closely and, hence, learn about the company's foreign operations.

Graduate programs abroad Every year, many of the Japanese multinationals surveyed send 10 to 20 career staff members to attend graduate business, law, and engineering programs overseas. The company will pay tuition and all expenses, in addition to the employee's regular salary. While attending graduate school, the Japanese employee is exposed to foreign principles of management, which will prepare him for eventual overseas assignment. Furthermore, during the two-year program, the Japanese employee gains a better understanding of the broad functioning of foreign societies.

In-house training programs Besides language training, the expatriates take courses in international finance and international economics, and are exposed to environmental briefings about the country of assignment.

Many Japanese companies now realize the importance of developing the management skills of expatriates to prepare them for the added responsibilities of overseas work. One study found that a principal reason for expatriate failure among Japanese multinationals was their inability to cope with the larger responsibilities of overseas work.[10] The situation arises because in a foreign assignment, the Japanese expatriate has to operate largely on his own, without the kind of close interaction he was accustomed to at home. To a Japanese who has been used to working in a group, this may pose a major problem of adjustment.

Outside agencies Besides the in-house training program, there are a number of institutes in Japan that prepare expatriates for overseas assignments. One such agency is the Institute for International Studies and Training, which was established under the auspices of the Ministry of International Trade and Industry. The Institute offers two types of residential programs: three-month and one-year. The Institute annually graduates 150–200 trainees, with the average attendee having six years of work experience in industry or government. The three-month program is designed for specialists and covers courses in English and international business transactions. The one-year program is designed to "foster generalists and internationally minded businessmen." Trainees enrolled in this program have to master English plus one other foreign language and receive intensive training in area studies. Classes are held from 9:00 a.m. to 4:00 p.m. In the evening, there are seminars given by ambassadors, ministers, foreign businessmen, and overseas researchers living in Japan. Besides the use of visiting professors from foreign countries, there is an exchange program so that students from other nations can share dormitories with Japanese trainees, thus facilitating the acquisition of foreign language skills and knowledge of foreign ways of life. The Institute has formal exchange programs with INSEAD (France), American University and American Graduate School of Management (United States), and Euro-Japanese Exchange Foundation (United Kingdom).

Support Systems in Corporate Headquarters

In general, both European and Japanese multinationals provide a more comprehensive support system to help allay expatriate concerns about problems of repatriation. One such mechanism is "parenting" or "mentoring," whereby an expatriate is paired to a superior in corporate headquarters who takes on the role of sponsor. The sponsor, who is usually a member of senior management, apprises the expatriate regularly about the situation at home, and has the responsibility of finding a position for the expatriate upon his return. Since the turnover rate at the senior management level in most European and Japanese firms is virtually nonexistent, the expatriate can feel secure that the sponsor will be there when he returns. In the words of a British petroleum executive, even though the sponsor may have taken up a new position elsewhere in the company, "The personal link is the vital thing, not the link by way of the role the general manager was at when the expatriates went out." This sentiment was echoed by a Japanese expatriate: "My boss will continue to be my boss for a long time. I know he will take care of me."

Where there is no sponsor-expatriate pairing, most companies have separate departments or divisions that are responsible for overseeing the material well-being and career path of expatriates. The expatriate is required to talk to personnel from these departments on his home leave, which is usually once a year. In addition, some companies have a senior manager in their overseas subsidiaries who has a "part time responsibility as a career manager or godfather." The expatriate community in foreign countries also plays a major role in reinforcing the support mechanisms provided by corporate headquarters. Given the longer history of overseas operations of European multinationals, their foreign subsidiaries are generally well established with a relatively large expatriate community. As such, the new arrivals are "fairly well looked after." In the case of Japanese multinationals, the "early settlers" will provide assistance to the new arrivals because of their commitment to a strong group orientation.

Qualification of Candidates

Given the importance assigned to the international market, both European and Japanese multinationals tend to send abroad their best people. In the words of a British executive, "We won't have any hope of acceptance in the host country unless [the expatriate] is visibly and perceptibly better than the local people." This theme was echoed by numerous executives from the United Kingdom, Italy, Switzerland, and Japan.

Restricted Job Mobility

Because of the smaller size of domestic markets in Europe, each country can generally support a limited number of firms in a given industry. This restricts job mobility, with the result that employees are generally more dedicated to organizational goals.

In Japan, this is reinforced by the traditional loyalty to one's company. According to many Japanese expatriates, one "has to endure" and do his best even if he does not like the overseas assignment. Under the system of life-time employment, a Japanese career staff member knows he must not disrupt the foreign operation because it will hurt his future career in the company.

While the values of Japan's younger generation may be changing (reflected in the findings of a 1979 survey by the Public Opinion Research Institute, in which respondents voiced a greater need to distinguish between work and personal lives), many executives indicated these findings can be partly attributed to a greater willingness of the younger generation to vocalize opinions and comments. Another more compelling reason to believe this changing trend may not have a negative effect on future performance of Japanese organizations can be ascribed to the projections by the Japan Ministry of Labor. These projections indicate that senior management positions in

Japanese companies will become more competitive in years ahead, particularly in light of the recent slowing down of the Japanese economy. Given the more limited chances of upward mobility and the overall competitiveness of the Japanese, it is unlikely this overall loyalty and commitment to their organizations will slacken as the younger generation matures.

FACTORS UNIQUE TO EUROPEAN MULTINATIONALS

International Orientation

Virtually all European executives interviewed for the study indicated that a primary reason for their success in expatriation is their employees' greater international orientation and outlook, compared with their U.S. counterparts. This accounts for the relative ease with which many European expatriates adapt to new cultural settings.

This spirit of internationalism can be ascribed to several factors. First, here is the smaller size of the European multinationals' domestic markets. In the United Kingdom, for example, one-third of the country's GNP is exported. This export mentality is best characterized by the British slogan, "Export or die." A company has to concentrate on overseas expansion to grow. For example, 98% of sales for a large Swiss chemical manufacturer are generated from abroad. This export mentality and heavy dependence on the international market stand in stark contrast to the situation in the United States, where multinationals typically derive a sizable portion of their sales and revenues from domestic operations. Second, because of the relatively small size of a European country and its physical proximity to others, most Europeans have greater exposure to foreigners and foreign ways of life. Third, executives from several European multinationals contend that the military and economic strength of the United States has led Americans to be too complacent about their own culture, which often is interpreted as arrogance and creates resentment among local people. Some British executives note that since World War II, the balance of economic and military powers has migrated westward across the Atlantic. This "humbling or sobering" experience, to quote one British executive, forced most Britons to make a more pragmatic assessment of their own limitations and adopt a "more realistic attitude overseas." In countries like Switzerland and Italy, where there is a history of emigration to improve one's fortunes, people have a more accepting attitude toward foreign lands. Fourth, there is the legacy of empire. In fact, many of the companies included in this study established their overseas operations during the height of European empire building. In the word of a British executive, "I suppose there is still a legacy of the empire on this side. It is a part of British culture to travel and work overseas. It is not unusual for many members of one's family to have been abroad or to know many people who have worked abroad." This theme was echoed by the executives in the German, Swiss, and Italian multinationals.

This spirit of internationalism has affected the human resource management practices of European multinationals in several ways. First, a greater value is placed on international experience and overseas assignments. In most of the companies studied, international experience is considered an important prerequisite for promotion to top management.

A second way in which this spirit of internationalism has affected human resource management practices in European firms is the recruitment of candidates for management level positions. Besides the criterion of technical competence, when recruiting candidates for management training programs many European companies seek "well traveled young graduates."

A third implication for human resource management practices is the heterogeneity or multinational composition of a management team to ensure an international perspective in all aspects of the company's operations. In a large British petroleum company, for example, there is a system of cross-country rotation of management personnel. Under this system, while most employees join a local operating company, they must have two to three years' experience in another overseas operating company before promotion to management level. Furthermore, each management team should normally have a foreign national who is on assignment from an overseas sister affiliate.

A fourth implication of the greater international orientation of Europeans is that spouses are typically more adaptive to foreign ways of life.

Longer History of Overseas Operations

As noted previously, many European firms surveyed expanded overseas in the heyday of European imperialism. This longer history of overseas operations has facilitated international human resource management in two important ways: First, the company has accumulated a wealth of experience in dealing with foreign nationals. Many companies have resident experts who can provide valuable advice, whether on a formal or informal basis, to the younger generation of expatriates. Second, foreign operations are generally already well established. Hence, in most cases, the expatriate moves into a developed operation abroad, which facilitates adaptation to the local environment.

Language Capability

Because of their close physical proximity to other European countries and the importance assigned to the international market, many Europeans are bilingual or even multilingual.

Knowledge of a foreign language may not always guarantee effective performance abroad, but it does facilitate adaptation by enabling the expatriate to develop a better rapport with co-workers, customers, and other members of the local community.

FACTORS UNIQUE TO JAPANESE MULTINATIONALS

Selection for Overseas Assignments

While a Japanese multinational may not administer specific tests to determine a candidate's adaptability prior to overseas assignment because of the unavailability of such tests in Japan, organization officials would carefully review every aspect of the employee's qualifications before making a final decision. This is possible because of the unique system of personnel management in Japan. The strong group orientation and the after-hours socializing among the male career staff enables the immediate supervisor in a Japanese company to become thoroughly familiar with an individual's family background, general preferences, and qualifications. Given such knowledge, the Japanese supervisor generally would not make unreasonable recommendations. Most Japanese companies also keep very detailed personal inventories on their career staff. These are compiled from the annual or semiannual performance evaluations completed by the individual, his immediate supervisor, and the chief of the division. In addition, candidates who are considered for an overseas assignment (excluding those who have been selected to study abroad) typically have been with the company for ten years. Hence, the company has ample time to assess capabilities and qualifications.

Role of the Family

A principal reason for expatriate failures in U.S. and European multinationals is the family situation factor.[11] Japanese wives, however, are generally more "obedient and dependent" than their American or European counterparts. Given the greater emphasis on face saving, a Japanese woman would not want to "fail" in her role as a wife by complaining about the problems encountered living in a foreign country.

IMPLICATIONS FOR U.S. MULTINATIONALS

Based on the foregoing analysis of expatriate assignments among a sample of European and Japanese multinationals, there appear to be common denominators to successful performance. Both European and Japanese multinationals benefit from the heavier emphasis placed on the international market and the adoption of long-term orientation with regard to overall planning in the area of international human resource management. These factors lead to a greater willingness to (1) sponsor rigorous programs preparing expatriates for cross-cultural encounters, (2) provide comprehensive support systems facilitating adaptation abroad, and (3) allay concerns about problems of repatriation. In addition, Europeans enjoy an inherent advantage of having been abroad longer, thus providing them with greater experience and a larger pool of in-house talent and resources. To compensate for their relatively recent entry into the international economic arena, the Japanese multinationals have acquired advantage by embarking on meticulous programs to prepare their expatriates for the challenges of living and working abroad. U.S. multinationals, on the other hand, possess neither the inherent advantage of the Europeans nor the acquired advantage of the Japanese.

Can this situation among U.S. multinationals be rectified? If so, how?

Based on the foregoing analysis, at least three primary implications for U.S. firms can be drawn.

First, U.S. multinationals should develop a longer-term orientation with regard to expatriate assignments, overall planning, and assessment of performance. While U.S. companies have traditionally espoused a short-term orientation, this strategy is incompatible with the evolving trend toward the globalization of industries, which necessitates greater international outlook among top management. This international perspective can be engendered through one or two tours of duty abroad. The solution, however, does not lie in short stints abroad. Even if the overseas assignment were undertaken primarily for career development purposes, it is doubtful that it would serve a useful purpose if the dismal performance abroad erodes the expatriate's self-confidence. Short stints abroad are not conducive to high performance because the expatriate barely has time to adjust before transfer home or to another location. To allay expatriate concerns that prolonged absence from corporate headquarters may negatively affect their chances of promotion within the corporate hierarchy, the implementation of some support mechanisms (similar to those found in European and Japanese multinationals) will help alleviate these fears. While individual mentoring may not be possible given the rapid turnover of American management personnel, multinationals might consider setting up separate departments or divisions whose sole function is to oversee the career paths of expatriates.

A longer-term orientation among U.S. companies may also engender greater commitment and loyalty among employees and increased willingness to undergo temporary inconveniences to advance the company's overall goals. Furthermore, increased loyalty on the part of employees may lower the turnover rate, which should result in a greater willingness by the company to invest in training programs.

Second, U.S. multinationals and U.S. society at large must develop a more international orientation and outlook. Without a fundamental change of attitude in this regard, the international market will continue to be relegated to a secondary role in the company's overall planning. Under these circumstances, it is unrealistic to expect that the company will devote sufficient attention to the area of international human resource management. Because of the narrowing technological gap among the United States, Europe, and Japan, U.S. multinationals can no longer rely solely on technology to gain a competitive edge in international markets. The successful operation of a multinational is contingent on the availability of additional resources, such as capital, know-how, and manpower. It is argued that manpower is a key ingredient in the efficient operation of a multinational because other resources are not as effectively or efficiently allocated to subsidiaries by corporate headquarters in the absence of a highly developed pool of managerial talent with international orientation.

The international competitiveness of U.S. multinationals has to depend on the ingenuity of its workers and, more important, the workers sent overseas as representatives of corporate headquarters. There are encouraging signs that the United States has finally awakened to this need, evidenced by the burgeoning interest in international business and cross-cultural programs at academic institutions, particularly at the university level. This is just a beginning, however, and much needs to be done.

Third, U.S. multinationals must provide more comprehensive training programs to prepare expatriates for cross-cultural encounters. Studies have shown that technical competence alone is a necessary but insufficient condition for successful operations abroad. Because of the greater mobility of the U.S. work force, American multinationals may be reluctant to sponsor more rigorous programs such as those found in the Japanese multinationals. However, programs along the lines of those offered by the Center for International Briefing at Farnham Castle in England should certainly be feasible. It is clearly impossible to prepare expatriates for all the contingencies of living and working abroad within the course of a program that lasts only a week. An executive with a large European transnational corporation suggests that a program like the one at Farnham can "at least dent people's over-confidence" in the superiority of their own ways of thinking and operating. Such programs emphasize that things are different in other countries and there is no way the expatriate can change that fact because it has been like that for centuries.

By examining and then implementing the aforementioned changes, the dismal record of U.S. expatriate performance can begin to improve.

NOTES

1. For a more detailed discussion of the questionnaire survey of U.S., European, and Japanese multinationals, see R. L. Tung's "Selection and Training Procedures of U.S., European, and Japanese Multinationals," *California Management Review*, 1982, 25(1), 57–71.
2. E. Harrari and Y. Zeira's "Training Expatriates for Managerial Assignments in Japan," *California Management Review*, 1978, 20(4), 56–62, contains the details of this study.
3. For an elaboration on this argument, see E. L. Miller's "The Selection Decision for an International Assignment: A Study of the Decision Maker's Behavior," *Journal of International Business Studies*, 1972, 3, 49–65.
4. Details of these findings can be found in R. D. Hays's "Ascribed Behavioral Determinants of Success-Failure Among U.S. Expatriate Managers," *Journal of International Business Studies*, 1971, 2, 40–46, and C. G. Howard's "Model for the Design of a Selection Program for Multinational Executives," *Public Personnel Management*, March-April 1974, 138–145.
5. For further information on this study, see R. L. Tung's "Selection and Training for Overseas Assignments," *Columbia Journal of World Business*, Spring 1981, 68–78.
6. J. Seward's "Speaking the Japanese Business Language," *European Business*, Winter 1975, 40–47, and T. E. M. Adams and N. Kobayashi's *The World of Japanese Business*, Tokyo: Kodnsha International, 1969, contain details of these findings.
7. See Tung (1982).
8. For a comprehensive description and analysis of the human resource management practices in Japanese and European multinationals, see R. L. Tung's *Key to Japan's Economic Strength: Human Power*, Lexington, Mass.: Lexington Books, D C Heath, 1984, and *Managing Human Resources in the International Context*, Cambridge, Mass.: Ballinger Publishers (in press).
9. See Tung (1982).
10. Ibid.
11. Ibid.

Rosalie L. Tung is professor of business administration and director of the International Business Center at the University of Wisconsin-Milwaukee.

Cases

A Management Dilemma: Regulating the Health of the Unborn
Donna M. Randall

One of the top ten mining production areas in the world is in northern Idaho's panhandle. The area, appropriately called the "Silver Valley," is a 30-mile stretch of land lying between two small Idaho towns, Cataldo and Mullan, and following the South Fork of the Coeur d'Alene River. The Silver Valley is a major U.S. supplier of lead, silver, zinc, and cadmium. To date, nearly $4 billion worth of mineral wealth has been extracted from the area.

The Bunker Hill Company, founded in 1887, was one of the first mining companies established in the Silver Valley. The main entrance to the underground mine, the famous Kellogg Tunnel, was constructed between 1893 and 1902. In May 1891 the Bunker Hill concentrator (which crushes the ore and separates the metal from waste rock), at the time the largest in the world, sent out its first trainload of ore to be smelted (i.e., melted and refined). The company built its own lead smelter in 1916.

With its lead industry expanding rapidly, the Bunker Hill–Sullivan Company (renamed after a merger) began to develop its zinc operations in 1926. The company completed construction of a zinc plant and began refining zinc in 1928. Throughout the 1930s and 1940s the company continued to expand. A research laboratory was added to the complex and the lead smelter was enlarged. By the early 1950s the company had grown to one of the largest mining operations in the country. In 1956 the company officially changed its name from Bunker Hill–Sullivan to the Bunker Hill Company.

Bunker Hill's growth pattern attracted the interest of a number of investors. In 1968 Gulf Resources, a small sulfur company based in Houston bought Bunker Hill for $80 million. The purchase proved a wise investment. The chairman of Gulf Resources, Robert Allen, claimed that Bunker Hill was one of his best and largest acquisitions. In fact, Bunker Hill was larger than Gulf Resources when purchased (Bagamery, 1981, p. 172). According to Gulf Resources President Frank Woodruff, revenues from the Bunker Hill Company exceeded $1.8 billion between 1968 and 1977 ("Kendrick, Woodruff tes-

---

For a fuller discussion of the issues involved in the Bunker Hill controversy, see Donna Randall, "Women in Toxic Work Environments: A Case Study and Examination of Policy Impact." In L. Larwood, A. Stromberg, and B. Gutek, Eds., *Women and Work, An Annual Review*. Beverly Hills: Sage, 1985.

Source: Reprinted by permission of the publisher from "A Management Dilemma: Regulating the Health of the Unborn" by Donna M. Randall, *Journal of Management Case Studies*, Vol. 1, No. 3, pp. 246–258. Copyright 1985 by Elsevier Science Publishing Co., Inc.

tify," 1981, p. 1). In 1980 the Bunker Hill Company contributed 66 percent of Gulf Resources' operating profits and 50 percent of Gulf Resources sales. With the revenue from Bunker Hill, Gulf Resources was able to develop into a large, diversified resources concern with $700 million in revenue (Bagamery, 1981, p. 172).

In the early 1980s the Bunker Hill Company produced 20 percent of the nation's primary refined silver, lead, and zinc. The company owned wholly, or in part, four major silver and lead mines: the original Bunker Hill mine, the Crescent mine, the Pend Oreille mine, and the Star mine. The largest of the mines, the Bunker Hill mine, is considered one of the world's largest underground lead, zinc, and silver mines. In addition to the mines, lead smelter, zinc plant, and research laboratory, the Bunker Hill Company operated three sulfuric acid plants that converted sulfur dioxide gas to liquid sulfuric acid, a tree farm located 3,000 feet underground in the Bunker Hill mine that produced seedlings, the Silverhorn Ski area in the mountains above Kellogg, and, in a joint venture with Stauffer Chemical Company, a plant to produce phosphoric acid and dry ammonium phosphate fertilizer.

The Bunker Hill Company, with about 1,700 hourly workers and 400 salaried workers, was not only the Kellogg area's largest employer (approximately 40 percent of the local population worked for the company) but also drew employees from all neighboring communities. Almost one-half of the employees in Idaho's Shoshone County employed in mining and smelting worked for Bunker Hill. Moreover, the company was the largest employer in the northern half of Idaho (Young, 1981, p. A1).

PROBLEMS AND CONTROVERSIES

The Bunker Hill Company has been beset by a variety of labor problems and embroiled in a number of controversies with regulatory agencies within the last decade over air and water pollution regulations and health and safety standards within the workplace. A major controversy erupted in 1974 when the Center for Disease Control revealed that the Bunker Hill lead smelter was the cause of elevated blood lead levels in approximately one thousand school children. In 1977 a serious labor dispute resulted in Bunker Hill's operations being closed for over four months. In 1981 the company was named a defendant in a $20-million lawsuit in which the parents of nine children alleged their children suffered physical and mental damage by living near Bunker Hill's lead smelter.

Of these controversies, one of the most significant and far-reaching concerns is an employment policy for women working in toxic work areas.

BUNKER HILL'S EXCLUSIONARY POLICY

Few women had been hired by Bunker Hill to work in production positions. Because of labor shortages during World War II, women were hired as production workers at the company, but immediately after the war all but two of the women who had been hired by the company discontinued their work. Employment opportunities for women in production remained limited for the next 20 years.

In 1972 a major change in Bunker Hill's hiring practices took place. Bunker Hill began to accept applications from women to work in production in response to pressure from the Equal Employment Opportunity Commission (EEOC). Over the next few years about 45 women were hired as production workers. Thirty of these women were placed in the lead smelter, the remaining 15 in the zinc plant. While both locations involved exposure to the toxic substance lead, there was little concern at the time about the possible negative health effects on women working in environments where they would be exposed to lead.

In early April 1975, however, Bunker Hill executives became very concerned about the possible consequences of exposing women to lead. One of the physicians on contract with the Bunker Hill Company had attended a lead industries conference in Florida where he was advised by a number of nationally known lead experts to encourage the company to remove women employees from the smelter because of potential harm to the unborn fetus (Tate, 1975, p. A1).

Upon his return to Kellogg, Idaho, the physician alerted the president of Bunker Hill at the time, James Halley, of the possible dangers of lead exposure to fertile women. Halley met with his lawyers and executive staff to consider what action the company should take. After a lengthy conference, Halley decided the company had no choice but to exclude all female workers who could become pregnant from areas of the plant where they would be exposed to lead. On the morning of April 14, 1975, Halley invited local union representatives to meet with him and his staff. At the meeting, union representatives of the United Steelworkers of America were informed that the company intended to exclude all fertile women from work places with lead exposure and would do so immediately.

In the afternoon of the same day, company management met with the 29 women currently employed in the lead smelter and the upper part of the zinc plant (where exposure to lead is the greatest). These women were informed they could no longer work in the lead smelter and zinc plant because of the possible harmful effects of lead on the health of the fetus. They were told that medical evidence had revealed women to be particularly susceptible to the effects of lead. In addition, the women were told that other firms had adopted similar policies that removed fertile women from working around lead.

The women were advised that an "exclusionary" policy had been put into effect. According to the policy set forth by the company, fertile women would no longer be permitted to work in the lead smelter and zinc plant. Those women desiring to maintain their jobs in the smelter and zinc plant would have to show proof of sterilization from their physician before they could return to their jobs. No other form of birth control would be viewed as acceptable to the company.

The women were informed that they could report back to the lead smelter and zinc plant only to clear out their lockers and that they would be temporarily reassigned to the mine yard crew (maintenance work) until permanent positions could be found for them in "safer" areas of the plant. Because they were being transferred from their departments, the women were informed that their department seniority would immediately end. Finally, they were told that if they disagreed with the exclusionary policy they would be fired.

The women affected by the policy were taken by total surprise when it was announced and were quite uncertain what to do. For some, the course of action was clear. At least six of them had previously undergone sterilization; they simply obtained a letter from their physician attesting to their operation and were able to return to their jobs in the lead smelter and zinc plant shortly afterward.

The decision was much more difficult for those women who had not been previously sterilized. Some of them underwent sterilization in order to return to their former jobs (Accola, 1980, p. 1A). Whereas the precise number of women who sought sterilization solely to keep their jobs is unknown, a female physician sent by Occupational Safety and Health Administration (OSHA) in 1980 to investigate the policy determined that at least three women obtained sterilization procedures within two to three months after the policy was enacted. These women informed the physician that they had consented to the operation solely to be allowed by the company to return to their former jobs. In total, 17 of the 29 women originally employed in the smelter and zinc plant returned to their former jobs.

The unsterilized women remained on the mine yard crew while the company attempted to place them in "safe" areas of the plant. However, the company had great difficulty finding areas of the plant without lead exposure. As the lead smelter and a major portion of the zinc plant were no longer open to fertile women, the women could be transferred only to the melting and purification plants, which had a limited number of openings. In an effort to place women in permanent positions, the company began to recruit women to work underground as miners in mid-September 1975 (Kuglin, 1977, p. 3A).

Despite the company's efforts to relocate the women, many of the women affected by the exclusionary policy were very upset about it and its effect on their lives. As a result, several women decided to take action to protest the company's policy. They first complained to their United Steelworkers of America (USWA) local. While the union was clearly sympathetic to the plight of the women, it did not have medical evidence to refute the company's policy and its efforts to protest the treatment of the women had little effect.

One woman filed a complaint with the Idaho Human Rights Commission (IHRC), which drew up a "Memorandum of Understanding" between the company and the women affected by the policy change. The document set forth an agreement about the use of exclusionary policies at Bunker Hill. Unfortunately, the approach was ineffectual as some of the company executives reportedly refused to sign the agreement.

Finally, 18 of the 29 women affected by the policy filed sex discrimination charges with the EEOC. An EEOC investigator met with each of the women and successfully negotiated individual monetary settlements. By mid-March 1976, all charges filed by the women with the EEOC were dropped, but not all the women were satisfied with the settlement. Some felt they had been "bought out" by the company and would have preferred for the EEOC to have made a policy decision on the legality of exclusionary policies.

The controversy over Bunker Hill's exclusionary policy did not end with EEOC's settlement. In April 1980, OSHA responded to a request by the union for an intensive investigation of health and safety conditions at Bunker Hill. On September 11, 1980, OSHA issued a citation against Bunker Hill for 108 violations of occupational safety and health regulations discovered during the inspection. One of those violations was for the maintenance of what OSHA called a "sterilization" policy. The proposed fine for this violation alone was $10,000.

Bunker Hill was not the first company to be cited and fined by OSHA for maintenance of an exclusionary policy. On October 9, 1979, OSHA had cited American Cyanamid for maintenance of a similar policy and had also proposed a $10,000 fine for the violation. After Bunker Hill was cited for the violation, OSHA's case against American Cyanamid was decided by the Occupational Safety and Health Review Commission (OSHRC). On April 28, 1981, the OSHRC determined the policy did not lie within OSHA's jurisdiction and the impact of the company's policy was outside the reach of the Occupational Safety and Health Act. OSHA lost its case against American Cyanamid. Because of the similarity of the Bunker Hill controversy to the American Cyanamid case, OSHA lawyers decided to drop the citation for the sterilization policy against Bunker Hill. On July 21, 1981, the citation against Bunker Hill for the exclusionary policy was officially dismissed.

THE AFTERMATH

Despite the attempts by the women, their union, IHRC, EEOC, and OSHA to change Bunker Hill's exclusionary policy, the policy remained in force. However, because of subsequent events at Bunker Hill, it is unlikely that the controversy over the policy will ever be reopened. On August 25, 1981, Gulf Resources, the owner of Bunker Hill, announced that it planned to close the plant owing to falling metal prices, the unavailability of ore to process, and the rising costs of labor, supplies, and meeting federal regulations. Bunker Hill had lost $7.7 million in the first six months of 1981 and the economy offered little hope of improvement. Today the plant is under the new ownership of Bunker Ltd. Partnership and currently remains closed.

While the controversy was finally resolved at Bunker Hill by the closure of the plant, the issue of whether exclusionary policies are an acceptable industry practice has not been settled. To understand fully the complex issues raised by the use of such policies, it is desirable to present various viewpoints on their use.

CONFLICTING VIEWPOINTS ON THE CONTROVERSY

The Company's Viewpoint

Bunker Hill maintained that its policy was defensible on medical, technological, and moral grounds. Top management felt that medical evidence clearly warranted exclusion of the female worker. Bunker Hill's president at the time, James Halley, claimed recent studies indicated, "There appears to be some physiological difference between a man and a woman that makes women more susceptible to the effects of lead in general" (Tate, 1975, p. 1). Similarly, Jack Kendrick, president of Bunker Hill during the OSHA investigation, explained, "The simple truth is that medical research, based on animal studies, has indicated prolonged exposure to chemicals or heavy metals may adversely affect a fetus" (Kendrick, 1980, p. 1).

The company also justified its policy on technological grounds. A company executive explained the difficulty in improving working conditions in the plant:

> The plant was constructed in the early 1920s and much of the original equipment and facilities still in use is not in the best physical condition. Maintenance dollars in many instances have been diverted to buy and install pollution control equipment. Expansion of production capabilities over the past 50 years has been achieved by adding equipment within existing plant areas or by modification of processes within processes. This has resulted in a plant layout which makes good housekeeping and maintenance most difficult. Thus, the company is faced with the requirement of revising old plants, equipment, and processes to meet the working area environmental standards expected of modern facilities and which can only be readily incorporated into a plant at the original design stage" (Fact File, 1975, pp. 8–9).

Top management felt that the technology simply did not exist that would make the work place safe for unborn children ("OSHA confronts Bunker Hill," 1980, p. 1). As an executive explained,

> People want an environment safe for males, females, and young children, too. That's impossible. You can't have a lead smelter and do that. Like you can't have Montana air in Los Angeles (Interview: Corporate official).

Finally, Bunker Hill defended its policy on moral grounds. Gulf Resources chairman, Robert H. Allen, charged that OSHA's use of "catchy buzzwords" like "sterilization" make for great headlines in the press. But, he asked, would anyone "reasonably suggest that these employees should be allowed, under some bizarre concept of freedom of choice, to continue in a position where there is a known risk to their health?" (Schlender, 1980, p. 25). Similarly, Halley felt that the moral course of action for Bunker Hill was to protect the health of the fetus:

> So am I supposed to put those women in the plant, or am I supposed to keep them out of the plant? Which is the more moral thing to do? If we don't put women in the smelter, that's going to mean fewer jobs for women. If we put a woman in the smelter, and she gets pregnant, we're liable to have a mentally retarded person born who otherwise would have been normal (Tate, 1981, p. 79).

Despite management's belief that the exclusionary policy was justified on these grounds, management also recognized the controversial nature of the policy. After the citation was dropped by OSHA, Bunker Hill management fully expected to be challenged again on its exclusionary policy by new female applicants or other federal agencies (Interview: Corporate official). A vice president of the company summarized the situation: "The issue is a political football and, therefore, it will not die" (Interview: Corporate official).

Industry's Viewpoint

Industry has an obvious economic interest in the health of unborn children of its work force. "When we remove a woman it is not to protect her reproductive capacity, but to protect her fetus," explained Bruce W. Karrh, medical director of E. I. du Pont de Nemours & Company (Shabecoff, 1981, p. 1). Industry may face legal liability if a female employee gives birth to a deformed child. Whereas some women may be willing to take the risk of pregnancy, industry representatives maintain that the women cannot legally waive the rights of the unborn children to sue for damages in the future. A child born with defects or diseases caused by parental exposure to toxic chemicals may bring personal injury actions against a company. Moreover, the media exposure and adverse publicity arising from a lawsuit involving a deformed child may be devastating to a company's image. After weighing the risks, Dr. Norbert J. Roberts, medical director of Exxon, concluded, "I would rather face an EEOC inspector than a deformed baby" (Pauly, 1976, p. 57).

The chemical companies and manufacturers of toxic substances contend that they have no choice but to remove women to protect them from toxic exposures. Like Bunker Hill management, industry representatives maintain that the technology does not presently exist to make work places, such as lead smelters, completely safe for either worker or fetus and that offering women affected by exclusionary policies equitable transfers to safer areas of the corporation is simply not economically feasible (Stillman, 1979, p. 601).

Furthermore, industry representatives claim that federal regulatory agencies have not given them sufficient guidance in the area of reproductive health and have actually placed them in the middle of a legal dilemma. Should the employer conform with the Occupational Safety and Health Act of 1970 (in which workers are given a right to a safe and healthy work place) or with Title VII of the Civil Rights Act of 1964 (in which workers are given a right to equal employment opportunties)? Industry representatives contend if the employer seeks to conform to OSHA's laws, the fertile female would be excluded from the work place to protect the fetus and equal employment laws would be violated. On the other hand, if the employer seeks to conform to EEOC's laws, the health of the fetus would be endangered and OSHA's standards would be violated. Hence industry representatives complain that industry has been left with a task of complying with conflicting regulations.

Women Employees' Viewpoint

The 29 women removed from their jobs in the lead smelter and zinc plant at Bunker Hill were very dissatisfied with the change in corporate policy for a variety of reasons. They were most upset at losing their departmental seniority. Seniority, as a union representative explained, is the "backbone of the system." It is the recognized way for an employee to advance in the company and to obtain more interesting, better-paying positions. By losing their departmental seniority, the women would lose all the rights and privileges they had worked to build up.

A number of the women were upset at the abrupt manner in which they were informed of the policy; they were informed of the new policy and removed from their jobs on the same day. Many felt the temporary work on the mine yard crew was demeaning. Removed from responsible positions, they were assigned to pick up gum wrappers and paint signs. Others enjoyed the work in the smelter and zinc plant and did not want to leave. These women felt they had worked hard to obtain their positions, had proven themselves, and had earned a right to stay in their jobs.

Many of the women transferred to the mine yard crew were upset with their new work schedules. Specifically, these women could no longer work evenings and nights to meet their families' schedules as they could in the smelter and zinc plant. The women were required to work from eight o'clock to five o'clock, five days a week. Moreover, work on the mine yard crew lacked night and holiday work, overtime opportunity, and incentive earnings offered in the lead smelter and zinc plant.

Other female employees felt their privacy was being invaded with the exclusionary policy. These women complained that in returning to the lead smelter and zinc plant, they were subjected to derogatory comments from their male co-workers. Women in other companies have voiced similar concerns, maintaining that an exclusionary policy

> subjects all women to special scrutiny about their childbearing intentions, sexual activities, and birth control methods and, thus, operates to invade their personal privacy in a most sensitive area. Any woman who remains in a restricted job is forced, per se, to publicly reveal her sterility. Men, on the other hand, are not asked if or when they intend to have children, even though their exposure to toxic substances could also result in injury to a future child (Clauss and Bertin, 1981, p. 22).

Finally, economic concerns were central to many of the women workers. About one-half of the women employed at Bunker Hill were single parents. Jobs were scarce in the Silver Valley and Bunker Hill was the largest employer. Women employees could have been replaced easily by men and could apply for only a limited number of openings as waitresses, bartenders, nurses, clerks, secretaries, teachers, and beauticians. All these positions meant substantial wage cuts from production work. For those women faced with a significant cut in income, a sterilization procedure that would allow them to keep their high-paying job became very attractive.

Women employees in other companies with exclusionary policies report similar economic pressure to consent to sterilization. A woman who applied to the Pittsburgh & Midway Coal Mining Company explained the economic pressure to get sterilized:

> It seemed that you could have a tubal ligation in a very short period of time. It cost about $800 and it seemed to be less than what one would pay for an employment agency to find you a job. ("A new twist ...," 1981, p. 7)

Women's Advocates' Viewpoints

Women's advocates maintain that widespread use of policies such as that adopted by Bunker Hill would significantly diminish women's employment opportunities in the lead industry. Hricko (1978, p. 400) estimated that if women of childbearing age were not allowed to work where there was lead exposure, almost two of every three female applicants for an estimated 1.3 million jobs would be turned away. Women's advocates point out that females can be easily discriminated against during periods of high unemployment and that they have been chosen by corporations to be economic scapegoats (Krekel, 1977, p. 125). Furthermore, exclusionary policies are perceived by some to be a "smokescreen laid down by male workers to obscure their self-interest in maintaining full employment for men" ("Do protective laws . . . ," 1980, p. 1).

While industry maintains that the technology does not presently exist to make work places such as lead smelters completely safe for either worker or fetus, Ann Trebilcock, an attorney for the United Auto Workers (UAW), asserts that the technology does exist to make the work place safe for the fetus, but employers would rather hire "superworkers" who can withstand toxic exposure instead of going to the expense of cleaning up the work place (Hyatt, 1977, p. 1). Women's advocates insist that exclusionary policies are much cheaper than instituting engineering controls that would protect both male and female workers. "The costs of such a policy," Win-O'Brien (1980, p. 509) points out, "are borne by the women who must leave their jobs in order to protect their ability to have children or the women who'll never be hired into these work places."

To support their claims of discrimination, women's advocates point to the different manner in which the issue of reproductive health is treated in hospitals, dental offices, beauty parlors, and the textile industry. In these areas where most of the employees are female, the employment of fertile women is unregulated although chemicals such as ionizing radiation are known to be dangerous (Stellman, 1977, p. 183). In addition, women have been barred from heavy industrial jobs entailing lead exposure, but not from lower-paying jobs in certain industries, such as pottery work, which also entail lead exposure (Stellman, 1977, p. 178).

Many women advocates feel that current medical research does not warrant exclusion of only women from the work place and point to research evidence which indicates that both male and female reproductive abilities are damaged by exposure to lead (see U.S. Department of Labor, 1979, pp. 186–187). According to available research evidence, occupational exposure of male workers to high levels of lead can lead to reduced sexual drive, impotence, decreased ability to produce normal sperm, and sterility (Gold, 1981, p. 10). Occupational exposure of females can lead to abnormal ovarian cycles, menstrual disorders, sterility, premature birth, miscarriage, and stillbirth (Hricko and Brunt, 1976, pp. C7–C8). Lead can also affect the nervous system of the developing fetus, resulting in learning disorders and psychological impairments. However, the precise nature of harm to the fetus and the level of lead exposure at which such damage occurs cannot be determined with certainty. Only limited medical research has been conducted on the effects of lead on male and female reproductive systems.

Despite the medical evidence indicating the susceptibility of both male and female reproductive systems to lead, women advocates complain that only women have been the objects of exclusionary policies and that the policies ignore the threat of damage to unborn children of male workers. Such policies assume that the future children of female workers are at a greater health risk than the unborn children of male workers.

Moreover, exclusionary policies are perceived to reject the female worker as a person with options. Surgical sterilization is required by the policies regardless of whether the female has chosen not to have a family, her sex partner has a vasectomy, or she is using another form of birth control (O'Brien, 1980, p. 509).

The impact of such policies may go beyond sex discrimination. Burnham (1976, p. 42) has pointed out that a policy that excludes one sex may also be used to exclude certain races from the work place. Lead may pose special health problems for blacks who might have sickle cell disease. Therefore, if fertile women can be excluded from toxic work environments on inconclusive medical evidence, the same type of evidence may be used in the future to exclude blacks.

Union's Viewpoint

The United Steelworkers of America (USWA) local sought to help the women affected by the exclusionary policy, but the local union did not possess enough personnel, medical expertise, and technological information to help the women. The local union consisted of 14 officers; only two (the president and financial secretary) were hired full time. The union had no medical evidence to prove that lead could harm male reproductive systems nor did it envision a technological solution to the dilemma. The officers believed it was impossible to clean up the work place to the point where it would be safe for fertile women.

However, the local union did offer some support to the women. They protested the company's failure to consider the wages, seniority, and benefits of the transferred women, assisted the women in filling out complaints to both EEOC and IHRC, tried to obtain medical research on the health effects of lead, and contacted the international headquarters of the USWA in Pittsburgh, Pa., for advice and information.

The efforts of the international union to protest the treatment of the women also had little effect. The international office could not maintain that a financial burden had been placed upon the women because the women had eventually been reimbursed by the company for lost wages. The union was also fearful of antagonizing Bunker Hill because the union wanted the company to continue to hire females as production workers. Moreover, Bunker Hill had decided that "it was easier to deal with union protests over the exclusion of women than with a damages trial in 1990 where a jury would be confronted by a horribly deformed human being" (Robinson, 1979, p. 4).

The international office of the USWA had filed a grievance against Bunker Hill for the sterilization policy. However, OSHA's dismissal of the citation against American Cyanamid and Bunker Hill destroyed the union's arguments. Several factors entered into the USWA's decision to withdraw its grievance against the company for the exclusionary policy: 1) the factual evidence was not that strong that the women at Bunker Hill were sterilized solely to keep their jobs, 2) the union would have legal problems in a suit since lead has not been proven to be a real hazard to the reproductive abilities of men, and 3) even the USWA's own doctors advised that pregnant women should not work around lead (Interview: International union official).

Other unions are resisting the transfer of women workers from hazardous jobs unless those transferred suffer no economic penalties. For instance, the United Auto Workers filed grievances against the General Motors Corporation, which barred fertile women from holding battery plant jobs where they may be exposed to lead in the air. Both the UAW and the USWA are insisting that women and other workers removed from certain jobs must not suffer loss of pay or seniority.

EEOC's Viewpoint

After EEOC "settled" the Bunker Hill controversy in 1976, the agency began to receive complaints of exclusionary policies from female employees in other companies. About fifty women filed complaints to EEOC that they were being involuntarily transferred from their jobs because of corporate exclusionary policies. The EEOC was uncertain about how to proceed with the new complaints; the agency had still not developed a policy to handle exclusionary policies and could deal with them only on a case-by-case basis. In fact, the year before the Bunker Hill controversy arose, EEOC had tacitly approved a similar corporate exclusionary policy maintained by the National Lead Industries (Freedom of Information Act: OSHA investigative file). However, the EEOC has warned employers that efforts to bar all women from certain jobs could violate federal civil rights legislation.

OSHA's Viewpoint

Bunker Hill is very visible in regard to environmental problems. By citing Bunker Hill, OSHA sought to pressure other companies into reducing lead levels in the work place (Harris, 1980, p. 1). OSHA believed its actions would give an incentive for companies to reduce lead exposure to safe levels and would discourage other companies from employing exclusionary policies. As Susan Fleming, a spokeswoman for OSHA, explained:

> Bunker Hill like a lot of other firms refuses to allow women who can bear children to work at lead smelting operations. OSHA is discouraging this policy. Employers should know that we're going to pressure them on the issue, and employees should know they needn't put up with this policy (Harris, 1980, p. 1).

While Bunker Hill officials view OSHA's accusations as an abuse of government power, OSHA sees its actions as incentives to industry to develop the necessary technology to reduce lead levels and maintains that the task is feasible ("OSHA confronts Bunker Hill," 1980, p. 1).

OSHA claimed that Bunker Hill could not legally seek to eliminate the health hazards lead presents to female employees "by compelling them to choose between their jobs and sterilization, thereby incurring serious and irreversible impairment to their reproductive systems" ("OSHA proposes . . ." 1980, pp.

1–2). The company's policy struck Marshall Saltzmann, who prepared OSHA's case, as "odious." "It seems so wrong," he said, "that it just has to be a violation of something" (Schlender, 1980, p. 25).

Eula Bingham, former head of OSHA during the Carter administration, maintained that industry must clean up the work place to make it safe for the fetus. "This business of having people go out and be sterilized — and I would feel the same way if it were men — to me it's like saying you're going to work on this machine and you might get your hand cut, so to prevent our liability, you'd better go out and have your hand amputated" (Tate, 1981, p. 80). Moreover, OHSA's area director in Boise, David M. Bernard, contended that there was a basic human right in question at Bunker Hill. He insisted, "Whether or not you want to limit your reproductive capabilities is your business. We don't feel it should be made a condition of employment" (Accola, 1980, p. 4a).

OSHA continues to be interested in exclusionary policies despite its failure to extend jurisdiction over the issue of exclusionary policies. OSHA officials do not believe the controversial issues raised by such policies will be resolved in the near future (Interviews: OSHA officials). One OSHA official describes the issue of exclusionary policies to be "a shaggy dog: it'll go on and on," and predicts that exclusionary policies will become one of the major regulatory issues in the 1980s (Interview: OSHA official).

Some question whether EEOC and OSHA should be involved in the regulation of reproductive hazards in the first place. Williams (1981, p. 652) observes, "To date the state has not prohibited women of childbearing capacity or pregnant women from smoking, drinking coffee or alcohol to excess, or taking aspirin — any one of which poses a greater hazard to fetal health than most jobs from which women have been excluded by protective employers."

Agreement on the rights and responsibilities of government, top management, industry, the union, and the female employee in the regulation of reproductive health does not exist. That some agreement be reached is critical, because it is highly likely that exclusionary policies will become common throughout industry. To prevent possible fetal damage, a number of major corporations have implemented corporate policies preventing female employees of childbearing age from working in positions where they would be exposed to the lead. Among these corporations are the General Motors Corporation of Canada and the United States; the DuPont Corporation of Wilmington, Del.; the Olin Corporation of East Alton, Ill.; and St. Joe's Mineral Corporation of Monoco, Pa. Exclusionary policies will undoubtedly be developed by other corporations not only to deal with lead but with a host of other toxins including benzene, beryllium, mercury, cotton dust, vinyl chloride, and ionizing radiation.

Dr. Corn of the National Institute of Occupational Safety and Health (NIOSH) identified the importance of this issue to Congress by observing, "We are in an area of social regulation, if you will, that has enormous ramification" (U.S. Congress, 1976, p. 411).

REFERENCES

Accola, J. Sept. 28, 1980. Women: company officials told us to "get fixed." *The Idaho Stateman*, p. A1.
A new twist to exclusionary policies: the case of

synfuels. 1981. *Coalition for the Reproductive Rights of Workers Newsletter* 1 (1), 3, 7.

Bagamery, A. 1981. Subtle charms. *Forbes* 128, 171–172.

Burnham, D. Mar. 14, 1976. Rise in birth defects laid to job hazards. *New York Times*, pp. 1, 42.

Clauss, C., and Bertin, J. 1981. *Brief of the American Civil Liberties Union Women's Rights Project, et al., Amici Curiae*. New York: American Civil Liberties Union Foundation.

Do protective laws hinder women on job? Oct. 26, 1980. *The Idaho Stateman*, p. 1.

Fact File. Feb. 14, 1975. *The Bunker Hill Company*.

Gold R. 1981. Women entering labor force draw attention to reproductive hazards for both sexes. *Family Planning/Population Reporter 10*, 10–13.

Harris, W. Sept. 16, 1980. OSHA fines Bunker Hill on sterility policy. *Metals Daily*, p. 1.

Hricko, A. 1978. Social policy considerations of occupational health standards: the example of lead and reproductive effects. *Preventive Medicine* 7, 394–406.

Hricko, A., and Brunt, M. 1976. *Working for Your Life: A Woman's Guide to Job Health Hazards*. Berkeley: Labor Occupational Health Program and Public Citizen's Health Resource Group.

Hyatt, J. Aug. 1, 1977. Work safety issue isn't as simple as it sounds. *Wall Street Journal*, p. 1.

Kendrick, J. Nov. 15, 1980. Smelter safety ensured. *The Idaho Stateman*, p. 1A.

Kendrick, Woodruff testify. Oct. 21, 1981. *Kellogg Evening News*, p. 1.

Krekel, S. 1977. A worker's viewpoint. In E. Bingham (ed.), *Proceedings: Conference on Women and the Workplace* (pp. 124–126). Washington, D.C.: Society for Occupational and Environmental Health.

Kuglin, J. Jan. 27, 1977. Women take plunge to work at Bunker Hill. *Lewiston Morning Tribune*, p. 3A.

OSHA confronts Bunker Hill. Sept. 25, 1980. Wallace, *Idaho Miner*, p. 1.

OSHA proposes $82,765 penalty for alleged health violations at Bunker Hill Company. Sept. 12, 1980. *U.S. Department of Labor News*, pp. 1–2.

Pauly, D. June 28, 1976. Women's work? *Newsweek*, pp. 56–58.

Robinson, G. 1979. The new discrimination. *Environmental Action* 10, 4–9.

Schlender, B. Dec. 9, 1980. Sterilization is main issue in OSHA suits. *Wall Street Journal*, p. 1125.

Shabecoff, P. Jan. 2, 1981. Industry and women clash over hazards in workplace. *New York Times*, p. 1.

Stellman, J. 1977. *Women's Work, Women's Health*. New York: Pantheon Books.

Stillman, N. 1979. The law in conflict: accommodating equal employment and occupational health obligations. *Journal of Occupational Medicine* 21, 599–606.

Tate, C. Apr. 17, 1975. Women shifted from Bunker Hill smelter jobs. *Lewiston Morning Tribune*, p. A1.

Tate, C. 1981. American dilemma of jobs, health in an Idaho town. *Smithsonian* 12, 74–83.

U.S. Congress. 1976. House Committee on Education and Labor, Subcommittee on Manpower, Compensation, and Health and Safety, 94th Congress, 2nd Session, Part 2. Statement of Dr. Morton Corn, Assistant Secretary, Occupational Safety and Health Administration. Washington, D.C.: U.S. Government Printing Office.

U.S. Department of Labor. 1979. Lost in the workplace: is there an occupational disease epidemic? *Proceedings from a Seminar for the News Media*. Washington, D.C.: U.S. Government Printing Office.

Williams, W. 1981. Firing the woman to protect the fetus: the reconciliation of fetal protection with employment opportunity goals under Title VII. *Georgetown Law Journal* 69, 641–704.

Win-O'Brien, M. 1980. Law in conflict: another view. *Journal of Occupational Medicine*, 22, 509–510.

Young, L. Aug. 26, 1981. Big mine firm plans to close. *Spokesman Review*, p. A1.

Donna M. Randall is in the Department of Management and Systems, Washington State University.

Decisions
Shannon Hines Ratcliff

Tony Quinn owns a small construction company. The company has been in business now for five years. Tony, who had always wanted to own his own company, is proud of himself and his business. After working construction for a number of years, he started Quinn Construct with 2 workers and a few pieces of second-rate equipment. As his contracts grew in size and number, so did the company. Quinn Construct now employs five work crews of 25 men each and has an impressive inventory of the finest construction equipment.

So far, the business has proved successful. Quinn Construct has an excellent reputation for performing high-quality work at competitive prices. Tony believes that one reason for the company's success is his close involvement with the business. He is in constant contact with his supervisors. He rotates visits with the work crews, often working side-by-side with them on various job sites. He knows most of his workers personally and feels he knows their work habits.

One day Tony decided to visit what he considered one of his best work crews. Lately their performance had dropped, and their supervisor had complained that the men did not seem to be as concerned as usual about the quality of their work. Several crew members were frequently coming to work late or not showing up at all. Job site accidents had increased for this crew by 200 percent. Nothing serious had happened, but the supervisor thought Tony should know about the recent occurrences.

After being on the job site for two hours, Tony went to visit the portable toilet. As he approached the building he noticed several workers hurrying back to work. When he entered the small building, he was almost overcome by marijuana smoke. On the floor he found a package of cigarette papers often used to roll "joints."

Tony was shocked. He tried to keep well informed about the construction industry by reading trade papers and magazines. He was aware of the high incidence of drug use among construction workers, but he never thought any of his crew members would use drugs — especially not on the job.

What was he going to do? He knew the hazards of performing construction work while "stoned." Someone could be seriously hurt or killed. Poor-quality work would ruin the reputation of his business. He had worked too long and hard to sit back and watch these things happen. Yet how should he handle the problem? Tony had read in one of the trade journals about testing workers for drugs. He had also read about potential problems in drug testing. As Tony walked back to the job site his mind was racing with questions: Should he force his employees to submit to drug tests? If so, what type of tests should he use? Who should be tested? Tony knew he had some decisions to make, and that they were not going to be easy.

Shannon Hines Ratcliff is affiliated with Texas A&M University.

"Decisions" by Shannon Hines Ratcliff is reprinted by permission of the author.

Readings for Professional Growth and Enrichment

Baird, L., and I. Mexhoulam (1984). "Strategic Human Resource Management: Implications for Training Human Resource Professionals." *Training and Development Journal* 38: 76–78.

Dyer, L. (1985). "Strategic Human Resources Management and Planning." In K. M. Rowland and G. R. Ferris (eds.), *Research in Personnel and Human Resources Management,* Vol. 3. Greenwich, Conn.: JAI Press.

Faley, R. H. (1982). "Sexual Harassment: Critical Review of Legal Cases with General Principles and Preventive Measures." *Personnel Psychology* 35: 583–600.

Folger, R., and J. Greenberg (1985). "Procedural Justice: An Interpretive Analysis of Personnel Systems." In K. M. Rowland and G. R. Ferris (eds.), *Research in Personnel and Human Resources Management,* Vol. 3. Greenwich, Conn.: JAI Press.

Gomez-Mejia, L. R., and T. M. Welbourne (1988). "Compensation Strategy: An Overview and Future Steps." *Human Resource Planning* 11: 173–189.

Gutek, B., L. Larwood, and A. Stromberg (1986). "Women at Work." In C. L. Cooper and I. T. Robertson (eds.), *International Review of Industrial and Organizational Psychology*. New York: John Wiley & Sons.

Ishida, H. (1986). "Transferability of Japanese Human Resource Management Abroad." *Human Resource Management,* 25 (Spring): 103–120.

Kozlowski, S. W. J. (1987). "Technological Innovation and Strategic HRM: Facing the Challenge of Change." *Human Resource Planning* 10: 69–79.

Lengnick-Hall, C. A., and M. L. Lengnick-Hall (1988). "Strategic Human Resources Management: A Review of the Literature and a Proposed Typology." *Academy of Management Review,* 13: 454–470.

Miles, R. E., and C. C. Snow (1984). "Designing Strategic Human Resources Systems." *Organizational Dynamics* 12: 36–52.

Wallace, M. J. (1983). "Methodology, Research Practice, and Progress in Personnel and Industrial Relations." *Academy of Management Review* 8: 6–13.